Inside UNIX

Chris Hare
Emmett Dulaney
George Eckel
Steven Lee
Lee Ray

NRP
NEW RIDERS PUBLISHING

New Riders Publishing, Indianapolis, Indiana

Inside UNIX

Chris Hare, Emmett Dulaney, George Eckel, Steven Lee, Lee Ray

Published by:
New Riders Publishing
201 West 103rd Street
Indianapolis, IN 46290 USA

Printed in the United States of America   3 4 5 6 7 8 9 0

Library of Congress Cataloging-in-Publication Data

```
Dulaney, Emmett.
    Inside UNIX / Emmett Dulaney, George Eckel, Chris Hare.
       p.    cm.
    Includes index.
    ISBN 1-56205-401-5
    1. Operating systems (Computers) 2. UNIX (Computer file)
I. Eckel, George, 1954-  . II. Hare, Chris, 1962-  . III. Title.
QA76.76.063D855  1994
005.4'3--dc20                                        94-37841
                                                        CIP
```

Warning and Disclaimer

This book is designed to provide information about the UNIX operating system. Every effort has been made to make this book as complete and as accurate as possible, but no warranty or fitness is implied.

The information is provided on an "as is" basis. The author and New Riders Publishing shall have neither liability nor responsibility to any person or entity with respect to any loss or damages arising from the information contained in this book or from the use of the disks or programs that may accompany it.

Publisher	Lloyd J. Short
Associate Publisher	Tim Huddleston
Product Development Manager	Rob Tidrow
Marketing Manager	Ray Robinson
Director of Special Projects	Cheri Robinson
Managing Editor	Matthew Morrill

About the Authors

Chris Hare started working with UNIX in 1986 as a programmer learning and writing C language code. Since that time, he has worked as a system administrator and written UNIX course materials, and numerous programs. In 1988, he became the first SCO Authorized instructor in Canada. He has spent the last few years focused on PERL and TCP/IP, while writing numerous technical articles for *Sys Admin* and testing programs for *UNIX World's* Wizard's Grabbag column. Chris currently is working as the Technical Services Manager for a Canadian software distributor and is studying Human Resource Management at Algonquin College in Ottawa, Canada.

Emmett Dulaney is a Product Development Specialist for New Riders Publishing. The author of several computer books, including *Voodoo NetWare* (Ventana Press) and *NetWare Solutions and Shortcuts* (M&T), he also is a contributing editor to *PCM* and frequent contributor to *SYS ADMIN*. An associate professor at Indiana University-Purdue University at Fort Wayne, he has taught continuing education classes in UNIX and writing, among other things, for the past five years.

George Eckel has worked as a collaborative author on other books published by Macmillan Publishing USA, including John Goodman's best seller *Memory Management For All Of Us* and Emmett Dulaney's *UNIX Unleashed*. George also has written a variety of software manuals for major corporations such as Hewlett-Packard and Informix.

Steven Lee is the Manager of Data Center Services for OpenSystems, Inc in Kirkland, Washington, where he is responsible for providing professional services for large, commercial installations of Sun Microsystems servers and workstations. Steve has worked with UNIX since 1987 as a Systems Engineer and consultant. He holds both Bachelor of Science and Master of Science degrees in Mechanical Engineering from Stanford University.

Lee Ray has been training users in the longs and shorts of UNIX for 10 years. He writes computer-based interactive training and articles about topics in UNIX. He administers systems used in support of research in digital audio and also operates a technical communications service in San Diego. He has a Ph.D. in Computer Music from the University of California and is a composer and performer.

Trademark Acknowledgments

All terms mentioned in this book that are known to be trademarks or service marks have been appropriately capitalized. New Riders Publishing cannot attest to the accuracy of this information. Use of a term in this book should not be regarded as affecting the validity of any trademark or service mark. UNIX is a registered trademark of X/Open Company Ltd.

Product Director
EMMETT DULANEY

Production Editor
CLIFF SHUBS

Editors
NANCY ALBRIGHT, AMY BEZEK
GENEIL BREEZE, KELLY CURRIE
LAURA FREY, JOHN KANE
SARAH KEARNS, PETER KUHNS
JOHN SLEEVA, ANGIE TRZEPACZ
LILLIAN YATES

Senior Acquisitions Editor
JIM LeVALLEY

Technical Editors
SCOTT ORR

Acquisitions Coordinator
STACEY BEHELER

Editorial Assistant
KAREN OPAL

Publisher's Assistant
MELISSA LYNCH

Cover Designer
JEAN BISESI

Book Designers
FRED BOWER, ROGER S. MORGAN

Graphics Image Specialists
CLINT LAHNEN, DENNIS SHEEHAN
SUSAN VANDEWALLE

Production Imprint Manager
JULI COOK

Production Imprint Team Leader
KATY BODENMILLER

Production Analysts
ANGELA BANNAN, DENNIS CLAY HAGER
MARY BETH WAKEFIELD

Production Team
GEORGIANA BRIGGS, MONA BROWN
MATT CURLESS, JUDY EVERLY
RICH EVERS, DAVID GARRATT
KIMBERLY K. HANNEL, ALEATA HOWARD
MICHAEL HUFF, LOUISA KLUCZNIK,
SHAWN MacDONALD, MICHELLE M. MITCHELL
SUSAN SHEPARD, JULIE SWENSON
SUZANNE TULLY, MARVIN VAN TIEM
DENNIS WESNER

Indexer
MICHAEL HUGHES

Acknowledgments

From Chris Hare

This is not the first time I've sat down to write a book, but it is the first time I've succeeded. With some gentle encouragement from Jim LeValley and Emmett Dulaney of New Riders Publishing after I initially declined the offer to work on this book, I sat down at the keyboard and burned a lot of candles.

This has been a fantastic learning experience and a chance to verbalize some of the obscure things that I have learned since getting involved with UNIX. For me UNIX is like a day without sunshine—you just can't bear to get out of bed when it is raining!

I would like to thank Jim LeValley and Emmett Dulaney at New Riders for their encouragement and support, as well as Martha Masinton and Robert Ward at R&D Publications who got me started in a writing career through *Sys Admin* magazine. Thanks also are extended to my uncle, Jim Hare, because if he hadn't pushed me hard in the beginning of my career, this book wouldn't be happening.

Finally, I need to acknowledge the loss of a husband and father during the last few months as I worked all day, then came home to write all night. To my wife Terri and my children Meagan and Matthew, I say thanks for putting up with being ignored, the late nights, and the grumpy Saturday mornings.

From Emmett Dulaney

I would like to thank Karen and Kristin for their patience and support and for not complaining too loudly when I fell asleep on the floor in the wee hours of the morning. So often, trains of thought that were estimated as taking "only 15 minutes more" to write, turned into hours. Without the understanding and support of my family, neither this, nor most other projects I undertake, would ever be completed.

From George Eckel

I would like to thank Sun Microsystems and Silicon Graphics for helping me capture many of the screen images used in this book. I also want to thank my family, Shirlee, Madeline, Nathalie, and Genevieve, for the support they gave me in completing this project, and Nancy Eckel, for starting things off right.

Contents at a Glance

Table of Contents

Introduction

Inside UNIX is designed for users and system administrators who plan to be working with the UNIX operating system. It is nonvendor specific, meaning that it strives to address as many different versions and flavors of UNIX as possible. Where there are major differences between the way a command works on different systems, those differences are noted.

Who Should Read This Book?

Inside UNIX is designed for advanced users and beginning system administrators of the UNIX operating system. The following chapters contain information and procedures for the average UNIX environment and are the product of many hours spent troubleshooting and administering said environment.

How *Inside UNIX* Helps You

The information presented in Part 1 provides an overview of the UNIX operating system and describes the differences between products and shells. These differences enable you to realize quickly the restrictions and benefits of the system you are working on and to concentrate on the commands and utilities available to you.

Part 2 moves through the major utilities and commands that are available from the command line. It shows the correct methods of creating files and directories, changing the permissions associated with them, as well as extracting data, sorting, redirecting, and comparing. The knowledge contained within Part 2 is essential to fully understanding the potential of the UNIX operating system.

Part 3 discusses the primary file editors within standard UNIX. Two chapters cover the functionality of vi—arguably one of the best editors ever created. The last chapter discusses the basics of ed—a line editor that has been around almost since the beginning of UNIX. While ed is not used any more than it absolutely has to be by most administrators, it is important to understand its workings, for quite often it is the only editor available after a system crash.

Graphic User Interfaces are the topic of Part 4, as it looks at X Windows, Motif, OpenWin, and Open Desktop—the four most common interfaces. More a saving grace for users than administrators, GUIs enable operations to be simplified from long, cryptic commands to simple clicks of an icon. These chapters walk through the interfaces and introduce the component essential in creating your own applications.

UNIX is divided into two key components—the kernel and the shell. Shells act as interpreters between users and the kernel, and are the most crucial addressable components of the system. Part 5 covers the core components and features of the shell. First, it explains the differences between the three available shells, then covers the features they offer, such as command-line history, job control, and command aliasing. With these concepts firmly in place, it then introduces shell scripts—automated routines that users and administrators write to simplify tasks.

Part 6 addresses the components of UNIX that only a system administrator could love. These include system-run levels and the logon process; methods of archiving data and performing backups; system security; and how to run processes at later points in time.

There are dozens of operating systems on the market that go by the name UNIX. Unfortunately, programs written for one UNIX do not run on another. Why? What are the differences? Part 7 reviews the differences in UNIX variants and flavors. All of the major UNIX products are broken into their platform and compared with all others. Nowhere else can this information be found, and it is invaluable to anyone who must work with more than one vendor's UNIX system.

Part 8 addresses means of communication—with other users and with the outside world. The Internet can be accessed through a variety of ways, and one chapter explores this issue. Internally and externally, electronic mail provides an excellent means of communication between users, and the second chapter discusses the means by which e-mail is utilized. The final chapter covers all means of communicating with users other than through mail—using the write utility, wall, talk, and others.

Part 9 covers the software aspects of connecting hardware together. This includes terminals, printers, DOS workstations, and TCP/IP networks.

Part 10 contains the Command Reference and Appendixes A and B, all of which are useful for quick reference.

The Command Reference details the key UNIX commands with proper syntax and options.

Appendix A compares the UNIX operating system with DOS and is intended for use in instructing DOS-based users how to transfer their knowledge over to UNIX.

Appendix B contains additional programs—in Perl and C language—that demonstrate how a shell archiver is written.

The accompanying disk contains ASCII copies of all the shell scripts discussed within the book. A separate subdirectory exists for each chapter containing scripts, and the scripts are stored by their addressed name in the book (usually also contained within the header).

New Riders Publishing

The staff of New Riders Publishing is committed to bringing you the very best in computer reference material. Each New Riders book is the result of months of work by authors and staff who research and refine the information contained within its covers.

As part of this commitment to you, New Riders invites your input. Please let us know if you enjoy this book, if you have trouble with the information and examples presented, or if you have a suggestion for the next edition.

Please note, however, that the New Riders staff cannot serve as a technical resource for UNIX or UNIX application-related questions, including hardware- and software-related problems. Refer to the documentation that accompanies your UNIX operating system or UNIX application package for help with specific problems.

If you have a question or comment about any New Riders book, there are several ways to contact New Riders Publishing. We will respond to as many readers as we can. Your name, address, or phone number will never become part of a mailing list or be used for any purpose other than to help us continue to bring you the best books possible. You can write us at the following address:

New Riders Publishing
Attn: Associate Publisher
201 W. 103rd Street
Indianapolis, IN 46290

If you prefer, you can fax New Riders Publishing at (317) 581-4670.

As well, you can leave a voice mail message to New Riders at (317) 581-3871.

You can send electronic mail to New Riders from a variety of sources. NRP maintains several mailboxes organized by topic area. Mail in these mailboxes will be forwarded to the staff member who is best able to address your concerns. Substitute the appropriate mailbox name from the list below when addressing your e-mail. The mailboxes are as follows:

ADMIN	Comments and complaints for NRP's Publisher
APPS	Word, Excel, WordPerfect, and other office applications
ACQ	Book proposals and inquiries by potential authors
CAD	AutoCAD, 3D Studio, AutoSketch, and CAD products
DATABASE	Access, dBASE, Paradox, and other database products
GRAPHICS	CorelDRAW!, Photoshop, and other graphics products
INTERNET	Internet
NETWORK	NetWare, LANtastic, and other network-related topics
OS	MS-DOS, OS/2, and all OS except UNIX and Windows
UNIX	UNIX
WINDOWS	Microsoft Windows (all versions)
OTHER	Anything that doesn't fit into the preceding categories

If you use an MHS e-mail system that routes through CompuServe, send your messages to the following:

>   *mailbox* @ NEWRIDER

To send NRP mail from CompuServe, use the following address:

>   MHS: *mailbox* @ NEWRIDER

To send mail from the Internet, use the following address format:

>   *mailbox*@newrider.mhs.compuserve.com

NRP is an imprint of Macmillan Computer Publishing. To obtain a catalog or information, or to purchase any Macmillan Computer Publishing book, call (800) 428-5331.

Thank you for selecting *Inside UNIX!*

Part I

UNIX Overview

Chapter Snapshot

The UNIX operating system was born in the halls of Bell Labs in the late 1960s. Since then, it has continued to prosper and grow with users and administrators who realize its potential. Other operating systems have tried to utilize the best features of UNIX, but none have incorporated all of them. This chapter discusses the following:

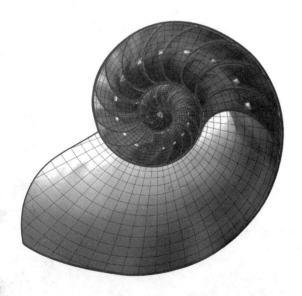

CHAPTER

1

History

This book does not purport to be an academic study. Instead of dwelling on who was the first user to realize that pressing U in vi undid all changes to the current line, this book devotes its pages to showing you how to perform those actions.

At the same time, no serious discussion on the workings of an open 8 rating system is complete without discussing what the operating system is and the history behind it. The purpose of this chapter is to fulfill those requirements and explain how UNIX came to be what it is today.

Understanding What UNIX Is

UNIX is a multiuser, multitasking, multithreading computer operating system that enables different people to access a computer at the same time and to run more than one program simultaneously. Since its humble beginning more than 25 years ago, it has been redefined and refined time and time again. Networking capabilities enhance the suitability of UNIX for the workplace, and support for DOS and Windows is coming in the 32-bit workstation markets.

When UNIX was first designed, emphasis was placed on keeping the system flexible and simple. Key components include a hierarchical directory tree that divides files into directories with intended purposes (executable files, user files, and so on), and real-time processing.

Going Back to the Beginning

The UNIX operating system came to life, as many things do, more or less by accident. In the late 1960s, an operating system called MULTICS was designed by the Massachusetts Institute of Technology to run on GE mainframe computers. Built on banks of processors, MULTICS enabled information-sharing among users, although it required huge amounts of memory and ran slowly.

Ken Thompson, working for Bell Labs, wrote a crude computer game to run on the mainframe. He did not like the performance the mainframe gave or the cost of running it. With the help of Dennis Ritchie, he rewrote the game to run on a DEC computer and, in the process, wrote an entire operating system as well. Several hundred variations have circulated about how the system came to be named what it is, but the most common is that it is a mnemonic derivative of MULTICS.

In 1970, Thompson and Ritchie's operating system came to be called UNIX, and Bell Laboratories kicked in financial support to refine the product—in return for Thompson and Ritchie adding text processing capabilities. A side benefit of this arrangement was that it enabled Thompson and Ritchie to find a faster DEC machine on which to run their new system.

Reviewing UNIX's Early Growth

By 1972, 10 computers were running UNIX, and in 1973, Thompson and Ritchie rewrote the kernel from assembly language to C language—the brainchild of Ritchie. Since then, UNIX and C have been intertwined, and UNIX's growth is partially due to the ease of transporting the C language to other platforms. Although C is not as quick as assembly language, it is much more flexible and portable from one system to another.

AT&T, the parent company of Bell, was not in the computer business (partially because it was a utility monopoly at the time and under scrutiny from the government) so it did not actively attempt to market the product. Instead, AT&T offered UNIX in source-code form to government institutions and to universities for a fraction of its worth. This practice led to UNIX eventually working its way into more than 80 percent of the universities that had computer departments. In 1979, it was ported to the popular VAX minicomputers from Digital, further cementing its way into universities.

Witnessing the Birth of a Commercial Product

The breakup of the AT&T monopoly in 1984 enabled the former giant to begin selling UNIX openly. Although AT&T continued to work on the product and update it by adding refinements, those unaffiliated individuals who received early copies of the operating system and could interpret the source code took it upon themselves to make their own enhancements.

Much of this independent crafting took place at the University of California, Berkeley. In 1975, Ken Thompson took a leave from Bell Labs and went to practice at Berkeley in the Department of Computer Science. It was there that he ran into and recruited a graduate student named Bill Joy to help enhance the system. In 1977, Joy mailed out several free copies of his system modifications.

While UNIX was in-house at Bell, enhancements to it were noted as version numbers—Versions 1 through 6. When AT&T began releasing it as a commercial product, system numbers were used (System III, System V, and so on). The refinements done at the university were released as Berkeley Software Distribution, or BSD (2BSD, 3BSD, and so on). Some of the more significant enhancements to come from Berkeley include the vi editor and the C shell. Others include increased file name lengths; AT&T accepted 14 characters for file names, and Berkeley expanded the limit to 25.

Getting a Giant Boost

Towards the end of the 1970s, an important moment occurred when the Department of Defense announced that its Advanced Research Projects Agency would use UNIX and would base its version on the Berkeley software. This achievement gave UNIX a national name and put a feather in the cap of the Berkeley version. One of the demands on the operating system placed by the DOD was for networking, and UNIX thus moved farther along the line of technological advancements.

Bill Joy, in the meantime, left the campus setting and became one of the founding members of Sun Microsystems. The Sun workstations used a derivative of BSD known as the Sun Operating System, or SunOS.

Exploring Recent History

One of the problems with so many different people enhancing the operating system has been a lack of uniformity among UNIX versions. A product that works on one vendor's UNIX might just as easily not work on another. Because both systems are UNIX, you would think that the application should work, but draw an analogy comparing a starter motor for a Cavalier to its counterpart for a Lexus. Although both the Cavalier and Lexus are cars, their applications/components are not interchangeable. The same can be said of UNIX operating systems, and several steps have been taken to correct this problem.

In 1988, Sun Microsystems and AT&T joined forces to rewrite UNIX into System V, release 4.0. Other companies, including IBM and Digital Equipment, fearful of losing their positions in the UNIX marketplace, countered by forming their own standards group to come up with a guideline for UNIX. Both groups incorporated BSD in their guidelines but still managed to come up with different versions of System V. One is governed by the Open Software Foundation, and the other by UNIX International. One of the first joint products created by the OSF was Motif, a tool kit for building X Window applications.

Watching Novell Enter the Picture

In April 1991, AT&T created a spin-off company called *UNIX System Laboratories* (USL) to market and continue development of UNIX. Immediately, Novell Inc., a leader in the field of DOS-based office networking, bought into the company as an edge against Microsoft's new NT operating system, originally feared by all as the operating system of total dominance. Later that year, a joint product, UnixWare, was announced that would combine UNIX with the features of NetWare. It finally came to market in November 1992, and in December of that same year, Novell purchased all of USL from AT&T.

Witnessing the End of BSD

In the early 1990s, Berkeley announced that it was in the business of providing education and was not a commercial software house—no more editions of BSD would be forthcoming. Sun Microsystems, one of the largest providers of UNIX in the world, quickly moved to the System V standards that had grown from enhancements to the original AT&T UNIX.

Predicting Future Directions

It is interesting to look at enhancements made in PC operating systems today and see the new additions each version brings. What makes it interesting is that these enhancements are marketed as wonderful and great when they have existed in UNIX for years. OS/2 386HPFS, for example, keeps track of file information by means of "fnodes." These fnodes are indexes to the physical data and contain all relevant information about data content. By having these indexes separate, the data can be a file, a directory, a link, or a device—facilitating the user's ability to move, delete, and modify on the fly. This same concept has been with UNIX since the beginning as "inodes."

Newer versions of DOS enable you to move files with one command, delete entire subdirectories with a single command, and create hidden files and directories. Again, UNIX users have enjoyed these features for years. NT and other operating systems use logins, passwords, and encryptions that UNIX has offered since early on.

For a long time, UNIX was thought to be confined to the mini-tower and the large workstation. People assumed that it would never be able to migrate to an end-user's desktop PC because the needs of the operating system were so great. For those users who were willing to give it a try, Microsoft created XENIX—a form of UNIX designed for the desktop PC—and later sold it to *Santa Cruz Operations* (SCO).

As time has passed, however, PCs have changed tremendously. A single PC can contain as much RAM and hard drive space as a mini-tower once did, and then some. As the personal computer has matured, UNIX has come more into favor as an operating system for it. SCO UNIX, as well as Sun's and Novell's entries, provide excellent operating systems for multiple-user environments.

Summary

UNIX is an operating system with a colorful past. The system has successfully migrated through the years and found its way from mini-towers to PCs. Its multitasking capabilities are surpassed by none. Built-in security features and networking are making UNIX a viable choice for businesses around the world. UNIX is now experiencing as much acceptance and growth as at any time in its past, and it is an operating system that is here to stay for a long while.

Chapter Snapshot

With all the features and utilities UNIX provides, they are meaningless if you lack access to the operating system. This chapter discusses how to login to the operating system and establish a session, including such topics as the following:

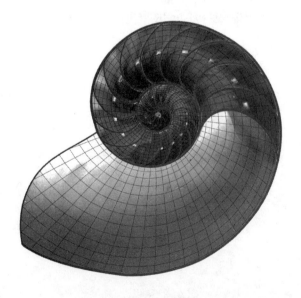

Gaining Access

Because it is such a secure operating system, you must identify yourself before you are able to operate within the UNIX system. You give your identification as two separate entities: a login ID and a password. You must know both, and the operating system must recognize them before you can use the commands UNIX offers.

This chapter covers the basic topics that you need to know to begin using the operating system successfully. You learn the rules of logging in, setting a password, and logging out.

Logging In

A UNIX session begins with the login prompt. This prompt appears on-screen, quite simply, as nothing more than `login:`. Other information (such as the name of the machine), might appear as well, but the prompt is of prime importance.

The system administrator must assign a login name and password to you before you can gain admittance to the system. After you have obtained both, enter the login name at the prompt, as in the following:

```
login:  karen  <Enter>
```

Next, a `password:` prompt appears. Enter your password here.

The prompt for a password appears regardless of whether you entered a valid login ID. By not rejecting invalid login IDs, the system provides a higher level of security—the entire login fails, and you do not know whether it was because you were wrong with the password or with the ID.

The first thing you might notice when typing is that the login name appears when you type it, but the password does not. Login names are common knowledge—words or names, such as karen, kristin, and so on. Passwords, on the other hand, are not common knowledge. They identify to the system that you really are who you say you are.

The second thing to note is that (on most systems) every character typed is interpreted as an entry. If you make a mistake and press the Backspace key to correct it, for example, the Backspace character is interpreted as part of the login or password, and the entry registers as incorrect.

If you mistakenly enter either the login ID or the password incorrectly, you receive a message that the login is incorrect, and the process starts over again.

After you correctly enter the login name and password, the shell prompt appears. The prompt is definable and can be anything, but the most common are the dollar sign ($) and the percent sign (%). UNIX contains various shells, or command interpreters. The % identifies that the C shell is in use, and the $ is used by most other shells. A pound sign (#), on the other hand, indicates that you have logged in with administrative (root) permissions.

Setting a Password

When an account is created, the administrator assigns a password for it. You should change this password fairly often to ensure security. After you have successfully logged in, you can change your password to anything you like—within reason. "Reason" would include restrictions, set up at a system level by the administrator, regarding password length and content.

Changing passwords is a straightforward process; you simply use the passwd command. After you have logged in, invoke passwd, which once more prompts you for your old password, then for a new password. Enter the new password, pressing Enter at the end of the line, and you are prompted to enter the new password again to verify it.

Both entries are accepted without being displayed; thus you cannot see what you are typing. Both entries must be identical, or UNIX informs you that they do not match, and no changes are made. If they do match, the password is changed to the new value.

The following code is a sample session during a password change. Several criteria have been established on a global level that prevent two of the changes from taking place. Remember that the actual entries typed do not appear on-screen and are shown here within braces {}.

```
$ passwd
passwd:  Changing password for karen
Old password:  {2Br02b}
New password:  {run4}
Password is too short - must be at least 6 digits
New password:  {runfast}
Password must contain at least two alphabetic characters and
at least one numeric or special character.
New password:  {run4it}
Re-enter new password: {run4it}
$
```

Any user can change his or her own password in this manner. The administrative (root) user, however, also has the ability to change anyone else's password. As the administrative user, you specify after the command the name of the user whose password is to be changed:

```
# passwd kristin
New password:  {she8aLL}
Re-enter new password:  {she8aLL}
#
```

Understanding the Importance of Good Passwords

The first line of defense in keeping an intruder from a system is a set of good passwords. As mentioned previously, to gain admission into a system, you must provide two things: the login ID and the associated password. Generally, login IDs are common knowledge. The ID for Madonna, for example, probably would be Madonna, madonna, donna, or any other similar representation. The password associated with the ID, however, should be known only by you and no one else. The more people who know your password, the more people who can enter the system, masquerading as you and gaining access to all of your files and objects.

An intruder masquerading as you can do damage, not only to your files/objects, but to your reputation if you don't catch it soon enough. Out of sheer maliciousness, an intruder can present an administrator and other bosses with the impression that it was you who screwed things up, in a manner similar to a credit card scam artist who gets *you* blamed for unpaid bills.

Because your password should be known only by you, it should be one that cannot be easily guessed. Users often do not pay enough attention to the manner in which they select their passwords. The system administrator has the responsibility of harping and nagging and educating users in the choosing of proper passwords.

The "Top 10" Password Ideas To Avoid

Anyone attempting to break into a system will try to do so in the easiest manner possible. A robber will break a window before renting a jackhammer and burrowing through the foundation. The following password ideas are among the first ones an intruder will try when attempting to masquerade as you. You should avoid these types of passwords at all costs:

10. Do not assign a password at all, just use the Enter key.

9. Repeat the login ID (login: karen; password: karen).

8. Spell your name backward (nerak).

7. Use the name of your spouse or children (bob), or spell the name backward (bob).

6. Use the name of your dog (pavlov).

5. Use a pet name for yourself (bones).

4. Use your social security number, phone number, birth date, or time card number.

3. Choose the name of a person you idolize (fabio). The same holds true for sports teams, movies, books, and so on.

2. Use any city with which you can be associated (sheboygan).

1. Use any word found in a standard dictionary.

Although the reasoning for the last point might not seem clear, many programs are available that can pull words from a dictionary and use them to guess passwords. It does take some time for an intruder to go through the entire dictionary, but an efficient program can reduce that time to almost nothing.

The "Top 10" Things To Do in Choosing a Good Password

Knowing what not to do is all well and good, but reviewing what constitutes a good password is important too:

10. Be original.

9. Think about the password you have chosen and ask yourself how difficult it would be for someone else to guess it. If it is too easy, change it.

8. Experiment.

7. Mix numbers and characters (2br02b).

6. Use upper- and lowercase characters (2Br02b).

5. Keep it less than eight characters long. The longer the password, the more possibilities for typing errors. Remember, what you are typing does not show on-screen.

4. Make it something of significance to you that you will not forget. Never write a password down—you defeat the whole purpose of being secretive if someone stumbles across the scrap of paper.

3. Don't be afraid to toss in punctuation and symbols (2Br_02b!).

2. Change the password regularly. Every three months is a good time frame, but also change the password anytime you suspect that someone might be trying to break in.

1. Choose a different password each time you change and never use the same password twice.

Logging Out

To end your session with the operating system, you need to leave the shell and return to the login. This task is known as logging out, or signing off. Several methods are available, depending on your software.

The preferred method is the exit command. An alternative is pressing Ctrl+D, which signifies the end of data input. Other commands that might exist on your system and perform the same function are logout, logoff, or log.

Summary

To begin a session with the UNIX operating system, you must identify yourself. You accomplish this step by providing a login ID and a password. If the two entries you give match an account established by the system administrator, a session begins.

Chapter Snapshot

Understanding the way UNIX creates and maintains files and directories is imperative to operating it successfully. Before you begin creating your own files and storing data, you must understand where the data should be saved and the conventions used by the UNIX to facilitate maximum ease of use. This chapter explores the file and directory structure, including the following topics:

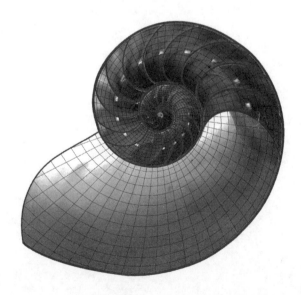

File and Directory Structure

he UNIX operating system uses an *inverted tree* structure, much the same as many other operating systems. In an inverted tree, one main directory branches into several subdirectories. Each subdirectory can then further branch into additional subdirectories.

This structure, although novel at the time UNIX first became available, is familiar now and commonplace with most operating systems. The purpose of each of the standard subdirectories and the method by which UNIX maintains files and directories, however, is vitally important.

Understanding the Root Directory and Its Branches

The *root directory* is the beginning, or first layer, of the file system. Symbolized as a forward slash (/), the root directory is the point from which all other subdirectories branch. Throughout UNIX, the word *root* is used to mean beginning or superior. A root user (also known as the *superuser*) has the ability to change anything related to the file system without question. This user can bring the system up, shut it down, and do everything in between. By no small coincidence, the home directory of this user is the root directory—from here, all information filters down. Figure 3.1 illustrates this by presenting the classic diagram of the UNIX subdirectory file system.

Figure 3.1
An inverted tree view of the UNIX file system.

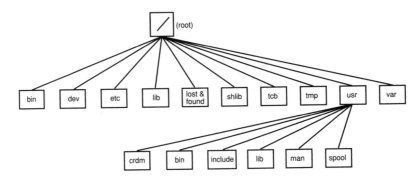

Only one file—unix —should be within the normal system's root directory. This is the actual, bootable, operating system file; in its absence, the operating system cannot come up after a restart. This file, also known as the *kernel*, is discussed in greater detail in Chapter 4, "Differences between Products and Shells."

In addition to the unix file, there are a number of subdirectories. Every system has unique ones created by an administrator for specific purposes, but the default ones created when a new operating system is installed are as follows:

bin

dev

etc

lib

lost+found

shlib

tcb

tmp

usr

var

The bin Directory

The bin directory contains binary files and executables. Many of the commands and utilities discussed throughout this book reside in the bin directory, including login, passwd, and other common commands such as the following:

cat

chgrp

chmod

chown

clear

cmp

cp

csh

date

df

diff

du

echo

ed

env

file

find

grep

head

hello

kill

ksh

ls

mail

mkdir

mv

pr

ps

pwd

rm

rmdir

sh

sort

tail

wc

who

Generally, every user has the right to read and execute files contained within the bin directory. Lacking these permissions, users are severely limited in what they can accomplish during a login session—providing they can log in.

The dev Directory

Within the dev directory resides all the device information for the system. Every piece of hardware constitutes a device that must be defined to the system—terminals, tape drives, modems, and so on. Key among these are the following:

✔ clock—The system clock

✔ dsk—The hard drive

✔ null—A dumping ground where output and errors can be redirected to, preventing them from writing to the screen or filling a file

The etc Directory

In writing, *etc.* is usually used to indicate something that continues on. In UNIX, etc is the directory that holds information specific to that machine. The password file (passwd) is here as well as other system files and tables that do not remain the same from one machine to another.

Because this information must be verified, at the very least, for each user, they have read and execute permissions to this directory as well. Some of the more important files that reside here are as follows:

✔ inittab — Information about what devices are enabled per each run state

✔ issue — Text that appears on each login screen

✔ magic — A database of what type files are recognized by the system.

✔ motd — A Message Of The Day that appears each time a user logs in.

✔ profile — Actions automatically executed with each login—usually includes checking for mail and setting the timezone

✔ shadow — The encrypted passwords from the passwd file

✔ TIMEZONE — Information about the local time zone

The lib Directory

The lib directory contains libraries of data for the various compilers on the system. Usually, these are used by C language routines.

The lost+found Directory

When a file becomes corrupted to the point that the system can no longer read it, it must be removed. This removal is done automatically when the system recognizes that a problem exists. (Many operating systems also perform a sanity check for problems with every boot.)

In the absence of a lost+found directory, the problem files are removed from the system completely during this cleansing process. In the presence of a lost+found directory, the files are dumped in there. Bear in mind that the system can no longer read the file, and what is dumped into lost+found is rarely usable. What this does, however, is inform you that a problem has occurred if you see entries in the lost+found directory. In a perfect system, the directory should always be empty. A less-than-perfect system will have entries in the lost+found directory. The dates and times associated with the files indicate when the file was dumped in the directory by the cleansing process.

By using the strings command, you can often view the files in the lost+found directory, and with some investigative work, you can ascertain what files the system had trouble with and removed.

The shlib Directory

The shlib directory contains shared library versions of programs used by compilers. Once again, these are generally C compilers included with individual vendor's versions of UNIX.

The tcb Directory

The Trusted Computing Base is not available with all versions of UNIX. tcb is a method of implementing system security beyond logins and passwords (see Chapter 27, "Security"). The files that tcb needs to implement this additional security are maintained within this directory.

The tmp Directory

When files are opened, or in use, the file system needs somewhere to store a copy of them; the tmp directory fulfills this need. Many other programs, such as the vi editor, also need locations to store original copies of files as they are being modified by users, and tmp is the location they use.

Files that you intend to keep should NEVER be stored in the tmp directory. Most systems have routines, either activated by cron or at startup, that empty the contents of tmp files to prevent them from overfilling the system.

The usr Directory

The User Specific Resources directory holds data (as in home directories) on individual users. Like the etc directory, information within usr is not standard across machines, but specific to each.

Besides containing user information and home directories, it also has several subdirectories beneath it of critical importance, as follows:

✔ adm—This is the main administrative directory. It is used for monitoring operations, process accounting, error reporting, and usage files. Among the entries here are sulog, which keeps track of each time a user invokes the superuser utility; installation scripts; and ctlog, which monitors ct usage.

I

✔ bin—This contains further binary executable files not in the standard bin directory. Executable utilities here include the following:

at

awk

banner

cal

cancel

compress

cut

diff3

disable

egrep

fgrep

join

logname

lpr

man

more

news

nl

paste

vi

✔ include—This holds the uncompiled routines used by UNIX, usually when compiling the kernel for the system.

✔ lib—This directory contains UNIX tables needed to keep the system running. Among the entries here are files or subdirectories affecting the operation of the keyboard, terminals, uucp, cron, and individual user accounts.

✔ man—This contains online manual entries describing the operations of each UNIX command.

✔ spool—This directory is used for temporary holding locations for data intended elsewhere. For example, when you print a file, the file is copied into the spool directory and then fed from the spool directory to the printer. In addition to the printer (lp), there are also entries for cron, mail, and uucp.

The var Directory

Whereas the usr subdirectory contains some information that differs from system to system, the var directory contains only information (files and subdirectories) that varies from one system to another. Traditionally, vendors add their enhancements to var, enabling administrators to quickly spot differences between UNIX products.

Moving Around the File System

As mentioned previously, the root directory is referenced by a single forward slash (/). Directories and files also are separated in an address by including a slash between them. Thus, to specify the root directory, simply enter the following:

```
/
```

To specify the lib directory, use this command:

```
/lib
```

And to specify the bin subdirectory, beneath the user directory, enter the following command:

```
/usr/bin
```

If you want to reference a file by the name of XYZ in the bin subdirectory of the usr directory, use this command:

```
/usr/bin/XYZ
```

Taking this one step farther, the command cd is used to change directories. From whatever subdirectory you may be in, issue the following command to immediately take you to the root directory:

```
cd /
```

Issuing the following command takes you to that directory—again regardless of where you may be at the time the command is issued:

```
cd /usr/bin
```

As a shortcut, the current directory can be referred to by a single period(.) and its parent by two periods(..). Thus, if you are in the /usr/bin subdirectory and want to move back one level to the usr directory, issue this command:

```
cd /usr
```

Or use the following:

```
cd ..
```

The first command moves back to the root level and then goes forward to usr, whereas the second just moves back one level from the current location. Likewise, from /usr/bin, you could move to root by specifying:

```
cd /
```

o r

```
cd ../..
```

The first command moves directly to root, whereas the second moves back one level, and then back another.

From the /usr/bin subdirectory, you can move to /usr/lib with the following command:

```
cd /usr/lib
```

Or this command:

```
cd ../lib
```

As you use the UNIX operating system and begin to use subdirectories farther from the root, the second alternative makes more sense and becomes easier to work with. Chapter 6, "Creating and Manipulating Files and Directories," addresses the topics of absolute and relative path names in greater detail and shows examples that bring this point home.

The True File System

File systems are groups of files that exist within a partition—either physical or logical—on a disk. Every file system has an initial sector on the disk where all files logically map to. This is known as the *superblock*.

The superblock—only one exists per file system—contains information about the file system and the physical data comprising it. In the PC world of DOS, the superblock is known as the *File Allocation Table*. Both serve the same purpose of mapping file locations to physical addresses.

The superblock, which is block 0 of the UNIX file system, is broken into smaller components, or individual entries for the file system, known as *inodes*. The physical location of the inode list directly follows that of the superblock. For every entry that shows up in a directory listing, there is a corresponding inode providing the information displayed for it. Inodes, or *index nodes*, each consist of between 64 and 200 bytes (depending upon the vendor), and are the focus of all file/directory activity in UNIX, functioning as pointers to the physical data.

Inodes can be thought of as address books giving information about the files. Just as one house can have two people living in it (two references in your address book for the same physical street address), one file can be referenced by several names (links). Two linked files will share the same inode number; thus, when you execute a link, the original set of data is pointed to and called.

Although the exact ordering of information occasionally differs by vendor, each inode entry consists of the following information about a file or directory:

1. A unique inode number

2. The type of entry it is; this can be broken into one of seven types, and each type is assigned a two-digit value as follows:

   01—A named pipe

   02—A character device file

   04—A directory

   06—A block device file

   10—An ordinary file

   12—A symbolic link

   14—A socket

3. The permissions on the entity. Permissions are four digits. The first indicates whether a special mode is set (1=sticky bit, 2=SGID, 4=SUID), and the remaining three tell read, write, and execute permissions.

4. Actual physical size of the file

5. Number of links to the entry

6. Owner of the file (often in numeric form—the information returned by the id command)

7. The group possessing the file—again, quite often, in numeric form

8. Times for creation or change, modification, and access. This is referenced in directory listings, as well as when the find command looks for files meeting a certain criteria.

9. The actual physical address where the file resides

As mentioned, these are the components of inode entries, but the ordering may be different from how they are presented in the preceding list. To see the ordering on your system, look for the file /usr/include/sys/inode.h.

Inode Information

Directories constitute nothing more than inode entries that pair their information with files. Structuring the file system in this manner makes it incredibly easy to move entire directories in UNIX. In reality, only the name associated with the inode is changed.

When files are linked, multiple references to the same inode occur. When you delete logical files, only the references are removed and not the physical data—if other files still point to it. During the linking process, the directory listing makes it appear as if more files are being created, but the inode numbers tell differently. The link numbers associated with the files tell differently as well.

> The inode numbers must be unique for physical data. This uniqueness is traditionally carried out by incrementing the number for each new entry. It holds true then that the first data placed on the file system has the lowest inode numbers.

The amount of space allocated for the inode table is determined when you make the file system (using the mkfs utility). If too much space is allocated, you are wasting room that can be used elsewhere. If not enough space is allocated, you will fill the table. The table contains entries—one for every piece of data out there—so it matters not if the hard drive has plenty of space left on it. If there are thousands of tiny files, those thousands of entries can fill the inode table. When an inode table is full, due to insufficient space being allocated for it during the build, you can do nothing but rebuild the file system.

Working with Other Operating Systems

UNIX vendors add enhancements to their product in attempts to make them better than the competition. In so doing, however, they succeed in making them incompatible with other versions of UNIX. Shell scripts and routines written on a Sun workstation probably do not work on an SCO machine. Executable files must be compiled natively to take full benefit of the operating system and environment.

Text files, on the other hand, can be safely imported and exported from one UNIX to another with minimal problems. They also can be imported and exported between DOS and most UNIX versions.

Today, it is fairly common to find a series of DOS utilities with UNIX, enabling you to interact between the two operating systems. Although each vendor names these utilities differently, they serve similar purposes. SCO, for example, enables you to copy files to a DOS floppy with the command doscp. Sun\Solaris allows similar actions with pcfs.

SCO, which is native to the Intel environment where DOS normally lives, offers a great many DOS-to-UNIX utilities, with names that are fairly descriptive. Among these are the following:

doscat

dosdir

dosformat

dosmkdir

dosls

dosrm

dosrmdir

Bear in mind when transferring files between UNIX and DOS that DOS terminates a line of text with a carriage return and linefeed, whereas UNIX uses a linefeed only. DOS also marks the end of a file with a Ctrl Z, whereas UNIX does not. Make sure that you check the vendor's manuals for the tools provided with your system to circumvent these problems. Using SCO as an example once again, the xtod utility transfers UNIX files to DOS format by placing a carriage return at the end of each line and a Ctrl Z at the end of the file. Conversely, dtox converts them from DOS to UNIX by stripping those characters.

Summary

This chapter examined the UNIX file and directory structure and looked at several factors that affect it. The directory structure is essentially an inverted tree, and the real information is maintained within index entries known as inodes.

The following chapter rounds out the overview section by looking at the differences between products and shells. Particular attention is paid to the kernel and why it figures so prominently in the UNIX operating system.

Chapter Snapshot

The UNIX operating system is made up of three subcompo-
nents—the kernel, shells, and utilities. This chapter examines the interaction between them and includes such topics
as the following:

The kernel serves as the go-between, controlling the interaction with the hardware. The shell works as the interpreter
between the kernel and the user, whereas the utilities enable
the shell to carry out actions specified by the user.

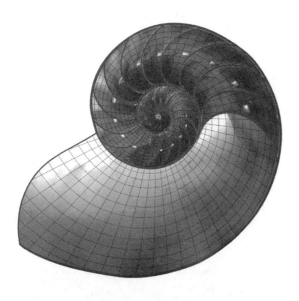

Differences between Products and Shells

The UNIX operating system is made up of several components. The kernel and shells are the most rudimentary. This chapter examines those components, as well as utilities, and introduces the differences inherent in different flavors of UNIX.

In its truest sense, the *kernel* is the UNIX operating system. It is the only file residing in the root directory, and it cannot be located anywhere else if the system is to be operable. When the system boots up, it boots this file, which stays active until the system is shut down.

The kernel interacts between the system hardware/physical devices and the system shells. The hardware understands machine language and micro programming. By giving the kernel sole responsibility for the interaction, it shields the user from the necessity of learning machine language and lets him interface more efficiently at a higher level.

When the UNIX operating system is installed on a machine, the kernel is built natively on that machine. In so doing, it takes into account all the hardware components and features, and builds a file designed to interact optimally with the machine. Any major changes to the file system (such as changing the number of allotted inodes, or other parameters) require a rebuilding of the kernel and a reboot for it to take the changes into account. Because of the complicated process involved, kernels are not rebuilt on a regular basis after installation except in lab settings.

Figure 4.1 illustrates the symbiotic relationship of the kernel to the user who is totally isolated from directly accessing it by the shell.

Figure 4.1
The kernel is isolated from the user by the shells.

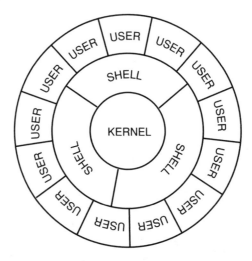

An important note that cannot be overlooked is that the kernel is the only part of the operating system that is loaded into memory at startup and remains there until shutdown. Every other process is called as needed, and stopped when not.

In addition to interacting with the hardware, the kernel is also responsible for managing memory, executing jobs, and managing the file system. In short order, the kernel does the following:

- ✔ Designates memory to programs

- ✔ Handles all input and output requests

- ✔ Partitions processing time and shares it between programs

To help the kernel monitor the system and execute jobs, it incorporates daemons. *Daemons* are kernel processes that are always active and on-alert for processes that need attention. Daemons exist for the print services, cron (automatic execution) jobs (also known as the scheduler), and others.

The kernel is written in the C language, which gives it an added benefit of portability because C code can be quickly re-engineered. This inherent portability has been one of the contributors to the acceptance of UNIX throughout the years.

Shells

Shells are command interpreters interacting between users and all aspects of the operating system, including the kernel. They accept input from the user in high-level language and determine what should be done with it. They are responsible for command substitution, wildcard expansion, and a whole host of responsibilities that are outlined in the next section of this book.

Sometimes the request can be answered quickly by the shell without the need to summon any further processing. Figure 4.2 shows a simple request made by a user to see the current process identification number. The shell needs to summon no other process for this and returns the number.

Figure 4.2
The shell answers a user request without calling any other processes.

If the request made by the user is more involved than the simple one illustrated in figure 4.2, then the shell must decide what is to be done with the request. It can either send the requests to be handled by other shells, or by the kernel. Figure 4.3 shows an example where a user asks for a listing of the files in the current drive. The shell recognizes this as a call to an executable utility and it spawns a child shell to execute the command. The child shell is born, runs the command, returns the answer to the parent shell, and goes away. The parent shell gives the user the answer to his or her request.

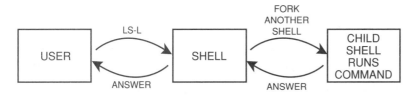

Figure 4.3
The shell summons a child shell to execute the request when it cannot be done internally.

If the user is running an application, for example a word processor or spreadsheet, the user is still running a shell and the shell is running the application. An extra process is added between the two shells for the application.

If the request requires interaction of a hardware component, then the shell must involve the kernel. Like an efficient secretary, the shell first tries everything it can to avoid having to get the boss (the kernel) involved. Only when things escalate to the point where the shell does not have the authority to act is the kernel brought in. Figure 4.4 shows a request to read a tape archive in. The user makes the request of the shell, and the shell, in turn, makes the request of the kernel. The kernel returns information to the shell and the shell, in turn, returns it to the user.

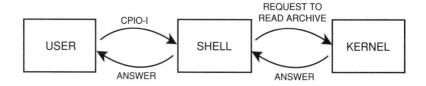

Figure 4.4
The shell must summon the kernel when hardware requests are made.

Shells must isolate the kernel from the user because UNIX is a multiple-user operating system (even if you are the only one on the system at the moment) and the kernel must devote its processing time as efficiently as possible.

These three examples, while very simplified, illustrate the interaction between user, shell, and kernel.

As defined, the purpose of the shell is to isolate the kernel from the user(s) and serve as an interpreter between the two. Several shells are in existence, and although all serve this purpose, each has features designed to make it more likable to the user than the other.

When UNIX was first created, the first interpreter to accompany it was the Bourne shell. The Bourne shell, abbreviated as sh, is the oldest one in existence and works as well today as it did years ago. Unfortunately, it has not been updated since then and lacks several features that make computing easier. Every version of UNIX currently marketed contains the Bourne shell, and it is the default shell for the root user and all processes that the system automatically executes in the background.

The second shell was the C shell, created at the University of Berkeley and based upon the C language. It incorporates such features as job control, command-line editing, and history. Unfortunately, it was developed independently and is not overly compatible with Bourne.

The Korn shell was developed to take the best of C shells features and mix them with Bourne compatibility.

Most UNIX versions today contain more than one shell and give the user the choice of which one they want to use. All of these shells are discussed in greater detail in later chapters of this book. Differences between the way a command executes as the result of a shell are also highlighted throughout the book.

The third part of the equation is the utilities. Utilities are commands which can be issued to UNIX that the shell does not internally understand. They are the executable files contained within the /bin and /usr/bin directories discussed in the preceding chapter.

System administrators and consultants purchase operating systems because of the computing potential they offer. They buy them for the utilities that come with the package and the internal structure on which the operating system runs. Users, department managers, and most other people are not particularly interested in the operating system. Their main concern is that when they want to do quick calculations, they can bring up a spreadsheet, get the figures they need, and move on to the next operation.

Current versions of UNIX come with approximately 300 utilities and commands built in. More important to the majority of users, however, is the wide number of applications available that will run on UNIX—everything from multiuser games to complex engineering programs.

UNIX is presently enjoying great popularity with graphic artists who are finding its abilities unparalleled. Complex renderings require a great number of resources as they formulate and gather the finished image to present to the screen. With UNIX's ability to multithread the requests, processing time can be exponentially reduced.

For the developer, the UNIX operating system offers a number of development tool kits that can be used to create custom applications and simplify life.

The kernel is a compiled executable file built natively on the machine to make it work optimally with the hardware present. There are three different shells that are standard with UNIX, and the one used is selected by the user.

The difference between vendor products usually amounts to a difference in the utilities that are included with the product. Which version of UNIX the vendor is basing its product upon (SVR4.2, BSD4.3, etc.) governs what standard utilities will be included. Beyond those standard utilities, vendors are free to add any enhancements and features that they feel will make their product better than the others on the market. For some, this is networking support, additional security features, or graphical interfaces. Chapters 28 and 29 explore, in detail, the differences between UNIX variants.

The heart of the UNIX operating system is the kernel. It controls all the hardware and manages memory, files, and security. All of these actions are cloaked from the user by means of the shell. The shell interprets high-level user commands into language understood by the kernel, and attempts to do as much as possible without involving the kernel. Utilities add commands that users can execute, but rely on shells and the kernel to fulfill their functions.

Part II

The Command Line

Chapter Snapshot

The shell is the command interpreter that accepts requests from users and passes them through to the UNIX operating system (the kernel). Understanding how to interact with the shell is essential in knowing how to use the operating system. This chapter discusses the basics of the shell, including the following:

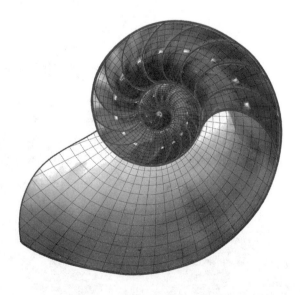

CHAPTER

Shell Basics

U NIX is one of the most fascinating operating systems in use today. One reason for the success of UNIX is the compartmentalized construction of the kernel and the tools. Of the tools that comprise UNIX, probably the most well-known is the *shell*. The *kernel* is the heart of UNIX. It provides process, memory, and hardware management functions, as well as ensuring that each user has fair access to the system resources.

The shell provides a number of components to the user (see fig. 5.1). The two major parts are the command interpreter and the command programming language. Why have a shell? Consider a real-life example. An oyster uses its shell to protect itself from outside predators. The UNIX shell wraps around the kernel and, to some degree, protects the kernel from its own predators—users. The user can be considered a predator because the kernel is the part of UNIX that handles the majority of the work that a user requests to have done. As such, an improperly written program can cause problems for other users on the system and, in drastic cases, for the kernel itself.

Figure 5.1
The shell
components.

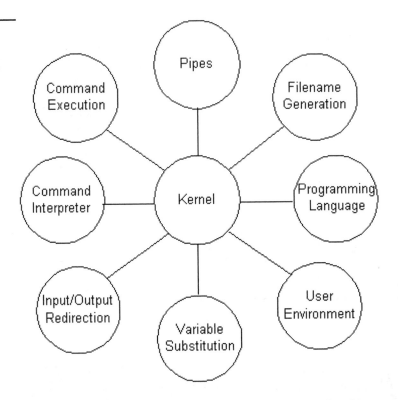

Figure 5.1 illustrates the services that the shell provides to the user and to the programs the user writes or executes. The shell, through its command interpreter component, prompts the user to enter a command, processes the instruction, and executes the appropriate command either from its internal language or from a command resident on the computer system's hard disk subsystem. The shell has a broad range of responsibilities, including program execution, variable and filename substitution, pipes, input/output redirection, user environment, and an interpreted programming language. All these topics are addressed in more detail later in this chapter.

Previewing the Services

To fully appreciate the services that are offered by the shell, it is important to look at each one of them separately.

Command Interpretation and Execution

Most people think of the shell for program execution. The shell is responsible for executing all the commands the user requests. It must determine if the command is built in to the shell, or it must locate it in the file system and start it. The shell assumes that each line you enter follows the same basic format:

```
program-name options arguments
```

This interface to the shell is typically known as the *command line* and is the most common way to interact with the shell. After typing the command, press the Enter key to instruct the shell to process and execute the command. The program name is the name of the command you want to run. Following are a few common ones:

```
ls

date

who

vi

cal

sh

ksh

csh
```

II

The Command Line

The simplest command is one word. The *options* are special *switches* or *flags* that change how the command works. An option is a character which is preceded by a hyphen. Many UNIX commands have a multitude of options, each of which change the way the command works. It has been said that the more options a command has, the less the programmer knows what he wants the command to do!

The options for any given command cannot be guessed, as there are no standards for options. One way to find out the options that are available is to use a character that is not likely used as an option. For example:

```
$ ls -?
usage: ls [-1CFRabcdfgilmqrstux] [files]
$
```

When a command encounters an unknown option, it terminates and prints a usage message. This usage message provides the proper syntax for the command as well as any options which are availble.

Other methods for determining the available options include consulting the online manual pages or the hardcopy manuals that were distributed with your UNIX system. The following is the ls command for my directory:

```
$ ls
cat          cdfs_mount   chmod        clri         cp
cc           chgrp        chpt         cmp          csh
```

But if the -l option is used on the ls command, then output is different and looks like the following:

```
$ ls -l
-rwxr-xr-x  1 root       28672 Mar 19  1991 cat
lrwxr-xr-x  1 root          13 Mar 20  1992 cc -> ../usr/bin/cc
-rwxr-xr-x  1 root       28672 Mar 19  1991 cdfs_mount
lrwxr-xr-x  1 root          16 Mar 20  1992 chgrp -> ../usr/bin/chgrp
-rwxr-xr-x  1 root       28672 Mar 19  1991 chmod
-rwxr-xr-x  1 root       32768 Mar 19  1991 chpt
-rwxr-xr-x  1 root       24576 Mar 19  1991 clri
lrwxr-xr-x  1 root          14 Mar 20  1992 cmp -> ../usr/bin/cmp
-rwxr-xr-x  1 root       28672 Mar 19  1991 cp
lrwxr-xr-x  1 root          14 Mar 20  1992 csh -> ../usr/bin/csh
```

Don't worry about what this output means yet—it is discussed in Chapter 6, "Creating and Manipulating Files and Directories." But notice that the use of the option changes the look of the output. Not all options change the way output looks. Some affect input; some affect how the program being executed processes the information given to it.

Finally, there are the arguments. The *argument* is information that you want the program to process. Following is the cal program, which prints the calendar for a given month and year. By default, cal prints the current month in the current year, as in the following example:

```
$ cal
    June 1994
 S  M Tu  W Th  F  S
           1  2  3  4
 5  6  7  8  9 10 11
12 13 14 15 16 17 18
19 20 21 22 23 24 25
26 27 28 29 30
```

But cal accepts arguments in the form of the month and year. The year must include the prefix (that is, 19), or the calendar will be wrong. The year 94 is not the same as 1994. The version of cal on the Digital Equipment Corporation DECStation 3100 accepts the month in numerical form, followed by the year, as in the following example:

```
$ cal 12 1994
   December 1994
 S  M Tu  W Th  F  S
              1  2  3
 4  5  6  7  8  9 10
11 12 13 14 15 16 17
18 19 20 21 22 23 24
25 26 27 28 29 30 31
```

Failing to include a month, as in the following example, prints the entire year:

```
$ cal 1994
```

It is important to note that the commands on your system all follow the same basic format. They may not include options or accept arguments, but they are all started the same way using the shell.

Variable Substitution

Variable and *filename substitution* enable the user to assign values to variables, which can later be referenced in shell scripts, by programs, or just by you. Filename substitution enables the user to present a partial file-name list to the interpreter, which then determines what files match the characteristics provided by the wild cards. The wild cards are the *, ?, and [], and are covered in more detail later.

Pipes

Pipes are a feature of the shell that allow the output of one command to be directly provided as input to another command. You can create very complex commands using pipes. They are a good feature to master because they eliminate the need for temporary files, which are then used by another command and later removed. The pipe character is the |, and on older systems the ^ (caret), although many newer systems understand both. When then shell interprets a command line such as who ¦ wc -1, the shell sees the pipe, connects the output of who to wc -1, then executes the commands. Only commands capable of reading from the standard input can be used at the end of a pipeline. (Standard input, standard output, and standard error are discussed in the next section.)

Input/Output Redirection

Input/output redirection enables the user to change where the output of a command goes and from where the input of a command comes. Input/output redirection relies upon the concepts of standard output and input as described later. This feature uses the metacharacters >, <, >>, and <<. Typically, the shell prints output and errors on the terminal and gets its input from the keyboard. This can be changed through the use of I/O redirection.

User Environment

The shell also provides environment variables that control not only the operation of the shell, but also of programs the user is executing. Your environment consists of your home directory, your login shell, and a list of directories to be searched whenever you ask the shell to execute a program for you.

Programming

Finally, the shell contains a programming language. This powerful, interpreted language is built into the shell and uses all the commands that you can type at the command line, although interactive commands, which are started from the shell script, are more difficult to utilize.

Three prominent shells are provided on most UNIX systems: the Bourne shell, the C shell, and the Korn shell. For the most part, they all provide the same components—a command interpreter and a command programming language. However, some differences exist in how they are implemented and how you, as the user, interact with them.

Filename Generation

The shell also provides a set of special characters called wild cards, which are used to permit a user to address more than one file at a time. Using these wild cards makes using UNIX more friendly because a command to copy ten files can be accomplished with just one command.

Interacting with the Shell

As mentioned in Chapter 2, before a user can interact with the shell, you must have a session with your UNIX host, which typically involves connecting to your system and logging in. A login session is established by entering your user name and password at a system prompt. The system then proceeds through a login procedure and starts the shell that the system administrator configured for you. Figure 5.2 shows several different methods of establishing a connection and a login session on a UNIX host.

Figure 5.2
Connecting
to UNIX.

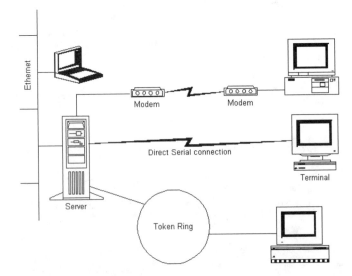

As illustrated in figure 5.2, an interactive login session can be established to the UNIX server through a wide variety of methods and from an equally wide variety of clients. Figure 5.2 illustrates connections through a modem, direct connection from a terminal, and network connections through Token Ring and Ethernet. The exact method used to connect to your UNIX system depends upon the type of communications interface used to make the connection.

As shown in figure 5.3, you see a login prompt after you are connected. In response to this prompt, enter the user name that the system administrator provided you. Typically, you also are prompted to enter your password. A *password* is a series of characters stored in a coded form on the computer. The combination of your login name and password identifies you to the system and restricts access to the server to authorized people only.

```
login: chare
Password:
```

Figure 5.3
Logging in.

Remember to keep your password a secret. It is the only thing that prevents another person from accessing the system with your user name. Chapter 27, "Security," discusses passwords and other system security issues in more detail.

Issuing Commands

Issuing commands to the shell is as simple as typing a command and pressing Enter; each command is terminated by the Enter key, which signals that the shell should process the instructions the user has typed and execute them. Although Enter is most commonly used, the semicolon can be used as a command terminator, too. The difference is that you can group more than one command on the command line when using a semicolon. The following example uses the semicolon:

```
who; date; ls
```

This executes the who command, followed by the date command, and then the ls command. Each command is executed as it appears on the command line and is equivalent to typing the command on separate lines.

The command notation used consists of a series of words or characters separated by whitespace. *Whitespace* is a non-alphabetic or non-numeric character. For example, a space, tab, and newline (the character generated by the Enter key) are all whitespace. Table 5.1 lists what each of these whitespace characters is used for.

Table 5.1
Whitespace

Character	Use
Space	Separates commands, options, and arguments
Tab	Separates commands, options, and arguments
Newline	Terminates a command

Prompts

The shell informs the user that it is ready to accept input through a prompt. The prompt on the Bourne shell is traditionally a dollar sign ($); for the C shell a percent sign (%); and the Korn shell a number followed by a dollar sign (4$), or just a dollar sign ($). In fact, each shell has several different prompts that inform you of different shell conditions, as illustrated in table 5.2. However, the prompts illustrated are the defaults and can be configured by the user and the system administrator, so what you see on your system might be very different.

Table 5.2
Shell Prompts

Prompt Name	Bourne Shell	C Shell	Korn Shell
PS1 (default)	$	not used	!$ or $
PS2	>	not used	>
PS3	not used	not used	#?
prompt	not used	%	not used

The names PS1, PS2, PS3, and prompt are the names of the shell variables which the respective shells use to identify each prompt. Using these variable names, the shell prompt can be changed. This is explored in Chapter 20, "Creating Basic Shell Scripts."

The PS1 prompt used in the Bourne and Korn shells is the standard prompt that the user sees. The standard prompt for the C shell is quite different; its name is prompt, and it is a percent sign. The PS2 prompt is used in the Bourne and Korn shells to indicate that the shell is expecting more input. For example, if you enter a command and press Enter before the shell thinks all the arguments are input, it presents this prompt. The PS3 prompt in the Korn shell prompts the user to enter a choice based upon the information provided in another Korn Shell command.

Here is an example of the PS1 and PS2 prompts in action.

In figure 5.4, the user struck the apostrophe key as he pressed Enter. This caused the shell to print the second prompt ">" because it was looking for the second apostrophe to complete the command. When mistakes such as this are made, it is useful to know the additional control or command keys that the shell uses (see table 5.3).

Figure 5.4

Typos can seriously affect your output.

Table 5.3
Special Keys

Special Key	Name	Explanation
Ctrl+D	End of File	Logs out or ends input operation
Ctrl+H	Backspace	Erases the previous key typed or Backspace
Ctrl+\	Quit	Interrupts the current command
Ctrl+C	Interrupt	Interrupts the current command or DEL
Ctrl+S	XOFF	Pauses output on the display
Ctrl+Q	XON	Restarts output on the display

You can find out what special keys are used on your system with the stty command, which is used to query and configure the system about the configuration of your connection session. The stty output looks like the following:

```
$ stty -a
line = NTTYDISC; speed 38400 baud
erase = ^h; kill = ^u; min = 6; time = 1; intr = ^c; quit = ^¦; eof =
^d;
eol <undef>; start = ^q; stop = ^s;
parenb -parodd cs7 -cstopb -hupcl cread -clocal -loblk
-ignbrk brkint -ignpar -parmrk -inpck istrip -inlcr -igncr icrnl -iuclc
ixon ixany -ixoff
isig icanon -xcase echo -echoe -echok -echonl -noflsh
opost -olcuc onlcr -ocrnl -onocr -onlret -ofill -ofdel tab3
```

You only need to notice a few things in this output. The -a option to stty instructs the command to print the information regarding your connection. The information that you are looking for is erase, intr, and quit. From this output, erase is Ctrl+H (^h), intr is

Ctrl+C (^c), and quit is Ctrl+l (^l). This information is important because the ability to stop an apparently hung command is useful. However, at this point, you could simply ask your system administrator which keys your system uses. Typically, SCO UNIX and AT&T/USL UNIX systems use the Del key to interrupt commands, whereas SUN and other BSD versions of UNIX use Ctrl+C.

Handling Mistakes

The shell also informs you when you make mistakes. If the command you enter is not available or doesn't exist, the shell informs you with a message like the one shown in figure 5.5.

Figure 5.5
Handling
mistakes.

```
$ daet
daet: not found
```

This message tells you that the shell cannot find the command you have asked it to execute. Sometimes this happens because you mistyped the command name, like in the example; other times it might occur because the command isn't installed on your system or because the shell hasn't been configured to look in the proper directories for the command. When you make a mistake typing a command, press the Backspace key to move the cursor back over your mistake so that you can correct it.

It is important to remember that the shell does not know how to interpret the control codes sent by the arrow keys on your keyboard. Consequently, these should not be used to correct mistakes.

Shell Features

The shell has a number of features that can be used on a regular basis without the need for the programming language. However, many users of the shell soon learn that the shell command language is an easy way to automate repetitive tasks. The command language is quite powerful. It includes variables and flow control, which are discussed later in the book.

The shell, depending upon which one you are using, might provide for wild cards, background job execution, job control, and more. These features are discussed in more detail in Chapters 18 and 19. However, it is essential that you develop a firm understanding of the shell's capabilities.

Wild Cards

Wild cards can be used to perform filename substitution. The wild cards used in filename substitution are the asterisk (*), the question mark (?), and the character class ([..]). Wild cards can be used anywhere in the file name and can be combined to produce some complex patterns. By using the wild card with some form of text, you "anchor" the pattern, meaning that the pattern match is restricted to those that meet the entire pattern. More examples of this are illustrated through this discussion.

The asterisk matches any character zero or more times. For example, if you enter the command ls -l *, then the shell will substitute all of the files for the asterisk.

```
$ ls -l *
-rw-------  1 chare    users       390 Aug 31 20:15 aba
-rw-------  1 chare    users       390 Aug 31 20:14 abc
-rw-------  1 chare    users       108 Aug 31 20:15 bab
-rw-------  1 chare    users       418 Aug 31 20:15 debbie
$
```

But the asterisk can be used in many other ways. What if the command ls -l a* were used on these files? This will list the files aba and aba only, as shown here.

```
$ ls -l a*
-rw-------  1 chare    users       390 Aug 31 20:15 aba
-rw-------  1 chare    users       390 Aug 31 20:14 abc
$
```

From this example, you can see that you could also look for file names using the asterisk first, then some text, or by enclosing the asterisk between some text. Following are illustrations of these two cases:

```
$ ls -l *b
-rw-------  1 chare    users       108 Aug 31 20:15 bab
$ ls -l *i*
-rw-------  1 chare    users       418 Aug 31 20:15 debbie
$
```

Table 5.4 provides some further examples and explanations for the different types of wild cards.

Table 5.4
Wild Card Examples

Example	Description
Asterisk Wild Card Examples	
a*	Matches all files starting with or followed by zero or more letters
*.doc	Matches any file names that end in .doc
text.*	Matches any file names that start with text
t*.doc	Matches any file names that start with t and end with .doc
Question Mark Wild Card Examples	
a?	Matches any file with two letters, the first one being an a
?.doc	Matches any file that has one letter followed by .doc
???	Matches any three-character file name
Combination Wild Cards	
a??.*	Matches any file that starts with "a", is followed by two letters, a period, and any other characters
*.??	Matches any text followed by a period and two more letters

The question mark matches one character only. Just as the * matches zero or more letters, there must be one character when the question mark is used. The command 'ls -l ?' lists only those files that have one character. The command ls -l ?? lists only those files that have two characters in their name. And the asterisk and the question mark characters can be combined to match very specific patterns, as shown under the *Combination Wild Cards* subheading.

The character class lists files that contain letters from a group of characters. The important thing to remember about the character class is that it matches one character of the group. The character class is used by listing the specific characters between left and right brackets ([]) as in [abf]. The character class is typically used with either the ? or * wild cards, unless you are working with short file names, because—like the ? wild card—the character can be combined to indicate more than one position to be matched. Table 5.5 illustrates the use of the character class, along with more wild cards.

Table 5.5
Character and More Wild Card Examples

Command	Description
Character Class Examples	
[abc]??	Matches any three-letter file name that starts with the letter a, b, or c
[Abc]*	Matches any file name starting with the letter A, b, or c
[abc][xyz]*	Matches any file name that starts with a, b, c, has a second letter of x, y, or z, and is followed by other letters
[abc]	Matches any single character file name which is a, b, c, or d.
[abc][ghi]	Matches any two character file name. For example, ag, ah, ai, bg, bh, or bi.
More Wild Card Examples	
ls *[!o]	Matches any file that doesn't end with an 'o'
ls *[\!o]	Matches any file that does not end with an 'o' (C shell example)
cat chap.[0-7]	Matches any file named chap. that ends with 0-7
ls [aft]*	Matches any file starting with either the letter a, f, or t
ls t??	Matches any three-letter file starting with t

Character classes can be much more complicated than this. What if you have a range of characters to include in the class, but don't want to type them all? How about if you have multiple ranges to include? These can be accomplished by combining all the letters in the []. To specify a range of characters, use the hyphen to separate the first and the last characters in the range. For example, to specify a range of a to t, use [a-t]. To list files that include a to f and j to p, use [a-fj-p]. The example [a-zA-Z0-9] matches any alphabetic and numeric character; it doesn't include punctuation. It is also possible to exclude characters from the match. For example, [!o] means match any character but the letter o. In this case, the ! negates the search. If you are a C shell user, then the exclamation mark (!) is special to the C shell. To use the exclamation mark to negate the character class, a backslash must be inserted prior to the exclamation mark, as shown in the following:

```
[\!o]
```

The backslash removes the special meaning of the exclamation point to the C shell. The backslash and the ! characters are discussed again in Chapter 18.

Character classes have other uses beside file name generation; they are discussed in Chapter 8.

Quotes

The shell also understands the different quotes that are available and that serve different purposes. The quotation mark characters are as follows:

    'text'   protects the contents

    "text"   expands the contents

    `text`   executes as a command

The single quotes (') instruct the shell to protect and not interpret the text between them. These quotes are typically only used in shell programs, which are called *shell scripts*.

The double quotes (") are used to group words together to form an argument to a command, or to form a sentence. By grouping them together, the shell does not interpret them as individual words, but rather as a group. These quotes are generally used in shell scripts, but also can be used by the ordinary user. This type of quote allows the shell to see the contents, and if a shell variable or wild card is present, interpret and expand it.

The easiest way to explain these two sets of quotes is with an example. The command tp is a shell program that lists the number of arguments and what they are. Consider the following example:

```
$ tp this is a test
Number of arguments = 4
argument = this
argument = is
argument = a
argument = test
```

No quotes are around the text provided to the tp command as an argument. As a result, tp saw four arguments. Consider the next example:

```
$ tp "this is a test"
Number of arguments = 1
argument = this is a test
```

Notice that in this example, the argument, this is a test, is enclosed in " ". This instructs the shell to group the words together and treat them as one argument. In this case, the double quotes and single quotes are equivalent. They differ in how they allow the shell to expand a shell variable. Like any programming language, the shell has variables that can be used in shell programs and are used to control the execution of other programs and the user's environment. This second form of variable is called an *environment variable*. Local and environment variables are covered in more detail in Chapters 18 and 20.

Consider the following example in which a variable named TERM is defined. To see the contents of a shell variable, reference the variable using its name preceded by a dollar sign.

```
$ tp "$TERM"
Number of arguments = 1
argument = ansi
```

In this example, the shell expands the variable $TERM and gives the value of the variable to the program tp. The next example illustrates how the single quote is different from the double. As mentioned, the single quote prevents the shell from being able to see inside the quotes—that is, the shell cannot interpret or expand anything between the quotes.

```
$ sh tp '$TERM'
Number of arguments = 1
argument = $TERM
```

In the preceding example, the shell cannot see that the $TERM in the quotes is supposed to be a variable, so it prints the literal $TERM instead. As you will see in Chapters 18 and 20, there are many different uses for these quotes, but those used in 18 and 20 are only the first two.

The final form of quote is the slanted single quote (`), often called a *backtick*. (The backtick is typically found on the same key as the tilde (~), which is above the Tab key on a PC-style keyboard.) These are used for command substitution. They enable the user either to execute a command and save the output in a shell variable or to execute a command and provide its output to another command. Consider the following example using the tp program:

```
$ tp `ls /bin/c*`
Number of arguments = 10
argument = /bin/cat
argument = /bin/cc
argument = /bin/chgrp
argument = /bin/chmod
argument = /bin/cmp
argument = /bin/cp
argument = /bin/csh
```

This example uses the command ls to list the files in the /bin directory that start with the letter c. The shell sees the command substitution quotes, executes the command, then puts the information returned on the command line for the shell. Only non-interactive commands can be executed in this fashion.

The backtick quotes also are used to put the output of a command in a shell variable. This is useful because information that might be needed again in a shell program can be easily accessed. Even at the command line this can be useful. For example, if you have a long directory path, you can store your current directory in a variable and change to that directory again without typing the path. As illustrated in Chapter 3, moving around the UNIX file system through directories is accomplished with the command cd. To save your current working directory in a variable called PWD, type the following command:

```
$ PWD=`pwd`
```

This causes the shell to execute the command pwd and puts the output of the command into the variable PWD. To print the contents of the shell variable PWD, use the command echo, as in the following example:

```
$ echo $PWD
```

Consider the following example. Start by executing the pwd command, which tells you that your current working directory is /usr/include/X11/extensions. Execute the command listed in the preceding example. When you print the contents of the variable, you see that it contains the current directory name.

```
$ pwd
/usr/include/X11/extensions
$ PWD=`pwd`
$ echo $PWD
/usr/include/X11/extensions
$ cd /tmp
$ echo $PWD
/usr/include/X11/extensions
$ cd $PWD
$ pwd
/usr/include/X11/extensions
```

Now change your current directory cd /tmp and again check the value of the PWD variable to find whether it is still the same. From the /tmp directory, execute the cd command with the variable PWD as its argument. The $ preceding the PWD instructs the shell to replace the variable with the value of the variable. Then when you check your current working directory, it is the value of the PWD variable, as you set it in the beginning.

Variables and the Environment

You have now had a brief introduction to shell variables, having looked at the PWD variable in the preceding example. Shell variables are a storage place for information, just like variables in any programming language. Just like other features of UNIX, variable names are case-sensitive. They can be any length, can be upper- or lowercase, and can contain numbers and some special characters; variable names cannot start with a number, nor can they contain the characters special to the shell—the asterisk, dollar sign, question mark, and brackets. The following are all valid variable names:

```
TERM

PATH

path

Visual_id

testDir
```

Access to the value stored in the variable is gained by prefixing a dollar sign to the name of the variable. Variables are assigned values by using a formula, as follows:

```
variable-name=value
```

No spaces should be around the equal sign, as illustrated. Including spaces causes the shell to misinterpret the command and report an error.

There are two types of variables called *local* and *environment*. To understand what local and environment variables are, first look at how the shell handles this information when starting a program. When the shell starts a new program, the user environment variables are copied to the environment for that program. The local variables are not copied to the new program so the information in those variables is not seen by the new program.

The only difference between local and environment variables is that environment variables can be seen by programs that you execute, whereas local variables cannot. This is accomplished because the status of a variable is adjusted by exporting the variable to the environment, much like a company or country exports products to other places in the world. To export a variable, the command export, followed by the name of the variable to be exported, is executed, as in the following example:

```
$ export PWD
```

Examining Existing Variables

To see the environment variables configured on your system, use the env or printenv command:

```
$ env
PATH=:/usr/ucb:/bin:/usr/bin
LOGNAME=chare
SHELL=/usr/bin/ksh
HOME=/home/chare
TERM=ansi
```

The user environment on this system lists five shell variables. Your system may have more or less, depending upon what the system administrator has configured. Environment variables are typically defined in the system setup files, which are processed when a user logs in, or in the user's own startup files. The following paragraphs discuss what these variables do.

The PATH variable contains a colon-separated list of directories that the shell uses to find commands. The PATH variable in the preceding example indicates that the shell looks in the current directory, then /usr/ucb, then /bin, and finally /usr/bin. If the command you entered doesn't exist in any of these directories, then the shell reports that it cannot find the command. The PATH variable is defined in your .profile file, discussed later in this chapter.

When a user logs in to a UNIX system, the system records the user's login name and saves it in the LOGNAME variable. This variable is used by many programs to determine who is running the command. The issues surrounding user names and security are discussed in more detail in Chapter 27.

The SHELL variable defines the name of the shell that the user is currently using as his login shell and is defined when the user logs in to the system.

The HOME variable defines what the user's home directory is. This variable is often used by UNIX commands to find out where information to this user should be written. Have you ever wondered how the cd command knows to put you in your home directory when you don't give an argument? It is because the cd command looks at the value of HOME.

The last variable shown in the preceding example is the TERM variable. Many UNIX commands depend upon knowing the terminal type the user is using. The terminal type is determined when the user logs in either through a system default or through customization of the user's startup files. Some systems prompt the user to enter the terminal type they are using. Programs such as Lotus 1-2-3, vi, and more require the terminal type. Without this, the program does not display properly, function keys don't work, and the user will be frustrated.

Before moving to the next section, first look at the variable syntax for the C shell because it differs from the Bourne and Korn shells.

C Shell Variables

The C shell was developed at the University of California at Berkeley, which is where BSD UNIX was born. It is traditionally available on BSD versions of UNIX and some UNIX derivatives, such as XENIX. When compared to the Bourne shell, the C shell has a different command structure for its programming language. At this point, you are most interested in how to deal with variables.

Variables are created by using the command set, followed by the variable name and the value, as in the following example:

```
set variable=value
set a=seahshell
```

C-shell variables are accessed in the same manner as the Bourne and Korn shells, by preceding the variable name with a dollar sign ($). The C-shell variables also support arrays, covered in Chapters 20 and 23. The C shell supports a different mechanism for assigning environment variables. As illustrated here, the C shell uses the command sentenv, followed by the name of the variable and value to be assigned. This places the variable in the environment, which operates similarly to the Bourne and Korn shells.

```
% setenv TERM vt220
```

Program Execution

As mentioned earlier, the shell is responsible for loading and starting the commands you execute. The shell uses the command line to collect from you the name of the command and the options, and arguments you want to pass to the command. The shell goes through several steps to execute a program, as illustrated in figure 5.6.

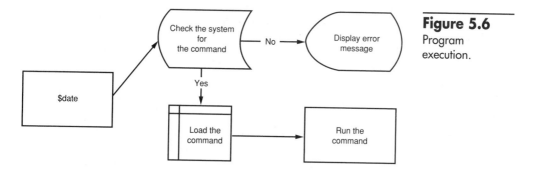

Figure 5.6
Program execution.

As illustrated in this figure, the user types the command date. The shell locates the command by looking in each directory listed in the PATH variable. If the command is not found, the shell prints an error message. If the command is located, the shell determines if the user can execute the command and, if so, loads the command into memory and requests the kernel to execute it. The end result is the output from the command, which, in this example, is the date.

This sounds like an amazing simplification, but in reality it isn't. The steps are the same, only the nitty gritty details are hidden from view.

The shell is a command, also. This means that you also can execute a shell when needed. A shell executed through the sh command is called a subshell. A subshell inherits its parent's environment, much like when a newborn baby goes home with his or her parents, the child inherits the home and loving environment from the parents. In the subshell's case, no feelings of love are involved, but all the environment variables discussed earlier are passed to the child. Variables that aren't part of the environment are local to the parent and are not seen by the child.

The subshell can manipulate these variables to suit its own needs, but these changes do not affect the parent's environment. The environments are tightly compartmentalized to prevent unwanted changes from being passed around. This mechanism is the same for any program that is executed, not simply the shell.

Program Grouping

Programs also can be grouped together to control how they are processed. Grouping is accomplished using the (...) and {...} constructs. The (...) construct causes the commands which are enclosed between the parentheses to be executed in a subshell. Therefore, when you are executing a group of commands that might alter your environment, use of the (...) construct is a prefered choice. The (...) construct starts a new version of the shell and executes the command in this new subshell. This can be useful to group a series of commands that you want processed on their own, or when you do not want to affect your current environment.

```
$ ( date; who; ls ) ¦ wc
      20      29     163
$
```

In the preceding example, the date, who, and ls commands are executed in a subshell, and the output of those commands is then processed by the command wc, which counts the lines, words, and characters in the output stream. The advantage in this situation is that the data output from all three commands is merged together and then sent to the wc command. The "¦" symbol indicates a pipe, which is presented later in this chapter.

The {...} construct instructs the shell to run the commands enclosed between the braces in your current shell. Any environmental changes that take place also affect your current shell. The following example illustrates the differences between these constructs.

```
$ var=1024                              set the value of var
$ echo $var                             print it
1024
$ (var=2048)                        in a subshell set var to 2048
$ echo $var                             print it
1024
$ (var=8192; echo $var)     in a subshell, set var to 8192 and print it
8192
$ echo $var                         print the current value of var
1024
$ { var=2048; }                 in this shell, change var to 2048
$ echo $var                             print it
2048
$
```

The semicolon in the { var=2048; } example is required because the {...} construction is considered a command, and when two commands are grouped on the same command line, they must be separated by a semicolon.

Background Jobs

Typically, commands that you execute are in the *foreground*, meaning that the program you are executing has control over your workstation. This is less of an issue now with X windows and TCP/IP than for terminal-based users. When you run an interactive command such as vi, or others, you interact with the command. This is *foreground execution*. With the exception of the Korn Shell, after the command is started, you cannot switch to another program without exiting the first. *Background execution* enables you to start a noninteractive command and send it to the background. This allows the command to continue execution and frees your login session so that you can run other noninteractive or interactive commands.

To execute a noninteractive command in the background, the command and its options and arguments are typed on the command line, followed by an ampersand (&), as in the following example:

```
$ long-running-command &
#PID
$
```

In the preceding example, long-running-command will execute until it completes, regardless of how long it takes. The #PID that is returned is the UNIX Process ID number assigned to this command. To get information regarding how this command is proceeding, you need this number. Background execution is not suitable for commands that require keyboard interaction. These commands do not execute properly in background mode. The Korn shell job control features are discussed in Chapter 19, "History, Aliases, and Job Control."

Input, Output, and Pipes

When you log on to UNIX, three files, or *data streams* are opened—standard input, standard output, and standard error. *Standard input* is typically the keyboard, or the source of data for the program. *Standard output* is typically the output device, or the output source for the program. *Standard error* is the error message stream. The standard output and error are separated so that programmers, users, and system administrators alike can all take advantage of the shell's powerful redirection facilities.

Input and Output

When you execute a command, the output of the command is written on standard output. When a command is executed, any output that the programmer wanted the user to see is written to standard output. Error messages, such as those printed when an invalid option is used, are generally written to standard error. In most cases, it will be impossible to tell one from the other because both standard output and error are generally printed on the terminal.

```
:
#
#
# @(#) termlist v1.0 - Show a list of supported terminals
# Copyright Chris Hare, 1989
#
# This script will occasionally generate some different looking results
# which is dependant upon how the termcap file is set up
#

:
#
# Get the system and release name
#
SYS=`uname -s`
REL=`uname -r`
echo "Supported Terminals for $SYS $REL "
echo "================================================="

grep '^..¦.*¦.*' /etc/termcap ¦
    sed 's/:\\//g
         s/^..¦//g
```

```
                     s/:.*://g' ¦
     sort -d ¦ awk '{ FS="¦"; printf "%-15s\t%-40s\n", $1,$NF }'
```

Any error messages are written to standard error, which appears the same as standard output because they both print on the terminal device.

The input/output redirection facilities enable you to change to where the input, output, and error streams are connected. This increases the level of flexibility in the operation of the system. For example, you can save the output of a command in a file without having to go through any difficult incantations to do so.

The syntax for redirection in the Bourne, Korn, and C shells are different in some respects in this area and are explained separately. Redirection allows the output of a command to be written in a place other than what is typical. You perform output redirection by writing the command and following it with a > and the name of a file to which the output should be written. The rule for redirection is that the output must be a file.

Following are several examples for standard output redirection. The object on the right hand side of the > sign, must be a file, as in the following syntax:

```
command  >  file
```

The following examples run the command who and save the output in a file.

```
$ who > /tmp/save
$ cat /tmp/save
chare     console Jun 25 16:36
```

Using the > file construct instructs the shell to create the file if it doesn't exist. If the file does exist, the information in the file is truncated, or lost. In many situations, this is not desirable. In fact, you might want to append information to the existing file for later comparison. If so, use >> rather than >, as in the next example:

```
$ date >> /tmp/save
$ cat /tmp/save
chare     console Jun 25 16:36
Wed Jun 29 09:53:47 EDT 1994
```

Notice that the file /tmp/save still has the information from the previously executed who command and the output from the date command. You also can redirect where the standard error messages are written. This uses a syntax similar to standard output redirection, but adds a file descriptor number, as shown in the following line:

```
command 2> file
```

Three file descriptors are associated with these data streams. Zero (0) is standard input; one (1) is standard output; and two (2) is standard error. This is why the number is present with the > in redirecting standard error. Redirecting standard error does not affect standard output. It is important to note that no space should be placed between the 2 and the >.

Abbreviations are often used to signify the three possibilities. Standard input is often abbreviated STDIN, standard output is STDOUT, and standard error is STDERR.

The following is an example of standard error redirection:

```
$ date -y 2> /tmp/save
$ more save
        date: illegal option -- y
        usage: date [-c ¦ -u] [+format] [[yy[mm[dd]]]hhmm[.ss][-
tttt][z]]
```

Standard input is generally associated with your keyboard because this is usually how people interact with UNIX. You also can redirect from where standard input comes by typing the command, followed by the < and a file, which has the input needed for the command. The following is an example:

```
command < file
```

Input redirection is used infrequently when compared with output redirection, but can be used to provide input to an interactive command. The following is an example of input redirection, with a list of words:

```
$ cat list
banana
apple
citrus
watermelon
lemon
orange
```

The sort command accepts its input and sorts the data. The following is an example of the sort command:

```
$ sort < list
apple
banana
citrus
lemon
orange
watermelon
```

In the preceding example, the command sort < list is equivalent to sort list. The sort command is discussed in Chapter 11, "Sorting and Comparing Files."

In the following example of input redirection, the command is sh, and the file you are using is called cmd, which contains a list of commands. As shown, when the command is started, all the output that normally is seen by the user is still present. It is not a good idea to redirect the input of your login shell from the keyboard because once redirected, your keyboard will no longer respond to commands.

```
$ cat cmd
date
who
ls
badcmd
$ sh < cmd
Wed Jun 29 10:46:33 EDT 1994
chare     console Jun 25 16:36
cmd                 save                stdout
list                smdb-:0.0.defaults
sh: badcmd: not found
```

In the preceding list of commands, three are valid commands, and one is not — badcmd. In the output, you see the results of the date, who, and ls commands, followed by the report that the shell couldn't find the badcmd command.

Using exec

Another method of input/output redirection is to use the exec command. The exec command redirects the data stream until told otherwise. The following example—used earlier in the chapter—performs the redirection only for this one command:

```
who > /tmp/save
```

But if you want to catch the output of a number of commands in a file, you can redirect the entire data stream. The following example redirects the standard output stream to the file /tmp/stdout:

```
$ exec > /tmp/stdout
$ date
$ who
$ ls
$ exec > /dev/tty
$ pwd
/tmp
```

In this example, the standard output is to be saved in the file /tmp/stdout. The shell still displays the prompt because it is displayed on standard error. The execution of the who, date, and ls command looks like no output is generated. Then you restore the standard output to the terminal by using a terminal device known as /dev/tty, which is a special name connected to the connection port you are using.

C Shell Differences

In the C shell, input and output redirection is slightly different, but the mechanisms work similarly. The C shell does not allow the use of numbers to differentiate between the redirection of standard output and standard error. Rather, an ampersand (&) is appended to the redirection symbol. This has the effect of redirecting both standard output and standard error to the same place. The following example redirects standard output and standard error in the C shell.

```
% who -Z >& /tmp/save
```

The C shell has an additional option that controls output redirection. This option is called *noclobber* and is discussed further in Chapter 18.

Pipes

A *pipe* (¦) is a mechanism that connects the output of the command to the input of another, much like a drain connects your sink to the sewer, and most UNIX systems still understand the old pipe symbol—the caret (^). The connection is between the standard output of one command and the standard input of another is illustrated in figure 5.7. By using pipes, you can build very powerful commands without having to learn a high-level programming language such as C. Commands must meet the following requirements to be used in a pipe:

✔ The command must write to standard output.

✔ The other command in the pipe must read from standard input.

Figure 5.7
Pipe connections.

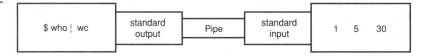

As you will recall, input and output redirection use files and any of the following formats:

```
command > file
command >> file
command 2> file
command < file
```

Pipes have a command on each side of the ¦ symbol, as in the following example:

```
command ¦ command
```

This is called a *pipeline*. Pipelines can be long and involved, or consist of only one or two commands. They are a convenient way for programmers and administrators to build shell programs without using intermediate files. The following program is an example of a complicated pipeline that uses the facilities of a number of common UNIX commands, which are discussed throughout this book. It is, however, a good example of a one-line program. Even though it is spread across multiple lines here, it is one large pipeline.

```
:
#
# Get the system and release name
#
SYS=`uname -s`
REL=`uname -r`
echo "Supported Terminals for $SYS $REL "
echo "==========================================================="

grep '^..¦.*¦.*' /etc/termcap ¦
    sed 's/:\\//g
          s/^..¦//g
              s/:.*://g' ¦
sort -d ¦ awk '{ FS="\"; printf "%-15s\t%-40s\n", $1,$NF }'
```

Pipelines do not need to be this complicated. You already saw them in some earlier examples. To illustrate standard input, output, and error and their interaction with pipes, look at the following small shell program. The first program in this example is called ax1 and is as follows:

```
$ cat ax1
# ax1 shell program

echo "This is being sent to standard output."
exit 0
```

ax1 simply prints the message This is being sent to standard output on the screen. If you were to run this at the command line, you would see the following:

```
 $ ax1
This is being sent to standard output.
$
```

So, in fact, it does write to standard output. The second command is called ax2 and is as follows:

```
$ cat ax2
# ax2 shell program

while read LINE
do
    echo "this came from standard input"
    echo "-> $LINE"
done
```

ax2 is a little more complicated. It reads standard input and prints each line that is read on the standard output device. If you run ax2 from the command line, the following happens:

```
$ ax2
this is a test
this came from standard input
-> this is a test
line 2
this came from standard input
-> line 2
this is for a sample pipeline
this came from standard input
-> this is for a sample pipeline
$
```

Because the ax2 command is reading from standard input, you must tell it when there is no more input to process. This is done using the special UNIX character, Ctrl+D, which is an End Of File marker that indicates that no more information is coming for commands that read from the standard input. Notice also that the standard error stream is not sent through the pipe with standard output. This allows the standard error stream to notify you of any errors that occur and allows any processing to happen without suffering ill effects caused by the error message.

For example, suppose that you are sorting a list of numbers, and one of the commands in your pipeline generates an error message. If the error message were sent through the pipe, your list of numbers would be corrupted by the text, and you would have to correct the problem and start over. By not sending the error message through standard output, you can see the message and decide if you need to start over. Perhaps the message is only informational and not an actual error.

Pipes are used in everyday situations. To find out how many files are in a directory, use the command ls ¦ wc -1. If you want to view all the files in a directory, but the list is too long, use ls -1 ¦ more. You can use pipes to do almost anything that involves a couple of commands.

Programming Language

The following list illustrates the sample tp program discussed earlier in the chapter. This is a very simple shell script. As you recall, it accepts an argument and then prints the number of arguments, as well as each of the separate arguments on the command line. This simple example demonstrates the structure to the shell programming language and includes both built-in and external commands.

```
$ cat tp
echo "Number of arguments = $#"
loop=1
num=$#
while [ $loop -le $num ]
do
    echo "argument = $1"
    shift
    loop=`expr $loop + 1`
done
$
```

The preceding listing also shows some control structures included in the shell language, such as while, for and do loops, if statements, and more. Chapters 20 and 23 cover programming in the shell in more detail. The versatility of the shell is illustrated by looking at some of the commands on your system. Most people think that the programs are all compiled C programs, but in fact, much of the UNIX operating system is shell scripts. Table 5.4 contains a list of shell programs in the /usr/bin directory of a DECStation running Ultrix 4.2.

Table 5.4
Sample Shell Scripts

Command	Shell Program Type
/usr/bin/basename:	/bin/sh script
/usr/bin/calendar:	/bin/sh script
/usr/bin/cflow:	shell commands
/usr/bin/ctc:	/bin/sh script
/usr/bin/ctcr:	/bin/sh script
/usr/bin/cunbatch:	/bin/sh script
/usr/bin/diction:	/bin/sh script
/usr/bin/diff3:	/bin/sh script
/usr/bin/dircmp:	/usr/bin/sh5 script
/usr/bin/explain:	/bin/sh script
/usr/bin/indxbib:	/bin/sh script

continues

Table 5.4, Continued
Sample Shell Scripts

Command	Shell Program Type
/usr/bin/install:	/usr/bin/ksh script
/usr/bin/lorder:	shell commands
/usr/bin/lp:	/bin/sh script
/usr/bin/lpstat:	/usr/bin/ksh script
/usr/bin/man:	shell commands
/usr/bin/nohup:	shell commands
/usr/bin/plot:	/bin/sh script
/usr/bin/ranlib:	/bin/sh script
/usr/bin/rnews:	/bin/sh script
/usr/bin/roffbib:	/bin/sh script
/usr/bin/spell:	/bin/sh script
/usr/bin/style:	/bin/sh script
/usr/bin/uam_home:	/bin/sh5 script

Table 5.4 was created using another UNIX command—file. The file command looks at the contents of a file to determine what type it is. For example, is it an ASCII file, a directory, a shell script, data, or more? In the version of file on the DECStation, it can distinguish between shell scripts for the C shell (/bin/csh), the Korn Shell (/usr/bin/ksh), the BSD version of the Bourne shell (/bin/sh), and the System V version of the Bourne shell (/bin/sh5).

To use the file command, simply list on the command line the file you want to examine as an argument. The file command can accept more than one file for arguments, so use those wild cards! The following is an example of file and its output:

```
$ file vmunix
vmunix: mipsel 407 executable not stripped - version 2.10
$ file home
home:   directory
```

A number of System V versions of UNIX also make wide use of the shell's powerful features. By doing so, programmers can write compact and powerful tools that can then be incorporated in a shell script that is easier to modify and maintain in the long run. For example, did you know that the custom program used to install SCO programs on SCO XENIX is a shell script? The shutdown command also is a shell script. On SCO UNIX systems, the haltsys command to stop the system is a shell script. As you can see from these examples, if you have an idea to make UNIX easier to use, it can probably be done as a shell script.

However, no matter how powerful or easy to use a language is, some things are better off done in other languages. The shell is no different. In return for the ease of use and the interactive, "don't compile me" nature of the shell's command language, you sacrifice speed. If you use many commands external to the shell, then each command has to be loaded and executed; you are at the mercy of the system in executing your commands. In the Bourne shell, arithmetic is a problem because it relies upon an external command called expr. However, the Korn shell addresses this problem by including integer math calculations in its programming language.

The language used for programming in the C shell is quite different from the other languages used in the other two shells; in fact, it resembles the C programming language. Because the C shell was initially only available on BSD versions of UNIX, it has not been as prevalent in the programming frontier because of compatibility and distribution reasons. Many programmers and system administrators learned to like the C shell for reasons other than its programming language, and many of those features are now incorporated in the Korn Shell.

Understanding the .profile File

The .profile file is the user's personal configuration management tool for his environment. It is the user equivalent of the system-wide /etc/profile, which is used by the system administrator to configure the environment for Bourne and Korn shell users. The .profile file is a shell program executed by the login shell when the user logs in. This environment includes information like terminal types, command search paths, and application-specific settings.

The .profile uses a period as the first character for a couple of reasons. First, UNIX treats files that use the period as the first character as special files. These are not shown in normal output from the ls command unless the option to ls is used to explicitly do so. Second, the programmers who have designed and modified the shells have deemed that the control and configuration files will be named with a leading period in the name. These are not configurable by the user.

The .profile file, which exists in the user's home directory, contains configuration information for the individual user's environment. It can be configured by the system administrator and the user to provide whatever additional commands and variables the user wants to have executed or set up when logging in. In fact, the .profile file can completely undo the configuration work done by the system administrator. The following example illustrates a small .profile file:

```
#
# This is my user profile
#
# Print the key configuration for erase, kill, and interrupt.
#
echo 'eerase ^?, kill ^U, intr ^C'


#
#Change the PATH to include some more directories.
#
PATH=/usr/ucb:/bin:usr/bin:/usr/local:$HOME/bin:
export PATH


#
# Change the prompt to show my user name, the host name, and the
# command number
# for the Korn shell
#
# If I change my mind to use the Bourne shell, then I can't use the
# command
# history in my prompt [!].
#
PS1="chare@wabbit [!]"
export PS1


#
# Configure some applications specific variables
#
UIMXDIR=/usr/lib/uimx
FMHOME=/usr/lib/frame
export UIMXDIR FMHOME


echo "Environment Configuration is complete."
```

Using the shell startup files to alter the environment or to undo configuration which has been defined by the system administrator might result in negative side effects. For example, commands might not work as expected, or worse, not work at all. Changes made to your shell startup files which could affect the currently defined environment should be checked with your system administrator.

Understanding the .login File

The .login file for C shell users is similar to .profile for the Bourne and Korn shells. The global initialization file is /etc/cshrc. The .login file is executed by the login shell to customize the login environment. The .login file is executed only by the login shell, while the second configuration file .cshrc is executed by every C shell. This mechanism is discussed in more detail in Chapter 18.

Summary

The shell is a powerful application program that enables the user to interact with the operating system to accomplish work. The shell has a wide variety of features and commands that create a rich environment for the user to experiment in and master. The generic nature in which the shell handles input and output allows the data to be redirected, and therefore creates a whole new realm of possibilities for commands and uses for UNIX.

Chapter Snapshot

To successfully interact with the UNIX operating system, you must know what files and directories are and how to manipulate them. This chapter examines those two entities through the following topics:

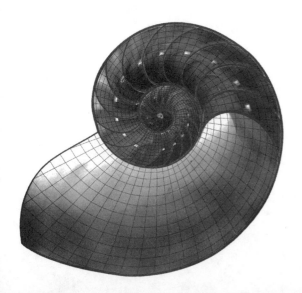

CHAPTER

Creating and Manipulating Files and Directories

Being successful in UNIX requires the mastery of some concepts and commands surrounding the file system, files, and directories. You need a good understanding of these things to get the maximum benefit from the rest of this book as well as from UNIX in general.

What is a File?

A *file* is a sequence of characters, or more specifically, bytes. When reading these bytes, the UNIX kernel places no significance on them at all; it leaves the interpretation of these bytes up to the application or program that requested them.

Consider then the password file. How does the kernel know when you have successfully logged in to the system? The kernel doesn't! The login program reads your password and verifies that it is indeed a correct match to the password stored in the system password file.

Additionally, the data files used by application programs are saved by the programs in a specific format that the application knows how to interpret. The kernel pays no attention to this format as it writes the information to the disk.

Understanding Directories

A *directory* is a file, meaning that it is just a sequence of bytes. But the directory has a format strictly controlled by the kernel. The information contained in a directory is the name of the file and an inode number.

An *inode* is like an index card that holds specific information about a file or other directory, including the following:

✔ Owner of the file

✔ Group that owns the file

✔ File size

✔ File permissions

✔ Data block addresses on the disk where the information is stored

As you saw in Chapter 3, the directory structure is part of the heart and soul of UNIX. If programmers were allowed to manipulate directories without kernel intervention, who knows what state your UNIX machine would be in right now?

The directory structure is dependent upon the version of UNIX you are using. System V derivatives, which do not support file names greater than 14 characters, have a simple structure consisting only of the inode number and the name of the file.

However, not many versions of System V UNIX are restricted to this file name length anymore. With the release of UNIX System V Release 3.2, UNIX vendors such as SCO started supporting extended length file names. The challenge for these vendors is to maintain backward compatibility with the existing software that expects the older directory format. System V Release 4 has the same concerns.

BSD UNIX systems have a different directory structure because this version of UNIX has always supported extended file names. The structure consists of an inode number, the length of the file name, and the file name itself. The exact mechanism used is beyond the scope of this book, but they did easily manage to maintain this compatibility.

You can think of a directory as a file folder, and the contents of the file folder (paper) are the files.

Special Files

UNIX also supports several types of special files, which fall into one of the following categories:

✔ Character device files

✔ Block device files

✔ Hard links

✔ Symbolic links

Because the kernel views everything as a file, including disk drives, terminals, modems, and network interface cards, the programmer can very easily develop applications independent of the device involved.

Character device files read and write data one character at a time. Figure 6.1 provides examples of character devices.

Figure 6.1
Sample character devices.

Block device files access a block of data at a time. A block is generally either 512 or 1,024 bytes, but other block sizes do exist. The kernel actually does read or write the device a character at a time, but the information is handled through a buffering process that only provides the information when there is a block. Example block devices are illustrated in figure 6.2.

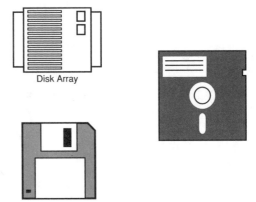

Figure 6.2
Sample block devices.

Disk Array

Disks appear as both block and character devices because, depending on the command in use, they function as either type of device. A wide range of devices is capable of acting as either type, depending on how they are being accessed.

A *hard link* is a special type of file that allows a single file to have multiple names. Have you ever photocopied some information so that you could place it in two files? Hard links have a similar idea; the file has two separate names. Hard links have the following two restrictions:

- ✔ The file and the second name must be part of the same filesystem.

- ✔ Hard links can only provide a second name for files. They do not work for directories.

Symbolic links serve the same purpose as hard links, but address the restrictions mentioned. Symbolic links can span filesystems, and they typically point to directories. You see how to create both hard and symbolic (or soft) links later in this chapter.

Moving around a Directory

Moving around in the directory structure requires that you know two commands: cd and pwd. The cd command is used to change from one directory to another.

cd

The cd command is used to move from one place to another in the file system. If the command cd is executed with no arguments, as in figure 6.3, then you are moved back to your home directory. The cd command uses the value of the environment variable HOME, which you saw in Chapter 5, to accomplish this.

```
$ pwd
/tmp
$ cd
$ pwd
/home/chare
$
```

When using cd with an argument, you add the name of the directory that you want to access. You can use either a full path name or a relative pathname to get to that directory. These are discussed shortly. The following are some examples of using cd with both types of pathnames:

```
$ cd /tmp
$ pwd
/tmp
$ cd
$ pwd
/home/chare
$ cd book
$ pwd
/home/chare/book
$ cd /usr
$ pwd
/usr
$
```

pwd

In the preceding examples, you saw the pwd command. pwd is an acronym for Print *Working Directory*. The pwd command accepts no arguments and prints the name of the directory you are currently working in. pwd always prints the directory name in an absolute format, as shown in the following example:

```
$ pwd
/home/chare/gopher2.012/doc
$
```

Understanding Absolute and Relative Pathnames

You can address files and directories under UNIX in two ways: absolute and relative pathnames. *Absolute pathnames* always start with a slash. Following is a list of some absolute pathnames:

/

/usr/spool/mqueue

/home/chare

/usr/mmdf

When using absolute pathnames with cd, enter the cd command followed by the name of the directory you want to go to, as in the following example:

```
$ cd /home/pat/shifty
$
```

In the preceding example, you are changing the directory to /home/pat/shifty, which is an absolute pathname. Relative pathnames, on the other hand, do not begin with a slash because the term *relative* means relative to the current directory. Absolute pathnames are absolute from the root directory. Look at a couple of sample directories in figure 6.3.

Figure 6.3
Start in the home directory, /usr/chare.

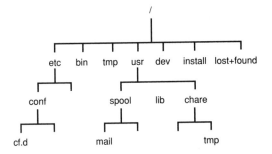

The following example introduces a new directory name. Each directory has at least two names: the real name and a dot (.). The dot is a relative name. For example, ./hello is a relative pathname because it is relative to the current directory. A connector, called dot-dot (..), is between each directory. This connector instructs the shell to move up one level in the directory structure. The preceding example starts in the directory /usr/chare, moves to tmp, and then moves back up to chare using the dot-dot format. This makes your working directory at this point the same as when you started out: /usr/chare.

```
$ cd tmp            relative - move to tmp
$ cd ..             relative - move up one level
$ cd /usr/spool     absolute
```

```
$ cd mail          relative move down to mail
$ cd ../..         relative - move up two levels
$ cd chare         relative - move down to chare
```

Listing Files and Directories

Obviously, one of the most needed commands in any operating system is one that lists the files found in a given part of the file system. UNIX is no different. In this section, you look at two commands that can help you navigate through the files and directories in your UNIX system.

The ls Command

The ls command lists the contents of a directory. It accepts arguments and has options that affect its operation. The following code shows some sample output of the ls command:

```
$ls
CrossRoads.DECterm       book
Mail                     gophermail.tar
News                     hch001.ps
WWW                      oreo.DECterm
adc                      shylock.DECterm
backup                   xgopher.1.3
$
```

In the preceding example, you see the files that ls displays. This is the form of ls found on BSD-type UNIX systems. System V UNIX lists all the files in a single column, which can be difficult to read. The ls command has a list of options that can alter the way it lists the files. The most common options are as follows:

-a	Lists all files, including hidden files
-C	Lists in columns
-F	Shows the file type (directory or executable)
-l	Lists in long format
-d	Shows directory names only
-R	Does a recursive listing

Now take a closer look at these options and the output they provide. The ls -a command lists all the files in the directory, including hidden files. A *hidden file* is one whose name starts with a period. As you remember from Chapter 3, every directory has two dot files. The current directory is indicated with a single dot (.), and the parent directory is shown as dot-dot (..). The following code illustrates the ls -a command:

```
$lx
gamma1    infra_red1    uvA          uvB      xray1      xray2
$ ls -a
.         .white        gamma1       uvA      xray1
..        .xray3        infra_red1   uvB      xray2
$
```

As you can see from the examples in the previous code, the first time the ls command was issued, no options were indicated and not all the files were listed. The second example added the -a option to the command, and you now see the hidden files as well.

The -C option to ls is the standard mode of operation for BSD systems. For System V systems though, you must specify the -C option to have the listed files appear in columns. The -C option often is combined with the -F option to see the executable files and directories in the file list. The following commands show an example of these two options:

```
$ ls -C
gamma1     infra_red1      uvA        uvB      xray1
xray2
$ ls -CF
gamma1*    infra_red1*     uvA/       uvB
xray1      xray2
$
```

In the second part of the previous code, some files are suffixed with an asterisk or a slash. The asterisk indicates that the file is an executable—that is, a program. The slash indicates that this is a directory.

The -l option lists the files and directories in a long format. This format provides most of the needed information to the user. Figure 6.4 illustrates this option.

Figure 6.4
BSD ls -l output.

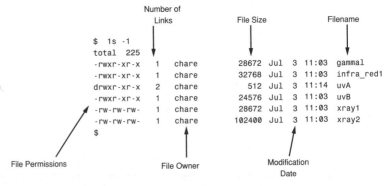

The information provided by ls -l as shown in figure 6.4 is explained in table 6.1.

Table 6.1
Columns in ls -l Listings

Column	Exaplanation
File permissions	Contains the file type and the permissions for the file or directory
Link count	Contains the number of names for this file or directory
Owner	Contains the name (or user number) of who owns the file
Group	Contains the name (or group number) of who owns the file
File size	Contains the size of the file in bytes
Access time	Contains the time the file was last accessed
Filename	Self-explanatory

The file type and file permissions make up the first part of the line in the output from ls -l. The file type is the first character of the line, and the file types are listed in table 6.2. By learning these file types, you can determine a file's type just by looking at the permissions field of the ls -l output. These file types are discussed again in Chapter 7, along with the file permissions.

When looking at your output from ls -l, the time field can show a date and time, such as date and year. If the file was accessed within the last year, the date and time will be printed. Otherwise, the date and year will be displayed.

Table 6.2
File Types

Symbol	Explanation
-	Regular file
d	Directory
c	Character special file
b	Block special file
l	Symbolic link
p	Named pipe (FIFO)

The example in figure 6.4 is the BSD version of ls. Figure 6.5 illustrates the System V output. The only difference is that by default the BSD version of ls doesn't list the group ownership, whereas the System V version does. BSD users can see the group by adding the -g option to the command line, as in ls -g.

Figure 6.5
System V ls -l
output.

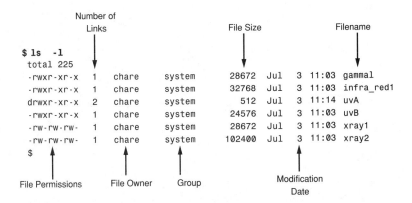

Sometimes, you must search through many files to find the existing directories. Although you can use the ls -CF command, it makes more sense to use an additional option to ls—the -d option. The -d option instructs ls to display only the directories and not the files. Generally, when you issue a command such as the following:

```
$ ls -l directory
```

ls responds by listing the contents of the directory specified. This might not be the desired behavior. The -d option instructs ls to print only the directory names and not the files. The following code illustrates the use of ls -d in the /usr/lib directory:

```
$ pwd
/usr/lib
$ ls -l tmac
total 4
-rw-r--r--  1 bin      bin         55 Jun  6  1993 tmac.an
-rw-r--r--  1 bin      bin         91 Jun  6  1993 tmac.m
-rw-r--r--  1 bin      bin         63 Jun  6  1993 tmac.osd
-rw-r--r--  1 bin      bin        289 Jun  6  1993 tmac.ptx
$ ls -d tmac
tmac
$ ls -ld tmac
drwxrwxrwx  2 root     users       96 Jun  6  1993 tmac
$
```

In the preceding example, the initial command shows the contents of the directory tmac. The second time the ls command was issued, only the -d option was used, which does not list the contents of the directory tmac, but simply prints the name of the directory. Finally, the ls command was issued with both the -l and -d options. This prints all the information on the tmac directory.

The last option discussed in this section is the -R option, which instructs ls to perform a recursive listing of the files in the directory. A recursive listing means that ls prints the files and the files within each directory it encounters. The following code shows using ls -R in a small directory structure:

```
$ ls -lR uvA
total 12
drwxr-xr-x  2 chare    users         48 Aug 24 17:53 micro_light
-rw-r--r--  1 chare    users        485 Aug 24 17:52 test1
-rwsr-xr-x  1 chare    users       4920 Aug 24 17:53 test3

uvA/micro_light:
total 1
-rw-r--r--  1 chare    users         29 Aug 24 17:53 sample3
$
```

As you can see, the -R command travels through several directories. It first looks in the uvA directory, lists the files and directories found, then does the same for any other directories found.

The file Command

The file command, as mentioned in Chapter 5, enables you to "peek" inside a file to see what it is. The file command uses a file called /etc/magic, or on some systems /usr/lib/file/magic, to tell it what to look for in the file that tells what type of file it is. This is called the *file signature*. Exactly how intelligent the file command is on your system is determined by the magic file and how many entries your vendor included in it. Following is a list of some responses that the file command gives you. The exact number is too great to list here.

```
ASCII text
symbolic link
shell commands
c program text
mipsel demand paged executeable
mc68k executable {shared library} (shared demand paged)
empty
Permission denied
cannot open
/bin/sh script
c-shell commands
```

```
English text
/bin/sh5 script
directory
rott, nroff, or eqn input text
data
```

The file command should be followed by a file or list of files that you want examined. The following example shows a sample of the file command in action:

```
$ file *
Filecabinet:    directory
MW.INI:         data
a.out:          mc68k executable not stripped (shared demand paged)
a1:             ascii text
b1:             c program text
brk:            commands text
city:           English text
hello.c:        c program text
list:           empty
$
```

Creating a File

You can create files in UNIX in a variety of ways. Files can be created by application programs through output redirection, or as temporary storage by commands such as language compilers. The following sections discuss at a few of these ways.

Using the touch Command to Create a File

One of the easiest ways to create a file is using the touch command. This command creates an empty file and can be used to update the file access times that UNIX tracks. The syntax of the command is as follows:

```
$ touch filename
```

The creation of a file using the touch command is illustrated in the following code:

```
$ touch new_file
$ ls -l new_file
-rw-r--r--  1 chare    users          0 Aug 24 17:59 new_file
$
```

The touch command creates a file in the current directory with the name specified on the command line. This newly created file is empty—that is, it has a length of zero bytes and has nothing in it. The touch command also is used for updating the access times on files.

UNIX keeps three separate times: one for last access, one for last modification, and one for the last time the inode was changed. The following code illustrates the changes that occur on the access times using touch:

```
$ touch /etc/passwd
touch: cannot change times on /etc/passwd
$ ls -l list
-rw-r--r--  1 chare    users       211 Aug 24 17:58 list
$ date
Wed Aug 24 18:01:14 EST 1994
$ touch list
$ ls -l list
-rw-r--r--  1 chare    users       211 Aug 24 18:01 list
$
```

The touch command tries to adjust the access times on the file /etc/passwd. The touch command informs you that you don't have the needed permission to make the changes. The second example starts with a file named list that was last accessed at 20:22 on Jul 3. After executing touch, the access time is changed to reflect the time that the command was executed, or 21:01 on Jul 3.

Because touch updates the last access time, it can be used to prevent the file from being removed using the find -time command because it hasn't been accessed.

Your Favorite Editor

Of course, you also can create files on UNIX by using your favorite text editor. Many text editors are available, and a number come with UNIX. Those that are typically part of UNIX distributions are ed, ex, vi, and in some cases, emacs. Many commercially produced editors for UNIX also are available. Some examples are commercial versions of emacs, Brief, and more. vi is introduced in Chapters 12 and 13; and ed in Chapter 14.

Output Redirection

As you learned in Chapter 5, files can be created using output redirection. To recap, output redirection enables you to change where the output of a command is sent. Rather than being written to the screen of your terminal, you can send the output to a file using the appropriate symbol for your shell. The following shows an example for the Bourne and Korn shells:

```
$ cal > /tmp/output
$ cat /tmp/output
   August 1994
 S  M Tu  W Th  F  S
    1  2  3  4  5  6
 7  8  9 10 11 12 13
```

```
14 15 16 17 18 19 20
21 22 23 24 25 26 27
28 29 30 31
$ ls -l /tmp/output
-rw-r--r--  1 chare    users          133 Aug 24 18:02 /tmp/output
$
```

As you can see, the output of the cal command is being redirected into the file /tmp/output, thereby creating a new file. The redirection symbol is the > between the command and the file name. The contents of the file /tmp/output are the output of the cal command. This new file can be seen by using ls to see the file information.

Making a Copy

Creating a file also can be done by making a copy of an existing file. This process involves the use of the command cp, which requires at least two arguments as illustrated in the following examples:

```
$ cp old_file new_file
$ cp file1 file2 file3 file4 ... directory
```

The first example of the command copies the old file to the new file. The following lines of code show an example of using this command in a real situation:

```
$ ls -l
total 3
-rw-r--r--  1 chare    users          211 Aug 24 18:04 list
-rw-r--r--  1 chare    users          133 Aug 24 18:05 output
-rw-r--r--  1 chare    users           36 Aug 24 18:05 sample
$ cp list new_file
$ ls -l
total 4
-rw-r--r--  1 chare    users          211 Aug 24 18:04 list
-rw-r--r--  1 chare    users          211 Aug 24 18:05 new_file
-rw-r--r--  1 chare    users          133 Aug 24 18:05 output
-rw-r--r--  1 chare    users           36 Aug 24 18:05 sample
$
```

As you can see, the user wants to make a copy of the file and name the copy. After the copy is done, list the directory to see that new_file exists.

The second format of cp enables the user to copy a number of files to a directory. You can name any number of files, but the directory must be the last argument on the command line. The following example illustrates copying a number of files to a directory:

```
$ cp list output uvA
$ ls -l uvA
total 14
-rw-r--r--  1 chare   users      211 Aug 24 18:07 list
drwxr-xr-x  2 chare   users       48 Aug 24 17:53 micro_light
-rw-r--r--  1 chare   users      133 Aug 24 18:07 output
-rw-r--r--  1 chare   users      485 Aug 24 17:52 test1
-rwsr-xr-x  1 chare   users     4920 Aug 24 17:53 test3
$
```

Here, you can see a copy of the files list and output being made from the current directory to the directory /home/chare/tmp/uvA. When the copy is complete, you can see
that the files were copied by issuing the ls command on the target directory, /home/
chare/tmp/uvA.

When a file is copied, the current time is used at the creation and the last access time. You
also become the owner of the file, and the permissions may be changed. This is different
from how the mv command operates, as you will see later.

Some versions of the cp command have the -R option, which can be used to copy an
entire directory structure. This will be mentioned again later in the chapter, as well.

Reading a File

Aside from using an editor to look at a file, a number of commands enable you to view
the contents of a file without using an editor. It is important that you make sure that the
file you want to view is indeed a text file. You can do this by using the file command. If the
file command returns a comment that includes the word text, then it is likely safe to view.

If the file is not a text file, the file itself may contain character sequences that cause your
terminal or terminal emulator to lock up. The only remedy to this may be to turn off your
terminal or cancel your session. The next three commands, cat, more, and pg, all do
similar things.

The cat Command

No, UNIX isn't going to the dogs. The cat command is used to view a small text file or to
send a text file to another program through a pipe. The cat command has no facility to
view the file in manageable chunks. The only way to do this is to use the Ctrl+S key to
suspend the output and Ctrl+Q to restart the output flow. Be warned though: If you are
connecting through a network, it is possible that the control commands will not be
processed quickly enough to avoid the "loss" of data off the screen.

The use of the cat command both to view a file and to send it to another program through a pipe is demonstrated in the following code:

```
$ cat fruits
apple
orange
lemon
lime
banana
kiwi
cherry
$ cat fruits ¦ sort
apple
banana
cherry
kiwi
lemon
lime
orange
$
```

In the first part, the cat command lists the contents of this (short) file to the screen. In the second part of the code, the cat command is used to give sort some input to sort. The sort command used in the previous code is discussed in more detail in Chapter 11.

To find out if the file has more information than you can handle on-screen, you can use one of the commands yet to be discussed—more or pg. You also can use the command wc to find out how big the file is.

The wc command is a word counter. It scans a given file and counts the number of lines, words, and characters in a file. The wc command uses whitespace to tell when a word starts and ends. This tells you whether you can use cat, or if you should use more or pg. The wc command uses the following format:

```
$ wc file
```

In this format, wc reports all three counts: lines, words, and characters, as demonstrated in the following code. The following example also shows how using the -1 option instructs the wc command to count only the number of lines:

```
$ wc a.out
     39    541  21959 a.out
$ wc -l fruits
      7 fruits
$
```

If the output from wc indicates that the file is more than 20 or 22 lines, then it is probably a good idea to use either more or pg to view the file.

The more Command

One alternative to the cat command is the more command, which has its roots in BSD UNIX. Because of its popularity, many other UNIX vendors started including the more command in their own distributions. The format of the more command is as follows:

```
$ more file
```

The more command displays the file one screen at a time, making it useful for viewing large files. As each screen is displayed, more pauses the display and prints a prompt on the last line of the screen, as seen in the following code:

```
$ more test3
total 220
drwxr-xr-x  2 chare   users      32 May 16  1993 Clipboard
-rw-r--r--  1 chare   users     126 Jun  5  1993 Environment
drwxr-xr-x  6 chare   users     272 May  3 07:47 Filecabinet
-rw-r----  1 chare   users      63 Jul 29  1993 MW.INI
drwx------  2 chare   users      32 Apr 30 06:37 Mail
drwxr-xr-x  2 chare   users      32 May 16  1993 Wastebasket
-rwxr-xr-x  1 chare   users   21959 May  8 07:01 a.out
-rw-r--r--  1 chare   users     290 Aug 19 07:59 a1
-rw-r--r--  1 chare   users     390 Aug 20 02:01 a2
-rw-r--r--  1 chare   users     418 Aug 19 08:40 a3
-rw-r--r--  1 chare   users     102 Aug 19 09:44 a4
-rw-r--r--  1 chare   users     108 Aug 19 10:58 b1
-rw-r--r--  1 chare   users     195 Aug 20 00:53 b2
-rw-r--r--  1 chare   users     245 Aug 20 00:33 b3
-rw-r--r--  1 chare   users     265 Aug 20 00:56 b4
-rwxr-xr-x  1 chare   users     232 Aug 12 20:59 brk
-rwxr-xr-x  1 chare   users       1 Aug 20 00:26 brk.awk
drwxr-xr-x  2 chare   users      96 Aug 24 18:05 chp6
-rw-r--r--  1 chare   users     109 Aug 19 01:03 city
-rw-r--r--  1 chare   users     128 Aug 20 01:58 city2
-rwxr-xr-x  1 chare   users     119 Aug 12 21:16 cont
-rwxr-xr-x  1 chare   users      68 Aug 11 22:17 cp2
--More--(35%)
```

As you can see, the last line in the display shows the --More-- (35%) prompt. By this, more tells you that it is waiting for a command, and that you have viewed 1 percent of the total file. The following code depicts a number of commands that more has built in to it:

```
Most commands optionally preceded by integer argument k.  Defaults in
brackets.
Star (*) indicates argument becomes new default.
------------------------------------------------------------------
```

```
<space>                    Display next k lines of text [current screen
                           ↦size]
z                          Display next k lines of text [current screen
                           ↦size]*
<return>                   Display next k lines of text [1]*
d or ctrl-D                Scroll k lines [current scroll size, initially
                           ↦11]*
q or Q or <interrupt>      Exit from more
s                          Skip forward k lines of text [1]
f                          Skip forward k screenfuls of text [1]
'                          Go to place where previous search started
=                          Display current line number
/<regular expression>      Search for kth occurrence of regular expression
                           ↦[1]
n                          Search for kth occurrence of last r.e [1]
!<cmd> or :!<cmd>          Execute <cmd> in a subshell
v                          Start up /usr/bin/vi at current line
h                          Display this message
ctrl-L                     Redraw screen
:n                         Go to kth next file [1]
:p                         Go to kth previous file [1]
:f                         Display current file name and line number
.                          Repeat previous command
-------------------------------------------------------------------
--More--(35%)
```

As you can see, more has flexibility built into it—from searching for text, to moving forward, to starting vi at the line that you are viewing. (Unfortunately, the editor started is not configurable.) As the help screen in the previous example shows, to view the next screen you simply press the spacebar. To view a line at a time, press the Enter key. Some of the commands are preceded by a colon; others are simply entered as is. Some commands can be preceded by a number. For example, you can tell more to move only 10 lines in the file by typing the digits 1 and 0 followed by the Enter key.

One of the more useful features likely is the search command. Pressing the slash (/) key tells more that you are going to enter a series of characters that you want it to search for in the file you are viewing. If the pattern is found, then more moves to that point in the file.

The pg Command

The pg command is like the more command, but has more System V background—although it is found on more and more BSD systems. The pg command accomplishes the same function as the more command: it enables the user to view a file one screen at a time. The command format for pg is the same as more, as shown in the following example:

```
$ pg file
```

The following list shows the help screen from the pg command:

```
- - - - - - - - - - - - - - - - - - - - - - - - - - - - - - - - - - - - - - - - - - - - - -
h             help
q or Q        quit
<blank>       or \n    next page
l             next line
d or ^D       display half a page more
. or L        redisplay current page
f             skip the next page forward
n             next file
p             previous file
$             last page
w or z        set window size and display next page
s savefile    save current file in savefile
/pattern/     search forward for pattern
?pattern? or
^pattern^     search backward for pattern
!command      execute command

Most commands can be preceded by a number, as in
+1\n (next page); -1\n (previous page); 1\n (page 1).

See the manual page for more detail.
- - - - - - - - - - - - - - - - - - - - - - - - - - - - - - - - - - - - - - - - - - - - -
```

The previous list shows some similarities between pg and more, but there are also some significant differences. For example, to view the next screen in the file, press Enter, not the spacebar. To view the next line in the file use the l key, not the Enter key. The following code shows the use of pg to view a file, which happens to be a directory listing, and how to use the l command to view a single line:

```
$ pg test3
total 220
drwxr-xr-x  2 chare    users          32 May 16  1993 Clipboard
-rw-r--r--  1 chare    users         126 Jun  5  1993 Environment
drwxr-xr-x  6 chare    users         272 May  3 07:47 Filecabinet
-rw-r-----  1 chare    users          63 Jul 29  1993 MW.INI
```

```
drwx-------2 chare    users         32 Apr 30 06:37 Mail
drwxr-xr-x 2 chare    users         32 May 16  1993 Wastebasket
-rwxr-xr-x 1 chare    users      21959 May  8 07:01 a.out
:l
-rw-r--r-- 1 chare    users        290 Aug 19 07:59 a1
:l
-rw-r--r-- 1 chare    users        390 Aug 20 02:01 a2
:l
-rw-r--r-- 1 chare    users        418 Aug 19 08:40 a3
:
```

With pg, you can easily move backwards line by line as well as forward line by line. In either case, precede the number of lines you want to move by either a + (forward) or - (backward) sign to instruct pg how you want to move. The choice between using cat, more, or pg is almost a personal one. Wars have been fought over which is better, more or pg. You have to choose for yourself.

Removing a File

Removing a file is a permanent process under UNIX. The file removal process under DOS is well known, documented, and some would say simplistic. The file removal process under UNIX is very different. When a file is removed, the inode number of the directory in which the file was is changed to zero. This means that there is no way to connect the file name to the actual information. And after this is done, you cannot effectively undo the erasure unless you have a backup copy of the file saved somewhere. So, consider removal of a file a permanent event.

The rm Command

Removing a file is done with the rm command, which has three options: -i, -f, and -r. The -i and -f options are discussed here; the -r option is covered later in this chapter. The format of the rm command is as follows:

```
$ rm file file file
```

Like most UNIX commands, you can specify any number of files on the rm command line, as illustrated here. To reiterate, after you press the Enter key, you have no way to undo the removal of the file. The following code shows removing a file and verifying that it has been deleted:

```
$ ls -l
total 13
-rw-r--r-- 1 chare    users         43 Aug 24 18:49 fruits
-rw-r--r-- 1 chare    users        211 Aug 24 18:07 list
```

```
drwxr-xr-x  2 chare   users       48 Aug 24 17:53 micro_light
-rw-r--r--  1 chare   users      133 Aug 24 18:07 output
-rw-r--r--  1 chare   users       36 Aug 24 18:49 sample
-rw-r--r--  1 chare   users      485 Aug 24 17:52 test1
-rwsr-xr-x  1 chare   users     3500 Aug 24 18:49 test3
$ rm output
$ ls -l
total 12
-rw-r--r--  1 chare   users       43 Aug 24 18:49 fruits
-rw-r--r--  1 chare   users      211 Aug 24 18:07 list
drwxr-xr-x  2 chare   users       48 Aug 24 17:53 micro_light
-rw-r--r--  1 chare   users       36 Aug 24 18:49 sample
-rw-r--r--  1 chare   users      485 Aug 24 17:52 test1
-rwsr-xr-x  1 chare   users     3500 Aug 24 18:49 test3
$
```

The code shows the way that file removals should be done. Use the pwd command to ensure that you know where you are in the directory structure. This helps prevent you from removing something that you don't really want removed. Next, list the files, and then type the rm command. Try to avoid wild cards in your filenames unless you use the -i option, discussed next. Avoiding wild cards helps to ensure that you don't remove something you want to keep.

The following list of code demonstrates the best way to remove files using wild cards. Use of the -i option puts rm into interactive mode. For each file on the command line, rm prompts you with the name of the file. If you specify **y** and press Enter, the file is removed.

```
$ ls -l
total 33
-rw-r--r--  1 chare   users    13874 Aug 20 05:13 a
drwxr-xr-x  2 chare   users       32 Aug 24 18:52 micro_light
-rw-r--r--  1 chare   users      133 Aug 24 18:02 output
-rw-r--r--  1 chare   users       76 Aug 24 05:59 sample
-rw-r--r--  1 chare   users      241 Aug 24 07:10 sed
-rw-r--r--  1 chare   users       77 Aug 24 07:20 test
$ rm -i *
a: ? y
rm: micro_light directory
output: ? y
sample: ?
sed: ? y
test: ?
$ ls -l
total 3
```

```
drwxr-xr-x  2 chare    users       32 Aug 24 18:52 micro_light
-rw-r--r--  1 chare    users       76 Aug 24 05:59 sample
-rw-r--r--  1 chare    users       77 Aug 24 07:20 test
$
```

If you type **n** or nothing and press Enter, the file is not removed. In this code, rm determined that micro_light was a directory and did not try to remove it. The rm command doesn't know how to remove directories, only files. Again, remember that when the file is deleted, it cannot be recovered without the use of a backup.

The -f option forces the removal of a file, regardless of the permissions. The use of this option requires that the user be the owner of the file, or root.

Creating a Directory

As you learned in Chapter 3, directories help you manage your files. You can make a directory named letters and put all your correspondence in it. As figure 6.6 illustrates, the system uses directories to organize information and programs in a common structure.

Figure 6.6
A sample
directory structure.

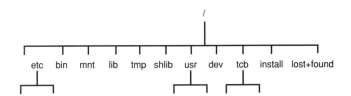

To make a directory, use the command mkdir, which accepts multiple arguments, each one being the name of a directory you want to create. Unless indicated by providing a full pathname, the directories are created in your current directory. It is also important for you to have permission to perform this task. Chapter 7 takes a thorough look at file and directory permissions.

The mkdir Command

The syntax for the mkdir is as follows:

```
$ mkdir directory_name
```

The same rules for file names apply for directory names. You can insert a space into a directory name, but it makes the name difficult to use because the entire name must always be enclosed in quotation marks. Avoid spaces in directory names; use an underscore instead. The directory name also cannot already exist as either a directory or a file. Both cases result in an error message.

The following shows some sample directories being created:

```
$ ls -l
total 5
-r--r--r--  1 chare    users       656 Aug 24 18:54 ax1
drwxr-xr-x  2 chare    users        32 Aug 24 18:52 micro_light
-rw-r--r--  1 chare    users        76 Aug 24 05:59 sample
-rw-r--r--  1 chare    users        77 Aug 24 07:20 test
$ mkdir new_dir
$ ls -ld new_dir
drwxr-xr-x  2 chare    users        32 Aug 24 18:54 new_dir
$ mkdir ax1
mkdir: file exists
$ mkdir /etc/chare
mkdir: Permission denied
$ mkdir "space dir"
$ ls -ld space dir
space not found
dir not found
$ ls -ld "space dir"
drwxr-xr-x  2 chare    users        32 Aug 24 18:55 space dir
$
```

In this code, you see a directory listing of the files in the current directory. The user successfully makes the directory new_dir, and then tries to make another directory called ax1. Of course this fails, and mkdir tells him that it failed because a file called ax1 already exists.

The user then tries to create a directory in /etc. This typically is not permitted because the /etc/directory, as you may recall, is used by the system as a place to store system administration commands and system configuration files. Next, is a directory name with a space in it. As you can see, using a space in the directory name can lead to all kinds of confusion. This is why you should avoid using spaces in both file and directory names.

Removing a Directory

Like anything else in this world, directories can outlive their usefulness. There comes a time when a directory needs to be removed. This is accomplished by using either the rmdir or rm -r commands. Both are discussed in this section.

The rmdir Command

The rmdir command also can accept multiple directory names like the mkdir command, but it has one requirement. The directory must be empty; it cannot contain any hidden files, files, or directories at all. You must remove these prior to using rmdir to remove the directory. If your directory has subdirectories that have subdirectories, removing them can be a tedious process. There is help, so don't worry. The following code illustrates the removal of a directory using rmdir:

```
$ ls -l
total 7
-rw-rw-rw-  1 chare    users        656 Aug 24 18:54 ax1
drwxr-xr-x  2 chare    users         32 Aug 24 18:52 micro_light
drwxr-xr-x  2 chare    users         32 Aug 24 18:54 new_dir
-rw-r--r--  1 chare    users         76 Aug 24 05:59 sample
drwxr-xr-x  2 chare    users         32 Aug 24 18:55 space dir
-rw-r--r--  1 chare    users         77 Aug 24 07:20 test
$ rmdir /etc
rmdir: /etc: Permission denied
$ rmdir space dir
rmdir: space nonexistent
rmdir: dir nonexistent
$ rmdir "space dir"
$ mkdir new_dir/test1
$ rmdir new_dir
rmdir: new_dir not empty
$
```

In this example, the user tried to create a subdirectory in the /etc directory. For the same reason that the user can't create a directory, the user can't remove /etc. Thank goodness! She then tried to remove that directory, which has a space in the name, and forgot about the quotation marks. This looked like two arguments to rmdir, which then complained that it couldn't find a directory named space, or dir. Then she remembered about the quotation marks and successfully removed the directory. However, the directory new_dir couldn't be removed because the directory isn't empty. And sure enough, when the directory is listed at least one thing is in it.

Although it was stated earlier that rm cannot remove directories, rm with the -r option can perform recursive removals of a directory structure, which includes all files and directories in that structure.

The rm -r command is very dangerous. Do not use it with wild cards unless you are prepared to live with the consequences. (This is particularly true if you are logged on as root—the system administrator.)

Unlike the regular rm command, rm -r accepts files or directories to be removed. If the argument is a directory, then rm looks through the directory, removes everything under it, then removes the directory itself. This is a fast process, and once started, some loss will occur even if you terminate the command before it completes.

The following code shows an rm -r command in action:

```
$ ls -l
total 6
-rw-rw-rw-  1 chare    users        656 Aug 24 18:54 ax1
drwxr-xr-x  2 chare    users         32 Aug 24 18:52 micro_light
drwxr-xr-x  3 chare    users        128 Aug 24 19:03 new_dir
-rw-r--r--  1 chare    users         76 Aug 24 05:59 sample
-rw-r--r--  1 chare    users         77 Aug 24 07:20 test
$ cd new_dir
$ ls -l
total 1
drwxr-xr-x  2 chare    users        112 Aug 24 19:03 test1
$ rm -ri test1
directory test1: ? y
test1/a.out: ? y
test1/a1: ? y
test1/a2: ? y
test1/a3: ? y
test1/a4: ? y
test1: ? y
$
```

The rm -r command in the preceding example has a slight twist to it. Unless you are sure about the directory to be removed or the directory it is very large, use the -i option to be prompted for verification that you want the file or directory removed. Simply using the rm -r command provides no output or error messages unless you do not have the permission to remove the directory tree. In these cases, rm reports the error message indicating that you don't have the needed permission.

From Here to There—Moving Things Around

Up to now, you have seen how to move around in the directory structure (cd, pwd), copy files, remove them, create and remove directories, and more. This section discusses moving files, renaming files, and using hard and symbolic links.

The mv Command

The mv command does two things: moves a file from one place to another and renames a file. This section discusses moving things around first. You already saw how to use the cp command to copy files from one directory to another. The disadvantage to this is that your file now takes up twice as much disk space. Sometimes you need this capability, but often you don't. You can move the file from one place to another instead. This saves some disk space and also some steps.

You can accomplish the same thing as the mv command does by copying the file and then removing the original. Or you can do it all in one neat command. On some versions of UNIX, the move command can only move files—you cannot move a directory and its underlying subdirectories and files (unless you are the system administrator). However, on other versions of UNIX, mv can move a directory. The syntax to move a file from one directory to another is like the cp command and is shown in the following example:

```
$ mv file file file .... directory
```

This syntax enables the user to enter at least one file name followed by the directory to move the file to. If more than one file is specified, and the last name is not a directory, the move fails and mv reports an error. The following code demonstrates the use of mv in this fashion:

```
$ ls -l
total 6
-rw-rw-rw-  1 chare   users        656 Aug 24 18:54 ax1
drwxr-xr-x  2 chare   users         32 Aug 24 18:52 micro_light
drwxr-xr-x  2 chare   users        128 Aug 24 19:05 new_dir
-rw-r--r--  1 chare   users         76 Aug 24 05:59 sample
-rw-r--r--  1 chare   users         77 Aug 24 07:20 test
$ mv s* t* /usr/tmp
$ ls s* t*
s* not found
t* not found
$ ls /usr/tmp
sample  test
$
```

This example shows the syntax for the mv command, as well as a successful move. Notice that several different types of wild cards are used in this example. In the first ls command, separate substitutions are made for the c* files and the s* files. The same substitution is made for the mv command. However, when it comes time to check the /usr/tmp/ directory, separate substitutions are not used; they are combined using a character class. This is file name substation in action, and it can simplify your life and reduce the keystrokes you need to complete your work. (I like them because I am less likely to make a mistake!)

The second format of the mv command enables you to change the name of a file. Again, you have two options. You can choose to change the name and leave the file in the current directory, or you can change the name and move it to another directory. The syntax for these cases follows:

```
$ mv old_name new_name
$ mv old_name /new_dir/new_name
```

The first example changes the file name and keeps it in the current directory. In the second example, the file name is changed and the file is put into another directory. The file can no longer be accessed by its old name or, if it was moved, in its old directory. The following sets of code illustrate both types of moves:

```
$ ls -l
total 6
-rw-rw-rw-   1 chare    users       656 Aug 24 18:54 ax1
drwxr-xr-x   2 chare    users        32 Aug 24 18:52 micro_light
drwxr-xr-x   2 chare    users       128 Aug 24 19:05 new_dir
-r--r--r--   1 chare    users       656 Aug 24 19:10 starter

$ mv ax1 junk
$ ls -l
total 6
-rw-rw-rw-   1 chare    users       656 Aug 24 18:54 junk
drwxr-xr-x   2 chare    users        32 Aug 24 18:52 micro_light
drwxr-xr-x   2 chare    users       128 Aug 24 19:05 new_dir
-r--r--r--   1 chare    users       656 Aug 24 19:10 starter

$ ls -l
total 6
-rw-rw-rw-   1 chare    users       656 Aug 24 18:54 junk
drwxr-xr-x   2 chare    users        32 Aug 24 18:52 micro_light
drwxr-xr-x   2 chare    users       128 Aug 24 19:05 new_dir
-r--r--r--   1 chare    users       656 Aug 24 19:10 starter
$ mv starter /usr/tmp/junk
$ ls -l /usr/tmp
total 4
-r--r--r--   1 chare    users       656 Aug 24 19:10 junk
-rw-r--r--   1 chare    users        76 Aug 24 05:59 sample
-rw-r--r--   1 chare    users        77 Aug 24 07:20 test
$
```

The example starts with a list of files. The first example with mv renames the file axl to junk. The second example shows that the file starter.doc is being moved to the /tmp directory, and its name is being changed to junk also. If you were to list the files in the current directory, you would see that the file tty_lines is missing, but a file named junk is there instead. In addition, when you look at the /tmp directory, you find a file named junk. If the situation arises in which you do not have the required permissions to complete the task, then mv informs you with the appropriate error message.

The ln Command

At times, you need to have the same file known by different names. This is possible without having to make a copy. As was explained earlier, the downside of making copies of a file is that it consumes the available disk space. Although this may not be a problem for a while, it will become one soon enough.

A hard link enables you to give a file another name. This is done by creating an entry in a directory; no additional disk space is consumed. Hard links cannot cross file system boundaries; however, most of the time your system administrator deals with them.

Creating a hard link is done with the command ln. The syntax of the command is much like cp and mv, as in the following example:

```
$ ln old_name new_name
```

The new name can be either an absolute or relative pathname. The following code illustrates the use of the ln command to create a hard link:

```
$ ls -l old_one
-rw-r--r--  1 chare     users        202 Aug 24 19:16 old_one
$ ln old_one new
$ ls -l old_one new
-rw-r--r--  2 chare     users        202 Aug 24 19:16 new
-rw-r--r--  2 chare     users        202 Aug 24 19:16 old_one
$
```

This code shows an ls -l listing of a file called old_one in the current directory. Notice the link count, which is the number immediately following the permissions (refer to figure 6.4 for a refresher). When the example began, the link count was one—that is, this file had one name. After the ln command was used to create another name for this file, the next ls shows a link count of 2, meaning that two directory entries in the system point to this file. As you can see, regardless of what name you use, the content of the file is the same.

Just as you can copy or move files anywhere you have the permission to, you can create links. The second kind of link, often used in Network File System (NFS) environments is the symbolic link. Symbolic or soft links can be used in non-NFS environments as well. They are often used for attaching a different directory name but also can be used for files, as shown in the following example:

```
$ ls -l
total 2
-rw-r--r--  2 chare   users      202 Aug 24 19:16 new
-rw-r--r--  2 chare   users      202 Aug 24 19:16 old_one
$ mkdir dir1
$ ln -s dir1 dir2
$ ls -l
total 4
drwxr-xr-x  2 chare   users       32 Aug 24 19:20 dir1
lrwxr-xr-x  1 chare   users       32 Aug 24 19:20 dir2 -> dir1
-rw-r--r--  2 chare   users      202 Aug 24 19:16 new
-rw-r--r--  2 chare   users      202 Aug 24 19:16 old_one
$ ln -s new before
$ ls -l
total 4
lrwxr-xr-x  1 chare   users      202 Aug 24 19:22 before -> new
drwxr-xr-x  2 chare   users       32 Aug 24 19:20 dir1
lrwxr-xr-x  1 chare   users       32 Aug 24 19:20 dir2 -> dir1
-rw-r--r--  2 chare   users      202 Aug 24 19:16 new
-rw-r--r--  2 chare   users      202 Aug 24 19:16 old_one
$
```

This code shows an example of creating symbolic links using the ln command. Not all versions of UNIX support this, and some versions restrict symbolic link creation to the system administrator. The syntax for ln -s is the same as for ln. In the previous code, you see two files. A news directory is created, and then a link to that directory is created.

Also in this example, a symbolic link to a file is created. In both cases, there was no difficulty in making the links. The ls -l output in the example shows that in the case of dir2, which is a symbolic link to dir1, the output reports a line like the following:

```
dir2 -> dir1
```

This means that dir2 is a symbolic link to dir1. Either name can be used to access the directory (or file), just like the hard link.

The copy Command

Some versions of UNIX also provide the copy command. copy and cp can be used to do the same thing—that is, to copy files. But copy is more notably used for copying an entire directory structure. The only version of UNIX on which I have seen this command so far is SCO UNIX.

Copy uses the same command format as the other commands that you have seen. But because it is typically used for copying a directory and its contents, this section looks at that format only. The copy command has a number of options used in the example shown in the following code. These options are -r, -o, -m, and -v. These instruct copy to do a recursive copy, retain the owner and last modification date, and to be verbose about what it is doing.

```
$ copy -romv ../andrewg .
examine directory ../andrewg/mail400
examine directory ../andrewg/mail400/mtaexe
copy file ../andrewg/mail400/mtaexe/mta-admin
copy file ../andrewg/mail400/mtaexe/mta
examine directory ../andrewg/mail400/uaexe
copy file ../andrewg/mail400/uaexe/mail400
examine directory ../andrewg/gopher
copy file ../andrewg/wsg-10.exe
$
```

This preceding notation tells the shell to go up one level and find the directory andrewg, and then copy it in the current directory. This is much easier than typing the entire pathnames out. The remainder of the example shows the output of the copy command. Copy, when using the -v option, informs you when it copies a file, or when it looks at a directory to see what there is to copy. In this example, copy finds four directories to search, but doesn't find any files to copy in many of them. This is not a problem because as the empty directory will be constructed in your directory anyway.

There are two other ways to copy a directory structure. One is to use the command cp -R on systems that support it, as shown here:

```
$ cp -R source destination
```

Here, the source directory structure is copied to a new directory called destination.

The second method uses the the command tar, which will be discussed more thoroughly in Chapter 26, "Archiving and Backup." The syntax of the command follows:

```
$ cd.source; tar cf - . ¦ (cd dest; tar xfBp - )
```

This uses the tar command to create an archive of the directory and to send it through a pipe to a subshell which, in turn, goes to the destination directory and uses tar to extract the archive. The result of this command is a copy of the original structure.

The importance of not becoming reliant upon copy—or any other command that is not part of standard UNIX—cannot be stressed enough. This is especially important if you are working on different vendors' implementations of UNIX. You should know a few different ways to accomplish these tasks because the command you use on one version may not be available on another.

Command Summary

The following is a list of the commands and options presented in this chapter:

Command	Explanation
cd	Changes directory
pwd	Prints working directory
ls	Lists the files in a directory
ls -a	Lists all files including hidden files
ls -C	Lists files in columns
ls -F	Lists files showing type
ls -l	Lists files showing full information
ls -g	Lists group owners (BSD only)
ls -d	Lists directory information
ls -R	Lists recursively
file	Determines file types
touch	Creates an empty file or resets access times
cal	Prints a calendar
cp	Copies files
cat	Views a text file
wc	Counts lines, words, characters
wc -l	Counts lines only
more	Views text files
pg	Views text files (System V)
rm	Removes a file
rm -i	Removes files interactively

continues

Command	Explanation
mkdir	Makes a directory
rmdir	Removes a directory
rm -r	Removes a directory and its contents
mv	Moves a file or renames a file
ln	Creates a hard link
ln -s	Creates a symbolic link
copy	Copies directory structures

Chapter Snapshot

Permissions control all actions in UNIX. They govern who owns a file, can view its contents, delete or modify it, or even execute it. This chapter explores the topic, specifically the following:

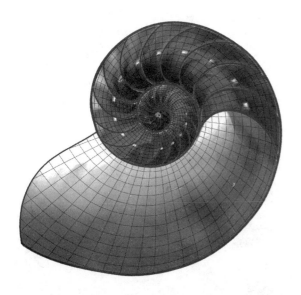

CHAPTER

7

Controlling Permissions to Files

Permissions are part of the UNIX security system. Although this chapter does not deal with security per se, you do have to know how to control file access and how you can make public, or very private, the information that you use.

Defining Permissions

The permissions that you grant your files and directories are much like the freedoms you grant to let others borrow or use your belongings. And just as you lock the front door of your house when you go to work in the morning, you also restrict who can access or modify the information that you value.

File and directory permissions form the combination lock around your data. However, even if you completely secure your information so that no other user can access it, on most systems the system administrator can still open and read your files. This is because someone has to be able to back up your files. So take warning: even though you can prevent the majority of people from accessing your files, you cannot prevent all of them. On more secure implementations of UNIX, not even the system administrator can open your files. This increases the level of security, but also can create other problems as well.

Before you can take a thorough look at how these permissions affect you and how you can take advantage of them, you must examine some relevant details.

The Password File

The basic information about who you are is stored in a file called the *password file*, which is typically found at /etc/passwd. On systems capable of higher levels of security, this information is found in other places, which are discussed in Chapter 28. The password file entry consists of seven fields, as illustrated in figure 7.1.

Figure 7.1
A password
file entry.

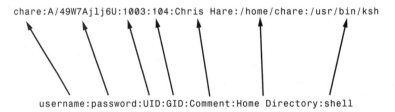

```
chare:A/49W7Ajlj6U:1003:104:Chris Hare:/home/chare:/usr/bin/ksh
```

```
username:password:UID:GID:Comment:Home Directory:shell
```

These entries are inserted when your account is created by the system administrator, and each tells UNIX something about you. The password file is colon delimited, which means that a colon separates each field in the file. The first entry is your login, or user name. This typically follows some convention for your site. These conventions usually are first name plus first initial of last name, first initial of first name plus last name, or simply initials. Some examples of user names are as follows:

chare

terri

jimh

rfh

All these are valid user names. The only restriction is that only the first eight characters in the name are significant. The second field in your password entry is the encrypted password. These passwords cannot be decrypted. When you log in, the password that you type is encrypted to see if there is a match. The password field can contain a number of things: the actual encrypted password, an asterisk meaning that the real password is stored somewhere else, or an 'x' that means the user cannot log in to the system. On some UNIX systems, the 'x' can mean that the password is stored elsewhere.

Any system capable of higher than traditional UNIX security, such as C2 or higher, does not store the actual encrypted passwords in the password file. The other location, which is more highly guarded, is used to store them. As you see during this chapter, the password file is used for more than just logging in.

The third field is your actual user number, or UID. This number uniquely identifies you to the system. The fourth field is your group number, or GID. This is your login group, and it identifies to which group of users you belong. This is explained in more detail shortly. The fifth field is a comment field. Generally, it contains your full name, but other information could be included, such as your phone number or office.

The sixth field in the password file is your home directory. When you log in to UNIX, it places you in a particular location of the directory structure. This is your home directory. From here, you can create and manipulate the data you want because it is yours. Anything outside your home directory you might not be able to modify. And the final, or seventh field, is your login shell. As you saw in Chapter 5, "Shell Basics," there are a number of shells that are available. The value of this field determines if you will be using the Bourne shell, the Korn shell, or the C shell.

The Group File

Just as your password file contains information about each user, the group file contains information about groups of users. Figure 7.2 has some group entries. Like the password file, the group file has a colon separating each field in the file, and there are four fields.

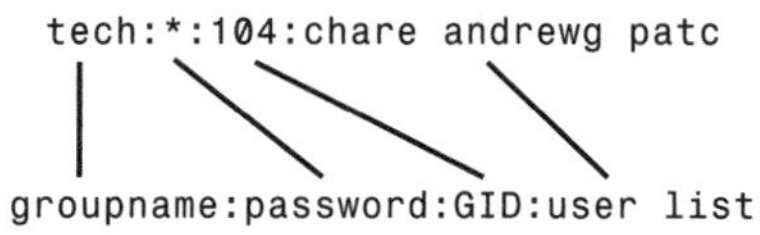

```
tech:*:104:chare andrewg patc



groupname:password:GID:user list
```

Figure 7.2
A group file entry.

The first field is the name of the group. Often, system administrators try to choose meaningful names for the groups so that it is clear who is entitled to what. The second field, which usually contains an x, is for a group password. This feature is generally not used. The third field is the actual group number, or GID, which identifies this group. The fourth field is a list of comma-separated user names. This list of user names specifies who belongs to each group. You can belong to more than one group: your user name simply has to appear in that group list. As you can see from our sample group file, some multiple group memberships exist.

User ID

As an individual, you get a Social Insurance Number or identification number that tells the organization who you are. You see them all the time: driver's licenses, credit cards, bank cards, even employee numbers! UNIX is no different. The only reason you have login names is to make it easier for you to use the operating system.

Each user is assigned a unique user id or UID that identifies him or her to the system. Tnis UID is stamped on everything you do. Every process you run, every file you create, is stamped with your UID. This UID is associated only with your user name. This ensures that you and only you can access what is rightfully yours.

Group ID

Just as your UID is like your Driver's License number, your Group ID, or GID, is like a driver's license from another province or state. You have one that you use most of the time (where you live), and another that you need to use other times (maybe where you work).

A group is a collection of users who may be assigned together so that they can access a common set of files or directories. This means that if they do not own the file, but are a member of the group who owns the file, they can still be allowed access to the file. You review this concept later in this chapter.

You can belong to as many groups as you need to. On older systems, you needed to execute a command when you wanted to change your group, but on most current systems, this is no longer required.

The id Command

Every once in a while, I like to look in my wallet and see who I am. The command id tells you the same information. As illustrated in the following code, id tells you your user name, UID, and GID. If your effective UID or your effective GID are different, these also are listed in the output of id.

```
$ id
uid=1003(chare)  gid=104(tech)
$
```

The id command is not to be confused with who. Who lists the users currently logged in to the system, whereas id tells you who is logged in at the terminal at which you type the command.

Reviewing the ls Command

You first saw the ls command in Chapter 6. As you recall, it is used to list the information for a file or directory, including the file type and the permissions for the file. Figure 7.3 reviews the output of ls.

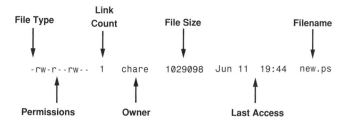

Figure 7.3
Sample ls output.

Recall from Chapter 6 that the file type is the first character in the permissions list, and nine characters represent the permissions bits. These permissions are represented as characters to make it easier to use this information and the file access security.

Understanding the Permission Bits

Nine permission bits are associated with each file and directory—three for the owner of the file, three for the members of the same group owner of the file, and three for everyone else. This means that if you are the owner of the file, those permissions affect your access. If you are not the owner, but you belong to the same group that owns the file, then the group permissions control your access. Finally, if you fit into neither of these categories, the final set of permissions control your access.

File Permissions

For each group of users (owner, group, others), there is a set of permission bits. These bits correspond to being able to read, write, and execute the file.

Figure 7.4 breaks down the permissions field into its three components and lists the right granted with each type of bit. Read permissions give the user the capability to open the file and view its contents. This could be done with any number of commands, for example, cat, more, and vi. Write permission gives a user the capability to open the file and replace or otherwise modify its contents. Finally, execute permission gives the user the capability to execute it as a command.

Figure 7.4
Permission bits.

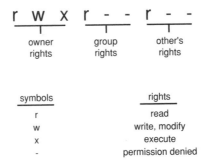

The following example illustrates permissions in action to control access to files:

```
$ ls -l output
--w------- 1 chare    users      236 Aug 24 20:13 output
$ cat output
cat: cannot open output
$ ls -l output2
-r--r--r-- 1 chare    users      236 Aug 24 20:15 output2
$ echo "new data" > output2
ksh: output2: cannot create
$ output2
ksh: output2: cannot execute
$
```

In the preceding example, you see how permissions affect file access. The first ls example shows the permissions on the file output. Notice that it has no read permissions for anyone. This means that when the user tried to read the contents of the file, the shell responded that the permission to do this is denied. Subsequently, the user tried to overwrite the contents of the file output2 using shell redirection. Because the file has read permission but not write permission, this action is denied, as is the user's request to execute the file.

Directory Permissions

The permissions on a directory work in concert with those for a file. As illustrated in figure 7.5 however, directory permissions mean slightly different things. When a user has read permission on a directory, the user can list the contents of a directory.

With write permission, the user can create new files, or delete existing files from the directory. The execute bit on a directory does not mean that you can execute the directory, but that you can use cd to go into the directory, or use a file in the directory. The following code illustrates the permissions on a directory in action.

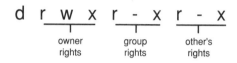

Figure 7.5
Directory
permissions.

symbols	rights
r	list the contents
w	add or delete files
x	cd to the directory
-	permission denied

```
$ ls -l a
a/list: Permission denied
$ ls -l
total 4
dr--r--r--  2 chare   users     48 Aug 24 21:09 a
drwxr-xr-x  2 chare   users     32 Aug 24 21:08 a2
drwxr-xr-x  2 chare   users     32 Aug 24 21:08 micro_light
-rw-r--r--  1 chare   users    133 Aug 24 21:08 output
$ cd a
ksh: a: bad directory
$ touch a/new
touch: a/new cannot create
$ cp output a2
$
```

On UNIX systems, the read bit enables the user to list the contents of the directory, but on DEC Ultrix systems, it takes more than the read bit to list the files. The execute permission bit restricts access to the directory by controlling if you can use the cd command to go into it. On SCO systems, for example, if you have the execute bit set and not the read bit, then you can cd into the directory and use a file if you know the name, but you cannot use ls to list the files. The write bit enables users to create or remove files in the destination directory.

Interactions

Interaction between the directory and the file can create problems. When a user wants to create a file, the permissions on the directory are checked. If the user has write permission on the directory, then the file will be created. Now, consider the following block of code. This illustrates a file that has write permission for all users, but no write permission on the directory. Can a user remove the file?

```
$ ls -l
total 4
dr--r--r--  2 chare    users        48 Aug 24 21:09 a
drwxr-xr-x  2 chare    users        48 Aug 24 21:12 a2
drwxr-xr-x  2 chare    users        32 Aug 24 21:08 micro_light
-rw-r--r--  1 chare    users       133 Aug 24 21:08 output
$ ls -ld a2
dr-xr-xr-x  2 chare    users        48 Aug 24 21:12 a2
$ls a2
output
$ rm a2/output
rm: a2/output not removed.  Permission denied
$ ls -l a2
total 1
-rw-r--r--  1 chare    users       133 Aug 24 21:12 output
$ date > a2/output
$ ls -l a2
total 1
-rw-r--r--  1 chare    users        29 Aug 24 21:14 output
$
```

As you see here, the user cannot remove the file using the traditional rm command. However, the file can essentially be removed because of the write permission on the directory. This is an example of when you think your data is protected, when in fact it isn't! As a result, you must be aware of the interaction between the directory and file permissions.

The chmod Command

Changing the permissions on a file or directory is done with the chmod command. chmod has a large number of options and selections that you will see here. The syntax of the command is as follows:

```
$ chmod mode file(s)
```

The mode is the permissions that you want to assign. You can write the mode in two ways. One is called *symbolic* and the other *absolute*. The symbolic format uses letters to represent the different permissions, and the absolute uses a numeric format with octal digits representing the different permission levels.

Bear in mind that only the owner of the file can change the permissions associated with it. Remember, though, that the super user or root can also alter the permissions as well.

Symbolic

The symbolic mode uses letters to represent the different permissions that can be assigned, as outlined in table 7.1.

Table 7.1
Symbolic Permissions

Symbol	Meaning
r	read
w	write
x	execute or search

As you recall, there are different groups of users to which you want to grant permissions. These are the owner (or user), members of the same group, and all other users. Each classification of user has a letter used in the mode to indicate which classification this permission change is for (see table 7.2).

Table 7.2
Symbolic Entities

Symbol	Meaning
u	owner or user of the file
g	members of the same group
o	all other users
a	all users

The final option in this table—all users—is the default action unless otherwise specified by use of one of these options.

Finally, three operators are used to indicate what is to be done with the permissions and the user group. These are identified in table 7.3.

Table 7.3
Symbolic Operands

Symbol	Meaning
+	Add the permission
-	Remove the permission
=	Set the permissions equal to this

Now, you must combine all this together to form the mode, as illustrated in figure 7.6.

To define a mode using symbolic format, you need to decide which users you will affect. The default is to make the desired changes for all users. After you select which users are to be affected, you need to decide if you are adding or removing the permission, and then what permission are you working with. Several examples are shown in the following code:

```
$ ls -l
total 8
dr--r--r--   2 chare     users          48 Aug 24 21:09 a
dr-xr-xr-x   2 chare     users          48 Aug 24 21:12 a2
-rw-r--r--   1 chare     users          25 Aug 24 21:28 alpha.code
drwxr-xr-x   2 chare     users          32 Aug 24 21:08 micro_light
-rw-r--r--   1 chare     users         133 Aug 24 21:08 output
-rw-r--r--   1 chare     users          29 Aug 24 21:28 test2
-rw-r--r--   1 chare     users          12 Aug 24 21:28 test_1
drwxr-xr-x   2 chare     users          32 Aug 24 22:19 uvA
$ chmod -r test2
$ ls -l test2
--w-------   1 chare     users          29 Aug 24 21:28 test2
$ chmod g+rwx test2
$ ls -l test2
--w-rwx---   1 chare     users          29 Aug 24 21:28 test2
$ chmod =r test2
```

```
$ ls -l test2
-r--r--r--  1 chare    users          29 Aug 24 21:28 test2
$ chmod u+rwx,g+r,o+r test2
$ ls -l test2
-rwxr--r--  1 chare    users          29 Aug 24 21:28 test2
$ ls -l test_1
---x--x--x  1 chare    users          12 Aug 24 21:28 test_1
$
```

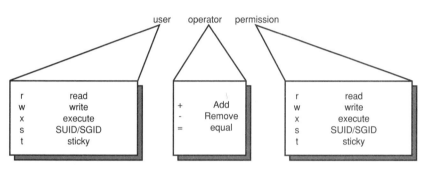

File/Directory Mode

Choose one from each

Figure 7.6
The chmod operators.

In the preceding examples, you have a user who makes consistent changes to the permissions on this file. The first example demonstrates the removal of read permission from the file test2. This results in the permissions being write-only for the owner. If you are a member of the group who owns this file, or any other user, then you have no access rights to this file.

The second example illustrates the addition of read, write, and execute permissions for the group owners. Notice that with the group option, the permission change doesn't affect any other users. The third example shows how to use the equals (=) operator. This instructs chmod to make the permissions on the file equal to whatever was indicated here. In this case, the permissions are made equal to read only for all users.

The next example illustrates how to make multiple changes at once. You could execute chmod three different times to make the desired changes, but it is less work to do it once. To make multiple changes, you include the complete information (user operator permissions) and separate each grouping with a comma, like the two last examples in the previous code block.

If chmod for any reason cannot access the file or make the requested change, an error message is printed to indicate the problem.

Absolute

The symbolic method of chmod is often easier to use than the absolute method, if for no other reason than the symbolic method enables you to change the permissions for a single group of users. The absolute method requires that the permissions for all users be specified, even for those that are not changing.

This method uses a series of octal digits to represent each of the permissions. The octal values are added together to give the actual permission. Figure 7.7 shows the octal representations.

Figure 7.7
Mapping
permissions and
values.

Notice in the following code that the read permission has an octal value of 4; write has a value of 2; and execute a value of 1. These values are used for both regular files and directories alike. To calculate the permissions, add the octal values for each group of users. The example in figure 7.7 has a value of 644. Then you run the chmod command using the value of 644 for the permissions instead of the symbolic values discussed earlier. The following code shows the same examples as seen earlier in the chapter, but using the absolute method of chmod.

```
$ ls -l
total 5
drwxrwxrwx  2 chare   users        48 Aug 24 21:12 a2
-rw-rw-rw-  1 chare   users        25 Aug 24 21:28 alpha.code
-rw-rw-rw-  1 chare   users        29 Aug 24 21:28 test2
-rw-rw-rw-  1 chare   users        12 Aug 24 21:28 test_1
drwxrwxrwx  2 chare   users        32 Aug 24 22:19 uvA
$ chmod 200 test2
$ ls -l test2
--w-------  1 chare   users        29 Aug 24 21:28 test2
$ chmod 270 test2
$ ls -l test2
--w-rwx---  1 chare   users        29 Aug 24 21:28 test2
$ chmod 444 test2
$ ls -l test2
-r--r--r--  1 chare   users        29 Aug 24 21:28 test2
$ chmod 744 test2
$ ls -l test2
```

```
-rwxr--r--  1 chare    users         29 Aug 24 21:28 test2
$ chmod 111 test_1
$ ls -l test_1
---x--x--x  1 chare    users         12 Aug 24 21:28 test_1
$
```

The commands are equivalent, so let's compare them.

chmod -r test2	chmod 200 test2
chmod g+rwx test2	chmod 270 test2
chmod =r test2	chmod 444 test2
chmod u+rwx,g+r,o+r test2	chmod 744 test2
chmod -r, -w, a+x test_1	chmod 111 test_1

You should have a good understanding of the symbolic method, so the absolute examples are further examined here. When changing the permissions, you must indicate all the permissions. In the first example, in which the permission mode is 200, you are assigning write only to the owner, and no permissions for any other users. In the second example, you assign write only to the owner, and read, write, and execute for the members of the same group, with no permissions for other users.

This method is considered more difficult because you have to translate the letters that represent the permissions to an octal value, and then execute the command. However, after some time, the octal values become second nature (particularly if you start doing system administration work).

Default File Permissions—umask

The default permissions for a file or directory are established when the file or directory is created. Figure 7.6 shows the default permissions, controlled by a value called umask. You can determine what the umask is by running the command umask. Figure 7.4 shows the default permissions for a file, and figure 7.5 for a directory, with a mask value as shown in the following:

```
$ umask
022
$
```

The umask command enables you to change the default file permissions assigned when you create a file or directory. To understand and change the umask, you must be able to think of permissions in the absolute sense. The umask is applied to the default permissions for a file and a directory. For example, the default file permissions for a file is 666, or read and write access for everyone on the system. This is not the most optimal thing to do, so apply the umask, which here is 022.

```
666
022
- - - -
644
```

The operation here is not subtraction although it appears that way. This is a bitwise exclusive OR (XOR) operation, but do not concern yourself with that too much. What is important here is for you to see the concept of what is happening and be able to apply it.

This example results in read and write for the owner, with read only for everyone else. The following example applies a umask value of 011.

```
666
011
- - - -
666
```

In this case, a umask value of 011 has no effect because the execute bits are not turned on. If you want read and write for the owner, with no access rights for anyone else, what would our umask value be?

```
666
066
- - - -
600
```

When the umask value is used, it removes the read and write bits for the group and other users, which leaves the read and write bits for the owner intact.

But the umask value applies to directories as well, so if you are going to customize the value, you must consider the impact on the directories also. The default permissions for a directory are 755 (after the umask is applied), which gives the owner read, write and search, with read and search for all other users. Like the file, the actual default is 777, so any user can do anything. So, apply the following umasks to your directory and see if you run into any problems.

```
777
022
- - - -
755
```

The preceding example shows us that the umask is working correctly. How about in the next case:

```
777
011
- - - -
766
```

This preceding example means that the group and other users can list files and create or delete them, but they cannot cd to this directory. This is not what you want to accomplish.

```
777
066
----
711
```

A umask value of 066 demonstrates how to allow people access to a directory while preventing them from creating, listing, or removing files.

In the situation where you want to prevent access by anyone except yourself, then you need to remove the read, write, and execute/search bits for all users except the owner. This is accomplished using a umask value of 077, which changes the default permission on the directory to 700.

```
777
077
----
700
```

In the preceding example, directories are protected by preventing access for any user but the owner. Does a umask value of 077 work to protect your files?

```
666
077
----
600
```

Yes it does! It works because you cannot mask off a permission bit that is not set. When applying the umask value of 077 to your default permissions of 666, the read and write permissions for the group and other users are removed. This results in the default permissions for your file being 600. The umask value also removes the execute bit, however. In the event that the permission you want to remove is not there, the umask value cannot change it.

Now that you have mastered the concept of umask and permissions, how do you change the umask? The command umask with no arguments prints the umask currently set. To change it, enter the command umask followed by the new umask you would like to have. This new umask is in effect until you log out. If you want this umask to be the default whenever you log in, insert it in your shell startup file, either .profile or .login in your home directory.

The following example completes this discussion of umask by illustrating how to change umask and that files and directories created have the new permissions.

```
$ ls -l
total 5
```

```
drwxrwxrwx  2 chare    users       48 Aug 24 21:12 a2
-rw-rw-rw-  1 chare    users       25 Aug 24 21:28 alpha.code
-rwxr--r--  1 chare    users       29 Aug 24 21:28 test2
---x--x--x  1 chare    users       12 Aug 24 21:28 test_1
drwxrwxrwx  2 chare    users       32 Aug 24 22:19 uvA
$ umask
022
$ umask 077
$ umask
077
$ mkdir new_dir
$ ls -ld new_dir
drwx------  2 chare    users       32 Aug 25 01:20 new_dir
$ touch new_file
$ ls -l new_file
-rw-------  1 chare    users        0 Aug 25 01:21 new_file
$
```

In this figure, you can see that after your umask was set to 077, the directory created had no permissions for anyone but the owner, and the same was true for the file.

Advanced Permissions

Several advanced permissions are available in UNIX. This section discusses two of them because they are the only relevant ones at this stage. These two permissions are called the Set User ID, or SUID, and the Set Group ID, or SGID. Interestingly enough, this concept has a patent number assigned to it—the first software patent number ever granted.

Two types of identification numbers are carried for you by the system: your real UID and your effective UID. The real UID matches the user name you logged in with. Your effective UID is your alias—who the system thinks you are. Sometimes when a command is executed, you must assume an identity other than your own for the period of time that the command executes. This is known as your *effective* UID.

File and directory permissions have been discussed at length, so now look at another example. The file /etc/passwd, which you know contains some information about your account, is protected by a set of file permissions. The following string shows those permissions:

```
-rw-r--r--  1 root        1364 Apr 14 10:45 /etc/passwd
```

Now, if the /etc/passwd file is not writable by anyone but root, then how can you change your password? Look at the passwd command, which is usually found in /bin, but may be located elsewhere, as in the following example:

```
-rwsr-xr-x  3 root      303104 Mar 19  1991 /usr/bin/passwd
```

Notice that the permission bits are different on this program. An 's' is where an 'x' would be in the owner's permissions. This is an SUID program. If you could run the id command while you were running the passwd command, you would see that your effective id is root. So, the SUID bit means that while you are running the program, you look like the owner of the program. When you run the passwd program to change your password, you look to the UNIX system like you are the root or super-user. A certain amount of UNIX is based upon this permission bit, and most potentially dangerous commands are often found to be controlled in this way.

The second advanced permissions discussed is the Set Group ID, or SGID. The SGID has the same function as the SUID, except that it is for the group. That is to say that when the command is executed, it appears to the system as if you are a member of the group, even if you are not. An example of an SGID command is shown as follows:

```
-rwsr-sr-x  1 root      kmem       180224 Apr  5  1991 /usr/bin/mail
```

This command, /usr/bin/mail, is an SGID program. This means that when the user runs /usr/bin/mail, he or she seems to be root and belong to a group called kmem. This means some things that would be difficult from a programming perspective are much easier. SGID is often used by application programmers to control access to files that are used by their application. By using SGID, the programmer doesn't have to ensure that all users on the system can read and/or write the files.

The SUID and SGID permissions are only for use on compiled or binary programs. Because of this, and the nature of the permissions, the process to allow this access with chmod is not discussed in detail. This is partly because the super user must assign this permission on some versions of UNIX.

The chown Command

The third of the advanced permissions is called the sticky bit. Since its inception, the sticky bit has evolved through different meanings.

The sticky bit was used as a memory management tool. When set, it instructed the kernel to keep a copy of the program in RAM, even if no one was using the program at the time. While this consumed memory resources, the command started execution very quickly.

When using directories. the sticky bit has different meanings on files and directories. It still prevents users from removing from public directories files that they do not own . The following example illustrates how this sticky bit is shown in ls:

```
$ ls -d /tmp
drwxrwxrwt ¦ root root    512 Aug 15 14:03
```

The sticky bit is shown by the letter 't' in the 'x' position of the 'other' permission bits. This means that even though the directory has read and write for all users, you cannot remove the file if you don't own it.

Every user on the system is assigned a unique UID that identifies them to the system. You will recall that every process, file, and directory created by this user has the user's UID stamped on it. At times however, you no longer need a particular file and want to give it to someone else. You can do this only if you are the owner of the file.

To accomplish the owner change, use the command chown, which has as the following command syntax:

```
$ chown user file(s)
```

The user name used in the chown command can be either a numerical UID, or the textual login name. In either case, the name or number must exist in the password file. The following code exemplifies chown in action.

```
$ touch new
$ /etc/chown patc new
chown: cant change ownership of new: Not owner
$
```

Take a note from this example. Some versions of chown are restricted—that is, if the user is not root, the super-user, then they cannot execute the command successfully. This is the circumstance for this example on a DEC Ultrix system, but is not the case on all UNIXes. This in itself is not a bad thing, because it helps prevent any possible loss of information through the improper use of this command, but it can prevent users from being able to do some of the things that they want to do with their files. However, even for other versions of UNIX, such as those that support C2 security or higher, the chown, chgrp, and chmod commands require special authorization from the system administrator in order to be able to execute them.

```
$ chown andreewg new
chown: unknown user id andreewg
$ chown andrewg new
$ls -l new
-rw-r--r--  1 andrewg    group         25 Aug 24 21:28 new
$
```

The file in this example is a sample chown from a version of System V UNIX. Notice that in this case, the use of chown is not restricted. On this system, which is SCO System V, it is possible to prevent a user from being able to execute this command.

The chgrp Command

Like chown, a command exists to enable users to change the group to which the file belongs. This can be useful if more than one person needs access to this file. Consider the following example. If you want to allow a group of users to access a file that is yours and they all belong to the same group, then you may change the group to be the same as theirs. Like the chown command, only the owner of the file may change the group name.

```
$ ls -l new
$ chgrp gopher new
chgrp: You are not a member of the gopher group.
$ chgrp tech new
$
ls -l new
```

The chgrp command gives a user the opportunity to change the group who owns the file. As illustrated in the previous code, the capability to change the group on a file requires that you also be a member of the group. As seen here, when the user tried to change the group ownership to gopher, she received an error message indicating that the request could not be completed. This behavior for chgrp is not consistent across all versions of UNIX. Many implementations will make the group change even though the user is not a member of the group.

Summary

This chapter discussed the protection of your information through one aspect of the UNIX System security—file permissions. The operation of this mechanism is very complex, and you should now be able to discuss and explain how permissions affect the access to information.

File Summary

/etc/passwd	Storage of user account information including passwords, user id numbers
/etc/group	Storage of information relating to group membership

Command Summary

id	Displays the user's real and effective ID
ls -l	Lists the contents of a directory.
chmod	Changes the permissions on a directory
umask	Lists or changes the default permissions
chown	Changes the ownership of a file
chgrp	Changes the group ownership of a file

Chapter Snapshot

Two of the most useful command-line utilities in UNIX are grep and find. grep enables you to search files for strings of text that meet your requirements, while find searches through directories for matching files. This chapter introduces these two tools with the following topics:

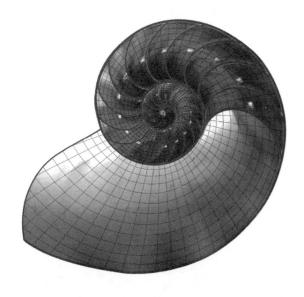

8

CHAPTER

grep and find

This chapter looks at two very powerful commands in UNIX: grep and find. For DOS users, they can be easily confused because grep is find under DOS.

Combined, these two utilities form a powerhouse of tools that can enable you to find all forms of data on your system. If you need to search for all occurrences of a phrase within a file, there is no easier tool to use than grep. Conversely, if you need to find all the files that were created within the last three days, find is the tool with unequaled searching capabilities.

Understanding the Difference between grep and find

As already mentioned, grep is equivalent to the find command under DOS. Both these commands look for text in a file. grep is one of three commands in the grep family, namely grep, egrep, and fgrep. Although these three commands are similar in what they do, how they do it is very different.

The find command on the other hand looks for file names in the directory structure based upon a wide range of criteria such as file name, file size, permissions, and owner.

Using Regular Expressions

Effectively using the grep family, as well as many other commands that search for text, is necessary to learn and understand regular expressions. A *regular expression* is a method of describing a string using a series of *metacharacters*, like in the shell. This is accomplished through a simple language.

The metacharacters are each assigned a special meaning when used in the regular expression context, but unfortunately, some of the metacharacters used in regular expressions overlap with the shell. The end result is that it is sometimes easy for a UNIX neophyte to get these confused. To combat this effect, take a good look at regular expressions.

Wild Cards and Metacharacters

The terms *wild card* and *metacharacter* are used interchangeable, and I have never heard anyone arguing the semantics of one versus the other. To look at how a regular expression is constructed, examine the wild cards presented in table 8.1.

Table 8.1
Wild cards and Metacharacters

Character	Description
c	Any non-special character; *c* matches itself
c	Turns off any special meaning for character *c*
^	Positions expression at the beginning of a line
^*c*	Any line in which *c* is the first character
$	Positions the expression at the end of a line

Character	Description
c$	Any line in which *c* is the last character
.	Any single character
[...]	Any one of characters in ...; ranges like a-z are legal
[^...]	Any single character not in ...; ranges are legal
\n	What the n'th \(...\) expression matches (grep only)
*r**	Zero or more occurrences of *r*
r+	One or more occurrences of *r* (egrep only)
r?	Zero or one occurrence of *r* (egrep only)
r1r2	*r1* followed by *r2*
r1|r2	*r1* or *r2* (egrep only)
\(*r*\)	Tagged regular expression
(*r*)	Regular expression *r* (egrep only)

Now take a careful look at these wild cards, and where appropriate compare them to those used in file name substitution by the shell. It is very important to note that in some cases, the way the wild cards are expanded can be very different because of how each shell processes the command line. This is discussed further in Chapter 18.

The ^ operator anchors a pattern (or expression) to the beginning of a line. For example, the pattern:

```
^the
```

matches occurrences in which the word "the" is at the beginning of a line. In fact, the "t" must be the first letter on the line. The letters "the" illiterate the first metacharacter listed in table 8.1, because they are not metacharacters. In this example, the letters "t h e" match themselves.

The $ operator anchors patterns to the end of a line, as illustrated in the following example:

```
the$
```

Although a special character that represents a newline does exist, no metacharacter is used to match only a newline. This operator does not count the newline in its search. Consequently, in the preceding example the word "the" is only matched when the letter "e" is in fact the *last* letter in the line.

In the shell's filename substitution, you saw that a ? is used to indicate a single character. This is not so in regular expressions. The single character wild card is a period (.). Consider the following example:

```
th.
```

This example matches any word that has the letters "t" and "h," followed by any character. Any number of "." can be put together to match a string. Two examples illustrating this and the metacharacters already discussed are presented in the following:

```
^the..
..th$
```

In these two examples, you are still looking for the occurrences of "th" and some letter. In these cases, both expect to find two letters before or after the "th". Notice that one pattern is anchored at the beginning of the line, and the other at the end.

The next metacharacter is the character class. The character class in regular expressions is the same as in the shell. Any single character in the group indicated in the class is matched. Table 8.2 shows some sample classes that can be used in either the [...] or [^...], which is discussed shortly.

Table 8.2
Expression Matches

Example	Description
[abc]	Matches one of a or b or c
[a-z]	Matches one of any lowercase letter between a and z
[A-Z]	Matches one of any uppercase letter between A and Z
[0-9]	Matches any one number between zero and nine
[^0-9]	Any character other than between zero and nine
[-0-9]	Any character between zero and nine, or a "-"
[0-9-]	Any character between zero and nine or a "-"
[^-0-9]	Any character other than between zero and nine and "-"
[a-zA-Z0-9]	Matches any alphabetic or numeric character

You saw character classes in action with the shell in Chapter 5, now look at the other character class in which you choose not to match certain letters. The [^...] operator indicates that you do not want to match certain letters, as in the following example:

```
th[^ae]n
```

This example does not match words like then and than, but does allow match for thin.

The next major operator in regular expressions is the *closure operator*, or the "*". This applies to the preceding pattern in the expression and collectively matches any number of successive occurrences of that pattern. This makes its operation here very different from the shell. For example, the following does not match chare like it does in the shell.

```
char*
```

This example matches "char," or "charr," "charrr," and so on. Now consider a few of other examples: [a-z]* matches any single character plus zero or more occurrences of that *same* character. Consider this: if the first letter matched from this class is an "r", then [a-z]* matches any number of the letter "r" after the first one.

To match any number of characters regardless of what they are, a combination of .* must be used. The period matches any single character, and the "*" matches any more occurrences of any single pattern.

This introduction to regular expressions is expanded and built upon during the balance of this chapter.

Understanding the grep Family

The grep family is a series of commands—grep, egrep, and fgrep—that all search for text strings within a file. The mechanisms and capabilities of the three commands are slightly different. This section examines these commands and how to use them with regular expressions. The power, flexibility, and capability of regular expressions cannot really be understood until you see them in action.

It is reasonable to ask why there are three very related commands. grep was reportedly the first of them and has very good capabilities. fgrep, although fast, cannot handle regular expressions, and this reduces its usefulness. egrep is probably a little harder to understand. Despite the extra features that it has, it is not much different from grep. During my career, I have yet to meet someone who uses egrep on a regular basis. Personally, I have rarely used it at all, opting to use grep instead.

This chapter examines regular expressions and grep, and takes a quick look at the capabilities of fgrep and egrep.

The grep Command

grep stands for *Global Regular Expression Print*. The command itself is a filter. It is designed to accept input and filter it like a sieve to reduce the output. To do so, grep can, like other filters, accept its input from either a file or through standard input. The standard input method can be either at the command line, or by sending information to grep through a pipe. To perform this task, grep accepts its input and compares the pattern to match with the input. If the pattern matches, then the line containing the match is printed. Otherwise, no output is generated. The following code illustrates using grep to extract information from the password file.

```
$ grep chrish /etc/passwd
$ grep chare /etc/passwd
chare:A/49W7Abjlj6U:1003:104:Chris Hare:/home/chare:/usr/bin/ksh
$
```

This illustrates the format of the grep command, which is as follows:

```
grep pattern file(s)
```

In the first line in the preceding example, the pattern is chrish, and the file is /etc/passwd. grep reads the contents of the file looking for chrish. Because grep did not print anything, you know that the file does not contain chrish. In the second line, the pattern is chare. In this case, grep prints one line from /etc/passwd. This is the entry for the user chare in the /etc/passwd file.

The patterns chrish and chare are very simple patterns. You are now going to look at using grep with more complex regular expressions.

Using grep

The grep command is a phenomenal tool when you consider the vast uses for it. We can search any file looking for text, given that you have the needed access to do it. grep's operation also can be changed through the use of options. Table 8.3 lists the options available for grep.

Table 8.3
grep Options

Options	Description
-b	Prints the line with the block number
-c	Prints count of matching lines only
-e pattern	Used when the pattern starts with a -
-f filename	Takes the pattern from the file

Options	Description
-h	Does not print the file name
-i	Ignores case of letters in the comparison
-l	Prints only filenames with matching lines
-n	Prints line numbers
-s	Suppresses file error messages
-w	Searches for an expression as for a word (DEC Ultrix)
-y	Ignores case of letters in the comparison (SCO XENIX, SCO UNIX)
-v	Prints non-matching lines
-x	Prints exact lines matched by their entirety (fgrep) (DEC Ultrix)

This chapter does not explore all the options available, but restricts examination to those more commonly used. Options for grep can also be combined. Care must be taken, however, because some options are complimentary, such as -icv, and other options oppose each other, such as -cn.

The chapter has already examined the grep command line; it now concentrates on using grep in some real-world situations and examples. For example, if you want to know who has sent you mail, you could easily run the mail program to read it. But suppose that you do not want to read it, you simply want to know who sent it. The following code illustrates two grep patterns that can be used to accomplish this.

```
$ grep From /usr/mail/chare
From uunet.ca!mail.uunet.ca!uunet.uu.net!rdpub!martha@gateway.UUCP Mon
Jul 11 19:21:23 1994
From: Martha Masinton <rdpub!martha@uunet.uu.net>
>from this text file.  I think that it would be best to replace it and
start over again with a graphic.
From uunet.ca!mail.uunet.ca!tpts1.seed.net.tw!idpt18@gateway.UUCP Fri
Jul 22 23:30:52 1994
From: idpt18@tpts1.seed.net.tw (PC_user)
From gateway!news Sun Aug 14 17:46:16 1994
From: nwishbow@bcarh79a.bnr.ca (Nina Wishbow)
From gateway!news Thu Aug 25 15:13:45 1994
From: bownes@emi.com (R.M. Bownes III)
From gateway!news Sat Aug 27 21:14:06 1994
From: don@ra.cs.umb.edu (Donald A. L'Heureux)
$
```

The preceding example simply uses the pattern "From" to select all the lines that contain this pattern. The downfall is that it gives you a large amount of information. Notice the two versions of the lines you see. Some lines use the pattern "From," and others use the pattern "From:". This match also produces a line from a message that contains the word from. So, the object is to restrict the output to only what you want. You can accomplish this by making the pattern more specific.

Because the lines that use "From:" in the example tell you more about who the message is from, use that one to narrow your search, as shown here.

```
$grep "From:" /usr/mail/chare
From: Martha Masinton <rdpub!martha@uunet.uu.net>
From: idpt18@tpts1.seed.net.tw (PC_user)
From: nwishbow@bcarh79a.bnr.ca (Nina Wishbow)
From: bownes@emi.com (R.M. Bownes III)
From: don@ra.cs.umb.edu (Donald A. L'Heureux)
$
```

The previous example narrows down your search quite a bit. Notice that the search pattern is enclosed in quotation marks. Quotation marks are not necessary unless there is a space or other characters that you do not want the shell to see, but using them is a good habit to get into. The output now is that you only have the lines that have the "From:" pattern in them. How about the converse? If you did not want the "From:" lines, you would restrict your search to eliminate those lines by changing your pattern to "From".

```
$ grep "From"  /usr/mail/chare
From uunet.ca!mail.uunet.ca!uunet.uu.net!rdpub!martha@gateway.UUCP Mon
Jul 11 19:21:23 1994
>from this text file.  I think that it would be best to replace it and
start over again with a graphic.
From uunet.ca!mail.uunet.ca!tpts1.seed.net.tw!idpt18@gateway.UUCP Fri
Jul 22 23:30:52 1994
From gateway!news Sun Aug 14 17:46:16 1994
From gateway!news Thu Aug 25 15:13:45 1994
From gateway!news Sat Aug 27 21:14:06 1994
$
```

The previous code illustrates the difference in the pattern between the previous examples, as well as the output. But now you have a different problem. You still have a line that is part of a message. How can you eliminate that? You do not see this line when you use the "From:" pattern because it does not match. But if you restrict your pattern match even farther by anchoring the pattern, you eliminate this unwanted line.

```
$ grep "^From"  /usr/mail/chare
From uunet.ca!mail.uunet.ca!uunet.uu.net!rdpub!martha@gateway.UUCP Mon
Jul 11 19:21:23 1994
```

```
From uunet.ca!mail.uunet.ca!tpts1.seed.net.tw!idpt18@gateway.UUCP Fri
Jul 22 23:30:52 1994
From gateway!news Sun Aug 14 17:46:16 1994
From gateway!news Thu Aug 25 15:13:45 1994
From gateway!news Sat Aug 27 21:14:06 1994
$
```

The previous example anchors the pattern to the beginning of the line, which then gets you only the output that you want. Listing 1 at the end of the chapter is a shell program that uses some concepts not yet discussed. chkmail is a program that does what has been discussed here thus far. It is an example of using grep in a program.

grep also can be used to find out if someone is logged on. On the UNIX system that I am using right now, it would be overkill as it only reports one user, but if you have 10 or 20 users, why read through the output when you can have the system do the work for you, as the following example illustrates:

```
$ who ¦ grep billj
billj     tty0d  Jul  7 21:14
```

Another interesting use for grep is to find files accessible by certain users. For example, consider the following example:

```
ls -l ¦ grep ^d
drwxr-xr-x 23 chare    users      416 Mar 23 23:31 Algonquin
drwxr-xr-x  2 chare    users      224 Jul  2 20:15 Bell
drwxrwxr-x  2 chare    users       32 Feb  5  1988 Clipboard
drwxrwxr-x  2 chare    users      448 May 23 05:30 bin
drwxr-xr-x  2 chare    users       80 Apr 19  1993 internals
drwxr-xr-x  2 chare    users      240 Jun 23 20:33 letters
drwxr-xr-x  2 root     other       80 Sep 27  1993 lp
drwxr-xr-x  2 chare    users       80 Apr 19  1993 memos
drwxr-xr-x  7 chare    users      192 May  3 18:40 perl
drwxr-xr-x  5 chare    users       96 Apr 18 19:39 publish
drwxr-xr-x  2 chare    users      224 Apr 19  1993 shells
drwxr-xr-x  8 chare    root       128 Apr 19  1993 tools
drwxr-xr-x  2 chare    users     1792 Apr 19  1993 tricks
$
```

The pattern used in the previous code anchors the letter "d" to the beginning of the line. The output is a list of the directories in your current working directory. The previous example shows how you could combine ls and grep to only list the directories. The following example illustrates how you can combine ls and grep to list the files that only you can access

```
$ ls -l ¦ grep "^.rw.------"
drwx------2 chare    users       32 Apr 30 06:37 Mail
```

```
-rw-------1 chare    users      21959 May  8 07:01 a.out
-rw-------1 chare    users        290 Aug 19 07:59 a1
-rw-------1 chare    users        390 Aug 20 02:01 a2
-rw-------1 chare    users        418 Aug 19 08:40 a3
-rw-------1 chare    users        102 Aug 19 09:44 a4
-rw-------1 chare    users        108 Aug 19 10:58 b1
-rw-------1 chare    users        195 Aug 20 00:53 b2
-rw-------1 chare    users        245 Aug 20 00:33 b3
-rw-------1 chare    users        265 Aug 20 00:56 b4
-rw-------1 chare    users        232 Aug 12 20:59 brk
-rw-------1 chare    users          1 Aug 20 00:26 brk.awk
$
```

The previous example combines the anchor and the period to create your pattern. You can also twist this around to see which files are accessible by everyone by using the same command and the -v option to grep as illustrated in the following example.

```
$ ls -l ¦ grep -v ^.rw.------
drwxr-xr-x  2 chare    users       32 May 16  1993 Clipboard
-rw-r--r--  1 chare    users      126 Jun  5  1993 Environment
drwxr-xr-x  6 chare    users      272 May  3 07:47 Filecabinet
-rw-r----   1 chare    users       63 Jul 29  1993 MW.INI
drwxr-xr-x  2 chare    users       32 May 16  1993 Wastebasket
drwxr-xr-x  2 chare    users       96 Aug 24 18:05 chp6
-rw-r--r--  1 chare    users      109 Aug 19 01:03 city
-rw-r--r--  1 chare    users      128 Aug 20 01:58 city2
-rwxr-xr-x  1 chare    users      119 Aug 12 21:16 cont
-rwxr-xr-x  1 chare    users       68 Aug 11 22:17 cp2
-rw-r--r--  1 chare    users      341 May  7 09:23 doc
-rw-r--r--  1 root     users      836 Jun  6  1993 exinit
-rwxr-xr-x  1 chare    users       94 Aug  9 21:55 fi1
-rwxr-xr-x  1 chare    users       38 Aug  9 22:59 fi2
$
```

This example shows the exact opposite of the previous one because the -v option instructs grep to print the lines that do not match the pattern.

With the use of complex regular expressions, grep becomes a powerful tool for shell programs and data manipulation. Remember from the discussion in Chapter 7 that the password file has seven fields, and the second field contains the user's password. (On many higher security capable systems, this example does not work because the password field is never empty.) If you want to know which users have no passwords, then you need to construct a pattern that checks to see if the second field is blank.

In the following example, the pattern used instructs grep to start its pattern match at the beginning of the line and match any character but a colon up to a pair of double colons.

If it finds this type of pattern, then grep should print the lines. So, those users listed in the following code do not have a password to access this machine. (So much for security!)

```
$ grep "^[^:]*::" /etc/passwd
uucp::5:6:uucp:/usr/spool/uucppublic:/usr/lib/uucp/uucico
nuucp::5:6:uucp:/usr/spool/uucppublic:/usr/lib/uucp/uucico
tutor::100:100:Tutorial:/u/tutor:
install::101:100:Administration Login:/u/install:
terri::102:100:Terri Hare:/u/terri:
meagan::103:100:Meagan Hare:/u/meagan:
matthew::104:100:Matthew Hare:/u/matthew:
$
```

The following examples show some of the other options to grep:

```
$ grep -c "[a-z].*" /usr/dict/words
24348
$ grep -c "^a.*" /usr/dict/words
1337
$ grep -vc "^a.*" /usr/dict/words
23137
$
```

The -c option instructs grep to count the number of times this pattern is matched and not to print the lines themselves. In the first example, grep informs you how many lines are in the file. The second example shows how many words that start with the letter "a" are in the dictionary. The last example here tells you how many words do not match the pattern specified.

Earlier, you saw that, by using a pattern such as `"^.rw----"`, you could list the files not accessible by anyone. In that example, you used a period as the first character of your pattern so it would match both directories and files. To allow for a match only on files, you need to add an option to the grep command. The option must be provided so that grep does not interpret the pattern as a list of options because it starts with a hyphen. This is illustrated in the following code:

```
$ ls -l | grep -e -rw.------
-rw------- 1 chare    users         21959 May  8 07:01 a.out
-rw------- 1 chare    users           290 Aug 19 07:59 a1
-rw------- 1 chare    users           390 Aug 20 02:01 a2
-rw------- 1 chare    users           418 Aug 19 08:40 a3
-rw------- 1 chare    users           102 Aug 19 09:44 a4
-rw------- 1 chare    users           108 Aug 19 10:58 b1
-rw------- 1 chare    users           195 Aug 20 00:53 b2
-rw------- 1 chare    users           245 Aug 20 00:33 b3
-rw------- 1 chare    users           265 Aug 20 00:56 b4
```

```
-rw------- 1 chare    users         232 Aug 12 20:59 brk
-rw------- 1 chare    users           1 Aug 20 00:26 brk.awk
$ ls -l ¦ grep "-rw.------"
grep: illegal option -- r
grep: illegal option -- w
grep: illegal option -- .
grep: illegal option -- -
grep: illegal option -- -
grep: illegal option -- -
grep: illegal option -- -
grep: illegal option -- -
grep: illegal option -- -
Usage: grep -blcnsvi pattern file . . .
$
```

In the first part of the example, the -e option allows grep to interpret the pattern correctly. Without this option, as shown in the second part, grep does not interpret the pattern correctly and misinterprets each of the hyphens as an option flag. This is the explanation for the error.

Using the fgrep Command

fgrep has a similar purpose to grep. In fact, they both do the same thing. The only difference between grep and fgrep is that fgrep searches for many literal strings simultaneously. This section looks at the fgrep command in action.

Unlike the grep and egrep commands, the fgrep command (fixed grep or fast grep) does not work with regular expressions.

It can only work with literal strings. The downside to this is that the matches are not anchored. For example, if your pattern list included the word *sign*, fgrep would also match *signal*, *signage*, and any other word that contained the word sign. As a result, you need to be prepared to see a good deal of output. The following code shows a short list of words and a search using fgrep in the dictionary, /usr/dict/words.

```
$ cat string
happy
emotion
$ fgrep -f string /usr/dict/words
emotion
emotional
happy
$
```

The example has been cut down to be something that could be shown easily and readily. For example, 21 words in the standard UNIX dictionary contain the word "sign!"

Using the egrep Command

egrep is the third command in the grep family. Like grep, egrep interprets and processes regular expressions, but egrep handles what Kernighan and Pike call "true regular expressions" (*The UNIX Programming Environment*, Prentice Hall 1984). They call them true regular expressions because egrep has an "or" operator and parentheses to group expressions for processing.

As you recall from table 8.1, egrep enables you to specify a string like the following, which tells egrep to match on the empty string, da, dada, dadada, and so on:

```
(da)*
```

egrep also has several other operators not found in grep. These include the "or" operator, which enables you to make a statement such as the following:

```
hello¦goodbye
```

This means that the match could be hello or goodbye.

grep and Pipes

Chapter 5 discussed redirection and pipes, and you examine them again in Chapter 10. But it is important to look at using grep with pipes. As mentioned earlier, grep is a filter: it accepts input through standard input and sends its output through standard output. This means that it can be in the middle of a pipe. In fact, some of the examples presented thus far showed grep in the middle of a pipe.

When you are going to use commands, think about using them in a pipeline wherever possible. This is easier for you the user and the system because the following example:

```
$ ls -l > files
$ grep "myfile" files
```

is equivalent to the following single command:

```
$ ls -l ¦ grep myfile
```

Consequently, there is less to type, which decreases the likelihood of a mistake. It also is easier for the system because, in the first example, a temporary file is made that the user might not remember to remove. Temporary files take up disk space, and if a process is large enough, can impact the performance of the system. The second case also uses a temporary file, but UNIX allocates the blocks and clears them after the operation is complete. This results in less disk space used over time, and is more efficient from the point of view of kernel and process resource allocation.

Some very complex commands can be built with pipes, and with the power of grep it is easier to harness those capabilities with a pipe.

The preceding example shows grep on the end of the pipe. But grep also can be in the middle of the pipe, as follows:

```
$ ls -lR ¦ grep "^.rw.------" ¦ sort ¦ tee ¦ lp
```

You have not seen many of these commands yet, but this is an example of a complicated pipeline, using some of the commands that you have seen thus far. The pipe does a recursive listing of all the files from where the user is now; sends the list through grep, which looks for files accessible only by the owner; sends the list to sort, which sorts it; and sends it through another pipe to tee, which prints the list on standard output and also sends the list to the printer via lp. This illustration ties five commands together. Not all commands can be in the middle of a pipe. The next section examines at a command that cannot be on the end of a pipe—only on the beginning.

Understanding the find Command

As mentioned earlier, the find command under UNIX is very different from find under DOS. First, the find command under MS-DOS essentially does what the grep command under UNIX does: searches for text within a file. The UNIX find command is useful to locate files within the directory structure, based upon a wide range of search criteria.

What is find?

Find is not a filter. It cannot be in the middle or at the end of a pipe. It can, however, provide information at the top of the pipe. Find is used to search the UNIX filesystem looking for files given a certain criteria. That criteria could be based upon file size, access time, name, file type, or more. The command syntax for find is as follows:

```
find path predicate-list
```

The path is from where find starts the search. It must be specified, because no default exists. The predicate list consists of the search criteria and command that you want find to do with the located files. The predicates available are listed in table 8.4.

Table 8.4
find Predicates

Predicates	Explanation
-atime days	True if the file was accessed in specified number of days
-cpio device	The file(s) found are written on the device indicated in cpio format

Predicates	Explanation
-ctime days	True if the file was changed in the specified number of days
-depth	Causes all entries in a directory to be processed before the directory itself; useful with cpio
-exec command {} \;	Executes the named command for each file
-group name	True if the file is owned by the specified group
-inum num	Tests true if the file has the specified inode number DEC Ultrix
-links num	True if the file has num links
-mount	True if the file is on the same filesystem as the starting pathname; ensures that the filesystem boundary is not crossed
-mtime days	True if the file was modified in the specified number of days
-name file	True if the specified name matches the name of each file
-newer file	True if the found file is newer than the specified file
-ok command	Like exec, except the user is prompted first
-perm octal	True if the found file has the permissions specified
-print	Prints the names of the files found
-size num	True if the file is the specified size in blocks (512 bytes per block)
-type flag	True if the file is of the specified type
-user name	True if the found file is owned by the specified user

Each option can be used singly or in combination and many of them are examined next.

Using the find Command

As mentioned, find is used to locate files. This is the extent of find's capability and use. This section looks at the find command options and how to combine them in practice.

The examples in the following code illustrate find in action. The -print option prints the names of the files that are found. If you do not include this option, find does not print the file names. When find exists, it sets a return code that tells the shell that it did find some files. The use of return codes are covered in Part V of this book.

```
$ find /usr -atime 10 -print
/usr/bin/id
/usr/bin/egrep
/usr/lib/ua/uasig
/usr/include/grp.h
/usr/include/pwd.h
/usr/include/stdio.h
/usr/include/sys/types.h
/usr/include/time.h
```

Apart from the -print option, the code also illustrates how to use the -atime option to find accessed files. Three separate times are stored in the inode for each file. These are the times the files were last accessed (read or executed), last modified (contents were written), and last changed (information in the inode was updated, like permissions, for example).

The find command in the previous code looks for files accessed in the last ten days. This does not mean files that were accessed in zero to ten days, but that were accessed ten days ago.

The following code illustrates two more options. The -name option requires an argument. This argument can use the file substitution wild cards, but if it does, it must be enclosed in quotes. This is because the shell expands the wild cards before find sees them. This example looks for files that end in ".ps". Notice that it starts from the current directory. After the files are found, you can print the names, and then write the file to the device specified with the -cpio option. In this case, the device is /dev/rmt0h. When all the file names are printed, the number of blocks written to the device is printed.

```
$ find . -name "*.ps" -print -cpio /dev/rmt0h
./a.out.ps
./a1.ps
./a2.ps
./a3.ps
./a4.ps
.
50 blocks
$
```

Another example of using find to back up a group of files is shown in the following code. In this case, the output of find, which is a list of file names, is sent directly to the cpio command so that the data can be written to the backup device. cpio is not discussed here, but is covered in Chapter 27.

```
$ find . -name "*.ps" -print | cpio -oBcv > /dev/rmt0h
a.out.ps
a1.ps
a2.ps
```

```
a3.ps
a4.ps
50 blocks
$
```

find also has two Boolean style operators, which provide the capability for find to match files based on one or more criteria. For example, the following example illustrates that files named care or ending in .bak are to be removed:

```
$ find /\(-name core -o -name "*.bak" \) -exec rm -f () \;
```

The following example looks at the -ctime option. You saw that -atime finds files accessed in the specified number of days. The -ctime option is only different in that it looks at the date the inode information was last changed. This information generally is the permissions on a file, but changes to other information can cause the inode change date to be updated.

```
$ find / -ctime 3 -print
/usr/adm
/usr/spool/lp/request/Epson
/usr/spool/uucp/SYSLOG
/usr/spool/uucp/o.Log-WEEK
$
```

You have seen that find can use the -cpio option to send the files directly to the cpio command. Using the -exec option, as illustrated here, you can execute any command on the found files:

```
$ find . -name "*.ps" -exec ls -l {} \;
-rw------- 1 chare    users       21959 Aug 25 19:25 ./a.out.ps
-rw------- 1 chare    users         290 Aug 25 19:25 ./a1.ps
-rw------- 1 chare    users         390 Aug 25 19:25 ./a2.ps
-rw------- 1 chare    users         418 Aug 25 19:25 ./a3.ps
-rw------- 1 chare    users         102 Aug 25 19:25 ./a4.ps
$
```

The previous code presents one of the more complicated options for find—the -exec option. This option instructs find to execute the named command on each file found. The tricky part is the syntax for the option. The syntax involves the command to be executed and its own options, a pair of curly braces, and a command terminator, as shown here:

```
-exec command {} \;
```

II

The Command Line

The curly braces instruct find to place the found file here, for example, the following code:

```
-exec ls -l {} \;
```

matches the file sampler.ps in the find statement, then the following exec instruction executes the command:

```
ls -l sampler.ps
```

The \; is used to terminate the instruction as it is passed to the shell. It cannot be omitted. In the -exec example, the command ls -l is executed for each file. Why wasn't the -print option included? If the -print option is included, find prints each of the files found that match the pattern. The ls -l being executed for each file is also executed. The end result is that for each file, two lines are printed: one printing the file name, and one for the ls -l output.

One of the biggest problems for new users is understanding where find starts looking for files. The first argument defines the start point. This can't be either an absolute or a relative pathname. For example, using a period instructs find to start searching from the current directory, but using a lone slash (/) instructs find to start searching from the root directory. Use of the slash and a path, as in /usr, instructs find to search from the /usr directory, in this case on files and directories under /usr and searched.

The following code examines finding files based upon the group that owns the file. This example looks for files that have a group ownership of mail. You can see the known groups on the system by looking at the file /etc/group, which was discussed in Chapter 7.

```
$ find / -group mail -print
/bin/mail
/bin/rmail
/u/chare/Filecabinet/choreo/policy/usr/itools/frame/dead.letter
/usr/mail
/usr/mail/uucp
/usr/mail/chare
/usr/spool/uucp/LOGDEL
/usr/spool/uucp/SYSLOG
/usr/spool/uucp/Log-WEEK
/usr/spool/uucp/o.Log-WEEK
/usr/spool/uucp/LOGFILE
/usr/local/elm
/usr/local/filter
$
```

The following example looks at the -ok option, which is like the -exec option. The difference is that while the -exec option simply executes the command, the -ok option asks the user if the command should be run.

```
$ find . -name "*.ps" -ok ls -l {} \;
< ls ... ./a.out.ps >?   n
< ls ... ./a1.ps >?   y
-rw------- 1 chare    users        290 Aug 25 19:25 ./a1.ps
< ls ... ./a2.ps >?   y
-rw------- 1 chare    users        390 Aug 25 19:25 ./a2.ps
< ls ... ./a3.ps >?   n
< ls ... ./a4.ps >?   n
$
```

The additional find options discussed here are -type, and -user. The -type option enables you to locate files based upon the file type. Table 8.5 lists the valid arguments for the -type option.

Table 8.5
File Types Used with find

Symbol	Description
b	block special file
c	character special file
d	directory
f	regular file
p	named pipes and FIFOs

As illustrated in the following example, you can find files that are only directories for example.

```
$ find . -type d -print
./Filecabinet
./Filecabinet/Profiles
./Filecabinet/c2
./Filecabinet/w
./Wastebasket
./Clipboard
./.elm
./Mail
./uvA
./uvA/micro_light
./chp6
$
```

This example lists all the directories in the directory structure below where you start from. The following example shows how you can use -type and -exec to correct the permissions on directories.

```
$ find . -type c -exec chmod 755 {} \; -print
./Filecabinet
./Filecabinet/Profiles
./Filecabinet/c2
./Filecabinet/w
./Wastebasket
./Clipboard
./.elm
./Mail
./uvA
./uvA/micro_light
./chp6
$
```

You can also use find to set the owner, group, and permissions for each file all at once. Try the following command:

```
$ find . -type d -exec chown USER {} \; -exec chgrp GROUP {} \; -exec
➡chmod 755 {} \; -print
```

This is one of the find command's major strengths. Grouping this type of activity like this means that you can accomplish the task in much less time than if you performed each one separately.

The final option discussed in this section is -user. Like -group, the -user command locates a file based upon the owner of the file.

The following code illustrates finding the files owned by a user named lslipp. The value following the -user on the command line can be either a valid UID, or a username. The username must be found in /etc/passwd. Using this option, you can find all the files owned by a user and archive them to tape before removing them from the system.

```
$ find /u -user terri -print
/u/terri
/u/terri/.profile
/u/terri/.phdir
/u/terri/Environment
/u/terri/Filecabinet
/u/terri/Filecabinet/Profiles
/u/terri/Filecabinet/Profiles/1200bps:Am
/u/terri/Filecabinet/Profiles/300bps:Am
/u/terri/Filecabinet/Profiles/9600bps:A2
```

```
/u/terri/Filecabinet/mydict.clm
/u/terri/Filecabinet/candy.pf0
/u/terri/Filecabinet/candy.rf0
/u/terri/.kshrc
/u/terri/Wastebasket
/u/terri/Clipboard
/u/terri/.othello.log
/u/terri/.caldir
$
```

The find Command and Pipes

As mentioned earlier, find cannot be in the middle or receiving end of a pipe. This is because it cannot read from standard input, but must have all its information present on the command line in order to complete. find is often used at the head of a pipe, as illustrated in some of the figures, to send information to another command for filtering, or direct processing.

Summary

Both grep and find are useful commands to search for text in files and to locate files on the disk. The powerful regular expression mechanism provides the basis for the flexibility of grep. With the wide variety of methods that can be used to search for files, the UNIX find command is the envy of computer users everywhere.

A good example of using grep is included in a shell program at the end of Chapter 24, "Run Levels and the Login Process." This program needs your mailbox to report who your mail is from.

Program Listing

```
chkmail (Version 1.0)
#!/bin/sh
# chkmail
# this program will print the From: or From line for the users from
# their mailbox.
#
# Chris Hare, 1994
# INSIDE UNIX
#
```

```
# Before doing any real work, we need to decide if the user has a
# mailbox
# configured. The shell variable MAIL usually indicates where the
# mailbox is.
#
# We want to use this mailbox value because the mailbox post offices
# are in
# either /usr/mail, or /usr/spool/mail, depending upon which version of
# UNIX
# is in use.
#
# Here is some sample output (default action)
#
# $ chkmail
# From: Chris Hare <chare@choreo.ca>
# From: root@choreo.ca
# From: System PRIVILEGED Account <root@choreo.ca>
# From: System PRIVILEGED Account <root@choreo.ca>
# From: Chris Hare <chare@choreo.ca>
#
# Here is some sample output using the -r option
#
# $ chkmail -r
# From chare Sat Jul  9 13:28:37 1994
# From root@choreo.ca Sat Jul  9 13:30:46 1994
# From daemon Sat Jul  9 13:31:49 1994
# From daemon Sat Jul  9 13:32:21 1994
# From chare Sat Jul  9 14:23:28 1994
#
# Is the MAIL variable defined?  We do this code section ONLY if the
# variable is
# NOT DEFINED.
#
if [ ! "$MAIL" ]
then
    if [ -d /usr/mail ]       # System V mailboxes (generally)
    then
        #
        # we will assume that the file spool files are here, and assign
        # the appropriate variables
        #
        MAIL=/usr/mail/$LOGNAME
        export MAIL
    elif [ -d /usr/spool/mail ] # BSD mailboxes. Also SCO.
```

```
    then
        #
        # we will assume that the file spool files are here, and assign
        # the appropriate variables
        #
        MAIL=/usr/spool/mail/$LOGNAME
        export MAIL
    else
        #
        # If we make it to here, then neither of the typical
        # directories
        # exist, and we don't know where to go looking. So, report an
        # error and exit.
        #
        echo "The location of your mail box is unknown."
        echo "Please contact your system administrator."
        exit 1
    fi
fi
#
# Do we want to see the From:lines, which is the default action, or the
# From lines (use -r).
# This section specifies the pattern which will be used with the grep.
#
if [ "$1" = "-r" ]
then
    PATTERN="^From "
else
    PATTERN="^From:"
fi
#
# Lets make sure we have a valid file, If the file doesn't exist, then
# we
# will report an error and exit.
#
if [ -f $MAIL ]
then
    #
    # Now we can search ....
    #
    grep "$PATTERN" $MAIL
else
    echo "Your mailbox ($MAIL) cannot be accessed."
fi
exit 0
```

Chapter Snapshot

The usefulness of data within a file is limited by its capability to be accessed and manipulated. This chapter introduces several utilities native to UNIX that serve to extract data from files. Topics discussed here include the following:

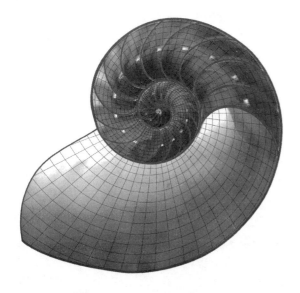

CHAPTER

Extracting Data

By the title, "Extracting Data," you might think this chapter is about retrieving information from a backup tape or other storage place. That is only partially correct. This chapter examines some commands that allow the manipulation of the data directly in files. Many complex commands and programs have been built with these tools.

Specifically, this chapter discusses controlling which part of a file you can look at using the commands head and tail; how to extract information from a file using cut; and put it back together again using paste. The join command is like paste but is used to join lines of text based upon a common field in each file.

Understanding the head Command

The head command is used to print the top of the file. By default, this command prints the top ten lines of the file. The command syntax for head is as follows:

```
$ head file(s)
```

or

```
$ head -num file(s)
```

The first format of the command prints the top ten lines of each of the named files, as illustrated in the following:

```
$ head /etc/passwd
root:HmILLEJdAnusE:0:0:Root:/:
daemon:NONE:1:1:Admin:/:
bin:NONE:2:2:Admin:/bin:
sys:NONE:3:3:Admin:/:
adm:NONE:4:4:Admin:/usr/adm:
uucp::5:6:uucp:/usr/spool/uucppublic:/usr/lib/uucp/uucico
nuucp::5:6:uucp:/usr/spool/uucppublic:/usr/lib/uucp/uucico
uucpadm:NONE:5:6:Uucp Administration:/usr/lib/uucp:
lp:NONE:71:1:Lp Administrator:/bin:
tutor::100:100:Tutorial:/u/tutor:
$
```

In the previous example, you see the first ten lines of the password file. However, often you don't want ten lines of output. The second format enables the user to control how much of the file they see. It is often useful to look at the first line of the file, as illustrated in the following example:

```
$ head -3 /etc/passwd
root:HmILLEJdAnusE:0:0:Root:/:
daemon:NONE:1:1:Admin:/:
bin:NONE:2:2:Admin:/bin:
$
```

From time to time, you want information from a command, but are not interested in looking at all the output. For example, as shown in the following code, some versions of UNIX, such as SCO and DEC Ultrix, have a command called pstat, which prints information on file and inode usage. pstat first prints how many files are open and then prints the file information. Typically, you do not want the file information, only the number of files open. By using the command in this code, you can strip out the unwanted information.

Not all versions of UNIX come with the head command; many only have tail. This is frequently a problem on System V UNIXes, including AT&T and UnixWare. The head command can be mimicked by using `sed -10q` which will print the first 10 lines and exit. The sed command is discussed in Chapter 22, "The sed Editor."

```
$ pstat -f ¦ head -1
135/600 open files
$ ps -ef ¦ grep chare ¦ head -2
  chare 1651    1  6 02:54:55 000  0:08 ksh
  chare 1951 1651 50 20:35:43 000  0:01 ps
$
```

The second command in the previous example shows using head in a similar fashion. First you get a list of the processess on the system, find those being executed by the user chare, and then list only the first two in the output. It is important to remember that some older versions of head limit the number of line that can be displayed to 99.

As you can see in these examples, head can function as a filter because it can read from standard input or a file. Because it writes to standard output, it can easily send its information down a pipe. But what if you want the information at the bottom of the file? Then use the opposite of head: the tail command.

Understanding the tail Command

The tail command does the same as head, but from the bottom of a file. By default, tail prints the last ten lines of the file. The command syntax is like head, as follows:

```
$ tail options file(s)
```

The options that tail has cover more than with head, as shown in table 9.1.

Table 9.1
tail Command Options

Option	Explanation
-f	Follows the growth of the file
+n bcl	Start reading at n+1 lines and print each until the end of the file
-n bcl	Reads from the end of the file, n blocks, characters, or lines

The first option discussed is -f. This is useful if reading a file that is growing and growing.

II

The Command Line

```
$ tail -f file
```

System administrators and programmers often use this command to watch a program write information to a log file. Normally, when tail prints the last lines of the file, it terminates. With the -f option, tail does not exit, but keeps reading information and printing it on standard output until the command is terminated with an interrupt signal. Because of the nature of this command, it is very different and difficult to view in a book. The program showtail, in Listing 1 at the end of the chapter, creates entries in a file so that you can use the tail -f command to see how it works.

The +n option instructs tail to skip a given number of lines and start printing the lines to the end of the file, as shown here:

```
$ tail +10 file(s)
```

As shown in the following example, tail skips the first five entries in the passwd file and continues to print until the end of the file.

```
$ tail +5 /etc/passwd
uucp::5:6:uucp:/usr/spool/uucppublic:/usr/lib/uucp/uucico
nuucp::5:6:uucp:/usr/spool/uucppublic:/usr/lib/uucp/uucico
uucpadm:NONE:5:6:Uucp Administration:/usr/lib/uucp:
lp:NONE:71:1:Lp Administrator:/bin:
tutor::100:100:Tutorial:/u/tutor:
install::101:100:Administration Login:/u/install:
terri::102:100:Terri Hare:/u/terri:
meagan::103:100:Meagan Hare:/u/meagan:
matthew::104:100:Matthew Hare:/u/matthew:
chare:tzxZUqZw4/2Ow:105:100:Chris Hare:/u/chare:/bin/ksh
catherine:npI.II95/xz8I:106:100:Catherine Agent:/u/catherin:
$
```

In this example, tail looks like head. The difference is that tail +n prints from the line specified through to the end of the file.

The tail command defaults to printing lines, but you can specify to print in blocks or characters. A block is defined as the amount of data stored in a block on the disk. As a result, it is reasonable to only use the block option with very large files. For example, the following example illustrates using tail -t look at the last line of the password file, and then the last 10 and 20 characters.

```
$ tail -1 /etc/passwd
catherine:npI.II95/xz8I:106:100:Catherine Agent:/u/catherin:
$ tail -10c /etc/passwd
/catherin:
$ tail -20c /etc/passwd
e Agent:/u/catherin:
```

Although it doesn't look like these lines have the correct number of characters, the file does in fact have some blanks at the end of each line that are accounted for.

The unfortunate problem with both head and tail is that you cannot look at lines farther in very easily. For example, what if you want the tenth line in a file? If you use head -10, then you have to look at the first nine lines. By combining head and tail, as shown in the following, you can become very selective.

```
$ head sample | tail -1
the dogs stood at the back door and watched this skunk who was sitting
on
$
```

The previous example illustrates how to accomplish this task. Using head, you get the first ten lines of the file, and by giving it to tail, tail prints the last line, which is the one you want to see. The same can be done with tail. Suppose that you want only the eleventh line from the end, as shown here.

```
$ tail -11 sample | head -1
place in or around my home.
$
```

In this case, you get the last eleven lines and give them to head, which gives you the line you want. As you can see, combinations of these commands enable you to pull the line you want out of the file.

Comparing Files and Fields

As you have seen, both head and tail work on lines in a file. But often you are interested in other items in a file. A file can consist of lines, words, and characters. Words are separated by whitespace or spaces, tabs, and newlines. Whitespaces are often referred to as *field separators*. The Bourne and Korn shells each use the *Internal Field Separator* (IFS) variable to specify the field separators in use. These field separators can be changed, but caution must be used because problems can be created later on. The cut, paste, and join commands all depend upon the contents of the IFS variable to work properly. The IFS is used to define what character separates each field in a file. IFS is explained fully in Chapter 18, "Bourne, CSH, and Korn Differences."

The default field separators for all the shells are the space, tab, and newline. These can be changed in the Bourne and Korn shells by adjusting the value of the IFS variable, as shown in the following:

```
$ echo ":$IFS:"
:
:
$ OldIFS="$IFS"
```

```
$ IFS="+"
$ echo ":$OldIFS:"
:
:
$ echo "$IFS"
+
$
```

As illustrated, it is important to save the real values in another variable so that they can be easily restored when you are done. Why would you want to change the field separators? Well, for processing files that contain fields separated by colons, commas, or anything other than the normal separators. With the next commands, you examine how you can process information contained in fields whether the separators are whitespace, or something else.

The cut Command

The cut command is used to cut information from files, based upon character position, or field within the file. The default delimiter for cut is a tab, but this can be changed by using the -d option to specify a different delimiter. The syntax for the cut command is as follows:

```
$ cut options files
```

The cut command is capable of reading from a file or standard input, and writes to standard output. As such, it is possible for cut to be a filter. Consider the following command line examples:

```
$ cut -c10-20 file
```

This option, as illustrated in the following example, instructs cut to cut characters 10 to 20 from each line of the input file, which is /etc/passwd. Any number of characters can be cut from each line. This is useful if you have a file that is fixed in length, like punch cards to use an analogy. The information produced as output from some database packages is in this format, so it is easy to cut out this information.

```
$ cut -c10-20 /etc/passwd
LEJdAnusE:0
NE:1:1:Admi
2:2:Admin:/
3:3:Admin:/
4:4:Admin:/
:uucp:/usr/
6:uucp:/usr
ONE:5:6:Uuc
```

```
1:1:Lp Admi
0:100:Tutor
101:100:Adm
2:100:Terri
03:100:Meag
104:100:Mat
ZUqZw4/20w:
:npI.II95/x
$
```

Ranges of either fields or characters can be specified with the -c and -f options. To specify a range, use the hyphen or the comma. For example, to cut the characters between 10 and 20 inclusively, use the range 10–20. To cut the 5, 10, and 20 characters from each line, use the range 5,10,20. Using the format 10- indicates that the cut should start at the tenth character or field, and go to the end of the line. These ranges can be combined to form a complex specification for cut. The range notation can be used for cutting characters, or fields.

```
$ cut -f3 file
```

The preceding example instructs cut to remove the third field from the file. Remember, in this case, the field delimiter is a tab. Normally cut passes through all lines, but the -s option instructs cut to ignore each line that does not have a delimiter, resulting in those lines not being included in the output.

The following example illustrates cutting fields from a file. In this case, the file is the password file, and you are extracting the information in the comment field, or field five. Notice that you also used the -d option to change the delimiter from the tab to a colon. The result is a list of names that all have accounts on the system. It is important to indicate that this list also includes some meaningless names because of the system accounts that exist.

```
$ cut -f5 -d: /etc/passwd
System Administrator
Mr Background
Ms Binary
System File Owner
Administration Manager
UUCP Account
Anonymous UUCP Account
Uucp Administration
Lp Administrator
Tutorial
Administration Login
Terri Hare
Meagan Hare
```

```
Matthew Hare
Chris Hare
Catherine Agent
$
```

The paste Command

The paste command does the opposite of cut. Whereas cut prints the information that you want to cut out of the original, paste enables you to paste it into some other existing file. The syntax of the command is as follows:

```
$ paste options files
```

Typically, paste takes the files and merges them together into columns. The who command prints five fields for each user logged in to the system. You can use cut to split this output into two files. The first file contains the user and terminal device. The second file contains the time the user logged in. The following code shows cutting the who output into the two files and pasting them back together again.

```
$ who
chare       tty000        Aug 25 18:48
root      w1              Aug 20 05:01
$ who ¦ cut -c1-17 > /tmp/who.1
$ who ¦ cut -c18- > /tmp/who.2
$ cat /tmp/who.1
chare       tty000
root      w1
$ cat /tmp/who.2
        Aug 25 18:48
        Aug 20 05:01
$ paste /tmp/who.1 /tmp/who.2
chare       tty000              Aug 25 18:48
root      w1                    Aug 20 05:01
$ paste /tmp/who.2 /tmp/who.1
        Aug 25 18:48    chare       tty000
        Aug 20 05:01    root      w1
$
```

The paste command can put these two files back together. For fun, the example shows assembling them backward, as well as forward, to demonstrate how paste works. It assembles lines by taking the first line of each file and putting them together. The line for the first file is separated by a tab, and then the line from the second file. After the line from the last file is processed, a new line is inserted.

The -d option on paste enables the user to change the delimiter to something other than a tab. For example, the following example illustrates the same process as the previous one, except that the delimiter is now a plus sign rather than a tab.

```
$ cat /tmp/who.1
chare       tty000
root        w1
$ cat /tmp/who.2
        Aug 25 18:48
        Aug 20 05:01
$ paste -d+ /tmp/who.1 /tmp/who.2
chare       tty000+     Aug 25 18:48
root        w1    +     Aug 20 05:01
$
```

The paste command has two other options, '-' and -s. The '-' tells paste to read from standard input for its files. The -s option tells paste to get all its input from the same file. For example, the following code shows the contents of a file, which is a list of names, one per line.

```
$ cat /tmp/who
Terri
Matthew
Meagan
Frank
Carol
Kim
Time
Allen
Kaitlin
Chris
$
```

With the -s option, paste is instructed to read only one file and use it as input for fields in the paste. The following shows that paste puts each of the names on the same line.

```
$ paste -s /tmp/who
Terri   Matthew   Meagan   Frank   Carol   Kim   Time   Allen    Kaitlin   Chris
$
```

The paste command compenmsates if any of the files specified do not have enough lines. Consider this example:

```
$ cat fileA
here
and
$ cat fileB
today
```

```
gone
tomorrow
$ paste fileA fileB
here      today
and       gone
          tomorrow
$
```

As shown in the previous example, the first file has fewer lines than the second. Consequently, paste insists nothing for the missing line in fileA. The result is only one word on the final line.

It is also possible to use more than two file names to paste together. Because paste simply pastes the files together, you can use as many as you want, which is shown in the following:

```
$ cat fileA
here
gone
$ cat fileB
today
tomorrow
$ cat file C
and
$ paste fileA fileB fileC
here      today     and
gone      tomorrow
$
```

The only issue about paste is that it is not intelligent. You cannot be selective about what to paste where, as so many users have become accustomed to in this age.

To wrap up this discussion of paste, a final example follows. You can get a quick list of users logged into the UNIX server and list them on one line. This combines who, cut, and paste. The source code for this example is included in Listing 2 at the end of this chapter.

```
$ who
chare        tty000        Aug 25 18:48
root         w1            Aug 20 05:01
$ qwho
chare    root
$
```

The join Command

The join command takes lines from two files and joins them together, based upon a common field or key. To use join, both files must share a common piece of data, called the *key* or *primary field*. The files must be in the same sorted order. (Consequently, the sort command is briefly discussed here, but Chapter 11, "Sorting and Comparing Files," is devoted to the subject.) As join assembles the lines, each field is separated by a tab or a series of spaces. Let's look at the source file for an example.

Listing 1

```
$ cat list1.txt
BC       604
ALTA     403
SASK     306
MAN      204
ONT      416,905,807,705
QUE      819,514,418,709
NS       902
NB       506
PEI      902
NFLD     709
YUK      403
NWT      403
$
```

Listing 2

```
$ cat list2.txt
BC       British Columbia
ALTA     Alberta
SASK     Saskatchewan
MAN      Manitoba
ONT      Ontario
QUE      Quebec
NS       Nova Scotia
NB       New Brunswick
PEI      Prince Edward Island
NFLD     Newfoundland
YUK      Yukon Territories
NWT      Northwest Territories
$
```

Anyone who knows geography can see that these are the provinces and territories in Canada. Listing 1 shows the telephone area codes used within these provinces. Listing 2 shows the actual names of the provinces. Because the common field between them is an abbreviation, this is the *key*. To ensure that things are in agreement, you must sort the two files, as the following shows:

```
$ sort list1.txt > list1.sort
$ sort list2.txt > list2.sort
$ cat list1.sort
ALTA    403
BC      604
MAN     204
NB      506
NFLD    709
NS      902
NWT     403
ONT     416,905,807,705
PEI     902
QUE     819,514,418,709
SASK    306
YUK     403
$
```

You sort the information to make sure that the keys in both files are in the same order. The sort is done using the same key as the join, which is typically the first field, although options on both commands enable you to change this. The following code shows using the join command to merge the two files and what the output looks like.

```
$ join list1.sort list2.sort > list
$ cat list
ALTA 403 Alberta
BC 604 British Columbia
MAN 204 Manitoba
NB 506 New Brunswick
NFLD 709 Newfoundland
NS 902 Nova Scotia
NWT 403 Northwest Territories
ONT 416,905,807,705 Ontario
PEI 902 Prince Edward Island
QUE 819,514,418,709 Quebec
SASK 306 Saskatchewan
YUK 403 Yukon Territories
$
```

It is essential to sort the input files because join will only connect the lines that have a matching key. The following example shows using one sorted file and one unsorted file:

```
$ join list1.sort list2.txt
BC    604    British Columbia
SASK  306    Saskatchewan
YUK   403    Yukon Territory
```

Notice that the level of output here is much less than our previous example—because these lines are in the position in both input files.

join has several options that alter how join operates. In some situations, there will be lines in either of the input files that have unpaired lines. The -a option, followed by either a 1 or 2, signifying either the first or second file, prints a line for each unpaired line. Use of the -a option is shown in the following example:

```
$ cat list2
#ALTA    Alberta
BC       British Columbia
$ cat list1
ALTA    403
BC      604
$ join list1 list2
BC 604  British Columbia
$ join -a2 list1 list2
#ALTA    Alberta
BC 604  British Columbia
$
```

In the previous example, when join is executed, the first line, only the line for BC is printed because there is no match for ALTA in list2. However, by adding the -a2 option, the line from list2, which is unpaired, also prints in the output.

Using the -j option enables the user to change which field is used to join a file on—for example—the following two files:

```
$ cat z3
403     ALTA
604     BC
204     MAN
506     NB
709     NFLD
902     NS
403     NWT
416,905,807,705 ONT
902     PEI
819,514,418,709 QUE
306     SASK
403     YUK
$ cat list2.sort
ALTA    Alberta
BC      British Columbia
MAN     Manitoba
```

```
NB      New Brunswick
NFLD    Newfoundland
NS      Nova Scotia
NWT     Northwest Territories
ONT     Ontario
PEI     Prince Edward Island
QUE     Quebec
SASK    Saskatchewan
YUK     Yukon Territories
```

If you look carefully at the two files, you will see that the changes happened in the first file—the files are reversed from the example that you looked at for join that used three files.

Now when you run the join command, you have to tell join which field to join on. This happens because join normally uses the first field as the key and the field to join. In the file z3, the filed to join on is not the first field. As a result, you have to use the following join command:

```
$ join -j1 2 z3 list2.sort
BC 604 British Columbia
MAN 204 Manitoba
NB 506 New Brunswick
NFLD 709 Newfoundland
NS 902 Nova Scotia
NWT 403 Northwest Territories
ONT 416,905,807,705 Ontario
PEI 902 Prince Edward Island
QUE 819,514,418,709 Quebec
SASK 306 Saskatchewan
YUK 403 Yukon Territories
$
```

This command means that when join processes file 1 (-j1), it should use field 2 as the field to join on. The end result is the output just shown. This output looks like the output that you saw earlier in this discussion on join.

The split Command

The split command takes a large file and splits it into smaller files, leaving the original file intact. This can be done out of necessity—because some programs cannot handle very large files, or because it is easier for you to work with a smaller amount of data. This is the first of two commands that can be used to split files.

The split command works by breaking a single file into chunks of equal sizes, but split cannot process multiple files. Unless specified, chunks of 1,000 lines are used. To change the size of the file, use a hyphen followed by the number of lines for the file size. The following code illustrates using split to break this large file into pieces.

```
$ wc -l filelist
   2733 filelist
$ split filelist
$ ls -l x*
-rw-r--r--  1 chare    users      46009 Aug 25 21:35 xaa
-rw-r--r--  1 chare    users      54791 Aug 25 21:35 xab
-rw-r--r--  1 chare    users      35208 Aug 25 21:35 xac
$
```

The files created by split use the name x with the letters aa, ab, ac, and so on, appended to the file name. You can change the file name prefix used for the new files by adding the new file name as the third argument on the command line, as shown in the following:

```
$ split -500 filelist YAK
$ ls -l YAK*
-rw-r--r--  1 chare    users      24026 Aug 25 21:40 YAKaa
-rw-r--r--  1 chare    users      21983 Aug 25 21:40 YAKab
-rw-r--r--  1 chare    users      27521 Aug 25 21:40 YAKac
-rw-r--r--  1 chare    users      27270 Aug 25 21:40 YAKad
-rw-r--r--  1 chare    users      24894 Aug 25 21:40 YAKae
-rw-r--r--  1 chare    users      10314 Aug 25 21:40 YAKaf
$
```

In the preceding example, you see an option to split that indicates the file should be split so each new file is 500 lines long. The third argument, YAK, is what the new files created should be named, in addition to the suffix that split appends to each name.

It is important to know that split pays no attention to where the file is broken. As a result, it is possible for the break to be in places where it is not practical to work on the file using another program: csplit.

The csplit Command

The csplit command varies from split by offering you a chance to split the file based upon the context. For example, say that you want to have a certain amount of information you want in a single file. The csplit command can be used in two ways. By providing a list of line numbers where you want the splits to be done, or a list of patterns which csplit should search for in the file.

The syntax for csplit is as follows:

```
$ csplit source line line line line ....
```

This instructs csplit to open the source file and to split it at the specified lines. So how do you get the line number information? Remember the grep command? grep has an option that prints the line number where the pattern was found. Suppose that you have a file containing a list of fruits, vegetables, and meats, as shown in the following:

```
$ cat foods
Meats
        Chicken
        Turkey
        Pheasant
        Beef
        Pork
        Ham
Fruits
        Banana
        Apple
        Orange
        Pear
        Watermelon
        Grape
Vegetables
        Tomato
        Beans
        Cucumber
        Lettuce
        Carrots
        Corn
$
```

You want to split this file into three files, one for each list. You can use egrep to find the line numbers for each of these as illustrated in the following code. Using this information, you can use csplit to separate the information using the line numbers from egrep. The end result is three files: one with fruits, one with vegetables, and one with meats.

```
$ egrep -n "Meats¦Fruits¦Vegetables" foods
1:Meats
8:Fruits
15:Vegetables
$ csplit foods 8 15
50
55
```

```
60
$ ls -l xx*
-rw-r--r--  1 chare    users         50 Aug 25 21:44 xx00
-rw-r--r--  1 chare    users         55 Aug 25 21:44 xx01
-rw-r--r--  1 chare    users         60 Aug 25 21:44 xx02
$ cat xx00
Meats
        Chicken
        Turkey
        Pheasant
        Beef
        Pork
        Ham
$
```

In this example all the line numbers are not specified. Because the first of the three groups is on line 1, it makes more sense to split the file at the other lines. If you were to include line 1 on the list, then you would have four files, with one empty. The output of csplit, which is printed on the screen are the file sizes of the newly created files. The advantage to csplit is that you can control where the split in the file takes place. Other than that, split is easier to use because it does not care where the file is split. The choice to use one or the other, depends upon how much effort you want to spend on it.

Command Summary

head [-num]	Lists the top num lines in the file; defaults to ten 10 lines
tail -f	Follows the end of the file
tail +num bcl	Lists the top num blocks, characters, lines in the file; defaults to ten lines
tail -num bcl	Lists the last num blocks, characters, or lines in the file; defaults to ten lines
cut -c	Cuts characters from the input
cut -d delim	Cuts with the specified delimiter
cut -f	Cuts fields from input
paste -	Pastes fields using standard input
paste -d delim	Pastes fields using the spcified delimiter
join	Joins lines of files using a common key
split	Splits a file into chunks of 1,000 lines

split -num	Splits file into smaller files of num lines
split source output	Splits the source file into 1,000 line chunks, using the filename output
csplit	Splits files based on user supplied context

Code Listings

The two sample programs here demonstrate several of the commands that were examined in this chapter. The first program provides a way to show how the tail -f command works, and the second provides a way of finding out who is logged onto the system

Listing 9.1.   tail -f example - showtail

The showtail command is used to demonstrate how tail -f works. To try this, type the program into a file and save it, then run showtail using the following command, which runs showtail as a background process:

```
$ sh showtail &
```

Now run the following command:

```
$ tail -f /twp/showtail
```

Now you can see tail -f in action.

```
#!/bin/sh
#
# showtail - Version 1
#
# This command will write its output to the file /tmp/showtail so it
# can be viewed eaily with tail -f
#
# The command will execute until it is stopped.
#
# Remember that exec redirectes standard output to the named file.
#
exec > /tmp/showtail
#
# The while command with a colon will loop forever. This will be
```

```
# discussed in a later chapter.
#
while :
do
    #
    # print some text
    #
    echo "Showtail -f"
    echo "`date`"
    echo "   This command will re-execute in 10 seconds ..."
    #
    # the sleep command suspends execution for the named period. In
    # this case, one second.
    #
    sleep 1
    echo "   8 seconds ..."
    sleep 1
    echo "   7 seconds ..."
    sleep 1
    echo "   6 seconds ..."
    sleep 1
    echo "   5 seconds ..."
    sleep 1
    echo "   4 seconds ..."
    sleep 1
    echo "   3 seconds ..."
    sleep 1
    echo "   2 seconds ..."
    sleep 1
    echo "   1 second ..."
done
```

Listing 9.2. qwho

The qwho command prints who is logged on, with the users names being shown. If who
gives the following:

```
$ who
chare    w1        Jul 18 11:31
steves   tty000    Jul 18 11:09
terri    ph1       Jul 18 08:14
$
```

Then qwho imparts this output:

```
$ qwho
chare steves terri
$
```

Here is Listing 2:

```
#!/bin/sh
# qwho Version 1
#
# This command prints the list of users who are logged into the
# system on one line.
#
# The cut command says "cut field one from the input, but use a
# space as the delimiter. Using the default tab doesn't strip anything
# as the who command inserts spaces between the fields in the output,
# not tabs.
#
who | cut -f1 -d" " | paste -s -
exit 0
```

Chapter Snapshot

By default, the results of every command's execution are displayed on the terminal screen. For simple operations, this is often sufficient. However, quite often, the output needs to be redirected, either to a file or to another command—a process known as *piping*. This chapter examines redirection and piping, specifically the following:

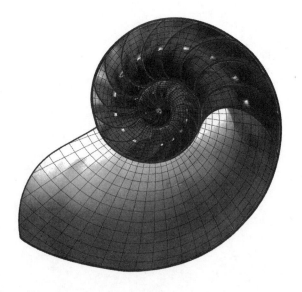

10
CHAPTER

Redirection and Piping

C hapter 5, "Shell Basics," discussed the issues surrounding redirection and piping within the shell. These services are provided by the shell that you are using, whether it be the Bourne shell, Korn shell, C shell, or any of the public domain shells available on the Internet.

As you recall, redirection is the process of sending the output of a command to a place other than the terminal. A pipe allows the output of one command to be sent directly to the input of another command.

Understanding Standard Input, Standard Output, and Standard Error

For every command, three files are opened: standard input, standard output, and standard error. Standard input is where the input for a command comes from. This is generally your keyboard, as most commands are interactive. However, some commands do not interact with the user directly, but require that a file be supplied that the command processes. For those commands, their standard input is connected to the file or files they are processing. Standard input has a numerical file descriptor of zero (0) and is often denoted as STDIN.

Standard output is where the output of a command is sent during processing, or after the process is complete. Standard output is generally the video device connected to your terminal or workstation. For commands that do not interact with the terminal, the standard output is connected to some other place, if used at all. The numerical file descriptor for standard output is one (1) and is often called STDOUT.

Standard error is separate from standard output, even though it generally sends its output to the same place. Standard error provides a mechanism for error messages to the user executing the command. Usually, these error messages are sent to the terminal from where the command was executed, even if the command is not interactive. Examples are when you run a command such as date, but provide invalid options. The result is an error message indicating what options are valid. The numerical file descriptor for standard error is two (2), but is often called STDERR.

The significance of these file descriptors is used with the Bourne and Korn shells. They are not used with the C shell, as you see again in this chapter.

Understanding Redirection

Redirection is useful in many different situations. You have seen it used on numerous occasions within the context of this book. Redirection enables you to save the output of a command in a file. The purpose for doing this is open for discussion. Perhaps you want to show someone else the output given a special set of circumstances. Maybe you want to include it in a report. Perhaps it is needed for further processing later. Perhaps you want to combine multiple files into one. Whatever the reason, it is there when you need it.

Recall that redirection is used to connect the output of a command to a file, as shown here in the following example:

```
$ command > file
```

It is pertinent to note that input and output redirection can be used at the same time; they are not mutually exclusive, as the following example illustrates:

```
sort < infile > outfile
```

Here, `sort` reads the data to be sorted from the file and saves the output in the file outfile.

Redirection does not interact with other commands like pipes. In the following sections, you look at some specific places in which redirection is used.

Command Line

You have seen redirection used on numerous occasions throughout this book, and most of the time it is used in places other than the command line. However, the command line is a popular place because it is here that you test instructions before incorporating them into a shell program or suddenly realize that perhaps you should save the output because you will need it later. The command line and shell scripts are the most common uses for redirection.

Shell Scripts

A shell script is a program written using the shell's built-in programming language. This interpreted language allows for heavy use of redirection. Redirection is useful for temporary files that must be processed in several different ways, or for log files that the script uses. Shell scripts are discussed in detail in Part 5 of this book.

The cron Command

When cron executes jobs that write output to standard output or standard error, cron saves this output and mails it to the user when the job completes. If the users on the system do not regularly use the e-mail facility within UNIX, the disk can eventually become clogged with e-mail messages. As a result, using redirection to send the output elsewhere is a major advantage in this situation. What cron does and how to do it are detailed in Chapter 25, "Processes Now and Later."

Output Redirection

There are two output streams, as you have seen, standard output and standard error. Here you see how to redirect the output streams to somewhere other than the screen.

Standard Output

As mentioned, output redirection is used to save the output of a command in a file. This is accomplished using the output redirection symbols, > and >>. The > symbol instructs the shell to create the file if it does not exist, or to truncate it if it does. This command also can be used in the Bourne and Korn shells to create an empty file, as illustrated in the following example:

```
$ ls -l
total 0
$ > newfile
$ ls -l
total 0
-rw-r--r--  1 chare   users         0 Aug 25 21:52 newfile
$
```

Overwriting the file and losing the contents is not always desired. In those situations, the redirection command >> is used. In this case, if the file exists, the new information is appended to the end of it, which causes the file to grow as more and more information is written to it. In the Bourne and Korn shells, if the file does not exist, it is created.

The C shell uses a variable called *noclobber* to control the operation of both the > and >> symbols. If noclobber has been set in the user's .cshrc file and the file exists when the > symbol is used, the file is not truncated and an error is reported. If the noclobber variable is not set, then the file is truncated. When using the >> symbol, the operation is similar, except that if noclobber is set and the file does not exist, an error is reported. It is possible to override the operation of noclobber by following the > or >> with an >!, as in >>!, or !>>. This operation is illustrated in the following code in which setting noclobber is illustrated, and in subsequent code, which demonstrates redirection in the C shell.

```
%
% set
argv    ()
cwd     /u/chare/new
home    /u/chare
path    (/bin /usr/bin /usr/ucb /usr/local /u/chare/bin )
prompt      %
shell   /bin/csh
status      0
term    vt220
user    chare
```

At this point, the noclobber option is not defined, as shown. The following set command enables the noclobber option, which is verified by executing the set command with no arguments.

```
% set noclober
set
argv    ()
cwd     /u/chare/new
home    /u/chare
```

```
        noclobber
        path    (/bin /usr/bin /usr/ucb /usr/local /u/chare/bin )
        prompt      %
        shell   /bin/csh
        status      0
        term    vt220
        user    chare
        $
```

Now that noclobber is defined, the following example illustrates using output redirection with the >! syntax.

```
        % ls -l
        total 0
        % date > newfile
        % cat newfile
        Thu Aug 25 21:59:32 EST 1994
        % pwd > newfile
        newfile: file exists
        % pwd >! newfile
        % cat newfile
        /u/chare/new
        % unset noclobber
        % date > newfile
        % cat newfile
        Thu Aug 25 22:00:46 EST 1994
        %
```

Versions of the Korn shell since 1986 also have the noclobber option. To enable noclobber in the Korn shell, the following command is used:

```
        $ set -o noclobber
```

This has the same effect as noclobber in the C shell. However, the syntax to negate the effect of noclobber in the Korn shell is different. To override the noclobber option, use of >¦ is required, as shown here:

```
        $ date >¦ /tmp/trey
```

The circumstances surrounding the operation of noclobber in the Korn shell is the same as in the C shell.

Standard Error

Standard error, as mentioned, does not follow the same path as standard output. With this facility, you can separate where the processed data goes and where standard error is sent. To redirect standard error, use the file descriptor 2 in the Bourne and Korn shells and a slightly different mechanism for the C shell. To illustrate the use of standard error, examine the following example, which shows that the error message printed by the command went to the file specified.

```
$ who -z
bad switch
Usage:  who [-rbtpludAasT] [am i] [utmp_like_file]

r       run level
b       boot time
t       time changes
p       processes other than getty or users
l       login processes
u       useful information
d       dead processes
A       accounting information
a       all (rbtpludA options)
s       short form of who (no time since last output or pid)
T       status of tty (+ writable, - not writable, x exclusive open, ?
        ➥hung)
$ who -z 2>err
$ cat err
bad switch
Usage:  who [-rbtpludAasT] [am i] [utmp_like_file]

r       run level
b       boot time
t       time changes
p       processes other than getty or users
l       login processes
u       useful information
d       dead processes
A       accounting information
a       all (rbtpludA options)
s       short form of who (no time since last output or pid)
T       status of tty (+ writable, - not writable, x exclusive open, ?
        ➥hung)
$
```

Did you notice that for this version of the data command, the error message regarding the option was saved in the file, but the usage message, which also is generally part of standard error, went to standard output? This is one of the many quirks that make up UNIX. But for the C shell, no file descriptors are allowed. Rather, an ampersand is placed immediately after the > or >>, as in >&, and both standard output and standard error are redirected to the file.

```
% who -z >& err
% cat err
bad switch
Usage:  who [-rbtpludAasT] [am i] [utmp_like_file]

r        run level
b        boot time
t        time changes
p        processes other than getty or users
l        login processes
u        useful information
d        dead processes
A        accounting information
a        all (rbtpludA options)
s        short form of who (no time since last output or pid)
T        status of tty (+ writable, - not writable, x exclusive open, ?
         ➥hung)
%
```

There are other situations where you want to redirect standard error: for example, if you execute a command in the background, and you don't want to see any error messages appear on your terminal; or the situation where you know there are going to be errors, but you want to ignore the text and keep working.

This demonstrates that even though the same facility is available, sometimes the mechanism for accessing or using it is very different. But at times, you might not want to save the output. You can accomplish this by using the /dev/null device.

The /dev/null Device

The /dev/null device is the answer to the problem of not wanting to save the output or error of a command. This is a special device that takes all its input and throws it away. If you write information to it from a C programming point of view, it writes zero bytes. If reading from it, it reads zero bytes. This special quality has earned /dev/null the name of *bit bucket*.

But why have /dev/null? Consider the example of cron earlier in this chapter. Saving the information in a file requires that you periodically remove this file. Failure to do so results in it eventually filling up your disk. Consequently, /dev/null has a nice quality about it. You can redirect the output of commands and programs there and never see anything again. Consider the following examples:

```
$ grep /dev/null /cronlist
15 0-23 * * * /news/bin/nntpsend.sh uunet.ca 2>&1 >/dev/null
```

```
$ grep /dev/null /etc/rc
        /etc/nfs_umount -b >/dev/null
$
```

The preceding illustration shows several examples of using /dev/null in standard output and standard error situations. The first one is from the cron file, which is used by root. The example shows redirecting standard error into the same data stream as standard out using 2>&1, and then redirecting standard output into /dev/null. This has the effect of not saving any output from the command, whether it be from standard output or standard error.

The second example within the code is from a DEC Ultrix system. This command is in the /etc/rc file, which is used to configure the system during startup. The command illustrated is part of the Network File System services, and it redirects any error messages generated to /dev/null.

Using Input Redirection

Input redirection is done far less frequently than output redirection. Most people use output redirection at least ten times a day, even if they do not know it. Input redirection is not the same, however. Recall from the preceding discussion that input redirection enables you to redefine from where the input for a command comes. If the command is interactive in nature, then normally the keyboard functions as the standard input.

You can change this and fool the command, however. The following example works with the command bc, which is a rudimentary calculator. (It does have some very impressive features to it, though.) This example has a file that contains a series of bc commands, which tell it how many decimal places to use and then to perform some arithmetic.

```
$ cat bc.cmd
scale=4
2+2
. * 3.1459
. + 1001
. * 4
. / 5
$ bc < bc.cmd
4
12.5836
1013.5836
4054.3344
810.8668
$
```

The command syntax for bc uses the . to mean the answer of the previous operation. When you tell bc to use this file for its instructions, it performs them as if you had typed each one because the < symbol informs the shell to tell bc that its input is coming from the file. Then the file is played just like an audio tape.

Input redirection can also be used to simply provide data to commands. For example, you just used the vi editor to create a file with some information that you want to mail to a user name meagan. The following command would do that for you:

```
$ mail meagan < file
```

In this case, mail reads the file to get its input, then mails the entire message to the user meagan.

For some commands, however, you should not use input redirection because you cannot anticipate all their commands. Input redirection is inflexible. The instruction given to the command must make sense at the time. So, the example in the previous code would have been very hard to do if you had decided that you would not divide by five if the answer was less than 5,000. For those situations, there is no equal to actual human intervention.

The Here-Document

Output redirection uses the >> symbol, but the << symbol indicates a *here-document*. This is used to accomplish input redirection, but the instructions are contained in the following lines, not in a separate file. The following example uses bc and the same instructions you saw in the previous one.

```
$ cat bc1
bc << !EOF
scale=4
2+2
. * 3.1459
. + 1001
. * 4
. / 5
!EOF
$ sh bc1
4
12.5836
1013.5836
4054.3344
810.8668
$
```

This example uses a file called bc1. In that file, you are going to execute the command bc and use a here-document to provide the instructions. This is typically how a hereis document is used. A command has a set of instructions to perform. Rather than put those instructions in a separate file, you can use the here-document to instruct the shell that the instructions come next. The syntax is as follows:

```
$ command << STRING
instructions
STRING
```

The pattern STRING indicates that the end of the instruction list has been reached. As with input redirection, only the commands that you can anticipate, or know what the response will be, are candidates for use with the here-document.

There is a variation to the here-document, although it is not supported by all shells. This variation uses the symbol <<-. It means that the command in the here-document can be tabbed in for clarity. For example, the following example is not as easy to read as the subsequent one:

```
cmd << EOF
newcmd
newcmd
EOF
```

Versus:

```
cmd <<-EOF
    newcmd
    newcmd
EOF
```

Although the here-document has its uses, it is not in widespread use. Many older shell scripts did use the here-document for presenting a list of choices to the user.

Understanding Pipes

As discussed in Chapter 5, pipes are a method of connecting the output of one command to the input of another. Although you can exist in UNIX without using pipes, you would have to use many temporary files with redirection. Suppose that you did not have any pipes, and you wanted to use the output of the tail command and give it to the head command. You would have to save the output of tail in a file, and then have head read that file. Finally, you must remember to remove the temporary file when you are done with it. This cumbersome process is illustrated in the following example:

```
$ tail sample > out
$ head -4 < out
```

Pipes are used everywhere: during system startup, execution of many commands that make up UNIX, as well as those commands that users themselves develop. The pipe is symbolized by a vertical bar (¦) that looks like a pipe. It connects the output of the command on the left of the pipe with the input of the command on the right.

Any number of commands can be grouped together in a pipe; you are not restricted to two or three commands. The following block of code illustrates some sample command lines using pipes. If you look back through the preceding chapters, you can see at least one example of a pipe every couple of pages.

```
$ grep "/u/" /etc/passwd ¦ sort ¦ head -5
catherine:npI.II95/xz8I:106:100:Catherine Agent:/u/catherin:
chare:tzxZUqZw4/2Ow:105:100:Chris Hare:/u/chare:/bin/ksh
install::101:100:Administration Login:/u/install:
matthew::104:100:Matthew Hare:/u/matthew:
meagan::103:100:Meagan Hare:/u/meagan:
$ ps -ef ¦ grep chare
   chare  1651     1  3 02:54:55 000  0:13 ksh
   chare  2084  1651 42 22:51:29 000  0:01 ps
   chare  2085  1651  5 22:51:29 000  0:00 grep
$
```

Connecting with Pipes

Not all pipes are created equal. Remember that the more commands that have to be executed, the longer it takes to do the work and get your output back. More important, many commands are capable of reading from standard input or from the files on the command line. Look at the following command:

```
$ cat file ¦ sort
$
$ sort file
$
$ sort < file
```

They all accomplish the same thing. The difference is that the first example must start the command cat, open the file, and pipe the output to sort, whereas the second and third examples simply open the file and sort it. Because the end result can be achieved with one command, it is inefficient to use the first type of example. Two processes have to be started, decreasing the system resources for other users, when one process is enough. Consequently, users should try to minimize the number of commands whenever possible. Many commands do more than one thing when options are added to the command line.

The tee Command

This is a good place to introduce and discuss the tee command, which is used in a pipeline to save the output in a file. Much like a plumbing fixture, tee sends a copy of its input to standard output, and another copy to the file named on the command line.

II

The Command Line

The following example illustrates the use of tee:

```
$ grep "/u" /etc/passwd ¦ tee pass1 ¦ sort ¦ tee pass2
adm:NONE:4:4:Administration Manager:/usr/adm:
catherine:npI.II95/xz8I:106:100:Catherine Agent:/u/catherin:
chare:tzxZUqZw4/2Ow:105:100:Chris Hare:/u/chare:/bin/ksh
install::101:100:Administration Login:/u/install:
matthew::104:100:Matthew Hare:/u/matthew:
meagan::103:100:Meagan Hare:/u/meagan:
nuucp::5:6:Anonymous UUCP Account:/usr/spool/uucppublic:/usr/lib/uucp/
➥uucico
terri::102:100:Terri Hare:/u/terri:
tutor::100:100:Tutorial:/u/tutor:
uucp::5:6:UUCP Account:/usr/spool/uucppublic:/usr/lib/uucp/uucico
uucpadm:NONE:5:6:Uucp Administration:/usr/lib/uucp:
$
```

The command shown above is an example of combining the tee command in a pipeline. Here, grep is used to find lines in /etc/passwd that contain the pattern /u. For each line, grep prints it to standard output, which has been connected by a pipe to the tee command. This first tee does two things. First, it saves a copy of everything it reads in the file pass1. Second, it prints the same information to standard output, which has been connected to the sort command through a pipe.

The sort command sorts the input file from the pipe and prints the sorted data on standard output, which has been connected to the tee command. This second tee saves a copy of its input in the file pass2 and prints the same information on the screen.

An innovative way to use tee is to show others what you are doing. For example, if you and a coworker are both on the same system, and you want him to see all the commands you type, then you should start a new shell and pipe the output through a tee to a file, like the following demonstrates:

```
$ sh ¦ tee /tmp/sh
```

Now, the other user uses the tail -f command to read the file, where she sees the same output that you do.

Tee is a useful command when the end result of the pipe is not what you were expecting. To solve this type of problem, inserting the tee command at various places in the pipeline enables you to look at the output of the different commands to determine what the problem is.

Command Summary

Here is a summary of the commands and options presented in this chapter.

>	Output redirection; creates the file if it does not exist, or truncates it if it does.
!>	Negates the effects of noclobber in the C shell.
>>	Output redirection; appends to the file if it exists, or creates it if it does not.
!>>	Negates the effects of noclobber in the C shell.
2>	Redirects standard error.
>&	Redirects standard output and standard error in the C shell.
2>&1	Redirects standard error into standard output.
<	Redirects standard input.
<<	Indicates hereis document.
|	Indicates a pipe, which connects the output of the command on the left to the input of the command on the right.
tee	Saves the input in a file and writes it to standard output.

Chapter Snapshot

This chapter introduces you to commands that help you organize and decipher similar files. Topics covered include the following:

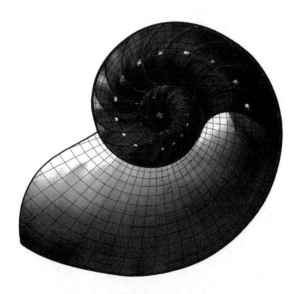

CHAPTER

Sorting and Comparing Files

I n this chapter, you look at how to get the output into the format you want. This chapter discusses sorting files, comparing them for differences, and removing common lines from the same file, to name a few topics. First, you learn about the sort command.

Sorting It Out

In many different situations, you need to sort information to make it easier to examine. You can sort information in a variety of ways—not to mention the fact that you can also sort upon multiple values within a file. The sort command is capable of reading from standard input or a file, and writing to standard output. This makes it behave like a filter. The command syntax for sort is as follows:

```
$ sort options file(s)
```

The sort command by default performs an ASCII sequence sort using the first field in the file. sort determines what the first field is by the delimiter currently in use, unless it is changed by an option on the command line. The following example shows the contents of a file and what happens when sort processes it.

```
$ cat fruits
apples
orange
lemon
lime
banana
Apples
watermelon
Kiwi
cherry
Pears
$ sort fruits
Apples
Kiwi
Pears
apples
banana
cherry
lemon
lime
orange
watermelon
$
```

The result after the sort is not what you might have expected. This is an ASCII sort, which means that the list is sorted according to the order established in the ASCII character definitions. This says that numbers come before uppercase letters, which come before lowercase letters. If you want the order of the file to be what you expected, you must use the -d option. This option instructs sort to sort the lists according to the rules used in the dictionary. That means that only letters, digits, and tabs are significant for the ordering. The following code shows the same file sorted in dictionary order.

```
$ sort -d fruits
Apples
Kiwi
Pears
apples
banana
cherry
lemon
lime
orange
watermelon
$
```

But the files are still ordered with the uppercase letters appearing first in the list. The -f option instructs sort to treat all letters as equals, as shown here:

```
$ sort -f fruits
Apples
apples
banana
cherry
Kiwi
lemon
lime
orange
Pears
watermelon
$
```

It is also possible to sort the file in reverse order. You can sort the file using the default rules, the dictionary rules, by treating upper- and lowercase letters as equivalents, and in reverse order.

The following listing shows numbers sorted in reverse order. This is an odd looking list because the numbers are not in an order that appears to make sense. Remember that sort, by default, uses ASCII order to sort the files. Because these are numbers, it is rare to see sort put them in the right order. The option -n instructs sort that the values being sorted should be treated as numbers. The subsequent listing shows the list in corrected sorted order and in reverse using the -r option.

II

The Command Line

```
$ cat nums
10
99
102
9999
7
18
582
$ sort nums
10
102
18
582
7
99
9999
$
```

```
$ sort -n nums
7
10
18
99
102
582
9999
$ sort -rn nums
9999
582
102
99
18
10
7
$
```

Despite these different features, the examples shown so far are simple files. The sort command uses the first field in the file as the sort key, which means that sort considers the file sorted when the first field is in the right order, as shown in the following example.

```
$ cat names
Kim Kirk
Chris Hare
```

```
Jim Hare
Tim Kirk
Frank Hare
Terri Kilmartin
Laurie McDougall
$ sort names
Chris Hare
Frank Hare
Jim Hare
Kim Kirk
Laurie McDougall
Terri Kilmartin
Tim Kirk
$
```

This isn't what you want at all—since when does a list of names use the person's first name? The sort command uses whitespace as field separators unless altered by the -t option, examined later. Suppose that you want to sort the file using the second field and then the first field. In sort, the first field is 0; the second field 1; and so on.

As with any command, sort can be used with output redirection or a pipe, or the -o option that enables you to specify the output file. This option accepts the name of a file to which the output is to be written, as illustrated in the following:

```
$ cat names2
Kim Kirk
Chris Hare
Jim Hare
Tim Kirk
Frank Hare
Terri Kilmartin
Laurie McDougall
Carol Cole
$ sort +1 -o names2.1 names2
$ cat names2.1
Carol Cole
Chris Hare
Frank Hare
Jim Hare
Terri Kilmartin
Kim Kirk
Tim Kirk
Laurie McDougall
$
```

II

The Command Line

In this example, the output file is a new file. However, it is possible to specify the same output file as the input filename through this mechanism. It cannot be done with the shell. For example, the following command does not work because the shell handles the redirection and truncates the file before sort has a chance to see the input data.

```
$ sort names > names
```

To use a different field as the sort key, use the + followed by a number to indicate which field is the first sort key. The following code reveals what the list of names looks like after the sort.

```
$ sort names
Chris Hare
Frank Hare
Jim Hare
Kim Kirk
Laurie McDougall
Terri Kilmartin
Tim Kirk
$ sort +1 names
Chris Hare
Frank Hare
Jim Hare
Terri Kilmartin
Kim Kirk
Tim Kirk
Laurie McDougall
$
```

In the previous list, the names are ordered by the last name, which is what you want. The +num indicates that sort should skip over the specified number of fields and then start the sort. The +field is further strengthened through the use of -num. As +num means sort should stop the sort at the specified field. Normally, all the information on the remainder of the line is used to sort the file. By using -num however, sort uses only the specified fields in the request.

Altering the key fields used in the sort is frequently accompanied by changing the delimiter used to separate the fields. This is accomplished with the -t option. The delimiter specified is placed immediately after the -t. sort then uses this character as the field delimiter instead of the default.

For example, to sort the /etc/passwd file, you need to use the -t option because the delimiter in this file is the colon. The following example sorts the file based upon the text in the fifth field.

```
$ sort -t: +4 -5 /etc/passwd
install::101:100:Administration Login:/u/install:
adm:NONE:4:4:Administration Manager:/usr/adm:
nuucp::5:6:Anonymous UUCP Account:/usr/spool/uucppublic:/usr/lib/uucp/
➥uucico
catherine:npI.II95/xz8I:106:100:Catherine Agent:/u/catherin:
chare:tzxZUqZw4/2Ow:105:100:Chris Hare:/u/chare:/bin/ksh
lp:NONE:71:1:Lp Administrator:/bin:
matthew::104:100:Matthew Hare:/u/matthew:
meagan::103:100:Meagan Hare:/u/meagan:
daemon:NONE:1:1:Mr Background:/:
bin:NONE:2:2:Ms Binary:/bin:
root:HmILLEJdAnusE:0:0:System Administrator:/:
sys:NONE:3:3:System File Owner:/:
terri::102:100:Terri Hare:/u/terri:
tutor::100:100:Tutorial:/u/tutor:
uucp::5:6:UUCP Account:/usr/spool/uucppublic:/usr/lib/uucp/uucico
uucpadm:NONE:5:6:Uucp Administration:/usr/lib/uucp:
$
```

In this example, the sort command has been altered to use the colon as the delimiter and
to start the search with field five (skip four fields), and do not use the remainder of the
line as search criteria, or stop the key at field six. Remember that counting fields starts at
zero for the first field. The result in this case is a version of the password file sorted by the
name in the fifth field.

You can be even more precise with sort. You can, in fact, limit the sort to not just a single
field, but to characters within the field. This is done by adding a digit of precision to the
field number as specified with the +num syntax. To do this, add the position of the
character to use as illustrated.

```
$ sort +1.0 -1.2 file
```

This restricts the sort criteria to the first letter in the second field of the file, as illustrated
in the following:

```
$ cat stuff
4-door  car
pickup  truck
panel   van
2-door  sedan
school  bus
pedal   bike
motor   cycle
kids    trike
```

II

The Command Line

```
air      plane
cruise   ship
$ sort +1.1 -1.2 stuff
pedal    bike
school   bus
4-door   car
motor    cycle
air      plane
2-door   sedan
cruise   ship
kids     trike
pickup   truck
panel    van
$
```

This example illustrates the use of characters keys within a field. The example shows using the second character in the second field as the sort key. This results in the output as shown and demonstrates very tight control on the sort order of the file.

What's the Difference?

With the sort command you can reorder the contents of a file or a data stream to process it with other tools. Some of those tools include this series whose purpose is to determine what the differences are between two files that appear to be the same. This section examines several commands that all do a similar job.

The diff Command

The diff command is used to determine the differences that exist between two files. The syntax of diff is as follows:

```
$ diff options file1 file2
```

The options are used to redefine some of the output presented by diff. A close examination of some UNIX manuals regarding diff explains that diff can be used to identify what lines must be changed to bring the two files into agreement. In the file names given to diff, one may be a directory. If that is the case, the other argument must be a file. The diff command looks in the named directory for a file with the same name as that specified and compares the two files. Otherwise, both arguments may be a file name. The following code shows the output of diff.

```
$ cat dfile1
This is a small file which will be used to test diff.
$ cat dfile2
```

```
This is a SMALL file that can be used to illustrate how diff operates.
$ cat dfile1 dfile2
1c1
< This is a small file which will be used to test diff.
—
> This is a SMALL file that can be used to illustrate how diff oper-
➥ates.
$
```

In this example, the first bit is a line of three characters, 1c1. This is the ed command, which is used to synchronize the two files. (ed is one of the three editors available on UNIX as delivered by a UNIX vendor. ed and the other editors are discussed in Chapters 12 to 15.) In this case, the command says that line one would be changed with line 1 of the other file. The lines after this command are the lines that would be affected by the command listed first. The lines in the first file are preceded by a <, and the lines in the second file are preceded with a >.

Several options can be used with diff. The first is -e. This option instructs diff to create an ed command script that recreates file 2 from file1. The -f option also creates a command script that recreates file1 from file2. This command script cannot be used with ed. The following example illustrates the use of the -e option and the output generated.

```
$ diff -e dfile1 dfile2 > cfile
$cat cfile
1c
This is a SMALL file that can be used to illustrate how diff operates.
$
```

An additional option worth mentioning is -h. This option cannot be used with either the -e or -f options, but is useful for very large files, or when the changes are grouped together.

The diff3 Command

The diff3 command is essentially the same as diff, except that it enables the user to compare a series of three files. The syntax for diff3 is as follows:

```
$ diff3 options file1 file2 file3
```

In diff, one of the arguments can be a directory. This is not the case with diff3—all the arguments must be valid files. diff3 attempts to print the differences between each of the files.

The following listing illustrates the output of diff3. diff3 initially reports one of several things using symbols as listed in table 11.1.

```
$ diff3 dfile1 dfile2 dfile3
====
1:1c
  This is a small file which will be used to test diff.
2:1c
  This is a SMALL file that can be used to illustrate how diff oper-
➥ates.
3:1c
  This is a small file which can be used to demonstrate the use of
➥diff3.
$ diff3 dfile1 dfile2 dfile1.save
====2
1:1c
2:1c
  This is a SMALL file that can be used to illustrate how diff oper
➥ates.
3:1c
  This is a small file which will be used to test diff.
$
```

Table 11.1
diff3 Symbols

Command	Explanation
====	All three files are different
====1	File 1 is different.
====2	File 2 is different.
====3	File 3 is different.

Using these symbols, the user gets a quick initial report on how closely the three files match. From the examples in the previous code listing, the first three files are all different; and in the second example, only the second file differs from the other two.

Like diff, diff3 also outputs the needed changes to bring the files into agreement. In the second example, because the contents of dfile1 and dfile1.save are the same, no output is generated by diff3 for the analysis of dfile1. diff3 also has three options that generate scripts for use with the ed command. These scripts create edits that incorporate the changes in file2 and file3 into file1.

The first option is -e, which like diff, creates the ed script to incorporate these changes. The -x option creates a script that incorporates the changes marked with '=====', indicating for all three files. And finally, -3 creates a script that only includes the differences marked with '=====3'. In this last case, only the changes marked for file 3 are included in the script. The following example illustrates the ed script generated for the files used in the previous sample listing.

```
$ cat dfile1
This is a small file which will be used to test diff.
$ cat dfile2
This is a SMALL file that can be used to illustrate how diff operates.
$ cat dfile3
This is a small file which can be used to demonstrate the use of diff3.
$ diff3 -e dfile1 dfile2 dfile3 > cfile3
$ cat cfile3
1c
This is a small file which can be used to demonstrate the use of diff3.
.
w
q
$ diff3 -x dfile1 dfile2 dfile3 > cfilex
$ cat cfilex
1c
This is a small file which can be used to demonstrate the use of diff3.
.
w
q
$ diff3 -3 dfile1 dfile2 dfile3 > cfile3
$ cat cfile3
$
```

The dircmp Command

Both diff and diff3 are used to compare the contents of files, but they do not tell you if two directory structures and related files are the same. This is the job of dircmp. dirmcp accepts as its arguments the names of two directories that it should compare. The syntax for dircmp is as follows:

```
$ dircmp directory1 directory2
```

dircmp generates tabular information about the contents of the directories. This information lists the files unique to each directory as well as common items. In addition, dircmp compares the files and reports if the contents are the same. It is a good idea if the output is going to the screen to pipe to more because the output is formatted with the pr command, and scrolls by very fast.

The following example lists the files not contained in both directories. In this case, the files all exist in the Chapter 11 directory, but not in the Chapter 5 directory. Because they do not exist in both places, these files are not compared with anything else.

```
Aug 26 03:38 1994  uvA only and /tmp/uvA only Page 1


./fruits                              ./new
./list                                ./old_one
./micro_light                         ./output
./micro_light/sample3                 ./output2
./sample                              ./who
                                      ./who.1
                                      ./who.2
```

The following listing, however, shows the files common between the directories. In this case, they are compared to see if their contents are the same and in this example, they are. If the -d option is given to dircmp as it was to generate the output seen in the subsequent example, a full diff is performed on the file if the contents are not the same.

```
Aug 26 03:39 1994  Comparison of uvA /tmp/uvA Page 1


directory      .
same           ./test1
same           ./test3
```

```
Aug 26 03:42 1994  Comparison of uvA /tmp/uvA Page 1


directory      .
different      ./test1
same           ./test3
```

The only other options for dircmp include -s, which suppresses the printing of duplicate filenames, and -w, which changes the number of characters in the output of the command. The default width of the report is 72 characters. To change this, use the following syntax:

```
$ dircmp -w 50 dir1 dir2
```

The following example illustrates the -s option. You are looking at the differences in the same directories as earlier. Only now, the files that are the same are not reported because of the -s option.

```
Aug 26 03:44 1994  Comparison of uvA /tmp/uvA Page 1



different     ./test1
```

Some Extra Goodies

The final commands examined in this chapter address handling data in a complimentary way to sort. These two commands—comm and uniq—are sometimes used in conjunction with sort to perform some additional filtering.

The comm Command

The comm command selects or rejects lines common to two files. The comm input files should have been processed by sort already, and that is why we have chosen to put them here rather than elsewhere. In the following code, you see two files, comm1 and comm2. They each have two entries in common.

```
$ sort c1 > c1s
$ sort c2 > c2s
$ cat c1s
apples
bananas
tomato
watermelon
$ cat c2s
apples
kiwi
passion fruit
watermelon
$ comm c1s c2s
                apples
bananas
        kiwi
        passion fruit
tomato
                watermelon
$
```

When they are processed through comm, comm prints three columns of output. The first column contains items in the first file, but not in the second. The second column contains items in the second file, but not in the first. The third column contains items in both files. The options to comm suppress what is printed in the output. Five options and option combinations to the command are demonstrated in the following example.

```
$ comm -1 c1s c2s
        apples
kiwi
passion fruit
        watermelon
$ comm -2 c1s c2s
        apples
bananas
tomato
        watermelon
$ comm -12 c1s c2s
apples
watermelon
$ comm -23 c1s c2s
bananas
tomato
$ comm -13 c1s c2s
kiwi
passion fruit
$
```

The first option, -1, prints only the items in the first file and common to both. The second example, -2, prints the items in the second file and those common to both. In both these examples, the common items are in the right-hand column. The third example combines the two, for an option of -12. This has the effect of selecting only the items common to the two files.

The option -23 only prints the non-common lines from the first file, just as the last example, -13 only prints the non-common lines from the second example. Using this combination, you can select lines that are either common to both files, or in one or the other only.

The uniq Command

Just as comm is meant to find the common items in two files, uniq is meant to find the repeated lines in a file. The uniq command reads the input and compares the adjacent lines looking for duplicate entries. Usually, the second and repeating lines of the file are removed. The remainder is written to either standard output or a file. The syntax for uniq is as follows:

```
$ uniq options input-file output-file
```

The output-file in the syntax is optional. If present, the output is there; otherwise, the output is written on standard output.

Because uniq looks at adjacent lines to find duplicates, the file must have been sorted first using the command sort. The default behavior of uniq is illustrated in the following:

```
$ sort c3 > c3s
$ cat c3s
apples
apples
bananas
kiwi
passion fruit
tomato
watermelon
watermelon
$ uniq c3s
apples
bananas
kiwi
passion fruit
tomato
watermelon
$
```

This example shows sorting the file comm3 and saving the output in comm3.sort. You then view the contents of comm3.sort to show that duplicated lines are in this file. Using uniq with only the filename removes the duplicated lines and prints only the unique ones.

The following example demonstrates three additional options to uniq. The -u option forces uniq to list only the lines not duplicated in the input, whereas the -d option prints only the duplicated lines. The normal output of uniq is a combination of the output from these options. The final option on uniq processes the file and prints each line along with a count of the number of times the item was found in the file. This can be useful if processing a large amount of common output. One example that comes to mind is taking an electronic vote.

```
$ uniq -u c3s
bananas
kiwi
passion fruit
tomato
$ uniq -d c3s
apples
```

```
watermelon
$ uniq -c c3s
   2 apples
   1 bananas
   1 kiwi
   1 passion fruit
   1 tomato
   2 watermelon
$
```

The subsequent example uses a sample shell script called vote. This shell script is included in Listing 1 at the end of this chapter. All this script does is accept either the word yes or no and record it in a file. After we ran the command a few times to collect some votes, we ran uniq. Notice the output? Because the file wasn't sorted first, uniq counted the lines as different each time it ran across a change in the voting pattern. When the file was sorted, it was clear to see the results—the "ayes" have it!

```
$ vote
Usage: vote choice
     choice is either yes or no
$ vote yes
$ vote no
$ vote no
$ vote yes
$ vote yes
$ vote no
$ vote yes
$ vote yes
$ vote no
$ uniq -c ballot.box
   1 yes
   2 no
   2 yes
   1 no
   2 yes
   1 no
$ sort ballot.box ¦ uniq -c
   4 no
   5 yes
$
```

Command Summary

sort	Sorts files using the default rules
sort -d	Sorts using a dictionary rule sort
sort -f	Sorts treating uppercase as lowercase
sort -n	Sorts treating numbers as numbers, not text
sort -r	Sorts in reverse order
sort -o filename	Sorts and sends the output to the specified file
sort -tdelim	Sorts using delim as the field delimiter
sort +num	Skips num fields for the sort key
sort +num -num	Limits the sort to a one field key
diff file1 file2	Locates the differences between the files
diff -e file1 file2	Locates the differences and creates an ed script
diff -f file1 file2	Locates the differences and creates a reverse ed script (Resulting script cannot be used with ed.)
diff -h file1 file2	Locates the differences between the files; useful for very large files
diff3 file1 file2 file3	Locates the differences between the three files
diff3 -e file1 file2 file3	Locates the differences and creates an ed script
diff3 -x file1 file2 file3	Locates the differences and creates an ed script
diff3 -3 file1 file2 file3	Locates the differences and creates an ed script
dircmp dir1 dir2	Compares two directories and their files
dircmp -s dir1 dir2	Compares two directories and suppresses printing of identical files
dircmp -d dir1 dir2	Compares two directories and performs a full diff on files that differ
dircmp -w num dir1 dir2	Compares two directories and changes the line length on the report to num characters

The Command Line

continues

comm file1 file2	Prints the lines in each file as well as those common to both
comm -1 file1 file2	Prints the items in the first file and common to both
comm -2 file1 file2	Prints the items in the second file and common to both
comm -12 file1 file2	Prints the items common to both files
comm -23 file1 file2	Prints the lines that appear only in the first file
comm -13 file1 file2	Prints the lines that appear only in the second file

Program Listings

Listing 1. vote

```
#!/bin/sh
# vote Version 1
# Chris Hare
#
# this command accepts a command line argument, either yes or no, and
writes
# that argument into a file called ballot.box.
#
if [ ! "$1" ]
then
       echo "Usage: vote choice"
       echo "       choice is either the word yes, or no"
       exit 1
fi
echo "$1" >> ballot.box
exit 0
```

Part III

Working with Editors

Chapter Snapshot

This chapter introduces you to all the basic vi and ex commands. With them, you can perform the following tasks:

Once you have read this chapter, navigating and editing text within UNIX will be old hat for you.

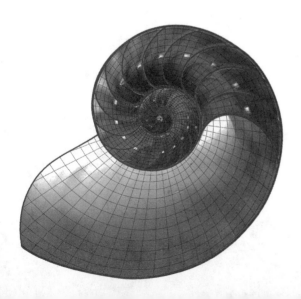

CHAPTER

vi: The Basics

Vi (pronounced vee eye) is one of the most common text editors on the UNIX platform. It was originally provided free of charge with the Berkeley flavor of UNIX. Its wide release made it the de facto UNIX text editor.

vi doesn't produce ornate documents. In fact, it can't even underline or italicize characters. But as a means of moving through a file of text, searching for words, and substituting corrections, vi provides a wealth of commands. For programmers, it provides all the tools needed for creating and editing applications.

This chapter introduces you to all the commands you use most often with the vi utility. You learn, for example, how to load and save programs, move through a file of text, search for words, and make corrections. Mastering the commands, however, comes from using them, not just reading about them. When you finish each section of this chapter, try the commands yourself.

After a short historical introduction to vi, the chapter discusses and shows examples of many vi commands that, with use, can become second nature to you.

Just as many flavors of UNIX are available, you can find many different versions of vi. All versions of vi work similarly. You might find, however, that one or two commands described in this chapter do not work on your system.

Reviewing a Short History of vi

To understand the origins of vi, you must travel back to the time when computers didn't look like the workstations used today. When Bill Joy, then a graduate student at the University of California at Berkeley, created vi, computers were just moving beyond the age of the teletype terminal—that Gatling-gun-sounding monster that ate and punched reams of paper tape. To appreciate what today would be considered a rudimentary editor, it's interesting to learn that vi was the culmination of all the editors that came before it.

In the beginning, no editors were available; users had only batch cards. You couldn't edit a batch card that was incorrectly punched; you could only throw it away.

Then came the age of the teletype terminal whose output medium was the printed page and paper tape. The only way to edit files on a teletype terminal was with a line editor. The editing procedure went something like this: First you printed a line of text, then you entered commands to edit the line, and then you reprinted the line to make sure that everything came out all right. This rather tortuous interaction was aided by the line editor. There were no cursors in the displayed text, so you had to specify words to change specifically. The following command, for example, substituted the word "cat" for "dog":

```
:substitute/cat/dog/
```

Some line-editor commands are quite efficient. Because vi is a superset of ex, a line editor, you can use all ex's line editor commands—a colon precedes ex commands. Many of vi's commands, however, supersede those in ex because of simplicity. Using vi's dd command to delete the current line, for example, is much easier than typing the ex command to do it.

The first CRTs—video terminals—enabled the line editor to edit text directly—if only on one line. Line editors enabled users to move back and forth on a line of text, deleting and adding words. After a line was committed to memory, however, changing it was not easy. It was tortuous to be unable to move up one line on the screen to correct the mistake dangling there.

The next generation of CRTs liberated the cursor from the bottom of the screen. Because the cursor could move around the entire screen, the concept of the screen editor was born. Text at the top and bottom of the screen—text in any part of a file—was eligible to edit. vi is a screen editor, but it also incorporates many line-editor and command-editor actions and conventions. In this way, vi is an amalgamation of all the text editors before it. It had something for everyone; every user could work the way he or she felt most comfortable: with commands, line editing, or screen editing.

vi, short for visual, is the screen-editor mode of the ex editor. ex, based on a previous editor called ed, has two other modes: *open* (a single-line form of vi) and *command* (a line-oriented editor). vi is a superset of ex and command. To use ex, the line editor, when you are in vi, you type a colon (:) in the command mode. To use command functions, you type a slash (/) or question mark (?) in the command mode. To return to vi, type **:vi**.

When Bill Joy created vi, he drew from the tradition of the line editor and the command editor to make programmers of that time feel comfortable. To users of today, vi looks unintuitive at first glance. The number of commands it uses is overwhelming. And because the keyboard is used in two completely different ways—sometimes for alphanumeric entry, sometimes for command entry—new users often get erroneous results.

In short, vi is not a word processor, nor is it a WYSIWYG tool. It does not, for example, provide any of the tools you use to format text, even something as simple as making a word bold. To add formatting to text, you have to use other programs, such as troff (pronounced, like a dinosaur, tee-roff). What vi does best is create simple documents and change existing ones. Software programs are good examples of what vi creates best.

vi does not have the buttons and scroll bars commonly found in graphical-user interfaces (GUIs), nor does it often use function keys or key combinations to accomplish single tasks. In general, one key, in command mode, accomplishes one action. The letter j, for example, moves the cursor down. You do not push the Enter key to initiate the action. Capital letters enact different commands than lowercase letters. The letter u, for example, undoes the last change, whereas the letter U undoes the changes to the current line.

In creating the command set, Bill Joy used mnemonics. The letter u, for example, stands for undo, and the letter o stands for open. He also used the characters themselves to suggest meaning. The right curly brace (}), for example, which resembles the head of an arrow, means to move to the next paragraph.

The fact that vi is one of the most widely distributed UNIX applications is one of its greatest attributes. It is the de facto word processor on the UNIX platform. Its commands are powerful and plentiful, but you don't need to memorize all of vi's commands at once. Like other applications, the commands you learn first are those you need to use most often. Learn the others on an as-needed basis. With repetition, the command interface becomes intuitive. The trick to learning vi is learning its jargon. Eventually, you'll learn to think of the word "backward" when you want to move to the previous word, and you'll associate the command letter b with that task automatically. At first, you might initially think of the word "left" or "last" and get erroneous results. The language of vi comes quickly with practice.

Starting and Stopping vi

Starting vi

You start vi by typing **vi** on the command line along with the name of a file to edit, as in the following:

```
% vi myFirstFile
```

myFirstFile is the name of a file. If the file is in a different directory from the current one, you have to supply the path to the file's directory before the name. In the following example, /usr/doc/myBook/ is the path to the text file:

```
% vi /usr/doc/myBook/myFirstFile
```

If myFirstFile does not exist, vi displays a column of tildes (~) signifying an empty file, as shown in figure 12.1.

Figure 12.1
An empty file.

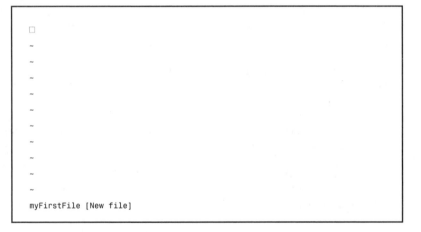

```
~
~
~
~
~
~
~
~
~
myFirstFile [New file]
```

If myFirstFile does exist, however, vi loads the file into a buffer and displays the file's contents, as shown in figure 12.2.

```
It was a dark and stormy night.  The rain on the roof droned like t
he monotonous rumble of a motor boat.□
I think it was before midnight when I languished into a state
of deep sleep— a sleep so deep that even the barking of a dog
could not wake me. It was in that sleep that the oddest dream
I have ever had happened; and it was as if I were there, in that f
ield of slaves whose faces I can even see now.
~
~
~
~
MyFirstFile [Modified] line 1 of 6 —16%—
```

Figure 12.2
Text in vi editor.

If you have trouble starting vi, the problem might be that vi does not know the type of terminal you are using. Although vi works with most terminals, specifying the wrong one in your .xlogin file (if you use csh) causes problems. To correct the terminal setting, change the environment variable in the C shell as follows:

```
% setenv TERM <teletypeName>
```

`teletypeName` specifies your terminal type, such as vt100 (VT-100). For other shells, use the following commands:

```
$ TERM = <teletypeName>; export TERM
```

After you start vi, you are automatically in command mode.

Stopping vi and Saving Files

You have many ways of getting out of vi, depending on whether you want to save the changes you made to the file. Table 12.1 shows some of these methods.

Table 12.1
Exiting VI

Command	Mnemonic	Description
:w	write	Save file to disk (and keep edits)
ZZ	—	Save file to disk and quit file
:wq	write/quit	Save file to disk and quit file
:q!	quit	Exit file (without saving changes)

Although the command ZZ doesn't have a mnemonic, the last letter of the alphabet (repeated!) symbolically suggests that it is the last command you can use in a vi session.

Remember that before you can execute any of the commands in table 12.1, you must be in command mode. If you are not, press Esc.

Fifteen commands are available for you to use to quit vi. Table 12.1 shows only the most common. The most important distinction between the commands is whether you want to keep the changes that you made while editing the file. If not, then quit the file without saving the changes.

The colon designates an ex command. As soon as you type a colon, the cursor jumps to the bottom of the screen—out of the file—and waits for a command. After typing a report called EndOf Year, for example, press Esc and type **:qw** (notice the capitalization). With all ex commands, you must use the Enter key to execute the command because ex uses key combinations. The only way vi can determine whether you are using a one- or two-letter command to execute a task is if you press Enter.

When you quit a file, vi provides a statistical snapshot of the file at the bottom of the screen:

```
"EndOfYear" [New file] 128 lines, 5849 characters
```

If you want to display this statistical summary at any point in an editing session, use the Ctrl+G command.

After you quit vi, the display returns to the UNIX shell command prompt. If you list the files in the directory, using ls, you find the file EndOfYear:

```
% ls
Book1     chapter6    EndOfYear
```

Saving Two Versions of a File

You often want to save the old and new versions of a file. The only way to do that is to save the new version under a different name. For this task, specify the name of the new file after the w command, as in the following example:

```
:w newFileName
```

newFileName is the name for the revised file. You also can use wq to rename a file, as in this example:

```
:wq newFileName
```

This command exits the editing session.

Comparing Two Files

You might be interested in comparing two files, perhaps old and new versions. You can do so by opening both files in vi at the same time, using the following syntax:

```
% vi fileName1 fileName2
```

To examine the differences between the files, you can use the UNIX command diff. To execute a UNIX command in vi, you must use the exclamation point (!), as follows:

```
:!diff fileName1 fileName2
```

The exclamation point creates a shell for the execution of the UNIX command. This command highlights the differences between the two files, as shown in figure 12.3.

```
It was a dark night.  The rain on the roof sounded like the rumble
of a motor boat.
I was in the middle of a large field of wheat.  The wind
swirled the long canes of corn and their clicking combined with
the low, gutterl singing of a mass of voices
reminded me of an ancient, tribal ritual— a ritual of
hope.  As the hands came down and scooped me up, I knew that day w
as my last.
It was just before midnight when I fell asleep— a sleep so
:!diff myFirstFile mySecondFile
```

Figure 12.3

Highlighting the differences between two files.

Figure 12.3
continued

```
e the rumble of a motor boat.
2c3
< I was in the middle of a large field of wheat. The wind
---
> I was in the middle of a large field of corn.  The wind
7c7
< hope. As the hands came down and scooped me up, I knew that day
was my last.
---
> sacrifice. As the hands came down and scooped me up, I knew t
hat day was my last.
[Hit return to continue]□□□
```

Another common use of UNIX commands in vi is displaying the date. To do so, use the following command:

```
:!date
```

Saving Part of a File

Just as sometimes you want to rename a file, at other times you might want to save only part of the original file as a separate file. vi enables you to save part of a file by specifying the line numbers you want to save.

Each line in a file has an associated line number. The first line is number 1, and so on. vi provides some special characters to help specify line numbers. The dollar sign ($), for example, represents the last line in the file. The dot (.) represents the current line. You can use these characters to specify parts of a file without knowing specific line numbers.

The syntax for saving only part of a file is as follows:

```
:first_line, last_linew newFileName
```

Note that the w (following last_line) is the write command, not a typo. This command saves the lines between the first and last line, inclusive, in a file named newFileName.

Table 12.2 shows examples of saving parts of files.

Table 12.2
Saving Parts of Files

Command	Description
:12, 35w version2	Saves lines 12 through 35 in a file named version2
:.,200w version2	Saves lines between the current cursor location and line 200 in a file named version2
:200, $w version2	Saves lines between 200 and the end of the file in a file named version2

Sharing Text between Files

At times you might want to add part of one file to a different file. For this task, use the UNIX redirect operator (>>), as follows:

```
:50, $w>>longFile
```

This command adds to the end of a file named longFile lines 50 through the end of the current file.

You can perform the inverse function, reading lines from another file into the current file, by using the r command (read), as follows:

```
:r otherFileName
```

Where otherFileName is the name of the other file you want to read into the current file. The effect of this command is to insert the entire file, otherFileName, into the current file after the cursor. So be careful to place the cursor correctly!

Using Command and Insert Modes

vi has two modes of operation: command and insert. vi automatically starts in command mode. You use command mode to move through a document and to make changes. In command mode, all the keys and key combinations, including the individual keys, the Shift+key combinations, and the Ctrl+key combinations, function as different commands.

In input mode, the keyboard acts just like a typewriter. You use insert mode to type your document or corrections.

III

Working with Editors

It would be nice if vi changed the shape of the cursor to indicate which mode you were in, but it doesn't. Often, new vi users unintentionally press the keys that switch them from one mode to another. If you get confused, press the Esc key several times to return to command mode and proceed from there.

Table 12.3 shows some of the commands you can use to change from command to insert text mode.

Table 12.3
Switching to Insert Mode

Command	Mnemonic	Description
i	insert	Inserts text before cursor
a	append	Inserts text after cursor
o	open	Opens a new line below the cursor
O	open	Opens a new line above the cursor

At first, you might think that having both commands, i and a, is repetitious and unnecessary. You will find the value of both input commands when, for example, you try to insert text at the end of a line. The cursor in vi does not skip from the end of one line to the beginning of the next, so you can't move beyond the last character in a line and begin entering text. In vi, the cursor usually comes to rest on the last character in the line. If you chose the command i, you would inadvertently insert characters between the last and second-to-last characters in the line. When you instead use the command a, even though the cursor is parked on the last letter of a line, the inserted information begins after the last character in the line.

In insert text mode, vi automatically wraps typing onto the next line by inserting its own carriage return. Press the Enter key only when you want to start a new paragraph. If you make a mistake while typing, move back to the incorrect entry and type over it.

To change from insert to command mode, press Esc.

Moving the Cursor

To edit a document, you first must know how to navigate on the screen. vi provides a wide variety of units of movement. You can move by the following increments:

- ✔ a single character at a time

- ✔ a word at a time

- ✔ a line at a time

- ✔ a sentence at a time

- ✔ a paragraph at a time

- ✔ a screen at a time

To move the cursor, remember to first press the Esc key to enter command mode. vi beeps when you try to move beyond the boundaries of the document, such as when you try to advance to the next paragraph when you are in the last paragraph of a document.

Moving One Character at a Time

Because moving one character at a time happens so often, Bill Joy put the motion commands right under your fingertips, as shown in table 12.4.

Table 12.4
Moving One Character at a Time

Command	Moves Cursor...
h	left one space
j	down one space
k	up one line
l	right one line

Figure 12.4 shows how these commands move the cursor.

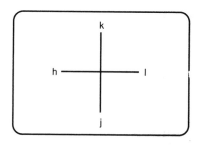

Figure 12.4
Moving the cursor one character at a time.

These commands do not have mnemonic correspondence. Originally, vi was developed on a terminal (the ADM3a) that had arrows on each of these keys. The placement of the keys, however, does relate to the action of the key. The "outside" keys, the "h" and "l," move the cursor one place to the left and right, respectively. The up and down keys, "j" and "k," respectively, are adjacent. Of course you also can use the four arrow keys to move the cursor, but they're generally out of the way or not available.

When you move the cursor up and down, the cursor moves to the position it last occupied on the line, not necessarily directly above or below the current location of the cursor. If the cursor was never on the line, it goes directly above or below the previous location of the cursor.

One frustrating limitation of vi is that moving the cursor continuously to the right, for example, moves the cursor, at most, to the end of the current line. The cursor does not skip to the beginning of the next line after moving to the end of the current one.

Moving One Word at a Time

You can move the cursor one word at a time by using the commands shown in table 12.5.

Table 12.5
Moving One Word at a Time

Command	Mnemonic	Moves Cursor...
w	word	to the beginning of the next word
W	word	to the beginning of the next word, ignoring symbols and punctuation marks
e	end	to the end of the next word
E	end	to the end of the next word, ignoring symbols and punctuation marks
b	backward	to the beginning of the previous word
B	backward	to the beginning of the previous word, ignoring symbols and punctuation marks

vi treats symbols and punctuation marks as though they were words. The following example shows where the cursor moves when you execute the w command 13 times.

```
The Red Baron, sweaty with anger, pulled hard on the stick and wrenched
his plane into a split S turn.
```

To ignore symbols and punctuation marks, use the W command. It moves the cursor to the beginning of words only, as shown in the following example.

```
The Red Baron, sweaty with anger, pulled hard on the stick and wrenched
his plane into a split S turn.
```

The e, E, b, and B commands work in a similar way. The E and B commands move the cursor ignoring symbols and punctuation marks, whereas the e and b commands treat symbols and punctuation marks as words.

Moving One Line at a Time

vi provides many useful commands for maneuvering to the beginning and ending of lines. Lines are defined as the text between carriage returns. A line is usually not a sentence. If you have autowrap turned on (:set wm=10), a line is at most 80 characters long. Autowrap inserts carriage returns automatically. If autowrap is turned off, lines can extend over several physical lines on the screen.

> You can see which physical lines are the start of new lines or continuations of previous lines by using the :set nu (set number) command. vi numbers the beginning of each new line.

You run into trouble with the definition of a line most often when you convert text generated from a word processor, such as WordPerfect, into a text-only format that vi can read. WordPerfect autowraps lines without carriage returns. As a result, entire paragraphs in WordPerfect, when displayed in vi, convert into one long line (occupying many lines on the screen). Line commands, in this situation, are less helpful because they don't move the cursor from one physical line on the screen to the next.

Table 12.6 shows the line commands you use to move the cursor.

Table 12.6
Moving One Line at a Time

Command	Moves Cursor...
0	to the beginning of the current line
^	to the first character of the current line (ignoring any spaces)

continues

Table 12.6, Continued
Moving One Line at a Time

Command	Moves Cursor...
RETURN	to the beginning of the next line
$	to the last position of the current line
+	to the first character of the next line
-	to the first character of the previous line

Again, these commands are not mnemonic. They are, however, symbolic of the action they perform. The command 0, for example, moves the cursor to the zero, or beginning, position on the line. The plus (+) and minus (-) signs, for example, increment or decrement, respectively, the position of the cursor to the next or previous lines.

The caret (^) command moves the cursor to the first alphanumeric character in a line; the 0 command moves the cursor to the first position in the line, regardless of the content. Likewise, the $ command moves the cursor to the last position in a line, regardless of the content.

What follows is an example of autowrap turned off.

```
1    It was a dark and stormy night. Our World War I
2    hero was entrenched behind enemy lines skillfully
     avoiding the ever watchful eyes of the enemy. Oh,
3    to see again the rustic interiors of the gay, French taverns.
```

The cursor is at the o in hero. If you use the $ command, the cursor moves to the comma after the word Oh, not to the y in skillfully.

```
1    It was a dark and stormy night. Our World War I
2    hero was entrenched behind enemy lines skillfully
     avoiding the ever watchful eyes of the enemy. Oh,
3    to see again the rustic interiors of the gay, French taverns.
```

Using the 0 command moves the cursor from its current position, the comma after h, to the h in hero, not to the a in the word avoiding.

Moving One Sentence and One Paragraph at a Time

The commands discussed up until now are the ones most frequently used to move the cursor throughout the file. At times, however, you might want to move more quickly through a document. vi provides the means to move the cursor in larger units, such as by sentence and paragraph.

vi recognizes the end of a sentence by finding a period followed by a space, or by finding the last nonblank character on a line. Table 12.7 shows the sentence commands you use to move the cursor.

Table 12.7
Moving One Sentence at a Time

Command	Moves Cursor...
(	to the beginning of the previous sentence
)	to the beginning of the next sentence

The shape of the parentheses, as though they were the heads of arrows, indicate the direction the cursor moves.

vi recognizes a paragraph as all the text occurring before the next blank line. Table 12.8 shows the paragraph commands you use to move the cursor.

Table 12.8
Moving One Paragraph at a Time

Command	Moves Cursor...
{	to the beginning of the previous paragraph
}	to the beginning of the next paragraph

Moving One Screen at a Time

Some documents are only a few lines long, but many are hundreds of lines long. A screen views only a limited number of document lines at once. If you think of a document as text written on a continuous sheet of paper, you can imagine a screen as a window looking at just a part of the text. To view different parts of the document, you use screen movement commands to scan up and down the document, as shown in figure 12.5.

Figure 12.5
A screen
displays part of
a document.

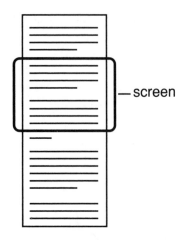

— screen

When reading a long document, the easiest way is to read one screen at a time. vi provides several commands to help you, as shown in table 12.9.

Table 12.9
Moving One Screen at a Time

Command	Mnemonic	Description
Ctrl+F	forward	Moves forward one screen
Ctrl+B	backward	Moves backward one screen
Ctrl+D	down	Moves forward one-half screen
Ctrl+U	up	Moves backward one-half screen
Ctrl+E	expose	Scrolls screen up one line
Ctrl+Y	—	Scrolls screen down one line

Ctrl stands for the Control key. To execute these commands, you press the Control key, the Shift key and the letter at the same time. The cursor appears at the first character in each new screen. Figure 12.6 shows the effects of executing the Ctrl+F command.

```
It was a dark and stormy night.  The rain on the roof droned like t
he monotonous rumble of a motor boat.

I think it was before midnight when I languished into a state
of deep sleep— a sleep so deep that even the barking of a dog
could not wake me. It was in that sleep that the oddest dream
I have ever had happened; and it was as if I were there, in that f
ield of slaves whose faces I can even see now.

It was in the middle of the hottest day of the year.  The wind
□wirled the long canes of corn and their clicking combined with
```

Figure 12.6
Moving forward
one screen.

Perform Ctrl+F.

```
□t was in the middle of the hottest day of the year. The wind
swirled the long canes of corn and their clicking combined with
the low, resonant voices of the soft spiritual being sung
reminded me of an ancient, tribal ritual— a ritual of
scarifice. As the hands came down and scooped me up, I knew that
day was my last.
~
~
~
```

III

Working with Editors

The up- and down-arrow keys and the j and k commands also scroll the screen one line at a time, but only when the cursor is at the bottom or top, respectively, of the screen. The Ctrl+E and Ctrl+Y commands scroll the screen regardless of the cursor's location. Although the Ctrl+Y command is not at all mnemonic, it was probably chosen because of its proximity to the U (for moving the window view "up") key.

The Ctrl+F and Ctrl+B commands are called paging commands because they advance through the documents almost one entire screen at a time. Actually, vi leaves the last line of the old screen as the first line on the next screen to provide continuity. The Ctrl+E and Ctrl+Y commands are called scrolling commands because they reveal the document one line at a time. These commands provide more continuity. Some users find the continuity important; others find scrolling annoying because the text bounces up the screen. Likewise, some users dislike the jump from one screen to another, and others find paging easier on the eyes. You'll quickly find out whether paging or scrolling suits you best.

Moving More than One Unit at a Time

vi enables you to combine movement commands with numbers to move a specified number of units. The command h, for example, is understood to mean 1h, which means to move the cursor one space to the left. If you want to move the cursor five spaces to the left, instead of repeating the h command five times, you can give the command 5h, as shown in figure 12.7.

Figure 12.7
Moving more than
one unit at a time.

```
It was in the middl□ of the hottest day of the year. The wind
swirled the long canes of corn and their clicking combined with
the low, resonant voices of the soft spiritual being sung
reminded me of an ancient, tribal ritual— a ritual of
scarifice. As the hands came down and scooped me up, I knew that
day was my last.
~
~
~
```

Perform 5h.

```
It was in the □iddle of the hottest day of the year. The wind
swirled the long canes of corn and their clicking combined with
the low, resonant voices of the soft spiritual being sung
reminded me of an ancient, tribal ritual— a ritual of
scarifice. As the hands came down and scooped me up, I knew that
day was my last.
~
~
~
```

Likewise, you can move more than one word, one line, one paragraph, and one screen at a time by using numbers, as shown in figures 12.8 and 12.9.

```
   It was in the □iddle of the hottest day of the year. The wind
   swirled the long canes of corn and their clicking combined with
   the low, resonant voices of the soft spiritual being sung
   reminded me of an ancient, tribal ritual— a ritual of
   scarifice. As the hands came down and scooped me up, I knew that
   day was my last.
   ~
   ~
   ~
```

Figure 12.8
Moving four words to the right by using numbers.

Perform 4w.

```
   It was in the middle of the hottest □ay of the year. The wind
   swirled the long canes of corn and their clicking combined with
   the low, resonant voices of the soft spiritual being sung
   reminded me of an ancient, tribal ritual— a ritual of
   scarifice. As the hands came down and scooped me up, I knew that
   day was my last.
   ~
   ~
   ~
```

```
It was in the middle of the hottest □ay of the year. The wind
swirled the long canes of corn and their clicking combined with
the low, resonant voices of the soft spiritual being sung
reminded me of an ancient, tribal ritual— a ritual of
scarifice. As the hands came down and scooped me up, I knew that
day was my last.

~

~

~
```

```
It was in the middle of the hottest day of the year. The wind
swirled the long canes of corn and their clicking combined with
the low, resonant voices of the soft spiritual being sung
reminded me of an ancient, tribal ritual— a ritual of
scarifice. As the hands came down an□ scooped me up, I knew that
day was my last.

~

~

~
```

Moving the Cursor within the Screen

Sometimes it is beneficial to move to different parts of the screen quickly—to the top or bottom of the screen, for example. Table 12.10 shows the commands that move the cursor to different locations in the same screen.

Table 12.10
Moving within a Screen

Command	Mnemonic	Description
H	home	Moves to the top line on the screen
M	middle	Moves to the middle line on the screen
L	last	Moves to the last line on the screen
nH	—	Moves n lines below the top line on the screen
nL	—	Moves n lines above the last line on the screen

Where n is an integer, a command such as 3H moves the cursor to the third line on the screen, as shown in figure 12.10.

```
It was in the middle of the hottest day of the year. The wind
swirled the long canes of corn and their clicking combined with
the low, resonant voices of the soft spiritual being sung
reminded me of an ancient, tribal ritual— a ritual of
scarifice. As the hands came down an□ scooped me up, I knew that
day was my last.
~
~
~
```

Figure 12.10
Moving the cursor within the screen.

Perform 3H.

```
It was in the middle of the hottest day of the year. The wind
swirled the long canes of corn and their clicking combined with
□he low, resonant voices of the soft spiritual being sung
reminded me of an ancient, tribal ritual— a ritual of
scarifice. As the hands came down and scooped me up, I knew that
day was my last.
~
~
~
```

Moving by Line Numbers

In the section "Moving One Line at a Time" you learned how to use the :set nu command to display a number beside each line in a file. In vi, you can use the Ctrl+G command to display at the bottom of the screen the name of the file, the current line number, the total number of lines in the file, and the percentage of lines in the file above the current line. If the current file name is myFirstFile, the Ctrl+G command might display the following line:

```
"myFirstFile" line 25 of 100  — 25% —
```

Table 12.11 shows the commands you use for moving the cursor to specific lines by using line numbers.

Table 12.11
Moving by Line Number

Command	Mnemonic	Description
*n*G	go	Goes to specified line number
:*n*	—	Goes to specified line number
"	—	Returns to beginning of original line
”	—	Returns to exact position on original line

vi provides the G (go) command to move the cursor to a specific line. 25G, for example, moves the cursor to the beginning of the 25th line in the file. You also can use the G command without a number. By itself, the G command moves the cursor to the end of the file.

After you go to another line, you sometimes want to return. Two single quotes (") return the cursor to the beginning of the line you were on originally. Two back quotes (”) work like an undo function; they return the cursor to the exact position it originated.

The G command is beneficial to users who want to move large blocks of text at a time, and to programmers because error messages from compilers refer to specific line numbers.

Using Markers To Move

Sometimes you know you want to return to specific locations in a document—you might need to add text, add figures, or check your writing. vi enables you to set markers, like bookmarks, to which you can return. Table 12.12 shows the marker commands you use to move the cursor.

Table 12.12
Using Marker Commands

Command	Description
m*x*	Marks current position as *x*
´x	Moves cursor to position *x*
´´	Returns to original position after a move

The variable *x* represents all letters, upper- and lowercase. One letter doesn't provide much room for making markers that remind you of bookmark locations. The variable does, however, provide 52 possible markers.

Moving by Searching

A powerful way to move the cursor to different words is by searching for them. If, for example, you discovered that you had incorrectly spelled the word "calendar," you might use the search command to advance the cursor to every instance of the word "calender" to correct it.

The search command begins with a slash (/). When you press the slash key, the cursor jumps to the bottom of the screen and waits for further input. After the slash, type the word or alphanumeric pattern you want to find, and press Enter. The syntax is shown here:

```
/text pattern <Enter>
```

All commands that you issue from the bottom of the screen are terminated by pressing Enter.

After you execute the command, the cursor moves to the first character in the next occurrence of the alphanumeric pattern. The search loops around to the beginning of the document automatically. If the pattern is not found, the message `Pattern not found` appears in the status line at the bottom of the screen.

Figure 12.11 shows several examples of searches.

```
It was in the middle of the hottest day of the year. The wind
swirled the long canes of corn and their clicking combined with
the low, □esonant voices of the soft spiritual being sung
reminded me of an ancient, tribal ritual— a ritual of
scarifice. As the hands came down and scooped me up, I knew that
day was my last.
~
~
~
```

Figure 12.11
Using the search command.

Figure 12.11

continued

```
It was in the middle of the hottest day of the year. The wind

swirled the long canes of corn and their clicking combined with

the low, resonant voices of the soft spiritual being sung

reminded me of an ancient, tribal ritual— a ritual of

scarifice. As the hands came down and scooped me up, I □new that

day was my last.

~

~

~
```

To move the cursor to the next instance of the text pattern, use the n (next) command. To find the next instance of the text pattern in the reverse direction, use the N command.

The text pattern remains in a buffer, so if you search for a text pattern, do some other work—you can search again for the same text pattern without reentering it by using n, N, /, or ?.

The slash (/), like n, asks vi to search forward from the current location of the cursor. To search backward and to loop from the beginning to the end of the document, if necessary, use the question mark (?) or N, as follows:

```
?text pattern <Enter>
```

vi displays the direction the cursor is searching in a status message in the lower left part of the screen.

You also can use wild cards to conduct searches. The asterisk (*) represents zero or more alphanumeric characters. The following words, for example, satisfy the *ing search criterion: saying, bathing, looking, king, and sailing.

Figure 12.12 shows the result of the following search:

```
/*ing <Enter>
```

If you want to look for a text pattern at the beginning of the lines, use the caret (^) command. The /^button command, for example, looks for the next instance of the word "button" at the beginning of a line. This command often helps you find words in highly structured documents, such as software applications where commands often start lines.

To search for words at the end of lines, use the dollar sign ($) command. The /button$ command, for example, looks for the next instance of the word "button" at the end of every line.

III

Working with Editors

```
of deep sleep— a sleep so deep that even the barking of a dog
could not wake me. It was in that sleep that the oddest dream
I have ever had happened; and it was if I wer ther, in that
field of slaves whose faces I can see even now.

It was in the mddle fo the hottest day of the year. The wind
swirled the long canes of corn and their clicking combined with
the low, resonant voices of the soft sprit<br>itual b□ing sung
reminded me of an ancient, tribal ritual— a ritual of
sacrifice. As the hands came down and scooped me up, I knew that
day was my last.
/.ing
```

Figure 12.12
Using wildcards
in searches.

Editing Documents

Everyone makes mistakes. Whether you are writing software applications or news articles, corrections are necessary to correct typos or improve the expression of ideas.

Most editing tasks are comprised of several basic components:

- ✔ searching for text
- ✔ deleting unwanted text
- ✔ changing current text
- ✔ inserting new text
- ✔ moving text
- ✔ copying text

The previous section described how to insert and search for words in a document. This section discusses how to perform the other editing tasks.

Changing Text

To change text in the document, you could either delete it all and then insert new text or, as a shortcut, use the change command, c. The c command takes care of putting you in the correct mode. When you use the c command, vi automatically puts you in insert mode.

In combination with other commands, you can identify many words as text to change. You don't need to input the same number of words as you delete, and you can enter as many (or as few) words as you like until you press the Esc key, ending the command.

You can use the c command in combination with all the movement commands discussed previously in this chapter. You also can use numbers, as explained in the section "Moving More than One Unit at a Time," to change more than one word at a time. Table 12.13 shows common examples of changes you might make.

Table 12.13
Changing Text

Command	Replaces...
cw	to the end of a word
c^	to the beginning of the line
c$	to the end of the line
4cw	the next four words
c}	the remainder of the paragraph
c)	the remainder of the sentence

To replace a word, move the cursor to the beginning of it. Use the command cw. vi places a dollar sign ($) at the end of the word to be replaced, as shown in figure 12.13.

Figure 12.13
Replacing a word.

```
It was a dark and stormy night.  The rain on the roof droned like
the monotonous rumble of a motor boat.

I think it was before □idnight when I languished into a stat$
of deep sleep— a sleep so deep that even the barking of a dog
could not wake me. It was in that sleep that the oddest dream
I have ever had happened; and it was as if I were there, in that
field of slaves whose faces I can even see now.
```

vi automatically puts you in insert mode, and you can type in the correction.

You can replace part of a word by positioning the cursor at the place in the word where you want to begin making a change, as shown in figure 12.14.

```
It was a dark and stormy night.  The rain on the roof droned like
the monotonous rumble of a motor boat.


I think it was before mid□igh$ when I drifted off into a
deep sleep— a sleep so deep that even the barking of a dog
could not wake me. It was in that sleep that the oddest dream
I have ever had happened; and it was as if I were there, in that
field of slaves whose faces I can even see now.
```

Figure 12.14
Replacing part
of a word.

Once again, vi uses a dollar sign to demarcate the text to be replaced.

An easier way to correct a single letter is the r command. It selects the character the cursor is on and replaces it with the character you type. r takes care of switching modes automatically. When you invoke the r command, vi switches automatically to insert mode. After you type the correct character, vi switches automatically to command mode. Changing modes automatically saves you many keystrokes.

The R command enables you to type over the existing characters starting at the position of the cursor.

Table 12.13 already showed some examples of how to replace all or parts of lines. vi has some special commands, however, to make line replacing even easier.

To replace an entire line, use the special command cc. vi selects the entire line the cursor is on as text to replace, regardless of the position of the cursor.

The C command is the equivalent of c$; it selects all the text between the cursor and the end of the line as the text to replace.

Deleting Text

You know that you use the change command, c, to replace text. At other times, however, you might just want to delete text. The delete command, d, works just like the c command. You use it in combination with movement commands to define how much text you want to delete. To delete a word, for example, position the cursor at the beginning of a word and then use the command dw, as shown in figure 12.15.

Figure 12.15
Deleting a word.

> It was a dark and stormy night. The rain on the roof droned like
> the ☐onotonous rumble of a motor boat.
>
> I think it was before midnight when I drifted off into a
> deep sleep— a sleep so deep that even the barking of a dog
> could not wake me. It was in that sleep that the oddest dream
> I have ever had happened; and it was as if I were there, in that
> field of slaves whose faces I can even see now.

Perform dw.

> It was a dark and stormy night. The rain on the roof droned like
> the ☐umble of a motor boat.
>
> I think it was before midnight when I drifted off into a
> deep sleep— a sleep so deep that even the barking of a dog
> could not wake me. It was in that sleep that the oddest dream
> I have ever had happened; and it was as if I were there, in that
> field of slaves whose faces I can even see now.

Table 12.14 shows common examples of deletion commands.

Table 12.14
Deleting Text

Command	Deletes...
dw	to the end of a word
d0	to the beginning of the line
d$	to the end of the line
4dw	the next four words
4dl	the next four letters

Command	Deletes...
db	the previous word or part of a word
d}	the remainder of the paragraph
d)	the remainder of the sentence

The command dw not only deletes the characters between the letters in a word after the cursor, but also deletes the space after the word. To delete only to the end of a word, use the de command, as shown in figure 12.16.

```
It was a dark and stormy night.  The rain on the roof droned like
the rumble of a motor boat.

I think it was before midnight when I drifted off into a
deep sleep— a sleep so deep that even the barking of a dog
could not wake me. It was in that sleep that the oddest dream
I have ever had happened; and it was as if I were there, in that
field of slaves whose faces I can even see now.

It was in the middle of the □ottest day of the year. The wind
swirled the long canes of corn and their clicking combined with
```

Figure 12.16
Deleting to the end
of a word.

```
It was a dark and stormy night.  The rain on the roof droned like
the rumble of a motor boat.

I think it was before midnight when I drifted off into a
deep sleep— a sleep so deep that even the barking of a dog
could not wake me. It was in that sleep that the oddest dream
I have ever had happened; and it was as if I were there, in that
field of slaves whose faces I can even see now.

It was in the middle of the hot□day of the year. The wind
swirled the long canes of corn and their clicking combined with
```

If you want to delete only a single character, use the x command. The x command deletes the character under the cursor, as shown in figure 12.17.

Figure 12.17
Deleting a single
character.

```
It was a dark and stormy night.  The rain on the roof droned like
the rumble of a motor boat.

I think it was before midnight when I drifted off into a
deep sleep— a sleep so deep that even the barking of a dog
could not wake me. It was in that sleep that the oddest dream
I have ever had happened; and it was as if I were there, in that
field of slaves whose faces I can even see now.

I□ was in the middle of the hot day of the year. The wind
swirled the long canes of corn and their clicking combined with
```

Perform x.

```
It was a dark and stormy night.  The rain on the roof droned like
the rumble of a motor boat.

I think it was before midnight when I drifted off into a
deep sleep— a sleep so deep that even the barking of a dog
could not wake me. It was in that sleep that the oddest dream
I have ever had happened; and it was as if I were there, in that
field of slaves whose faces I can even see now.
```

To delete the character before the cursor, use the X command. You can combine both the x and X commands with numbers to delete the specified number of characters. The 8x command, for example, deletes the character under the cursor and the seven characters to the right of it. 8X deletes the eight characters to the left of the cursor, as shown in figure 12.18.

```
It was a dark and stormy night.  The rain on the roof droned like
the rumble of a motor boat.

I think it was before midnight when I drifted off into a
deep sleep— a sleep so dee☐ that even the barking of a dog
could not wake me. It was in that sleep that the oddest dream
I have ever had happened; and it was as if I were there, in that
field of slaves whose faces I can even see now.

I was in the middle of the hot day of the year. The wind
```

Figure 12.18
Deleting a
specified number
of characters.

Perform 8X.

```
It was a dark and stormy night.  The rain on the roof droned like
the rumble of a motor boat.

I think it was before midnight when I drifted off into a
deep sleep— a slee☐ that even the barking of a dog
could not wake me. It was in that sleep that the oddest dream
I have ever had happened; and it was as if I were there, in that
field of slaves whose faces I can even see now.

I was in the middle of the hot day of the year. The wind
swirled the long canes of corn and their clicking combined with
```

Table 12.14 shows some of the commands you can use to delete some or all of a line. vi, however, has some special commands for deleting lines. The dd command, for example, deletes the line the cursor is on, regardless of the position of the cursor.

You can combine the dd command with numbers to delete more than one line at a time. Figure 12.19 shows an example of deleting three lines at once, using the 3dd command.

III

Working with Editors

Figure 12.19

Deleting more
than one line
at a time.

```
It was a dark and stormy night.  The rain on the roof droned like
the rumble of a motor boat.

I think it was before midnight when I drifted off into a
deep sleep— a slee□ that even the barking of a dog
could not wake me. It was in that sleep that the oddest dream
I have ever had happened; and it was as if I were there, in that
field of slaves whose faces I can even see now.

I was in the middle of the hot day of the year. The wind
swirled the long canes of corn and their clicking combined with
```

Perform 3dd.

```
It was a dark and stormy night.  The rain on the roof droned like
the rumble of a motor boat.

I think it was before midnight when I drifted off into a
□
I was in the middle of the hot day of the year. The wind
swirled the long canes of corn and their clicking combined with
the low, gutterl singing of a mass of voices
reminded me of an ancient, tribal ritual— a ritual of
sacrifice. As the hands came down and scooped me up, I knew that
day was my last.
```

To delete the text from the cursor to the end of the line, use the D command, as shown
in figure 12.20.

```
It was a dark and stormy night.  The rain on the roof droned like
the rumble of a motor boat.

I think it was before midnight when I drifted off into a



I was in the middle □f the hot day of the year. The wind
swirled the long canes of corn and their clicking combined with
the low, gutterl singing of a mass of voices
reminded me of an ancient, tribal ritual— a ritual of
sacrifice. As the hands came down and scooped me up, I knew that
day was my last.
```

Figure 12.20
Deleting the remainder of a line.

```
It was a dark and stormy night.  The rain on the roof droned like
the rumble of a motor boat.

I think it was before midnight when I drifted off into a

I was in the middle□
swirled the long canes of corn and their clicking combined with
the low, gutterl singing of a mass of voices
reminded me of an ancient, tribal ritual— a ritual of
sacrifice. As the hands came down and scooped me up, I knew that
day was my last.
```

Unlike the dd command, you cannot combine the D command with numbers.

Moving Text

When you delete (or change) a word or a line, the text remains in a buffer until you delete (or change) another word or line. To insert the deleted text elsewhere in the document, use the movement commands to navigate to the new location, and then use the put command, p, to insert the contents of the buffer after the cursor. To insert the contents of the buffer before the cursor, use the P command.

Suppose, for example, that after reviewing a document, you decide that the order of two paragraphs should be reversed. Figure 12.21 shows how to switch the positions of the paragraphs.

Figure 12.21
Cutting and
pasting text.

```
the rumble of a motor boat.

☐t was just before midnight when I fell asleep— a sleep so
deep that even barking dogs did not wake me.

I was in the middle of a large field of corn.  The wind
swirled the long canes of corn and their clicking combined with
the low, gutterl singing of a mass of voices
reminded me of an ancient, tribal ritual— a ritual of
sacrifice. As the hands came down and scooped me up, I knew that
day was my last.
```

Perform c}.

```
the rumble of a motor boat.

    ☐

I was in the middle of a large field of corn.  The wind
swirled the long canes of corn and their clicking combined with
the low, gutterl singing of a mass of voices
reminded me of an ancient, tribal ritual— a ritual of
sacrifice. As the hands came down and scooped me up, I knew that
day was my last.
```

Perform p.

```
I was in the middle of a large field of corn.  The wind
swirled the long canes of corn and their clicking combined with
the low, gutterl singing of a mass of voices
reminded me of an ancient, tribal ritual— a ritual of
sacrifice. As the hands came down and scooped me up, I knew that
day was my last.

☐t was just before midnight when I fell asleep— a sleep so
deep that even barking dogs did not wake me.
```

To reverse the position of adjacent letters, use the command sequence xp. The x command deletes the character under the cursor. The next character moves under the cursor. Then the p command places the deleted character after the cursor, as shown in figure 12.22.

```
I was in the middle of a large field of corn.  The wind

swirled the long canes of corn and their clicking combined with

the low, gutterl singing of a mass of voices

reminded me of an ancient, tribal ritual— a ritual of

sacrifice. As the hands came down and scooped me up, I knew that

day was my last.


☐I was just before midnight when I fell asleep— a sleep so

deep that even barking dogs did not wake me.
```

Figure 12.22
Reversing the position of two characters.

Perform xp.

```
I was in the middle of a large field of corn.  The wind

swirled the long canes of corn and their clicking combined with

the low, gutterl singing of a mass of voices

reminded me of an ancient, tribal ritual— a ritual of

sacrifice. As the hands came down and scooped me up, I knew that

day was my last.


☐t was just before midnight when I fell asleep— a sleep so

deep that even barking dogs did not wake me.
```

Using the p command does not flush the buffer, so you can insert the same deleted text repeatedly until the next delete or change command.

Copying Text

A command related to the move command is the copy command, y. Y? Bill Joy already had used the letter c to stand for change, so he stretched his imagination and came up with the command y, which is either the last letter in the copy command, or the first letter in the mnemonic yank; use the memory trick that works best for you.

When you move text, you first must delete it from its original context. When you copy text, however, you copy text into the buffer but leave it intact in its original context. After copying text to the buffer, you then move the cursor to another location in the document and use the put command, p, to place the contents of the buffer into the document.

You can combine the yank command with all the movement commands described earlier in the chapter. Table 12.15 shows some common applications of the yank command.

Table 12.15
Copying Text

Command	Copies...
yw	to the end of a word
y0	to the beginning of the line
y$	to the end of the line
4yw	the next four words
4yl	the next four letters
yb	the previous word or part of a word
y}	the remainder of the paragraph
y)	the remainder of the sentence

Table 12.15 shows a number of ways to copy all or parts of lines. vi, however, provides a special command for copying an entire line: yy. The yy command copies the entire line the cursor is on, regardless of the position of the cursor on the line.

The Y command is the equivalent of the y$ command—the command copies the text from the cursor to the end of the line, as shown in figure 12.23.

Figure 12.23
Copying part
of a line.

```
I was in the middle of a large field of corn.  The wind
swirled the long canes of corn and their clicking combined with
the low, gutterl singing of a mass of voices
reminded me of an ancient, tribal ritual— a ritual of
sacrifice. As the hands came down and scooped me up, I knew that
day was my last.

It was just □efore midnight when I fell asleep— a sleep so
deep that even barking dogs did not wake me.
```

Perform y$ then p.

```
I was in the middle of a large field of corn.  The wind
swirled the long canes of corn and their clicking combined with
the low, gutterl singing of a mass of voices
reminded me of an ancient, tribal ritual— a ritual of
sacrifice. As the hands came down and scooped me up, I knew that
day was my last.

It was just before midnight when I fell asleep— a sleep so
deep that even barking dogs did not wake me.
before midnight when I fell asleep— a sleep so □
```

You can combine the y command with numbers to copy more than one word, line of text, or paragraph. To copy two lines of text, for example, use the command 2yy, as shown in figure 12.24.

```
I was in the middle of a large field of corn.  The wind
swirled the long canes of corn and their clicking combined with
the low, gutterl singing of a mass of voices
reminded me of an ancient, tribal ritual— a ritual of
sacrifice. As the hands came down and scooped me up, I knew that
day was my last.

It was just □efore midnight when I fell asleep— a sleep so
deep that even barking dogs did not wake me.
```

Figure 12.24
Copying two lines of text.

III

Working with Editors

Perform 2yy then p.

```
I was in the middle of a large field of corn.  The wind
swirled the long canes of corn and their clicking combined with
the low, gutterl singing of a mass of voices
reminded me of an ancient, tribal ritual— a ritual of
sacrifice. As the hands came down and scooped me up, I knew that
day was my last.

It was just before midnight when I fell asleep— a sleep so
deep that even barking dogs did not wake me.


□t was just before midnight when I fell asleep— a sleep so
deep that even barking dogs did not wake me.
```

The buffer is not flushed when you execute the put command, so you can copy a selection of text repeatedly until you execute the next change, delete, or yank command.

Using Different Buffers

You have seen that the delete, change, and yank commands read the selected text into a buffer. You then can insert the contents of the buffer into the document. Whenever you execute the next delete, change, or yank, however, the contents of the buffer are replaced with the new text selection.

At times, storing more than one buffer of information is important. vi makes that task easy by supplying the following commands: "cY and "cP. "cY yanks the line the cursor is on and places it in the buffer labeled c. Because c can take any alphabetical value between a and z, the c value has 26 possible values. You then use "cP to place the contents of buffer c, where c is a value between a and z.

Searching and Replacing Text

At times you need to replace one piece of text with another. A product might change its functionality, for example, so that the number 320 Hz must replace the number 280 Hz wherever it appears. Finding each occurrence of the number and changing it is a slow process. Instead, vi uses the ex command s (substitute) to find and replace text, as follows:

```
:first_line, last_line s/old_text/new_text/
```

The first two values, first_line and last_line, specify the range of line numbers to search in the current text. The last two values, old_text and new_text, specify that new_text should replace old_text. The following command tells vi to search through lines 15 through 134 inclusive and substitute 320 for every occurrence of 280.

```
:15, 134s/280/320/
```

Remember that every line in vi is numbered. You can display line numbers by executing the :set nu command.

Instead of specifying line numbers, you can specify the range of lines to search by supplying a beginning and ending text pattern. Use the following syntax:

```
:/text_pattern1/,/text_pattern2/s/old_text/new_text
```

This command searches the current file between the first instance of text_pattern1 to the first subsequent instance of text_pattern2 and substitutes new_text for old_text. You might use text patterns as search criteria when, for example, you want to search the text between two section headings but don't know their line numbers.

When you execute a search and replace, vi replaces only the first instance of old_text with new_text. For example, the command

```
:1, 2s/cat/dog/
```

produces the subsequent text:

```
The darn dog ate the cat food
when she wasn't supposed to.
```

To replace every instance of old_text with new_text on a line, you must add g to the end of the command, as follows:

```
:1, 2s/cat/dog/g
```

Now, the same text would read

```
The darn dog ate the dog food
when she wasn't supposed to.
```

Making global replacements sometimes produces unexpected results. After the previous search-and-replace command, for example, you might read through your document and see the following:

```
I ordered the dress from the dogalog.
```

The word "catalog" was unexpectedly changed. You can try to catch such mistakes by adding a space after "cat" and "dog" in the command, as follows:

```
:1, 2s/cat /dog /g
```

Although adding the space eliminates the problem of changing words like "catalog," the command misses such instances as "cat," and "cat." To solve this problem, vi uses the greater-than and less-than symbols (<>). When they bracket a word, they indicate that only whole words should be replaced regardless of adjacent punctuation. So the correct form of the search and replace is as follows:

```
:1, 2s/<cat\>/dog/g
```

The backslash (\) identifies the next character as an ordinary character. The <cat command means that the word must begin with "cat." The word "concatenate," for example, would not be a match. cat\> enables the following matches: "cats," "cat." and "cat,".

Nevertheless, you might find it more comforting to validate each substitution before vi makes it. To do so, use the c command at the end of the line, as follows:

```
:1, 2s/cat/dog/gc
```

Whenever vi encounters the target word, "cat" in this case, it places carets (^) under it, as follows:

```
The darn cat ate the cat food
            ^^^
```

vi asks you to press y (and Enter) if you want to replace the word. Entering anything else, including pressing Enter, does not perform the replacement.

Using Wild Cards in Defining Ranges of Lines

Having to know actual line numbers to perform searches is a nuisance—why should you have to know the number of the last line in a file if you want to extend your search to it? Well, you don't. vi provides wild cards to help you specify ranges of line numbers to search. Table 12.16 describes the wild cards.

Table 12.16
Using Wild Cards To Define Ranges

Wild Card	Destination
.	The current line
$	The last line
%	The entire file

To search a file from the location of the cursor to the end of the file, for example, use the following command:

```
: ., $s/old_text/new_text/
```
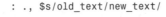

Using Wild Cards To Specify Words

Wild cards are like variables; they represent a variety of values. The asterisk, for example, represents zero or more characters. The search expression **ing* would match the following words: sorting, beginning, laughing, flying, eating.

vi provides a wide variety of wild cards to aid in your text searches. Table 12.17 describes some of these.

Table 12.17
Using Wild Cards To Specify Words

Wild Card	Description
.	Represents any single character
*	Represents zero or more characters
[...]	Represents any character in the bracket; for example, [mnp] would generate matches for any instance of m, n, or p
[..-..]	Represents any character in the specified range; for example, [a-w] would generate matches for any instance of a lowercase letter between a and w, inclusive; [2-9] would generate matches for any instance of a number between 2 and 9, inclusive

Using Other Helpful Commands

Several other commands can save you significant time. This section describes those commands.

Reusing Commands

When you execute a command, the command is saved in a buffer. It remains in the buffer until you execute another command. You can execute the command stored in the buffer by using the dot (.). Figure 12.25 shows an example of reusing your command.

You can use numbers with the dot to execute the last command more than once. If the last command given was cc, for example, 3. replaces the cursor's line plus the next two lines after the cursor.

Figure 12.25
Reusing a command.

```
day was my last.

It was just before midnight when I fell asleep— a sleep so
deep that even barking dogs did not wake me.

It was just before midnight when I fell asleep— a sleep so
deep that even barking dogs did not wake me.

□t was just before midnight when I fell asleep— a sleep so
deep that even barking dogs did not wake me.
```

Undoing Commands

To reverse the effect of a command, use the u command (undo). The position of the cursor is insignificant for the u command.

A similar command is the U command. It undoes all the edits made on the cursor's line. vi records all the edits made to a single line until the cursor moves off it. vi then sends the contents of the line buffer to the file buffer; consequently, you cannot return to a line and undo previous line edits by using U.

Joining Lines

Occasionally you need to join two lines. Going to the beginning of the second line and pressing the Del key, however, doesn't join the lines. To join consecutive lines, place the cursor in the first line and use the J command, as shown in figure 12.26.

Figure 12.26
Joining two lines.

```
it was a dark and stormy night. The rain on the roof droned like
the rumble of a motor boat.
   □
I was in the middle of a large field of corn. The wind
swirled the long canes of corn and their clicking combined with
the low, gutterl singing of a mass of voices
reminded me of an anciet, tribal ritual— a ritual of
sacrifice. As the hands came down and scooped me up, I knew that
day was my last.
```

```
It was a dark and stormy night. The rain on the roof droned like
the rumble of a motor boat.


☐ was in the middle of a large field of corn. The wind
swirled the long canes of corn and their clicking combined with
the low, gutterl singing of a mass of voices
reminded me of an anciet, tribal ritual— a ritual of
sacrifice. As the hands came down and scooped me up, I knew that
day was my last.


It was just before midnight when I fell asleep— a sleep so
```

Figure 12.26
Continued.

Summary

This chapter has introduced you to all the basic vi and ex commands. With them, you can ably perform the following tasks:

- ✔ Start and stop vi

- ✔ Share text between files

- ✔ Move the cursor one or more letters, words, lines, sentences, paragraphs, and screens at a time

- ✔ Move to specific line numbers and markers

- ✔ Move by searching for text patterns

- ✔ Change, delete, move, and copy text

- ✔ Search and replace text patterns

The commands that accomplish these tasks are summarized in table 12.18.

Table 12.18
Using vi Editing Commands

Command	Description
Start/Stop	
vi	Begins vi
:w	Saves file

Working with Editors

continues

Table 12.18, Continued
Using vi Editing Commands

Command	Description
:wq	Saves file and exits document
:q!	Exits without saving changes
ZZ	Saves file and exits document

Moving

h	Moves left one character
j	Moves down one line
k	Moves up one line
l	Moves right one character
w	Moves to beginning of next word
b	Moves to beginning of previous word
e	Moves to end of a word
+	Moves to next line
-	Moves to previous line
(	Moves to beginning of sentence
)	Moves to end of sentence
{	Moves to beginning of paragraph
}	Moves to end of paragraph
Ctrl+F	Moves forward one screen
Ctrl+B	Moves backward one screen
Ctrl+D	Moves down one half screen
Ctrl+u	Moves up one half screen
Ctrl+f	Scrolls down one page
G	Moves to end of line
nG	Moves to nth line of file

Command	Description
/*pattern*	Searches for text *pattern* after cursor
?*pattern*	Searches for text *pattern* before cursor

Editing

x	Deletes character under cursor
dd	Deletes cursor's line
D	Deletes to end of cursor's line
cw	Replaces a word
dw	Deletes a word
c4w	Deletes next four words
r*x*	Replaces character with *x*
y	Copies (yanks) text to buffer
p	Inserts (puts) contents of buffer after cursor
P	Inserts (puts) contents of buffer before cursor
s	Substitutes

Inserting

a	Inserts after the cursor
i	Inserts before the cursor
o	Opens new line below
O	Opens new line above

Miscellaneous

J	Joins two adjacent lines
u	Undoes the effect of the previous command
U	Undoes all changes on current line
.	Repeats previous command

III

Working with Editors

You can combine vi commands with movement commands to complete sophisticated tasks. Table 12.19 shows some common combinations.

Table 12.19
Using Command Combinations

Operates on...	Copy	Delete	Change
next line	y+	d+	c+
next sentence	y}	d}	c}
one word	yw	dw	cw
end of line	y$	d$	c$
beginning of line	y0	d0	c0
end of file	yG	dG	cG
line number 5	y5G	d5G	c5G

Having now learned about all of vi's basic commands, you can see how vi is an amalgam of many different editor interfaces. vi uses the line-editor interface (all commands beginning with the colon), the command interface (all commands using the slash or question mark), and the screen-editor interface (all commands not beginning with a slash or question mark).

The next chapter introduces you to many advanced features of vi to make your task of editing files easier.

Chapter Snapshot

Continuing the discussion of vi from the last chapter, this chapter is aimed at system adiministrators and those who need to know vi intimately. Topics covered include the following:

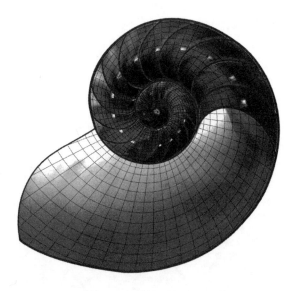

13

CHAPTER

vi: Advanced Topics

The last chapter introduced you to the vi editor and its functions. This chapter
continues on that topic and covers some of its more advanced features.

The set Commands

There are a number of options that can be established inside an editing session to affect the way the display is shown. All of these are invoked from command mode by typing a colon (:), then typing the appropriate command:

✔ **set number** numbers each line of the display. The default is for this not to take place. Once numbering has been invoked, it can be turned off with set nonumber.

✔ **set showmode** indicates, in the bottom right corner, the mode you are in—I or INSERT for insert, A for append, and so on. The default is off, and it can be turned off with set noshowmode.

✔ **set ignorecase** ignores case sensitivity in all searches, thus MODEMS is found when looking for modem. To reenable the case sensitivity, use set noignorecase.

✔ **set terse** provides shortened error messages. The default is noterse, and it can be reenabled with set noterse.

You can see the present value of any option by typing its command, followed by a question mark. For example, typing **set terse?** returns noterse, meaning that terse is not active. Were it active, the returned response is terse.

To see options that you have set individually, type **set** by itself. The following example indicates that upper- and lowercase distinction is ignored, that redraw is slow, which terminal type it is, and that terse is now on:

```
ignorecase slowopen term=vwpt60 terse
```

To see all variables affecting your editing session, type **set all**, and a display similar to the following appears:

noautoindent	nomodelines	noshowmode
autoprint	nonumber	noslowopen
noautowrite	nonovice	tabstop=8
nobeautify	optimize	taglength=0
directory=/tmp	paragraphs=IPLPPPQPP	tags=tags
noedcompatible	prompt	term=vwpt60
noerrorbells	noreadonly	noterse
noexrc	noredraw	timeout
flash	remap	ttytype=vwpt60
hardtabs=8	report=5	warn
noignorecase	scroll=8	window=16
nolisp	sections=HUuhsh+c	wrapscan

```
nolist          shell=/bin/sh       wrapmargin=0
magic           shiftwidth=8        nowriteany
nomesg          noshowmatch
```

Most of these defaults are true for all vi sessions on the system, but all can be set individually by a users for their defaults, or sessions. Many of them are discussed elsewhere in this chapter, but a brief description follows. The listing is in alphabetical order, ignoring the no that may precede each. The listing (with or without the no) is shown in the format of the usual default. For example, the normal value of `autoindent` is `noautoindent`, and it is listed that way. The normal value for `autoprint` is just that (the opposite of which is `noautoprint`):

- ✔ **noautoindent**—When turned on, each time a new line is created with insert, append, or any other operation, vi spaces it the same number of characters as in the preceding line. Abbreviations: `noai` and `ai`, for `noautoindent` and `autoindent`, respectively.

- ✔ **autoprint**—This variable displays the current line after yank and put operations. Abbreviation: `ap` or `noap` to turn off.

- ✔ **noautowrite**—When enabled, it automatically writes buffer contents to the current file when other commands (such as !) are used. Abbreviations: `aw` or `noaw`.

- ✔ **nobeautify**—When active, it ignores all control characters in the files except tabs, white space, carriage returns, and formfeeds. Abbreviations: `bf` and `nobf`.

- ✔ **directory**—This variable specifies the directory where temporary files are created during the session. Abbreviation: `dir`.

- ✔ **noedcompatible**—When active, it remembers whether g or c was used on the last substitute command and uses it again until it is turned off. Abbreviation: none.

- ✔ **noerrorbells**—When turned on, it precedes the display of an error message with an error bell. Abbreviations: `eb` and `noeb`.

- ✔ **noexrc**—This variable indicates whether an exrc file is used. This is discussed later in this chapter.

- ✔ **flash**—When it is enabled, the screen flashes on an error. Abbreviation: none.

- ✔ **hardtabs**—This variable specifies the number of characters for each tab. Abbreviation: `ht`.

- ✔ **noignorecase**—During search operations, it ignores upper- and lowercase sensitivity to find matches, except for specifications contained within brackets. Abbreviations: `ic` and `noic`.

III

Working with Editors

✔ **nolisp**—This variable indicates whether `autoindent` should be active for LISP code. Abbreviation: none.

✔ **nolist**—This variable indicates whether lines should be displayed with tabs and carriage returns. Abbreviation: none.

✔ **magic**—This variable governs the number of metacharacters that are interpreted in regular expressions. If the value is `nomagic`, only the dollar sign ($) and carat (^) are still interpreted as special search characters. Abbreviation: none.

✔ **nomesg**—If enabled, `mesg` enables other users to write messages to you with the write command while you are editing files (not a good idea). Abbreviation: none.

✔ **nomodelines**—This variable indicates whether mode lines will be shown at the bottom of the screen. Abbreviation: none.

✔ **nonumber**—`number` turns on line numbering within the editor. Abbreviations: `nu` and `nonu`.

✔ **nonovice**—This variable is similar to `showmode`, and it makes vi "friendlier" for those who are new to it. Abbreviation: none.

✔ **optimize**—The terminal does not do automatic carriage returns on lines longer than one screen width; thus, the performance time is increased. Abbreviations: `opt` and `noopt`.

✔ **paragraphs**—This variable gives the delimiter that is used between { and } operations, in terms of nroff macros. Abbreviation: `para`.

✔ **prompt**—When this variable is enabled, a colon appears as the command mode prompt on the status line. This can be turned off with `noprompt`. Abbreviation: none.

✔ **noreadonly**—This variable indicates whether the file being edited is read-only or can be modified and saved. Abbreviation: none.

✔ **noredraw**—If enabled, the dumb terminal emulates a smart terminal. This slows processing down considerably. Abbreviation: none.

✔ **remap**—This variable indicates whether map commands are enabled (see the section on maps later in this chapter).

✔ **report**—This variable indicates the number of changes a command can make before it causes feedback. On a global change, for example, it reports how many items can change before notification of the scope is reported.

✔ **scroll**—This variable indicates the number of lines that scroll when a redraw operation is requested.

✔ **sections**—This variable indicates the nroff macros that are used to delimit sections of code, marked by [[and]].

✔ **shell**—This is the pathname used for commands that start with an exclamation point. Abbreviation: sh.

✔ **shiftwidth**—This is the width of a tab stop, in the number of characters to take when doing a reverse tab. Abbreviation: sw.

✔ **noshowmatch**—When this variable is enabled, typing } or) flashes the cursor quickly on the corresponding { or (if it exists within the file. Abbreviations: sm or nosm.

✔ **noshowmode**—When this variable is active, the phrase INPUT MODE appears when the insert mode is active (whether with I, i, O, o, A, or a). Abbreviation: none.

✔ **noslowopen**—When enabled, it slows down the update of the display when insertions are in the process (with i, a, or any other insert combination). Abbreviation: none.

✔ **tabstop**—This variable indicates the number of white spaces to account for with each tab that is found in the file. Abbreviation: ts.

✔ **taglength**—This variable indicates the number of characters to ignore in a tag name. Zero implies that all characters are important. Tags are traditionally created with ctags. Abbreviation: tl.

✔ **tags**—This is the path to tag files (usually created with ctags) used for the tag command. If no path is specified, the search is done on the current directory and /usr/lib.

✔ **term**—This variable indicates the terminal type in use.

✔ **noterse**—Shorter diagnostic screens are provided when terse is turned on. Abbreviation: none.

✔ **timeout**—This variable indicates the number of milliseconds to wait for input characters in multicharacter sequences. Abbreviation: to.

✔ **ttytype**—This variable indicates the type of terminal; it should be identical to term. Abbreviation: none.

✔ **warn**—If a shell command is attempted (!) and there have been changes made to the file that have not been saved, a warning message appears. Abbreviation: none.

III

Working with Editors

✔ **window**—This variable indicates the number of lines in a text window. This is usually a condition of the speed of the connection: 8 for slow speeds, 16 for medium, and `full-screen` for higher.

✔ **wrapscan**—This variable indicates whether searches should wrap around lines when looking for regular expressions. For example, when looking for `rolling stone`, if `rolling` is the last word in a line, this variable indicates whether the search should look at the first word of the next line for `stone`). Abbreviations: `ws` and `nows`.

✔ **wrapmargin**—This variable indicates the margin for automatic insertion of new lines during input. Abbreviation: `wm`.

✔ **nowriteany**—This variable indicates whether a check should be done before the execution of a write command to see whether system protection is on. Abbreviations: `wa` and `nowa`.

Editing Multiple Files

More than one file may be edited at a time with vi. To do so, specify all files that you want to open on the command line:

```
vi fileone filetwo filethree
```

And so on. The first file specified is brought up on the screen.

If you then go to command mode (by typing the colon), then type **n**, vi leaves the current file and starts up the next one.

Chapter 12 addressed using different (named) buffers to store information. Recall that they are named buffers because they use an alphabetic character to distinguish them from everything else and maintain their contents throughout the entire vi session—not just on the current file. Because this is so, you can copy a paragraph from the `fileone` file into a named buffer, start up the `filetwo` file, and place the paragraph in that file.

Jumping to the Shell

In the last chapter, you also learned how the date command is initiated:

```
!date
```

Any valid command can be run while inside vi by preceding it with the colon prompt. For example, to write to another party without quitting the editing under way, the following command starts up the write interaction:

```
!write kristin /dev/tty07
```

When you finish (by pressing Ctrl+D), you are automatically returned to the document and editing.

Typing **sh** at a command (colon) prompt within vi does not call a command, however—it calls another shell. In such a way, you can leave vi without exiting the document and perform other tasks. To return to the document, type **exit,** and you are returned to vi and the file on which you were working.

Using the abbr Variables

Variables can be assigned values to be substituted automatically within vi sessions, using the abbr command. When such a variable is assigned, the second value (usually longer in length) replaces the first when it is typed in the text. The following command automatically converts LAN to Local Area Network when the text is typed within the text.

```
abbr LAN Local Area Network
```

The unabbreviate command (which also can be specified as una) is used to cancel the abbreviation substitution without exiting the vi session:

```
una LAN
```

The map and map! Commands

Mapping enables you to create aliases for character and escape sequences within vi sessions. Similar in nature to abbr, mapping is more flexible in that it enables you to define character sequences and not just word substitutions. For example, if the company name is General Computing Services, mapping one key to that phrase enables vi to do the substitution and saves a considerable number of keystrokes. map commands are given at the command mode and take this syntax:

```
map {keystroke} {value}
```

Thus, to map the company name to Ctrl+G, use the following command:

```
map ^G General Computing Services
```

Quite often, keystroke savings can be gained by mapping commands to aliases. For example, Ctrl+O (O for out) can be mapped to the :q! sequence. It is important to notice that for the quit-and-not-save sequence to take effect, however, it must include a carriage return on the end. This must be hard-coded into the string, as with any other command sequence. A carriage return is denoted in vi as Ctrl+M. You tell vi that it is to take the next character at face value with Ctrl+V. Thus, the full command is the following:

```
map ^O :q!^V^M
```

This maps Ctrl+O to the quit sequence, complete with carriage return on the end.

Commands, or aliases, that are defined using the map command are effective only when in command mode. The cousin of map is map!, which defines substitions that take place in insert mode.

To cancel a map without exiting a session, use the unmap command. unmap cancels any character or escape definitions defined with the map command. An important note, however, is that unmap does not affect definitions established with map!. The only way to lose these definitions is to exit the session and restart.

The exrc File

When Bill Joy first created vi, it was based on the most popular line editor at the time—ex. Evidence of this persists in many of the commands given in command mode and in the naming of a key file—exrc.

This file can be equated with the profile or login file that exists for each user. With those two, list commands are automatically executed each time a user logs in. The exrc file contains commands that are executed each time a vi session is started.

Settings that are changed with the set command, maps that are created with the map command, and substitutions made with abbr are active only for the duration of the vi session. In order to enable them for each session, they must be included in the user's exrc file.

If the file contains the following commands each time a vi session is started, the lines are numbered and terse mode enabled.

```
set number
set terse
```

This example can be shortened to one line and fulfill the same purpose:

```
set number terse
```

The exrc file should be placed in each user's home directory, and provides an efficient means by which to customize operations and include map statements.

Quick Tips

The following miscellaneous commands increase efficiency and may be used often within your scope of operations:

✔ **s** was demonstrated in the last chapter for substituting words and phrases. With the same syntax, but using S (uppercase), you can substitute entire lines.

✔ **J** is used to join two lines previously separated by a carriage return.

✔ **x** is used to delete a character at the cursor. Using X, you can delete the character before the cursor.

✔ **z** redraws the screen, putting the current line at the top of the screen.

✔ **z-** redraws the screen, putting the current line at the bottom of the screen.

✔ **z.** redraws the screen, putting the current line at the middle of the screen.

✔ **z10.** redraws the screen and sets the window size to ten lines.

Fun with vi

You can start vi several ways. The first is the standard line:

```
$ vi {filename} {filename .....}
```

Other choices include the following command, which brings the file up in read-only mode—preventing changes from being made:

```
$ view {filename}
```

The following command brings the editor up with showmode and novice mode set. It denotes when insert, append, and so forth are on, and is intended to make vi easier to use for beginners.

```
$ vedit {filename}
```

The following command begins the editor with a window size of ten lines:

```
$ vi -w10 {filename}
```

The following example starts the editor on the seventh line of the file:

```
$ vi +7 {filename}
```

The following opens the file and starts the editor on the first occurrence of the word within the file:

```
$vi +/{word} {filename}
```

The following command starts the editor with read-only status, preventing changes from being saved:

```
$ vi -R {filename}
```

The following example encrypts the file when it is written, and requires a password to decrypt it when it is read again:

```
$ vi -x {filename}
```

Finally, the following command opens the file and runs the specified command. The command must be a vi operation, such as search or delete.

```
$ vi -c {command} {filename}
```

Command Summary

Chapter 12 ended with a partial listing of the available commands in vi. Table 13.1 summarizes those not previously shown. Combining the two lists provides a complete listing of all vi commands.

Table 13.1
More vi Commands

Command	Function
	Starting/Stopping
:sh	Runs shell, then returns
:!cmd	Runs given command, then returns to editor
:n	Edits next file

Command	Function
	Moving
H	Goes to top line on screen
L	Goes to last line on screen
M	Goes to middle line on screen
^	Goes to first nonwhite
0	Goes to beginning of line
$	Goes to end of line
f*x*	Finds *x* forward
F*x*	Finds *x* backward
t*x*	Goes to *x* forward
T*x*	Backs up to *x*
	Adjusting the Screen
z	Redraws, placing current line at top of window
z-	Redraws, placing current line at bottom of window
z.	Redraws, placing current line at center of window
z*n*.	Uses a window of *n* lines

Summary

This chapter covered advanced vi commands and features. These commands can be incorporated into .exrc files and active for each vi session or changed on a session-by-session basis.

Chapter Snapshot

The ed text editor is one of the oldest editors for the UNIX operating system. It has been available nearly from the start, and it still ships with many versions today. In this chapter, you learn how to execute the following ed tasks:

This chapter presents ed from a need-to-know basis. It walks you through the most basic operations and introduces you to the functions ed offers.

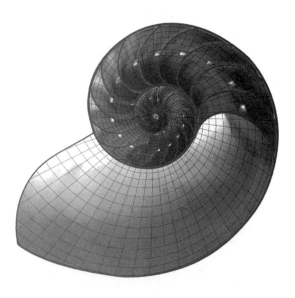

CHAPTER

A Quick Look at ed

I n the days before visual editors, there were line editors. Line editors, predecessors to visual ones, are much more difficult to work with, and far less intuitive in operation. ed was one of the first line editors included with UNIX, and it still ships with most versions today. Most users prefer to stick with vi, emacs, or another more perceptive editor, but administrators should be familiar with ed and know where to find information on it, should they need it.

ed requires far less memory than most editors, and does not utilize extraneous files and directories. After a system crash, it quite often is the only editor that can be started on system files. After key files are restored, the system can be brought up further and a visual editor used on other files.

Starting ed

You start ed by typing **ed** on the command line along with the name of a file to edit. In this example *FileName* is the name of a file in the current directory:

```
$ ed FileName
```

If the file is not in the current directory, you supply the entire path to it.

A byte count will appear denoting the number of bytes in the file. If the file does not exist, you see the file name once more, preceded by a question mark (*?FileName*). In either case, you are greeted with the "invisible" prompt, unlike visual editors that display the file.

The byte count indicates that the editor has read the entire document and is now awaiting a command from you. If you press Enter without entering any commands, a question mark (?) is displayed indicating that ed failed to understand what you requested.

Stopping ed

Leaving ed is as simple as typing **q** and pressing Enter. If no changes were made or the file is empty, the command prompt returns immediately. If you made any changes that were saved, ed warns you with a ? warning. Typing q a second time tells the editor that you confirm the transaction and enables you to exit without saving the changes.

If you know that you have made changes and want to exit without saving them, you can save yourself from typing two q sequences by using Q. This tells the editor to abandon all changes made since you last saved the file.

To get around some of the cryptic question mark prompts, you can turn on human-readable mode by entering an **H** at any command prompt. If you made changes and did not save them, this turns the question mark following q into a warning: `w.`

Saving Changes

The w command writes the file back to the hard drive, whether changes have been made or not. When you want to save the document, enter the w command, and a new byte count, representing the physical size of the file now, is displayed.

Most saves are done when exiting the file. If you use the command wq, the file is written to disk and then the editor quits.

Viewing Lines

When a file comes up in the editor, there is no indication of the current content of the file. Having read the entire file sequentially, the editor is now on the last line, but that might not always be the one you want to address; or, it might be nice to see what currently exists before making changes.

The p (print) command prints a block of text and accepts a range of addresses preceding it. To see all lines in the file, you use the following:

```
,p
```

or

```
1,$p
```

Both show the entire file because 1 is the first line in the file and $ represents the last line in the file. (A , by itself is an abbreviation for 1,$ in ed.)

> The ed commands often use the syntax of having a starting line number, a delimiter, an ending line number, and the command.

You also can use *absolute addressing* by including the line numbers of the lines that you want. The following example prints the first through seventh lines of the file, inclusively:

```
1,7p
```

Relative addressing is also available, which takes the current line and works in either direction from it. Here are some examples. The first lists lines 7 through 9:

```
7,7+2p
```

The following is a shorter way of writing the last command:

```
7;+2p
```

The semicolon (;) forces ed to make the current line the result of the first address. If the current line is 15, the following commands can be read:

```
2;+2p    display lines 2-4
2,+2p    display lines 2-17
```

The current line is always signified by a period (.) in ed, so you can show the current line with the following:

    .p

Or even shorten it to this:

    p

Displaying and Numbering Lines

In addition to displaying lines, you also can number them in relation to their position in the file. To do so, substitute the **n** command in place of p, and all else holds true. The following example displays all lines above the current line with line numbers:

    1,.n

Calling Lines by Number

The final way to see the contents of a line is to enter the number of that line and press Enter. This makes that line the current one in the editor and displays its contents. For example, to move to line 7 and show its contents, press 7, then Enter.

Creating a New File

The following example creates a new file called waterfall with only the word escher in it. The a command stands for add and enables keyboard input to the file until a period is pressed—at that point, ed changes from input mode to command mode.

    $ ed waterfall
    ?waterfall
    a
    escher
    .
    w
    7
    q
    $

Because the file is new, its name, preceded by a question mark, is displayed where a byte count normally is. The a command places it into insert mode, the text **escher** is entered, then typing the period returns you to command mode. The file is written with w and a byte count returned—7 due to the inclusion of a carriage return on the end. Finally, the editor is quit by typing **q**, and you are returned to the shell prompt ($).

Suppose that additional lines are to be added to the file:

```
$ ed waterfall
7
a
hands
(c)1948 M.C. Escher
.
w
34
1,p
escher
2,3p
hands
(c)1948 M.C. Escher
q
$
```

The file now exists and the editor shows the byte count when it is started. The a command begins adding, or appending, after the last line, because that is where the editor now resides. Two lines are added and stopped with the period. Next, the file is written to the drive and a new byte count returned. The p command is used to show the contents of the file, and the q command quits the editor and returns to the shell prompt.

Adding Text

When creating a file from scratch, the a command adds new lines to the buffer. When working with a file that already has data in it, you want to know both the a (append) command (insert a line after the current line and go into input mode) and the i (insert) command (insert a line above the current line and go into input mode).

Addresses can be used with both the a and i commands to insert text. Some useful combinations of addresses and a are shown in table 14.1.

Table 14.1
Adding Text with Addressing

Address	Function
0a	Add text to beginning of file
$a	Add text to end of file
i	Add text above current line
-a	Add text above current line
a	Add text below current line
9a	Add text below line 9

Deleting Text

Deleting lines of text is an easy operation in ed, but deleting portions of a line can prove more difficult.

Deleting Lines

The d command provides an easy mnemonic for line deletion, and can be done on the active line, or by specifying a series of addresses. To delete the current line, merely type **d** and it is gone.

The delete command also accepts the same addressing scheme enabled by the p command. By using addressing, you can delete blocks of text with a single command. Thus, to delete line 19, use the following:

    19d

And to delete lines 13 and 14, use the following:

    13,14d

Deleting Text Within a Line

Deleting text within a line—without deleting the entire line—involves finding the value you want to delete and substituting it with nothing. The identical search feature is used as in vi, encompassing the value within slashes (/*value*/). The s command is used to signify substitution.

If a line contains the phrase `Inside UNIX Shell Programming`, for example, and you want to change it to `Inside Shell Programming`, the command is the following:

```
s/ UNIX//
```

or

```
s/UNIX //
```

But `s/UNIX//` does not work properly, however, because it leaves two spaces in the sentence—the one that existed before the word, and the one that existed after the word.

> As with vi, it's possible to search for strings as part of an address by using the /re/ (search forward) or ?re? (search backward) commands.

Undeleting

As with vi and most other editors, the u command undoes the last editing change that was made. If you delete lines 7 through 10, then type the u command, these lines are restored. If you enter u again, the lines are deleted once more. u does nothing more than switch the last action taken; for this reason, you cannot undo multiple actions. Only the last change to the file, whether it was a deletion or insertion, can be switched with the u command.

Changing Text

There also are two ways to make changes to lines in ed. The first is to change the entire line, and the second is to change a portion of the line.

Changing an Entire Line

The c (change) command is used to change complete lines of text. Using the earlier example, if you want to change `Inside UNIX Shell Programming` to `LAN Server Certification Guide`, the sequence is the following:

```
7p
Inside UNIX Shell Programming
c
LAN Server Certification Guide
.
7p
LAN Server Certification Guide
```

The hardest part of dealing with ed is remembering to enter a period to leave any insert mode and return to command mode. The period ***must*** be used with the a, c, i, or any other command that places you in a mode wherein you can enter text into the file from the keyboard.

Changing Portions of a Line

Previously, when discussing the deletion of text within a line, the substitute command was used to accomplish the task. The old value was replaced with a null value. When changing portions of a line, the s command is also used—now changing the old value to a new value.

The syntax is the following:

```
s/old value/new value/g
```

The g on the end of the syntax tells the editor to make the change globally throughout the line. In its absence, the first change in the line is made, and it is the only one for that line. Thus, if you have the sentence All's well that ends well, and you want to change well to good, the following changes the sentence to All's good that ends well:

```
s/well/good/
```

And this example changes the sentence to All's good that ends good:

```
s/well/good/g
```

Combining Multiple Files

In addition to adding text from the keyboard, you can use the r (read) command to read text from another file and import into the one with which you are presently working. Specifying the following reads the entire file named october and imports it into the file you currently have open:

```
r october
```

The file is copied into the existing one after the line where you are currently working. Thus, if you are on line seven of the existing file, the contents of october are copied beginning at line eight.

If you want to position the imported text elsewhere, put an address in front of the r to tell ed which line to follow with the import. 9r *file* puts the contents of *file* between lines 9 and 10.

When used in conjunction with an exclamation mark, the r command also can be used to execute shell commands and place the output into the file. For example, to insert the output of the process status command, use the following:

```
r !ps -ef
```

Cutting and Pasting

The m (move) command enables you to move lines from one part of the file to another. The syntax is the following:

```
{start address},{stop address}m{line to follow}
```

Thus, to move lines 10-20 after line 50, this is the command:

```
10,20m50
```

This removes the eleven lines in question and places them after the current line 50. Counting as an editing command, the u command reverts the file to its original state if you make a mistake.

Copying

The capability of manipulating text can be divided into two steps—cutting and copying. The m command enables you to cut, and the t (transfer) command enables you to copy. The syntax for t is the following:

```
{start address},{stop address}t{line to follow}
```

Thus, to copy lines 10-20 after line 50, use this command:

```
10,20t50
```

The original eleven lines are left exactly where they were and are now replicated as lines 51 to 61. This also constitutes an editing action, and in the event of an error, u restores the file to the way it was before the action took place.

This chapter does not address all the features and functions of ed. Because it is a line editor, it is rarely used on a global scale anymore. It uses little memory, however, and does not require extraneous files, so it is important to know the rudimentary operations of it should a system crash and its files need to be rebuilt. Table 14.2 summarizes the most important ed commands.

Table 14.2
Important ed Commands

Command	Function
.	Quit input (or append) mode
a	Append text
c	Change
d	Delete
H	Make error messages readable
i	Input
m	Move
n	Number lines
p	Print
q	Quit
r	Read
s/old/new/	Substitute
t	Transfer
u	Undo
w	Write

Part IV

Graphic User Interfaces

Chapter Snapshot

This chapter covers the basics of X Windows, including the following:

After reading this chapter, you should feel comfortable using X clients and customizing them. It's impossible to cover the functionality of all the widgets in X. However, you should be able to interact effectively with new unfamiliar widgets based on the exercises you practice in this chapter.

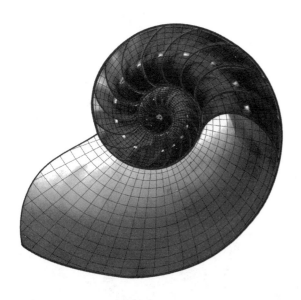

15

CHAPTER

Using X Windows

X Windows is not a user interface in itself, but a library of graphics routines you can use to create a GUI. UNIX GUIs ride on top of X Windows.

There are two X libraries: the X Toolkit Intrinsics (Xt) and the Athena widget set (Xaw); together they are called the X Toolkit. The X Toolkit Intrinsics library helps build and use widgets. Athena widgets are user interface objects, such as menus, dialog boxes, scroll bars, and buttons. These basic graphical tools provide the developer an easy way to create an interface.

This chapter introduces you to the basic architecture, widgets, and operation of X Windows. As you might expect, X has gone through a number of revisions since 1984. The latest version, version 11, was released in 1987. Since that time, version 11 has gone through a number of different releases. The release discussed in this book is number 5.

The Architecture of X

Most windowing systems are intimately tied to the operating system itself. For this reason, they can only work on one type of platform, such as a RISC workstation. When an operating system or application can only work on one platform, it is called *non-portable*. Non-portable systems require programmers to write different code for each platform on which the operating system and application run.

X, on the other hand, is a *portable* system. It is not tied to any operating system and is not hardware specific. X bases its operation on the client-server model. The server part of X works with user input and display. The client part of X works with applications that require the operating system (and consequently the hardware) to execute specific tasks, such as iconify a window.

The X Server

The server part of X sits between input and display hardware (such as a keyboard, a mouse, and a monitor) and running X applications. The X server tracks data sent from input devices and sends that information to the appropriate client application. The X server also tracks the output of running X client applications and updates the display accordingly. For example, when a user moves the mouse, the hardware sends that information to the X server. The X server then leaves a message with the running application that the user moved the mouse. After processing the event, the running client application sends a request, which the X server implements, to move a window to the location specified by the mouse.

Information, like keystrokes and mouse actions, are called *input events*. An event is an instruction that a client application must process. When a client application receives an event, it processes the event and issues a request to the server to update the display accordingly. Servers can run on many systems, such as workstations, PCs, and X terminals.

Advantages of the Client/Server Architecture

There are many advantages to breaking X into two distinct parts, including the following:

✔ You can put the client and server parts of X on different machines.

✔ You can access more than one computer at a time.

✔ You can spread one display across more than one monitor.

✔ You can send the display of an application to more than one monitor.

✔ You can easily port X client applications to other systems.

You can put the client and server parts of X on different machines as long as the machines are connected by a network using X protocol. A common example is to put the X server on a local workstation or PC and the client on a remote, powerful system. In this example, the X server accepts all user input and display output locally while the client program runs on the faster system.

You would choose to run the client on a remote machine only if the remote machine offered some features unavailable to your local machine. For example, the remote machine might be faster or contain large databases that would take too long to transfer across a network. Another common reason for remote clients is if the remote machine uses a different architecture that better supports a specific task. By using the networking capabilities of X, you can access these remote computers and see the results locally.

X provides a variety of display options. You can access more than one computer at a time and have each computer display its output in a different window in the display. The display can be on one or more monitors—control mechanisms can appear on one monitor while output data appears on another monitor. X can also facilitate broadcasting one display across a network to many monitors, which is extremely useful in an educational setting.

The final advantage of the client-server architecture pertains to the portability of X applications. Because the X server program is only concerned with computer hardware, machine-specific details are hidden from X client applications. To an X client application, all computers (running the X server) look the same. This makes X client applications portable across systems.

Understanding X Clients

The current release of X includes over 50 clients. xterm is used most often, but other clients are familiar, such as the mail program, the calculator, the clock, and the system load monitor. Clients appear in their own windows and all clients can run simultaneously. In fact, they always do. You wouldn't, for example, want the clock to stop while you worked in an xterm window. The system load monitor wouldn't mean much if it stopped working while you were loading or compiling in another window. Clients that run simultaneously enable you to do two things at the same time, such as look at your mail while a file copies over the network to the local floppy.

X, by itself, is not a standard interface. Users can customize the clients on each server. (You see how to do this in later sections.) For that reason, the clients might look different from server to server. In addition, servers must be customized to the display hardware they interact with. Consequently, the clients might look different according to the demands of the hardware.

Each X client stores information about itself, such as the name of the application running in its window, in a small file associated with it on the X server. This small file is called the *property* of the client, and is very similar to extended attribute files in OS/2 (and HPFS). Properties make available to all other X clients information about the X client they can use. In this way, X clients communicate with one another. For example, an X client might use its properties to tell the window manager where to locate its icon. Or, when a client is iconified, the window manager looks on the server for the client's property called WM.NAME to find the name of the application and puts that name in the title bar of the icon.

To display the property of a client, you first specify the client, either by specifying its name, process id (obtained with *xwininfo*), or by using the pointer to highlight the window, and using the command *xprop*. For example, if the window is at the root, you could display its name with the following command:

```
xprop -root WM_NAME
```

If you want to display all the properties of a window whose process id is # 0x100032, use the following command:

```
xprop -id 0x100032
```

Understanding Specific X Clients

Three X clients are used frequently: the Window Manager, the xterm Terminal Emulator, and the Display Manager. This section briefly looks at each of these clients and then lists other clients you use often.

As mentioned previously, windowing systems that are integrated with operating systems (in kernel mode) are not customizable. X Windows, on the other hand, is not tied to the operating system, and therefore is customizable. The window manager sets the variables that determine the windowing system's look and feel.

The window manager that ships with OSF/Motif is called mwm. It performs all the tasks discussed earlier, such as moving, sizing, iconifying, shuffling, and creating windows. The X Consortium specified the standard interactions between window managers and X clients in a document called the *Inter-Client Communication Conventions Manual* (ICCCM). mwm conforms to those standards. These standards are necessary because, in their effort to make X flexible, MIT engineers did not make X specify how a window manager had to accomplish basic tasks, such as installing color maps, changing window focus, or communicating data between applications. The ICCCM standard, however, allows all window managers that conform with it to work together on the same server. Other window managers include olwm (from OPEN LOOK™), awm (from Ardent™), and rtl (from Siemen's Research and Technology Laboratories). By early 1995, as UNIX vendors migrate to OSF/Motif, almost certainly you'll be using mwm.

X Windows provides bitmapped graphic elements, such as buttons, clocks, and frames, for a user interface. This is helpful unless you want to type. The xterm terminal emulator provides a standard alphanumeric terminal interface in a window. Consequently, any task you might normally perform on a terminal you can perform in an xterm window, which is the reason it is called a terminal *emulator*. The xterm window emulates a Tekronix® 4014 or a DEC® VT 102 terminal. It is in xterm windows that you execute UNIX commands.

An xterm (terminal emulator) is a computer within a computer. You can connect xterm windows to a variety of computers and display each on your monitor at the same time. Or, each xterm window can display different applications multitasking on the same computer simultaneously. For example, in one xterm you can work on the code of an application, while in another xterm, you can write the user guide for the application. (That's called being up against a deadline!)

The display manager, xdm, automatically starts (from the /etc/rc UNIX system file) and keeps the X server running. The display manager can do as little at startup as conduct a basic login session, prompting the users for their names and passwords. On the other hand, xdm can start multiple clients and fetch personal resources, such as display characteristics (for example, screen color, border width, and the presence of a scroll bar), depending on how the clients are customized. If the screen is bare when you start your UNIX workstation, the xdm is doing little. If, on the other hand, a clock, an xterm window, a performance monitor, and a mail icon appear when you start your workstation, you know xdm is performing a variety of tasks.

X includes a variety of other clients, too plentiful to discuss in depth in this book. Table 15.1, however, summarizes the functions of some of these clients.

Table 15.1
Standard X Clients

X Clients	Usage
Desktop Objects	
xbiff	Mailbox
xclock oclock	Clock

continues

IV

Graphic User Interfaces

Table 15.1, Continued
Standard X Clients

Desktop Objects

xcalc	Calculator
xload	Monitor for system load
xman	Browser for manual pages

Display and Input Setup

xmodmap	Maps keys and pointer buttons to specific functions
xset	Sets up various display and input defaults, such as cursor acceleration, screen saver options, and speaker volume
xsetroot	Sets up the color, background pattern, border width, and other features of the root window

Font Controls

fs	Provides access to fonts over a network (stands for font server)
fslsfonts	Lists the fonts provided on a remote computer
showfont	Shows, in ASCII format, the contents of a compiled font file
xfd	Lists the characters in a particular font
xfontsel	Lists available fonts and enables you to choose one for an application
xlsfonts	Lists the fonts provided on the local computer

Graphic Controls

atobm, bmtoa	Translates ASCII characters to bitmaps, or bitmaps to ASCII characters, correspondingly
bitmap	Editor for bitmap
xmag	Magnifier

Printing Programs

xwd	Transfers a window image into a file
xpr	Converts the image in a file to a particular format, for example, PostScript®, for printing on different printers
xwud	Displays the image saved in a file

Window Management

xdpyinfo	Lists display characteristics
xkill	Stops a client application
xlsclients	Names the clients running in the display
xprop	Displays the properties of the window
xwininfo	Displays the general characteristics of a window

Resource Management

appres	Displays the resources available to a specific client
editres	Enables you to test and change resource variables
xrdb	Loads into the X server customized client preferences often found in the .Xresources or .Xdefaults files in the user's home directory (xrdb stands for X resource database)

Starting X Windows

X Windows may start automatically on your workstation. If it doesn't, you can start it manually. Before you can execute the command to start X Windows, you must first make sure that the X11 directory is in your path.

X clients are generally in the directory /usr/bin/X11. To add this directory to your path, use vi, or another text editor, to open the .profile file, if you are using the Bourne shell, or the .cshrc file, if you are using the C shell. Edit the path statements, as follows:

✔ For Bourne shell:

```
PATH=/usr/bin/X11: ...
export PATH
```

✔ For C shell:

```
set path=( /usr/bin/X11 ...)
```

No doubt you will find many other directories in the path statement. Do not erase them. Simply add the X11 directory to the statement.

Directories are searched from left to right; that is, the directory closest to the path statement is searched first for a command, then the directory to the right of the first is searched second, and so on. For this reason, don't put the X11 directory too far to the right in the path statement.

For the revised path statement to take effect, you must log off and log back on. On some workstations, the command rehash accomplishes the same task.

To start X Windows, you enter the following command at the system prompt:

```
% xinit
```

This command starts the X server and displays an xterm window.

Starting X Windows Automatically

Manually starting X Windows and all the X clients you customarily use is not necessary. Instead, you can create a script that starts X Windows and your favorite X clients.

If xdm starts X Windows on your system, create an executable called .xsessions that contains the script of the X clients you want to run. Put this file in your home directory—$HOME/.xsessions. The xdm command automatically runs .xsessions files on start up. If .xsessions doesn't exist, xdm displays an xterm window by default.

If you use xinit to start X Windows, you must save the script as .xinitrc. Unlike .xsessions, .xinitrc is not an executable. Put this file in your home directory.

In addition to other things you might want in your .xsessions file, you want to load the X resources file by entering the command:

```
xrdb $HOME/.Xresources
```

You also will want to load some favorite X clients by entering these commands:

```
#clock
xclock -digital -update -1 &
#xterm
xterm -geometry 80x20-12-12 &
#console
xconsole
#calculator
xcalc -geometry -0+90 &
```

Some commands must run in the foreground; others, in the background. Commands that you want to execute until they are completed, such as xrdb, should run in the foreground. xrdb exits as soon as the X resources are loaded so that the remainder of the startup script can execute. Other commands, such as xclock, must run in the background because they do not exit unless a user specifically kills the client. Waiting for xclock to exit in the foreground would hang the startup script.

Using Basic X Windows Features

MIT developed X Windows in 1984. Since then, many large companies, including AT&T, Hewlett-Packard, DEC, Sun, and IBM— collectively called the X Consortium—have funded and contributed to X's development.

Using a Typical X Display

X enables you to view more than one running application at a time by creating a window for each application. The application running in the window can be anything. No doubt you're accustomed to seeing clocks, performance indicators, and calendars as windows. X provides a variety of standard desktop objects, such as trash cans and calculators.

Many people wrongly attribute the desktop metaphor to Apple. Although Lisa and Macintosh were the first computers to successfully implement a graphical user interface commercially, the operating system for these computers owes its design philosophy to a research company.

In 1973, engineers at Xerox's research center, called Palo Alto Research Center, or PARC, for short, created a computer called Alto. It had a high resolution monitor, a mouse, and its operating system was the very first GUI. At that time, the command line was the only interface of operating systems, similar to UNIX and DOS.

IV

Graphic User Interfaces

The GUI was as radically different in look as it was in its conceptual approach to user interfaces. It enabled users to manipulate file folders, in/out boxes, and other common desktop objects to accomplish tasks. When Steve Jobs saw the Alto in 1979, he immediately decided to base the Lisa computer on it. When Bill Gates, co-founder of Microsoft, saw the Alto only a few months later, he decided to create a new operating system that he called Windows.

The windows you use most often, however, are terminal emulators, called xterm windows, for short. An xterm15 is a standard blank page in which you can perform a variety of operations according to the application running. For example, in an xterm you can enter commands, write and compile programs, and edit documents.

All windows are related in a hierarchy. The gray background behind the windows is called the *root window*. It is the parent to all the other windows on the display, which are called *child windows*. All application windows 15 are child windows of the root window.

In X, the term "screen" does not mean "display." Some applications use two screens (monitors) for each display, with each monitor showing different parts of a single display (see fig. 15.1).

Two screens (monitors) can also show different parts of the same display. The term "screen" is synonymous with "monitor." All the screens together present a single display. Both displays use a single keyboard and pointer. This means that a single pointer can move sideways (back and forth) between monitors.

Figure 15.1
A display that uses two monitors.

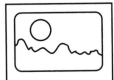

Child windows can also spawn children. Applications often display menus, dialog boxes, or message windows that all relate to the application window. These grandchildren of the root window are one step further down the hierarchical line from the application window. The litmus test for determining hierarchy is discovering what windows on the display disappear when a window is closed. Closing a parent window closes all of its child windows as well.

Not only will the different windows allow you to watch your computer multitask applications, X allows you to log in remotely to another computer. You might do this to complete tasks not accessible on your machine or to spread the processing load of your computer across those in the network. You can operate a remote computer from your terminal and see the result of its work on your display. This capability demonstrates that X is a networked-based graphics library. For more information about the networking qualities of X, see the section called, "The Architecture of X," earlier in this chapter.

Setting Preferences

The term "setting preferences" can mean deciding what color to make the border of a frame that is in focus, or the background color of the root window, or the font used in window titles, or the use of the bell. For many people, the default settings are adequate. X Windows provides a wealth of commands, however, to change even the finest graphical details of windows, including the meaning of the keys on the keyboard. This section looks at some of the more common preferences you might like to edit.

To edit preferences, you use the xset client. To make your customized interface take effect, include xset in your .xsessions file.

To see the current values set by xset, use the q option (query) with xset, as follows:

```
% xset q
```

Controlling the Bell

It's not really a bell anymore. Teletypes had bells. Workstations now have some sort of buzz, or chord. Regardless of the sound, the function remains the same from the days of teletypes: the bell requires the immediate attention of the user.

Using the b option with xset controls the bell. Some people simply want to turn off the bell. You can do that by executing the following command:

```
% xset b off
```

Another command to turn off the bell is the following:

```
% xset b 0
```

Still another way to turn off the bell is the following:

```
% xset -b
```

The last xset example shows a common feature of xset commands; you can disable features by placing dashes in front of options that are by themselves.

To turn on the bell to the default volume, execute this command:

```
% xset b on
```

To control the loudness, note, and duration of the bell, use the following syntax:

```
% xset b loudness note duration
```

Where *loudness* is a number between 0 and 100; *note* is in hertz; and *duration* is in milliseconds. Start with the following setting and then modify it to your tastes:

```
% xset b 40 2500 90
```

Controlling the Mouse Cursor Speed

You use the m (movement) option with the xset command to set the speed of the mouse cursor:

```
% xset m speed limit
```

Where *speed* is the multiple of the base speed the cursor normally moves; *limit* is the number of pixels the cursor must move before the cursor moves faster than the base speed.

For example, if you set the cursor speed as follows when you move the mouse cursor more than 20 pixels, the cursor moves four times the number of pixels on the screen that the mouse moves on the mouse pad.

```
% xset m 4 20
```

To use the default value for the limit, but change the speed, simply enter one number:

```
% xset m 4
```

To use the default value for the speed, but change the limit, use the word default, as follows:

```
% xset m default 20
```

Controlling the Screen Saver

Screen savers are common nowadays. They prevent burn in on the monitor by changing or turning off the image on the monitor. To set the screen saver, use the s option (screen saver) with xset and the following syntax:

```
% xset s interval shift
```

Where *interval* is the number of seconds before the screen saver takes effect; *shift* is the number of seconds that transpire before the image on the screen is moved.

If the display can blank the screen, the second argument is disregarded; the screen simply goes blank after interval seconds. If the display cannot blank itself, after interval seconds, the image on the monitor is moved one pixel in a random direction every shift seconds. Using the following example, the screen saver is invoked after five minutes, and, if the screen does not go blank, the image moves one pixel every 2 seconds.

```
% xset 300 2
```

The original contents of the screen are restored whenever the user hits a key or uses the mouse.

To return the arguments to their default values, use the following command:

```
% xset default
```

To turn off the screen saver, use the following command:

```
% xset off
```

Controlling the Key Repeat Feature

Whenever a key is held down, the keystroke is repeated. You can disable this function by using the r option (repeat) with xset as follows:

```
% xset r off
```

Another way to disable key repeat is to use the command:

```
% xset -r
```

To turn on the key repeat function, use the following command:

```
% xset r
```

Another way to turn on this function is to use the command:

```
% xset r on
```

Controlling the Root Window Appearance

To control the appearance of the root window, use the xsetroot client. As with xset, the best way to control the root window is to include xsetroot in your .xsessions (or .xinitrc) file.

The standard pattern of the root window is a gray mesh. You can change the pattern of the window by using the -bitmap option, as follows:

```
% xsetroot -bitmap bitFileName
```

Where *bitFileName* is the name of the file containing the bitmapped image that will be tiled across the root window. Standard bitmap can be found in /usr/include/X11/bitmaps.

Note You can even create your own bitmaps using the bitmap client.

To set the colors of the pattern, use the -fg and -bg options to set the foreground and background colors, respectively. Here is an example:

```
% xsetroot -bitmap bitFileName -fg yellow -bg purple
```

To display a grid on the root window, use the -mod option, as follows:

```
% xsetroot -mod x y
```

The x and y arguments specify the number of pixels between vertical and horizontal lines, respectively. The largest value of x and y is 15. The larger the x and y values, the more apparent the grid.

To set the root to a solid color, use the -solid option with the following syntax:

```
% xsetroot -solid color
```

where *color* is the color you would like to use in the root window.

Changing the Pointer in the Root Window

The default shape of the mouse cursor when it is in the root window is X. You can change the shape to one of the standard cursor shapes provided in /usr/include/X11/cursorfont.h, using the following syntax:

```
% xsetroot -cursor_name standard_name
```

where *standard_name* is the name of a cursor, such as box_spiral.

You can also change the cursor to one of the bitmapped shapes supplied in /usr/include/X11/bitmaps, using the following syntax:

```
% xsetroot -cursor bitmapFile outlineFile
```

where *bitmapFile* is the name of the file containing the bitmapped cursor; *outlineFile* is the name of the file containing the same image as the bitmapped image, except it is one pixel larger in width and length. The outline image goes directly underneath the cursor to set it off from the root window.

Modifying the Keyboard

Different keyboards have different modifier keys. *Modifier keys* modify, or change, the normal function of other keys. Besides being able to capitalize letters, modifier keys are most often used to execute functions. Ctrl+C, for example, often interrupts a process.

Common to all keyboards are the modifier keys Shift, Caps Lock, and Control. PCs have the Alt key. Macintosh's™ have the Fan key. Sun workstations have Left, Right, and Alternate keys. Writing an application is difficult when you don't know what keys will be on the user's keyboard. To respond to this problem, X uses "logical" modifier keys that users can map to any physical key on their keyboards. The most commonly used logical modifier key is called the Meta key. Again, you won't find a key labeled Meta on any keyboard, but you might find it assigned to the Fan key or the Alt key, depending on the keyboard and the user's preference.

X supports eight logical modifier keys, including Shift, Caps Lock, Control, Mod1 (referred to as Meta), Mod2, Mod3, Mod4, and Mod5. Mod2 through Mod5 are not commonly used.

You can map the function of any key. For example, on your keyboard, the Control key might be in an inconvenient location. If you had another key, perhaps the Alt key, in a more convenient location, you could map the functions associated with the Control key to the Alt key.

The xmodmap client provides the mechanism to map functions to physical keys. Although you can use this client for ridiculous results, such as displaying "P" when you press the key labeled "M," you'll normally use this client only to remap modifier keys.

One reason you might remap the function of a physical key is to bring your keyboard more in line with others you've worked with. For example, some users have set up the backspace and the delete key to perform identical operations. To make this change, you'd use the following command:

```
% xmodmap -e 'keysym BackSpace = Delete'
```

To check the functionality of these two keys, you might print out the key assignments with the delete function by using the following command:

```
% xmodmap -pke ¦ grep Delete
```

The output from such a command might be similar to the following:

```
keycode 45 = Delete

keycode 67 = Delete
```

The numbers 45 and 67 are the key codes of the keys marked "Delete" and "<—," (back space).

Each key on a keyboard generates a value. That value is called its *keycode*. The value of the "c" key, for example, might be 109. You cannot change the keycode of a key. You can only change the function of the key.

The function of the key is specified by *keysym* (key symbol). Each key has a keysym, a function that generally corresponds to the label on the physical key. For example, "g" is the keysym for the "g" key by default. This is not always true, however, as shown in the previous example where you reassigned the keysym of the Backspace key the keysym "Delete." In this case, the Backspace key no longer means backspace; it means delete.

You might also change the function of physical keys to create a more efficient keyboard layout, such as the Dvorak keyboard layout, to replace the QWERTY layout customary on keyboards.

Each X server has a default map assigning shift, caps lock, and control functions to their corresponding physical keys. Finding the Meta key, however, is less obvious. xmodmap (with the -pke option) enables you to print current modifier key assignments.

Besides mapping modifier keys and remapping physical keys, xmodmap also can map the functionality of the buttons on the mouse. The left button generates what is called button code 1, the middle generates button code 2, and the right button generates button code 3. In xterm windows, the default functionality of button code 1 is the copy-to-buffer function. When you drag the mouse over text, mwm copies that text to the buffer. The default functionality of button code 3 is paste-from-buffer. When you move the cursor to a new location and press the right button, the contents of the buffer are pasted after the cursor.

If you are left handed, you might want to reverse the functionality of these buttons with xmodmap:

```
% xmodmap -e 'pointer = 3 2 1'
```

You can return to the default button assignment by substituting the word "default" for "3 2 1" in the preceding statement.

Using the Pointer

To use X windows, you must have a mouse. The mouse cursor changes as it passes over different parts of the screen. For example, when the pointer is over an xterm window, it looks like a capital I. This shape is called an *I beam* because it resembles the steel girders used to build skyscrapers. When the pointer is over the root window, it looks like an "X."

X Windows provides 77 different pointer shapes. Table 15.2 shows the most common pointers from the standard set, plus one used in Motif, as well as the reasons they appear.

Table 15.2
Common X Windows Pointers

Pointer	Name	Appears when...
X	X	The pointer is over the root window
I	I beam	The pointer is over an xterm window
●	Stop	You try to click on something outside a window that requires immediate action
↖	Upper left	You resize the window in the direction of the arrow
→|	Right	You resize the window in the direction of the arrow
↔	Cross	You move a window across the screen

You can only type in a window when the pointer is in it and the window is in *focus*. The window that you can operate in is said to be *in focus*. Normally, the frame of the window in focus is lighter in color than the other frames (you can customize this visual feedback to any color/hue combination, however). You can only operate in one window at a time; thank goodness. You probably don't want to type the same word in six different windows at the same time.

There are two ways to bring a window into focus: you either click on the window or you simply move the pointer to it. If the window comes into focus when you move the pointer into it, the focusing style is called *real-estate-driven*. If you have to click in the window, the focusing style is called *click-to-type*. Click to type is generally the preferred style and is the default in Motif. With a real-estate-driven setup, it's easy for the user to lose track of the pointer. Often, the pointer ends up outside the active window. If it ends up on another window and the user starts typing, the text will go into the highlighted window, not the window the user expected. If the pointer is in the root window, the text is simply lost.

In click-to-type, there is far less chance of this error occurring. The focus doesn't change until you actually click in another window. Some people find click-to-type extra work. For touch typists who often don't look at the screen, only a couple errant inputs will justify the use of click-to-type.

You can switch from click-to-type to real-estate-driven focusing.

The other drawback of real-estate-driven focusing is that often there is a lag time between moving the pointer to a window and having it come into focus. This is a result of the programming overhead of mwm. As you might expect in this situation, some of the initial keystrokes might not enter the expected window.

Focus and Display Stacks

In the preceding section, you saw that there are two ways of establishing focus: click-to-type, in which you must click on some part of a window for it to receive focus, and explicit, in which the pointer merely needs to be in the window for it to receive focus. Both icons and windows can receive focus, which is usually portrayed by displaying larger, different colored borders around a window or icon.

Icons or windows in focus rise to the top of the stack of icons and windows in the display automatically. The resource variable *focusAutoRaise* controls this functionality. Only windows or icons in focus can receive input. Appropriate inputs for icons are shortcut key commands from the Window Menu for icons, such as Alt+R, for Restore.

You can manipulate the stack of windows and icons using the key combinations shown in table 15.3.

Table 15.3
Stack Manipulation

Key Combination	Effect
Meta+Esc	Raises a window to the top of the stack.
Meta+Shift+Esc	Lowers a window to the top of the stack.
Meta+Tab	Moves the window currently on top of the stack to the bottom. The new window on top receives focus.

Key Combination	Effect
Meta+Shift+Tab	Moves the window currently at the bottom of the stack to the top and receives the focus.

Remember, mwm considers the Meta and Alt keys the same; you can substitute one for the other.

To determine the Meta key assignment on your keyboard, use the xev client located in the /demos directory. When you type xev at a prompt in an xterm, an xev window appears, as shown in figure 15.2.

Place your pointer inside the small box in the window and begin pressing keys one at a time. For each key pushed, xev prints the key's keysym and keycode in the xterm window where you started xev. The output might look like the following:

```
... keycode 135 (keysym oxffe1, Lock) keycode 136 (keysym
    ➥0xffe9, Meta) ...
```

In this output, xev displays the keycode as a decimal and the keysym as both a name and a hexadecimal. By typing keys you suspect might be the Meta key, you can find it relatively easily.

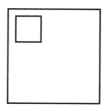

Figure 15.2
The xev client.

Generally, child windows follow the parent window in the stack. If the parent window rises in the stack, the child windows follow. This need not always be the case, however. Version 1.2 of mwm enables you to manipulate the parent and child windows independently by using the actions f.lower, f.raise, and f.raise_lower.

A window on top of the stack does not necessarily have focus. For example, if you move the top window that had focus to the bottom of the stack with the keystrokes Meta+Esc, the window still has focus. Similarly, executing Meta+Shift+Esc does not shift the input focus from the window that was on top of the stack.

IV

Graphic User Interfaces

If a window or icon is terminated, the focus shifts back to the window or icon that had it previously. If the window manager itself dies, focus normally reverts to pointer focus. To restart window manager, type its name, such as mwm or twm, in an xterm. This doesn't always work because of a bug in mwm. If no window has focus, display the Main Options menu of an xterm by making sure the pointer is in an xterm window, and then hold down the Ctrl key while pressing the left mouse button. Use the Secure Keyboard item to restore focus.

Creating Function Keys

If you use a number of operations often, you might want to make function keys for them. Function keys initiate operations, such as saving files, with a single keystroke. Function keys are normally named F1, F2, F3, and so on.

To define a function key, you would use the following syntax:

```
[object][*subobject...]*Translations: #override\
 [modifier]<Key>F1: string("command")[ string(keycode)] \n\
```

or

```
[modifier]<Key>F1: function() \n\
```

where *command* is the operation you want to initiate, such as lpq -Pprinter3; *keycode* is the hexadecimal code for any key on the keyboard. If you press the F1 function key in this example, the *command* prints on the command line. To initiate the function, you must press Enter. To include a return in the F1 function, you specify the hexadecimal keycode for the return key, 0x0d, in *keycode*, as shown in the following example:

```
xterm*Translations: #override\ <Key>F2:    string("cd /usr/yourFiles")
string(0x0d) \n\
```

These lines define the F2 function key to change the directory (cd) to *yourFiles*. The second string enters a return character so that the function key automatically initiates the cd command.

If you want to use functions that the X client recognizes, you can use the alternate syntax that specifies a function. If, for example, you want to use Ctrl+f for moving ahead one page in the Text X client, you would specify the following translation:

```
*Text*Translations: #override\
    Ctrl<Key>f: next-page() \n\
```

To find out what functions X clients recognize, find a reference manual about X clients.

Controlling Functionality from the Command Line

X provides a command, -xrm, that enables you to change resource specifications from the command line. Sometimes this is easier than opening and editing a resource file. -xrm uses the following syntax:

```
% object -xrm  'object [*subobject...]*resource: setting'  &
```

To set the background in an xterm to black, you could use the following line:

```
% xterm -xrm  'xterm*Background: black' &
```

This specification is not saved in the resource database. It applies only to the current instance of the application. In addition, a specification made on the command line will not take precedence over resource specifications that are more specific.

X also enables you to create different versions of X clients by using the -name option in the following syntax:

```
% object -name newName &
```

You might, for example, create different xterm windows for different applications. In your resource file, you could put the following descriptions:

```
XTerm*geometry:          80x35
tinyXterm*geometry:      80x20
hugeXterm*geometry:      80x50
```

After entering this information, when you input the following command at the prompt the resource manager displays a small xterm:

```
% xterm -name tinyXterm &
```

You can substitute hugeXterm for tinyXterm in the same command line to display a large xterm. You can also change the fonts, foreground colors, background colors, and so on for each xterm window.

Customizing Functionality Using xrdb

The xrdb program loads your resource files. Before Release 4, if you ran clients on more than one machine, your resource files had to be resident on each machine. xrdb eliminates this irritation. It stores the resource files on the X server so that all clients can use them. Actually, the resources are stored in a data structure called the RESOURCE_MANAGER, which is at the root window of screen 0 of the X server.

You can either make xrdb part of your .xinitrc or .xsession files so that your resources are loaded during login, or you can use xrdb as a command at a prompt. It has the following syntax:

```
xrdb [options][filename]
```

This section discusses some of the common options, such as -merge, -load, and -query. For a complete list of options, consult an X command reference manual.

The `filename` argument identifies the file from which the resources should be read. The two most common file names to which people save their resources are .Xdefaults and .Xresources. If you don't include a file name, xrdb expects you to enter resource descriptions from the keyboard. You see examples of this shortly.

Examining Your Resources

You might like to see what resources are presently active. You can use the -query option of the xrdb command to see these resources:

```
% xrdb -query
```

The computer will display your current resources, as in this example:

```
XTerm*geometry:        80x35
tinyXterm*geometry:    80x20
hugeXterm*geometry:    80x50
```

Of course, if xrdb hasn't been run, resources won't be set, and you won't get an output.

If xrdb hasn't run, then RESOURCE_MANAGER on the X server isn't loaded with the resource settings. The local resource manager looks instead in the local resource file, often called .Xdefaults, in the home directory. The resources in this file, however, only pertain to the local machine.

Resources are loaded into the resource manager in the following order:

1. The client application's default settings are loaded from the /usr/lib/X11/app-defaults directory.

2. The client application's default settings are loaded from any application-specific resource files specified by XUSERFILESEARCHPATH, and XAPPLERESDIR.

3. The resource files loaded by xrdb in the RESOURCE_MANAGER property. If xrdb hasn't run, then the resource manager looks in the .Xdefaults file.

4. The SCREEN_RESOURCES property (loaded by xrdb).

5. Any environmental variable specified by XENVIRONMENT. If XENVIRONMENT isn't defined, then the resource manager looks in the .Xdefaults-hostname file.

6. Any resource settings entered at the command line.

There are often other default settings for X clients set in the directory /usr/lib/X11/app-defaults. To see all the resource settings an X client uses, X provides the appres (which stands for application resource) option using the following syntax:

```
appres Xclient
```

For example, to see all the resources an xterm client can use, type the following line at the prompt:

```
% appres XTerm
```

XTerm is the class name xterm windows, so the output would show what all xterms use as resource specifications. You can also use an instance of xterm, but that display would not show the system-wide default resource settings.

Loading Resources

To load a file of new resources, use the -load option with the following syntax:

```
xrdb -load resourceFile
```

You would substitute the real name of the file that contained the resources for *resourceFile*.

You can also load new resources from the command prompt by substituting the resource specification in place of *resourceFile*, as shown in the following example:

```
% xrdb -load
xterm*foreground:  Black
```

This entry changes the foreground of all xterms to black. That is, unless there is a more specific resource description. Remember, the more specific a resource description, the higher priority it receives. So, for example, the previous resource description would not take precedence over the following line:

```
xterm*vt100.foreground:   White
```

Graphic User Interfaces

If you simply want to add resource descriptions rather than replace descriptions, you can use the -merge option of xrdb using the following syntax:

```
xrdb -merge newResources
```

As in the -load option, *newResources* can either be a file of resource descriptions or a single resource entered at the command prompt.

Saving New Resources

The -load option replaces the old resource values so the revised values become the default values of RESOURCE_MANAGER. New values you've merged (using -merge), however, are not retained unless you specifically save them. To do this, use the -edit option of the xrdb command from the command line with the following syntax:

```
xrdb -edit ~/resourceFile
```

For example, if you store your resources in .Xdefaults, you would type at the prompt:

```
% xrdb -edit ~/.Xdefaults
```

This line saves the contents of the RESOURCE_MANAGER (where the loaded and merged resources reside) into the .Xdefaults resource file in your home directory.

You might like to return to previously set resource descriptions. You can do this by using the -backup option. To save a current version of .Xdefaults, you would use the following line:

```
% xrdb -edit .Xdefaults -backup old
```

The -backup option appends old to .Xdefaults so that the current resource file is duplicated in a file called .Xdefaults.old.

Deleting Resources

If you want to delete the resource definitions from the RESOURCE_MANAGER (on the X server), you use the -remove option of xrdb with the following syntax:

```
xrdb -remove
```

This command deletes the entire resource file. There isn't an option that selectively removes single lines from the file. To remove single lines, you need to display the resource settings using the -query option, then edit the file using vi, or another editor, and then save the revised file to the RESOURCE_MANAGER using the xrdb -load option.

Summary

Although it's impossible to cover the functionality of all of X's widgets, this chapter covered widgets you may have been unfamiliar with before. As you progress to the next chapter, you have a better understanding of the architecture of X Windows, how to start X Windows, setting preferences, changing focus, and customizing functionality.

Chapter Snapshot

This chapter covers the basics of how to use the Motif GUI, from using the frame and hidden menus to using a variety of widgets and customizing the Motif Window Manager. Topics include the following:

After reading this chapter, you will feel comfortable using the Motif GUI. Covering the functionality of all the widgets in Motif is impossible, but you will be able to interact effectively with unfamiliar widgets based on the widgets discussed here.

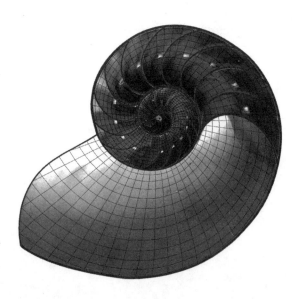

16

CHAPTER

Motif

As all vendors developed their own version of the UNIX operating system, so, too, did they develop their own graphical-user interface to accompany it. When the standards committees began meeting to try and define a common set of ground to call UNIX, one of the first issues they tackled was that of the GUI. The Motif interface grew from these committees as a common interface that could be ported and available on any vendor's UNIX.

A Short History of UNIX GUIs

For most of UNIX's 25-plus years, the UNIX interface has been the command line. To work in UNIX, you had to learn arcane abbreviations such as cp, grep, mv, ls, and rm, along with their associated flags and options. With more than 200 commands, and with some commands using more than 10 different options, the task of mastering UNIX was formidable.

Many people, once they have mastered it, rejoice in the obscurity of the command set. UNIX is, after all, a terrifically powerful operating system. After you learn the cryptic commands, you can accomplish powerful tasks very quickly. You don't need to traverse multiple levels of menus or windows. Expert users appreciate the speed available from typing a command and getting an instant answer. But the command set creates problems for nonexpert users. When you know UNIX, you belong to a select group of people who can manipulate the UNIX system in dramatic ways. When you don't know the UNIX command set, the obscurity of the commands presents a significant challenge. In addition, UNIX doesn't help the novice user much. It gives you a list of flags and a syntax statement when you incorrectly use a command, but its error messages convey failure, not suggestions on how to do it better.

Although a certain camp of users treat UNIX reverently, other people choose not to use UNIX at all. Because these preferences obviously affect the sales of operating systems, it was only a matter of time before someone came up with a means of executing UNIX graphically instead of through the command line.

With the skyrocketing popularity of the *graphical-user interface* (GUI) in the 1990s, a proliferation of UNIX GUIs hit the marketplace. Although most share a similar look and functionality, enough differences exist among the GUIs to make using different ones confusing.

The most popular GUIs are Motif, by *Open Software Foundation* (OSF), and Open Windows, by Sun Microsystems. Other common UNIX GUIs include NeXTSTEP, by NeXT, and Open Desktop, by SCO. UnixWare can use two GUIs: Open Windows and Motif. All these GUIs were built with X Windows tools. X Windows is not an interface in itself but a library of graphic routines you use to create a GUI. UNIX GUIs ride on top of X Windows.

In the second quarter of 1993, many large corporations, including Hewlett-Packard, DEC, IBM, Sun, and SCO, decided that the multitude of GUIs was hurting the success of UNIX. UNIX users were limited in their choice of applications by their choice of GUI. Faced with competition from Windows NT, the corporations decided to unify UNIX GUIs. This is not to say that all the flavors of UNIX are now the same. Although they are all compatible on a systems level, each corporation maintains its own flavor of UNIX and touts its advantages. But at least all the flavors look the same to users.

The agreement among the corporations is called COSE (pronounced "cozy"), which stands for Common Operating System Environment. Instead of creating a new, vanilla interface, the corporations agreed to standardize on Motif.

Motif has always been one of the most popular UNIX GUIs. What prevented companies from standardizing on Motif in the past was the high fees that OSF charged. In exchange for the standardization on Motif, OSF agreed to revise the licensing fees and to modify Motif so that it complies with version 11, release 5 of X Windows. As a result of COSE, many other UNIX interfaces will slowly begin to disappear.

> As of this writing, Novell and Sun Microsystems ship Motif as the default interface of UNIX. You can, however, revert to NetWare or Open Look if you choose.

This chapter discusses Motif from a user's point of view. The scope of this book prevents an exhaustive discussion of Motif, but included is more than enough to acquaint you with the skills you need to use Motif.

Using the Motif Interface

Many of the X clients customized by Motif have a similar functionality. This section describes the basic means of interacting with Motif clients.

Using the Frame

The window manager, called *mwm* (for Motif window manager), is the mechanism that enables you to move, resize, and shuffle windows. X windows can overlap (as well as tile—sit one next to another) without interfering with the applications running in them. Manipulating windows is important because the advantage of X is that you can see more than one application at a time. For this reason, X often runs on 17-inch monitors or larger. You might like to see multiple applications at the same time, for example, if you want to cut and paste between two documents or compare a spreadsheet with another document.

The window manager provides the *frame* for each window, which provides some standard functions. The frame is shown in figure 16.1.

Figure 16.1
The frame of an X
window.

window menu
button

title bar

minimize and
maximize buttons

data field

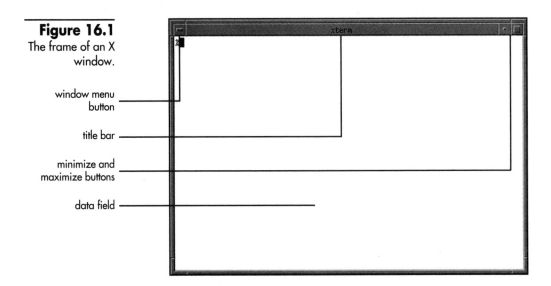

Most of the functionality is graphically embedded into the upper side of the frame, called the *title bar*, which is larger than the other sides by necessity. The title area in the title bar gives the developer an opportunity to identify the window. The default name that mwm automatically supplies is xterm. The buttons in the upper-right corner, when clicked on, minimize and maximize the window. The button in the upper-left corner of the frame displays the Window menu and closes the window if you double-click on it. You also can pull the sides and lower corners of the frame to resize the window. You examine all these features in greater depth later in this chapter.

The mwm uses shading to create a three-dimensional look to the frame. This feature is functional, not just an aesthetic artifice. Notice in figure 16.1 that buttons appear to be at different heights. The small square in the Minimize button, for example, appears higher than the square on which it sits. The mwm achieves this appearance by placing white lines on the upper and left sides of objects and black lines on the right and lower sides of objects. It reverses this color scheme to make the objects look indented. In this way, the shading is functional.

The benefit you get from real-looking objects is that the learning curve for the interface is minimized; you do not have trouble remembering that a depressed-looking button means that you've initiated the associated function.

The entire frame appears beveled, which helps distinguish it from the background. It also gives you the feeling that the frame contains the data field, like walls contain water in a pool. By putting the data "down in" the frame, the mwm conveys the sense that the frame remains constant even though the data field often changes. The frame is like a looking glass into an application. In a word processing document, for example, if you imagine each page of your document joined end to end, the frame is your field of vision through which you scroll up and down those pages.

The mwm was designed to be used with Motif, but other window managers are on the market. The original window manager supplied with X from MIT is called twm, for Tom's window manager, named after Tom LaStrange, the developer of twm. This window manager, like the others, provides a different look and feel. One example is that twm does not frame the application. It provides only a title bar, different from mwm's. It does, however, provide similar window management functionality.

Using Iconified Windows

An *iconified window* is a window that has been reduced to a small square with a graphic and title. These icons are slightly larger and more richly detailed than those found in other window managers.

An application continues to run while iconified. Some icons can provide progress reports on the application running "inside" the icon. If the application is faxing a document, for example, the icon can show the percentage of the document faxed. Double-clicking on the icon restores the window to its previous size, either full screen or smaller. Clicking on the window displays the Window menu for icons, which is discussed later in the chapter.

You iconify windows to save screen space. Sometimes, too much is on the screen. When that happens, windows get buried so deep you can't access them. By iconifying windows, you know exactly where to access the application, or you uncover windows by eliminating windows you're not using immediately. You can move icons around the screen just as you can active windows.

Using Hidden Menus

By default the mwm provides two hidden menus, called the Window menu (for windows and icons) and the Root menu. You access these menus with keystrokes or, more commonly, by pointing to and clicking on different parts of the display.

The Window Menu

You access the Window menu by clicking once (not holding the button down) on the square on the left side of the title bar. As shown in figure 16.2, a menu drops down with a box drawn around the current selection.

IV

Graphic User Interfaces

Figure 16.2
The Window
menu.

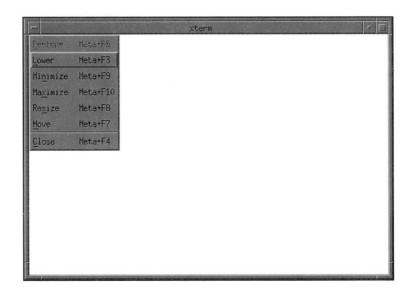

The Window menu options have the effects described in table 16.1. Menu items that appear grayed out on the menu are not presently usable.

Table 16.1
Using Window Menu Options

Option	Effect
Restore	Changes an icon back into a window the size it was when it was iconified
Move	Enables you to move the entire window
Size	Enables you to resize the window
Mi**n**imize	Reduces the window to an icon
Ma**x**imize	Makes the window as large as the root window
Lower	Buries the icon or window behind other windows and icons
Close	Terminates the window and the application or process in it

You can initiate any of these options by clicking on it; by dragging the pointer down to the option and releasing the mouse button; by holding down the Alt key and pressing the letter key indicated by the option's underlined letter, called the *mnemonic* (for example, press Alt+R for **R**estore); or by pressing the option's keyboard shortcut, called the *accelerator* (for example, press Alt+F5 for **R**estore). The advantage of using accelerators is that you needn't display the Window menu to initiate a function (although accelerators also work when the Window menu is displayed).

The Window menu displays the accelerators as combinations of the Alt key plus a function key. The Alt and Meta keys are equivalent to mwm. As a result, to use accelerators, you can use Alt or Meta in the keystroke combinations.

These options function in predictable ways. When you choose **M**ove, for example, the pointer changes to cross-arrows and moves to the center of the window. When you then move the mouse, the window moves correspondingly, and when you choose **S**ize, the pointer changes again to cross-arrows. When you move the pointer to the borders or corners of the frame, the pointer changes to a vertical or diagonal arrow, and you can "push" or "pull" the borders or corners in the direction the mouse moves.

You can accomplish some of the tasks of the Window menu options by using graphical features of the frame and mwm, as summarized in table 16.2.

Table 16.2
Equivalent Actions of Window Menu Options

Option	Equivalent Action
Restore	Double-click on an icon
Move	Click and hold on the title bar of the frame, and move the pointer
Size	Click and hold on the bottom, a side, or a corner of the frame, and pull or push the window to the size you want
Mi**n**imize	Click on the first of the two buttons on the right of the title bar
Ma**x**imize	Click on the second of the two buttons on the right of the title bar
Lower	No equivalent
Close	Double-click on the button that displays the Window menu

Double-clicking on the button on the left side of the title bar is the equivalent of issuing an xkill command at the prompt. (If you type **xkill** at the prompt, the pointer changes to a "draped" box. You then click on the window you want to kill.) This method is a convenient way of ridding yourself of a stubborn window whose process is hung. But repercussions result from such a drastic action.

continues

IV

Graphic User Interfaces

First, data is not saved before the process terminates. Second, the executing process simply stops; it does not clean up after itself. This situation might affect underlying system processes, such as reading from or writing to a socket, or it might affect processes visible to the user, such as an editing session. For these reasons, use xkill as a last resort. Before resorting to xkill, try the following methods in the following order:

1. Type the command you use to log off the system, such as **exit**.

2. Use special keystroke combinations, such as Ctrl+C.

3. Remove xcalc and bitmap xterms by typing **q** or **Q**.

4. Use application-specific commands, such as quit, Send HUP Signal, and Send TERM Signal, in the Main Options menu of xterm.

5. Choose **C**lose from the Window menu.

6. Double-click on the button on the left of the title bar.

7. Type **xkill** at the prompt.

8. Use the UNIX kill command with the ID number of the client's process (use ps to find the ID number).

9. For xterm windows, choose Send KILL Signal from the Main Options menu of the client.

The two options that work in the most opposite manner are **S**ize and **M**ove. When you choose either option from the Window menu, you simply move the pointer to resize or move the window and then click to complete the action. With the equivalent actions shown in table 16.2, you must click and hold the mouse button on a graphical object—the title bar for **M**ove or the side or corner of the frame for **S**ize, and release the button to complete the action.

The equivalent actions listed in table 16.2 are often more direct than performing the same functions through the Window menu. As a result, you might find that you don't use the Window menu much.

The only function you can't perform graphically is **L**ower. If you find that you use this function often, but you object to the time required to access the Window menu option, and you find that pressing the keyboard shortcut Alt+F3 is awkward, you can customize the system.mwmrc file to define a keystroke-button combination to perform the **L**ower function. A later section in this chapter, "Customizing mwm," tells you how.

The mwm program also displays the Window menu when you click once on an icon. Sometimes the mwm has difficulty distinguishing between a double-click and two single clicks. You might double-click on an icon to restore it, for example, but see only the Window menu appearing. At that point, clicking on the **R**estore option is just as easy as double-clicking again on the icon.

To close the Window menu without making a selection from it, click somewhere outside it.

The Window Menu and Icons

When you click once on an icon, the mwm displays the Menu window. The options are the same as for a window, but some options, such as **S**ize and Mi**n**imize, don't apply. Table 16.3 summarizes the effects of these options.

Table 16.3
Effects of Window Menu Options on Icons

Option	Effect
Restore	Changes an icon back into a window the size it was when it was iconified
Move	Enables you to move the icon
Size	Not available
Mi**n**imize	Not available
Ma**x**imize	Makes the icon as large as the root window
Lower	Buries the icon or window behind other windows and icons
Close	Terminates the icon and the application or process in it

These options have the same mnemonics and accelerators as the corresponding options in the Window menu for windows. To use mnemonics and accelerators, the icon must have focus. When you bring an icon into focus (by clicking on it), its border and title enlarge. The icon remains in focus until you click on another window or icon.

You can manipulate icons graphically in much the same way as you manipulate windows graphically. To raise an icon to the top of the stack of icons and windows on the display, for example, click on the icon. (Clicking on it also displays the Menu window.) You can move an icon by clicking and holding the mouse button on it and then moving the mouse. And you can restore (or de-iconify) an icon by double-clicking on it. This action returns the window to the size it was when it was iconified, not necessarily the size of the root window.

The only difference between icon and window management is that the mwm doesn't enable icons to overlap; windows can overlap icons, but icons can't overlap icons. This safety net prevents you from mysteriously losing iconified applications.

The Root Menu

You display the Root, or master, menu by placing the pointer over the root window and clicking and holding the right mouse button. Figure 16.3 shows the Root menu.

Figure 16.3
The Root menu.

The Root menu is the main menu of mwm. Whereas the Window menu pertains only to its associated window, the Root menu pertains to everything on the display. Table 16.4 describes the options on the menu and their effects.

Table 16.4
Effects of Root Menu Options

Option	Effect
New Window	Opens a new window, an xterm window by default, usually on the local display, unless the DISPLAY environmental variable is set to a remote display. The new window automatically has focus.
Shuffle Up	Moves the window or icon at the bottom of the stack on top of all other windows and icons on the display.
Shuffle Down	Moves an icon or window to the bottom of all other windows and icons on the display.
Refresh	Redresses the contents of the display. It buries system messages that obscure the contents of the display.
Pack Icons	Arranges the icons in an icon box evenly. (Icon boxes are discussed later in this chapter in the section called "Customizing mwm.")
Restart...	Initiates any changes you make to the system.mwmrc (or .mwmrc) file.

Because stopping and restarting the mwm is more drastic than the other actions, note that a line separates the Restart option from the other options. Also, as the elipsis (...) after the option name implies, you must confirm your selection. mwm displays a dialog box with two buttons: Cancel to cancel the selection, and OK to initiate Restart. If you choose OK, the screen goes blank, an hourglass appears, and the mwm restarts with its initial display.

You can accomplish some of these tasks in different ways. To refresh the display, for example, you can type **xrefresh** in the xterm window at the prompt. To shuffle up a window, simply click on it. Because this method is easier than using the Root menu option, you might not want to use Shuffle Up unless the window or icon is entirely obscured. Then, it's a valuable option.

As in the Window menu, you can customize the options offered in the Root menu by changing the configuration information in the .mwmrc file, as explained later in this chapter.

Using Motif Applications

As mentioned previously, X is not a graphical-user interface (GUI). X provides the mwm, but the window manager is only a part of the GUI. The look and feel of the GUI also come from the widgets (and gadgets) that an application uses. The X Toolkit enables programmers to create their own widgets.

Widgets are graphical tools you use to perform common tasks. Common examples of widgets include scroll bars, buttons, menus, and text windows, as shown in figure 16.4.

Figure 16.4
Common Motif widgets.

A few widgets don't accomplish tasks. The separator widget, for example, is a line that separates items on a menu. The separator widget is used in menus to demarcate groups of functionally related menu options.

Many widgets are just combinations of more elementary widgets. A scrolled list, for example, is made of a text window and a scroll bar.

If you've used any graphical interface, you already know the kinds of widgets common to many applications—even if the widgets have a different look and feel. Scroll bars, for example, might look different in Motif and Microsoft Windows, but their functionality is similar.

The X Toolkit contains two subroutine libraries: the X Toolkit (Xt) Intrinsics and the Athena widget set (Xaw). The X Toolkit gives you the tools to create widgets, such as menus, buttons, dialog boxes, and scroll bars. The Athena widget set is a ready-made set of widgets that programmers can use. GUIs, like Motif, use some Athena widgets, parallel other Athena widgets, and create entirely new widgets.

Open Software Foundation, the creator of Motif, created the Motif Toolkit. It is based on the Xt Intrinsics tool set and on tool kits originally developed by Digital Equipment Corporation and Hewlett-Packard. Motif widgets look like the IBM/Microsoft Presentation Manager.

Although many Athena and Motif widgets appear to be similar, some important differences exist. Athena widgets are basically two-dimensional, and Motif widgets appear three-dimensional (see fig. 16.5).

Figure 16.5
Comparing Athena and Motif widgets.

```
                                    xterm
!!
!! Button Binding Description(s)
!!

Buttons DefaultButtonBindings
{
        <Btn1Down>        icon|frame        f.raise
        <Btn3Down>        icon|frame        f.post_wmenu
        <Btn3Down>        root              f.menu   DefaultRootMenu
}

Buttons ExplicitButtonBindings
{
        <Btn1Down>        frame|icon        f.raise
        <Btn3Down>        frame|icon        f.post_wmenu
        <Btn3Down>        root              f.menu   DefaultRootMenu
  !     <Btn1Up>          icon              f.restore
        Alt<Btn1Down>     window|icon       f.lower
  !     Alt<Btn2Down>     window|icon       f.resize
  !     Alt<Btn3Down>     window|icon       f.move
}

Buttons PointerButtonBindings
```

continues

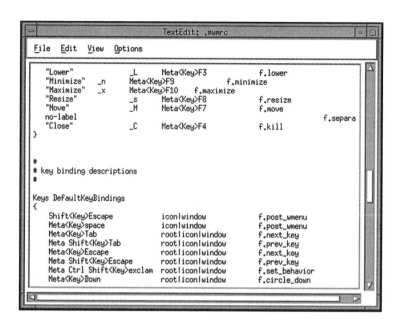

Figure 16.5

continued

To display Athena menus, you must click and hold the mouse button on the title of the menu. In Motif, you need only click on the menu title. The menu remains until you click once again. To choose a menu option in Athena menus, you must drag the pointer down and release the mouse button on the option you want. Motif enables you to choose an option in various ways, such as pressing Enter on the default option, clicking on the option, and so on.

Also, you'll notice, back in figure 16.5, that the Athena scroll bars are simply rectangles within rectangles.

Motif scroll bars look and behave quite differently. You can use Athena scroll bars only one way: you use the pointer to grab the dark rectangle (called the thumb) and move it left and right or up and down in the scroll region. You can use Motif scroll bars in a variety of ways. You can click on the arrows to scroll through the screen a line at a time. You can click on the scroll region to advance (backward or forward) a window at a time. Or you can use the pointer to grab the slider and drag it through the scroll region to move correspondingly through the windows, just as you can with Athena scroll bars.

These are just some of the appearance and functional differences between Athena and Motif widgets. As you learn about other Motif widgets in this section, you explore how they differ from Athena widgets.

Graphic User Interfaces

Using Menus

Motif provides three types of menus:

✔ Pop-up

✔ Pull-down

✔ Option

Pop-up menus are so called because they are invisible until you display them. In effect, they pop out of nowhere. The Root menu, discussed previously, is a good example of a pop-up menu. To display a pop-up menu, you put the pointer in a defined area and click or hold down the third mouse button. To display the Root menu, for example, you place the pointer in the root window and click (or hold down) the third button.

To choose options from a pop-up menu, you can drag down to or click on an option.

The problem with pop-up menus is their invisibility. Novice users of applications might never know of the existence of a pop-up menu. For that reason, you often can accomplish the tasks carried out by pop-up menu options in different, often more circuitous, ways.

Expert application users appreciate pop-up menus because they don't take up screen real estate and they offer shortcuts.

Pull-down menus, by contrast, have some graphic element always displayed. It might be a button, like the button on the left of the title bar that displays the Window menu, or simply the title of the menu in the menu bar. A menu is called pull-down because when you click on the graphic element, the menu pulls down from it, as shown in figure 16.6.

Figure 16.6
A typical pull-down menu.

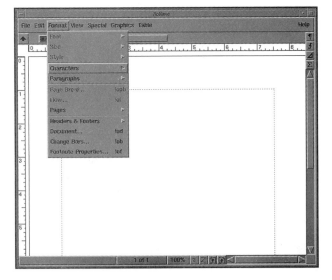

Notice that each menu title has one letter underlined. This letter is the menu's mnemonic. You can display a pull-down menu by holding down Meta and pressing the mnemonic. You can invoke a menu option without even displaying the menu by pressing the accelerator key combination. These key combinations are displayed next to menu options in menus. You might initiate a save function, for example, by pressing Alt+S. Each application specifies its accelerators, but most applications follow de facto standards established by the current body of applications.

Besides using accelerators, you can choose menu options in the following ways:

✔ Press Enter if the (default) highlighted option is the one you want.

✔ Click on the option.

✔ Press the mnemonic key. You might, for example, press O for **O**pen.

✔ Drag the pointer down and release the button on the option you want.

An *option menu* is one that displays when you click on a button. This type of menu looks and behaves like the pull-down menu, as shown in figure 16.7.

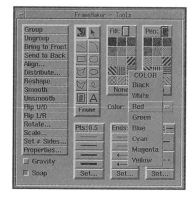

Figure 16.7
An option menu.

All three types of menus can also be tear-off menus. Normally, when you choose a menu item, the menu disappears, and some action starts. A tear-off menu can remain visible and be used repeatedly until you decide to close it.

A tear-off menu is denoted by a perforated line, as shown in figure 16.8.

Figure 16.8
A tear-off menu
before and after it
is torn off.

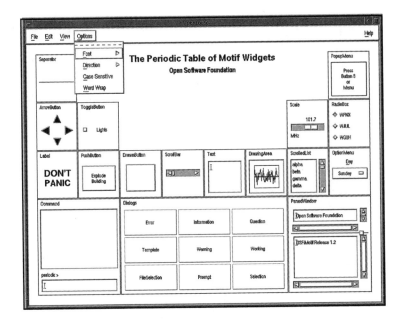

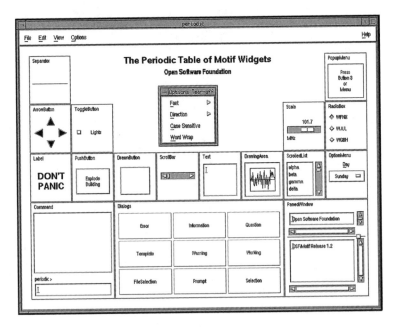

Menus that you use on a continuing basis are good candidates for tear-off menus.
FrameMaker, for example, provides tear-off menus for formatting paragraphs and fonts,
so that you don't have to repeatedly display and use the menu.

You tear off a menu by clicking on the perforated line. When you do, a frame forms around the menu. Its functionality is restricted. It has a Window menu button in the upper-right corner of the title bar. You can move the menu by clicking and holding the first mouse button on the title bar and moving the mouse. You can resize the menu by pulling or pushing the corner.

To close a tear-off menu, you can double-click on the Window menu button, single-click on it and choose **C**lose, type the mnemonic or accelerator for **C**lose, or press the cancel key, which is often Esc.

Using Push Buttons and Drawn Buttons

You initiate actions with push buttons by clicking on them. (Remember that in Motif, the PushButton widget appears to depress because of subtle shading. This graphical representation of pushing a button is easy to remember and gives you important feedback. If you don't see the button depress, you know that the action described by the label on the button hasn't executed.)

Push buttons are square and make exclusive selections—that is, you can choose only one button in a group of buttons. (To make more than one selection in a group, you use check boxes, which are discussed later in this chapter's section on "Using Radio Boxes, Check Boxes, and Toggle Buttons.")

Default buttons are gray; you can choose them by pressing Enter. Athena and Motif push button widgets are identical except for this feature. Only Motif buttons work with Enter.

Although the push button "depresses" when you click on it with the mouse button, the action doesn't take effect until you release the button. Suppose, for example, that in the middle of choosing a button, you change your mind. As long as you haven't released the mouse button, you can move the pointer off the push button and cancel the activation of its function.

A button related to the push button is called the *drawn button*. Instead of having a button label, the drawn button has a bitmapped picture on it. When you choose the button, the picture often changes. Besides the picture, the functionality of the drawn and push buttons are identical.

Using Radio Boxes, Check Boxes, and Toggle Buttons

You also make exclusive selections by using radio boxes. *Radio boxes* are columns of diamond-shaped toggle buttons that appear to depress when you click on them (and pop up when you click on them a second time). Figure 16.9 shows some typical radio boxes.

IV

Graphic User Interfaces

Figure 16.9
Radio boxes.

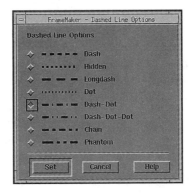

A similar widget is the check box. A *check box* is a column of toggle buttons that look like squares (rather than diamonds). You can check more than one toggle button in a check box, as shown in figure 16.10.

Figure 16.10
Check boxes.

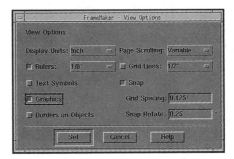

A *toggle button* is like a check box except that it has only one toggle button in it, as shown in figure 16.11.

Figure 16.11
A toggle button in
the lower left.

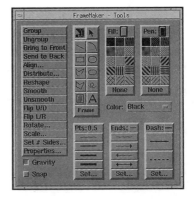

The appearance of the toggle buttons in all these widgets is the same. They appear depressed when you click on them, and pop up when you click on them a second time.

Using Text Windows

A variety of Athena widgets accept text, such as xterm, xman, bitmap, and xedit. Likewise, Motif provides a variety of text windows. Some are only one line long. Other larger ones enable you to access any part of a file by using a scrollable control.

The caret is the standard cursor in text windows for Athena widgets, except for xterm, which uses an I beam. Motif widgets use the I beam as well, as shown in figure 16.12.

Figure 16.12
A typical Motif text widget.

You use the mouse to perform many text manipulations. To erase a selection, you move the pointer over the selected text while holding down the first mouse button. This action highlights the text. When you press Del, the highlighted selection disappears. This method is a great deal more convenient than using repeated backspaces.

To move or copy selections of text (or pictures or button labels), you again move the pointer over the selected text while holding down the first mouse button. Then you move the pointer to the place where you want to copy or move the text.

To copy the text, you click the second mouse button. You can continue to copy the selection throughout a document by clicking the second mouse button in various locations as long as the original selection remains highlighted.

To move the text (erase it from its original location and copy it to a new location), you click the second mouse button while holding down the Shift key.

You also can use these techniques to copy or move text (or pictures) between applications. The selection moved between applications must be compatible with the new application. You can't move a picture, for example, to a text-only widget.

To abandon the copy or move function, simply click the first button. The selection loses its highlighting. To move the cursor to a new location but keep the selection highlighted (and not copy or move the selection), click the first mouse button while holding down the Ctrl key.

Another, perhaps more visual, way of moving text is called drag and drop. This feature enables you to grab text that you've highlighted and drag it to a new location. When you reach the destination, you drop the text. Drag and drop works with pictures as well as text.

To drag a selection, first highlight the selection by moving the pointer over the text while holding down the first mouse button. (The only exception is a button label—you don't need to select it.) Then place the pointer on the selection and hold down the second button. A drag icon, which represents the text, appears. Use the mouse to move the drag icon to the new location. The drag icon changes shape, usually to a negation symbol, when it is not over a valid drop site. To copy the text, simply release the second button at the drop site. To move the selection to the new site, hold down the Shift key when you release the second button.

To abandon the drag-and-drop function, press the key that performs the cancel function, usually the Esc key, while continuing to hold the second button.

You can use various standard keystrokes to move the cursor around the text widget. Table 16.5 summarizes these keystroke commands.

Table 16.5
Cursor Movement in Text Widgets

Keystroke	Cursor Movement
↑	Up one line
↓	Down one line
→	Right one character
←	Left one character
Ctrl+↑	Up one paragraph
Ctrl+↓	Down one paragraph
Ctrl+→	One word to the right
Ctrl+←	One word to the left
PgUp	Up one window
PgDn	Down one window

Using the Command Box

A *command box* enables you to type in commands and see a history of the commands you've typed. It consists of two text windows: a large one called the history window, and a smaller one called the command window, as shown in figure 16.13.

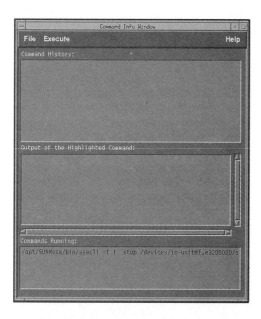

Figure 16.13

Entering commands in the command box.

When you type a command in the one-line text window at the bottom and press Enter, the command disappears in the one-line text window and reappears in the history window. You continue to execute commands by typing them in the command window. You also can execute a command by highlighting one in the history window. When you do, it appears in the command window. You then can edit the command (you can't in the history window) if you need to, and press Enter to execute the command. This method saves you some typing.

Using the Scale Widget

A *scale widget* enables you to choose a value from a spectrum of values. The values can be numeric, colors, or shading, depending on the application. Often the selected value appears in the scale widget along with a horizontal slide box and a slider, as shown in figure 16.14.

Figure 16.14
A typical Motif
scale widget.

Scale widgets might or might not be interactive. If not, the scale widget simply indicates a value and its position relative to the scale of available values. If the scale widget is interactive, you have three ways to adjust the values:

✔ You can click on the slider with the first button, on its left or right side, and move the slider one unit to the left or right correspondingly.

✔ You can click on the slide box with the second button. The slider moves immediately to that position.

✔ You can click and hold on the slider with the first button. When you move the mouse, the slider moves correspondingly.

Some scale widgets also have arrows at the ends of the slide box. With this type of scale widget, you can click on the arrows to move the slider back or forth through the slide box one unit at a time.

Using Dialog Boxes

Motif provides nine different types of dialog boxes: error, question, information, template, warning, working, file selection, prompt, and selection. The first six are message dialog boxes.

Using Message Dialog Boxes

A *message dialog box* presents you with a message, sometimes a question, an icon, and one or more push buttons. The icon gives you a visual clue to help you immediately understand the kind of message being presented. A warning dialog box, for example, presents an exclamation-point icon. A question dialog box presents a question-mark icon (inside a human head). Figure 16.15 shows some of the message dialog boxes.

Figure 16.15
Message dialog boxes.

Many message dialog boxes contain only one button. The message usually presents important information that you confirm you've read by clicking on the button, perhaps marked OK. Other dialog boxes ask you to confirm decisions you've made. Before executing dramatic actions such as erasing files or reformatting disks, for example, good applications ask you to confirm (or cancel) the task.

In Motif dialog boxes, unlike Athena dialog boxes, one of the push buttons can receive focus by default. The button that receives focus is normally the most likely answer to a message, or the least destructive answer. If the message asks whether you want to reformat drive C, for example, the Cancel button should receive default focus. You can easily choose the default button by pressing Enter. To choose any other button, you must click on it (assuming that you're using explicit [click-to-type] focus).

Athena dialog boxes work just like Motif dialog boxes, except Athena dialog boxes don't display default button choices.

Using Prompt Dialog Boxes

A *prompt dialog box* normally asks you to supply a short answer to a question that it poses. The box usually contains a question, a one-line text window in which to reply, and two buttons: one marked Cancel, and another marked OK. Figure 16.16 shows a typical example of a prompt dialog box.

Figure 16.16
A typical Motif
prompt box.

Using Selection Dialog Boxes

A *selection dialog box* enables you to choose one item from a list of choices. To accommodate that functionality, the selection dialog box contains a list box, a scroll bar for the list box, a text window—usually one line long, and two or more push buttons to accept or cancel the selection or the selection process. Figure 16.17 shows a typical example of a selection dialog box.

Figure 16.17
A typical Motif
selection
dialog box.

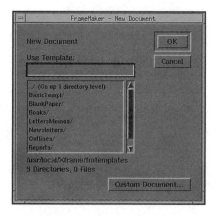

You can make a selection from the list of choices in two ways. Because the default position of the cursor is in the one-line text window, you can immediately begin typing the selection in the text window. You also can click on one of the choices. (If the selection you want is outside the list box, you use the scroll bar to move the list up or down until your selection appears.) When you click on the option, it appears in the one-line text window. You then click on the appropriate push button to accept or reject the selection. Often the default button choice is OK or Accept. You can press the Enter key to initiate these button actions.

Using the File Selection Dialog Box

You use the *file selection dialog box* to specify particular files on disk. The file selection dialog box is an amalgamation of many different widgets, and the box varies in form from application to application. A normal implementation might include two list boxes, with accompanying horizontal and vertical scroll bars, two one-line text windows, and two or more push buttons. Figure 16.18 shows a typical file selection dialog box.

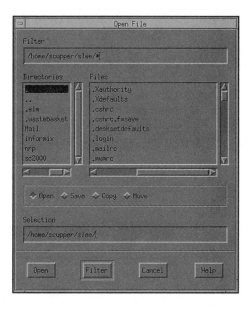

Figure 16.18
A typical Motif file selection dialog box.

In figure 16.18, the first one-line text window acts as a filter for the directories listed in the first list box. The filter is a path description that restricts the directories listed in the directory list box to those further down the path. If you don't specify a filter, the directory list box displays all the directories on a drive. If the directory you're looking for isn't displayed, change the filter.

To choose a directory in the directory list box, click on that directory. The file list box then displays the files in the selected directory. To choose a file, click on it in the file list box. The file then appears in the second one-line text window labeled File Selection. At that point, you click on the appropriate push button to initiate the selection.

If you know the name of the file to begin with, you can just type it in the File Selection text window and click on the appropriate push button.

Customizing mwm

The mwm window manager is flexible. You can customize just about everything about it. You can, for example, change the arrangement of icons in the display, the shape of window frames and icons, and the menu selections in the Root menu and the Window menu; you can even create new menus to appear in the root window. You manage mwm's features through two files: the system.mwmrc file in your home directory and the .Xresources file (or any other file that contains resource specifications).

The system.mwmrc file controls the default operation of mwm. This file specifies, for example, the key combinations you use to execute tasks and the contents of the Root and Window menus. In this section, you look at ways of customizing this file so that mwm better suits your tastes. You don't want to lose the system.mwmrc file, however. Before customizing it, you should create a copy of it in your home directory and title it simply .mwmrc.

In addition to modifying the .mwmrc file, mwm enables you to customize many application resources. Discussing all these customization options is not practical here, nor do you want to bother customizing all of them. For these reasons, the text discussion is limited to some of the more useful resources you might want to customize.

You should remember that any changes you make to the .mwmrc and .Xresources files are not reflected until you restart mwm. Having to wait to see the fruits of your labor, continuously restarting mwm to see whether the changes you make to the files are really what you want, is a bit frustrating. But that's the way it works. You restart mwm by choosing Restart in the Root menu.

When you make changes in the .Xresources file, you need to load these changes into the resource database by using the following command:

```
% xrdb -load .Xresources
```

where .Xresources is the file that contains the resource information. This command replaces all the present settings in the resource database with the new ones in the .Xresources file you customized. If you just want to add new settings to the .Xresources file, use the -merge option. Again, after you change the .Xresources file, you need to restart mwm to let the changes take effect.

Hard as it is to believe, sometimes the fruits of your labor aren't so great. X gives you a reprieve, however. You can revert to the system default resource specifications by using

the keystroke combination Shift+Ctrl+Meta+1. In response to this action, mwm displays
the dialog box shown in figure 16.19.

Figure 16.19
Toggling between
default and
customized
resource
specifications.

Using the keystroke combination enables you to switch back and forth between your
customized specifications and the default resource specifications. mwm uses the function
f.set_behavior to do the switching.

If you plan to do a lot of customizing, you might like the toggle function
available to you in the Root menu. Actually, the function is written into the
default .mwmrc file but is commented out. To add the menu item Toggle
Behavior to your Root menu, simply remove the comment marks in the .mwmrc
file. Make sure that you also add the option to your customized .mwmrc file;
otherwise, you still have to use Shift+Ctrl+Meta+1 to get from the customized to
the default .mwmrc file.

Understanding the system.mwmrc File

Although it's long, the system.mwmrc file isn't difficult to read. The options are grouped
according to menu, keystroke, or button functionality. Lines that start with a pound sign
(#) or an exclamation point (!) are comment lines. Lines that start with a backslash (\) or
a code continuation character (➡) are continuations of the previous line.

The following list is the system.mwmrc file shipped with release 1.2 of OSF's Motif.
Remember, before you change parameters, make a copy of this file called .mwmrc in your
home directory. Otherwise, you might get stuck retyping this long file.

```
!
! (c) Copyright 1989, 1990, 1991, 1992 OPEN SOFTWARE FOUNDATION, INC.
! ALL RIGHTS RESERVED
!
!
! Motif Release 1.2
!


!!
!!   DEFAULT Mwm 1.2 RESOURCE DESCRIPTION FILE (system.mwmrc)
!!
```

```
!!  NOTE: To personalize this file, copy this file before editing it.
!!        Personalize copies of the Mwm resource file typically
!!        reside as:
!!
!!        $HOME/.mwmrc
!!


!!
!! Root Menu Description (this menu must be explicitly posted via
   ➡f.menu)
!!

Menu DefaultRootMenu
{
    "Root Menu"         f.title
    "New Window"          f.exec "xterm &"
    "Shuffle Up"         f.circle_up
    "Shuffle Down"          f.circle_down
    "Refresh"         f.refresh
    "Pack Icons"          f.pack_icons
    "Toggle Behavior..."     f.set_behavior
     no-label         f.separator
    "Restart..."          f.restart
    "Quit..."          f.quit_mwm

}

Menu RootMenu_1.1
{
    "Root Menu"          f.title
    "New Window"          f.exec "xterm &"
    "Shuffle Up"          f.circle_up
    "Shuffle Down"          f.circle_down
    "Refresh"          f.refresh
!    "Pack Icons"          f.pack_icons
!    "Toggle Behavior"      f.set_behavior
    no-label     f. seperator
    "Restart . . . "     f. restart
}


!!
!! Default Window Menu Description
!!
```

```
Menu Default Window Menu
}
    Restart    R    Alt<Key>F5     f. restore
    Move       M    Alt<Key>F7     f. move
    Size       S    Alt<Key>F8     f. resize
    Minimize   n    Alt<Key>F9     f. minimize
    Maximize   x    Alt<Key>F10     f. maximize
    Lower      L    Alt<Key>F3     f. lower
    no-label                       f.seperator
    Close      c    Alt<Key>F4     f. kill
}
!!
!! Key Binding Description
!!


Keys DefaultKeyBindings
{
    Shift<Key>Escape       window¦icon         f.post_wmenu
    Alt<Key>space          window¦icon         f.post_wmenu
    Alt<Key>Tab         root¦icon¦window    f.next_key
    Alt Shift<Key>Tab      root¦icon¦window    f.prev_key
    Alt<Key>Escape         root¦icon¦window    f.circle_down
    Alt Shift<Key>Escape    root¦icon¦window    f.circle_up
    Alt Shift Ctrl<Key>exclam root¦icon¦window    f.set_behavior
    Alt<Key>F6         window          f.next_key transient
    Alt Shift<Key>F6   window          f.prev_key transient
    Shift<Key>F10       icon           f.post_wmenu
!    Alt Shift<Key>Delete   root¦icon¦window    f.restart
}


!!
!! Button Binding Description(s)
!!


Buttons DefaultButtonBindings
{
    <Btn1Down>     icon¦frame     f.raise
    <Btn3Down>     icon¦frame     f.post_wmenu
    <Btn3Down>     root       f.menu     DefaultRootMenu
}
```

```
Buttons ExplicitButtonBindings
{
     <Btn1Down>     frame¦icon     f.raise
     <Btn3Down>     frame¦icon     f.post_wmenu
     <Btn3Down>     root           f.menu     DefaultRootMenu
!    <Btn1Up>       icon           f.restore
     Alt<Btn1Down>  window¦icon    f.lower
!    Alt<Btn2Down>  window¦icon    f.resize
!    Alt<Btn3Down>  window¦icon    f.move


}

Buttons PointerButtonBindings
{
     <Btn1Down>     frame¦icon     f.raise
     <Btn3Down>     frame¦icon     f.post_wmenu
     <Btn3Down>     root           f.menu     DefaultRootMenu
     <Btn1Down>     window         f.raise
!    <Btn1Up>       icon           f.restore
     Alt<Btn1Down>  window¦icon    f.lower
!    Alt<Btn2Down>  window¦icon    f.resize
!    Alt<Btn3Down>  window¦icon    f.move
}


!!
!!  END OF mwm RESOURCE DESCRIPTION FILE
!!
```

The first half of the system.mwmrc file defines the contents of the Root and Window menus. It pairs the menu option with the function. All the functions begin with the letter f. The function names are self explanatory. f.move, for example, moves a window. Some functions might be puzzling. In the list of menu options in the DefaultRootMenu menu, for example, you see the option no-label and the associated function f.separator. This function draws a line in the menu separating the last option, Quit, from the others.

To display menus with keystrokes or buttons, use the f.menu function along with the menu's name. You also use this function to create submenus.

Figure 16.4 shows one version of the Root menu, entitled DefaultRootMenu. But another version of the Root menu is entitled RootMenu_1.1. This menu is the Root menu for version 1.1 of the mwm. RootMenu_1.1 is not bound to any button or keystroke combination, so it's never displayed. You can display it, of course, by customizing the system.mwmrc file. But because the menu's functionality is duplicated with DefaultRootMenu, you have little reason to use RootMenu_1.1.

The syntax in DefaultRootMenu is simple:

```
"label"     function
```

The menu option Quit, for example, invokes the f.quit_mwm function on the Root menu. In the menu structure, the label invokes the associated function, and words in quotes display in the menu listing. You can see that adding or subtracting menu options is as easy as adding or deleting (or commenting out) label-function pairs.

The syntax in DefaultWindowMenu is slightly different:

```
label    mnemonic    shortcut key    function
```

Examine the following line:

```
Restore    _R        Alt<Key>F5    f.restore
```

The **R**estore menu option invokes the f.restore function, which you also can invoke by using the shortcut key Alt+F5 or the mnemonic R. The mnemonic invokes the function only when the menu is displayed. In this example, the R in **R**estore is underlined in the menu list. Pressing R after the menu is displayed invokes f.restore.

After the menu definitions come the key binding descriptions. The term binding simply means association. These descriptions associate keystroke combinations with predefined functions. Also listed are the places where the pointer must be for keystroke combinations to work. Those places are window, icon, and root.

The syntax in DefaultKeyBindings, then, is as follows:

```
Modifier Key<Key>Physical Key    place        function
```

More than one modifier key can exist. The term <Key> denotes that the following key name is the physical key (and last key) in the sequence. Examine the following line:

```
Alt<Key>Tab        root¦icon¦window    f.next_key
```

This line shows that pressing Alt+Tab invokes the f.next_key function (which moves the top window to the bottom of the stack) regardless of where the pointer is (root, icon, or window).

The title of the menu, DefaultKeyBindings, is listed in the .Xresources file. You can create a new menu of key bindings and refer to it rather than the default by changing the line in the .Xresources file to the following:

```
Mwm*keyBindings:        YourKeyBindings
```

You can even customize the bindings for specific clients. You can change the key bindings just in xterm windows, for example, by adding the following line to the .Xresources file:

```
Mwm*xterm*keyBindings:     YourXtermBindings
```

YourKeyBindings would remain valid for all clients other than xterm.

Following the key binding section is the button binding section. Its syntax is similar to the syntax for key bindings:

```
Modifier Key<Key>Button     place          function
```

Again, zero or more modifier keys might be associated with each button function.

The major difference from key bindings is that the pointer can be in more places. The valid locations of the pointer for buttons are window, icon, root, title, frame, border, and app. Title refers to the title bar. Border refers to the border of the frame but doesn't include the title bar. Frame refers just to the frame of the window. App refers just to the application area of the window. Window refers to frame and app put together. This wide variety of options provides great functional flexibility.

Notice that three sets of button bindings are listed. You specify the one you want to use in your .Xresources file in the following line:

```
Mwm*buttonBindings:     YourButtonBindings
```

The default button bindings setting specified in .Xresources is, not surprisingly, DefaultButtonBindings.

Changing the Root Menu

Now that you are familiar with the syntax of the .mwmrc file, you can change the menu options in the Root, Window, and Icon menus. You might, for example, add an option called Time that invokes the function f.exec "xclock&" to open a clock in the display. You can even use bitmapped icons rather than words as menu options. You can insert the picture of a mailbox in a menu, for example, by preceding its file name with the at (@) sign, in the following way:

```
@flagup     f.exec "xbiff&"
```

The file flagup contains a bitmapped picture of a mailbox. By selecting it in the menu, you invoke the xbiff client, which is the mail facility. Such pictures are generally in the /usr/include/X11/bitmaps directory. If a picture isn't there, you must provide the full path name to the picture file or change the default directory for bitmaps. You do so by changing the bitmapDirectory value in the .Xresources file.

As mentioned previously, some options in DefaultRootMenu are remarked out. To include the Toggle Behavior or Quit options, for example, simply erase the exclamation point (!) at the beginning of their respective lines.

Making New Menus and Submenus

Sometimes creating new menus instead of altering old ones makes more sense. Creating new menus is not difficult as long as you strictly follow the syntax of the menu structures in the .mwmrc file, and, of course, you need to invoke defined functions. If you make a mistake and mistype a defined function, or you choose the function f.nop (which means no operation), the corresponding menu option appears lighter than the other options, otherwise known as being "grayed out."

To display a menu by using the second button in the root window, you would add to the .mwmrc file the following line:

```
<Btn2Down>       root       f.menu       NewMenuName
```

You would then define NewMenuName in a menu structure by providing the menu options and their corresponding functions.

Sometimes, you might want to create a submenu (sometimes called a cascading menu) that appears to the right and slightly below the selected menu option. For this task, you first define the submenu just as you would a menu: by providing the menu options and their corresponding functions in a menu structure in the .mwmrc file. Next, you must add the f.menu function to the parent menu, as follows:

```
"Games"     f.menu       GamesMenu
```

Games is but one of a list of options in the parent menu. When the user chooses Games, mwm displays the GamesMenu submenu, as shown in figure 16.20.

Figure 16.20
A cascade menu.

Notice that f.menu also inserts an arrow to the right of Games in the Root menu. This character leads the user, correctly, to suspect that a submenu follows when the Games option is chosen. You can attach submenus to submenus forever, theoretically. In practice, however, the better approach is to keep the number of submenus to a minimum.

Customizing mwm Resources

You can change three kinds of things when you customize mwm:

✔ The appearance of the window frame, icons, and menus

✔ The functionality of components such as focus, key bindings, and button bindings

✔ The functionality of one or a class of X clients

Many resources are associated with each of these categories—far too many to discuss in this chapter. In the following paragraphs, however, you look at some of the more useful resources in each category.

Changing the Appearance of mwm Components

The mwm program controls the appearance of a variety of graphical and nongraphical elements, including dialog boxes, icons, windows, frames, and menus. The syntax of the line in the .Xresources files is as follows:

```
Mwm*[element]*[subelement]*feature:    selection
```

If you want to color the title bar of an xterm yellow, for example, you use the following description in the .Xresources file:

```
Mwm*client*title*background:    yellow
```

If you want to color the Games menu red, you use the following description:

```
Mwm*GamesMenu*background:    red
```

If you want everything to have a white background, use the following description:

```
Mwm*background:    white
```

As you can see from the examples, you specify the exact element you want to modify; otherwise, as in the last example, the resource affects all graphical objects. In the last example, all backgrounds, including the backgrounds of menus, X clients, title bars, frames, scroll bars, and windows, are turned white.

To make the background of the window in focus different from the backgrounds of all the other windows, you use activeBackground rather than background in your .Xresources file.

The names for many resources are transparent, as shown in table 16.6.

Table 16.6
Resource Names

Feature	Resource Name
Title bar	title
Menu	menu
Icon	icon
Client window frame	client
Dialog box	feedback

Changing the Functionality of mwm Components

You can change the functionality of all X clients through the .Xresources file. You can, for example, choose a set of buttons to use, define whether you will use explicit or pointer focus, or choose a set of key bindings.

The syntax to do such things follows:

```
Mwm*resource_variable:    setting
```

Remember, for example, that three sets of buttons are defined in .mwmrc: DefaultButtonBindings, ExplicitBindings, and PointerButtonBindings. To choose one of them, you must use the following line in the .Xresources file:

```
Mwm*buttonBindings:    PointerButtonBindings
```

This line activates the button set called PointerButtonBindings (which uses the pointer focus policy).

You use the same procedure to define key bindings. Because .mwmrc contains only one set of key bindings, the keybindings resource automatically defaults to this set, called DefaultKeyBindings.

The last two examples point out the importance of coordinating the .mwmrc and .Xresources files. Although you might change settings in one set of button bindings in .mwmrc, they don't take effect unless that set is specified in the .Xresources file.

Another popular resource to set is the focus policy. As you might remember, you can choose *explicit*, in which you give focus to a window by clicking in it, and *pointer*, in which you give focus to a window simply by moving the cursor into it. The default in mwm is explicit. The line that defines that setting in .Xresources follows:

```
Mwm*keyboardFocusPolicy:        explicit
```

To change the keyboard focus policy to pointer, simply change the explicit setting in this line to pointer.

Changing the Functionality of Specific X Clients

You can change the functionality of one, a class, or all X clients by using .Xresources. You might, for example, elect to eliminate some of the functionality of the frame for some X clients. You might elect to eliminate the Maximize button on X term windows. Or you might choose to add a Maximize button to an oclock window.

You also can alter the appearance of specific X clients. You can, for example, define the bitmapped image that appears in icons for each X client.

The syntax to perform such tasks is as follows:

```
Mwm*XclientName*resource_variable:    setting
```

XclientName is the name of the X client, or the group of X clients, affected. The resource_variable defines the element being customized. And setting defines the value of the resource variable—for example, true or false.

If you don't know the name of the X client, run xprop and click on the X client. The name is contained in the WM_CLASS property. If the window manager doesn't know the name of the X client (a rare occurrence), you can still manipulate the functionality of the client by using the literal **defaults** for the name of the application. Of course, all X clients whose names are not known to the window manager also inherit the new functionality.

If you want to set a resource variable for all X clients, you simply omit the XclientName. The syntax then is

```
Mwm*resource_variable:    setting
```

Perhaps the most commonly used resource variable is focusAutoRaise. You use this resource to define whether or not a window rises to the top of the stack of windows and icons when it is in focus. To raise a window to the top of the stack when the window receives focus, for example, you use the following description:

```
Mwm*focusAutoRaise:    true
```

The variable focusAutoRaise does have several defaults. It defaults to true when you are using explicit (click-to-type) focus, and false when you are using pointer focus. Those settings are probably the ones you want. For kicks, you can change the variable to true when using pointer focus. That means that whenever the pointer drifts over a window, it rises to the top of the stack. When you move the pointer around the screen, windows reshuffle madly. Of course, the entertainment lasts for only a few minutes. After the thrill is gone, you can see how miserable such a setting would be in which to work. Likewise, setting the variable to false when using explicit focus requires additional work—and is not nearly as amusing.

You also can specify focusAutoRaise differently for clients. You could change the focus policy for the mail client, for instance, by adding the following description:

```
Mwm*xbiff*focusAutoRaise:    false
```

Although setting focus policies separately is possible, it's not practical. Making the focus policy of clients inconsistent would primarily cause confusion and frustration. Unless you have an overwhelming need, keep X client functionality consistent and easy.

Creating Icon Boxes

An *icon box* contains icons of all active windows. Without an icon box, icons appear on-screen only when you iconify a window. With an icon box, an icon appears for each active window whether or not it is iconified.

The display for an iconified window and a restored window differs. When a window is iconified, the icon appears three-dimensional. It has bold outlines. The title of the icon occupies its own (connected) box, and the frame of the icon is shaded. When a window is present in the display, the corresponding icon appears smaller and flatter. The frame of the icon is not shaded, and the title of the icon is not set off by itself. Figure 16.21 shows an icon box with one iconified and two maximized windows.

Figure 16.21
Three- and two-dimensional icons in the icon box.

To turn on the icon box, you must add the following line to your .Xresources file:

```
Mwm*useIconBox:    true
```

This command displays an icon box every time mwm starts. The default size of the icon box is six icons across, one icon high. The default position of the icon box is the lower left corner of the display. You can change the size of the icon box by using the mouse pointer to pull or push the sides and corners of the box. When you restart mwm, however, the icon box returns to its default location and size.

To change the default size of the icon box, use a command similar to the following:

```
Mwm*iconBoxGeometry:    4x2+0-0
```

This line makes an icon box that is four icons wide by two icons high.

To change the default location of the icon box on the display, use a command similar to the following:

```
Mwm*iconBoxGeometry:    4x2-0+0
```

This line positions the same four by two icon box in the upper right corner. The first plus or minus sign specifies the right (-) or left (+) side of the display, and the second plus or minus sign specifies the top (+) or bottom (-) of the screen. If you intend to leave the box in its default position (+0-0, lower left corner of the display), you don't even need to include the +0-0.

You operate on the icons in the icon box by single- or double-clicking on the icons. If you use the left (or first) mouse button to double-click on a three-dimensional icon, the window it represents is restored, the icon becomes flat, and the restored window rises to the top of the stack and takes the focus. If you double-click on a two-dimensional icon, the window it represents rises to the top of the stack. The icon box, however, retains focus.

If you use the left (or first) mouse button to single-click on an icon, mwm displays the Window menu for icons. The Window menu for icons contains the same menu options described previously, including **R**estore, **M**ove, Ma**x**imize, and **C**lose, as shown in figure 16.22.

Figure 16.22
The Window menu
of an icon in an
icon box.

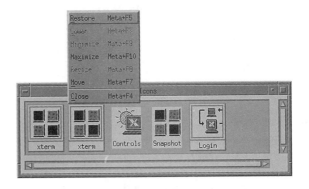

The **R**estore command redisplays the iconified window. The **M**ove option enables you to move the icon in the icon box. You might like to rearrange icons in groups that make sense, for example, grouping together different word processor applications. Because you can move an icon by clicking and holding down the first mouse button, however, you don't have much need for the **M**ove option. The Ma**x**imize option increases the size of the corresponding window to the full size of the screen. The **C**lose option terminates the window process, and both the icon and the window (if it's in the display) disappear. (Note that if the corresponding window is already displayed, only the **M**ove and **C**lose options are available. The others are grayed out.)

The icon box itself has some functionality. First, you can see in figure 16.22 that the icon box has both horizontal and vertical scroll bars. Thus, many icons in the icon box might be out of sight. Simply move the scroll bars to display all the icons in the icon box.

The icon box has the same Window menu as the icons, except that instead of having a <u>C</u>lose option, the menu has a Pack Icons option (Shift+Alt+F7). The Pack Icons option simply moves together the icons in the icon box. When you close X clients, the icon disappears, which leaves a blank space in the icon box. You could move the remaining icons to fill the hole or, more easily, use the Pack Icons option. When you choose Pack Icons, mwm fills all blank spaces.

You might also use the Pack Icons option when you resize the icon box. If, for example, you add more rows of icons to the icon box, you can use the Pack Icons option to fill the second and subsequent rows in the icon box, or you can tediously move the icons yourself. Figure 16.23 shows the icon box before and after the Pack Icons option is chosen.

Figure 16.23
The icon box before and after the Pack Icons option is chosen.

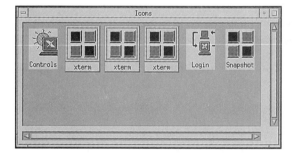

Customizing Resources

You can customize the appearance and functionality of mwm resources, such as the color of the frame of an xterm, or the focus policy. You can customize a class of re-sources or specific instances of resources. You can color the background of all menus white, for example, or you can color the background of each menu differently.

You can customize resources individually from the command line. When you have a lot of resources to modify, however, the command line is an impractical means of entering the changes. Instead, X provides resource files, called .Xdefaults or .Xresources. In these files the resource variables are set equal to boolean values, such as true/false, or string constants, such as blue or red. By collecting all the resources into one file, you can easily modify many resources at once.

Note If you do change resource settings on the command line, the changes take precedence over the settings in the resource files.

These resource files are automatically read at system startup and user login by the resource manager. The resources are read from general to specific so that you can set defaults and then modify individual resources. You might color the foregrounds of all buttons white, for example, but set the foreground color of the help button to blue. You can even color the foreground of all resources on a single line.

The resource files are in the home directory. They specify the appearance and functionality of all the X clients you run. The system administrator also can set up default resource settings for the system or create default resource settings for each machine or for groups of machines on a network, using the xrdb (which stands for X Resource DataBase manager) program.

The resources that each X client uses varies. To learn about the specific resources that an X client uses, you must consult a reference book about the X client. Although X clients use a variety of resources, most are written to use the X Toolkit.

The *X Toolkit* provides the programmer with a standard set of widgets, such as buttons, menus, dialog boxes, and scroll bars. The Toolkit saves programmers from performing redundant work. It also gives all applications a consistent look.

The syntax for resource settings is also consistent across X clients. The following line shows the syntax of resource settings:

```
[X client]*resource_variable:      setting
```

The brackets mean that the enclosed parts of the statement are optional. With that in mind, the simplest resource setting is as follows:

```
*resource_variable:    setting
```

The following line, for example, makes the foreground of all X clients white:

```
*foreground:    white
```

If you change the line to the following:

```
xterm*foreground:     white
```

Then the line pertains only to xterms.

Finally, you could change the line to the following:

```
xterm*Menu.foreground:     white
```

This line makes the foreground of the menus in xterms white. You can continue going down the hierarchy until you reach an atomic unit—for example, the color of the option Chess on the Games menu in the xterm. Rather than provide examples *ad nauseam,* you can see the pattern of proceeding down through the widget hierarchy until you reach the one whose attributes you want to set. Perhaps the most descriptive syntax statement for setting a resource is expressed by the following line:

```
[X client]*[object] [.subobject...] [.] resource_variable:     setting
```

You use the single period in brackets whenever you specify an object. If you don't specify an object, you don't need the period. You can substitute periods for asterisks and asterisks for periods depending on the widget hierarchy.

You have the option of specifying the resource setting of each subobject or, if the subobjects are instances of the same class of objects, specifying the resource setting of all the instances by setting the class of the objects. The color of the pointer, foreground, and cursor, for example, are instances of the class Foreground. The next two groups of settings are thus equivalent:

```
*foreground:       black
*pointerColor:       black
*cursorColor:       black
```

is the same as

```
*Foreground:       black
```

Notice that class names start with a capital letter, and instances begin with lowercase letters. In compound words like cursorColor, however, the first letter of each new word is capitalized. The capitalization is for reading purposes only. It has nothing to do with class names.

You use class names to set resource defaults for an entire class of objects and instances of objects to modify specific objects. You might, for example, use the following settings:

```
*Foreground:           black
xterm*pointerColor:       red
```

In this example, the first line makes the foreground, pointer, and cursor color of all widgets (that have those objects) black. The second line changes the color of the pointer in xterms to red.

Now that you understand the meaning of the asterisk, you can understand why a resource setting that doesn't specify an X client, such as `*Foreground:` `black`, must start with an asterisk. It connects the Foreground class variable to all X clients.

You might wonder when you should use an asterisk (*) and when to use a period (.) in a resource statement. Each represents a different type of *binding*, a term that refers to the proximity of the objects on either side of the period or asterisk. The asterisk represents a loose binding. The period represents a tight binding. If you use a period, the objects on either side of the period must be adjacent in the hierarchy of widgets. If you use the asterisk, the objects on either side can be near or far from one another in the widget hierarchy. In this sense, the asterisk is like a wild card: it enables you to traverse the intervening layers of widgets without specifying them. (Don't use the asterisk as you would in C, where it means zero or more alphanumeric characters!)

You don't get extra points for using periods instead of asterisks. To be safe, using asterisks makes sense. Also, if a programmer decides to put a new layer of objects into the widget hierarchy, you have to go back and change all the resource settings that use a period.

If you choose to use periods, be careful. The resource manager doesn't provide error messages. Your resources therefore might not function as you expect. `xterm.scrollbar:true`, for example, is an invalid statement because `xterm` and `scrollbar` are not adjacent in the widget hierarchy. The resource manager, however, would not tell you so. The scroll bar simply wouldn't appear in the xterm.

Using Wild Card

You saw previously how the asterisk works something like a wild-card connector. As of release 5, X also includes the question mark (?) wild card. Again, its usage is different from that in C. In C, the question mark can represent any single alphanumeric character. In X, the question mark represents any widget. Generally, you use the question mark with tight bindings when you want to affect many widgets in a particular layer of the widget hierarchy. Look at the following line as an example:

```
xterm.?.?.foreground:        black
```

This line specifies that the foreground color of all widgets two levels below xterm is black. But the line pertains only to the grandchildren of xterm, not the levels below it.

If, instead, you want the foregrounds of the grandchildren of xterm, as well as all great-grandchildren further down the hierarchical line, to be black, you use an asterisk in the following way:

```
xterm.?.?*foreground:        black
```

In this line, an asterisk replaces the second period. This loose binding connects the attribute `foreground` to all the grandchildren and further descendants of xterm.

From this example you can see that both the question mark and the asterisk are wild cards that connect one layer of widget hierarchy to another. The question mark connects widgets across one layer. The asterisk connects widgets across multiple layers of hierarchy.

Determining the Precedence of Resource Settings

In preceding examples, you've seen that having conflicting resource settings is perfectly okay. The following lines, for example, set the default foreground colors for all X clients and the color of pointers in xterm windows:

```
*Foreground:           black
xterm*pointerColor:    red
```

These settings obviously conflict. A general rule determines which setting has precedence: the more specific the definition of the widget, the higher its precedence. In the preceding example, the instance pointerColor is more specific than the class name Foreground, so pointerColor takes precedence over Foreground. This order of precedence is the way you want things to work because you can specify default settings and then make specific modifications. If the precedence worked in the opposite direction, you would have to specify every resource setting.

You can generalize the precedence from a number of common types of resource conflicts:

✔ **An instance takes precedence over a class.** `*foreground`, for example, takes precedence over `*Foreground`.

✔ **Tight bindings take precedence over loose bindings.** Tight bindings are far more specific than loose bindings and therefore take precedence. `xterm.?.scrollbar` is more specific, for example, and therefore takes precedence over `xterm*scrollbar`.

✔ **A line that specifies an X client takes precedence over one that doesn't.** `xterm*foreground`, for example, takes precedence over `*foreground`.

✔ **A specific X client or a specific widget takes precedence over a wild card.** `xterm*foreground` takes precedence over `?*foreground`, for example, and `xterm*help.foreground` (help is an instance of the Button class—it's the help button) takes precedence over `xterm*?.foreground`.

Presenting in this chapter all the available resources in the X Toolkit is impossible. Table 16.7 presents some of the resources used most often.

Table 16.7
Common Resources in the X Toolkit

Class	Instance	Default	Definition
BorderWidth	borderWidth	1 pixel	Width of the border
BorderColor	borderColor	Black	Color of the border
Class	Instance	Default	Definition
Background	background	White	Color of the background
Foreground	foreground	Black	Color of the foreground

Customizing Functionality

Just as you can modify the appearance of X clients, you can alter their functionality. User input information, such as keystrokes and mouse actions, is passed from server to X client in the form of messages, also called *events*. Events tell the X client that it needs to respond to something—for example, a keystroke. The resource manager can match events with appropriate actions. This matching process is called *translating*.

Actually, messages convey information other than just user input. In fact, most of the messages an application sends are invisible to the user. Because the interest in this section is only in the functionality of the user interface, the text discussion of messages is limited to those of which the user is aware, namely, user input and the actions taken in response to those inputs.

Because each X client has to respond to many different events, the resource manager uses a table listing many event translations. Each X client comes with a default translation table. In an xterm window, for example, you can select and copy text to the Clipboard by using the mouse. The actions are listed in the following chart:

Event	Translation
1. Click first mouse button	Deselect anything else and begin selecting new text.
2. Move mouse over text	Define section, using inverse video.
3. Release button	End selection and copy selection to Clipboard.

Notice how atomistic this approach is in describing a simple event. Translation tables are similarly atomistic. The section of the translation table for the xterm client pertinent to this event follows:

```
<Btn1Down>:      select-start()\n\
<Btn1Motion>:      select-extend()\n\
<Btn1Up>:          select-end(PRIMARY,CUT_BUFFER0)
```

You see that the translation table is also grouped into *event-action* pairs.

Translation tables are embedded in the X client and for that reason can't be modified. To modify event or action definitions, you must create your own translation table that supersedes the settings in the default table. You do so by using the following syntax:

```
[object][*subobject...]*Translations:       #override\
   [modifier]<event>:    action
```

Notice that each line except the last one terminates with a backslash (\), which means that the next line is a continuation of the previous line. This design is necessary because elements in the translation table must comprise a single string.

The `modifier` can be a key or a mouse button. The reserved words, `Translations` and `#override`, tell the resource manager to modify the translations for `object`. Events are superseded only if they match identically the default events in the translation table; otherwise, their functionality is appended to the default translation table. In the preceding example, if you replace Btn1 with Btn2, Btn1 maintains its default functionality. If, however, you change the actions of Btn1 events, you override the default translations.

If you're left handed, you might like to make the following translation modifications:

```
xterm*Translations:           #override\
   <Btn3Down>:      select-start()\n\
   <Btn3Motion>:      select-extend()\n\
   <Btn3Up>:          select-end(PRIMARY,CUT_BUFFER0)
```

With this modification, you can now use the third button on the mouse to perform a copy operation. This translation replaces any other functionality of the third button. The first button, at this point, retains its default functionality.

To paste the selection, you use a line similar to the following:

```
Ctrl <Btn1Up>:    insert-selection(PRIMARY, CUT_BUFFER0)
```

This line inserts the contents of PRIMARY, or, if it is empty, CUT_BUFFER0, at the cursor when you hold down the Ctrl key and click the first button (the up, not the down, movement of the button causes the paste). Although you haven't explicitly redefined `<Btn1Down>`, you no longer want its default action, which is to deselect everything and begin a select action, as explained previously. For this reason, you should redefine `<Btn1Down>`.

Summary

This chapter has covered the basics of how to use the Motif GUI, from using the frame and hidden menus to using a variety of widgets. After learning about the basics, you looked at customizing the Motif Window Manager.

After reading this chapter, you should feel comfortable using the Motif GUI. Covering the functionality of all the widgets in Motif is impossible. But you should be able to interact effectively with unfamiliar widgets based on the widgets discussed in this chapter.

Chapter Snapshot

Sun Microsystems created the OpenWindows interface and continues to ship it with every graphical version of their product. Several other vendors also include it with their UNIX versions. This chapter walks through the OpenWindows interface and addresses by covering the following topics:

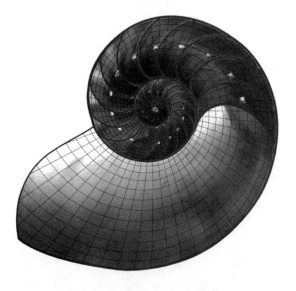

CHAPTER

OpenWin - Desktop

When the *graphical-user interface* (GUI) became popular on UNIX workstations, many companies created their own GUIs. In the last chapter, you learned about Motif, which is not associated with any computer platform. Open-Windows is another GUI that accomplishes many of the same tasks as Motif. Open-Windows, however, is specific to Sun Microsystems' computer platforms. It is a robust interface that includes plenty of helpful widgets.

Sun Microsystems continues to distribute OpenWindows; but because of the COSE agreement, Sun makes Motif the default GUI on their workstations. Users can, if they prefer, switch to OpenWindows.

This chapter introduces you to the operation of all the major OpenWindows tools.

Understanding OpenWindows Basics

Many of the windowing concepts presented in the preceding two chapters apply to OpenWindows. Even if the names of objects or tasks in OpenWindows differ from those in Motif, they perform the same function. For example, what Motif calls the *root window*, OpenWindows calls the *Workspace*—a more appropriate name because the Workspace doesn't behave at all like a window. Or, for example, to exit a window in Motif, you double-click on the icon on the left side of the title bar; in OpenWindows, you click on the push pin on the left side of the title bar.

Windows function the same in OpenWindows and Motif. In OpenWindows, as in Motif, you can move, resize, iconify, restore, and exit window—and you use similar means to accomplish these tasks. So, you already know how to perform many important functions in OpenWindows.

Starting OpenWindows

To start OpenWindows, enter the following command at the command prompt:

```
% openwin
```

Depending on your setup, many OpenWindows widgets might appear on the Workspace. As is the case in all windowing systems, each application appears in its own window. The File Manager, for example, occupies its own window. To exit the File Manager, you can close its window by double-clicking on the Window Menu button on the left side of the title bar. Just as in Motif, all windows have similar functionality. You can perform the following tasks on all windows:

- ✔ Move a window by grabbing the title area with the left mouse button

- ✔ Raise a window to the top of the stack by clicking on the title area

- ✔ Resize a window by grabbing a corner of a window and pushing or pulling

- ✔ Iconify and restore a window by clicking on the push pin (so it comes out) and by double-clicking on an icon, respectively

In this chapter, the term *grab* means to click and hold down the mouse button. For example, grabbing the title area of a window means to place the mouse cursor on the title area of the window and click and hold down the mouse button.

Somewhat different from Motif, however, is that OpenWindows has two kinds of windows: base and pop-up. These windows are discussed at greater length later in the chapter.

Using the Mouse

You can't use OpenWindows effectively without using a mouse. Each button on the mouse performs a different task. OpenWindows gives each button a name; from left to right, the button names are Select, Adjust, and Menu, as shown in figure 17.1.

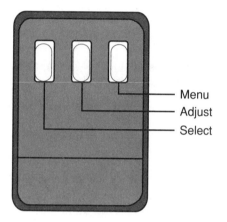

Figure 17.1
Mouse button names.

Menu
Adjust
Select

The *Select* button is the workhorse of the three. You use it to select objects, such as desktop widgets, menu items, and text. You also use the Select button to initiate actions by, for example, clicking on buttons. Finally, you use the Select button to move and resize desktop objects.

When this chapter instructs you to click on an object, use the Select button unless otherwise stated.

The *Adjust* button adjusts selections made with the Select button. You can either select additional items or deselect items using the Adjust button.

The *Menu* button pops up hidden menus according to the location of the mouse cursor. To pop up the Workspace menu, for example, click the Menu mouse button anywhere on the Workspace, and the Workspace menu pops up at that location.

IV

Graphic User Interfaces

Understanding Mouse Cursors

OpenWindows uses a variety of mouse cursors to give the user immediate feedback about the work the mouse is performing. Table 17.1 describes some of the most common mouse cursors.

Table 17.1
Common Mouse Cursors

Cursor	Description
Arrow	The default cursor that selects objects
Clock	Tells the user to wait because the application the mouse cursor is on is busy
Question	Indicates that the selection made by the mouse is incorrect
Text move	Appears as an arrow pointing away from a selected object; shows the object is ready to move using the mouse
Drop pointer	Appears as crosshairs when a desktop object is dragged over a place where it can be dropped

Window Functionality

Just as in Motif, the frame of a window embodies a great deal of functionality. Most tasks you accomplish using the frame are similar to those performed in Motif. The graphical tools, however, that accomplish those tasks are different.

This section examines some tasks you are familiar with from working with Motif. For example, to display the Window menu, use the Menu mouse button to click on the Window Menu button in the upper left corner of the window. If you click on this button with the Select button on the mouse, you execute the menu's default function, usually to close the window.

You also can click on any part of the border with the Menu button to display the Window menu. This functionality is valuable whenever the top part of the window is covered.

The pane in which the application's data is displayed has its own pop-up menu that you display by clicking on the pane with the Menu mouse button. This functionality is explored in greater detail later in this chapter.

Tip — If you hold down the Alt key while pressing the Menu mouse button over the pane, the Window menu displays.

Under the pane is the area that displays feedback and error messages.

The Scroll Bar

More functionality is hidden in the scroll bar than many people recognize. You use the scroll bar to move the contents in the pane left, right, up, or down according to the action you take with the scroll bar. You can operate the scroll bar in many ways:

✔ Grab the center of the slider and move the mouse in the appropriate direction: left or right, for horizontal scroll bars; up or down, for vertical scroll bars.

✔ Click on one of the arrows on the slider to move the slider one step at a time.

✔ Grab one of the arrows on the slider to scroll in the direction of the arrow.

✔ Click on the scroll bar, but not on the slider, to move the slider one screen at a time.

✔ Grab the scroll bar, but not on the slider, to scroll through a file a page at a time.

✔ Click on the boxes at the extremes of the scroll bar to go to the extreme of the scroll bar all at once, for example, on a vertical scroll bar, clicking on the bottom box in the scroll bar makes the slider jump to the bottom of the scroll bar.

✔ Click on the slider or scroll bar with the Menu button to display the Scroll bar pop-up menu and select an action on it.

On either side of the slider in the scroll bar is a dark line that indicates what percentage of the entire file is in the pane.

For example, if the dark line is long, the text displayed in the pane represents a large percentage of the entire file. If you were writing a book, the line would start out very long, but as you added pages to your book, the line would grow shorter and shorter.

Resizing Windows

In Motif, you can't tell whether you can grab a corner of a window and resize it. OpenWindows, however, marks corners that you can resize with what looks like a metal corner. Only corners drawn with metal corners have resize functionality.

IV

Graphic User Interfaces

To resize a window, grab a resizable corner with the Select button and move the mouse to resize the window. If you press and hold down the Ctrl key before clicking on the corner, the window resizes in only one direction: the direction you move first, either horizontally or vertically.

Closing Windows

The push pin in the upper left corner of window provides the graphical representation of whether the window is "pinned up" in the Workspace. The push pin has three states: stuck in, pulled out, and pulled out (sic). Really! It's a bit confusing. When the pin is stuck in, the window is there to stay regardless of what you do in it. If you click on a stuck-in pin, the pin pulls out, and the window disappears. So far, so good. Some windows appear with the pin already pulled out.

The pin pulled out means that the window will close when you perform an action in the window, for example, clicking on a button. To close such a window without completing an action in it, you click on the pin, which sticks it into the window, and then click on it a second time to pull it out.

Using Pop-Up Windows

Many windows in OpenWindows have additional window associated with them. Unlike pop-up menus, these windows persist when the mouse button is released. You generally move them off to the side or close them after using them. They are children of the main window, so if the main window is either iconified or closed, the associated pop-up windows iconify or close as well.

Table 17.2 describes three types of pop-up windows.

Table 17.2
Pop-up Window Types

Window Type	Description
Execution	Sets parameters, sets properties of objects, or executes commands that affect the content of the pane
Help	Displays useful information about the functionality of OpenWindows components
Status	Stops the application to provide vital information and may ask for user confirmation

Execution windows generally display when you click on buttons that have a name plus an ellipsis (...). They look exactly like a normal window. In the window, you execute a function, such as searching for a word.

Help windows are context-oriented. When a desktop object is highlighted or the cursor is over a specific desktop object, the Help window displays information relevant to the highlighted object.

You display Help windows by pressing the Help key on the keyboard. After you are in the help system, you can navigate to other topics for additional reading.

Status windows require immediate user input. All input is disabled except for the input fields or buttons on the Status window. A common example of a Status window is a window that confirms that you want to erase a file.

Pop-Up Menus

OpenWindows provides three hidden pop-up menus, as follows:

- ✔ Workspace menu

- ✔ Window Manager menu

- ✔ Pop-up menu

You access each one by pressing the Menu mouse button while the mouse cursor is over the Workspace, title area, or pop-up window, respectively.

Workspace Menu

When you click on the Workspace with the Menu mouse button, the Workspace menu appears.

Notice that the first item in the list of menu options is circled. The circle designates the default option of the menu. You can execute the default option without displaying the Workspace menu. For example, to execute the Program option, the default of the Workspace menu, double-click in the Workspace using the Select button.

When an arrow appears beside a menu option, clicking on the menu option opens a child menu of the first. For example, when you click on the Program menu option, the Programs menu appears.

IV

Graphic User Interfaces

The Programs Menu

Clicking on the Programs option in the Workspace menu displays the Programs menu. The Programs menu contains many of the desktop tools you use every day. Many are important applications, such as the clock, calendar, mail icon, and snapshot. Other menu items are important management tools, such as the File Manager and the Print Tool.

The last item on the menu displays a child menu of demonstration programs, such as solitaire, Xsol.

The Utilities Menu

Clicking on the Utilities option in the Workspace menu displays the Utilities menu. Table 17.3 explains the menu items on the Utilities menu.

Table 17.3
Utilities Menu Options

Menu Option	Description
Refresh	Redraws all the graphical objects in the Workspace
Reset Input	Resets input from the keyboard
Window Controls	Displays a pop-up menu with the following options: Open/Close, Full/Restore Size, Back, and Quit
Save Workspace	Saves all the windows and icons displayed in the workspace in their present sizes and locations
Lock Screen	Covers the workspace with a white screen and a request to enter a password
Console	Opens a console, as a command tool, in which warning and error messages are displayed

You use the Refresh option when, for some reason, the windows on the Workspace are incorrectly drawn.

The menu options in the Window Controls pop-up menu are a subset of those in the Window menu, discussed later in this chapter.

The Save Workspace option enables you to run favorite applications automatically at the start of OpenWindows. Simply open all the widgets you always like displayed, such as the clock, the performance meter, and the File Manager, and click on the Save Workspace option. To edit the initial setup of your Workspace, open or close widgets and click on the Save Workspace option.

The Properties Option

The Properties Menu provides many ways for you to set the properties of the environment, such as colors and mouse actions. This is discussed in more detail later.

The Help Option

Choosing the Help option opens the Help Viewer window.

Each entry represents a chapter in a book. To turn to a specific chapter, double-click on it. Help is context-specific, so if you seek help while a particular window is in focus, the Help Viewer displays information about the content of that window.

The Exit Option

Choosing the Exit option quits OpenWindows and returns you to a shell prompt.

Using the Window Menu

The Window menu offers options that manipulate the window, not the application running in the window. The options enable you to move, close, and resize the window.

The Close Option

Selecting the Close option iconifies the window—that is, the window and all its associated pop-up windows disappear, and an icon, representing the window, appears in the Workspace. You use the Close option when you need more room in the Workspace but don't want to exit an application.

The Close option is the menu default. Using the Select button to click on the Window menu button iconifies the window.

The Full Size Option

Selecting the Full Size option expands the window to the size of the entire screen. When the window fills the screen, the menu option changes to Restore. Selecting the Restore option changes the window back to its previous size.

You can expand a window to the size of the screen, or conversely, change it back to its previous size by double-clicking on the title or border area of the window.

IV

Graphic User Interfaces

The Move Option

You have little need to select the Move option because you can grab and drag the title area of a window directly. OpenWindows, however, does offer more sophisticated moves. For example, to move more than one window at a time, use the Select button to highlight the first window; then use the Adjust button to highlight more windows. Now when you move a window, all highlighted windows move correspondingly.

 When you move a window, OpenWindows displays an outline of the window for you to move. To move the window itself, hold down the Shift key while you grab and drag the window.

To make a window move only horizontally or vertically, hold down the Ctrl key as you grab and drag a window.

The Resize Option

You probably will not use this option either. The metal-looking corners on windows that identify them as resizable enable you to resize windows directly. You can accomplish the same task by using the Resize option. After selecting it, use the arrow keys on the keyboard to shrink or expand the window. When you are finished, press Enter.

The Back Option

Selecting the Back option moves the window behind all others in the display. To move a window to the top of all other windows, click on the window's title bar.

The Refresh Option

The Refresh option redraws all the windows in the display. Use this option if, for some reason, all the windows are not displayed fully.

The Quit Option

Select the Quit option when you want to exit an application.

Using the Pop-Up Menu

Display the pop-up menu by pressing the Menu button while the cursor is on a pop-up menu.

The Dismiss Option

The Dismiss option is the default. When you select the Dismiss option, OpenWindows displays a child window with two options: This Window and All Pop-ups. The first option exits the current pop-up window. The second option makes all the pop-ups on the Workspace exit.

The Move Option

When you select the Move option, you can move the pop-up window in the same way that you would move a base window: grab and drag it around the Workspace.

The Resizing Option

You resize pop-up menus just as you would base windows: grab a corner and push or pull. Like base windows, you can only resize pop-up menus that have the metal-looking corners. If the pop-up menu does not have metal corners, the Resizing option is grayed out.

The Back Option

Use the Back option to move the pop-up menu underneath other windows. Use this option to display buried windows.

The Refresh Option

The Refresh option redraws all the windows in the display. You use this option if, for some reason, all the windows do not display fully.

The Owner? Option

The Owner? option shows you which base window owns the pop-up window. When you select the Owner? option, the title area of the parent window flashes five times.

Using Important OpenWindows Tools

Now that you have control over the pop-up menus and the tasks performed by the mouse, you are well prepared to interact with the other tools provided by OpenWindows. Providing an exhaustive discussion of any one tool is beyond the scope of this book. This section does provide, however, more than the basic information you need to know to effectively operate in the OpenWindows environment.

Using the File Manager

You use the File Manager to copy, move, delete, and organize your files. The organization model is to group together files that have a similar purpose; for example, you might group together the chapters of a book where each chapter is a separate file. OpenWindows uses the desktop metaphor to represent the tools that groups files: the folder. The folder in OpenWindows is equivalent to a directory in other environments. By opening and closing a folder, you go "down" or "up" the hierarchy of files, respectively. The folder metaphor has the advantage of being graphical: a folder you can portray as open or closed; a directory has no such visual counterpart.

Files are arranged in a hierarchy. The highest level is called the *root directory*, or *root folder*. It is represented by a forward slash (/).

For the remainder of the chapter, unless stated to the contrary, slash means forward slash.

The root folder can hold files as well as folders. In other systems, these folders would be called *subfolders*. These folders can, in turn, contain folders and so on. The end result is a hierarchical tree of files and folders. Figure 17.2 shows such a hierarchy.

Figure 17.2
Hierarchy of files
and folders.

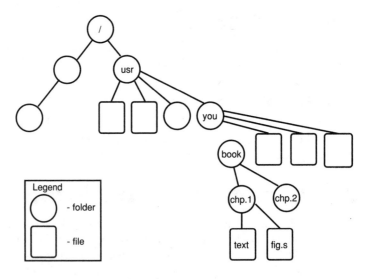

Notice that as you navigate "up" the tree—toward the root folder—the folder topics become more generic. This pattern is the organizational principle of a hierarchy: from generic (top) to specific (bottom).

As you move down the tree, selecting one branch after another traces a path of folders until you end with a file. This path is called the *pathname*. The *absolute pathname* includes the entire path of folders from the root to a specific file, for example:

```
% cd /usr/you/book/chp.1/text
```

A *relative pathname* designates a file in the current directory, for example:

```
%cd text
```

The File Manager displays graphical representations of files and folders within folders.

The File Manager window has several important areas, as follows:

- ✔ Menu buttons access the File Manager's functionality.

- ✔ Line of folders shows the absolute pathname to the current folder.

- ✔ File pane shows the files and folders in the current folder.

The last folder in the line of folders is the current folder.

You open files by double-clicking on them. Move down the file tree by double-clicking on—opening—folders in the file pane; move up the file tree by clicking on a folder in the line of folders.

Another way to change the directory you are in is by typing the name of the new directory in the Goto field located in the Menu bar.

When you click on the Goto button, the drop down menu displays the nine folders you most recently used.

If you want to go back to any of those folders, double-clicking on the appropriate entry transports you to that folder and file.

Starting File Manager

To start the File Manager, you can either enter the following command at a system prompt, or you can use the Menu mouse button to display the Workspace menu and select Programs; then select File Manager from the Programs menu.

```
% filemgr &
```

The Wastebasket Icon

To delete files from the File Manager, drag them down to and drop them on the Wastebasket icon. The icon changes from "empty" to "full." The Wastebasket is not the final resting place of files and folders, however. By double-clicking on the icon, you can display

IV

Graphic User Interfaces

the contents of the wastebasket in the Wastebasket window. By holding down the Menu mouse button on the Wastebasket window, you can display the Wastebasket pop-up menu.

Many of the menu options are familiar; several, however, are not. Table 17.4 explains the function of those options.

Table 17.4
Wastebasket Menu Options

Option	Description
Empty Wastebasket	Permanently removes all files and folders in the wastebasket—be careful!
Delete	Permanently removes highlighted files and folders from the wastebasket
Undelete	Retrieves highlighted files and folders from the wastebasket and places them back in the File Manager

The wastebasket is OpenWindows' way of forgiving you for throwing away the wrong file because the file sits in the wastebasket until you empty it. When you remove a file or folder from the wastebasket, however, it is effectively gone.

You also can drag files and folders out of the wastebasket and drop them back in the File Manager to recover them. This procedure is more direct than using the Undelete option in the Wastebasket menu.

Selecting Files and Folders

You already saw that one way to select a file or folder is to click on it. Double-clicking on a file or folder either executes the file, if it is executable, or opens the folder, in which case the contents of the File pane change to the contents of the selected folder, and the new folder is added to the line of folders.

You can open more than one file at a time in the following ways:

✔ Use the Select and Adjust mouse buttons

✔ Draw a rectangle around the file names with Select or Adjust

✔ Use the Select All option in the File pane

✔ Use the Goto field

After highlighting a file or folder with the Select button, you can use the Adjust button to select, or deselect, additional files and folders.

You can use the Select mouse button to draw a rectangle with dashed lines around a number of contiguous file and folder icons to select them.

This action also deselects all icons outside the rectangle.

You can use the Adjust mouse button in the same way to create a rectangle, however, the action does not deselect highlighted icons not in the rectangle.

To select all the files and folders in the current folder, use the Select All option in the File Pane window. You display the File Pane window by holding down the Menu mouse button in the File pane.

Finally, you can use the Goto field in the menu bar to select files in the File pane. You type the name of the file in the field and press the Return key. The File manager highlights the specified file. This method is valuable when you have quite a few files in a folder.

You also can use wildcard searches in the Goto field. The most common wildcards include the following:

* * stands for zero or any number of alphanumeric characters
* ? stands for one alphanumeric character
* [] selects those files with names that include one or more of the alphanumeric characters within the braces

For example, typing ***.doc** in the Goto field selects all files with the extension .doc. Typing **example?.c++** selects such files as example1.c++, example2.c++, exampleA.c++, and so on. Typing **example[135].c++** selects such files as example1.c++, example3.c++, and example5.c++.

After selecting all the files and folders you want, you can perform on them any commands provided in the menus. For example, you can open or delete them.

Viewing the Files and Folders

The File Manager can display the contents of folders in a variety of ways. The View menu on the File Manager window enables you to select the display you like best. Table 17.5 describes the different options in the View menu.

IV

Graphic User Interfaces

Table 17.5
Menu Options on the View Menu

Menu Option	Displays...
Icon by Name	Large icons alphabetically
Icon by Type	Large icons arranged by file type, for example, all word processing document icons are listed together
List by Name	Small icons alphabetically
List by Type	Small icons arranged by file type
List by Size	Small icons arranged by size with largest files displayed first
List by Date	Small icons arranged by date with most recent files displayed first

Creating and Renaming Files and Folders

You create new files and folders in the current folder by selecting, from the File menu, either the Create File or Create Folder menu options. The File Manager displays either a file or folder icon, respectively, in the File pane. The new icon is highlighted. At this time, it is easy to change the name of the icon from its default, NewDocument, to a more specific name. If the name of the icon is not already highlighted, use the Select mouse button to select it. When it is highlighted, type a new name and press the Return key for it to take effect. If you do not press the Return key, the icon reverts to its previous name.

Make sure that you are in the correct folder before using the Create File or Create Folder options. Otherwise, you have to take the unnecessary step of moving them to the correct folder.

Moving, Copying, and Linking Files

When you move a file, you actually delete it from one folder and add it to another. When you copy a file, the file remains in the original folder, and a copy of it is added to a new folder. When you link a file, you add to a folder a reference, or pointer, to a file in another folder. If you need two versions of the same file, then copy the file. If you want to avoid version conflicts but want easy access to a file from different folders, use a link.

To move a file from one folder to another, follow these steps:

1. Display the file in the File pane.

2. Grab the file icon and drop it onto a folder icon in the File pane or onto a folder in the line of folders.

The procedure is the same whether icons or lists are displayed.

You also can use the Cut and Paste menu options on the Edit or File Pane menus to copy files, as follows:

1. Select one or more files.

2. Select the Cut option.

3. Open the folder where you want to move the file.

4. Select the Paste option.

To copy one or more files, follow these steps:

1. Select one or more files to copy.

2. Select the Copy menu option in the Edit or File Pane menu.

When you select the Copy option, a cascade menu displays, giving you the option of copying the file (the File option) or copying a pointer to the file (as a Link option).

3. Select the File option.

4. Select the folder where you want the copy of the file.

5. Select the Paste option from the Edit or File Pane menu.

You also can copy files graphically by using these steps:

1. Hold down the Control key.

2. Display the file in the File pane.

3. Grab the file icon and drop it onto a folder icon in the File pane or onto a folder in the line of folders.

IV

Graphic User Interfaces

Use the following steps to place a link to a file in a different folder:

1. Select one or more files to link.

2. Select the Copy menu option in the Edit or File Pane menu.

3. Select the *as a Link* option from the cascading menu.

4. Open the folder where you want the copy of the file.

5. Select the Paste option from the Edit or File Pane menu.

You also can copy files to different machines connected in a network. Other machines appear as folders. So you can use all the techniques described earlier for moving, copying, and linking files to different machines.

If navigating through menus is too tedious for you, you can use the Remote Copy option in the File menu. When you select Remote Copy, the Remote Copy window displays.

Setting Permissions on Files

You can give (or not give) read, write, and execute permissions to yourself, a group, and everyone else. Read permission means that you can read a file (only). Write permission means that you can edit a file. Execute permission means that you can execute a file, usually an executable.

You restrict other people's permissions to prevent them from changing the content of a file. If you do not grant others any permissions, you can effectively hide the file from them.

To assign permissions to the owner, group, and everyone else, use the File Properties window.

To display this window, click on the Props button with the Menu mouse button and drag down to select the File option. Much of the information in the window is provided by the File Manager and cannot be changed. The fields you can change are the following:

✔ Name

✔ Owner

✔ Group

✔ Permissions

If you select many files to set permissions, fields on the File Properties window that have different values for different selected files appear dim. When you set a value for a field, that value applies for all the selected files.

Designing Your Own Commands

You can customize the File manager by adding your own set of commands. To create a command, follow these steps:

1. Use the Menu mouse button to click on the File menu button.

2. Drag down to the Custom Commands option.

3. On the cascading menu that displays, drag down to and select Create Command.

The File Manager displays the Create Command window.

4. Click on the New Command button in the Create Command window.

5. Fill in all the appropriate fields, described in table 17.6.

Table 17.6
Fields on the Create Command Window

Field	Description
Menu Label	Contains the name of the command
UNIX Command	Contains the UNIX equivalent of the command
Prompt Window	Determines whether to display a prompt window when the command is executed
Prompt	Contains the text to display in the prompt window
Output Window	Determines whether to display an output window

The Output window can display the output of the command.

For example, you could type the command name, List, in the Menu Label field. In the UNIX Command field, you would type ls. Select the No button for the Prompt window and leave the Prompt field empty. Select the Yes button for the Output Window so it can display the list.

Using Other Tools on the Desktop

The File Manager is only one of many widgets provided by OpenWindows to fill the desktop. It's beyond the scope of this book to cover all the others in detail, but table 17.7 provides a brief description of many of the widgets you most likely will use.

Table 17.7
OpenWindows Tools

Tool	Description
Audio Tool	Plays, records, and edits audio
Binder	Associates files with icons, print methods, and open methods
Calculator	A calculator
Calendar Manager	A calendar that records and prompts you for appointments
Clock	A clock
Command Tool	A text window with a scroll bar and more menu options than the Shell Tool
Console	A text window that receives error messages from the system
Icon Editor	Creates and edits icons
Mail Tool	A tool to send, receive, and organize e-mail
Performance Meter	Displays CPU usage
Print Tool	Prints files, selects printers, controls print options
Shell Tool	A text window without buttons
Snapshot	Takes pictures of all or part of the screen
Tape Tool	Controls tape and disk drives often for archiving
Text Editor	A GUI word processor

You can access all these tools either from the command line or from the Program menu. For example, when using the command line, enter the following commands:

```
% mailtool &
% printtool &
% snapshot &
```

To display the Program menu, click on the Workspace with the Select mouse button, and select the Program's menu item on the Workspace menu.

Some of these tools, such as the Clock, Calculator, Audio Tool, and Calendar look and work like their real-world counterparts. Menu options provided with these tools accomplish familiar tasks, such as looking at a calendar a day, or a month at a time.

The Shell and Command Tools are text windows. In them you can execute UNIX commands, start applications, and start other tools. The Command Tool has slightly more functionality than the Shell Tool, but both operate according to the basic operating instructions presented at the beginning of this chapter. For example, both have pane pop-up menus that you display by clicking on the Menu mouse button in the pane; both have hidden Window menus that you display by clicking the Menu mouse button on the left of the title bar; both can be iconified; and both can be resized.

Using Simple Tools

Other tools, including the Console, Performance Meter, Tape Tool, Snapshot, and Print Tool are important but largely one-dimensional. They perform single functions without a sophisticated interface. Because they are important, and perhaps one step removed from a real desktop, it's important to say a couple of words about each.

The Console Window

Always have a Console window open so that you can receive error messages. Both system and application error messages display in the Console. You also can use the Console like a Command Tool, but because the Console has little functionality, it's easier to use a Shell or Command Tool.

The Performance Meter

The Performance Meter graphically displays CPU usage.

The Performance Meter's greatest value is user feedback. Sometimes when you execute a command, perhaps to start an application, nothing happens. You automatically wonder if your connection to the server died, or if you have a locked window. The Performance Meter shows you whether the CPU is working. If the CPU usage is high, just wait a little longer for the application to start. If the CPU usage is low, something is wrong. Try closing the window or starting the application again.

IV

Graphic User Interfaces

The Tape Tool

The Tape Tool is important for archiving and dearchiving files to and from tape.

Archiving files to tape is just like copying files: you drag selected files from the File Manager to the Tape Tool window. To read files from the tape, use the Read menu and select one of the following three menu options:

- ✔ **Selected**, to read files selected in the Tape Contents/Files to Read list

- ✔ **Entire List**, to read all the files on the list

- ✔ **Entire Tape**, to read all the files on the tape

To list the files on the tape, click on the List button.

Snapshot

Snapshot is a great utility for capturing all or part of the screen in an image file.

These images are stored as data in files that you can import into word processing files, mail to others, or print. Using Snapshot is simple. After selecting the delay time before the picture is taken, and selecting how much of the screen you want to capture, you click on the Snap button. If capturing a window, the cursor changes to crosshairs. Click on the window that you want to capture and it will be saved. To save the image in a specific file, click on the Save button and specify the file. Snapshot captures images only in the raster format. Snapshot, however, can display two file formats: GIF and raster; raster is the default. Snapshot decompresses images automatically, so you need not run decompression programs, like pkZip, on image files.

The Print Tool

The Print Tool enables you to specify one or more files to print, select the printer to print them on, and view the progress of their printing.

You can specify the files to print on the File: line, or by dragging a file icon from the File Manager onto the Print Tool and dropping it in the upper left corner.

The Printer drop-down menu button displays all the printers available to you. If no printers display, ask your system administrator to assist you in connecting to printers on your network.

The list on the bottom of the window is the print queue. It displays all the print jobs pending for the selected printer. If many jobs are pending, you might select a different printer for faster results. You also can highlight your print job in the print queue; click on the Stop Printing menu button; and cancel the print job. You also can click on the Stop Printing menu button to cancel all print jobs in the queue.

Using Sophisticated Tools

The Text Editor, Mail Tool, and Binder are sophisticated GUI applications that each deserve a chapter of explanation. The basic functions of each application presented in this section, however, are easy to understand.

The Text Editor

The Text Editor provides most of the basic functionality you expect from a GUI word processor.

For example, you can cut, paste, copy, move, and delete text. Many options in the menus are the same as or similar to menu options in other word processors, such as Microsoft Word. Armed with this knowledge, you can operate all the basic features of the Text Editor without trouble.

The Mail Tool

The Mail Tool enables you to send and receive letters, files, voice mail, and screen captures across a network.

The Mail Tool uses the following three windows:

✔ Mail Queue window

✔ View Message window

✔ Compose Message window

The Mail Queue window shows the mail, both read and not read, in your mailbox. When you double-click on one of the entries in the mail queue, the entry is displayed in the View Message window. To read the next entry in the queue, click on the Next button.

To erase an entry, highlight it and click on the Delete button.

To reply to the letter writer, click on the Reply button, and the Compose Message window displays with the To: and Subject: fields appropriately filled. To include the original letter in the reply, click on the Include button. To send the letter, click on the Send button.

To write a letter (not reply to a letter), click on the Compose menu button and pull down to New. In this case, the Compose Message window displays without any fields filled in.

IV

Graphic User Interfaces

To add an attachment, such as a file, an image, or an executable, select the Add option from the File menu and specify the absolute pathname of the attachment in the Add Attachment window.

To send voice mail to someone else, use the Audio Tool to record a message and then add the audio file to a letter as an attachment.

The Mail Tool provides more functions, but the functions described in this section are the ones you use most.

The Binder

The Binder is a tool that defines a miscellany of elements used to describe a file and its icon. Table 17.8 describes all the properties defined by the binder.

Table 17.8
Binder Properties

Property	Description
Icon	Displays icon and file type, for example, document
Image File	Displays name of file containing icon
Mask File	Displays name of file containing the mask image of the icon
Foregr Color	Displays the color that fills the icon
Backgr Color	Displays the color behind the icon but in front of the black mask
Application	Displays application name to start when icon is double-clicked on
Print Method	Displays program run when file is printed

Customizing OpenWindows

You can customize many of the tools presented in this chapter as well as the look of all the windows. This section describes the most important customization features.

Customizing the Workspace

You can customize the look and operation of many basic features in OpenWindows by clicking with the Menu mouse button on the Workspace and selecting the Properties button on the Window menu. The Workspace Properties window enables you to customize six attributes, as described in table 17.9.

Table 17.9
Workspace Properties Options

Property	Description
Color	Controls the colors of the workspace and window border
Icons	Specifies the location on the screen for icons
Menus	Specifies the behavior of the Select button on menus
Miscellaneous	Sets scroll bar placement, beep usage, and focus policy
Mouse Settings	Enables you to set the speed of the mouse and the interval between clicks that defines a double-click
Localization	Specifies the language used in the system

Setting Colors

When you choose Properties on the Workspace Menu, the Workspace Properties window displays; its default is the Color settings.

Use the Color setting to select a color for the Workspace and for the border of window. The Custom button enables you to make your own colors by controlling hue, saturation, and brightness.

You also can use the palette of colors presented in the Workspace Properties window by clicking on the Palette button, the default.

After deciding on a color for the Workspace and for the window, simply click on the Workspace or Window button; click on a color; and click on the Apply button. The Workspace Properties window displays a confirmation screen to make sure that you want to make the changes.

IV

Graphic User Interfaces

Setting Fonts

When you click on the Category button, you can select the Fonts option. The Workspace Properties window for icons enables you to determine which fonts are used.

Setting Menu Properties

The Workspace Properties window for menus enables you to adjust two menu properties: the distance in pixels you must drag the mouse to the right before a cascading menu displays, and the function of the Select mouse button.

Whenever a menu option has an arrow to its right, you know that selecting the option displays a cascading menu. The cascading menu displays when you move the mouse cursor toward the arrow. The default is set to 100 pixels—that is, after moving the mouse cursor 100 pixels to the right, the cascading menu displays.

When the mouse cursor is over a menu button, the Select mouse button can either select the default option on the menu without displaying the menu, or display the menu (just like the Menu mouse button). You can make that choice by clicking on the Select's Default or Display's Menu buttons.

Mouse Settings

The Workspace Properties window for Mouse Settings enables you to set mouse pointer functionality and placement and define a double-click.

With the Scroll bar Pointer Jumping checkbox checked, the display jumps forward (or backward) a screen at a time when the Select mouse button is clicked on the scroll bar.

With the Pop-up Pointer Jumping checkbox checked, the mouse cursor jumps to the default button when a window displays.

By sliding the slide bar left or right, you define how quickly you must click for the system to understand that you intended to double-click.

Setting Miscellaneous Properties

The Workspace Properties window for the Miscellaneous option enables you to adjust how often the beep is used, the focus policy, and the placement of the scroll bar.

You can restrict the number of times the beeper is used by clicking on the Notices Only button, which allows beeps only when notices are displayed; or on the Never button, which turns off the beeper. The Always button places no restriction on the use of the beeper.

Window can receive input focus in one of two ways: the user clicks within the window, or the mouse cursor moves onto the window. The Click SELECT and Move Pointer buttons reflect those choices, respectively.

Placing the scroll bar is as simple as clicking on the Left or Right button.

Localization Settings

The Workspace Properties window for Locale enables you to set display and input languages, time, and numeric format.

When you click on the Basic Setting button, a drop-down menu enables you to choose between U.S.A., Japan, Korea, China, and other countries. Your choice sets the other fields appropriately. For example, when you choose U.S.A., only one choice of time format is available. When you choose Japan, however, you get a choice of two time formats.

Changing the .Xdefaults File

All the customization features made available by the Workspace Properties window actually add to or modify the .Xdefaults file. Instead of working through the Workspace Properties window, you can edit the .Xdefaults file directly.

The .Xdefaults file is not read by OpenWindows. Instead, it is loaded by the X Window server into the X resources database, xrdb. After making changes to the .Xdefaults file, to make the changes take effect in the current session, use the following command:

```
% xrdb -load .Xdefaults
```

Clicking on the Apply button in the Workspace Properties window executes this command.

You can see what is currently loaded in to xrdb by using the -query option, as follows:

```
% xrdb -query
```

Setting Colors

In the Workspace Properties window, you saw that it is possible to set the color of the Workspace and all the window. You can set the color of the window of a particular application by using the -xrm option, as in the following example:

```
% <application> -xrm 'OpenWindow.WindowColor: <color>'
```

IV

Graphic User Interfaces

This is illustrated by the following:

```
% mailtool -xrm 'OpenWindow.WindowColor: salmon'
```

You can specify the color by name or by its hex equivalent. The names of the colors reside in $OPENWINHOME/lib/rgb.txt. The hex numbers specify the red, green, and blue intensities in hex numbers from 0 to ff (0 to 255). For example, #0fa533 specifies a red intensity of 0f, 15; a green intensity of a5, 181; and a blue intensity of 0x33, 51.

To change the color of the Workspace, modify the following line in the .Xdefaults file:

```
% OpenWindow.WorkspaceColor: wheat
```

To set the color of the text areas in text panes, modify the following line in the .Xdefaults file:

```
% *Background: green
```

To set the color of the text in text panes, modify the following line in the .Xdefaults file:

```
% *Foreground: lavender
```

To set the color of window borders, modify the following line in the .Xdefaults file:

```
% OpenWindow.BorderColor: yellow
```

To change the display in text window to reverse video—where the background and foreground colors switch—modify the following line in the .Xdefaults file:

```
% *ReverseVideo: TRUE
```

You can combine some or all of these commands for a particular application, as in the following example:

```
% mailtool -xrm '*Background: black' -xrm 'Foreground:wheat'
```

Setting Icon Properties

Working in the .Xdefaults file provides more options than the Workspace Properties window. Whereas in the Workspace Property window, you can set the location of the icons and the direction in which the icons are saved, for example, right to left, by using the following command:

```
OpenWindow.IconLocation: <placement order>
```

The possible values of <placement order> are shown in table 17.10.

Table 17.10
Icon Locations

Position	Description
top-rl	Top, starting right, adding icons to the left
top-lr	Top, starting left, adding icons to the right
bottom-lr	Bottom, starting left, adding icons to the right
bottom-rl	Bottom, starting right, adding icons to the left
left-tb	On left, starting top, adding icons below
left-bt	On left, starting bottom, adding icons above
right-tb	On right, starting top, adding icons below
right-bt	On left, starting bottom, adding icons above

Setting Window Properties

Many window functions that people take for granted are, in fact, resources that can be changed.

To change the focus policy of a window, set the following line to FALSE if you want a window to receive focus only after it has been clicked in. Set the following line to TRUE if you want a window to automatically receive focus when the mouse cursor is in it:

```
OpenWindow.AutoInputFocus: TRUE
```

To raise a window to the top of the stack on the screen when a mouse cursor is in it, set the following line to TRUE:

```
OpenWindow.AutoRaise:TRUE
```

The default is FALSE: only when you click on a window does it rise to the top of the stack on the screen.

To show the entire window as you drag it, rather than an outline of the window, use the following setting:

```
OpenWindow.DragWindow: TRUE
```

The default is FALSE.

To make the window appear three-dimensional, set the following resource:

```
OpenWindow.Use3DFrames: TRUE
```

The default is FALSE.

Setting Fonts

You can set the fonts of the following objects:

ButtonFont—Sets the font of menu items

TitleFont—Sets the font of window titles

IconFont—Sets the font of an icon

For example:

```
OpenWindow.ButtonFont: helvetica-bold-12
```

or

```
OpenWindow.TitleFont: lucidasans-italic-12
```

You can change the point size of fonts in applications to one of four values—small, medium, large, extra_large—as in the following example:

```
% snapshot -scale large
```

The default is medium.

You also can change the font used in an application by using the -font option, as follows:

```
% snapshot -font adobe-courier-bold-o-normal--18-180-75-75-m-110-
➥iso8859-1
```

To find out which fonts are available, use the following command:

```
% xlsfonts
```

You might want to pipe the command through more because many fonts usually are on a system.

Summary

This chapter gave you a whirlwind tour of OpenWindows—from operating its most basic features to customizing resources. The operating system is robust in the number of tools it offers users; many of them are discussed in this chapter.

It is impossible in one chapter to describe all the tools available in OpenWindows, or even all the functions of the tools presented. This chapter does, however, present the tools and functions you use most frequently. Learn the material in this chapter, and you will be well on your way to mastering OpenWindows.

Part V

Mastering the Shell

Chapter Snapshot

There are three primary shells available for use with UNIX today. The Bourne shell was the first shell and has been around since the beginning. The C shell incorporated many enhancements, but was incompatible with Bourne. The Korn shell came about as an attempt to combine the best of the other two. This chapter examines the following:

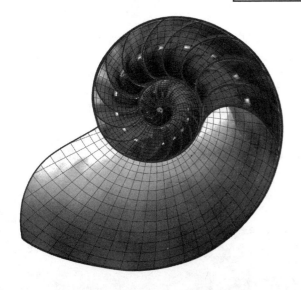

Bourne, CSH, and Korn Differences

As you saw in Chapter 5, "Shell Basics," the *shell*, or command interpreter, is the major interface between the user and UNIX. Aside from starting a specific application program when you log in, the user interacts with the shell to one degree or another. There are those users who can't live without it, and others who don't want to be bothered with it. In this chapter, you examine the history of the different shells, the major differences between the shells, and how they each process the command line.

The Shell History

Each of the shells was designed for a specific purpose. What were the motivators behind the design? The original UNIX shell, /bin/sh, was designed by Stephen Bourne while working at AT&T Bell Laboratories in the mid-1970s. As a programming language, it contains numerous constructs to develop intricate programs using the built-in primitives and variables. As a command language, it provides an interface to the process-related facilities of UNIX, resulting in the execution of other commands in the system.

The C shell, /bin/csh, was written by Bill Joy while he was at the University of California at Berkeley with the group of users and sharp programmers responsible for the development and evolution of the *Berkeley Software Distribution* (BSD) UNIX. The C shell was meant to provide a more superior shell to the Bourne shell and provide features that the users wanted, such as command editing, command history, and job control.

Although the C shell was growing in popularity, the major disadvantage of it was that it wasn't as widely available as the Bourne shell. Combined with the fact that the command and programming languages for each of them are so different, it was a major task to switch from one to the other. Despite these stumbling blocks, the C shell gained a large following because of what it offers.

In the late 1980s, the Korn shell, /bin/ksh, entered the picture. Written by David Korn of AT&T Bell Laboratories, this shell is completely compatible with the programming language of the older Bourne shell, but also includes many features found in the C shell—and then some. These are the major reasons why people have flocked to the Korn shell; it provides the flexible, well-known, and utilized command language of the Bourne shell, and the extended capabilities of the C shell. What *are* the real differences?

The Shell Game

The following table shows the features available for the operating system, and whether or not they are available when using that shell.

Table 18.1
Shell Comparisons

Feature	Bourne Shell	C Shell	Korn Shell
Environment variables	Yes	Yes	Yes
Global variables	Yes	Yes	Yes
File-name substitution	Yes	Yes	Yes
Wild cards	Yes	Yes	Yes

Feature	Bourne Shell	C Shell	Korn Shell
Command completion	No	Yes	No
Command history	No	Yes	Yes
Command editing (vi)	No	Yes	Yes
Command editing (emacs)	No	Yes	Yes
Job control	No	Yes	Yes
Command substitution	Yes	Yes	Yes
Pipes	Yes	Yes	Yes
I/O redirection	Yes	Yes	Yes
Shell functions	Yes	No	Yes
Aliases	No	Yes	Yes
cd spell checker	No (Yes on SCO)	Yes (In some shells)	No (Yes on SCO)
Built-in arithmetic	No	Yes	Yes
Built-in arrays	No	No	Yes

A quick study of the table and it is hard to see why anyone would want to use the Bourne shell. Yet, many system utilities depend upon its use. For example, the superuser, root, generally has a Bourne shell on System V systems. Under System V, much of the operating system expects root to have the Bourne shell. Furthermore, some System V vendors will not support you if you change root's shell to something other than /bin/sh. The cron command expects the use of /bin/sh, and tells you so if you are using the C or Korn shells. (See Chapter 25, "Processes Now and Later," for a discussion of cron and other process tools.)

The superuser on the BSD-based systems typically uses the C shell. This could be because the C shell was designed by its programmers, and not dependent upon a format designed by someone else. It also is a known fact that the BSD distribution contains no AT&T System V code.

It's clear that the Korn shell does all that the Bourne shell does and more. Why can't you use the Korn shell as root? Parts of the UNIX operating system expect that root's working shell will be the Bourne shell. Some vendors strongly advise against changing the shell for root from the Bourne shell. Rather, they recommend that an alternate user should be created, using the alternate shell.

Even though you will examine many features of the different shells over the next few chapters, let's take a moment to look at the major differences and what they mean for you.

Command Completion

Command completion is a feature available only in the C shell. It enables you to enter a unique part of a command and have the shell complete the command name. In order for this to work, you must have entered enough of the command name for it to be unique. If the terminal beeps at you, the characters specified are not unique enough, and you must specify more. You can generate a list of options at this point with Ctrl+D. This causes the shell to print a list of options. You must enter enough characters to complete the command:

The file completion feature of C shell is not immediately active in all implementations by default. In SunOS, for example, you have to set a shell variable—filec—to make it active.

```
% du[ESC]
(beep)
[CONTROL]d
du  dump
% du
1    ./.elm
1    ./Mail
986   ./tcsh
26   ./book
1226  .
%
```

Command History

Command history is available with the Korn and C shells, but not with the Bourne shell. Command history enables you to reexecute previous commands without having to enter the complete command line. Each of these two shells performs the function differently.

In either shell, you access the history list through the command history. The exact mechanism used to store the history is different, and is discussed in Chapter 19, "History, Aliases, and Job Control." The following illustrates the output of the history command:

```
% history
    1     set prompt = "% "
    2     lc /bin
    3     du
    4     du
    5     du
    6     du
    7     history
    8     cd tcsh
    9     lc
   10     more tcsh.man
   11     lc
   12     history
%
```

The C shell requires that you enter the history command using a "bang-style" syntax, meaning that the command to be executed is preceded by an exclamation mark (see Chapter 19 for more detail):

```
% history
    1     set prompt = "% "
    2     lc /bin
    3     du
    4     du
    5     du
    6     du
    7     history
    8     cd tcsh
    9     lc
   10     more tcsh.man
   11     lc
   12     history
% !6
du
986
%
```

The Korn shell uses a different syntax, as shown in the next example. This syntax uses the r command and the command number to accomplish the same result. As you will see in Chapter 19, the r command is an alias for the command fc, which is responsible for other tasks, such as command editing.

```
$ history
    1    pwd
    2    lc /bin
    3    du
    4    du
    5    du
    6    du
    7    history
    8    cd tcsh
    9    lc
   10    more tcsh.man
   11    lc
   12    history
$ r 6
du
986
$
```

Command Editing

Command editing is also a feature available only in the Korn and C shells, and, again, the approaches are different. Whereas command history enables us to reexecute the same command with the same arguments, you can use command editing to change some part of the command before executing it. One form of command editing in the C shell is to use the caret (^) replacement technique:

```
% daate
daate: Command not found.
% ^aa^a
date
Sat Jul 30 10:14:53 EDT 1994
%
```

In this example, which replaces aa with a, the caret is used to start the old pattern and the new pattern. When the substitution is performed, the command is properly executed. With this format, you can edit only the command just executed. Many C shells also offer other forms of command-line editing, including using vi or another editor to edit the command line of any command that can be accessed from the history list.

However, in the Korn shell, the form of command-line editing is through an editor, as discussed in Chapter 19. This uses the command fc and the command number to start the editor, which has been configured in the shell. By default, this is the ed editor, but it can be changed. The next example demonstrates using the ed editor to correct a similar error:

```
25$ daate
26$ fc 25
6
p
daate
s/aa/a/
p
date
w
5
q
date
Fri Aug 5 20:35:10 EDT 1994
27$
```

As you will see in Chapter 19, it is possible to change the editor used to correct your errors.

Job Control

Job control is another feature that is restricted to the C and Korn shells. The job control features must be fully supported by the implementation of the operating system in use. Otherwise, only portions of the job control services can be used. This service enables you to suspend a job that is running on your terminal and place it in the background, thereby enabling you to run other jobs on your terminal session.

The commands used are the same in both of the shells. To suspend the job, you use Ctrl+Z, which places the job in the background. From there, you can list the current jobs, kill jobs, move jobs into the foreground, and wait until they complete. You explore this service thoroughly in the upcoming chapters.

Functions and Aliases

An alias is another name for something. A function is a program to perform some task. The Bourne shell has functions, and the Korn and C shells have aliases. In many respects, they accomplish the same purpose: to define commands during your login session. You create aliases and functions differently between the shells.

Functions are created in the Bourne shell using the following syntax:

```
name()
{
commands
}
```

The *name* before the parentheses is the name that you use to execute the command. The *commands* contained between the braces are the actual UNIX or shell commands that will be executed when you enter the function name. The following is a sample function:

```
stats()
{
who
df -v
}
```

It is worth noting that not all Bourne shells include the capability of creating and using shell functions. You should be particularly aware of shells called /bin/sh and /bin/sh5 on BSD systems. The /bin/sh shells on these systems often do not support functions, but the /bin/sh5 shells generally do.

Aliases, although they accomplish the same result as functions, are established quite differently. They are created in the C shell using the syntax shown in the following example:

```
% alias name command
% alias stats "who;df -v"
```

In the Korn shell, aliases are created using the following syntax:

```
$ alias name=command
$ alias stats="who;df -v"
```

In both cases, the aliases are created and inserted into your environment. They are not permanent, unless they are added to your customization files (discussed in Chapters 19 and 20).

The cd Spell Checker

The cd spell checker is a feature often associated with the C shell, but many vendors are adding this capability to the Bourne and Korn shells. It is also not available in all vendors versions of C shell, even though it is a C shell feature.

This feature catches the mistakes that you make when entering a directory name. The shell prompts you with the correct directory name, if one exists in the path specified. This is illustrated in the following:

```
% cd /tmo
/tmp? y
ok
%
```

Many versions of the shell do not have this feature. However, it is worth mentioning, because more and more of the vendors are adding support for this feature.

The Shell Variables

Each of the shells has a specific environment configured when you log in. In this part of the chapter, you are going to look at the environment that is established and the environment variables that are typically defined.

The Bourne and Korn Shell Login Environment

The Bourne and Korn shells share two configuration files, which define the global configuration and the user's specific configuration. The /etc/profile, which is configured by the system administrator, is used to define the global system configuration for both the Bourne and Korn shell user. Remember, the Korn shell can process the Bourne shell commands. Your configuration file, profile, is found in your home directory. Between these two files, you end up with a configured environment. The following is a sample profile:

```
#
# We must trap the exit of the shell so we can simulate the .logout
# like that which is used in the C shell
#
trap "$HOME/.checkout" 0

TERM=vt220;export TERM
stty intr
stty erase
```

The Korn shell uses a second configuration file, called kshrc. This file is also found in your home directory. The kshrc file typically contains Korn shell specific configuration, such as prompts and aliases. The following is a sample kshrc file:

```
322$ more .kshrc
set -ao vi
PATH=$PATH:$HOME/bin:/usr/games:/usr/lib:/etc/lddrv
PS1="$LOGNAME ! > "
PS2="$LOGNAME ? "
PS3="$LOGNAME # "
EXINIT="set ai aw sm"
FCEDIT=/usr/bin/vi
alias h='fc -l ¦ tail -23 ¦ more -c'
alias c=clear
alias j=jobs
alias x='fc -e "cat >/dev/null" $1 $2'
alias w='whence -v'
alias log='tail -f /usr/spool/uucp/LOGFILE'
323$
```

When you look at this file, you can see the configuration of a number of aliases. The primary reason for putting this information in a file other than profile is that there is common use of this file between the Bourne and Korn shells. You look at these configuration files in Chapter 20.

The Common Environment Variables

This section examines the environment variables that exist between the Bourne and Korn shells. Most of the environment variables that are found in the various versions of the Bourne and Korn shells are listed; however, your specific version may not have all of them.

"Underscore (_)"

The underscore is a temporary variable used in the Korn shell to represent the last argument of the previous command. Here is how it works:

```
$ print hello world
hello world
$ print $_
world
```

CDPATH

This variable is not set by default. It is used by the Bourne and Korn shells to look for a directory name when a relative pathname is used. It is important to remember to include the current directory when setting this variable. Here is an example:

```
CDPATH=.:$HOME:$HOME/tcsh
```

This means that when we issue a command such as the following, the shell processes CDPATH to see whether the directory is in one of those listed:

```
$ cd bin
```

If so, the shell changes to that directory, even if it is in another place in the file system. Like the PATH variable, this one is a list of colon-separated directories. It is easier to see how CDPATH works by looking at the following example:

```
$ CDPATH=.:$HOME:$HOME/Filecabinet:/tmp:/usr
$ export CDPATH
$ pwd
/u/chare
$ cd lib
/usr/lib
$
```

COLUMNS

This is a Korn shell variable used to define the width of the terminal output device.

EDITOR

This is a Korn shell variable used to define the editor that will be used for editing the history list. It is used interchangeably with the VISUAL variable. It is /bin/ed by default.

ENV

This is a Korn shell variable that specifies the name of the Korn shell environment file, kshrc.

ERRNO

This variable is set to the system error number after a failed command. It is primarily used in debugging a shell program. Unfortunately, however, with the differences between UNIX implementations, its practical use is limited because there are no standards regarding error message numbers. To make the situation worse, not all implementations of the Korn shell support its use.

EXINIT

This variable is used by the shell to provide configuration information for the ex and vi commands.

FCEDIT

This is the variable that defines which editor to use when performing command-line edits using fc. The default is /bin/ed.

HISTFILE

The Korn shell normally uses the history file $HOME/.sh_history. Defining this variable causes the Korn shell to use an alternate file.

HISTSIZE

This is the number of commands that will be stored in HISTFILE.

HOME

This is the user's login directory, set for the user from the information provided in the /etc/passwd file. The cd command uses the value in this variable to go to your home directory when you do not provide an argument.

IFS

This defines the Internal Field Separators, which are used by the shell to delimit words on the command line. They are also used in other situations. The default values are the space, tab, and newline.

LINENO

The Korn Shell keeps track of each line in the script by assigning the line number to this variable. In this way, ksh can tell you the line number where it is in the script. Like the ERRNO variable, older versions of the ksh do not support this variable.

LOGNAME or USER

This variable defines the login name of the user who is logged in on the port. It is generally set at login time through the results of the command logname.

MAIL

This variable defines the location of the user's mailbox. On System V, the login process sets this variable to /usr/mail and the user's login name; on XENIX and BSD systems, the value is set to /usr/spool/mail and the login name.

MAILCHECK

The Korn and Bourne shells periodically check to see whether you have new mail in your mailbox. If so, a message is printed telling you that new mail has arrived. This check is done at the time interval specified here in seconds. It is important to note that this check is done by the shell, so you are not informed automatically if you are using an application program.

MAILPATH

This variable provides a list of colon-separated files, which the shell checks to see whether new mail or text has arrived. A custom message can be printed by adding it behind a ?[ac] in the Korn shell, and a %[ac] in the Bourne shell. The following is an example of the MAILPATH variable:

```
329$ MAILPATH=/usr/mail/chare?(')New Mail!('):/etc/motd?(')New MOTD!(')
330$ MAILCHECK=10
331$ export MAILPATH MAILCHECK
332$ date
Thu May 12 19:44:11 EST 1994
New Mail!
333$
```

OLDPWD

This is the value of the user's working directory prior to the last cd command:

```
$ pwd
/tmp
$ cd $HOME
$ pwd
/u/chare
$ echo $OLDPWD
/tmp
```

OPTARG

This is used by the getopts program, which is used in a shell script to collect and validate options and their needed arguments. Only the newer versions of ksh support this variable.

OPTIND

This variable is used to set the index for finding the next option as defined by getopts. Like its counterpart OPTARG, it is available only in the newer versions of ksh. Both the OPTARG and OPTIND variables are presented with the getopts command in Chapter 23, "Advanced Shell Techniques."

PPID

This variable is the process ID number of the parent process of the shell.

PS1

This is the primary prompt string. It is typically defined as the dollar sign ($) followed by a single space, and can be changed.

PS2

This is the secondary prompt string. This prompt is used when the shell is expecting additional input. For example, if you are entering a command and forget to insert a quote, as shown in the next example, the shell responds with the PS2 prompt to inform you that it is looking for more information:

```
$ date'
> '
ksh: date^J: not found
$
```

In this example, the user accidentally pressed the single quote when pressing the Enter key. The shell initially responded with the > prompt, and the user entered a second quote to complete the command. Because the shell sees the Enter key as part of the command, it fails to find a command with this name, so reports an error and issues a new prompt.

PS3

This is the tertiary prompt used in the Korn shell. It is used with the select command in the Korn shell programming language.

PS4

This is a debugging prompt, and is rarely used except when writing shell scripts.

PWD

This is the value of the current working directory, as illustrated with the following example:

```
$ pwd
/u/chare
$ echo $PWD
/u/chare
```

RANDOM

This is a random number generator. The RANDOM variable has the integer attribute set for it. Each time that you access the RANDOM variable, a different number between the range of 0 to 32767 is printed. This generator can be seeded, which produces a different set of random numbers.

One method of randomizing the output is to seed the generator with the process id of the shell, or the command that is accessing it. This seeding is done by assigning a value to the variable.

```
$ RANDOM=$$
$ print $RANDOM $RANDOM $RANDOM
21285 32239 31965
```

SECONDS

This contains the number of seconds since the Korn shell was invoked.

SHELL

This variable is assigned by the system login process. It contains the name of the shell that was started as your login shell. The login shell definition comes from your /etc/passwd file entry. Normally, you wouldn't change this variable, because it is used to provide information about which shell to start up when you select a shell escape in an application.

TERM

This variable contains the name of the terminal type that you are using. Because many of the full-screen commands that are part of UNIX (vi for example) and other applications need to know what type of terminal you are using, this variable must be set upon login.

TMOUT

If this variable is nonzero, the Korn shell exits if there is no terminal activity for the specified number of seconds. Here is an example:

```
$
$ TMOUT=30
$ export TMOUT
$
shell time out in 60 seconds
ksh: timed out waiting for input
Logging out chare on /dev/tty000 at Thu May 12 20:18:21 EST 1994

Logout successful.

Welcome to the AT&T UNIX pc
Please login:
```

If there is no activity for the specified amount of time, the shell prints a warning that the shell will exit unless you press the Enter key within 60 seconds. In this example, the Enter key was not pressed, so the logout was successful.

TZ

This variable contains the time zone information. Many commands use the TZ variable to format information properly. For example, the date command uses the TZ variable to ensure that the correct time is printed. The value consists of three components: the standard time zone, the number of time zones west of Greenwich Mean Time, and the daylight savings time zone (EST5EDT). The following shows how the value of TZ affects the output of the date command:

```
$ echo $TZ
$ EST5EDT
$ date
Thu May 12 21:33:00 EDT 1994
$ TZ=PST8PDT
$ export TZ
$ date
Thu May 12 18:33:13 PDT 1994
```

VISUAL

This is a Korn shell variable, which is equivalent to the EDITOR variable. It specifies which editor is to be used for editing the history list.

The C Shell Login Environment

The C shell uses different control and configuration files from those used by the Bourne and Korn shells. The global file used is called /etc/cshrc, and is used to set the default values for the C shell. The login file that is in the user's home directory is read-only and instructs the login shell how to configure the environment, such as the path and term variables. Here is an example:

```
#
# This is the global initialization file for C shell users
#
echo "Initializing ...."
#
# Set the initial search path
#
set PATH = ( . /bin /usr/bin /usr/ucb /usr/local )
#
# Who is this?
set LOGNAME = `logname`
set USER = $LOGNAME
#
# What version of the Operating System are we running? This may have to
# be modified depending upon the version of UNIX in use. Most versions
# of UNIX have a uname command that provides information like this
#
#    ULTRIX wabbit.Choreo.CA 4.2 0 RISC
#    $1     $2       $3 $4 $5
#
set OP = `uname -a`
#
# Print a welcome message. This is formatted differently for the C
# shell because the C shell uses an array to hold the results of
# command substitution.
echo "Welcome to $OP[1] $OP[3] $OP[4] ($OP[5])"
#
```

```
# Report and record our login
#
echo "   Logged in on `date` on `tty`"
#
# This shows when we last logged in This is performed by some versions
# of UNIX, but not all.
#
echo "Last logged in on `cat -s $HOME/.lastlogin`"
#
# This saves the date and terminal port that the user logged in to a
# file in the users home directory.
# We must set and then unset noclobber to make sure that the state is
# where we want it.
#
set noclobber
unset noclobber
echo "`date` on `tty`" > $HOME/.lastlogin
#
# Set the users mailbox
set MAIL = /usr/spool/mail/$LOGNAME
#
# Now set some other flags
#
# HISTORY—the size of the history list
set history = 20
#
# NOTIFY—inform the user when a background job has completed
set notify
#
# PROMPT—set the prompt for the user
# Select the default prompt for the system by adjusting the comments
# print the command number for history
#
# set prompt = "[\!] "
#
# print the default prompt
#
set prompt = "% "
#
# the end
```

The cshlogin file is a sample; the actual one on your system may be very different. The layout and further discussion is presented in Chapter 24. The login file, which is the second configuration file processed, is included in the following:

```
#
# This is a login file for the C shell.
#
# Customize this ourselves ...
#
# Our TERM type is ALWAYS vt220 ...
#
setenv TERM vt220
#
# Add a directory to our PATH
#
set PATH = ( $path $HOME/bin )
#
# I want a different prompt!
#
set prompt = "chare [\!] "
echo "Login Environment Configuration complete."
```

The third file is the .cshrc file, which is read for each C shell. This file usually contains information, such as aliases, which you want subshells to be able to access. A sample .cshrc file is shown in the following:

```
alias lc ls -CF
alias printenv env
alias h history
```

These three files are discussed in more detail in Chapter 24, which focuses on the login process, and in Chapter 20, which discusses basic shell programming.

The Common Environment Variables

As with the Bourne and Korn shells, the C shell environment contains a number of variables. Again, some of these are defined on some systems, but not on others.

cdpath

This is analogous to the CDPATH variable in the Bourne shell, which was discussed previously. The definition of this variable is put in the cshrc file so that it is available for every C shell that is executed. In the Bourne shell, only the cd command recognizes the CDPATH variable. For the C shell, the cd, popd, and pushd commands all recognize cdpath.

cwd

Many implementations of the C shell store the current working directory in the variable cwd. This makes it easy to set your current working directory as your prompt on these systems. To include your current working directory in your prompt, you must use an alias for the cd command, as in the following:

```
alias cd'cd\!*; set prompt="`echo $cwd`> "'
```

This works by creating a version of the cd command, which is executed in place of the normal cd command. The alias performs the cd to the directory named on the command line (\!*), and then sets the prompt to be the current directory. This is shown in action in the next example:

```
% alias cd'cd \!*; set prompt="`echo $cwd`> "'
% cd /tmp
/tmp> cd
/usr1/chare> cd /usr/lib
/usr/lib>
```

histchars

This enables you to change the characters used to define history commands to something other than the default ! and ^ (caret). Any new definition of these characters should be put in the cshrc file so that it is available in all C shells. There are real examples of why you would want to change the history characters. If you execute a lot of UUCP commands, which use the ! in the command, you could be predisposed to a change. Here is an example:

```
/usr/lib> !!
cd /usr/lib
/usr/lib> cd /tmp
/tmp> set histchars="#^"
/tmp> ##
set histchars="#^"
/tmp>
```

Notice that there are two characters specified. To change one, you must specify both.

If you change the history character from a ! to a #, as shown in the previous example, any aliases that depend upon the ! character no longer work. They need to be rewritten to support the new # character.

history

This variable sets how many commands the C shell remembers when you use the history command. If this variable is not set, the default is to remember only the last command executed. Most people set this value to 20 or so to prevent scrolling off the screen when executing history. Alternatively, you can set the history list to be larger, and use the history *number* command to restrict the history list print.

home

This variable is analogous to the Bourne and Korn shell variable HOME. Normally, you should not adjust the value of home.

ignoreeof

If you set this variable in your login file, the C shell ignores attempts to log out using the Ctrl+D command. You have to type exit or log out to terminate your login shell. If you want subshells to ignore Ctrl+D, put ignoreeof in the .cshrc file also.

```
/tmp> set ignoreeof
/tmp> ^D
Use "logout" to logout.
/tmp>
```

mail

This variable combines the Bourne/Korn shell MAIL, MAILPATH, and MAILCHECK variables into one. The files that are specified in the variable are checked, by default, every 10 minutes. Here is an example of setting the variable:

```
/tmp> set mail = (/usr/mail/chare2 /usr/mail/chare )
```

You can change the check interval for some or all of the files. The check interval is measured in seconds, and is placed before the file that is to be checked:

```
% set mail = ( 180 /usr/mail/chare2 60 /usr/mail/chare )
```

In this example, the C shell checks the mailbox /usr/mail/chare2 every 180 seconds, or 3 minutes, and the /usr/mail/chare file every 60 seconds. If new mail arrives, the C shell shows this by printing the message You have new mail on the terminal device.

noclobber

Setting this variable affects how the C shell operates input/output redirection and enables the creation or truncation of files when using the > and >> directives.

path

The path variable is analogous to the PATH variable in the Bourne/Korn shells. The PATH variable is also available in the C shell, but the information in the two variables is formatted differently. The shell also updates the value of the variables as needed. The formats are shown in the following:

```
% echo $PATH
.:/bin /usr/bin:/usr1/chare/bin
% echo $path
. /bin /usr/bin /usr1/chare/bin
% set path = ( /bin /usr/bin /usr/local )
% echo $path
/bin /usr/bin /usr/local
% echo $PATH
.:/bin:/usr/bin:/usr/local
%
```

prompt

The prompt variable controls what the user sees as the primary prompt string. By default, it is a percent sign (%) followed by a space. You can include the history command number in your prompt:

```
% set prompt="[!]% "
New mail in /usr /mail/chare.
[51]%
```

This example shows the history command number in the prompt. It also illustrates how the shell informs you when new mail arrives. This is the result of the mail variable discussed earlier.

savehist

Setting savehist in the cshrc file defines the number of commands that you want the C shell to save to disk. Normally, the C shell saves its history in memory and not on disk, so it is lost when you log out. This variable saves the specified number of commands in a file called history in your home directory. This file is read when you log in, and those commands in the history file are added to your history list for that session.

shell

This variable names the shell that is in use. Normally, you wouldn't change this variable, because it is used to provide information on what shell to start up when a user selects a shell escape in an application.

term

Like the Bourne/Korn shell variable TERM, this defines the terminal type that you are using for your session. This is generally set in the login file upon login to the system.

time

Setting this variable in the cshrc file causes the C shell to print timing statistics for each command executed. The following example shows this variable in action:

```
[52]% du
1     ./.elm
1     ./Mail
1043  ./tcsh
9     ./book/chap21
15    ./book/chp22
1     ./book/chap23
26    ./book
1283  .
[53]% set time
[54]% du
1     ./.elm
1     ./Mail
1043  ./tcsh
9     ./book/chap21
15    ./book/chp22
1     ./book/chap23
26    ./book
1283  .
0.01u 0.35s 0:00.36 100.0%
[55]%
```

The first part of this example illustrates running the command with times not set. After setting times, and running the same command, there is information showing the user, system, and real time. The actual timing output varies somewhat in the different shell implementations. In this case, the time usage is very low, and it would be considered very "noisy" to have this output for every command. By setting a value for time, as in the next example, you instruct the shell to print timing statistics only for commands that take more than the specified amount of time. The value is in seconds:

```
[55]% set time = 3
[56]% find / -name "core"
0.86u 11.85s 0:23.10 55.0%
[57]%
```

In this case, the command took more than three seconds to complete, so the shell reports the timing information.

There may be more variables defined by the C shell than are defined here. Remember that vendors often make their own enhancements—thus "breaking the mold."

Processing Input

It is important to know how the different shells process the command line so that you can understand the steps involved, and why some things don't work properly.

The Bourne Shell

The Bourne and Korn shells process the command line in the following order:

1. Command substitution

2. Parameter expansion

3. Word splitting

4. Pathname expansion

5. Quote removal

Command Substitution

During command substitution, the shell executes the indicated command and replaces it with the results of the command on the command line. In this fashion, you can use existing commands to print values:

```
echo `date`
```

In this example, the shell executes the command date and replaces it with the output of the command. After this is done, the command line looks like this (in its intermediate stage):

```
echo Sun Aug 7 18:13:01 EST 1994
```

Once the command substitution is complete, you can proceed to expanding any parameters on the command line.

Parameter Expansion

At this stage, the shell scans the command line, looking for dollar signs ($) that are not quoted. If any are found, the shell examines the name following the $. If it matches a currently defined parameter (or variable), the value is substituted for the $ and variable name. Using a variable that is undefined results in a space being inserted for the variable. Dollar signs that are contained in quotes are interpreted later in the process.

Word Splitting

Now that the command and parameter or variable substitution have been performed, the shell splits the command line into individual words, using the value of the IFS variable to provide the template. Normally, IFS is set to a space, tab, and newline, so the shell splits the command line in this fashion. If the value of IFS is different, the command line is split differently.

For example, if the value of IFS is a colon, a line in /etc/passwd is split properly. If the value of IFS is a space, you end up with something very strange.

Suppose you have a shell program that contains the following lines. First, you set IFS to be a colon and not the default. Next, you get a line from /etc/passwd using the grep command, and break it into its positional parameters using the command set. Then, you print the line from /etc/passwd with an _ (underscore) between each field instead of a colon:

```
IFS=":"
set `grep chare /etc/passwd`
echo "$1_$2_$3_$4_$5_$6_$7"
chare_u7mHuh5R4UmVo_105_100_Chris Hare_/u/chare_/bin/ksh
```

The end result is shown as a properly formatted entry from the /etc/passwd file.

However, if you run the same command using the default IFS values, you get the following:

```
set `grep chare /etc/passwd`
echo "$1_$2_$3_$4_$5_$6_$7"
chare:u7mHuh5R4UmVo:105:100:Chris_Hare:/u/chare:/bin/ksh___
```

This output doesn't make a lot of sense, however, because the line was split using the spaces that exist in the password file. For this entry, the first space was between the user's first and last names. The next splits were made at the end of the line for each space that existed. As you can see from this example, splitting the line with the wrong IFS values can have a serious impact on the outcome of the script.

Pathname Expansion

It is at this stage that the shell expands the file name substitution wild cards: *, ?, and []. If none of these characters are present, this step is skipped. Otherwise, the pattern is expanded. Examine the following:

```
$ ls -d boo*
book
boor
boot
```

This example uses the asterisk to list any files or directories existing in the current directory that begin with boo. This generates three names. The shell expands the pattern and provides the filenames as arguments to the command. Consequently, this command actually goes through the following phase before resulting in ls printing the list:

```
$ ls -d boo*
        ls -d book boor boot
book
boor
boot
```

The indented line is what the ls command actually sees on the command line. Consider this pattern:

```
$ ls -d boo[!st]
book
boor
$
```

This example looks for files that start with boo, but do not end in the letters s or t. When the shell expands this, it provides the files book and boor to ls, but doesn't include boot because it doesn't match the specification. Once all the wild cards are expanded, you proceed to the next step.

Quote Removal

The final step before the shell actually executes the command line is to process and remove any quotes. Here, the special characters |, ô, and æ are removed unless they are also quoted, and null arguments that are enclosed in double quotes are preserved. This is important to remember later when you deal with advanced shell programming techniques in Chapter 23, "Advanced Shell Techniques."

The Korn Shell

With a few exceptions, the Korn shell processes commands by following the same order as the Bourne shell:

1. Alias expansion

2. Tilde expansion

3. Command substitution

4. Parameter expansion

5. Word splitting

6. Pathname expansion

7. Quote removal

You can see right away that the major difference is that there are two steps earlier in the process. Let's look at these two steps, because they are the major differences from the processing described previously for the Bourne shell.

Alias Expansion

When the Korn shell processes the command line, it examines the command name to see whether it is a defined alias. If it is a defined alias, the shell replaces the alias name with the value of the alias. This is done internally: the shell does not change what the user sees on the terminal. Consider this example:

```
$ alias bar="hello world"
$ alias foo="echo "
$ foo bar
          echo hello world
hello world
```

Here, the shell expands the alias foo to be echo, followed by a space, and then expands bar to hello world. Before you see the output, the shell sees the command line that is indented. In the Korn shell, alias expansion is always done first.

Tilde Expansion

The second step in the Korn shell is to check to see whether any of the expanded aliases begin with an unquoted tilde (~). If so, ksh looks up to the first / to see whether it matches one of the criteria mentioned in the following list:

~ (by itself)	The tilde is replaced by the value of $HOME.
~+	The value of $PWD is substituted.
~-	The value of $OLDPWD is substituted.
~login name	The home directory of the named user is substituted.
~anything else	No substitution is performed.

The tilde is a method of addressing certain commonly used variables in a shorthand notation. These expansions are illustrated by the following:

```
$ echo ~
/u/chare
$ echo ~+
/tmp
$ echo ~-
/u/chare
$ echo ~terri
/u/terri
$ echo ~%
~%
```

Once the tilde expansions are performed, the Korn shell continues its command-line processing in the same fashion as the Bourne shell.

What About History?

Command-line history is not implemented in the same way as it is for the C shell. The commands that access the history in the Korn shell are, in fact, aliases to a single command: fc. Once the alias is expanded to the appropriate value, the command is executed, using any additional arguments that you supply.

The C Shell

The C shell follows a similar order when processing the command line:

1. History substitutions

2. Alias substitution

3. Variable substitution

4. Command substitution

5. Filename substitution

6. Input and output

7. Expressions

8. Control flow

Once the command line is processed, the C shell determines whether the command to be executed is a built-in command or an external command. Built-in commands are executed directly by the shell, but those that are not built-in commands must be processed further. The extra processing involves finding the command to execute. This is discussed in the next section, "Order of Execution."

The sample filename substitution, which was examined earlier in the discussion on Bourne and Korn shells, does not work in the C shell because of the way the C shell performs the substitutions. Before examining why, let's see what the result is of this command:

```
% ls -d boo*
book
boor
boot
% ls -d boo[!st]
st]: Event not found.
%
```

Why does the C shell respond in this fashion? To see why, let's expand the line, using the order seen here. The first thing the C shell does is to expand any history access. Remember, you access history by using the ! symbol. When the C shell encounters the !, it interprets the subsequent characters as the historical event, or command, which is to be re-executed. Because the shell cannot find an event in the history list, it reports an error.

Order of Execution

All the shells follow the same basic procedure to locate and execute commands that are not built in. This additional processing involves searching through the path variable if the command does not start with an absolute path. For example, to execute the command date, how does the shell find it?

The shell looks through the path variable and checks in each of the defined directories to see whether there is a file named date. If there is, and it is an executable file, the file is opened, and the instructions are executed (see fig. 18.1).

This figure illustrates how all the shells conduct the search for a file. Returning to the example of how the shell finds the command date, assume that your path variable contains the following directories:

```
PATH=.:/bin:/usr/bin:/usr/local
```

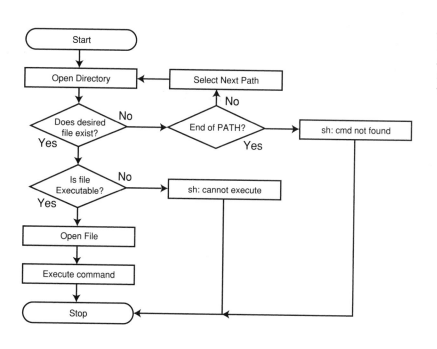

Figure 18.1
A flowchart showing a shell's file search.

Also assume that your current directory is your home directory. When you type the command date, the shell processes the PATH statement (or path statement) in the order of the directories. Using the flowchart illustrated in figure 18.1, the shell proceeds in this order:

1. Select the next directory, which is a period, to indicate the current directory.

2. Look in the current directory for a file named date, if, and only if a period (.) is specified as one of the fields in $PATH.

3. Did you find one? No.

4. Are you at the end of your PATH? No.

5. Select the next directory, which is /bin.

6. Look in /bin for a file named date.

7. Did you find one? Yes.

8. Is it executable? Yes.

9. Load the command and transfer execution to it.

The end result is that you get the date from the system. If the command cannot be found, and the path has been exhausted, the shell reports that the command can't be found.

Summary

In the end, the choice of which shell to use is yours. When you look at the information presented in this chapter, however, it is easy to conclude that the Bourne shell is the major loser when it comes to neat features. Despite this lack of features, the Bourne shell still remains a major player in the UNIX game today.

Chapter Snapshot

Three features that every user wants after he or she learns of the benefits they provide are command history, command aliasing, and job control. This chapter explores those three topics with such subjects as the following:

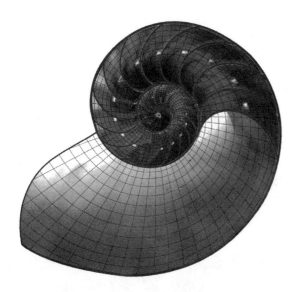

History, Aliases, and Job Control

n the last chapter, you looked extensively at the shells, and you will examine the programming languages in Chapters 20 and 23. This chapter focuses on command history, aliases, and job control within each of the shells.

Examining the Command History Feature

Command history is a feature of a shell that enables you to recall and reexecute a command without having to type the entire command again. Often this mechanism includes command editing, the ability to edit the recalled command prior to executing it.

Lack of History in the Bourne Shell

These features—command history and command editing—are not part of the Bourne shell. Even so, it is probably the most-used shell today because it is a good learning tool for users who are unfamiliar with the intricacies of the operating system. In addition, the superuser, or root, account is configured with the Bourne shell on all System V UNIX systems. And cron also uses the Bourne shell to execute the commands that are scheduled through this facility. For those of you who want command history and command editing features, turn to the Korn shell to provide them—and other features—for you.

History in the Korn Shell

The Korn shell, or *ksh*, records the commands that you execute, enabling you to retrieve and execute those commands later. ksh saves the commands, defined functions, and aliases in the history file. This history file is defined in your environment with the HISTFILE variable. To access your command history, use the history command, as illustrated in the following example.

```
$ history
871      vote yes
872      vote no
873      vote no
874      vote yes
875      vote yes
876      vote no
877      vote yes
878      vote yes
879      vote no
880      uniq -c ballot.box
881      sort ballot.box ¦ uniq -c
882      clear
883      z()
         {
         date
         who
         }
884      date
```

Mastering the Shell

```
885     su
886     history
$
```

Notice in the previous example where a function called z was defined? The HISTFILE variable is used to define where the ksh history file is located, and HISTSIZE defines the limit on how many commands the history file can access. ksh itself imposes no limit on how big the history file can be. The following example illustrates what these variables are on a sample. The HISTFILE itself is written in plain text, so it is viewable as a list.

```
$ echo $HISTFILE $HISTSIZE
/u/chare/.kshistory 128
$ ls -l /u/chare/.kshistory
-rw———  1 chare   users       8917 Aug 28 20:45 /u/chare/.kshistory
$
```

The history command accepts a number of options. To see the last 20 commands, for example, enter this command:

```
$ history -20
```

To see the commands between a certain range, enter the upper and lower numbers, as in the following example:

```
$ history 10 18
```

The final method is simply to put on the history command line the number of the command that you want to see, as in the following:

```
$ history 20
```

This command would show command 20 in the history list.

The value of HISTSIZE determines how far back into the history list you can access commands. In the previous example, you can go back only 128 commands in the history list. If you try to access a command that is outside the range addressable by the history command, ksh responds with an error.

```
$ history 20
ksh: fc: bad number
$ history 880
880     uniq -c ballot.box
881     sort ballot.box ¦ uniq -c
882     clear
883     z()
        {
        date
        who
        }
```

```
884     date
885     su
886     history
887     echo $HISYFILE $HISTSIZE
888     echo $HISTFILE $HISTSIZE
889     ls -l /u/chare/.kshidtory
890     ls -l /u/chare/.kshistory
891     history 20
892     history 880
$
```

But wait! The message says fc: bad number. Aren't you running the history command? As you find out shortly, history is a command alias (for the fc command).

Accessing History

Now that you know how to find out what commands are in your history list, you might be wondering how you can access those commands and how you can keep track of what command number you are currently executing. Look at the second issue first. In the shell command prompt, you can insert the ! symbol. This symbol instructs the shell to insert the command number in the prompt. Consider the shell prompt in the following example:

```
$
$ echo ":$PS1:"
:$ :
$
```

This shell prompt shows a user name and a number. If you simply press the Enter key, the number doesn't change. If you enter a command, however, the prompt number changes. This number is the command number. By looking at your PS1 variable, you can see that it contains the ! symbol. Change the prompt to something other than what it is, but keep the command number in the prompt.

The following example shows the current prompt and then the use of the PS1 variable to change the prompt. The new prompt simply shows the command number.

```
$ PS1="[!] "
[897] export PS1
[898]
```

You next need to know how to access your commands. To access and manipulate the history list, you use the command fc. As mentioned previously, the history command is indeed an alias. When you run history, you are in fact running the command fc -l. fc also enables you to execute commands from the history list and edit those commands. Most commonly, you execute commands from the history list by using the command r, which is another alias for fc. The r command expects to have an argument, but if one is not supplied, it defaults to the last command.

The following shows an example of using the r command to run the previous command, without an argument specified. The command tried to run command number 375 but didn't succeed. When you use the r command, it prints the name of the command that you asked it to execute. In this example, the command fails because it is trying to access a command on the history list that is beyond the accessible list.

```
[898] date
Sun Aug 28 20:49:23 EST 1994
[899] who
chare       tty000      Aug 25 18:48
root        w1          Aug 20 05:01
[900] r
who
chare       tty000      Aug 25 18:48
root        w1          Aug 20 05:01
[901] histroy 20
ksh: histroy:  not found
[902] r 898
date
Sun Aug 28 20:50:09 EST 1994
[903]
```

Alternatively, you can specify part of the command name. Suppose that you are a C programmer, and you want to execute the last command to compile your program. You can put part of the actual command you used, typically the beginning of the command, and ksh will execute it. An example is shown in the following:

```
[906] cc hello.c
[907] date
Sun Aug 28 20:52:51 EST 1994
[908] pwd
/u/chare
[909] r cc
cc hello.c
[910]
```

This syntax is different from what you use for the C shell, which is investigated later in this chapter (see "History in the C Shell").

Using Command Editing

The Korn shell has two command-line editors available: one resembles emacs, and the other vi. The commands available for editing these commands are extensive. But the default editor for the command line is, believe it or not, /bin/ed. The editor used is controlled by the shell variable FCEDIT. When you want to edit a command, enter the following:

```
$ fc cmd#
```

The following example shows the end result of the edit. The prompt has been changed. After you changed the command by using vi, ksh executed the command, and the prompt change was made.

```
[910] echo $FCEDIT
/usr/bin/vi
[911]

[911] PS1="Whadda ya want? [!] "
Whadda ya want? [912] export PS1
Whadda ya want? [913]
```

On several occasions in this text you have encountered the term "aliases," so the following sections give you a look at what they are and how to create them.

History in the C Shell

The history mechanism in the C shell (csh) is different again from the Korn shell. As in the Korn shell, you use the ! to substitute a command number in a prompt. But the ! also instructs csh to substitute history information into the current command. For this reason, when adjusting the csh prompt to include the command number, you must use a format like that shown in the following example:

```
set prompt = "chare[\!] "
```

The backslash in front of the ! escapes, or removes, the special meaning of the ! to the shell. Thus, when the shell issues a prompt, the command number is then inserted. You can follow the ! in a command line by a command number, a number relative to the current number, or a string, meaning to run the most recent command that is of string.

As with ksh, you need to know how to access the history list. The command used in the C shell is also called history and is illustrated in the following:

```
% history
901     histroy 20
902     date
903     lc
904     l *.c
```

```
905     cc heloo.c
906     cc hello.c
907     date
908     pwd
909     cc hello.c
%
```

Accessing History

Using history in csh is the same as in ksh, except the method of addressing the command is different. All commands that are to access the history list (which is not stored in a file as in ksh) use the command !. You have a choice of what follows the initial !, as shown in table 19.1.

 Under most circumstances, the C shell doesn't store history commands into a file like the Korn shell. If $savehist is set (to a non-zero value), the current history list is stored in $HOME/.history when $USER logs out. During $USER's next login, this file is read and the current history list updated.

Table 19.1
! Symbol Options

Command	Action
!num	Execute command *num* from history
!-num	Execute the command that is *num* previous
!string	Execute the last command called *string*
!?string	Execute the last command that contains *string*
!!	Execute the last command

 !string is indeed used to execute the last command called string. Although this implies that you need to type in the entire command name, in reality, it is the last command executed that starts with the given string. If you wanted to rerun the last command that started with the letter c, you could type !c at the prompt.

The following example illustrates using the command history features in the C shell:

```
12% !2
grep prompt .*
```

```
.login: # I want a different prompt!
.login: set prompt = chare [\!]
13% !-2
date
Sun Aug 28 21:06:35 EST 1994
14%
```

The history mechanism in the Korn shell is much more complex than the history mechanism in the C shell at this level. But the command-editing component of the C shell is different from that of the Korn shell.

Command Editing

As you have seen, command editing enables you to edit a command in the shell and then reexecute the command. One of the most commonly used forms of command editing uses the caret (^) symbol. In this case, it works only on the last command edited. You type a caret, the old text, a caret, and the new text, and press Enter. The new text replaces the old text, and the command is re-executed.

```
14% daate
daate: Command not found.
15% ^aa^a
date
Sun Aug 28 21:08:12 EST 1994
16%
```

Using Aliases

Webster's dictionary defines an alias as "a false or assumed name." From a UNIX perspective, this definition is true because an alias is another name for a command. In all cases, these alias definitions are not saved unless they are stored in the shell start-up files. In the following paragraphs, you examine aliases and learn how you can create, modify, and use aliases in each of the shells.

The Korn Shell Alias

You can create, list, and remove aliases in the Korn shell. First you need to know how to find out what aliases are currently defined. For this task, you use the alias command. This command prints a list of all the currently defined aliases, some of which are shown in the following example.

```
[910] alias
pwd=print - $PWD
r=fc -e -
rm=/bin/rm
sh=/bin/sh
```

```
sort=/bin/sort
split=/usr/bin/split
su=/bin/su
tail=/bin/tail
true=:
type=whence -v
uniq=/usr/bin/uniq
vi=/usr/bin/vi
w=whence -v
wc=/bin/wc
who=/bin/who
x=fc -e "cat >/dev/null" $1 $2
[925]
```

This list is not complete because more than a screenful are configured in this shell.

Two kinds of aliases exist in the Korn shell. The *tracked aliases* are typically full path-name commands—those that are not built into the shell. The other form is the exported alias. An *exported alias* remains in effect across the different commands and shells that are executed.

With the alias command, you also can see the definition of a specific alias. In the previous example you saw a list of aliases, but suppose that you want to see the definition for a single alias. To do so, issue the alias command with the name of the alias, as shown in the following:

```
[925] alias history
history=fc -l
[926] alias r
r=fc -e -
[927] alias lc
lc=/bin/lc
[928]
```

You use the alias command not only to list the aliases but also to create them. Use the following syntax with the alias command:

```
$ alias [-t] [-x] alias definition
```

To create a tracked alias, add the -t option, or use -x for an exported alias. The following illustrates the creation of an alias to report the date and to report who is on the system.

```
[928] alias mydate="date;who"
[929] mydate
Sun Aug 28 21:17:52 EST 1994
chare      tty000      Aug 25 18:48
root       w1          Aug 20 05:01
[930]
```

An important note when creating aliases: If you want the value expanded only when the alias is executed, enclose the value in single quotes. If your alias includes a shell wild card, for example, unless the alias is enclosed in single quotes, the wild card will be expanded when the alias is created, not when it is executed.

The history command, you may recall from earlier in this chapter, is an alias of fc. The r command is also an alias of fc.

The C Shell Alias

The C shell offers the alias and unalias commands to manipulate its aliases. You can use the alias command to create and list the aliases that are currently defined. As in the Korn shell, the alias command can list all the aliases that are defined, or only a specific one. To use the command this way, enter the alias command with no argument for all the defined aliases, or specify an alias name. If the alias is defined, its definition is printed, as in the following:

```
28% alias
h     history
lc    (ls -CF)
printenv    env
29% alias lc
ls -CF
30%
```

The alias command also creates new aliases. The syntax is different from the Korn shell. The syntax to create an alias in the C shell is as follows:

```
% alias name [as]command[as]
```

The value for alias name cannot be alias or unalias, because these words are reserved and will cause problems with the definition of your alias. Notice that you use no equal sign as you do in the Korn shell. The definition of an alias is illustrated in the following example.

```
31% alias clear "tput clear"
32% alias
clear     tput clear
h         history
lc     (ls -CF)
printenv        env
33%
```

The unalias command removes the alias definition from the shell. To use this command, simply add the alias names that you want to remove. The syntax is as follows:

```
% unalias name
```

And an example would be:

```
34% unalias h
35% alias
clear     tput clear
lc        (ls -CF)
printenv          env
36% unalias *
37% alias
38%
```

In this example, the command first removed the alias h; then the asterisk was used to indicate that all the aliases should be removed. As you can see, this command is a legal one that removes all your aliases. Don't use this command unless you are absolutely sure that it is what you want.

The Bourne Shell "Aliases"

The Bourne shell doesn't have aliases. But you can make it look as if you have aliases, using shell functions. You look at shell functions in great detail in Chapter 23, "Advanced Shell Techniques," including adding them to start-up files. But for now, what is a shell function?

A *shell function* is a command that is built into the shell and specified by the user. The syntax for the function is as follows:

```
$ command_name()
{
valid shell and UNIX commands
}
```

Now whenever you type the name of the command you specified, the commands you specified between the curly braces are executed. This command is now "built into" the shell for your current login session. (When you log out, the function is lost. You find out how to correct this problem in Chapter 23.) The following example demonstrates the creation of a shell function and the resulting output of the command.

```
[917] mydate()
chare ? {
chare ? date
chare ? who
chare ? }
[918]
[918] mydate
Sun Aug 28 21:10:10 EST 1994
chare     tty000      Aug 25 18:48
root      w1          Aug 20 05:01
[919]
```

In the preceding example, you see the syntax to create the function and then when to execute the function; the shell runs the commands you specified. If you want to know what functions, or "aliases," are defined, you use the set command, which lists the currently defined variables and, at the end of the output, the shell functions, as seen in the following:

```
PPID=1
PS1=[!]
PS2=chare ?
PS3=chare #
PWD=/u/chare
SHELL=/bin/sh
TERM=vt100
TMOUT=0
TNAME=vt100
TTY=/dev/tty000
TZ=EST5
mydate(){
date
who
}
z(){
echo "a ha!"
}
[923]
```

Here you see two shell functions defined: mydate and z. The z function simply prints a ha! on the user's terminal, then the shell returns to a prompt.

Process Management: Using the Job Control Feature

The Korn and C shells have another nice feature that the Bourne shell lacks: job control. This job control in the Korn shell consists of the commands bg, fg, jobs, kill, and wait. Before looking at these commands, you need to take a moment to find out what job control is. (This chapter addresses job control for both the C and Korn shells because they use similar commands. With the exception of a section on the Korn shell specifics, the two versions operate the same.)

Job control is a mechanism that enables you to control foreground and background tasks fully. Some systems support only a subset of the functions, and you should bear this in mind if something you learn in this section doesn't work on your system.

Addressing Korn Shell Specifics

Before delving into the discussion, you need to examine some aspects of job control. The Korn shell contains a flag called monitor. This flag determines whether the job ID numbers are printed for each command that is executed in the background. This number is printed in [] and is assigned for each job. If the monitor flag is turned off, these job numbers are not printed. When turned on, the job numbers are printed when the background job is started. In fact, for job control to be fully active, the monitor option must be turned on. On systems that have full support for job control, the monitor is implicitly turned on for every interactive ksh, even if it is reported off.

Don't confuse the job number printed in [] with the process ID number or PID. They are not the same.

The monitor flag is not turned on by default. To find out whether the flag is turned on or off, use the command set -o, as shown in the following example.

```
[930] set -o
Current option settings
allexport       on
bgnice          off
errexit         off
emacs           off
gmacs           off
ignoreeof       off
interactive     on
keyword         off
markdirs        off
monitor         off
noglob          off
noexec          off
nounset         off
restricted      off
trackall        on
verbose         off
vi              on
viraw           off
xtrace          off
[931]
```

As you can see, the value for monitor is turned off. To turn it on, use the command set -o monitor, which instructs ksh to turn monitor on. The following example illustrates the changes this makes in the settings:

```
[931] set -o monitor
[932] set -o
Current option settings
allexport        on
bgnice           off
errexit          off
emacs            off
gmacs            off
ignoreeof        off
interactive      on
keyword          off
markdirs         off
monitor          on
noglob           off
noexec           off
nounset          off
restricted       off
trackall         on
verbose          off
vi               on
viraw            off
xtrace           off
[933]
```

When the monitor option is on, ksh also reports each background job that has finished before issuing a new prompt. Each process created is considered a job, and each job can be referred to by process ID (PID) or by job number. Table 19.2 shows a number of methods that you can use to address a job.

Table 19.2
Korn Shell Job Variables

Variable	Explanation
%number	Refers to the job by job *number*
%string	Refers to the job whose name begins with *string*
%?string	Refers to the job whose name contains *string*

Variable	Explanation
%+ or %%	Refers to the current job
%-	Refers to the previous job

You look at these variables while you consider the various commands that are part of the job control mechanism.

Suspending Jobs

On systems that support full job control, you can suspend a process that is running in the foreground with the suspend command, normally Ctrl+Z. When you use Ctrl+Z, ksh issues a message indicating that the job has stopped and then displays a prompt. A job that is currently running in the background normally stops whenever it tries to read from your terminal. By using the command stty tostop, the command also stops when it tries to write to your terminal.

Not all UNIX systems support the tostop mode on stty, and so they also do not support the Ctrl+Z feature, which depends on the availability of the suspend command. You still, however, can use some of the features of job control on these systems.

The availability of the fg and bg commands depends on the host UNIX supporting full job control. If the host does not, the ksh supports only partial control with the jobs, kill, and wait commands.

The bg Command

You use the bg command with the suspend Ctrl+Z to place a suspended job into the background. Consider the following example:

```
[10] sleep 60
[control]-z
^Z[1] + Stopped          sleep 60
[11] bg
sleep 60&
[12] jobs
[1]  + Running           sleep 60
```

Here the sleep job is started, then suspended and moved to the background to continue running until it expires.

The fg Command

The fg command does the opposite of bg. It brings into the foreground a job that is running in the background and starts executing it. Using fg with no arguments brings the most recent background job back into the foreground.

The jobs Command

You can use the jobs command even on systems that do not support full job control. This command displays information on the currently running jobs that the current ksh has started. The jobs command reports on the following information:

✔ **The job number that is displayed in [].** If the job is the current job, a + sign follows the job number. If it is the job just preceding the current job, a - sign appears after the job number.

✔ **The status of the job.** The status can be running, stopped, done, or terminated. If a number appears after the word "done," this number indicates the exit code from the job. If no exit code exists, the command had an exit code of zero.

✔ **The command line.** ksh reads the command line from the history file. Consequently, if the line is blank, ksh cannot access the needed entry from the history file.

The jobs command is illustrated in the following:

```
[933] jobs
[934] sleep 60 &
[1]     2414
[935] sleep 5000 &
[2]     2415
[936] jobs
[2] + Running                sleep 5000 &
[1] - Running                sleep 60 &
[937]
```

The wait Command

Not restricted to the Korn shell, you use the wait command to wait for all jobs or for a specific job to complete executing. If you specify a job or process number, which you had to do for early versions of ksh, the shell suspends until those jobs complete. The wait command on the newer ksh also accepts the command with no arguments. In this case, as illustrated in the following, ksh suspends all execution until all the jobs have completed.

```
[937] jobs
[2] + Running                sleep 5000 &
[1] - Running                sleep 60 &
[938] wait
```

On some systems, using the interrupt key while ksh is waiting for the process to complete terminates the wait.

The kill Command

The final command in the job control arsenal is kill. kill, like wait, is not restricted to the Korn shell, but is available in all three. This command enables you to terminate jobs and could send a signal to the specified process to terminate. You can send the signal in either a numerical or a name format. kill -l lists the signals that the kill command in your ksh understands. The following demonstrates the kill command listing the signals and stopping a job.

```
[939] kill -l
EXIT HUP INT QUIT ILL TRAP IOT EMT FPE KILL BUS SEGV SYS PIPE ALRM
TERM USR1 USR2 CLD PWR ERR
[940] jobs
[2] + Running                sleep 5000 &
[941] kill %2
[2] + Terminated             sleep 5000 &
[942]
```

Summary

This chapter focused on the three features that set shells apart from each other—job control, command history, and command aliasing. Focus was on the Korn shell, yet many of the commands given also work with the C shell.

V

Mastering the Shell

Chapter Snapshot

Every operating system worth its salt has a means by which you can automate processes and tailor the operating system to work more efficently with you. In DOS, this is done through batch files. In OS/2, it is accomplished with REXX scripts. In UNIX, shell scripts perform this function. This chapter examines the ways in which you can create your own scripts, including the following:

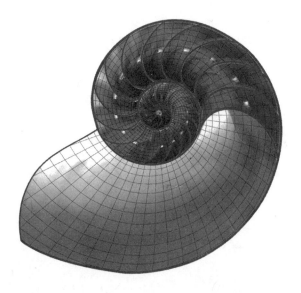

Creating Basic Shell Scripts

You have interacted with the shell in almost every chapter in this book. You now know that the shell accepts one command at a time from the command line. Why should you restrict yourself to entering commands in this fashion? A *shell script* is a file that contains a sequence of commands executed by the shell. The following example shows a shell script in its simplest form–only one line.

```
$ pwd
/u/chare/c21
$ ls -l
total 1
-rwxr-xr-x  1 chare   users        26 Aug 30 21:37 simple
$ cat simple
find / -user chare -print
$
```

Most shell scripts are typically many lines long, and many of the commands you have seen so far are actually shell scripts, as illustrated in the following.

```
$ file /bin/* ¦ grep command
/bin/basename:      commands text
/bin/false:    commands text
/bin/l:                commands text
/bin/lc:       commands text
/bin/lorder:   commands text
/bin/mc68k:    commands text
/bin/pdp11:    commands text
/bin/true:     commands text
/bin/u370:     commands text
/bin/u3b:      commands text
/bin/vax:      commands text
$
```

The shell script is essentially plain text. The difference is that most shell scripts have the execute bit turned on so that the file can be executed like a command. This chapter will examine how the shell processes the commands in your script, some rules and guidelines on writing your scripts, as well as an introduction to the constructs and commands used in building simple shell scripts. The chapter focuses primarily on the syntax and rules for the Bourne shell because virtually all the shell programs in existence use this language rather than the C shell. Bourne shell scripts will not run in the C shell, but they are processed without difficulty in the expanded environment of the Korn shell.

How Does the Shell Process a Script?

Shell scripts are not compiled languages like C or PASCAL. Rather, they are more like BASIC in that the interpreter reads the file one line at a time and executes the lines. Shell scripts process the lines sequentially. For each command that is not built into the shell, the shell starts a new process and waits for the command to complete before continuing the processing of the script. A shell script can start other shell programs. In fact, if the execute bit is turned on, the shell script has no way of knowing whether the command that it is starting is a compiled program like ls, or a shell script like dircmp.

You can execute a shell script in one of two ways: turn on the execute bit with chown, or run the command /bin/sh (or /bin/csh, or /bin/ksh), as seen in the following example.

```
$ ls -l
total 2
-rwxr-xr-x  1 chare    users         6 Aug 30 21:40 mycmd
-rwxr-xr-x  1 chare    users        26 Aug 30 21:37 simple
$ sh mycmd
```

```
    UID   PID  PPID  C   STIME  TTY   TIME COMMAND
   chare  2427    1  8  Aug 28  000  0:07 ksh
   chare  2857 2427 13 21:40:52 000  0:00 sh
   chare  2858 2857 60 21:40:52 000  0:01 ps
$ chmod +x mycmd
$ mycmd
    UID   PID  PPID  C   STIME  TTY   TIME COMMAND
   chare  2427    1 10  Aug 28  000  0:07 ksh
   chare  2860 2427 13 21:41:04 000  0:00 ksh
   chare  2861 2860 57 21:41:04 000  0:01 ps
$
```

The preceding example illustrates executing the shell script both ways. They both do the same thing. The difference is that when you run the command sh mycmd, it starts the command sh, which runs the commands in mycmd. In the second form, the execute bit is turned on and the login shell executes the command directly, by starting a copy of itself to run the commands.

Shell Script Etiquette

There is an etiquette to writing good shell scripts. Any programmer knows the importance of documentation, and good documentation within your shell script makes it easier to remember how it works later, when you or someone else has to modify it. The following example has a sample header that I use when writing any shell script that is longer than about 10 lines.

```
$ cat header
:   # or #!/bin/sh if your system supports it!
#
# @(#) command name - Version #
# Author:
# Date  :
# Description of the script
#       Indent one tab for readability
#
# Revision History
# Num   Date    Who     Description
# -------------------------------------------------------------
# 0     940724  C.Hare  Sample revision entry
#
# -------------------------------------------------------------
$
```

The preceding example illustrates several rules of etiquette. First, all Bourne shell programs should start with either a colon (:) as the first character on the first line, or #!/bin/sh. In either case, a Bourne shell will be started if it is not your default shell. If the shell script is for use in a C shell, then #!/bin/csh should be used; #!/bin/ksh would be used for the Korne shell. The syntax #!, if supported, specifies the name of the program that should be started to interpret and process the commands in the script. For example, PERL programmers know that they use #!/usr/local/perl to start the PERL interpreter.

The preceding example also illustrates how comments are inserted in a shell script. The pound symbol (#) is a comment indicator. It tells the shell that all text to its right is to be ignored. The comment indicator can appear anywhere on a line; it can be at the beginning of the line or somewhere else because of its position as the first line of the preceding example.

There can never be too many comments in a script or program because a program is only as good as the documentation that goes with it. If your script depends on a command working in a specific fashion, then you should indicate as such by comments in the script.

Variables

Every programming language has variables of one sort or another. The shell is no different. The variables do not have a type associated with them because the shell treats everything as text. Variables are created by defining a name and value for the variable.

One important concept to remember is that variable names are case-sensitive just as many things in UNIX are. For example, $USER is not the same as $user.

A good rule of thumb that generally holds true is that while most UNIX commands are lowercase, variables are virtually always UPPERCASE.

Creating Variables

All variables are assigned with the following syntax:

```
*** begin code ***
$ VAR=value
*** end code ***
```

The equal sign should have no spaces around it. The shell will not interpret the command as a variable assignment, but rather as a command that has two arguments. This is illustrated in the following example:

```
$
$ x = 100
x: not found
$ x=100
$
```

Variables can be assigned from other variables, from the output of programs, directly by the programmer, or even internally within the program.

In the C shell variables are defined using the command:

```
*** begin code ***
% set VAR = value
*** end code ***
```

Notice the distinct difference in how the assignment is performed. This is the first of many differences in how the shells work.

Variable names can consist of any combination of alphabetic and numeric characters, including the period (.) and underscore (_). The exception is that they cannot start with a number. Avoid characters that are special to the shell, such as the asterisk (*),the question mark (?), and the space. This is shown in the following example.

```
$ _gamma="Radiation!"
$2be=bad
2be=bad: not found
$ echo $x $_gamma
100 Radiation!
$
```

Accessing Variables

It is okay to create variables for other reasons, but the primary reason for so doing is to be able to access them later. To access the contents of a variable, use the dollar sign ($) in front of the variable name. This causes the shell to replace the variable name with the value of the variable. This use of the dollar sign is called *referencing*, and is illustrated in the following example:

```
$ x = 100
x: not found
$ x=100
$ echo $x
100
$ echo $HOME
/uchare
```

```
$ echo $PATH
:/bin:/usr/bin:/etc:/usr/local::/u/chare/bin:/usr/games:/usr/lib:/etc/
lddrv
$
```

The command echo will print the arguments that it is given. In this case, the argument is not the variable $x, but the value 100. The shell resolves the reference to the variable x, and puts the value of x on the command line for echo to print.

The ${} construct

There are times when the shell gets confused when it is expanding a variable reference. Suppose you want to rename a file from $filename to $filenameX. When the shell attempts to expand the value of $filename, it retrieves whatever the value is. When the shell attempts to get the value of $filenameX, it cannot because the shell has no knowledge of a variable named filenameX. In this situation, the use of the ${} construct is desirable. The following example illustrates this. The `${filename}` tells the shell where the variable name ends, and the text to be added begins. As a result, the shell correctly expands the value of `${filename}X`.

```
$ ls -l
total 2
-rwxr-xr-x  1 chare    users          6 Aug 30 21:40 mycmd
-rwxr-xr-x  1 chare    users         26 Aug 30 21:37 simple
$filename=simple
mv $filename $filenameX
mv: Insufficient arguments (1)
Usage: {mv¦cp¦ln} f1 f2
       {mv¦cp¦ln} f1 ... fn d1
       mv d1 d2
$ mv $filename ${filename}X
$ ls -l
total 2
-rwxr-xr-x  1 chare    users          6 Aug 30 21:40 mycmd
-rwxr-xr-x  1 chare    users         26 Aug 30 21:37 simpleX
$
```

It is a good habit to learn to use the ${} construct with all variables, or at the very least, with anyone that may be confused by the shell when it is being expanded.

Filename Substitution and Variables

It is possible to assign a list of files to a variable by using the shell's filename substitution wild cards. For example, consider the following example which shows that you can use this filename substitution to assign a list of files to a variable. The first example shows the use of the asterisk to match all the files, and the second to assign the files using a combination of the character class and the asterisk.

```
$ l
total 3
-rw-r--r--  1 chare    users        412 Aug 30 21:51 header
-rwxr-xr-x  1 chare    users          6 Aug 30 21:40 mycmd
-rwxr-xr-x  1 chare    users         26 Aug 30 21:37 simpleX
$ y=*
$ a=[hs]*
$ echo $y
header mycmd simpleX
$ echo $a
header simpleX
$
```

A question when looking at these examples is when did the shell insert the list of file names into the variable? The answer is when the variable is referenced. The shell does not do wild card expansion when being assigned to a variable. Interestingly enough, the shell performs the following steps when processing the first portion of the preceding example.

1. The shell scans the line and substitutes the asterisk for the value of y.

2. The shell rescans the line and sees the asterisk. At this point it replaces the asterisk with the list of file names.

3. The shell then runs the echo command, giving the file names as the arguments.

Understanding the Use of Quotes

The quoting mechanism in the shell, which you read about in Chapter 5, can be a source of confusion to new shell programmers. A simple rule can be observed: if in doubt, use quotes! The trick is in knowing when you want to use a single quote and when you want a double quote. This next part of the chapter looks at the quoting mechanisms. The most common use for quotes is to keep text that contains whitespace together.

The following example shows that the script is looking for the words Operating System in the file cshlogin. grep gives back an error because the shell separates arguments with whitespace. Because there is a space between the words Operating and System, grep thinks that System is the name of a file that should be opened. The result is that grep reports an error because it cannot open a file named System, but it does find the desired text in the file cshlogin. Quotes enable you to correct this type of behavior.

```
$ grep Operating System cshlogin
grep: can't open System
cshlogin:# what version of the Operating System are we running?  This
may have t
o be
$
```

The Single Quote

The purpose of the single quote is to hide any special characters from the shell. The preceding example shows grep reporting an error because the shell misinterpreted what you wanted it to do. You can use the single quotes to protect the space and group these two words together, which causes it to look like one argument, as shown in the following example.

```
$ grep Operating System cshlogin
grep: can't open System
cshlogin:# what version of the Operating System are we running?  This
may have to be
$ grep `Operating System´ cshlogin
# what version of the Operating System are we running?  This may have
to be
$
```

The major advantage of the single quote is that it protects the shell from seeing and interpreting characters that would otherwise be expanded by the shell. Put your text in a variable, as in the following example, to see what happens.

```
$ search="Operating System"
$ echo $search
Operating System
$ grep ´$search´ cshlogin
$
```

You were expecting grep to find the text, right? The shell did not see that there was a variable to expand because it ignores the text that is between the single quotes. The following example shows that there is one irritating problem with single quotes however.

```
$ a=´I feel really good today.´
$ echo $a
I feel really good today.
$ b=´* means list all of the files´
echo $b
Mail book cshlogin profile tcsh means list all of the files
$
```

Here you are reminded of how the shell processes the information you give it. The asterisk is not expanded when the variable is assigned, but expands later when the variable is referenced. The only way to effectively handle this situation is by using the double quotes.

One word of caution. The single quote is the character on the keyboard which slants from the top right to the left. This character is entirely different from the back quote, which starts at the top left and slants to the right.

They are interpreted entirely differently by the shell, and it is important to use the correct one. The use of the back quote is explained later on in this chapter, as command substitution.

The Double Quote

The double quote normally serves the same purposes as the single quote. The difference is that the double quote instructs the shell to ignore most special characters; the single quote ignores all of them. Specifically, the shell does not ignore the following characters when they are in double quotes:

- ✔ Dollar signs

- ✔ Back quotes

- ✔ Backslashes

Variable expansion, command substitution, and special character escapes are performed. All other special characters to the shell are ignored. Look at the preceding example. If you do it again with double quotes, will the result be different?

You can see in the next example that when you print the value of the variable b with no quotes, a list of file names plus your text appears. When you put single quotes around the variable, only the name of the variable appears because the shell does not know that it is supposed to expand it. With the double quotes, the asterisk is printed as an asterisk because the shell does not expand this character when it is between double quotes.

```
$ a="I feel really good today."
$ echo $a
I feel really good today.
$ b="* means list all of the files"
echo $b
Mail book cshlogin profile tcsh means list all of the files
$ echo '$b'
$b
```

```
$ echo "$b"
* means list all of the files
$
```

Just for fun, enclose the string you are printing in quotes for emphasis. This is accomplished by using the alternate set of quotes. Suppose you want the string to be surrounded with single quotes. The entire string, including the single quotes, is now surrounded by double quotes. If you want double quotes around the text, the entire string must be enclosed in single quotes. These possibilities are illustrated in the next example.

```
$ d1="`this is in single quotes`"
$ d2=`"This is in double quotes"`
$
$ echo $d1
`This is in single quotes`
$ echo $d2
"This is in double quotes"
$
```

Command Substitution

Command substitution is performed whenever the command is enclosed in back quotes. These quotes instruct the command to execute the command first, and then perform the remainder of the line. In the next example, you see two versions of command substitution.

```
$ DATE=`date`
$ echo $DATE
Tue Aug 30 22:21:34 EST 1994
$
$ echo "The current date and time are `date`"
The current date and time are Tue Aug 30 22:21:50 EST 1994
$
```

The first example demonstrates the use of command substitution to save the output of a command in a variable; the second example shows command substitution within another command. The remainder of this chapter shows more examples of when command substitution is useful.

You can create a small shell script that displays the current status of your system. The actual code for this command is included at the end of this chapter; the output is shown in the next example.

```
$ info
Current System Date is : Tue Aug 30 22:24:27 EST 1994
Users logged in are :      2
USERNAME    WHERE       WHEN
chare       tty000      Aug 30 21:34
root        w1          Aug 20 05:01
Current Disk Space status:
             Actual Disk Space free
/mnt     :      0.28 MB of   0.30 MB avail (92.92%).
/        :     16.99 MB of  35.07 MB avail (48.44%).
Total    :     17.27 MB of  35.38 MB avail (48.82%).
$
```

This command, called info, provides statistics on the system. These include the date and time, how many users are logged on and who they are, and how much disk space remains on the system.

The Backslash

The effects of the backslash are similar to putting single quotes around a single character. Occasionally, you may want to use a character, but do not want the shell, or some other command to place any meaning on it. One common example is the dollar sign. The shell uses the dollar sign to indicate that a variable expansion should occur. As you read in Chapter 8, regular expressions use the dollar sign to anchor a pattern to the end of a line. How do you list all the shell variables in a shell script if the dollar sign will be interpreted in one fashion or another?

The next example shows how the use of the backslash solves this problem. Put the backslash in front of the dollar sign, which removes the special meaning from it for the shell and for the grep command. The result is a list of where the variables are referenced in the script. This example is a tricky one because the backslash cannot do it all on its own. For the command to be successful, you must enclose the pattern in single quotes. This is because the shell removes the special meaning associated with the backslash when it is being expanded. As a result, the backslash is still needed to grep that the dollar sign has no special meaning in this case.

```
$ grep '\$' profile
USER=${LOGNAME}
#          $1          $2          $3  $4  $5
set $OP
echo "Welcome to $1 $3.$4 ($5)"
echo "Last logged in on `cat -s $HOME/.lastlogin`"
echo "`date` on `tty`" > $HOME/.lastlogin
MAIL=/usr/spool/mail/${LOGNAME}
case `basename $SHELL` in
```

```
        PS1="$ "
        PS1="$ "
$ grep "\$.*" profile
USER=${LOGNAME}
#          $1          $2          $3  $4  $5
set $OP
echo "Welcome to $1 $3.$4 ($5)"
echo "Last logged in on `cat -s $HOME/.lastlogin`"
echo "`date` on `tty`" > $HOME/.lastlogin
MAIL=/usr/spool/mail/${LOGNAME}
case `basename $SHELL` in
        PS1="$ "
        PS1="$ "
$
```

The second example accomplishes the same output, but uses double quotes and an additional pattern to match the variables. The first example is too generic to be able to work properly without the single quotes.

Adding It Up

Even in simple shell scripts, you want to be able to perform some measure of arithmetic. In the Bourne shell, this is accomplished with the command expr because the Bourne shell has no built-in mechanism for arithmetic calculations. The Korn and C shells, however, have their own mechanism for performing arithmetic.

The expr Command

The command expr, which can do more than math (shown in Chapter 24) is used to do math calculations in the Bourne shell. It can be used without difficulty in both the C and Korn shells, but they have their own built-in mechanism for performing rudimentary math functions.

The shell assumes that even numbers are letters, so how does it handle math? Not very well as you can see in the following example.

```
$ a=1
$ b=$a+1
$ echo $b
a+1
$
```

When execution of the statement that looks like addition is performed, the shell simply adds the text +1 to the existing contents of variable a. To achieve what you want in the preceding example, you must use the command expr. The expr command evaluates the expression that was provided on the command line and returns the result. It can be used for more than just math. For example, it can be used to measure the length of a string. This discussion, however, focuses on its arithmetic capabilities. It is important to note that expr can only perform integer arithmetic functions. Floating-point calculations require the use of the command bc. The next example shows how to add the expression from the preceding example using expr.

```
$ b=`expr $a + 1`
$ echo $b
2
    $
```

In the preceding example, you see that expr accepts as arguments variables or values each separated by an operator. The operators expr knows are standard ones: the plus sign (+) indicates addition; the minus sign or hyphen (-) indicates subtraction; the asterisk (*) means multiplication; and the slash (/) means division. The modulus, or remainder operator is the percent sign (%). The next example illustrates the use of each of these operators with expr.

```
$ expr 10+2
10+2
$ expr 10 + 2
12
$ expr 10 -2
expr: syntax error
$ expr 10 - 2
8
$ expr 10 * 2
expr: syntax error
$ expr 10 \* 2
20
$ expr 10 / 2
5
$
```

In the preceding example, you see that the expression syntax for expr is very precise. Each part of the expression is considered an argument, so there must be a space between every operand and operator. In the first example, expr simply displayed the argument that you provided because there were no spaces to indicate what each argument was.

In the subtraction example, the spacing was altered to show how expr handles errors like this. In this case, expr sees the arguments as 10 and -2, not as 10, minus, and 2. Notice the multiplication example. What happened? The asterisk is expanded by the shell to mean the files in the current directory. As a result, expr reports an error. To be able to use multiplication properly, it is necessary to escape the asterisk with the backslash. This removes the meaning from the asterisk, and the shell ignores it.

Math in the Korn and C Shells

Both of these shells are capable of processing arithmetic without the need for expr, although they each have a slightly different syntax. The next example shows some integer arithmetic in the C shell using the built-in support.

```
% @ A = 1
% @ b = 100
% @ c = $a + $b
101
% @ c = $c - 50
% echo $c
51
% @ c = $c / 2
% echo $c
25
% @ d = $c * 4
% echo $d
100
%
```

In the preceding example, the use of the at symbol (@) instructs the C shell that the variable named after the symbol is to be used for integer mathematics. With the obvious exception of not having to use the backslash with the multiplication operator, the operation is equivalent to using expr.

One of the primary reasons users move from the Bourne shell to Korn, or another, is its ability to manipulate variables and understand them as items other than text. The following script increments from 1 to a number specified on the command line in the Korn shell.

```
# increment from 1 to whatever number is specified on the command line
typeset -i x y
x=$1
y=1
unitl [ "$y"="$x"]
do
print $y
let y="$y+1"
done
print $y
```

This can also be accomplished in the C shell with the following:

```
#!/bib/csh
set x= $1
set y = 1
while ( $y != $x )
        echo $y
        @ y  += 1
end
echo $y
```

Shell Arguments

When you write shell scripts, eventually you will want to pass arguments to the command. Arguments enable you to build a more powerful script that is flexible and responsive to the arguments, giving the impression that the command was written specifically for them.

Positional Parameters

The shell uses ten positional parameters and several special variables for use with arguments that come in through the command line or when you set them. These positional parameters are numbered from 1 to 9, and are accessed by putting a dollar sign in front of the number. For example, $2 will access the second positional parameter. If there is no value for the parameter specified, then the value is null.

The following example shows the output of a shell script that collects arguments and prints the values of all ten positional parameters. Notice that the actual values have been delimited with > and < signs. These characters help you see more easily which values were empty. The first example shows that there were not ten arguments provided on the command line. In the second, there were twelve arguments. The shell cannot process more than ten positional parameters at one time. The command shift is used to move the positional parameters to the left. Because shift is of limited value unless some other shell constructs such as looping have been presented, shift is saved for Chapter 23.

```
$ args  CHris Terri Matt Meagan
1 = >CHris<
2 = >Terri<
3 = >Matt<
4 = >Meagan<
5 = ><
6 = ><
7 = ><
8 = ><
9 = ><
```

```
$ args Jim Laurier Josh Kim Tim Allan Kaitlin Frank Carol Ashley Amber
1 = >Jim<
2 = >Laurier<
3 = >Josh<
4 = >Kim<
5 = >Tim<
6 = >Allan<
7 = >Kaitlin<
8 = >Frank<
9 = >Carol<
$
```

Several other shell variables are related to the command-line arguments. Table 20.1 lists these similar variables.

Table 20.1
Command-Line Variables

Variable	Explanation
$#	Number of arguments on the command line
$*	All arguments on the command line
$@	All arguments on the command line, after quotes have been placed around each of them

The best way to see what these variables do is to add them to your command args. The next example shows what arguments display after you add the $# variable, which explains how many positional parameters are not null. This is accomplished with a shell script aptly named args.

```
$ args one two three
There are 3 positional paremeters set.
They are:
1 = >one<
2 = >two<
3 = >three<
4 = ><
5 = ><
6 = ><
7 = ><
8 = ><
9 = ><
$
```

The $# variable provides an easy method for you to know how many positional parameters are set. As you will see in Chapter 23, this variable is useful for checking to see if the needed arguments are provided for those commands that must have them.

The next variable is the $*, which addresses all ten of the positional parameters. Add it to your args program to see if your output looks like the following example.

```
$ args one two three go!
The command line is:
one two three go!
There are 4 positional paremeters set.
They are:
1 = >one<
2 = >two<
3 = >three<
4 = >go!<
5 = ><
6 = ><
7 = ><
8 = ><
9 = ><
$
```

With the addition of this variable to the command, you can see what exactly has been provided on the command line. Now you have seen what the positional parameters are, but the $* variable is all of the positional parameters. This variable is also useful for processing a list of arguments, as you will read in Chapter 23.

Putting an End to It

As with all good things, shell scripts must end. The exit command obviously ends a shell script. This ensures that a return code is provided to the parent. For most cases, exit is used with the argument of zero. This indicates to the program that started your shell script that the command executed and exited successfully. Chapter 24 looks at exit more closely and introduces looping and decision making in your shell scripts. The programs included here end with the exit command.

Summary

This chapter introduced many aspects of the operating system shell and the scripting language. Three scripts follow to illustrate the means by which simple commands are used to construct them. Chapter 23 explores this concept further and covers the remainder of the scripting language.

Some Sample Scripts

The following scripts illustrate the use of the scripting language and show how it is implemented in the real world. Some of the concepts shown may not have been introduced here, but will be in Chapter 23. The important thing is to illustrate how complex scripts are created from simple commands.

Do remember that all scripts are contained on the companion disk to save you the necessity of typing them in should you wish to try them. Their inclusion here is merely for purposes of illustration and enlightenment.

Listing 1. info

```
:  # or #!/bin/sh if your system supports it!
#
# @(#) info - Version 1.0
# Author: Chris Hare
# Date : July 24, 1994
# Description of the script
#    this script will report on some system statistics. Most noteably,
#    they are:
#        the current system time and date
#        how many users are logged in on the system
#        who is logged in
#        the current disk space free.
#
# Revision History
# Num  Date  Who   Description
# ------------------------------------------------------------------
# 0    940724 C.Hare Sample revision entry
#
# ------------------------------------------------------------------
#
# Report on the current system time and date. This uses command
# substitution
# to include the date in the echo statement.
#
echo "Current System Date is : `date`"
#
# find out how many users are currently logged in.
# Doing the variable assignment and then printing the variable is not
# any slower than putting the pipe in a command subsstitution in the
  echo
```

```
# statement.
#
NUM='who ¦ wc -l'
echo "Users logged in are : $NUM"
echo "USERNAME  WHERE     WHEN"
who
#
# Now we report disk space.
#
echo "Current Disk Space status:"
#
# Use df -v if you have it. Alternatively, you could use ordinary df,
# or some other command, such as dfspace under SCO UNIX.
#
dfspace
exit 0
```

Listing 2. args

```
:   # or #!/bin/sh if your system supports it!
#
# @(#) args - Version 1.0
# Author: Chris Hare
# Date : July 24, 1994
# Description of the script
#    Print the ten positional parameters from the command line.
#
# Revision History
# Num  Date  Who   Description
# ------------------------------------------------------------------
# 0    940724 C.Hare Initial Version
# 1    940724 C.Hare Added line to print how many positionals are set
# 2    940724 C.Hare Added line to print the command line arguments
#
# ------------------------------------------------------------------
echo 'The command line is (using $*):'
echo $*
echo "There are $# positional parameters set."
echo "they are: "
echo "1 = >$1<"
echo "2 = >$2<"
echo "3 = >$3<"
echo "4 = >$4<"
echo "5 = >$5<"
```

```
echo "6 = >$6<"
echo "7 = >$7<"
echo "8 = >$8<"
echo "9 = >$9<"
exit 0
```

Listing 3.   header

```
:   # or #!/bin/sh if your system supports it!
#
# @(#) command name - Version #
# Author:
# Date :
# Description of the script
#     Indent one tab for readability
#
# Revision History
# Num  Date  Who   Description
# ----------------------------------------------------------------------
# 0    940724 C.Hare Sample revision entry
#
# ----------------------------------------------------------------------
```

Chapter Snapshot

awk is one of the most useful utilities in the UNIX operating system. While it can be called a utility by its inclusion in the standard directories, in reality it is a powerful programming language that performs functions no other UNIX utility can. Discussed in detail here, the topics include the following:

The awk Processor

Awk is a programming and data-manipulation language. It is named after its creators Alfred Aho, Peter Weinberger, and Brian Kernighan. Using awk's programming language, you can create short programs that read input files, sort data, process it, perform arithmetic on the input, and generate reports. awk makes heavy use of regular expressions and comparison operations on strings and numbers.

One of the uses of the shell is to prototype other programs using the rich standard command set. The same is true for awk. Because of the shortness of the programs that you can create with awk, it is a good prototype tool. Part of the ease of use in the prototype is on the command line. Once a program has been prototyped in awk, it is easy to port it to the C language and create a compiled executable.

Running an awk Program

You can start awk programs in one of two ways. You can place the commands to be executed on awk's command line, or you can put them in a file by themselves. In small awk programs, you often place the commands on the command line, but awk programs that are larger in size are generally put in a file to facilitate debugging and future revisions of the program.

Only three command-line arguments are available for use in awk:

✔ -Fc —Specifies an alternate field separator, using character c

✔ -f prog —Reads the file prog to get the program instructions to be executed

✔ - —Reads the standard input for the files to process

To put the program on the command line, you must enclose the commands for awk in single quotes to ensure that awk gets the program as a single argument, and that it is not processed in some manner by the shell. Consider the following example:

```
$ awk ´commands´ file(s)
```

Few small programs, however, are one line long, so you must have a way to have awk read multiple program lines from the command line. You accomplish this task by simply pressing Enter between each of the commands that are being given to awk, as in this example:

```
awk ´
        {
          command(s)
}´ files
```

For most situations, awk is instructed to get its information from a file that contains the instructions that awk is to execute. By using the -f flag on the command line, you instruct awk to read its instructions from the file that is named after the -f, as illustrated in this example:

```
$ awk -f cmd.awk
```

Understanding the Structure of the awk Language

The awk language has a specific structure. Although it resembles the shell programming language in many areas, awk's syntax is very much its own. awk was originally designed to work in the text-processing arena and is well suited to this and other applications because

of how it handles the incoming data. The awk language is based on executing a series of instructions whenever a pattern is matched in the input data. The syntax of the language is as follows:

```
pattern { action }
```

where *pattern* is what awk is looking for in the input data, and *action* is the series of commands that are executed when awk finds a match between the pattern and the input data.

An awk command doesn't always need a pattern. The simplest awk program would simply print every line in the given input stream. This program doesn't match any text, it just prints it all. Consider this example:

```
{ print $0 }
```

Curly braces are not always required around your program, but you can use them to group a series of instructions based on a specific pattern. Consider the following example:

```
$3 == 0 { print $1 }
```

In this case, if the third field has a value of zero, awk prints the first field. If no pattern is indicated, the instructions are executed for all input lines.

An awk program also can be missing the action portion.

When reading your program file, awk evaluates it to ensure that no syntax errors exist. If it finds syntax errors, awk issues error messages. Assuming that no syntactical errors are found, awk reads the data input one line at a time and evaluates each of the patterns in order. For each pattern that matches, the associated commands are executed. In situations where no pattern is specified, the actions are processed for each input line. When awk finds a pattern-action statement that is missing the action, awk simply prints the matching lines on standard output.

The awk language consists of a wide variety of pattern-matching formats, actions, input and output control, flow control, and functions. The built-in functions include both string and arithmetic operators such as sine and cosine capabilities.

Like most programming languages, awk also includes support for comments. You indicate comments in your awk program with the pound (#) symbol, like that used in the shells. You see examples of comments later in this chapter. The primary advantage to using copious quantities of comments in some of the programming languages, which at times border on the purely esoteric, is to enable easier modification and review of what the program does six weeks (or six months) from now.

Before you can start to take a detailed look at the command syntax and learn how to build an awk program, you must examine how awk handles input data files.

Working with Records, Fields, and Separators

As awk processes each input line, it deals with records and fields. A *record* is considered each individual line of input. One of the most important features of awk is that it splits each input record into fields using the current field separator. The default field separator is a space or a tab, and the record separator is a new line.

You use two kinds each of record and field separators. The record separator, RS, is used for input files, and the output record separator, ORS, for creating the output records. It is possible and entirely reasonable for the input and output record separators to be different if required.

The following shows how to change the record separator:

```
RS = "\n"
```

(In awk, you use several special characters to represent other special characters. One such character is \n, which represents a new line. You learn about the others when you look at creating output.)

The field separator, FS, is like RS. It is the field separator for the input records. Likewise, OFS is the output separator for the output records. The field separator is defined in the variable FS, and you can change it by using an assignment statement. To change the field separator to a colon, for example, insert the following line in your awk program:

```
FS = ":"
```

Table 21.1 lists these special variables, their meanings, and default values.

Table 21.1
Field and Record Separators

Separator	Meaning	Default Value
FS	(Input) Field Separator	space, tab
OFS	Output Field Separator	space
RS	(Input) Record Separator	new line
ORS	Output Record Separator	new line

The awk variable $0 refers to the entire record. As awk reads the input, the entire record is assigned to the variable $0. Each field, as split with the field separator, is assigned to the variables $1, $2, $3, and so on. A line contains essentially an unlimited number of fields, with each field being accessed by the field number. When you examine how to create output by using awk, you look at these variables in more detail.

Recognizing the Built-in Variables

awk has a number of built-in variables. You have already seen four of them (FS, OFS, RS, and ORS). The others are used to provide the name of the file that is currently being processed (FILENAME), the record number (NR), and the number of fields in the input records (NF).

The NF variable holds the number of fields in the input record. If five fields exist, NF is 5. If 10 fields exist, NF is set to 10. Notice that in these two cases, you do not use the $ symbol to access the value of NF. Using $NF provides the value of the last field on the input line, not the number of fields.

The NR variable holds the current input record number. With this variable you can keep track of how many records have been processed through the awk script. Finally, you use the FILENAME variable to provide the name of the current input file. This variable can be useful if you specified multiple input files on the command line. Like NF, neither NR nor FILENAME is used with the dollar sign ($). You look at these variables again in the next section.

Creating Simple Output

The simplest form of output for an awk program is to print every input line. The following command instructs awk to print each input line:

```
{ print }
```

Consider this example:

```
$ awk ´{ print }´ users
root
service
chare
jonh
andrew
beccat
terri
frankh
$
```

The print command has two major forms in awk:

```
print expr1, expr2, ..., exprN

print ( expr1, expr2, ..., exprN )
```

Unlike the shell, where $0 means the name of the program, $0 in awk means the whole line input record. Using { print } is thus the same as using the instruction { print $0 }.

Remember that using the print instruction on its own prints the entire record. If you want to print a blank line, you must use the following command:

```
print ""
```

You also can choose to print only certain lines, or fields within certain lines. awk uses the same syntax as the shell for addressing fields. To access a field, precede the field number with a dollar sign, as in the preceding example, $0. If you want to access field 12, use the notation $12. Unlike the shell, the number of fields on a line has no limit. As you saw in the preceding section, awk uses a calculated variable to keep track of how many fields are on a line. This variable is NF.

If you want to know how many fields are on a line, use the variable NF. In the following example, each value is the number of fields that are on each line in the file proc:

```
$ awk '{ print NF }' proc
1
14
15
5
0
2
1
7
$
```

To know the value of the last field, use the variable $NF. These two commands are not equivalent, as illustrated in the following example:

```
$ awk '{ print NF, $NF } ' proc
1 i
14 real
15 source
5 program.
0
2 oops
1 a
7 branch
$
```

To reiterate, NF is the number of the last field in the record. $NF, on the other hand, is the value of that last field.

Suppose that you have a list of cities and their distance from your location, as in this example:

Ottawa 0

Toronto 300

Montreal 175

Nepean 15

Orlando 1300

Halifax 1200

Syracuse 300

With this file, you look at the first part of simple output. First, suppose that you want to print only the city names. The city is the first field in each record. Because each field is addressed by the field number for the record, the following program prints the city names:

```
$ awk '{ print $1 }' city
Ottawa
Toronto
Montreal
Nepean
Orlando
Halifax
Syracuse
$
```

You learned in the preceding section that awk has several built-in variables. One of these variables is NR, which holds the record number of the current file. You can add this variable to the output of your program by separating each print argument with a comma, as shown in this example:

```
$ awk '{ print NR, $1 }' city
1 Ottawa
2 Toronto
3 Montreal
4 Nepean
5 Orlando
6 Halifax
7 Syracuse
$
```

This command successfully, and sequentially, numbers each line of the output. The print command inserts the OFS, or output field separator, between each of the print values. In this case, because it has not been defined, the default of a space is used. awk knows that it should insert the OFS because of the common separator between the arguments. If you do not include the comma in the code, however, awk prints the output without a space, as in the following:

```
$ awk '{ print NR $1 }' city
1Ottawa
2Toronto
3Montreal
4Nepean
5Orlando
6Halifax
7Syracuse
$
```

What if you want to print the distance between here and your destination without printing the city name? You would simply change the $1 to $2, as in the following:

```
$ awk '{ print $2 }' city
0
300
175
15
1300
1200
300
$
```

The approach here is the same as when you printed only the city name. But what do you do when you want to print a different character between the fields in your output? You have a couple of choices. One option is to insert the character in your print statement, as shown in this example:

```
$ awk '{ print $1 ":" $2 }' city
Ottawa:0
Toronto:300
Montreal:175
Nepean:15
Orlando:1300
Halifax:1200
Syracuse:300
$
```

Here, you put the colon in quotes between the fields that you want printed. You must enclose the colon in quotes; otherwise, awk generates an error.

The alternative solution is to adjust the value of the OFS, as in this example:

```
$ awk '{ OFS=":"
> print $1, $2
> }' city
Ottawa:0
Toronto:300
Montreal:175
Nepean:15
Orlando:1300
Halifax:1200
Syracuse:300
$
```

Here you see two things different from the other awk programs you have seen so far. The first difference is that this program spans multiple lines. You can set up the program this way because awk continues accepting commands until it sees the entry of the second single quotation mark on a line. The second difference is that this program illustrates how to change the way awk works by altering the OFS variable. The comma in the code between $1 and $2 is now no longer equal to the default space character, but a colon instead.

These examples demonstrate about the highest level of output you can get using the print command. You can, however, create much fancier output by using the command printf.

Creating Practical Output

Often, the simple output that you have seen so far can't handle the intricate detail that you frequently want in your programs. The more complex output is handled with the command

```
printf( format, value, value ...)
```

Like the print command, printf doesn't have to be enclosed in parentheses—they are optional—but using them is a good practice. When making the decision to use the parentheses, be consistent when using print or printf.

This syntax is like that of the printf command in the C language, and the specifications for the format are the same. You define the format by inserting a specification that defines how the value is to be printed. The format specification consists of a % followed by a letter. Table 21.2 lists the various specifications that are available for the printf command.

Table 21.2
Specifications for printf

Specification	Description
%c	Prints a single ASCII character
%d	Prints a decimal number
%e	Prints a scientific notation representation of numbers; format is [-]d.dddddE[+-]dd
%f	Prints a floating point representation; format is [-]ddd.dddddd
%g	Prints %e or %f; whichever is shorter
%o	Prints an unsigned octal number
%s	Prints an ASCII string
%x	Prints an unsigned hexadecimal number
%%	Prints a % sign; no conversion is performed

You can supply some additional formatting parameters between the % and the character. These parameters further refine how the value is printed (see table 21.3).

Table 21.3
printf Formatting Parameters

Parameter	Description
-	Left-justifies the expression in the field
width	Pads the field to the specified width as needed (a leading zero pads the field with zeros)
.prec	Maximum string width or the maximum number of digits to the right of the decimal point

The printf command enables you to control and, where needed, translate the value from one format to another. When you want to print the value of a variable, you must provide a specification that instructs printf how to print the information. You normally enclose the specification in double quotes. You must include a specification parameter for each variable that is being passed to printf. If too few specification parameters are included, printf does not print all the values.

To better look at how printf works, reconsider an example that you have seen already in this chapter:

```
$ awk ´{ printf "%s", $1 }´ city
OttawaTorontoMontrealNepeanOrlandoHalifaxSyracuse$
```

This output is probably not what you would expect. Note that the specification is enclosed in quotes and appears first on the command line. The %s indicates that this is a string to be printed by awk. The variable is $1, which is the name of the city from your file. Why did awk print the city names all on one line? Like the printf command in the C programming language, the printf statement in awk does not print a new line unless explicitly told.

You can include two special characters in the format component of the printf statement. These characters are \t for a tab, and \n for a new line. The use of the new line is illustrated in the following example:

```
$ awk ´{ printf ( "%s\n", $1 ) }´ city
Ottawa
Toronto
Montreal
Nepean
Orlando
Halifax
Syracuse
$
```

You saw earlier in this chapter that you can add the record number to your output by using the variable NR in the printf statement. In this example, you take your first look at printing numbers and using both the tab and new line in your output:

```
$ awk ´{ printf ( "%d\t%s\n", NR, $1 ) }´ city
1       Ottawa
2       Toronto
3       Montreal
4       Nepean
5       Orlando
6       Halifax
7       Syracuse
$
```

Here, the first output field, which is a number, is specified in the format with a %d. This specification means that the corresponding value is an integer or decimal number. The second value is a string, which is the city name. A tab (\t) is used to separate the fields, and a new line (\n) is used to terminate each output record. In many cases, if the data that you want to print is not of the same format, awk translates the value into the appropriate format.

Have a closer look at printing numbers. Examine table 21.4.

Table 21.4
printf Options

Format	Value of $1	Results of printf (format,$1)
%c	101	e
%d	101	101
%5d	101	101
%05d	101	00101
%e	101	1.010000e+02
%f	101	101.000000
%7.2f	101	101.00
%g	101	101
%o	101	145
%04o	101	0145
%x	101	65

When you examine this table carefully, you can see that the number 101 has been represented in many different ways, not only in the traditional decimal number systems, but also in hexadecimal and octal. When a zero follows the percent sign, the printf statement is instructed that the number is to be padded to the specified length using leading zeroes. If zeroes are not specified, the padding is done with spaces.

%7.2f, for example, instructs awk to print the number as a floating point, with a maximum size of seven characters including the decimal point. Because the decimal point on the format has the digit 2 on the right of the decimal, the number which that is printed also will have two decimal places.

The final item to call to your attention is that you are not restricted to printing numbers with numbers. Using the %c format, printf translates the given number into the corresponding character on the ASCII table. This ASCII character is what is printed, not the actual number.

Printing strings with printf is also easy, and the %s format for strings offers several variations, which are listed in table 21.5.

Table 21.5
Results of printf Formatting

Format	Value of $1	Result of printf (format, $1)
l%sl	January	lJanuaryl
l%10sl	January	l Januaryl
l%-10sl	January	lJanuary l
l%.3sl	January	lJanl
l%10.3sl	January	l Janl
l%-10.3sl	January	lJan l
%%	January	%

For the most part, the examples presented here are self-explanatory. But several bear particular mention. When you add a level of precision to a string by using `width.precision`, you are instructing awk to print a field that is `width` characters in length but that uses only the `precision` number of characters from the variable. When you instruct printf with the specification %10.3, for example, you create a field that is padded with spaces to be 10 characters in length, but that has only the first three characters of the variable. Lastly, if you simply want to print a percent sign on its own, you indicate such an instruction by including two percent indicators in your format statement.

The print and printf commands that you have seen thus far write their information to standard output. You can change or redirect that operation to some extent. In the next section, you look at how awk handles output to places other than standard output.

Files and Pipes

With awk, you have the ability to send your output to both files and pipes. If you can, you should try to use standard output, because it enables you to create an awk program that can function as a filter, thereby increasing the usefulness of your program.

Output to Files

Like the shell, awk uses the output redirection operators > and >> to put its output into a file rather than onto standard output. Look at the following example:

```
$ awk '{ printf ( "%d\t%s\n", NR, $1 ) > "/tmp/z" }' city
$ cat /tmp/z
1       Ottawa
```

```
2        Toronto
3        Montreal
4        Nepean
5        Orlando
6        Halifax
7        Syracuse
$
```

When you examine the format of the statement, you can see that the output redirection is done after the printf statement is complete. The > and >> symbols react like their counterparts in the shell, so > creates the file if it doesn't exist, and >> appends to the existing file.

You must enclose the file name in quotes, or else it is simply an uninitialized awk variable, and the combination of instructions generates an error from awk. The preceding example demonstrates using printf, but you can use redirection with the print command, following the same format.

The only caveat that you need to remember about the redirection symbols is that if you use them improperly, awk gets confused about whether the symbol means redirection or is a relation operator. This situation usually occurs when awk cannot tell the difference in the print statement. Consider this example:

```
{ print $1, $2 > $3 }
```

Does this mean that the values of $1 and $2 are to be sent to $3, or that $2 should be printed only if greater than $3? To resolve this type of problem, you must use parentheses to group the relational operator, as in this example:

```
{ print $1, ( $2 > $3 ) }
```

Output to Pipes

Output into pipes in awk is not that different from the way you accomplish it in a shell. To send the output of a print command into a pipe, follow the print command with a pipe symbol (|) and the name of the command, as in the following:

```
print expr ¦ command
```

The following example illustrates using pipes in awk:

```
$ awk '{ print $1 ¦ "sort" }' city
Halifax
Montreal
Nepean
Orlando
Ottawa
Syracuse
```

```
Toronto
$
```

As you saw in output redirection, you must enclose the command in quotes. In fact, the name of the pipe is the name of the command that is being executed. In most circumstances, a pipe or file is opened once, although you can close and reopen it during the course of the script. That you can close and reopen redirectors is important because awk sets out certain limits on what you can do. These limits are presented at the end of the chapter in the Summary.

Output to Standard Error

When you use awk to create output, you always send it to standard output. Because the awk program might be sending information to a file or pipe internally, or because the output might be going through an external pipe, you need a different path for error messages or diagnostics. This different path is through the standard error device that is associated with the terminal.

Several different methods are available for sending the output to standard error.

This example opens a pipe to the cat command, where the standard output is redirected to standard error:

```
print message ¦ "cat 1>&2"
```

The following example redirects the output of the print command to go directly to the terminal:

```
print message > "/dev/tty"
```

The end result is the same in both cases. The output that would normally be printed on standard output and be missed in the execution of the awk program is actually printed elsewhere.

Closing Files and Pipes

The last issue to deal with while you examine files and pipes is how to close these files and pipes. The reason for closing the files and pipes when they are not required is to ensure that you do not exceed the system-imposed limits. You are generally allowed 15 open files and one pipe per awk program, although different implementations might change these limits.

To close a file or pipe, you use the close command with the name of the file or pipe to be closed. The name, or expression that is the name, is the same name used when the file or pipe was opened. Consider this example:

```
print $1 > "/tmp/log"
.....
```

```
close( "/tmp/log" )
```

This close command closes the file opened in the print statement. Likewise, when using the print command with a pipe, you use the name of the command that was on the other end of the pipe, as in this example:

```
print $1 ¦ "command"
...
close( "command" )
```

In both cases, the file or pipe is closed and the resources used are freed for later use in your program.

Up to now, you have closely examined the structure of an awk program and how to create output. Much of the power of the awk language comes not from the output it generates, but from its powerful pattern-matching features.

Making Selections by Comparison

You have seen that the basis of the awk language is a pattern-action pair, and you have seen some of the possible actions, that being output. What you are going to examine now is the powerful pattern-matching features of awk.

Matching Numerical Values

Patterns can consist of several different formats, such as numbers or strings. For matching numerical values, you use the comparison operators listed in table 21.6.

Table 21.6
Numerical Comparison Operators

Operator	Meaning
==	Equal to
<	Less than
>	Greater than
>=	Greater than or equal to
<=	Less than or equal to
!=	Not equal to

These operators enable you to select input lines based on the successful comparison of a field to a numerical value. The comparison operator is part of the pattern, along with two operands.

The sample city files used throughout this chapter (and listed again for you here) are the source for the simple, one-line example programs that follow.

```
$ cat city
Ottawa 0
Toronto 300
Montreal 175
Nepean 15
Orlando 1300
Halifax 1200
Syracuse 300
$
```

The following example shows a series of operations being conducted on the text shown previously as being in the city file:

```
$ awk '$2 < 50 { print $1 }' city
Ottawa
Nepean
$ awk '$2 > 1000 { print $1 }' city
Orlando
Halifax
$ awk '$2 == 300 { print $1 }' city
Toronto
Syracuse
$ awk '$2 >= 1000 { print $1 }' city
Orlando
Halifax
$ awk '$2 <= 500 { print $1 }' city
Ottawa
Toronto
Montreal
Nepean
Syracuse
$
```

In all these cases, the programs are making a comparison between the second field in the file and a specific number. If the pattern evaluates as true, that is to say a match occurs, the action is executed. In these cases, the value of the first field, the city name, is printed. These programs represent your first look at using patterns to perform an action. You can create a more complex version of these commands to combine them all into one program.

Consider the following examples:

```
$ cat a1
$2 < 50 { printf "%s is less than 50 miles from here\n", $1 }
$2 > 1000 { printf "%s is more than 1000 miles from here\n", $1 }
$2 == 300 { printf "%s is 300 miles from here\n", $1 }
$2 <= 500 { printf "%s is less than 500 miles from here\n", $1 }
$2 >= 1000 { printf "%s is more than 1000 miles from here\n", $1 }
$
```

When you look at this program and the contents of the file, some of the data lines are likely to match multiple entry patterns in the program. Later in this chapter, you see how you can skip the remaining lines after a match is made. For now, however, what do you see when you run the program? The following lines show the program's output:

```
$ awk -f a1 city
Ottawa is less than 50 miles from here
Ottawa is less than 500 miles from here
Toronto is 300 miles from here
Montreal is less than 500 miles from here
Nepean is less than 50 miles from here
Nepean is less than 500 miles from here
Orlando is more than 1000 miles from here
Orlando is more than 1000 miles from here
Halifax is more than 1000 miles from here
Halifax is more than 1000 miles from here
Syracuse is 300 miles from here
$
```

As expected, the lines in the data file matched more than one pattern. (This example is somewhat far-fetched.)

Remember that these operators are for comparing numbers. You cannot use them to compare strings.

Matching Strings

Matching strings is slightly different from matching numbers or numerical expressions. The operators used to match strings are listed in table 21.7.

Table 21.7
String Comparison Operators

Operator	Meaning
==	Matches the string exactly
/regex/	Matches the string exactly or matches the regular expression
expression ~ /regex/	Matches if the string in expression contains a substring matched by regex
expression !~ /regex/	Matches if the string in expression does not contain a substring matched by regex

Notice that awk understands the powerful regular expression language that grep and other UNIX commands use. The following example illustrates using the string-matching commands in awk:

```
$ awk '/.a./ { print $1 }' city
Ottawa
Montreal
Nepean
Orlando
Halifax
Syracuse
$
```

In this first example, the pattern is to match the regular expression pattern .a. You might recall from Chapter 8, "grep and find," that a period in a regular expression indicates that a character must be found. In this example, you are looking for words where a character is followed by the letter a and then any character. As a result, when you run the command, it matches virtually all the entries in the file.

```
$ awk '/or/ { print $1 }' city
Toronto
$
```

Here, any line that contains or anywhere within the line is matched and the first file printed.

The next example shows the other way to use this operator. It matches either the specified pattern, as in this case, or a regular expression, as in the previous example. The second string comparison operator applies the specified regular expression to the pattern. If a match occurs, the expression evaluates true, and the actions are executed.

```
$ awk '$1 ~/on/ { print $1 }' city
Toronto
Montreal
$
```

Here you are looking for expressions that contain the specified pattern in the regular expression between the slashes. In this case, you have only two matches in your city file. If the left-hand value contains the regular expression on the right-hand side, the expression evaluates as true. As well, if the regular expression on the right is found anywhere in the value on the left, the expression also evaluates as true. Only when the first field matches the specified value is an entry printed.

The final string comparison operator is the negation or not-equal-to operator. Using this operator, you want to find those entries that do not include the pattern or regular expression. Consider the following example:

```
$ awk '$1 !~/on/ { print $1 }' city
Ottawa
Nepean
Orlando
Halifax
Syracuse
$
```

The negation operator, !, indicates to awk that it is not to match the pattern specified. Here, all lines not containing "on" in the first field are considered matches and are printed.

Now you know how to compare the incoming data with numbers and strings on the basis of one pattern at a time. Sometimes, however, you need to be able to combine patterns to have more control over the operation of your program.

Combining Patterns

The patterns you have seen so far have been relatively simple, matching either numerical or string expressions. Being able to match more than one expression at a time would prove valuable in complex awk programs. You can use several operators for combining patterns. These operators are listed in table 21.8.

Table 21.8
Combination Comparison Operators

Operator	Meaning
expr && *expr*	Both expressions must match

Operator	Meaning
expr ¦¦ *expr*	Either expression can match
¦	Alternation operator

Using these logic patterns, you can combine as many patterns as you need. Go back and examine the example program you saw previously in this chapter:

```
$ cat a1
$2 < 50 { printf "%s is less than 50 miles from here\n", $1 }
$2 > 1000 { printf "%s is more than 1000 miles from here\n", $1 }
$2 == 300 { printf "%s is 300 miles from here\n", $1 }
$2 <= 500 { printf "%s is less than 500 miles from here\n", $1 }
$2 >= 1000 { printf "%s is more than 1000 miles from here\n", $1 }
$
```

You can combine some of the patterns in this program to improve its operation. Consider this example:

```
$ cat a1
$2 < 50 { printf "%s is less than 50 miles from here\n", $1 }
$2 > 50 && $2 <= 300 { printf "%s is %d miles from here\n", $1, $2 }
$2 >= 1000 { printf "%s is more than 1000 miles from here\n", $1 }
$
```

When you look at this program, you see the first of two operators that are used to combine patterns (&& and ¦¦). The && operator means that both expressions must be true for the actions to be executed. If the first expression is false, the second is not evaluated. If the first expression is true, but the second is false, the actions are not executed.

In this example, if the value of the second field is greater than 50 and less than 300, the action is executed. When you run this program, this is your output:

```
$ awk -f a1 city
Ottawa is less than 50 miles from here
Toronto is 300 miles from here
Montreal is 175 miles from here
Nepean is less than 50 miles from here
Orlando is more than 1000 miles from here
Halifax is more than 1000 miles from here
Syracuse is 300 miles from here
$
```

The second operator is the ||, although the && symbol essentially means "and," and the || symbol means "or." Consider the following example:

```
$ awk ' $1 ~/n/ ¦¦ $1 ~/o/ { print $1 }' city
Toronto
Montreal
Nepean
Orlando
$
```

In this example, you are examining the first field of the city file, looking for names that contain the letter n or the letter o. When awk processes this statement, it evaluates the first expression. If it is true, the second is not evaluated, and the actions are executed. If the first expression is false, the second expression is evaluated. If the second expression is false, no action is taken. If the expression is true, the actions are executed. In this situation, if either expression is true, the actions are processed.

You can use the && operator to instruct awk that both patterns must be matched before the instructions can be executed. A match of only one of the conditions is not acceptable. The alternate is the || operator, which instructs awk that if either of the expressions is a match, the instructions following should be executed.

In cases where both of the patterns you want to match are string expressions, you can simplify the pattern match by using the | operator. Consider the following example:

```
$ awk '$1 ~ /awa¦pe/ { print $1 }' city
Ottawa
Nepean
$
```

This operator indicates to awk that the pattern match can be either of the patterns. In fact, saying the following:

```
$1 ~ /awa/ ¦¦ $1 ~ /pe/
```

is the same as saying:

```
$1 ~ /awa¦pe/
```

awk executes both commands in approximately the same amount of time. In fact, if no other fields exist in which these patterns can match, you can write them without the field specified, as in this example:

```
/awa/ ¦¦ /pe/
```

or use the alternation operator, as in the following:

```
/awa¦pe/
```

The issue is not one of speed but one of clarity in writing your code. If you choose one way over the other, be consistent when writing your code. This consistency makes it easier to see what the program is doing later when you or someone else has to modify it.

Using awk for Data Verification

You can use awk to validate the incoming data and take no action or report errors when the incoming data doesn't meet some qualification. Consider this example:

```
$ cat a2
NF > 2 { print "Line ", NR, ":", $0, ": too many fields." }
NF < 2 { printf "Line %d : %s : has too few fields\n", NF, $0 }
$2 > 10000 { print $0, ": The distance seems out of bounds." }  $ awk -
➥f a2 city
Line  4 : Nepean 15 4 : too many fields.
Line 1 : Tulsa : has too few fields
Miami 12000 : The distance seems out of bounds.
$
```

This example shows the output of a small awk program to verify the incoming data. You see how you can take different actions based on different comparisons, which is one of the powerful uses of awk.

Many programs require the input data to be in a specific format. Using awk, you can build a program to validate the format of the input file. With your program, you not only can detect bad data, but you also could possibly correct it and save the input line. When you examine flow control in awk, you consider how you can make these kinds of corrections and rebuild your distance data verify program.

Changing the Field Delimiter

The examples you looked at in the preceding section illustrate using awk for data verification, using one-word city names, and using a space as the delimiter between the fields. But not all city names are only one word. What if you add a couple more? In the next example, a new city and distance have been added: San Francisco.

```
$ cat city2
Ottawa 0
San Francisco 3000
Toronto 300
Montreal 175
Nepean 15 4
Orlando 1300
Halifax 1200
```

```
Syracuse 300
Tulsa
Miami 12000
$
```

But when you run the verify program, it complains about the entry for San Francisco. How can you change the program?

```
$ awk -f a2 city2
Line  2 : San Francisco 3000 : too many fields.
San Francisco 3000 : The distance seems out of bounds.
Line  5 : Nepean 15 4 : too many fields.
Line 1 : Tulsa : has too few fields
Miami 12000 : The distance seems out of bounds.
$
```

What you need to do is change the field delimiter that awk uses so that you can use city names that have spaces in them. Then you have to change the format of your file so that it uses the same character for the field separator. Remember that normally awk uses the standard field delimiter of a space to separate fields, and new lines to separate records. If you change the field delimiter to a colon, you need to tell awk that the colon is now the delimiter. The following example introduces two new components—FS and BEGIN:

```
$ cat a2
{ FS=":" }
NF > 2 { print "Line ", NR, ":", $0, ": too many fields." }
NF < 2 { printf "Line %d : %s : has too few fields\n", NF, $0 }
$2 > 10000 { print $0, ": The distance seems out of bounds." }
$
```

In this program, you use the built-in variable FS to change the field delimiter from a space to a colon. As you have already learned, FS is the Input Field Separator that is used by awk to break the input record into fields. By performing other actions when FS is set, you can begin to use city names that have more than one word. When you run this program with the modified city files as shown, your output looks like this:

```
$ cat city2
Ottawa:0
San Francisco:3000
Toronto:300
Montreal:175
Nepean:15:4
Orlando:1300
Halifax:1200
```

```
Syracuse:300
Tulsa:
Miami:12000
$ awk -f a2 city2
Line 1 : Ottawa:0 : has too few fields
Line  5 : Nepean:15:4 : too many fields.
Miami:12000 : The distance seems out of bounds.
$
```

But why does the awk program complain about the first line in the file? This line has only two fields. The catch is that in order for the change in FS to be made for each of the records, you must alter how you change the FS variable. This change is best done through a special pattern, BEGIN.

Using BEGIN and END

The BEGIN clause is a predefined pattern whose actions are executed when the awk program starts executing. Likewise, END is executed immediately before awk exits. Using these constructs, you can have special variables set or output headers printed before the real processing begins. Consider the following example:

```
$ cat a2
BEGIN { FS=":" }
NF > 2 { print "Line ", NR, ":", $0, ": too many fields." }
NF < 2 { printf "Line %d : %s : has too few fields\n", NF, $0 }
$2 > 10000 { print $0, ": The distance seems out of bounds." }
$
```

In the preceding example, you changed the field delimiter from a space to a colon, but the program didn't quite work. By changing the program to set FS in a BEGIN clause and then execute it, the output is slightly different and is in fact what you want to see.

As you can see in the following output lines, no warning messages appear for any lines other than those that are in fact matches for the patterns for which you wanted to search.

```
$ awk -f a2 city2
Line  5 : Nepean:15:4 : too many fields.
Miami:12000 : The distance seems out of bounds.
$
```

As mentioned, the END pattern is processed just before the awk program is about to complete. Often, END is used to print totals at the end of a report. You can use it to print other types of information also. You can add END to the a2 verification program, for example, to report on how many records were processed.

```
$ cat a2
BEGIN { FS=":" }
NF > 2 { print "Line ", NR, ":", $0, ": too many fields." }
NF < 2 { printf "Line %d : %s : has too few fields\n", NF, $0 }
$2 > 10000 { print $0, ": The distance seems out of bounds." }
END { printf "\n%d records processed.\n", NR }
$
```

In this sample program, awk prints the number of records that have been processed by
the program before it exits, as you can see in the following output:

```
$ awk -f a2 city2
Line  5 : Nepean:15:4 : too many fields.
Miami:12000 : The distance seems out of bounds.

10 records processed.
$
```

By using an extra new line before printing the number of records, you can create some
output that is easier to read because it is separated from the main body of output. From
these lines, you now know that you processed 10 records, but the program didn't like two
of them. Suppose, then, that you also want the program to report how many good and
bad records were in that list. You can determine that information by using a simple
mathematical operator.

Doing the Math

Performing arithmetic operations in awk is easier than in the shell. You can perform the
calculations and print the result, or store it in a variable. Aside from the standard arithmetic functions listed in table 21.9, awk also has some other operators for performing
advanced mathematical functions, including comparison, logical, and assignment
operators and built-in functions.

Performing Elementary Math Operations

As in most programming languages, elementary mathematical functions as well as
advanced functions are included in awk. The typical elementary operations are those
shown in table 21.9.

Table 21.9
Basic Math Operators

Operator	Description
=	Makes simple assignment
var += value	Adds value to var and assigns the new value to var
var -= value	Subtracts value from var and assigns the new value to var
var *= value	Multiplies var by value and assigns the new value to var
var /= value	Divides var by value and assigns the new value to var
var %= value	Takes the modulus of value and assigns the new value to var
var ^= value	Uses value as an exponent to var and assigns the new value to var
++n	Increments n before using
n++	Uses n and then increments
- -n	Decrements n before using
n - -	Uses n and then decrements

These are the typical assignment operators found in the C language. They enable you to use a shorter form of writing an expression. For example, the following:

```
myvar = myvar + $3
```

becomes this:

```
myvar += $3
```

In the former, you add 3 to the value of myvar and then assign the new value to the variable myvar. The latter example does the same thing but uses a more concise method of performing the calculation.

The equal sign (=) performs a simple assignment of a value to a variable. You can have a variable on both sides of the equal sign. Notice that the variables are not accessed with the dollar sign. This feature is standard for awk. The only place the dollar sign is used is on specific variables such as positional parameters and the NF, NR built-in variables.

In all the operations where the operator and the equal sign are combined, the operation is performed and applied to the named variable, and the resulting value is assigned to the variable.

The a2 verify program offers a practical example. By adding a simple counter in the action fields of the a2 verify program, you can calculate how many bad records have been processed.

```
$ cat a2
BEGIN { FS=":" }
NF > 2 { print "Line ", NR, ":", $0, ": too many fields."
        bad += 1 }
NF < 2 { printf "Line %d : %s : has too few fields\n", NF, $0
        bad += 1 }
$2 > 10000 { print $0, ": The distance seems out of bounds."
        bad += 1 }
END { printf "\n%d records processed.\n", NR
        printf "\t%d bad records found\n", bad
        printf "\t%d good records found\n", NR - bad }
$
```

This modified a2 verify program illustrates two new things. First, you now have actions that consist of more than one line. The action is started with the opening curly brace and is terminated with the corresponding closing curly brace.

The program also illustrates how to calculate the number of bad records. Because three of the patterns can result in a bad record, the code to calculate the bad records is duplicated. In a situation such as this one, that code is not too significant. If you are working on a large program, however, it might be to your advantage to create a variable that is set to a pattern, and then create a new action that is executed. This approach is shown in the following example:

```
$ cat a3
BEGIN { FS=":" }
NF > 2 { print "Line ", NR, ":", $0, ": too many fields."
        BAD = "YES" }
NF < 2 { printf "Line %d : %s : has too few fields\n", NF, $0
        BAD = "YES" }
$2 > 10000 { print $0, ": The distance seems out of bounds."
        BAD = "YES" }
BAD ~/YES/ { bad += 1
        BAD = "NO" }
END { printf "\n%d records processed.\n", NR
        printf "\t%d bad records found\n", bad
        printf "\t%d good records found\n", NR - bad }
$
```

In this case, when a bad record is found, the variable BAD is set to have a value of YES. As awk reads the next pattern, it eventually finds a pattern that matches the value of BAD. When the action is executed, the value of bad is incremented to track how many bad records are found. In addition, the value of BAD is set to NO so that the good records are not improperly counted. When you run these two modified versions of the program, the end result is the same:

```
$ awk -f a3 city2
Line  5 : Nepean:15:4 : too many fields.
Miami:12000 : The distance seems out of bounds.

10 records processed.
        2 bad records found
        8 good records found
$
```

The format you choose to use depends on the size of the program and your own programming style.

Another thing worth noting about these programs is that you are using an expression in the printf command that is part of the END pattern. In the last line of the END block, a calculation is done to subtract the number of bad records from the total number of records. Although you can make this calculation separately and save the result in a variable, a computation and assignment can be saved by doing the calculation when the value is to be printed.

Advanced Math Capabilities

The advanced math services available in awk consist of logical operators and built-in math functions. The logical operators are shown in table 21.10.

Table 21.10
Logical Operators

Operator	Description
expr1 && expr2	expr2 is not evaluated unless expr1 is true.
expr1 || expr2	expr2 is not evaluated if expr1 is true.
expr1 ? expr2 : expr3	If expr1 is true, expr2 is used for the output of the expression. If expr1 is not true, expr3 is used for the output of the expression.

These operators enable the logical evaluation of expressions in the program, to aid in the control of the logic flow. You have been introduced to the use of && and || in the pattern-matching services of awk. You can use these logical operators in the logical evaluation of numerical or string values. The one that you have not looked at before, the last entry in the table, is a conditional operator. Consider this example:

```
{ print ( $1, $1 < 1000 ? "is less than " : "is greater than", "1000" ) }
```

When you run the preceding awk program, using the numbers 100, 30,000, 9, and 123 in a file called num, you see these results:

```
$ awk -f z num
100 is less than  1000
30000 is greater than 1000
9 is less than  1000
123 is less than  1000
$
```

This type of operator is useful when you want to take two different actions depending on how an expression is evaluated. In many respects, this operator is like the if-else construct that you examine later in this chapter (see "Controlling the Flow").

awk also includes a set of built-in arithmetic functions, as shown in table 21.11.

Table 21.11
Built-in Math Functions

Function	Description
atan2(y,x)	Calculates the arctangent of y/x in the range of -pi to pi
cos(x)	Calculates the cosine of x, with x in radians
exp(x)	Calculates the exponential function of x
int(x)	Calculates the integer part of x, truncated toward 0 when $x > 0$
log(x)	Calculates the natural (base e) logarithm of x
rand()	Calculates the random number r, where $0 <= r < 1$
sin(x)	Calculates the sine of x, with x in radians
sqrt(x)	Calculates the square root of x
srand(x)	Provides x as a new seed for rand()

These functions enable you to construct a complex set of applications. The following example shows a simple program that prints the square root for a list of numbers:

```
$ cat square
{ print "square root of ", $1, "is", sqrt($1) }
$
```

This tiny program reads a list of numbers and prints the number and its square root, as shown in the following lines:

```
$ awk -f square num
square root of  1 is 1
square root of  16 is 4
square root of  32 is 5.65685
square root of  256 is 16
square root of  144 is 12
chare 415 >
$
```

These advanced math functions are in the trigonometric area of mathematics, but they can be useful when building more complex tools that are to analyze some form of input data.

Controlling the Flow

At this point in the chapter, you're ready to look at the flow-control structures that exist in the awk language. Three primary flow-control constructs are available: if-else, while, and for. Each accomplishes the same type of goal as its shell equivalent, which you review in more detail in Chapter 23, "Advanced Shell Techniques."

The if Command

The if-else construct follows the same syntax as its C language equivalent. The syntax is as follows:

```
if ( expr)
        commands
else
        commands
```

If more than one command is to be executed, you need to enclose the commands in curly braces. Consider the following example:

```
if ( var > 4 )
{
```

```
tmp = tmp * var
}
```

For this discussion of the if command, reexamine a previous example. The following example is from the section on conditional expressions:

```
{ print ( $1, $1 < 1000 ? "is less than " : "is greater than", "1000" )
}
```

You can write this expression by using an if statement, as in the following:

```
{
if ( $1 < 1000 )
        {
        print $1, "  is less than 1000"
        }
else
        {
        print $1, "is greater than 1000"
        }

}
```

These two statements accomplish the same goal: They both execute statements based on a condition. In this example, the if clause is strengthened with the addition of the else statement. If the expression in the if clause is true, the commands within the braces following the if command are executed. If not, and the else clause is present, the commands within the else clause are executed. In either case, awk starts executing the commands right after the closing brace.

The while Command

The while construct executes the instructions in the loop while a condition is true. The syntax follows:

```
while ( expr )
{
commands
}
```

In the following example, the expression must evaluate true. As soon as it does not, the while loop is exited.

```
        {
a = 1
while ( a <= $1 )
    {
```

```
        printf ( "record %d: value = %d  loop=%d\n", NR, $1, a)
        a += 1
        }
   }
```

The preceding example illustrates using a while loop to process information that has come in from a file. When you execute this program, you see the following output, assuming that the values you provide as input are 1, 2, and 4:

```
$ awk -f b1 num
record 1: value = 1  loop=1
record 2: value = 2  loop=1
record 2: value = 2  loop=2
record 3: value = 4  loop=1
record 3: value = 4  loop=2
record 3: value = 4  loop=3
record 3: value = 4  loop=4
$
```

The program ph.awk in Listing 21.2 at the end of the chapter illustrates how to use the while loop to solve a real problem with formatting telephone numbers.

The for Loop

The final construct is the for loop. The awk's version does not resemble the for loop that is available in the Bourne and Korn shells, but rather it resembles the C shell and C language for loops. The syntax follows:

```
for ( var = value; var expr value; expr )
{
commands
}
```

In the for loop, you must have a variable with an initial value assigned in the first part of the statement. In the second component, you must establish the limit of the loop—for example, a < 10. The final expression indicates how the value is changed. The expression might be an increment, a decrement, or some other calculation that adjusts the number for the loop. Unlike the while loop, with the for loop you can accurately predict how many times the loop will be processed. Consider the following example:

```
{
a=4
for ( x = 1; x <= $1; x++ )
        {
        print "x = ", x, " value = ", $1, "calc = ", x * a
        }
}
```

Execute this example to see what it does, and you get the following results:

```
$ awk -f b2 num
x =  1  value =  1 calc =  4
x =  1  value =  2 calc =  4
x =  2  value =  2 calc =  8
x =  1  value =  4 calc =  4
x =  2  value =  4 calc =  8
x =  3  value =  4 calc =  12
x =  4  value =  4 calc =  16
$
```

Putting a Stop to It

Using these three control structures—if-else, while, and for—you can build some powerful applications. But how do you handle things when you want to break out of a loop? Sometimes, when you have a loop of some kind controlling the flow of your script, you might need to break out of the loop because of some other condition that has been satisfied. You can break out of loop by using one of several commands: break, continue, or exit.

The break Command

The break command causes awk to exit the loop and start processing at the first command following the closure of the loop. Consider the following program:

```
{
a = 1
while ( a <= $1 )
   {
   printf ( "IN LOOP: record %d: value = %d  loop=%d\n", NR, $1, a)
   if ( a == 3 )
      {
      print "executed break!"
      break
      }
   a += 1
   }
print "first command following the loop prints this"
}
```

In this example, the script processes the input and loops until the value of *a* is greater than the number read from the file. In the loop, a test is included to see whether the value of the loop counter *a* is equal to 3. If it is, the script exits the loop and prints the line of text in the command following the loop closure.

When you run this script, the results look like the following:

```
$ awk -f b3 num
IN LOOP: record 1: value = 6  loop=1
IN LOOP: record 1: value = 6  loop=2
IN LOOP: record 1: value = 6  loop=3
executed break!
first command following the loop prints this
IN LOOP: record 2: value = 2  loop=1
IN LOOP: record 2: value = 2  loop=2
first command following the loop prints this
IN LOOP: record 3: value = 4  loop=1
IN LOOP: record 3: value = 4  loop=2
IN LOOP: record 3: value = 4  loop=3
executed break!
first command following the loop prints this
$
```

The output generated by this script makes clear that no matter what value is in your output, if it is greater than 3, the loop executes only three times. In the second iteration of the loop, the value is 2, and so the break is not executed.

As you can see with the break statement, execution of the script continues at the first command following the loop. Sometimes, however, you want to skip the remaining commands in the loop and start the loop over again. For this task, use the continue command.

The continue Command

You use the continue command to force processing to the top of the current loop. When awk reaches this statement, the program ignores the statements following the continue command. In the following example, the continue command is used to prevent execution of the remaining commands in the loop:

```
{
a = 1
while ( a <= $1 )
   {
   printf ( "IN LOOP: record %d: value = %d  loop=%d\n", NR, $1, a )
   if ( a == 3 )
      {
      print "executed continue!"
      a += 2
      continue
      }
   a += 1
```

```
        }
        print "first command following the loop prints this"
    }
```

In this script, the commands in the if block are executed when a has a value of 3. In this case, however, the program prints a message indicating that it is going to execute the continue. Instead of adding 1 to the value of a, the script adds 2 to the value of a. This action has the effect of stepping through the loop faster. The results look like the following:

```
$ awk -f b4 num
IN LOOP: record 1: value = 6   loop=1
IN LOOP: record 1: value = 6   loop=2
IN LOOP: record 1: value = 6   loop=3
executed continue!
IN LOOP: record 1: value = 6   loop=5
IN LOOP: record 1: value = 6   loop=6
first command following the loop prints this
IN LOOP: record 2: value = 2   loop=1
IN LOOP: record 2: value = 2   loop=2
first command following the loop prints this
IN LOOP: record 3: value = 4   loop=1
IN LOOP: record 3: value = 4   loop=2
IN LOOP: record 3: value = 4   loop=3
executed continue!
first command following the loop prints this
$
```

In this example, the continue branch is executed twice. When you look at the values printed for loop, you see in the first example that the value went from 3 to 5. In the final example where the continue branch is taken, the loop is terminated early because the value of the loop counter a has a value greater than the input value.

The continue command has the opposite effect of break. Although break causes execution of the loop to terminate, continue causes execution to start over again at the top of the loop. To exit the script altogether, use the exit command.

The exit Command

The exit statement causes awk to jump immediately to the END action and continue processing. If no END action is there, or the exit statement is found in the END action, the script exits immediately. You can include an expression as an argument to exit, which is provided as the exit status to the operating system. Consider this example:

```
$ cat a2
BEGIN { FS=":" }
```

```
NF > 2 { print "Line ", NR, ":", $0, ": too many fields."
        bad += 1 }
NF < 2 { printf "Line %d : %s : has too few fields\n", NF, $0
        bad += 1 }
$2 > 10000 { print $0, ": The distance seems out of bounds."
        bad += 1
        exit }
END { printf "\n%d records processed.\n", NR
        printf "\t%d bad records found\n", bad
        printf "\t%d good records found\n", NR - bad }
$
```

An exit statement has been added to this script, which you saw earlier in this chapter. The exit statement is executed if the input data has a distance that seems out of bounds to the script. In this situation, the commands in the END statement are executed. The results are as follows:

```
$ awk -f a2 city2
Miami:12000 : The distance seems out of bounds.

4 records processed.
        1 bad records found
        3 good records found
$
```

Here you see that the script exited when it found the distance bounds error. In this case, the exit code of the script is zero. But you can use a more appropriate exit code, which could be the number of bad records that were found. To use this code, you need to change the script, as follows:

```
$ cat a2
BEGIN { FS=":" }
NF > 2 { print "Line ", NR, ":", $0, ": too many fields."
        bad += 1 }
NF < 2 { printf "Line %d : %s : has too few fields\n", NF, $0
        bad += 1 }
$2 > 10000 { print $0, ": The distance seems out of bounds."
        bad += 1
        exit }
END { printf "\n%d records processed.\n", NR
        printf "\t%d bad records found\n", bad
        printf "\t%d good records found\n", NR - bad
        exit bad }
$
```

Here the expression bad was added to the exit statement. This change has the effect of exiting the awk script with the value of bad as the return code. Study the following results:

```
$ awk -f a2 city2
Miami:12000 : The distance seems out of bounds.

4 records processed.
        1 bad records found
        3 good records found
$ echo $?
1
$
```

Note that the script still exits in the same place. But when you test the shell variable $?, which contains the exit status of the last command, you see that the script exited with a value of 1.

The break, continue, and exit commands all provide improved flexibility in the control of the program flow within an awk script, including breaking out of a loop early, starting the next iteration of a loop, and exiting a script.

Using the Built-in String Functions

In order to provide the same level of support for strings as for numbers, the awk language includes a number of built-in string support functions. These functions are listed in table 21.12. In this table, r represents a regular expression, s and t represent strings, and I and n represent integers.

Table 21.12
Built-in String Functions

Function	Description
gsub(r, s, t)	Globally substitutes s for each substring of t that is matched by the regular expression r. If t is omitted, uses the contents of $0.
index(s, t)	Returns the location where t is found in s. If t is not found in s, returns 0.
length(s)	Returns the length of the string s.
match(s, r)	Returns the index of where s matches r, or 0 if no match occurs.

Function	Description
sub(r, s, t)	Substitues s for only the first matched substring of t that is matched by the regular expression r.
substr(s, i, n)	Returns the n character substring of s starting at position i. If n is omitted, returns the string from position i to the end of the string.

To complete the discussion of strings, considering an example of each of these functions might be helpful. The following sample list of city names is used for the examples in this section.

```
$ cat list
Toronto
Vancouver
Paris
London
Edmonton
Regina
Halifax
$
```

In some situations, you want to know the specific location of a string inside another string. The index function is handy for this task. The index function requires two arguments that provide the source string and the substring.

The following script, for example, reads the list of city names, looking for the pattern *on*. When it finds a match, the program prints the city name and the position where the pattern starts.

```
$ cat z

{
   pos = index( $1, "on" )
   if ( pos > 0 )
      {
      printf "%s matched 'on' at position %d\n", $1, pos
      }
}
$
```

The return of the index function is an integer that is saved in the pos variable. The value of pos is evaluated to see whether the value is greater than zero. If so, a match is found for the pattern in the input pattern. The city name and the position where the match is found are printed. When you execute the script, the output looks like the following:

```
$ awk -f z list
Toronto matched 'on' at position 4
London matched 'on' at position 2
Edmonton matched 'on' at position 4
$
```

You determine the length of a string with the length function. This function requires a single argument: the string to be measured. The following script prints the length of each of the city names in the sample list:

```
$ cat z1
{
    printf "%s: length is %d\n", $1, length($1)
}
$
```

The results are as follows:

```
$ awk -f z1 list
Toronto: length is 7
Vancouver: length is 9
Paris: length is 5
London: length is 6
Edmonton: length is 8
Regina: length is 6
Halifax: length is 7
$
```

Before you examine the sub and gsub functions, the substr function bears scrutiny. You use the substr function to return a portion of the string, which is provided as the first argument. The other two arguments define the start position of the substring and the length of the substring. If you do not provide the length of the substring, the substring starts at the specified position and goes to the end of the string. Look at the following example:

```
$ cat z2
{
    printf "%s: substring 1 to 3 is %s\n", $1, substr($1,1,3)
    printf "%s: substring 4 to end is %s\n", $1, substr($1,4)
}
$
```

In this script, the first execution of substr extracts a three-character string starting at position 1 of the source string. The second execution of substr extracts a substring starting at position 4 and includes all characters to the end of the source string. When you execute this script, the output looks like the following example:

```
$ awk -f z2 list
Toronto: substring 1 to 3 is Tor
Toronto: substring 4 to end is onto
Vancouver: substring 1 to 3 is Van
Vancouver: substring 4 to end is couver
Paris: substring 1 to 3 is Par
Paris: substring 4 to end is is
London: substring 1 to 3 is Lon
London: substring 4 to end is don
Edmonton: substring 1 to 3 is Edm
Edmonton: substring 4 to end is onton
Regina: substring 1 to 3 is Reg
Regina: substring 4 to end is ina
Halifax: substring 1 to 3 is Hal
Halifax: substring 4 to end is ifax
$
```

The final string function you need to look at is gsub. gsub and sub are essentially the same, except that gsub performs a global substitution, and sub performs a substitution on only the first match.

Remember the script that you saw earlier in this chapter, where you indexed the string on into the source file? Now you can use gsub to replace the substring on with some other text. Look at the following lines:

```
$ cat z4
BEGIN { printf "%15s\t%15s\t%15s\n\n", "BEFORE", "GSUB", "SUB" }

{
        save = $1
        printf "%15s\t", $1
        gsub( /on/, "ON", $1 )
        printf "%15s\t", $1
        sub( /on/, "ON", save )
        printf "%15s\n", save
}
$
```

This sample script illustrates how sub and gsub work and also shows the differences between them. It first prints the headings. Then, for each input record, it prints the original value, followed by the value after the global substitution with gsub, and then the simple substitution with sub.

```
$ awk -f z4 list
         BEFORE              GSUB              SUB

         Toronto           TorONto          TorONto
       Vancouver         Vancouver        Vancouver
           Paris             Paris            Paris
          London            LONdON           LONdon
        Edmonton          EdmONtON         EdmONton
          Regina            Regina           Regina
         Halifax           Halifax          Halifax
$
```

Notice that with gsub all occurrences of the pattern in each input line are replaced, and with sub, only the first occurrence is replaced. These operators enable you to perform substitutions based on specific criteria.

Summary

The awk programming language is an interesting and powerful language with which you can construct complex data reduction and report tools. It is a language characterized by its powerful pattern/action construct and flexibility.

awk hasn't met with the popularity of many of the newer UNIX programmers because of the insurgence of languages such as PERL, which incorporate the major features of awk and other UNIX commands into one rich set.

Example awk Programs

These two sample programs illustrate the use of awk in some different situations. The first program scans the /etc/termcap file and prints the names of the different terminal types that are supported. The second program demonstrates how you can use awk to format a phone number.

Listing 21.1. termlist

Before you examine the listing, look at this sample of what the output from termlist looks like:

```
Supported Terminals for UNIX SYSTEM5
```

```
=======================================================
1620-m8         diablo 1620 w/8 column left margin
2621-48         48 line 2621
2621-ba         2621 w/new rom, strap A set
2621            hp 2621
2621k45         hp 2621 with 45 keyboard
2621-nl         hp 2621 with no labels
2621-nt         hp 2621 w/no tabs
2621-wl         hp 2621 w/labels
2640b           hp 264x series
2640            hp 2640a
3045            datamedia 3045a
33              model 33 teletype
37              model 37 teletype
382             dtc382
4025-17         tek 4025 17 line window
4025-17ws       tek 4025 17 line window in workspace
4025            tektronix 4024/4025/4027
4025-cr         tek 4025 for curses and rogue
```

The script works only on systems that have the /etc/termcap file. Note that although many systems still have this file, the newer systems are using the terminfo database almost exclusively.

```
:
#
#
# @(#) termlist v1.0 - Show a list of supported terminals
# Copyright Chris Hare, 1989
#
# This script will occasionally generate some different-looking re-
sults,
# depending on how the termcap file is set up
#

#
# Get the system and release name
#
SYS=`uname -s`
REL=`uname -r`
echo "Supported Terminals for $SYS $REL "
echo "================================================="
```

```
grep '^..¦.*¦.*' /etc/termcap ¦
   sed 's/:\\//g
        s/^..¦//g
            s/:.*://g' ¦
sort -d ¦ awk '{ FS="¦"; printf "%-15s\t%-40s\n", $1,$NF }'
```

Listing 21.2.   ph.awk

This awk script formats phone numbers. A phone number such as 14032461111 is formatted by this script to look like 1-403-246-1111. Following are a couple of examples:

```
$ ph.awk 14032461111
1-403-246-1111
$ ph.awk 7371111
737-1111
$ ph.awk 13591329
1-359-1329
$
```

Note that the following program is a shell script that incorporates an awk program to format the phone number:

```
:
#
# @(#) ph.awk - Split a phone number into readable format
# Copyright 1990 Chris Hare
#


#
# This script accepts as its only argument a nonformatted phone
# number, which then is split into a formatted version. The rules
# used are
#        - if the number starts with a 1, it is long distance
#        - insert a hyphen after a long-distance prefix
#        - insert a hyphen after the first three numbers (area code)
#        - insert a hyphen after the NXX (Number Exchange)
#
# This script does not know how to handle INTERNATIONAL calls.
#


#
```

```
# If we don't have enough arguments, return an error.
# If more than one argument is submitted, process only the
# first one.
#
if [ $# -lt 1 ]
then
    echo "`basename $0` : not enough arguments"
    echo "                  : require an unformatted phone number"
    exit 1
fi


#
# Run the following awk(C) script to parse through the input data
#
echo $1 ¦ awk '
    {
    SRC=$1
    while ( length(SRC) > 0 )
        {
        #
        # If the first number is a 1, it is a long-distance call
        # put in the 1 then a -
        # 1-xxx
        #
        if ( substr( SRC, 1, 1) == "1" )
            {
            PHONE=PHONE "1-"
            SRC = substr( SRC, 2, length(SRC) - 1 )
            LONG_DIST="YES"
            }
        #
        # If more than four digits are left, insert another
        # dash
        # (1-)234-
        # If the call value LONG_DIST is set, omit the leading
        # dash
        JUNK=length(SRC) - 3
        if ( JUNK >= 4 )
            {
            if ( LONG_DIST == "YES" )
                {
```

```
            PHONE=PHONE "" substr( SRC, 1, 3 )
            LONG_DIST = ""
            }
        else
           if ( PHONE == "" )
               PHONE=PHONE "" substr( SRC, 1, 3 )
           else
               PHONE=PHONE "-" substr( SRC, 1, 3 )
        SRC = substr( SRC, 4, length(SRC) - 3 )
           }
    #
    # We are working on the last four digits, insert the hyphen and
then
    # the digits
    #
    if ( length(SRC) == 4 )
       {
       PHONE=PHONE "-" SRC
       SRC = ""
       }
    }
#
# print the new value back to standard out
#
print PHONE
}´
```

Chapter Snapshot

If you were stranded on a deserted island and could take only two UNIX utilities with you, undoubtedly they would be awk (discussed in the last chapter) and sed. sed enables you to perform mass edits on files without the need for interaction, as this chapter details. Topics discussed include the following:

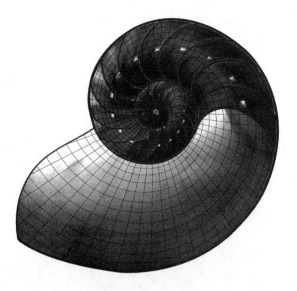

22
CHAPTER

The sed Editor

Sed is an editor. In addition to not being screen-oriented, it is non-interactive. This means you have to insert commands to be executed on the data into a file or onto the command line, in much the same way you did with awk.

What is sed?

sed is well-suited for performing global substitutions on files, or stream editing to change the contents of a file. sed can read its input from both standard input and from a file, and it always writes to standard output unless redirected. This means sed can function as a filter, which is how it often is used. This chapter introduces sed and illustrates how it can help you in your work.

The Differences

sed is not like the other editors distributed as part of UNIX. It has the following three primary uses:

✔ To edit files that are too large for comfortable, interactive editing

✔ To edit any size of file when the sequence of editing commands is too complicated to be comfortably typed in interactive mode

✔ To perform multiple "global" editing functions efficiently in one pass through the input

Other editors (like ed, which you looked at in Chapter 14, "A Quick Look at ed") can accomplish some of these things. But the reason most people learn sed is because of the third point listed above. sed is much faster than other editors in non-interactive mode, and it can perform all of the instructions given in one pass through the input. This means that no matter how many instructions you give, sed only goes through the data once.

How Does sed Work?

sed works by applying all of its instructions to each line of input as it is read. This means that if the instructions for sed consist of 20 lines of pattern matches and substitutions, each of these instructions is applied to the given line of input before processing to the next one. By taking this approach, sed only needs one pass through the input to process it and make all the changes and modifications.

sed has been used in many ways. It can reduce text, explode text, and even replace existing text with new text. As sed reads each line and applies the desired changes, each line, changed or not, is written to the standard output. Because sed writes to standard output, the input data is not changed.

Using sed

The syntax for sed is as follows:

```
$ sed 'commands' filename(s)
```

Where *commands* uses the following generally accepted format:

```
[ address [ , address ] ] function [ arguments ]
```

The address components specify a range of lines to which the function is applied, `function` is the command to be applied, and `arguments` is the text to be searched for and replaced, for example. The address component typically specifies a range of lines to which the sed commands are to be applied. For example, the address command 1,5 instructs sed to process only lines 1 to 5, inclusive. All other lines would be ignored. Function is one of the commands that are explained and illustrated later in this chapter. The argument list is specific to each sed command.

To illustrate the use of sed, the following file will be used in the examples:

```
$ nl text
1
2 The sed command
3
4 This is a test document which we will use to illustrate the sed command on.
5 sed is a very powerful command which is only one of several hundred
6 commands which make up the UNIX operating system.
7
8 the sed command allows for the user to insert, delete and substitute text
9 as needed.
```

sed has several command-line options, as illustrated in the following table.

-f file	Take the sed commands from the named file
-n	Suppress the default output

The -f file option instructs sed to read the commands from the named file. You can look at this feature of sed later in this chapter. Like awk, most sed commands are included on the command line, unless they are a larger and more complex set of instructions.

It was mentioned earlier that sed prints all the input lines regardless of whether or not the line was changed. There are situations in which you might want to be more restricted in your command and what you have output. To jump a little ahead, the following command prints only lines 1 to 4 of the file.

V

Mastering the Shell

```
sed -n '1,4p' text
```

This is demonstrated in the following example.

```
$ sed -n '1,4p' text

The sed command

This is a test document which we will use to illustrate the sed command on.
$
```

If the -n option were not used, then not only would these lines be specifically printed, each line in the file also would be printed. The end result is that some lines are printed twice. Now that you have seen the options for sed and how the commands are formed, you can start your examination of the commands that are part of the sed editor.

Using the Command Line

The command line is often where small scripts are placed. This is done by enclosing the instructions in single quotation marks. Single quotes are used to avoid having the shell process any commands or wildcards that may be included in the instructions. This is illustrated in the following example:

```
$ sed '2D' sample
```

The instructions provided on the command line can be much more complex than this, as you see later in this chapter. You can put more than one command on sed's command line. However, the more complicated the list of instructions, the easier it is to make a mistake. Consequently, it is better to put larger instruction sets into a file.

Using a Command File

The following example illustrates using a command file. A command file is a file that contains a list of sed instructions. Each of these instructions is processed for each line of input, unless the command is restricted to a list of line numbers.

```
$ cat s1
1a\
The SED Command\

3i\
INSERTED TEXT

$
```

When you look at this command file, two separate commands exist. The first one adds a new line, and the second inserts some additional text. The backslash is used because the command is terminated at the first newline. Breaking up each of the lines of text with the backslash enables you to insert the text the way you want it. You also can add multiple lines at one pass, instead of having an append command for each line to be added. The next section describes the append command and other sed commands.

sed Commands

Table 22.1 lists the various commands that are part of sed. While this chapter does not examine all of them, the entire list is included for your reference.

Table 22.1
sed Commands

Command	Arguments	Explanation
a	text	Appends the specified text in the specified place.
b	label	Branches to the : command with the specified label.
c	text	Changes the text by deleting the pattern space and inserting the text. (Pattern space is discussed later.)
d		Deletes the pattern space.
D		Deletes the initial pattern space to the first newline.
g		Replaces the pattern space with the hold space.
G		Appends the pattern space with the contents of the hold space.
h		Replaces the hold space with the contents of the pattern space.
H		Appends the hold space with the contents of the pattern space.
i	text	Inserts the text in the standard output.
l		Lists the pattern space on the standard output and prints non-printing characters spelled in two-digit ASCII.
n		Copies the pattern space to standard output. It then replaces the pattern space with the next line of input.

continues

Table 22.1, Continued
sed Commands

Command	Arguments	Explanation
N		Appends the next line of input to the pattern space with an embedded newline.
p		Prints the pattern space on the standard output.
P		Prints the initial segment of the pattern space through the first newline of the standard output.
q		Quits sed by branching to the end of the sed script.
r	file	Reads the contents of file and places them on the output before the next input line.
s		The argument is /search pattern/replacement/flags. This substitutes the replacement strings for the search pattern, which can be a regular expression. Flags can consist of the following: ✔ **n=1 to 512**—Substitute for just the nth occurrence of the pattern. ✔ **g**—Globally substitutes for all non-overlapping instances of the regular expression. ✔ **p**—Print the pattern space if a replacement was made. ✔ **w file**—Write the patterns space to file if a replacement was made.
t	label	Branches to the : with the name label if any substitutions have been made.
w	file	Writes the pattern space to the named file.
x		Exchanges the contents of the pattern and hold spaces.
y	/str1/str2/	Replaces all occurrences of characters in str1 with the corresponding characters in str2. The lengths of str1 and str2 must be the same.

Command	Arguments	Explanation
!function		Applies the function only if the lines are not selected by addresses.
:	label	Bears a label for the b and t commands.
=		Prints the line number on the standard output as a line.
{		Executes the commands through to the next } as a group, only when the pattern space is matched.

This is a very large list of commands, but it illustrates the overall versatility of the sed command. This chapter discusses a number of these commands as well as how you can use sed to build some tools.

Inserting Lines and Text

Some of the most common uses for an editor are inserting, deleting, and substituting text. This section examines inserting text. Inserting text can be done with several commands: a, i, and in some ways, r. The first command is illustrated next.

For the purposes of the text, the following illustrates the source file used as input for sed in our examples.

```
The sed command

This is a test document which we will use to illustrate the sed command on.
sed is a very powerful command which is only one of several hundred
commands which make up the UNIX operating system.

the sed command allows for the user to insert, delete and substitute text
as needed.
```

The next example adds a new line to the output of this text.

```
$ sed '1a\
> Welcome to UNIX
> ' text

Welcome to UNIX
The sed command
```

```
This is a test document which we will use to illustrate the sed command on.
sed is a very powerful command which is only one of several hundred
commands which make up the UNIX operating system.

the sed command allows for the user to insert, delete and substitute text
as needed.

$
```

Here you instruct sed to add a new line after the first line of the file. If the digit 1 in the command is changed to 5, then the line would be inserted after the fifth line in the file as shown here.

```
$ sed '5a\
> Welcome to UNIX
> ' text

The sed command

This is a test document which we will use to illustrate the sed command on.
sed is a very powerful command which is only one of several hundred
Welcome to UNIX
commands which make up the UNIX operating system.

the sed command allows for the user to insert, delete and substitute text
as needed.
$
```

The a command cannot be used with a range of addresses, as shown in Table 22.1. The second command is i, which inserts text into the output.

The i command is used to place the accompanying text preceding the indicated line. Like the a command, using i requires the use of the backslash command.

```
$ sed '2i\
> INSERTED TEXT
> ' text

INSERTED TEXT
The sed command
```

```
This is a test document which we will use to illustrate the sed command on.
sed is a very powerful command which is only one of several hundred
commands which make up the UNIX operating system.

the sed command allows for the user to insert, delete and substitute text
as needed.

$
```

Here sed is directed to insert the text prior to the second line. Given that the second line is, in fact, where the text The sed command is, you can verify where the text is inserted.

How do you put these two commands together? This is illustrated in the following example, which shows how to link the commands together on the command line. This is the first step to building some complex sed commands.

```
$ sed '5a\
> Welcome to UNIX
>
> 2i\
> INSERTED TEXT
>
> ' text

INSERTED TEXT
The sed command

This is a test document which we will use to illustrate the sed command on.
sed is a very powerful command which is only one of several hundred
Welcome to UNIX
commands which make up the UNIX operating system.

the sed command allows for the user to insert, delete and substitute text
as needed.

$
```

The following example demonstrates using a file to include both of these commands to process the file.

```
$ cat s1
5a\
Welcome to UNIX\

2i\
INSERTED TEXT

$
```

With this command file, you can accomplish the same result as in the preceding figure by putting the commands on sed's command line.

Both of these commands enable you to insert one or two lines in the output. However, the r command enables sed to read the contents of another file into the output. This is shown in the following example.

```
$ cat s1
5a\
Welcome to UNIX\

2i\
INSERTED TEXT

7r sample
$
```

When you look at this command file, you see that a new command has been added to it. The r command requires the name of a file that is to be inserted in the output. The command enables a line number to be specified where the output is to be inserted. In this case, the contents of the file sample are inserted at line 7. The file name specified can be either a relative file name, indicating that the user must be executing the awk command where the file is, or an absolute file name, as shown in the following.

```
$ cat s1
5a\
Welcome to UNIX\

2i\
INSERTED TEXT

7r /tmp/sample
$
```

In either case, when you run this command, the following is what your output looks like:

```
$ sed -f s1 text

INSERTED TEXT
The sed command

This is a test document which we will use to illustrate the sed command on.
sed is a very powerful command which is only one of several hundred
Welcome to UNIX

commands which make up the UNIX operating system.

THIS IS FROM THE FILE NAMED SAMPLE.
the sed command allows for the user to insert, delete and substitute text
as needed.

$
```

Through the examples in this chapter, you can build on both your text file and your script file, which contains the instructions that you want sed to process.

Deleting Lines and Text

Being able to delete text is also a requirement for any text editor. This can be accomplished in sed using the d command. The following illustrates the d option.

```
$ sed '5d' text

The sed command

This is a test document which we will use to illustrate the sed command on.
commands which make up the UNIX operating system.

the sed command allows for the user to insert, delete and substitute text
as needed.

$
```

This is the first of two ways to use the d command. The second is to perform the deletion of the line by specifying a pattern for which to search. Up to now, line numbers have been specified for commands because that is how these commands operate. Many of sed's commands also work with patterns. In these cases, sed looks for the pattern, and when matched, performs the specific command. The following illustrates using the d command with a pattern.

```
$ sed '/sed/d' text


commands which make up the UNIX operating system.

as needed.

$
```

When sed encounters a pattern like this one, it first locates the pattern between the two slashes. Once the pattern is matched, the command is executed. In this case, the pattern is sed, and lines that contain this pattern are deleted. Either way, the end result is the same: lines that contain the pattern, or that are specified by address, are deleted. The lines that match the pattern are deleted before they are automatically printed. Most typically, however, sed is used for substituting one series of characters or patterns for another.

Substitutions

Substitution is probably the most common usage of sed—to process a file, or input stream, and substitute a set of strings with another set of strings. This is easy for sed to do, and it can handle multiple substitutions simultaneously. The following is an example of a simple substitution.

```
$ sed 's/sed/"sed"/g' text

The "sed" command
This is a "sed" test document which we will use to illustrate the "sed" command on.
"sed" is a very powerful command which is only one of several hundred
commands which make up the UNIX operating system.

the "sed" command allows for the user to insert, delete and substitute text
as needed.

$
```

In the previous example, you have your first look at performing substitutions with sed. The substitute command has a specific syntax, consisting of the following:

```
s/search pattern/replacement/flag
```

In the example, the g flag is used, which instructs sed to replace every occurrence. If the g flag is not used in this example, then only the first occurrence of the pattern on each line is replaced. The difference in operation with and without the g flag is illustrated next, where the g flag is not used.

```
$ sed 's/sed/"sed"/' text

The "sed" command

This is a "sed" test document which we will use to illustrate the sed command on.
"sed" is a very powerful command which is only one of several hundred
commands which make up the UNIX operating system.

the "sed" command allows for the user to insert, delete and substitute text
as needed.

$
```

In this case, only the first occurrence of the word sed on each line is replaced with `"sed"`. On the first line of the preceding main paragraph, there are two occurrences of the word sed. Notice that only the first one has been changed to be in quotes. The second occurrence is left as is. This is the difference between using the g, or global change, flag and not using it.

The sed command also can be used to mimic the delete command. The delete command you saw earlier enables you to delete lines by specifying a line or range of lines, or by specifying a pattern for which to search. Using sed, you can selectively delete characters or words without deleting the entire line.

```
$ echo "alpha-beta" | sed 's/.//'
lpha-beta
$
```

In this example, sed replaces the first character, regardless of what it is, with the null string. The substitute command here has no value for the replacement string, which causes sed to delete the specific text. The pattern that is to be matched can contain the typical regular expression syntax, shown in the following:

```
$ echo "alpha-beta" | sed 's/-.*$//'
alpha
$
```

In the previous example, sed replaced only the first character. In the preceding example, sed replaces any and all characters up to the end of the line in the text, starting with a hyphen. You should recall from the discussion on regular expressions that the dollar sign ($) is the symbol that means the end of the line.

You have seen how to remove characters from the pattern, but how about adding characters?

```
$ echo "alpha-beta" ¦ sed 's/./& /g'
a l p h a - b e t a
$
```

In this example, sed is used to "explode" the pattern. sed is instructed to replace any character with the same character and a space. The ampersand instructs sed to use the current character in the replacement pattern. When the g flag is used with this command, the spaces are inserted in the entire pattern.

Another commonly used flag with the substitute command is 'p,' which prints the lines that have changed. In the following example, all the lines were printed, not just those that were changed.

```
$ sed 's/sed/"sed"/p' text

The "sed" command

This is a "sed" test document which we will use to illustrate the sed command
on.  "sed" is a very powerful command which is only one of several hundred
commands which make up the UNIX operating system.

the "sed" command allows for the user to insert, delete and substitute text
as needed.

$
```

Here the 'p' flag instructs sed to print the lines that have changed. However, sed prints all of the lines automatically, so the 'p' flag serves little purpose without using the -n option to the command as shown in the following.

```
$ sed -n 's/sed/"sed"/p' text
The "sed" command
This is a "sed" test document which we will use to illustrate the sed command
on.  "sed" is a very powerful command which is only one of several hundred
```

```
the "sed" command allows for the user to insert, delete and substitute text
$
```

In the preceding example, the -n option was added to sed. Normally, sed prints each line regardless of a match. Using the -n flag instructs sed to only print the lines it is told to. The result is that only the modified lines are printed. Using the -n option with the /pattern/p command enables you to create a grep-like command.

Multiple substitutions also can be placed on the command line to process a file, as shown next. All of these substitutions are processed at the same time and on each line of data processed by sed.

```
$ sed 's/sed/"sed"/g
> s/test/TEST/g' text

The "sed" command

This is a "sed" TEST document which we will use to illustrate the "sed" command
on.  "sed" is a very powerful command which is only one of several hundred
commands which make up the UNIX operating system.

the "sed" command allows for the user to insert, delete and substitute text
as needed.

$
```

In this example, providing multiple substitutions on the command line is demonstrated again. Here both changes are applied at the same time. But what if you look at the command file you created earlier and include these two substitutions? What is the output going to look like?

Following is the command file with the added substitutions.

```
$ cat s1
5a\
Welcome to UNIX\

2i\
INSERTED TEXT

7r /tmp/sample
```

```
s/sed/"sed"/g
s/test/TEST/g
$
```

Here is what the output of this command file looks like.

```
$ sed -f s1 text

INSERTED TEXT
The "sed" command

This is a "sed" TEST document which we will use to illustrate the "sed" command
on.  "sed" is a very powerful command which is only one of several hundred
Welcome to UNIX

commands which make up the UNIX operating system.

THIS IS FROM THE FILE NAMED SAMPLE, which is being used to demonstrate
sed.
the "sed" command allows for the user to insert, delete and substitute text
as needed.

$
```

When you examine the output created here by sed, you can see where the text was inserted, added, deleted, and read in from a file. You also can see the substitutions that changed sed to "sed," and test to TEST. But did all of the occurrences get changed? In fact, they did not. Text that has been inserted into the output stream through the a, i, or r commands is not processed by the substitution commands because these lines are not part of the input stream. It is important to remember these considerations when designing complex sed programs.

It also is possible to restrict the lines that sed processes with the substitute command. This is done by indicating the lines, or range of lines, that are to be processed. This is illustrated in the following example:

```
$ sed '1,3s/sed/"sed"/g' text

The "sed" command

This is a sed test document which we will use to illustrate the sed command
```

```
on.  sed is a very powerful command which is only one of several hundred
commands which make up the UNIX operating system.

the sed command allows for the user to insert, delete and substitute text
as needed.

$
```

Here the substitutions are restricted to lines 1, 2, and 3 in the input stream. When you examine the output, it is clear that only one substitution took place—the one on the second line of the input. As you can see, the substitute command is probably the most versatile and well-used command in the sed repertoire, but many more also can be used to your advantage.

Translating Text

You have seen elsewhere in this book how you can translate characters and cut and paste based upon field separators and delimiters. sed also provides the facilities to perform character translation. Recall, for example, that the password file /etc/passwd is delimited by colons. You can use sed to create a file that has all of the colons removed. While you could use the s command to perform a substitution, you also can use the y command to perform direct translation, as shown in the following example on the /etc/passwd file:

```
$ sed 's/:/ /g' /etc/passwd
root HmILLEJdAnusE 0 0 Root /
daemon NONE 1 1 Admin /
bin NONE 2 2 Admin /bin
sys NONE 3 3 Admin /
adm NONE 4 4 Admin /usr/adm
matthew  104 100 Matthew Hare /u/matthew
chare tzxZUqZw4/2Ow 105 100 Chris Hare /u/chare /bin/ksh
$
```

The following example is how you would accomplish this with the s command. The syntax for y is the same, except the y command enables you to change more than one character at the same time.

```
$ sed 'y/:0/ !/' /etc/passwd
root HmILLEJdAnusE ! ! Root /
daemon NONE 1 1 Admin /
bin NONE 2 2 Admin /bin
sys NONE 3 3 Admin /
adm NONE 4 4 Admin /usr/adm
```

```
matthew  1!4 1!! Matthew Hare /u/matthew
chare tzxZUqZw4/20w 1!5 1!! Chris Hare /u/chare /bin/ksh
$
```

The y command must provide a pattern list and a replacement list. The command works by replacing the character in the pattern list with the corresponding character in the replacement list. When you look at the lists, you see that the colon is to be replaced with a space, and the number zero is replaced with an exclamation mark. If you wanted to perform both of these as substitutions, you would need to use two separate substitution commands: one for the colon, and one for the zero.

In order for the y command to work, the replacement list must have the same number of characters as the pattern list. If the pattern list has three characters, for example, then the replacement list must have three characters also. It is also plain to see that situations exist where use of the y command in sed is more efficient than using the s command to perform the substitutions.

Printing Lines and Text

It has been mentioned several times that sed automatically prints all of the input lines, plus any that are added, onto the standard output. You can control what is actually printed by sed through two commands: p and w. These commands are typically used with the -n option, which causes sed to print nothing on standard output unless explicitly instructed, as depicted in the following example:

```
$ sed -n "s/test/TEST/" text
$
```

Even though the change may have taken place, you have no way of knowing! This is where to use the p command. The p command instructs sed to print the line when it is matched. This is demonstrated in the following example.

```
$ sed -n 's/test/TEST/p' text
This is a sed TEST document which we will use to illustrate the sed command
$
```

You do not have to use the p command with a pattern or as part of a substitute command. The head command, for example, prints the top 10 lines of a file. You can mimic the head command using sed with the command shown in the following example.

```
$ sed -n '1,10p' /etc/passwd
root:HmILLEJdAnusE:0:0:Root:/:
daemon:NONE:1:1:Admin:/:
bin:NONE:2:2:Admin:/bin:
sys:NONE:3:3:Admin:/:
adm:NONE:4:4:Admin:/usr/adm:
```

```
uucp::5:6:uucp:/usr/spool/uucppublic:/usr/lib/uucp/uucico
nuucp::5:6:uucp:/usr/spool/uucppublic:/usr/lib/uucp/uucico
uucpadm:NONE:5:6:Uucp Administration:/usr/lib/uucp:
lp:NONE:71:1:Lp Administrator:/bin:
tutor::100:100:Tutorial:/u/tutor:
$
```

In this example, sed is simply told to print lines 1 to 10 and nothing else. This is a similar type of behavior as the head command.

The w command is the opposite of the r command, which we saw earlier to load some information into the output stream. The w command is used to write information to the named file.

```
$       sed -n "/sed/w /tmp/sed" text
$ cat /tmp/sed
The sed command
This is a sed test document which we will use to illustrate the sed command
on.  sed is a very powerful command which is only one of several hundred
the sed command allows for the user to insert, delete and substitute text
$
```

Here the w command is used to save the lines that contain the pattern sed to the file /tmp/sed. No lines are printed on standard output, and sed only handles the lines that contain the pattern sed. Even these lines are written to the file specified, not the standard output.

The use of these two output statements can be combined, as shown in the following example.

```
$ sed -n '/test/w /tmp/test
/sed/p' text
The sed command
This is a sed test document which we will use to illustrate the sed command
on.  sed is a very powerful command which is only one of several hundred
the sed command allows for the user to insert, delete and substitute text
$ cat /tmp/test
This is a sed test document which we will use to illustrate the sed command
$
```

In this example, you are printing to standard output only the lines that contain the pattern sed, and printing the lines that contain the pattern test to the file tmp/test. Once the sed command has terminated, you can check the contents of /tmp/test and find that it does indeed contain the line you are expecting it to contain.

This section illustrated that with the sed command you write, you can control what sed prints and where it prints it. Up to now, you have mostly used the command to create your sed commands, but how should you build your command files?

sed Script Files

With sed's ability to read its commands from a file, large, complex scripts can be built using this type of arrangement. This is an advantage if you use a set of sed commands frequently, or if one is complex enough that it may require some editing or refinement to get it right. Unfortunately, sed has no concept of comments, so you cannot explain what your sed script is doing inside it. This is rather unfortunate, because for the uninitiated, reading a sed command file is almost a heart stopper!

The files you build should ideally perform all the substitutions, deletions, and changes first, followed by whatever lines are being inserted. Why should you do it this way? Well, consider this example you have seen previously.

```
$ cat s1
s/sed/"sed"/g
s/test/TEST/g
5a\
Welcome to UNIX\

2i\
INSERTED TEXT

7r /tmp/sample

$
```

This file has been changed to put the substitutions first. This is an advantage because now it is easier to ensure the substitutions are done and done correctly. By adding text after the substitutions, it is easier to debug the script when you think some substitution is not being performed.

```
$ sed -f s1 text

INSERTED TEXT
The "sed" command
```

```
This is a "sed" TEST document which we will use to illustrate the "sed" command
on.  "sed" is a very powerful command which is only one of several hundred
Welcome to UNIX

commands which make up the UNIX operating system.

THIS IS FROM THE FILE NAMED SAMPLE, which is being used to demonstrate
sed.
the "sed" command allows for the user to insert, delete and substitute text
as needed.

$
```

You have in your script, for example, the command to read in the contents of a file called /tmp/sample. When you look at the output, an instance of the word sed is not in quotes. If you did not quite understand how things are processed, or had your commands all intermixed in your script, it becomes harder to mentally process the steps sed goes through when processing the data.

Flow Control

A couple of commands enable us to control how sed flows through the input data, although it is probably not a good idea to count on sed to write large-scale applications requiring lots of movement around a script. However, you have used sed to manipulate large amounts of data in a very short time. The commands used for flow control are the b, t, and q commands. In order for the b and t commands to work, you must insert a label into your script, using the : command. The label is text that follows the colon. This is illustrated in your script in the following example.

```
$ cat s1
s/sed/"sed"/g
s/test/oops/g
5a\
Welcome to unix\

2i\
INSERTED TEXT

7r /tmp/sample

/oops/boops
```

```
:oops
7a\
This was added by the oops branch in our sed script.

$
```

Here you have added a branch called :oops at the end of your script. In the next section, you see how to utilize this.

The Branch Command

At the beginning of your sed script, you told sed that if it finds the pattern oops, it should branch to this label. The result is that a line is printed in the output to show that sed transferred execution to that point. This means other changes that had not yet been done are skipped, but are processed again for the current input line when sed exits from the branch. The next example illustrates the resulting output of your branch.

```
$ sed -f s1 text

INSERTED TEXT
The "sed" command

This is a "sed" oops document which we will use to illustrate the "sed" command
on.  "sed" is a very powerful command which is only one of several hundred
Welcome to UNIX

commands which make up the UNIX operating system.

THIS IS FROM THE FILE NAMED SAMPLE, which is being used to demonstrate
sed.
This was added by the oops branch in our sed script.
the "sed" command allows for the user to insert, delete and substitute text
as needed.

$
```

The Quit Command

The quit command is not different from a branch, except that execution of the script is terminated. If you tell sed to execute a quit instruction when it finds the word stop, for example, sed stops when it has found the text. The next example shows adding the instruction to your file, and the following example shows the output when the script is executed now.

```
$ cat s1
/oops/boops
/stop/q
s/sed/"sed"/g
s/test/oops/g
5a\
Welcome to UNIX\

2i\
INSERTED TEXT

7r /tmp/sample
:oops
7a\
This was added by the oops branch in our sed script.

$
```

Here you have added the quit command to your script. When sed executes this script, it
looks for the pattern stop. When it finds it, sed quits the current script and exits to the
shell prompt, as shown in the following example.

```
$ sed -f s1 text

INSERTED TEXT
The "sed" command

This is a "sed" oops document which we will use to illustrate the "sed" command
on.  "sed" is a very powerful command which is only one of several hundred
Welcome to UNIX

commands which make up the UNIX operating system. stop
$
```

When you examine the output at this point, some things were not done. Your oops
branch was not executed, for example, and your file was not read in. This occurred
because sed exited before these events could be triggered by the input stream.

But the quit command can be used in other situations. You used the y command earlier,
for example, to translate the colon to a space in the password file entries. You could do
the same thing with the q command, as shown in the following:

```
$ sed 1q /etc/passwd
root:HmILLEJdAnusE:0:0:Root:/:
$ sed 5q /etc/passwd
root:HmILLEJdAnusE:0:0:Root:/:
daemon:NONE:1:1:Admin:/:
bin:NONE:2:2:Admin:/bin:
sys:NONE:3:3:Admin:/:
adm:NONE:4:4:Admin:/usr/adm:
$
```

In both of these cases, sed is used to print some number of lines and exit without processing any remaining data in the file. Here is another way to mimic the operation of the head command. Earlier you saw using the print command in sed to mimic head by adding in a start and end address. This is even easier because sed automatically prints the lines. So your sed version of head would actually be:

```
$ sed 10q file
```

Unfortunately, no easy way exists to start at the end of the file using sed, because it does not have the capability of moving through the file more than once. But now that you have seen how you can further control how sed works and processes its input, where do you generally see sed being used? In shell scripts.

Pattern and Hold Spaces

Before the discussion of sed is concluded, it must briefly address the issues of pattern and hold spaces, even though they will not be examined in detail. The pattern space is used to make edits on while sed works. If sed is instructed to substitute one pattern for another, for example, this substitution takes place in the pattern space. The hold space is used to make a copy of the pattern so that the original can be saved. Here is an analogy to illustrate the point. Leonardo da Vinci created a number of precious works of art. While a lot of people in the world would like to own one, they all cannot as there is only one original.

As a result, someone makes copies of the artwork so that the original can be stored in a safe place like a museum (the hold space), and copies are distributed around the world (the pattern space).

Summary

In conclusion, you have taken a look at what sed can do and how you can use it to accomplish a wide variety of tasks. In fact, sed is so versatile that it could replace other commands, should you be so inclined to use it in that fashion. sed also has very powerful substitution and translation facilities, which is where sed is most often used. Its ability to function as a filter and data reduction tool is well-known and utilized. Like awk, however, sed is a tool that the majority of people who use it only scratch the surface of its capabilities.

Mastering the Shell

Chapter Snapshot

Chapter 23, "Advanced Shell Techniques" introduced the concept of shell scripts. Such scripts enable you to combine multiple commands into a single executable file. This chapter returns to that topic and shows how logic can be applied within those executable files. The topics include the following:

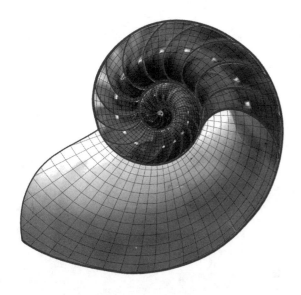

CHAPTER

Advanced Shell Techniques

This chapter examines the more advanced features of the shell programming language, such as flow control and decision making, and provides more detail on input and output. The introduction in Chapter 20, "Creating Basic Shell Scripts," provided you with a good foundation in the shell's programming language. That introduction, coupled with the look at awk and sed and the information in this chapter, now give you the capability to build effective and complex shell scripts.

As in Chapter 20, this chapter focuses primarily on the Bourne shell because it is the most prominently used in the UNIX environment, and because of the limitations imposed by the operating system.

Understanding Shells and Subshells

How does the shell execute the commands that it is asked to? Chapter 19 explained how the shell processes the individual commands. But what about shell scripts? The following code shows a simple shell script that prints the value of a variable. The following program prints the value of the variable a, which is initially defined:

```
$ cat var
echo :$a:
$ a=50
$ var
::
$
```

When executing the program, it doesn't know the value of a, so the value is null. As a result, the shell prints the two colons side by side. The following example shows another version of this command:

```
$ cat var2
a=100
echo :$a:
$ a=1
$ var2
:100:
$
```

In the second example, the shell script sets the value of a to 100 and then prints the value. We change the value of a to be 1, and then execute the program. What is the value of a at this moment? One? 100? In actual fact, the value of a is one.

```
$ echo :$a:
:1:
$
```

But why? This is because the programs var and var2 are executed in a subshell. A subshell is in fact a new version of the shell as created by the login shell to execute the desired program. The variables local to the shell are not passed on to the subshells. This is discussed in Chapter 21, "The awk Processor," regarding parent and children processes.

The program var2 has no local variables visible to it. When it runs, it assigns the value 100 to the variable a, prints it, and exits. As you have learned, a child process, or in this case a subshell, cannot affect the variables that its parent process has defined. Quite often there is a necessity to have the current shell process the commands that you want executed and prevent subshell execution when we want to. In reality, there are several methods available to accomplish this.

The . and source Commands

The . command is used in the Bourne and Korn shells to have the current shell read the file and execute the commands in the current shell, not in a subshell. Using this technique, you can alter the value of a variable even though the commands are in a separate file. For example, following is the var2 program, which is executed in the current shell.

```
$ echo :$a:
:1:
$ . var2
:100:
$ echo :$a:
:100:
$
```

This example uses the . command to execute the commands in the var2 script. The current shell executes the commands. The value 100, therefore, is assigned to the variable a, which is then printed. The value of a when the shell script exits is 100 because the instruction to assign the variable was executed in the current shell, not in a subshell.

The . command can be used to load a list of aliases or shell functions. Shell functions are examined at the end of this chapter. In addition, this command can be used to load a series of configuration variables from within a shell program, as in the following example:

```
$ cat list
var1="This"
var2="is"
var3="a test"
$ cat pgm
. list
echo "$var1 $var2 $var3"
$ sh pgm
This is a test
$
```

The preceding example sets three variables in the file list. The file pgm contains a command that includes the . and the name of the file pgm. This has the effect of "loading" the variables into the pgm environment. When the variables are printed, they are now local to the shell that is executing the instructions, just as if the variable assignments had been part of the pgm file.

The equivalent of the . command in the C shell is the source command. They both accomplish the same function. The following example illustrates using the source command in the C shell:

```
$ csh
% pwd
```

```
/usr1/chare
% source .login
Initializing ....
Welcome to unilabs R3V4.8 920715 (M68020)
     Logged in on Tue Aug  2 20:49:48 EDT 1994 on /dev/console
Last logged in on Tue Aug  2 20:07:25 EDT 1994 on /dev/console
Login Environment Configuration complete.
chare [4]
```

The (...) and {...;} Constructs

You can instruct the shell to execute the commands in two other ways. You can use the (...) construct, which instructs the shell to execute the commands between the parentheses in a subshell; and the {...} construct executes the commands in the current shell. Take another look at the var2 commands:

```
$ cat var2
a=100
echo :$a:
$ a=1
$ var2
:100:
$
```

The preceding example executes the command var2 in a subshell; this program assigns the variable a and then prints the value. You can do something similar using (...), as shown in the following example:

```
$ echo :$a:
::
$ (a=100)
$ echo :$a:
::
$
```

Using (...) in this example, the variable assignment is done in a subshell. Consequently, when you print the value, the variable has no value. You might want to use the (...) construct in the programs if you want to execute commands without affecting the current environment, or to submit a group of commands to be executed in the background, such as in the following example:

```
$ ( sort data -o output; mycmd output ) &
1825
$
```

This submits the commands and executes them in the background, while ensuring that the order in which they were submitted is preserved. The number returned, 1825, is the *process id* (PID) of the process running the commands in the background. That number will always be different.

The {...} construct tells the shell to execute the identified commands within the current shell. This means that if you want the commands executed to alter variables within your environment, then the . or {...} constructs are better used.

```
$ echo :$a:
::
$ { a=100; }
$ echo :$a:
:100:
$
```

In the preceding example, the {...} construct is used to set the value of a. Notice that the use of the {...} construct requires a distinct format. A space must follow the left brace, and if the right brace is included on the same line as a command, a semicolon must follow the command before the right-hand brace. Aside from setting variables, or forcing execution of a command in the current shell, the {...} construct is useful for connecting the output of a group of commands to the same file, as in the following example:

```
$ { cmd1; cmd2; cmd3; } 2> errors
```

The preceding example runs each of the commands in sequence, writing any errors to the same file. The down side to this example is that using the {...} with I/O redirection or pipes causes a subshell to be executed for the grouped commands.

The Art of Decision Making

In any programming language, the capability to make decisions and alter the program flow based upon those decisions is a requirement to perform any work. This section examines the commands that enable you to control the flow of the scripts by making decisions.

The if Command

Most decisions—whether in day-to-day life or in a program—involve choosing between two things. Exactly what the options are is inconsequential: you simply have to make a choice. This is done with the if command, which has the following syntax:

```
if expression then
    commands
fi
```

Or

```
if expression
then
    commands
fi
```

In either case, if the expression evaluates as true, then the commands in the block are executed. It is easy to see where the end of the if block is because it is terminated with a backwards if, or fi command. The expression in the command can be a standard UNIX command, or some other built-in command. The following code shows some examples of the expression:

```
if grep "chare" /etc/passwd > /dev/null
then
    echo "Chris"
fi
if touch /tmp/x
then
    echo "file created"
fi
```

In both of these examples, the commands evaluate true if they execute successfully. As you saw in Chapter 21, if a command has an exit code of zero it has executed successfully, thus meaning that the command evaluates as true. Any nonzero number is considered false in the comparison. In the first example, the command grep requires the output redirection to the null device. This redirection is required because the grep command prints the line that is matched by the pattern. For example, execute the command in the first part of the example:

```
Chris
```

In the preceding example, you see that the command prints only the text on the echo statement in the command block. If you were to remove the output redirection, the command and output would look like the following:

```
if grep "chare" /etc/passwd
then
echo "Chris"
fi
chare:lc9yhXbXIqCyE,M4/I:215:100:Chris Hare:/usr1/chare:/bin/sh
chare2:rg.0X/55wUgzA:215:100:Chris Hare:/usr1/chare:/usr1/chare/tcsh/
tcsh
20166::20166:1:BBS Account for test:/usr1/chare/term/bbs/bbs:/bin/sh
Chris
```

In this case, the matching lines from the /etc/passwd file are printed as a result of the grep command; then the commands within the block are executed, resulting in the "Chris" being printed after the matched password file lines. If you want to match on other criteria, it is necessary to use the test and [commands.

The test and [Commands

You can further use the if statement to control the flow of the program by combining it with the test command. The [command is another name for test, but uses a slightly different syntax. The syntax for test and [is as follows:

```
test expression
[ expression ]
```

In both cases, test evaluates an expression and returns true or false. If it is used in conjunction with the if command, then you can have extensive control over the program flow. However, as you see later in this chapter, you do not have to use the test command with the if construct. Use of either the test or [commands requires an expression. The expression is typically a comparison of either text, numerals, or file and directory attributes. This expression can consist of variables, constants, and operators. The operators can be string, integer, file, or Boolean operators. Each of these is examined in turn before moving on to the next part of the if command.

The File Test Operators

The list of file operators for the test and [command are shown in table 23.1.

Table 23.1
File Operators for the test and [Commands

Parameter	Test
-b file	True if file is a block special file
-c file	True if file is a character special file
-d file	True if file is a directory
-f file	True if file is an ordinary file
-g file	True if file has its SGID bit set
-k file	True if file has its sticky bit set
-p file	True if file is a named pipe
-r file	True if the file is readable by the process
-s file	True if file has nonzero length
-t fd	True if fd is an open file descriptor associated with a terminal; fd is 1 by default.
-u file	True if file has its SUID bit set

continues

Table 23.1, continued
File Operators for the test and [Commands

Parameter	Test
-w file	True if the file is writeable by the process
-x file	True if the file is executable

With these operators, you can take different actions within the program, depending upon the file type. The next example writes a new version of the more command, which can determine if it should show the file:

```
     :

     #
     # If the first argument is a directory, then report that it is a
     #directory, and exit.
     #
     if test -d $1
     then
             echo "$1 is a directory"
             exit 1
     fi
     #
     # If the first argument is executable, then run the command
     #
     if [ -x $1 ]
     then
             $1
             exit
     fi


     #
     # If the first argument is a file, then run the more command on the
     # file.
     #
     if [ -f $1 ]
     then
             more $1
             exit 0
     fi
```

The preceding example shows three different test commands using the test and [commands. The operators used work on the file. In the script, if the file is a directory, then it is reported that the named file is a directory and the script is exited. If the file is executable, then iot is executed. Finally, if the file is a regular file, then the more command is used to view the contents of the file. The following code shows the output from the command and gives an example for each of the three tested types:

```
$ rat chap21
chap21 is a directory
$ rat /etc/group
root::0:root
other::1:
bin::2:root,bin,daemon
sys::3:root,bin,sys,adm
adm::4:root,adm,daemon,listen
uucp::5:uucp,tventure,choreo,goofy
wizards::100:chare
weanies::101:terri,frankh
bbs::2000:bbs
$ rat /bin/date
Tue Aug  2 23:12:25 EDT 1994
```

In the rat program, you can only look at the first argument on the command line. As you work through this chapter, you make more changes to the rat program to enable you to work through as many files as supplied on the command line. Before moving on with the rat program, look at examples for each of the other operators. The following code provides examples in which the operators return true:

```
if [ -b /dev/hd00 ]    This is a block device file.
if [ -c /dev/tty ]     This is a character device file
if [ -d /tmp ]         This is a directory.
if [ -f /unix ]        This is a regular file.
if [ -g /usr/bin/mailx ]    This file has the Set Group ID
                            (SGID) bit turned on, as seen here.
$ ls -l /usr/bin/mailx
-r-xr-sr-x   1 bin       mail      104024 Nov 10  1991 /usr/bin/mailx
if [ -k /usr/bin/perl ]      This file has its sticky bit turned on,
➥ as seen here.
$ ls -l /usr/bin/perl
-rwxr-xr-t   3 root      other     337708 Aug  3 1992 /usr/bin/perl
if [ -p /usr/spool/lp/FIFO ]    This file is a named pipe using the
➥ line printer system. The file information looks like this.
$ ls -l /usr/spool/lp/FIFO
prw-------   1 lp        bin            0 Jul 30 09:27 /usr/spool/lp/FIFO
if [ -r $HOME/.profile ]        If the file is readable by the user
➥ running the process, this test is true.
This test file looks like ls -l $HOME/.profile
-rw-r--r--   1 chare     wizards      187 Jul 23 11:14 /usr1/chare/
➥ .profile
```

```
if [ -s /etc/wtmp ]    If the file has a size of zero, the then test
➥will fail. In this case, if the file size is greater than zero, the
➥test will pass.
$ ls -l /etc/wtmp
-rw-rw-r--   1 adm        adm        2090196 Aug  3 20:41 /etc/wtmp
if [ -t 2 ]    If the file descriptor specified is associated with a
➥terminal, then the test is true. The default file descriptors are 0,
➥1, 2.
if [ -u /bin/login ]    If the file has its Set User ID bit turned on,
➥this test is true.
$ ls -l /bin/login
-r-sr-xr-x   2 root       bin          28232 Nov 10  1991 /bin/login
if [ -w /tmp/ok ]        If the file is writable by the user who is
➥running the command, the test will be true. Here are the permissions
➥on the file for the test to pass.
$ ls -l /tmp/ok
-rw-r--r--   1 chare      wizards          0 Aug  3 20:52 /tmp/ok
if [ -x /bin/date ]    If the file has its execute bit turned on, then
➥this test will pass.
$ ls -l /bin/date
-r-xr-xr-x   1 bin        bin          17788 Nov 10  1991 /bin/date
```

Up to now, you have looked at some of the features of the test command. Before examining the rest of the test operators, take a look back at the rat command. The preceding examples provide an argument on the command line. But, what happens if you run the rat program without providing an argument as in the following example:

```
$ rat
rat: test: argument expected
$
```

The preceding error message from the shell script is the result of the first test in the program. This line reads as follows:

```
if test -f $1
```

The test command expects to find an argument on its command line. Remember that when the shell has no value for a variable, the variable is considered null. This means that when the script reaches the test command and there is no argument, the test command reports this error.

You can resolve this problem and tell the user when he or she does it wrong by enclosing the argument within double quotes. The shell then expands the variable and if no value exists, shows a null value to the test command. You also can add another test to see if the first command-line argument is set. If not, then the script can tell the user that it needs an argument, and then exit. The following code shows the changes you could make to the rat program:

```
:
#
# If we have no files, then report an error
#
if [ ! "$1" ]
then
        echo "Usage: `basename $0` file"
        exit 1
fi
#
# If the first argument is a directory, then report that it is a
# directory, and exit.
#
if [ -d "$1" ]
then
        echo "$1 is a directory"
        exit 1
fi


#
# If the first argument is executable, then run the command
#
if [ -x "$1" ]
then
        $1
        exit
fi


#
# If the first argument is a file, then run the more command on the
# file.
#
if [ -f "$1" ]
then
        more $1
        exit 0
fi
```

When you run this command with the changes, the following happens:

```
$ rat
Usage: rat file
$
```

Now look at the first part of the preceding script, which is where the major change takes place. The following line tests for the existence of the variable $1 first:

```
if [ ! "$1" ]
```

As you saw in Chapter 20, the $1 variable is a positional parameter. It is one of the nine that contain the command-line arguments available to pass information to the scripts. The preceding instruction checks for the existence of a value in the variable. The ! sign is a negation operator to test. This means that you want to know if the variable is not set; that is to say—that the variable does not have a value. If the variable has no value, then the usage message is printed. Now the script can tell if the user has given us anything to process.

The String Comparison Operators

Before you move on to the other instructions associated with the if command, look at the remainder of the operators used with the test command. Table 23.2 lists those operators used for evaluating strings.

Table 23.2
String Comparison Operators

Operator	Function
string	Tests to see if strings is not null.
-n string	Tests to see if the string is not null; string must be seen by test, typically by enclosing it in double quotes.
-z string	Tests to see if the string is null; again, the string must be seen by the test command.
string1 = string2	Tests to see if string1 is identical to string2.
string1 != string2	Tests to see if string1 is not identical to string2.

You have seen the first string test in action. You can test any variable to see if it is not null simply by placing it on the test command line, as in the following example:

```
if test "$var"
```

Normally, tests like this are done with the variable enclosed in double quotes, which allows the shell to see the variable, even if it is null. To some degree, the -n string and string tests are equivalent, as you can see in the following example:

```
if test -n "$1"
then
    echo "$1"
fi
```

If you execute the code in the preceding example, you see the following result:

```
$ fi2 testing
testing
$
```

The program code in the preceding example executes the commands following the if expression if the value of the variable on the command line is not null. This is the same as using the format illustrated by the following code:

```
if test "$1"
then
    echo "$1"
fi
```

When you run this preceding program, the results are the same as the program shown in the next example.

```
$ fi3 testing
testing
$
```

You can add a twist to the testing by changing the operator used with test. Instead of using the -n option, you can use the -z option to see if the value is null. Consequently, you can write the argument testing code at the top of the rat program, shown earlier, by using the -z option, and still maintain the correct operation.

The code fragment shown in the following example says that you want to execute the code within the if block if the expression evaluates true. In this case, you want the expression to evaluate true if there is no value:

```
if [ ! "$1" ]
then
        echo "Usage: `basename $0` file"
        exit 1
fi
```

You can, however, use the third string operator with test to evaluate if the variable is null. The -z option is used to perform this, and is shown in the following example:

```
if test -z "$1"
then
    echo "no value was given"
fi
```

When you run this program with no command-line argument, the expression evaluates true, so the text within the block is executed. If the user provides a value on the command line, the script exits, doing nothing, as the expression does not evaluate as true. The following code illustrates executing the program in the preceding example both with an argument and without an argument.

```
$ fi4
no value was given
$ fi4 testing
$
```

The next two string operators test for equivalence and inequivalence of two strings. Both cases have a "[" pattern that the variable is tested against. The pattern itself may be contained within a variable. The following examples test for equivalence:

```
if [ $1 = "Sample" ]
then
     echo "we have contact!"
fi
pattern=sample
if [ $1 = $pattern ]
then
     echo "we have contact"
fi
```

In either case, the result is the same. If the variable $1 contains the value sample, then the expression evaluates true. You have seen this expression in the rat program already. But, how do you test for non-equivalence? You do this by using the negation operator as you saw earlier to show inequality. This is illustrated in the following code:

```
if [ $1 != "sample" ]
then
     echo "Your answer is not appropriate."
fi
pattern=sample
if [ $1 != $pattern ]
then
     echo "You can't say that!"
fi
```

The Integer Comparison Operators

In the examples in this section, the expression evaluates true if the variable does not contain the value sample. If the variable contains the word sample, then expression evaluates false. These two operators are for evaluating strings. They do not work with numbers. Table 23.3 lists another set of options for evaluating integers.

Table 23.3
Another Set of Options for Evaluating Integers

Test	Action
int1 -eq int2	True if int1 is equal to int2
int1 -ge int2	True if int1 is greater than or equal to int2
int1 -gt int2	True if int1 is greater than int2
int1 -le int2	True if in1 is less than or equal to int2
int1 -lt int2	True if int1 is less than int2
int1 -ne int2	True if int1 is not equal to int2

These integer comparison operators do not work with strings, just as the string operators do not work with numbers. The comparison, like strings, can be with a variable and a constant, or with two variables. The following code uses the integer operators:

```
if [ $1 -eq 2 ]
then
    echo "You entered $1 as an argument."
fi
num=2
if [ $1 -gt $num ]
then
    echo "Your entry was larger than $num."
fi
```

You will use these operators on many occasions throughout this chapter.

The $# Variable

This is a special shell variable that holds the number of arguments present on the command line. You can write a small script that looks like this:

```
:
echo $# arguments
```

When you run this command, the script prints how many arguments are on the command line. The following code illustrates using this script:

```
$ fi5 1 2 3 4 5
5 arguments
```

```
$ fi5 hello world
2 arguments

$ fi5 This "is a" test
3 arguments
```

Here the $# variable holds the number of arguments on the command line. Did the third example in the preceding code surprise you? If you remember back to Chapter 21 when quoting was discussed, you will know that the quotes tell the shell that the words "is a" are treated by the shell as one argument. This variable is introduced here because it is frequently used with the integer operators to test if the correct number of variables is on the command line.

For example, the cp command requires two arguments on the command line. The first is the source file, and the second is the destination file. You can simulate the behavior of cp with the command cp2, shown in the following example:

```
:
if [ $# -ne 2 ]
then
        echo "$0: src-file dest-file"
        exit 1
fi
```

If you run the preceding script with two arguments, then you see nothing. However, if you run it with only one or more than two arguments, the script issues an error, as illustrated in the following code:

```
$ cp2 fileA fileB
$ cp2
cp2 : src-file  dest-file
$ cp2 fileA
cp2 : src-file  dest-file
$
```

The Boolean Operators

The final set of operators is the Boolean operators. Table 23.4 shows the three Boolean operators.

Table 23.4
Boolean Operators

Operator	Function
! expr	True if the expression evaluates false
expr1 -a expr2	True if expr1 and expr2 evaluate true
expr1 -o expr2	True if expr1 or expr2 evaluates true

You saw the Boolean operator ! earlier in the evaluation of a variable. The following code is another example of using this operator. Again, it negates the normal test:

```
if [ ! "$testvar" ]
then
      echo "testvar is not defined"
fi
```

In the preceding example, the test without the negation operator evaluates true only if the variable is defined—that is, the variable has a value. With the addition of the negation operator, the test is opposite. If the variable has a value, the test fails. If the variable has no value, the expression evaluates as true as illustrated in the following example:

```
$ fi6
testvar has no value
$ testvar=12
$ fi6
$
```

When fi6 is first executed, there is no value for it, so the test expression evaluates as true, and the echo statement is executed. After testvar is assigned a value and the command is run, no output is generated because the test expression fails.

The first of the other two Boolean operators is the -a or AND operator. For the expression to evaluate true, both expressions must evaluate true. If one evaluates false, then the test evaluates as false. Consider the next example:

```
if [ $# -lt 2 -a $1 -ne 1 ]
then
      echo "Sorry, you cannot run this command."
fi
```

In this example, the expressions $# -lt 2 and $1 -ne 1 must both evaluate true. If either expression evaluates false, then the entire test fails, as shown in the following example:

```
$ fi7 4 4
$ fi7 4
```

```
Sorry, you cannot run this command.
$ fi7 1
$
```

In the earlier example of code, the first execution fails because more than one argument is on the command line. Thus, the first component of the test fails, and the echo statement is not executed. The second invocation has less than two arguments, and the first argument is not equal to 1, so the echo statement is printed as both tests are true.

The third time we pass the first expression, but fail on the second because the value of the first parameter is 1. It sneaks past the test, but still is not meeting the desired criteria. Using the Boolean AND operator, you can ensure that code is executed only when two conditions are met.

The final operator to the test command is the Boolean OR operator. This operator, -o, instructs test to evaluate true if *either* expression evaluates true. What would happen to the following code if you use the OR operator?

```
if [ $# -lt 2 -o $1 -ne 1 ]
then
    echo "Sorry, you cannot run this command."
fi
```

The code itself hasn't really changed, but when you execute with the same arguments as before, it is clear that you have definitely changed the meaning:

```
$ fi8 1 3
$ fi8 1
Sorry, you cannot run this command.
$
```

But wait! When this instruction was used with the Boolean AND operator, you received no response when you used a single argument of 1. Why do you see one here? In the -o expressions, the second expression is not evaluated if the first expression is true because if the either expression is true, then the code inside the if is executed. If the first test fails, then the second test is evaluated. If neither evaluates true, then the code following the if is not executed.

So far you have looked at one form of the if command. You learned how to use if to control execution of a shell script through the use of test and command evaluation. Can you improve the limited control that we have in the current form of if?

The if-else Construct

The answer is yes. Several additional constructs can be used to assist in the execution control. The first twist to the if statement is the if-else construct. The syntax is as follows:

```
if expression; then
        commands
else
        commands
fi
```

The first part of the construct is the same as the if command that you just saw. The purpose of the if-else construct is to further control the program flow. In the event that the if expression is false, the commands following the else statement are executed. Consider the following example:

```
:
if [ -f "$1" ]
then
        echo "$1: regular file"
else
        echo "$1: not a regular file"
fi

exit 0
```

When you execute this file with the argument being the name of a file, the expression on the if command is true, and the commands following them then are executed. Otherwise, the commands following the else are executed, as illustrated in the following:

```
$ fi1 /etc/motd
/etc/motd: regular file
$ fi1 /tmp
/tmp: not a regular file
```

Looking at the output of this code example, the first execution using a regular file prints what you expect—as does the second execution. The only difference is what is executed. The first example executed the code from the if block, whereas the second executed the code in the else block. You can make this even easier for yourself by introducing another component to the if construct.

The elif Construct

The elif construct, when added to the if construct, enables you to create an even more complex series of tests. With the elif, representing else if, the syntax becomes the following:

```
if expression
then
        commands
elif expression
```

```
        commands
else
        commands
```

Any number of elif expressions can be in the if block. If the expression on the initial if statement is false, then the code proceeds to the next elif statement. If that expression is true, then the commands following are executed. If false and there are additional elif statements, those are evaluated. If none of them evaluate true, then the final block, else, is executed. You can see the use of elif more clearly by looking at the rat program again using elif and else:

```
:
# rat version 2
#
# If we have no files, then report an error
#
if [ ! "$1" ]
then
        echo "Usage: `basename $0` file"
        exit 1
fi
#
# If the first argument is a directory, then report that it is a
# directory, and exit.
#
if [ -d "$1" ]
then
        echo "$1 is a directory"
        exit 1
#
# If the argument is executable, then run the command
#
elif [ -x "$1" ]
then
        $1
        exit
#
# If the first argument is a file, then run the more command on it.
elif [ -f "$1" ]
then
        more $1
        exit 0
else
```

```
                echo "Sorry, I don't know what to do with this file."
        fi
```

In this command, you see a series of if statements, but with a twist. In the original program given earlier, each if statement is executed one after the other. By using elif, the subsequent expressions are only evaluated if the preceding one is false. For example, if the file is a directory, then only the first if statement is evaluated. If the file is not a directory, then it is evaluated to see if it is executable. If so, the program tries to run the command. If not, the program checks to see if it is a regular file. If it is, the program attempts to view it. If none of these tests evaluates as true, then the code in the else statement is executed.

```
$ rat2
Usage: rat2 file
$ rat2 Mail
Mail is a directory
$ rat2 a.out
Hello World
$ rat2 /usr/spool/lp/FIFO
Sorry, I don't know what to do with this file.
$ rat2 hello.c
main()
{
printf ("Hello World\n");
}
$
```

 In the above example, a.out is an executable which echoes\prints the result above, `hello.c` is a nonexecutable file and is "more'd" to the screen.

In the preceding example, you see the if-elif-else code at work. There can be an infinite number of elif branches, but only one if and one else block in the group. However, using this format for a large number of options can be tedious to write as well as to maintain properly. As a result, you can use the case command.

The case Command

The case command is a great way to simplify complex if statements. The syntax for case is as follows:

```
case value in
    pat1)
        command
```

```
            command
            ;;
      pat2)
            command
            command
            ;;
      esac
```

The case command, like if, uses the command name spelled backwards to signify the end of the command. In case, a value is compared against each of the patterns until a match is found. If a match is found, then commands following until the first double semicolon is found are executed. At that point, the case loop is exited and processing continues at the first command after the esac.

If no patterns match the value, then no commands in the case are executed. The default pattern of this *) is provided to allow for this instance. It should always be the last pattern in the case because the asterisk matches everything if it is first, resulting in other patterns in the case being considered.

Unlike the other commands that you have looked at in the shell programming language, the patterns in this case can use the shell's metacharacters, *, ?, and {...} along with the requisite meanings. Additionally, the ¦ symbol is used to *or* two patterns together.

```
      case "$1" in
          -a)     aOpt=TRUE;;
          -b)     bOpt=TRUE
             ;;
          *)      echo "Unknown Option"
      esac
```

The preceding example shows a small case command. If the value of $1 is -a, then the instructions following the a) up to the first semicolon are executed. If the pattern is -b, then the second set of instructions is executed. The double semicolons in the -b section are on a line by themselves. This is equivalent to putting them at the end of the last command. Many people feel that this is easier to read because the blocks are more visible, although it creates a program with longer lines.

As mentioned, case patterns also can use the shell wildcards: ? to match a single character; * to match zero or more characters; and [...] to match any one character. The range of combinations available for the characters class on the command line is similar here:

```
      case "$1" in
          [1-9])     validNum=TRUE;;
          a¦A)       drive=A;;
          b¦B)       drive=B;;
```

```
        /dev/*)     drive=$1;
    esac
```

If $1 is a number other than zero, the first item is executed. If it is a lowercase a or uppercase A, the second item is executed, and so on and so forth.

The preceding example illustrates using the different types of ranges with the case command. Case is very useful for testing and evaluating command-line arguments, and is used all the time. It will be of limited value for the rat program, however, because the rat command depends upon the use of the test command and not on matching a specific pattern.

The null Command

There is always a time and a place where you want to test for the occurrence of something, but not really do anything at the time you wrote the program. The : command is a *no-op*. This means that the shell does nothing when it encounters this command. It is often used as the first line of a Bourne or Korn shell program because the C shell uses this character to indicate that it is a Bourne shell program. Some people also use the colon to indicate comments in their shell scripts. This should not be done because the shell interprets each colon and then does nothing, whereas it recognizes that the comment symbol (#) is in fact a comment, and it ignores it.

You have seen the null command at the top of many of the shell script examples thus far. Frequently, the null command can be used to hold spaces in shell scripts. For example, as you test the script and insert if statements, you can use the null command as the command to be executed in the if statement while you test things.

```
    if [ ! $1 ]
    then
            :     # We'll add this code later
    fi
```

This is evaluated by the shell because the : is considered a command. If you were simply to insert comments in place of the null command, the shell complains that there are no commands to be executed. You see more the of the null command as you progress through this chapter.

The && and || Constructs

These commands control execution. The && executes the command following the && when the previous command returns true. For example:

```
    who ¦ grep "chare" 2>/dev/null && echo "Chris is logged on"
```

If the first command returns true, as it would if the user chare is logged on, the echo statement is printed informing the user running the command that the user is on the system. The ¦¦ is used when the command on the left of the symbol returns a false value.

```
who ¦ grep "chare" 2>/dev/null ¦¦ echo "Chris is not logged on"
```

In the preceding example case, if the user chare is not logged on, the echo statement is printed. Frequently, these are used with the test command to execute a command if the test returns true or false.

In other words, the second part of the statement executes ONLY if the first part is unsuccessful.

```
[ -f $file ]  && more $file
```

The preceding line executes the more command on the specified file if the test command says that it is a regular file.

By now, you have seen how to test files, strings, and integers; compare variables; and control program flow using the if command along with && and ||. A number of other commands, however, can be used to control program flow.

Going in Circles

At this point, you must be able to change the flow of commands within the scripts and to execute the same commands over and over again. The commands that you can use are while, for, and until.

The for Command

The for command is used for processing a list of information. The syntax of the command is as follows:

```
for var in word1 word2 word3
do
    commands
done
```

Each word on the command is assigned to the variable var. The commands between the so and done statements are then executed. This process continues until no more words are left to process. When the last word is assigned and the commands are processed, the for loop is terminated, and execution continues at the first command following the done.

```
for var in one test three four five
do
        echo "var = $var"
done
```

When you run this sample code, the for command assigns each word to the variable var, and then runs the echo command. It looks like the following when you run it:

```
$ for1
var = one
var = test
var = three
var = four
var = five
```

When the loop finishes, processing continues at the first command following the done. If there are no commands, the shell script terminates. This command has several special formats, which indicate the use of the positional parameters currently assigned, or the files in the current directory.

```
for var
do
        commands
done
```

is equivalent to

```
for var in $*
do
        commands
done
```

In both cases, the variables $1 to $9 are assigned to the variable var in turn. This is useful for processing the arguments on the command line, as shown in the following example:

```
for var in $*
do
        echo "var = $var"
done
```

When you execute this with some command-line arguments, it looks like the following:

```
$ for2 This is a sample script
var = This
var = is
var = a
var = sample
var = script
```

If you do not provide any arguments, the script does nothing. In addition to processing command-line arguments and positional parameters, you also can process the files in a given directory using the filename substitution wildcards seen earlier:

```
for file in *
do
        echo "Found $file"
done
```

This example produces a list of the files in the current directory, one per line. You can consider it a lengthy form of ls! The asterisk could be replaced with commands such as the following:

```
for file in *
...
for file in [ab]*
...
for file in a??
...
```

In each of these examples, the files listed by the for command are provided by the shell using the filename substitution. The for command continues execution until no more arguments are left to process. Now you can add the for command to the rat program, so that you can work on multiple command-line arguments. This new version of rat is as follows:

```
:
# rat version 3
#
# If we have no files, then report an error
#
if [ ! "$1" ]
then
        echo "Usage: `basename $0` file"
        exit 1
fi
#
# Loop around each argument on the command line
#
for file in $*
do
#
# If the first argument is a directory, then report that
# it is as such
#
if [ -d "$file" ]
then
echo "$file is a directory"
#
# If the argument is executable, then run the command
```

```
        #
        elif [ -x "$file" ]
        then
                $file
        #
        # If the first argument is a file, then run the more command on
        # it.
        elif [ -f "$file" ]
        then
                echo "===== $file ===== "
                cat $file
        else
                echo "Sorry, I don't know what to do with this file."
        fi
done
$
```

The preceding example changes the rat program to include the for command. This enables you to specify more than one file on the command line and have the rat program process it. Prior to adding this, the rat program could only process the first file on the command line. Now, no matter how many files are provided, the rat command can process them all.

Bear in mind, however, that there is no way to accurately predict how many times the loop will execute. For that you use the commands discussed: while and until.

The while Command

The while command is used to execute a series of commands a specific number of times. The syntax for the command is as follows:

```
while   expr
do
    commands
done
```

The expression expr is evaluated at the top of each loop. If the expression evaluates as true, then the commands between the do and done are executed. At the bottom of the loop, processing returns to the top, and expr is evaluated again. This process continues until the expression at the top of the loop evaluates false.

You can execute a loop a specific number of times by using the command expr:

```
loop=1
while [ $loop -lt 10 ]
do
```

```
        echo "loop = $loop"
        loop=`expr $loop + 1`
done
```

The output of this command shows the process that the while command goes through:

```
$ while1
loop = 1
loop = 2
loop = 3
loop = 4
loop = 5
loop = 6
loop = 7
loop = 8
loop = 9
$
```

Because the script said to continue while the value of loop is less than ten, the last time the value of loop is seen, the value is nine. This is because after the echo statement is printed, the value of loop is incremented. When the value of loop is tested again at the top of the while loop, the value of loop is ten. Because the test expression at the top of the while loop indicates that the value of loop must be less than ten, you don't execute the commands.

The until Command

With the while command, the loop is executed until the expression evaluates false. Another way to think of this is while the expression evaluates as true, execute the commands. The until command, however, executes the commands until the expression returns true. The format of the until command is as follows:

```
until expr
do
        commands
done
```

Like the while command, if the expression evaluates as false, the commands between do and done are executed. When the expression evaluates true, the commands are no longer executed. What happens if you use the same commands as you saw earlier to accomplish the same result?

```
loop=1
until [ $loop -eq 10 ]
do
        echo "loop = $loop"
```

```
        loop=`expr $loop + 1`
    done
```

Notice that because the command structure has changed, you need to change the expression so that it evaluates false until you reach the limit of the execution.

```
$ until1
loop = 1
loop = 2
loop = 3
loop = 4
loop = 5
loop = 6
loop = 7
loop = 8
loop = 9
$
```

In this case, the expression is evaluated at the top. If the expression is false, as it is for the first nine instances of the loop, the instructions within the loop are executed. When the tenth instance is processed, the value of loop is ten, so the expression evaluates as true. When this happens, the until loop exits, and processing continues at the first command following the loop.

Thus far you have seen how to perform a task repeatedly. But how do you then break out of the loop prematurely should the need arise?

Breaking It Up

Two commands affect the execution of a loop: continue and break. They can be used with any of the looping mechanisms discussed thus far.

The break Command

The break command is used to exit the current loop. For example, if you are processing a while loop with a secondary condition in the middle of it, use the break command when that condition is satisfied, and the loop must be exited:

```
$ cat brk
loop=1
var=2
while [ loop -lt 10 ]
do
        echo "loop = $loop \c"
var=`expr $var \* $loop`
        if [ $var -ge 15 ]
```

```
          then
                  echo "Top reached!"
                  break
          else
                  echo "  var = $var "
          fi
          loop=`expr $loop + 1`
done
echo "End of Loop!"
exit 0
$
```

The use of \c in echo statements doesn't work in some implementations of UNIX.

The preceding example shows a sample script that loops around ten times using a while loop. Within the while loop, a new variable, called var, is calculated. This variable is multiplied by the value of loop. When var reaches the upper value of 15, the loop is exited by using a break command. The execution of this program is as follows:

```
$ brk
loop = 1    var = 2
loop = 2    var = 4
loop = 3    var = 12
loop = 4 Top reached!
End of Loop!
$
```

Here you see the rapid increase of the var variable compared to the loop variable. As you can quickly surmise, there is no hope of the loop variable reaching its maximum. When the loop is exited, processing continues at the first command following the loop.

The while command can be combined with the null command to create a loop that continues forever. This type of loop depends upon the use of the break and exit commands to control the exit of the script. A sample is illustrated here:

```
while :
do
        commands
        if [ expr ]
        then
            break
```

```
        fi
done
```

This sample script illustrates using the null command to create this forever loop and how break is integrated into this scenario.

The continue Command

The other command used is the continue command. Break causes the shell to exit the loop and continue processing at the command following the done. But the continue command shifts execution back to the top of the loop. For example, if a command-line argument is incorrect or invalid, but you want to continue processing the remainder of the arguments, then use the continue command to shift processing to the next argument:

```
$ cat cont
for num in $*
do
        if [ $num -lt 5 -o $num -gt 10 ]
        then
                continue
        fi
        echo "arg= $num. value is within range"
done
$
```

This script processes the command-line arguments looking for numbers outside the specified range of 5 to 10. If an invalid number is found, then the script executes the continue command, which moves the processing to the top of the for loop. If the number is within the range, the echo statement is printed to indicate that it is a valid number.

```
$ cont 1 3 6 7 11
arg= 6. value is within range
arg= 7. value is within range
$
```

The preceding code is the execution of the earlier script. As you can see, only two of the numbers were actually within the range that the script is looking for. In the invalid cases, the echo statement is not executed because the test evaluates true, and the continue is executed to start the loop with the next value.

Using the flow control constructs with the break and continue statements results in considerable capability to develop complex programs with in-depth flow control. The most important thing to remember about using them is that they can speed up the execution of scripts by preventing the shell from having to execute unneeded code.

Both break and continue can accept an integer indicating the number of loops to exit.

Background Execution of a Loop

Normally loops are executed in the foreground of the current shell. This can be changed however, by placing an ampersand on the last command in the loop, which is a done. For example:

```
for var in 1 2 3 4
do
        echo "processing $var"
done &
```

When this is done, the loop is processed in a subshell in the background. The process id number is returned like any background job. This is applicable to either the for, while, or until loops.

I/O Redirection and Loops

Dealing with input and output through redirection and pipes can be a challenge. Notice that input from the user hasn't been mentioned yet. This is addressed in the next section of this chapter. When using input redirection on a loop, all the commands that get their input through standard input receive their data from the redirected source.

```
for file in *
do
        commands
done < source
```

This means that each command in the loop reads its input from the specified source. This is not the same as specifying an input source for a specific file as in the following example:

```
for file in *
do
        commands < source
done
```

The second example allows each command to get its input from a different place, whereas the first does not. The same is true for output redirection. If output redirection is applied to the loop, then all the commands in the loop have their output redirected to that file:

```
for var in 1 2 3 4
do
        echo "$var"
done > output
```

In situations like this one where it is important to print something on the terminal so that the user knows what is happening, you can use the generic tty device, /dev/tty, as the output file. This puts the information you want on the terminal where the command was being run. If the command is being executed by cron, then the output is saved and mailed to the user upon completion of the command.

```
for var in 1 2 3 4
do
        echo "Processing $var" > /dev/tty
        commands
done > output
```

The examples here have only redirected standard input or output. In fact, standard error also can be redirected using the same type of approach.

You also can pass information to or from the loops through pipes. By placing the pipe either before the loop command such as for, or after the done command:

```
ls ¦ for file in *
do
        file $file
done
```

The preceding example illustrates piping data into a command, whereas the following one illustrates getting information into a pipe at the end of the loop:

```
for file in *
do
        echo $file
done ¦ wc -l
```

This second example prints the file names and pipes them to wc -l, which counts how many files there are. Reading the information piped into a loop can be accomplished with the read command.

Reading Data

One command (read) is used to directly read data from a user, or other source, and a second command (exec) can be used to adjust where the output or input comes from for a specific script or series of commands in a script.

The read Command

The first of these commands is the read command, which accepts on its command line a list of variables into which the information is to be placed. Each whitespace delimited word is put into a separate variable. If fewer variables than words exist, then the excess words are stored in the last variable. The syntax for read is shown here:

```
read vars
```

The read command works by waiting for the user to enter some text, which it accepts up the newline.

```
$ read num street
2735A 103rd Street
$ echo ">$num< >$street<"
>2735A< >103rd Street<
$
```

Here you see where the user is prompted to enter some text, which will be assigned to the variables num and street. The first word is assigned to the variable num, and because there are more words than variables, the remaining words are assigned to the street variable. It is important to note that using only one variable on the line for read has the effect of assigning the entire line to the variable. The following example assigns the information to a single variable.

```
$ read info
CF-18A Hornet
$ echo $info
CF-18A Hornet
$
```

Now read also can be used to accept input from a pipe in a loop. This is particularly noticeable when working with the while command as in the following code:

```
ls fi* ¦ while read file
do
        echo $file
done
```

In this example, the ls command provides a list of files that is fed to the while loop using a pipe. For each file name, it is read using the read command and saved into the variable file. In this case, the read command knows when no more data exists, and so it exits, allowing the loop to continue. When the incoming input is exhausted, the while loop terminates.

You can add the read command to the rat script to prompt the user for some action when an executable file is found. The following new version of rat uses read to prompt the user to decide if he or she wants to execute an executable file:

```
:
# rat version 4
#
# If we have no files, then report an error
#
if [ ! "$1" ]
then
      echo "Usage: `basename $0` file"
      exit 1
fi
#
# Loop around each argument on the command line
#
for file in $*
do
    #
    # If the first argument is a directory, then report
    # it as such
    #
    if [ -d "$file" ]
    then
            echo "$file is a directory"
    #
    # If the argument is executable, then run the command
    #
    elif [ -x "$file" ]
    then
                echo "Enter y to execute the command"
                read answer
                if [ "$answer" = "y" ]
                then
                        $file             # user entered y
                else
                        continue          # user did something else
                fi
    #
    # If the first argument is a file, then run the more command
    # on it.
    elif [ -f "$file" ]
    then
                echo "===== $file ====="
                more $file
     else
                echo "Sorry, I don't know what to do with this file."
```

```
        fi
done
$
```

The following code shows the operation of rat with the prompt:

```
$ rat4 a.out
Enter y to execute the command
y
Hello World
$ rat4 a.out
Enter y to execute the command

$
```

Here, when you execute the new version of rat and give an executable file as the argument, you are prompted to execute the program. If you enter a **y**, then press Enter, then the command is executed for you. Any other key followed by Enter results in the script returning to the top of the loop as a result of the continue statement.

The exec Command

The exec command can be used to do several different things depending upon the arguments given to it. These things include the following:

✔ Replace the shell with a specific command

✔ Redirect input or output permanently

✔ Open a new file for the shell using a file descriptor

Each of these is examined in turn to see how you can maximize the shell programming efforts through the exec command.

First off, exec is most commonly used to replace the current shell with another program. This is often done in the user's login file (.profile or .login) to replace the login shell with an application. This means that when the user exits the application, their session to the system is terminated. In effect, the application or command now replaces the login shell.

```
$ exec /bin/date
Fri Aug 12 22:46:52 EST 1994
Welcome to AT&T UNIX
Please login:
```

The preceding code is an example of using exec to replace the current login shell with the program /bin/date. After the command exits, the user must log in again. This format of exec is most often used in a user's .profile to start an application and do away with the shell completely.

The second use for exec is to redirect where input or output is to be sent on a semipermanent basis. Inside the shell script, you can include a line such as the following:

```
'em begin code 'em
exec > /tamp/trace
'em end code 'em
```

that instructs the shell that all text destined for standard output will be instead written to the file /tmp/trace. This remains in effect until the script exits, or the following command is executed to send the output back to the terminal:

```
exec > /dev/tty
```

Standard error can similarly be redirected using the following command:

```
exec 2> /tmp/log
```

And finally, input also can be redirected using the following format, although it is indeed much rarer:

```
exec < /tmp/commands
```

Unless these commands are typed directly at the command line, they remain in effect only until the shell exits. Even after these commands are issued, they can be overridden. They set the default action for input or output. By specifying where the output is to go, you can override this action. For example, consider this code fragment:

```
....
exec > /tmp/report
echo "Date : `date`"                # Written to /tmp/report
echo "Processing report ... please wait ...." > /dev/tty
# written to the terminal
...
```

In the preceding example, the default action is to write text destined to standard out into the file /tmp/report. However, by specifying that you want the progress report sent to /dev/tty, the user gets to see what is happening.

The final case for exec is when you want other files to open for input or output besides the standard three that each shell gets. In the script, you need to use the following format:

```
exec fd mode file
```

in which fd is the file descriptor number. Remember that 0, 1, and 2 are already used. The maximum value that a file descriptor can be is nine. Mode indicates the redirection symbol to accomplish the task you want, and file specifies the name of the file you want to interact with.

```
$ cat sam
:
# Keep track of any errors which we generate
exec 2>/tmp/errors
# use this file for writing the standard log messages
exec 3>/tmp/log
# we can still write info messages to the terminal without
# interference!

echo "Processing ...."
echo "Start at `date`" >&3        # this goes into the log file

phase=1
while [ $phase -le 5 ]
do
        echo "   Phase $phase ... please stand-by ..."
        echo "Phase $phase started at `date`" >&3
        phase=`expr $phase + 1`
done

echo "Processing Complete."
echo "Complete at `date`" >&3
exit 0
$
```

The preceding is a sample program that illustrates how you can use a different file for writing information to, and still leave standard output for the terminal. When you run this command, the output that you see on the terminal is like this:

```
$ sh sam
Processing ....
   Phase 1 ... please stand-by ...
   Phase 2 ... please stand-by ...
   Phase 3 ... please stand-by ...
   Phase 4 ... please stand-by ...
   Phase 5 ... please stand-by ...
Processing Complete.
$
```

When this command runs, you can see from the initial exec lines that you will be creating a new file called /tmp/errors for recording the error messages in. In addition, you will be creating a file called /tmp/log for writing the informational and log messages in. When you want to access this file, simply append the file descriptor to redirect this message. Recall that the file descriptors are assigned the values 0, 1, and 2 to standard input, standard output, and standard error. After you run the command, the contents of the log file, which is opened using file descriptor three, look like the following:

```
$ cat /tmp/log
Start at Fri Aug 12 23:40:43 EST 1994
Phase 1 started at Fri Aug 12 23:40:44 EST 1994
Phase 2 started at Fri Aug 12 23:40:44 EST 1994
Phase 3 started at Fri Aug 12 23:40:45 EST 1994
Phase 4 started at Fri Aug 12 23:40:46 EST 1994
Phase 5 started at Fri Aug 12 23:40:47 EST 1994
Complete at Fri Aug 12 23:40:47 EST 1994
$
```

You know from the shell script what you expect to find in here. However, in a complex script that is dependent upon data in certain formats it is a valuable tool to have in the back pocket.

Shell Functions

Earlier chapters have discussed shell aliases and functions. It is worth having another look at shell functions simply because they can play an invaluable part in writing shell scripts. This is because you can write a smaller module to perhaps do logging of certain information and status conditions to a file or the terminal depending upon severity. Instead of having to have multiple occurrences of this code in the file, and slowing the execution time by waiting for other shells to start, you can define a function in the script that executes when you need it.

A shell function is defined following a specific syntax, as indicated here:

```
function_name()
{
        commands
}
```

The function name can be any series of characters and letters, following the same rules as for variable names. It is best to not use a function name that is the same as a command because this can cause problems for other shell scripts that see the function rather than the command as it is found on the disk. In some respects, the function is like a Korn shell or C shell alias. However, functions are available in most Bourne shells- and are in Korn shells. For diehard Bourne shell users, it is the only way to build-in commands to the shell.

```
# @(#) search - search for a file from $HOME
#           Usage search filename
search()
{
if test $# -lt 1
    then
```

```
        echo "Usage : search FILENAME"
        return 1
fi

FILE=$1

echo "searching..."
find $HOME -name $1 -print

echo "search complete."
return 0
}
```

The preceding is a sample shell function that accepts as an argument the name of a file to search for. The function uses the find command to locate and print the name of the file. When looking at this function, note that the exit command is not used. When using functions, the current shell executes them. This means that an exit command has the effect of logging the user off the system. As a result, use the return command, which exits the function and provides a return code back to the system. The return and exit commands serve the same purpose, but the first is for a script, and the second is for a function.

Because a function is executed in the current shell, functions are much faster to execute than starting another shell program to perform some repetitive task. For example, say that you need to be able to prompt the user with some text and collect a variable. Here is how you could do it using a shell function:

```
$ cat func
:
prompt()
{
# The first argument is the text to prompt the user with.
echo $1 > /dev/tty
# we need this to send the output to the right place
read tmpvar
echo "$tmpvar"
return 0
}

# Here is my code
name=`prompt "Enter your Name: "`

echo "Your name is $name"

$
```

Notice that the shell function is defined first. This must be done for the shell to know of the function. Because the shell doesn't read the entire file and then start processing, the functions used in the script must be declared first. In fact, it is possible to have a file with a common set of functions, and you use the . command to load the functions into the current shell right at the beginning of the script.

If you execute the preceding code, this is what you see:

```
$ func
Enter your Name:
Chris
Your name is Chris
$
```

In the preceding example, you see the prompt, which was passed to the function; the user entered his name; and the script printed the text the user entered. Looking further at the earlier example, you see that the information that the user enters is simply echoed to standard output. As a result, you must use command substitution to save the information into a variable. This again is important because it is the typical way of executing functions.

Shell Archives

A shell archive is a shell program that contains other programs and files. It is often created by a shell program itself, but many are created by some very sophisticated programs. The major advantage to a shell archive is that it creates a file that is easily mailed or transmitted to another user via UUCP. And for the recipient, it isn't any more difficult to extract the files than typing the command sh and the name of the shell archive file. Listings in Appendix B contain two shell archive makers. The first listing is a C program, whereas the second is for PERL.

Both create complex archives that include directories, special files, and binary programs, which a simple shell archive program cannot handle. A sample shell archive looks like the following:

```
if test -f fi3 -a "$1" != "-c"
then
    echo "shar : will not overwrite fi3 "
else
    echo "extracting fi3 (35 bytes)"
    cat > fi3 << \!END_OF_FILE!

if test "$1"
then
    echo "$1"
fi
```

```
!END_OF_FILE!
fi # end of overwrite test
    if test "`wc -c fi3`" -ne "35 fi3"
    then
echo "WARNING fi3 : Extraction Error"
    fi
```

In the preceding example, you see some shell code that uses a hereis document to include the file and then extracts it on the recipient's machine when they issue the appropriate command. Shell archives are typically used for mailing information from one user to another, which allows for the easy extraction of the files on the recipient's end.

Summary

When considering all this information, bear in mind some advice that I learned long ago. I have found that this holds true for shell scripts and C language programs, as well as other languages. I haven't always followed this advice, and it occasionally has caused me trouble:

✔ You can never have too many comments.

Comments are the best way to keep track of a program's flow and to document specific things of importance in the script or program. As a teacher, I have always found that the comments are one of the best ways to learn about programming in any language.

✔ Write clear, concise code.

One of the best signs of a capable programmer is not just the number of comments but how clear the code is. By using as little confusing code as possible, you minimize the chance of you or someone else getting it wrong in the future.

✔ Break a larger program into smaller ones.

I have always found this to be the most valuable. For shell scripts, write small scripts or shell functions that perform a specific function. Then reuse them whenever you can. Why reinvent the wheel when you already have four?

You have had a very fast look at the capabilities and commands that make up the shell's built-in programming language. It is a versatile environment that is useful for prototyping, resolving little problems quickly, and building large scale production programs.

Command Summary

(...)	Executes the specified commands in a subshell.
{...}	Executes the specified commands in the current shell.
if expr; then commands fi	Executes commands if expression evaluates as true.

if expr; then
    commands
else
    commands
fi
	If the expression is true, execute the commands following the then statement. Otherwise, execute the commands following the else statement.

if expr; then
    commands
elif; then
    commands
else
    commands
fi
	If the initial expression is true, execute the commands following the initial then statement. Otherwise, test the expression on the next elif clause. If the expression evaluates true, execute the code following its then clause. If no expressions evaluate as true, execute the default, which is the else clause.

test expr	Test the expression to evaluate true.
[expr]	A synonym for the test command.
expr && expr2	Execute expr2 if expr evaluates true.
expr || expr2	Execute expr2 if expr evaluates as false.
:	The null command. Do nothing.
for var in word word word do commands done	Process each word in the list according to each command specified between the do and done commands.
while expr do commands done	Process the commands between the do and done statements while expr evaluates as true.

continues

until expr do commands done	Process the commands between the do and done until the expr evaluates as true. (We want it to evaluate as false to execute the commands.)
continue	Continue execution at the top of the loop.
break	Break out of the loop and restart execution at the first command following the loop.
read var var	Read data and assign it to variables.
exec	Replace the shell with a program, open files, perform semi-permanent redirection.
name() { commands {	Define a shell function.

Part VI

Administration

Chapter Snapshot

There are various run levels that control the portions of UNIX that are active at the time. This chapter examines those, as well as the entire logon process, and what becomes active at each step of the process. The discussion includes the following:

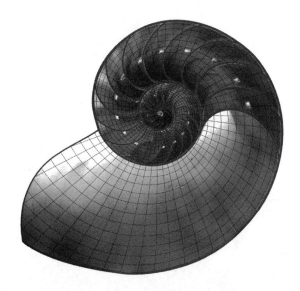

Run Levels and the Login Process

This is the first of three chapters focused on access to the system, processes, and security. These three issues are, for this discussion, very closely related. Unless you can get access to the system, you can't run processes and get your work done. In addition, this chapter takes a detailed look at the files used to customize your login environments.

The Login Process

The login process in this chapter examines the process that occurs on the console of the UNIX server, or a terminal. You will also look at how it works for network logons. For a direct connection to the system, the logon process involves three phases. These involve the following commands: getty, login, and init. For network connections, the commands telnetd or rlogind provide the network login session. These are discussed later.

Initialization

The initialization for a terminal session is started by the init command. init is the first UNIX process and is, at one time or another, the parent of all processes running under UNIX. In this case, init is responsible for starting the `getty` command to listen on a terminal port for an incoming connection. init does not work on network terminal ports, only on those that are directly connected to the machine.

init accomplishes this task by looking at the /etc/inittab file on System V UNIX systems, and the /etc/ttys file on BSD-based systems. The /etc/inittab file, which follows, shows a sample initialization line used to start `getty`.

```
11:23:respawn:/etc/getty tty11 9600 # VT420 workstation
```

This example shows a sample entry from a System V inittab indicating that this `getty` should be respawned each time it exits. That means when the user's login shell exits, a new `getty` should be started. The following example shows the output of the ps command, where you see that this system has a couple of getty programs running.

```
$ ps -ef
    UID   PID  PPID  C   STIME   TTY  TIME  COMMAND
   root     0     0  0  Aug 31     ? 1561:35 swapper
   root     1     0  3  Aug 31     ? 0:01  init
   root     2     0  0  Aug 31     ? 0:00  pagedaemon
   root     3     0  0  Aug 31     ? 0:03  windaemon
   root    77     1  3  Aug 31    w1 0:01  getty
  chare   172     1  5  Aug 31   000 0:06  ksh
  chare   334   172 58 17:37:28  000 0:01  ps
   root    65     1  3  Aug 31    w4 0:01  wmgr
     lp    57     1  3  Aug 31     ? 0:00  lpsched
   root    62     1  3  Aug 31    w3 0:01  .phclr
   root    69     1  3  Aug 31    w5 2:09  smgr
$
```

The exact syntax of the /etc/inittab and /etc/ttys files are beyond the scope of this book, and they are included here, as is the previous example, for completeness in the discussion. The following code shows a sample entry from the /etc/ttys file, which is used in a BSD environment.

It is worth noting that on old SunOS (since replaced by Solaris), this file is actually /etc/ttytab. The /etc/ttys file is actually created at boot by the init after init reads /etc/ttytab.

```
console "/etc/getty std.9600" vt100   off   secure # console terminal
```

In this line of code, init will run a getty command using the terminal settings as defined, called std.9600, using a default terminal type of vt100. The remainder of the line is not relevant to this discussion.

Login Phase 1: getty

When you press Enter on your terminal, the system responds with a login prompt. This prompt informs you that the system is ready for you to log in. The login prompt typically looks the same for both network and direct connection login. The program responsible for printing the login prompt is the command getty (get a tty). getty prompts for the user's login name, as shown in the following:

```
Welcome to UNIX
Please Login:
```

This login name has been assigned by the system administrator. The name can be up to eight characters in length and can consist of a wide variety of possibilities. Often the login name is the user's initials, their first name, or first name and first initial of their last name, just to name a few. The following example illustrates the user chare logging in to this machine:

```
Welcome to UNIX
Please Login: chare
```

The prompt printed by getty is different depending upon the machine in use. Some of the system prompts are quite lengthy, whereas others are very terse—they may be only the word "login." Once the user has entered their login name, getty spawns, or starts, the login command, which is Phase 2 of the process.

Login Phase 2: login

The second phase of the process involves the command login. login prompts the user to enter his or her password by printing a prompt as illustrated in the following example. The user enters the password which does not print on the screen. The password isn't printed on the screen for security reasons. On some systems, not necessarily UNIX, a letter or group of letters is printed on the screen as the user enters the password. This is a security problem because it lets someone watching know how many characters are in the user's password.

```
Welcome to UNIX
Please Login: chare
Password:
```

Passwords, which are discussed in detail in Chapter 27, "Security," are the weakest link in the security of any computer system, not just UNIX. However, bearing that in mind, the remainder of that discussion is saved for Chapter 27.

If the user enters the password incorrectly, the system responds with a generic message, `Login incorrect`, as shown in the following example. The reason for this generic message is simple. The problem could be that the user name does not exist or that the password for a valid user name is incorrect. Why aid in the successful breach of your system by telling the would-be cracker that the password is wrong or the user name doesn't exist?

```
Welcome to UNIX
Please Login: chare
Password:
Login incorrect
login:
```

The login command accepts the password entered by the user and encrypts it using the same mechanism used by the passwd command to put the password in the /etc/passwd file. If the encrypted values match, the password is correct. Otherwise, the password entered by the user is incorrect. The login command cannot decrypt the password once it has been encrypted. When the password is entered properly, the next phase of the login process is entered.

The /bin/login executable is started by getty. It is this executable which encrypts the password, checks it against the password file, and updates the system files. The system files that are updated are dependent upon the UNIX version, but can include /etc/wtmp, /usr/adm/lastlog, and /etc/utmp.

Login Phase 3: Login Shell

The third phase of the process is entered after the user has entered the correct password for the login. This phase sets the parameters around which the user is set up. For example, their login shell is started, and they are placed in the home directory, as this information is stored in the /etc/passwd file. The init command starts the user's login shell as specified in the /etc/passwd file. The user's initial environment is configured, and the shell starts executing. This process is illustrated in the following:

```
Welcome to the AT&T UNIX pc

Please login: chare
Password:
Starting login procedure ...
```

```
Please type the terminal name and press RETURN:  vt100

        48% of the storage space is available.


$
```

Once the shell is started, the user executes the commands as he wants. When the user logs out, the shell exits, init starts up getty again, and the process loops around again. This loop is illustrated in the following:

```
Welcome to UNIX
Please Login: chare
Password:
Login incorrect
login:
```

Logging In through telnetd and rlogind

When users want to log in to a system through a TCP/IP network, there are two primary access methods. One uses the telnet protocol, and the other uses the rlogin protocol. telnet and rlogin use a process on the UNIX system called a *server*. This server is started when an incoming connection for the specified protocol is received. In both cases, these commands act like getty and login. They prompt for the user's login name and the password. If the user doesn't enter the password correctly, these commands handle this situation also, just as login would.

Once the user has entered a valid login and password combination, telnetd and rlogind start the user's shell and accomplish the same tasks as init. When the terminal connection is terminated, however, these commands terminate until the next connection is made.

The Global Initialization Files

There are two global initialization files used for the Bourne, Korn, and C shells. These initialization files are executed for each user who logs in to the system, regardless of their permissions and user level.

The /etc/profile File

This shell script is executed for the users of the Bourne and Korn shells only. A sample /etc/profile is included at the end of this chapter in Listing 24.1. The profile file is executed for each user when they log in. Many sites have site-dependent information in them, like that illustrated in Listing 24.1. The profile file is a shell script, so learning how to read it will help you create your own profile and customize your environment.

The output shown in the following list illustrates what the /etc/profile is doing. It prints some welcome text and configures the user's environment. You will see the profile files again later in this chapter.

```
Welcome to the AT&T UNIX pc

Please login: chare
Password:
Starting login procedure ...

Please type the terminal name and press RETURN:  vt100

          48% of the storage space is available.

      Logged in on Thu Sep  1 18:18:15 EST 1994 on /dev/tty000
Last logged in on Thu Sep  1 18:17:44 EST 1994 on /dev/tty000
$
```

Customizing the User Login Files

There are a number of files that are user-dependent and can be modified to create an environment more suited to the user's tasks. These include the .profile file and a handful of others.

The .profile File

The .profile file is equivalent to the /etc/profile file, except that it enables the user to customize and alter the configuration established by the system administrator. A sample user profile is shown in Listing 24.2 at the end of the chapter, which illustrates adding to the configuration that was performed in the /etc/profile script. To show that the processing of both of these files is done, the .profile prints several lines. One lists the keys that are configured for the erase, interrupt, and kill commands, which are part of the terminal driver. The line that shows that the process is complete is the last line in the .profile file.

The .profile can contain any valid UNIX or shell command. This should be evident at this stage by looking at the commands that are in both of these shell scripts.

The C Shell .login File

When a user logs in to the system and his shell is the C shell, a file called .login is executed. This file can contain any valid UNIX or C shell command. The example in Listing 24.3 at the end of the chapter illustrates a C shell startup file equivalent to the /etc/profile, which is called for this example /etc/cshlogin. The accompanying .login file in Listing 24.4 shows the global file used to save on the duplication of globalized code.

The .login file typically contains commands regarding the terminal configuration, as well as options for the terminal driver, such as the erase character and the interrupt character for some.

The C Shell .logout File

The .logout file is executed when the login shell is terminated. When the user types the command logout or exit, the shell terminates and executes the commands that are in the .logout file. The following illustrates the execution of the commands in the .logout file:

 It is mentioned that telnet and rlogin act like getty and login. Actually, these two programs also act a great deal like getty. Like getty, telnet and rlogin execute /bin/login to continue the login process.

```
%
% logout
logged out chare at Thu Sep  1 18:20:56 EST 1994

Welcome to UNIX
Please Login:
```

The commands that are output in this figure are illustrated in Listing 24.5 at the end of this chapter.

The C Shell .cshrc File

The .cshrc file is executed each time a new C shell (/bin/csh) is started. The .cshrc file typically contains commands that are loaded for each shell. Examples are prompts and information regarding aliases. An *alias* is another name for a command. For example, if your system doesn't have the command lc, you could create an alias in the C shell to define lc as ls -CF. This is discussed in Chapter 20, and a sample .cshrc file is included at the end of this chapter in Listing 24.6.

A .logout File for the Bourne and Korn Shells

The Bourne shell and Korn shell do not have the equivalent of a .logout file, although this facility can be easily mimicked by using the shell's capability to trap signals. As you saw in Chapter 23, the shells are capable of catching signals from the user or from various events that occur during operation. One of these signals is generated when the user requests a logout.

In the following example, you see the same type of output that you saw with the sample .logout. In fact, the files could be the same, as long as there were no shell-specific commands in them. You can simulate the .logout file by adding the following lines to the .profile file in the user's home directory. This line catches, or traps, when the user requests the logout, and it executes the commands in the .checkout file.

```
trap $HOME/.checkout 0
```

The sample .checkout code used here is illustrated in Listing 24.7 at the end of this chapter.

Run Levels Under System V

The init program that performs most of the system startup and initialization is init, and you have seen one of its major functions in handling the startup of the getty program. Run levels have not been around since UNIX was designed. In fact, they are a recent development to System V. Early versions of System V did not have the concept of run levels. A *run level* is an operating state that determines what facilities are available for use. There are three primary run levels, although there can be more.

The run level is not adjustable by the user, so the focus is on what a run level is, what the primary run levels are, and how to tell what run level the system is operating in right now.

Examining the Run Level: who

The command who, aside from showing you who is logged on the system, is also capable of showing the run level in which the system is currently operating. This run level is viewed with the option -r. The output of this command is shown in the following:

```
$ who -r
   .        run-level 2  Aug 31 15:31    2    0    S
$
```

When you look at the output of who -r, you see that your current run level is 2. The date is when you entered that run level, and the digits to the right show the current, oldest, and last run level, in that order. Now take a brief look at the three major run levels in System V UNIX.

Run Level 0

This is the shutdown state. When the system is in transition to run level zero, the system administrator has issued a shutdown command to halt the operating system. When this occurs, the processes running are stopped, and the CPU is halted.

Run Level 1 or S

This is single-maintenance mode, or single-user mode. In this mode, only the console of the system is operational, enabling the system administrator to make changes, solve problems, or install software without having to worry about users working on the system. At this point, neither terminal connections nor network connections to the system are permitted.

Run Level 2

This is multiuser mode, which is the normal operating mode. During run level 2, all of the non-root file systems are mounted, user processes such as the line printer daemon are started, and login sessions are permitted. Although other potential multiuser modes are available, this is the usual one.

Run Levels Under BSD

BSD, XENIX, and early UNIX systems, such as the Version 6 and UNIX systems, do not use run levels. They have two modes of operation: single-user, and multiuser. Many of these systems enter multiuser mode automatically when the system starts up, but others have to be switched to multiuser mode during system startup.

Code Listings

The following code listings illustrate some of the concepts discussed in this chapter. They are also contained on the companion disk to save the necessity of typing them in by hand.

Listing 24.1. A sample /etc/profile file.

```
#
# This is the global initialization file for Bourne Shell users
#
echo "Initializing ..."
#
# Set the initial search path
#
PATH=:/bin:/usr/bin:/usr/ucb:/usr/local
#
# Who is this?
#
```

continues

VI

Administration

Listing 24.1. continued

```
LOGNAME='logname'
USER=${LOGNAME}

#
# What version of the Operating System are we running? This may have to
# be modified depending upon the version of UNIX in use. Most versions
# of UNIX have a uname command which provides information like this
#
#       ULTRIX wabbit.Choreo.CA 4.2 0 RISC
#     $1    $2    $3  $4   $5
#
OP='uname -a'
set $OP
#
# Print a welcome message
#
echo "Welcome to $1 $3.$4 ($5)"


#
# See if there is a message for us from the system administrator
#
if [ -f /etc/system.news ]
then
 more /etc/system.news
fi


#
# Report and record our login.
#
echo "  Logged in on `date` on `tty`"
#
# This shows when we last logged in. This is performed by some
# versions of UNIX, but not all.
#
echo "Last logged in on `cat -s $HOME/.lastlogin`"
#
# This saves the date and terminal port the user logged in to a
# file in the user's home directory.
#
echo "`date` on `tty`" > $HOME/.lastlogin
#
```

```
# Set the user's mailbox
#
MAIL=/usr/spool/mail/${LOGNAME}


#
# Check for new mail every 300 seconds (5 minutes)
#
MAILCHECK=300


#
# Set the Internal Field Separator
#
IFS="   "


#
# Perform some instructions depending upon the shell in use
#
case 'basename $SHELL' in
        sh)
        #
        # The unset is done this way because the /bin/sh
        # on BSD systems cannot do an unset.
        # This needs to be modified for System V systems.
        :
        PS1="$ "
        PS2="> "
        ;;
        sh5)
        #
        # The unset is done this way because the /bin/sh
        # on BSD systems cannot do an unset.
        # This needs to be modified for System V systems.
        unset OP
        PS1="$ "
        PS2="> "
        ;;
        ksh)
        #
        # The unset is done this way because the /bin/sh
        # on BSD systems cannot
        # This needs to be modified for System V systems.
        unset OP
```

continues

VI

Administration

Listing 24.1. continued

```
                PS1="[!] "
                PS2="> "
                FCEDIT=/usr/ucb/vi
                ;;
esac
#
# Put these variables into the shell environment
#
export PS1 FCEDIT PS1 PS2 IFS MAIL MAILCHECK LOGNAME USER
#
# the end
#
```

Listing 24.2. A sample .profile file.

```
#
# This is my user profile
#
# Print the key configuration for erase, kill, and interrupt.
#
echo 'erase ^?, kill ^U, intr ^C'


#
# Change the PATH to include some more directories.
#
PATH=/usr/ucb:/bin:/usr/bin:/usr/local:$HOME/bin:
export PATH


#
# Change the prompt to show my user name, the hostname, and the command
# number for the Korn Shell
#
# If I change my mind to use the Bourne shell, then I can't use the
# command history in my prompt [!].
#
PS1="chare@wabbit [!]"
export PS1


#
# Configure some application specific variables
#
```

```
UIMXDIR=/usr/lib/uimx
FMHOME=/usr/lib/frame
export UIMXDIR FMHOME
echo "Environment Configuration is complete."
```

Listing 24.3.   A sample /etc/cshlogin file.

```
#
# This is the global initialization file for C shell users
#
echo "Initializing ...."
#
# Set the initial search path
#
set PATH = ( . /bin /usr/bin /usr/ucb /usr/local )
#
# Who is this?
set LOGNAME = 'logname'
set USER = $LOGNAME


#
# What version of the Operating System are we running? This may have to
# be modified depending upon the version of UNIX in use. Most versions
# of UNIX have a uname command which provides information like this
#
#   ULTRIX wabbit.Choreo.CA 4.2 0 RISC
#   $1      $2      $3  $4  $5
#
set OP = 'uname -a'
#
# Print a welcome message. This is formatted differently for the C
# shell because the C shell uses an array to hold the results of
# command substitution.

echo "Welcome to $OP[1] $OP[3] $OP[4] ($OP[5])"


#
# See if there is a message for us from the system administrator
#
if ( test -f /etc/system.news )
then
```

continues

Listing 24.3. continued

```
    more /etc/system.news
endif


#
# Report and record our login
#
echo "   Logged in on `date` on `tty`"
#
# This shows when we last logged in This is performed by some versions
# of UNIX, but not all.
#
echo "Last logged in on `cat -s $HOME/.lastlogin`"
#
# This saves the date and terminal port that the user logged in to a
# file in the user's home directory.
# We must set and then unset noclobber to make sure that the state is
# where we want it.
#
set noclobber
unset noclobber
echo "`date` on `tty`" > $HOME/.lastlogin


#
# Set the user's mailbox
#
set MAIL = /usr/spool/mail/$LOGNAME


#
# Set the Internal Field Separators
#
set IFS = ""


#
# Now set some other flags
#
# HISTORY - the size of the history list
#
set history = 20
#
# NOTIFY - inform the user when a background job has completed
#
```

```
set notify
#
# PROMPT - set the prompt for the user
# Select the default prompt for the system by adjusting the comments
# below
# Option 1 - print the current working directory
#
# set prompt = "$cwd> "
#
# Option 2 - print the command number for history
#
# set prompt = "[\!] "
#
# Option 3 - print both current working directory and command number
#
# set prompt = "$cwd [\!] "
#
# Option 4 - print the default prompt
#
# set prompt = "% "
#
# the end
#
```

Listing 24.4.   A sample .cshrc file.

```
alias lc ls -CF
alias printenv env
alias h history
```

Listing 24.5.   A sample .login file.

```
#
# This is a login file for the C shell.

#
# Call the systemwide /etc/cshlogin file
#
source /etc/cshlogin
```

continues

Listing 24.5. continued

```
#
# Customize this ourselves ...
#
# Our TERM type is ALWAYS vt220 ...
#
setenv TERM vt220

#
# Add a directory to our PATH
#
set PATH = ( $path $HOME/bin )

#
# I want a different prompt!
#
set prompt = "chare [\!] "

echo "Login Environment Configuration complete."
```

Listing 24.6.   A sample .logout file.

```
#
# A sample .logout file for the C shell
#
clear
echo "Logged out $LOGNAME at `date` on `tty`"
exit 0
```

Listing 24.7.   A sample .checkout file.

```
#
# This is a sample file which simulates the .logout file
# for the Bourne shell
#
clear
echo "Logged out $LOGNAME at `date` on `tty`"
exit 0
```

Summary

This chapter discussed run levels and the logon process. It is important to know what transpires when you logon, so you know where to begin troubleshooting when problems arise. It is also important to understand run levels and how they affect other processes to which the system is attending.

Chapter Snapshot

Processes and jobs need not always be started at the command line by a user typing them in. It is also possible to have jobs execute automatically at certain times as one-time shots, or on a regular basis. This chapter examines means by which such can be accomplished, including the following:

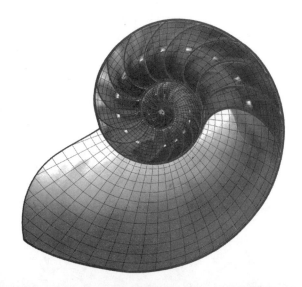

CHAPTER

Processes Now and Later

Throughout this book, you have seen how you can interact with UNIX to get your work done. You have seen how to run commands in the foreground, and how to run them in the background. You have even seen how to keep them running if you log out. But what if you want to run a command while you aren't there to type it? Is it even possible? That is the focus of this chapter.

You are going to examine three facilities that exist in UNIX to run jobs when you aren't around, when the load permits, or over and over again. The specific facilities mentioned are at, batch, and cron.

The ABCs of Processes

These three commands all belong to the same family. In fact, to some degree they all perform the same function: the execution of a command or commands without user intervention. I am going to look at each of these commands in detail regarding what they are and how to use them.

At What Time?

The at command is used to run a single command at a specific time. The typical UNIX command reference says that at is to run commands at a later time. With the at command, you must specify not only the command to be executed, but also the time at which the command must be run. Look at the syntax of the command:

```
at time [ date ] [ increment ]
```

The time is not optional on the command line, but you can optionally specify the date the command should be run or an increment from the current time. I will look at each of these options shortly. The commands are entered on lines one after the other until a Ctrl+d is entered.

Setting the Time

The time component for at may be specified as one, two, or four digits. If only one or two digits are used, the time is assumed to be hours. In the case of four-digit numbers, a colon may be used. In any case, an hour digit number consists of hours and minutes. The user can also specify the hours in the standard 12-hour notation format by using the a.m. or p.m. symbols, or with the 24-hour clock. The user can also indicate to at that the command should be run at Greenwich Mean Time instead of local time, by adding the keyword zulu to the command line. Some valid times are listed here:

1 a.m.	0100	11 p.m.	23:00
2:25 p.m.	9	07:15 zulu	1718

at also understands four plain words that can be used to provide the time frame, or increment. These are as follows:

now

midnight

noon

next

Based upon this simple understanding, you can now look at some simple at commands:

```
$ date
Sat Aug  6 20:02:49 EDT 1994
$ at 2004
date
Ctrl+d
job 776217840.a at Sat Aug  6 20:04:00 1994
$
```

In the preceding list, you checked the date and time to ensure that you set your job up appropriately. The command line to at indicates that you want to run the job at 2004, or 8:04 p.m. The command you want to run is date. You can enter as many commands as you want. Each of them will be executed in sequence. Once all the commands to execute have been entered, press Ctrl+d on a new line. This informs at that no more commands are going to be entered. Before terminating, at prints out a job number for the newly queued job. This job number can be used to find out information on the job in the future.

The job number is actually the number of seconds since the epoch, which is known as January 1, 1970, when the command will be executed. Although no system utilities are available to print the actual date from the number provided by at, Listing 25.1 at the end of this chapter includes the C language source code for a program called gtimes, which does just that. A sample of gtimes is illustrated as follows:

```
$ gtimes 776217840
Clock : 776217840
Date  : Sat Aug  6 20:04:00 1994
$
```

Controlling Output

Where does the output from your jobs go? If you are logged on, the output could be sent to your terminal, but that might cause other problems with the application you could be using at the time; alternatively, you might not be logged on, so where does at send the output? Normally, at saves all output from the commands queued unless the output is redirected somewhere else. The output is then mailed to the user who queued the job after it has completed. Here is the mail message for the command executed in the previous listing:

```
From root Sat Aug  6 20:13:15 1994
Return-Path: <root@UniLabs.ORG>
Received: by unilabs.UniLabs.ORG
         (/\==/\ Smail3.1.24.1 #24.6 conf:93-09-06/16:45 Motorola 8000
    ➥(UNIX)
```

```
            id <m0qWvid-0000VdC@unilabs.UniLabs.ORG>; Sat, 6 Aug 94 20:04
            ➥EDT
Message-Id: <m0qWvid-0000VdC@unilabs.UniLabs.ORG>
Date: Sat, 6 Aug 94 20:13 EDT
From: root (Unilabs System Manager)
To: chare
Status: R


Sat Aug  6 20:04:00 EDT 1994



****************************************************
Cron: The previous message is the standard output
      and standard error of one of your cron commands.
```

Aside from all of the electronic mail headers, you have the output of your date command. In addition, there is some text indicating that this mail message originated from a queued job. Notice, however, that the text doesn't mention that the output is from at, but from cron. As you will see later, cron is related to at, and is the actual process responsible for running it.

Being More Precise

At this point, you can see that at is useful for running a single job, or a group of jobs once. If it is something more routine, or that must done time and time again, then at is not a good choice. You will revisit this theme when you look at cron later in this chapter.

The at command will also accept a date to be more precise on when the commands should be scheduled. The date information can be a full date with month, day, and year, or a day of the week. Two special keywords, today and tomorrow, are recognized. (Yesterday is not understood.) If no date is given and the hour is greater than the current hour, today is assumed by at. If the hour is less than the current hour, tomorrow is assumed. The following code illustrates valid date formats for use with at, by presenting some acceptable command lines.

```
at 22:05 today          at 1 pm tomorrow      at 11:30 Jan 24
at 1201 am Jan 1, 1995  at 4:30 pm Tuesday
```

These are all valid dates for use with at. Once the job is scheduled, it will remain until it is removed, it is executed, or the system is reinstalled. The final command-line argument available for at is an increment. This increment is used to add the prescribed time period to the time and date specification. For example:

```
at now + 1 week
```

Instead of having to fill in all the blanks, including the date, the system can figure it out for you. The keywords recognized by at are minutes, hours, days, weeks, months, and years. A sample of the increment is shown here:

```
$ at now + 1 week
echo "this is a test"
job 776824920.a at Sat Aug 13 20:42:00 1994
$ at 1201 am Jan 1, 1995
echo "Happy New Year!"
job 788936460.a at Sun Jan  1 00:01:00 1995
$
```

This listing illustrates submitting two jobs with at. You have spent a great deal of time looking at input and output redirection as it is handled by the shells. What you have looked at is one method of placing a job into the at queue. In fact, the job can be submitted from within a shell or some compiled program. This is done by using either of the methods shown here:

```
at 1715 <<!EOF
date
echo "It is time to go home"
!EOF
at 1715 < atjob
```

Both are acceptable. The first inputs the job to at through the use of a Bourne or Korn shell hereis document, and the second uses input redirection to provide the commands in the file atjob to at.

If the at command schedules your jobs to run at some time in the future, how can you monitor these job or remove them sometime in the future? The answer is simple: Use the same command you used to put them into the queue to begin with.

Listing at Jobs

The at command has several other options used to list the contents of the at queue and to remove jobs. The -l option will instruct at to list the contents of the at queue. This will list only the jobs that have been queued by the invoking user. This means that one user cannot see the at jobs queued by another user. The use of this option is shown here:

```
$ at -l
776824920.a     Sat Aug 13 20:42:00 1994
788936460.a     Sun Jan  1 00:01:00 1995
$
```

The output generated lists the job number and the date when the job is to be executed. There is no way for the user to find out what commands are being run for each job.

Removing at Jobs

The at command also provides the -r option, which is used to remove queued jobs from the at command queue. To do this, you must know the job number of the job to remove, which you can determine by using at -1. The -r option requires that you provide the job number. Using the at -r command is illustrated next:

```
$ at -l
776824920.a      Sat Aug 13 20:42:00 1994
788936460.a      Sun Jan  1 00:01:00 1995
776222460.a      Sat Aug  6 21:21:00 1994
$ at -r 776222460.a
$ at -l
776824920.a      Sat Aug 13 20:42:00 1994
788936460.a      Sun Jan  1 00:01:00 1995
```

As a user, it is important to note that you will be able to remove only the jobs that you scheduled. You will not be able to remove someone else's scheduled job. This can be done only by the system administrator.

To conclude this discussion of at, you know that at can be used to schedule a job once. The job will be run at the specified time, and the output will be mailed to the invoking user. But will the machine be capable of handling the load of your job at the time? I don't know. However, the batch command allows for job execution when the system permits.

 at commands are actually stored as files in /usr/spool/cron/atjobs, and some portion of them can be viewed with the cat command (such as who requested, etc.)

Interactive versus batch

As you have seen, at will run a job once, at a specified time. However, if you are working on a machine that is heavily used, it may be advantageous to allow the system to decide when the job should be run. Such is the case with the batch command.

With batch, the commands are executed at a time when the system is free enough to handle such requests. For example, if you have a major program compile to do on a busy system, and you can afford to wait for it to complete, using batch may be the nicest thing you can do for yourself and your fellow users.

Commands are given to batch in the same format as with at. Commands are entered at the command line, with a Ctrl+d entered on a new line to terminate the command list.

This is illustrated in the following:

```
$ batch
date
who
df
pwd
Ctrl+d
job 776222586.b at Sat Aug  6 21:23:06 1994
$
```

Here you have scheduled these commands to be executed by way of batch. Like at, batch prints a job number using the same format, except that the letter following the job number is a **b** instead of an **a** as it is with the at command.

The output of the commands is saved and returned to the user through the electronic mail system on the UNIX system. If the command has been written to save its output somewhere else, or if the output is redirected, there will be no mail message. The output from the batch command in the previous example is shown next.

```
From root Sat Aug  6 21:25:30 1994
Return-Path: <root@UniLabs.ORG>
Received: by unilabs.UniLabs.ORG
        (/\==/\ Smail3.1.24.1 #24.6 conf:93-09-06/16:45 Motorola 8000
        ➥UNIX)
        id <m0qWwxL-0000VmC@unilabs.UniLabs.ORG>; Sat, 6 Aug 94 21:23
        ➥EDT
Message-Id: <m0qWwxL-0000VmC@unilabs.UniLabs.ORG>
Date: Sat, 6 Aug 94 21:25 EDT
From: root (Unilabs System Manager)
To: chare
Status: R

Sat Aug  6 21:23:18 EDT 1994
chare         console      Aug  6 20:02
/         (/dev/dsk/m323_0s0):      5468 blocks      2732 i-nodes
/usr      (/dev/usr      ):     52188 blocks     11781 i-nodes
/usr1     (/dev/usr1     ):    110296 blocks     14113 i-nodes
/tmp


***************************************************
Cron: The previous message is the standard output
      and standard error of one of your cron commands.
```

Again, in the output from your batch-submitted jobs, you see the message that the output was a result of a cron job. This makes sense, because at and batch are closely related. In a moment you will see why.

Alternatively, the list of commands can be entered into a file, and that file can be read by batch through the input redirection capabilities of the shell. With batch, there is no real way to predict when the commands will be executed. In fact, they might be executed right away, with no delay to the user submitting them, or they might not execute for hours.

To see the jobs that are queued with batch, use the at command. The at jobs are listed with the letter *a* following the job number, and the batch jobs are found by looking for those jobs that have the letter *b* following the job number. batch jobs are removed by using the at -r option. Unfortunately, it is very difficult to get a system that will hold on to a batch job long enough to use these commands to interact with it.

batch is little used in today's computing environment. However, there are situations when batch can be an advantage. As mentioned, one such case is if you have a large, complex job that will require considerable CPU resources to complete. If you can spare the time, getting the extended resources when they are available may help you get your job completed faster than if you shared the CPU with everyone else.

To finalize this discussion, batch is used to submit jobs that will be executed when the system decides, based upon the load level.

Running the Job Over and Over Again

In both at and batch, you have little control if you want to automate a job, or want it executed on a regular basis. But there is yet another command in this series, called cron. cron is designed to execute commands at specific times, based upon a schedule. This schedule is known as a crontab file because of the command that is used to submit it to cron. You will see how to do this shortly.

The cron command is not actually executed by a user. It is started when the system is booted and remains running until the system is shut down. It executes commands for all of the users on the system who have scheduled jobs through its service.

Before you can successfully navigate through the land of cron, you must learn how to give cron the information it wants.

The crontab File

The crontab file is used to provide the job specifications that cron uses to execute commands. A user has one crontab file that can contain as many jobs as required.

This file has a very precise format, as shown in the following:

```
minutes    hours    day of month    month    day of week    command
```

Each line in the crontab file looks like this. There can be no blank lines, but comments are allowed, using the shell comment character, #. The first five fields are integer fields, and the sixth is the command field, which contains the command information to be executed. Each of the five integer fields contains information in several formats and has a range of legal values. The legal values are listed in the following table.

minutes	hours	day of month	month	day of week
0-59	0-23	1-31	1-12	0-6 0=Sunday

Each of these integer fields has a series of formats that are allowable for their values. These formats include the following:

✔ A number in the respective range. For example, a single digit.

✔ A range of numbers separated by a hyphen, indicating an inclusive range. For example, 1-10.

✔ A list of numbers separated by commas, meaning all of these values. For example, 1,5,10,30.

✔ A combination of the previous two types. For example, 1-10,20-30.

✔ An asterisk, meaning all legal values.

It is through the combination of these values that the user defines to cron when each command should be executed. Before moving onward, look at some sample commands from a crontab file:

```
0 * * * 0-6 echo "\007" >> /dev/console;date >> /dev/console; echo >> /
➡dev/console
0,15,30,45 * 1-31 * 1-5 /usr/local/collect.sys > /usr/spool/status/
➡unilabs
0,10,20,30,40,50 * * * * /usr/local/runq -v9 2>/dev/null
5,15,25,35,45,55 * * * * /usr/lib/uucp/uucico -r1 -sstealth 2>/dev/null
```

These four entries are from a crontab file on a real system. They illustrate the different values that each of the integer fields can contain. What is important here is to be able to look at the line and tell what in fact it is doing. Examine the first line:

```
0 * * * 0-6 echo "\007" >> /dev/console;date >> /dev/console; echo >> /
➡dev/console
```

This line means that the command will be executed at the 0 minute of every hour because the minute's field is zero, and the hour's field, which is the second from the left, is an asterisk, meaning all legal values. This is done for every day of the month, for every month of the year—both of these fields, the third and fourth, contain asterisks also. The fifth integer field contains the values 0-6, which indicates that this is done for each day of the week.

The second line is similar:

```
0,15,30,45 * 1-31 * 1-5 /usr/local/collect.sys > /usr/spool/status/
unilabs
```

The minute's field indicates that this command is executed every 15 minutes. Because there is no abbreviation for this type of information, it must be indicated by listing the specific times, separated by commas. The asterisk in the second field means that this is done for every hour of the day. The third field, which is the day of the month, indicates that this command is to be run on every day of the month. However, when you look at the fifth field for the days of the week, you see that this command is restricted to Monday through Friday. So, if the day of the month is in the range 1 to 31, and the day of the week is in the range of Monday to Friday, then the command will be executed.

The following example creates a number of problems:

```
* * * * * any command
```

This has the effect of overloading your system very quickly because the command is executed every minute of every hour, of every day, of every month. Depending upon the command, this could bring your system to its knees very quickly. Please be careful to avoid crontab entries like the preceding one.

Any asterisk (*) in the minute field is a horrible idea. This allows the command to execute every minute for as long as the other conditions defining the time are true. In the case of the following, the command would execute every minute of every hour, all day long on October 31st.

```
* * 31 10 * any command
```

It is far more preferable to restrict the minute (and hour) whenever possible to prevent overloading a system.

Consider an example of your own. On the first day of every month, you want to send yourself a reminder to change the calendar on your desk:

```
0        0        1        *        *        mycmd
```

The command runs at midnight (0 hours, 0 minutes), on the first day (1) of any month (*), on any day of the week (*). This means, however, that even if the first day of the month is a Saturday, the command will be executed.

The sixth field in the file is the command to be executed. The command can be any valid UNIX command or shell script. However, commands that require keyboard interaction will need to have their input come from elsewhere. These commands are generally not good programs for use with cron. This command can use redirection of either input or output, and you can decide where to send the data.

Creating a crontab File

crontab files are created with your favorite text editor. Do not use word processors, because they insert special characters and control codes. The file must be plain text, such as that which is created with the vi editor. Each field should be separated by a space or a tab. Blank lines are not allowed; they cause the crontab command to complain, as you will see subsequently. Comments are allowed, and as always, I urge you to make good comments for clarity later. The comment symbol is the same as that used for the shells, the pound symbol (#).

You should save your crontab file in a place where you will remember where it is, such as your home directory. The file can be named anything you want. There are no forced names for this file.

Submitting the crontab File

The crontab file, once created, is submitted to cron through the use of the command crontab. The only argument crontab needs to submit a cron job is the name of the file that contains your specifications. An example follows:

```
$ cat cronlist
#
# This job is executed to remind me to go home
#
15 17 * * 1-5 mail -s "time to go home" < /dev/null
$ crontab cronlist
$
```

This demonstrates a successful submission to cron. But it is not uncommon to make mistakes, as shown here:

```
$ cat cronlist
#
# This job is executed to remind me to go home
#
15 17 * * 1-5 mail -s "time to go home" < /dev/null
```

```
$ crontab cronlist

crontab: error on previous line; unexpected character found in line.
$
```

In the preceding example, there is a blank line at the end of the file. When crontab reads the file to ensure that its format is correct, it sees the blank line and reports that there is an error in the file. This is the same error message that crontab will print if there aren't enough fields on the line. However, integers that are outside their boundaries are reported, as seen in the following:

```
$ cat cronlist
#
# This job is executed to remind me to go home
#
99 17 * * 1-5 mail -s "time to go home" < /dev/null
$ crontab cronlist
99 17 * * 1-5 mail -s "time to go home" < /dev/null
crontab: error on previous line; number out of bounds.
$
```

If crontab doesn't report any problems when you are submitting your file, then it has been taken care of successfully.

Making Changes

The crontab command has two options that can be used to make changes to your submitted jobs. The first is -r. This option instructs crontab to remove the existing crontab file. The contents of the file that is used by cron are destroyed. Unless you still have the copy from which you started, the jobs specifications that were used by cron are lost. The second option is -l, which lists the jobs that are currently know to cron for the invoking user. These options are illustrated in the following:

```
$ crontab -l
#
# This job is executed to remind me to go home
#
15 17 * * 1-5 mail -s "time to go home" < /dev/null
$ crontab -r
$ crontab -l
crontab: can't open your crontab file.
$
```

This example demonstrates that by using crontab -l you were able to see the commands that you previously submitted to cron. With the -r option, you removed those specifications, which you were able to see because no output was generated when you next ran the `crontab -l` command. In the final part of this example, `crontab` tells you that it cannot open your crontab file. This should be indicator enough that you don't have one.

The files used by cron are stored in the directory ./usr/spool/cron/crontabs. You would be well advised not to edit the files in this directory. If you want to make a change to your crontab file, please follow the steps outlined here to prevent causing yourself frustration.

1. `crontab -l > $HOME/cronlist`

   This retrieves the job specifications that cron currently has and saves them in the file cronlist, in your home directory.

2. `vi cronlist`

   Once you have this information, you must edit it to reflect the changes you want to see. Edit the file using your favorite text editor, make the changes, and save the file.

3. `crontab cronlist`

   Next execute the crontab command with your newly changed cronlist file. This has the effect of replacing the current information with your new specification. It also signals to cron that there is a new crontab file to be read and processed.

Output: Where Did It Go?

Like at and batch, if the commands you asked cron to execute send any output to standard output or standard error, cron saves this and sends it to you via electronic mail once the command has completed. Like any command that could be entered at the command line, you can choose to redirect the output of your command to other files or through a pipe as appropriate.

Controlling Access to at, batch, and cron

The job of controlling who gets access to these services and how to do it is the responsibility of the system administrator. The following code illustrates the various messages if the needed authorization is missing.

```
$ at now + 2 minutes
at: you are not authorized to use at.  Sorry.
$ batch
```

```
at: you are not authorized to use at.  Sorry.
$ crontab $HOME/cronlist
crontab: you are not authorized to use cron.  Sorry.
```

Should you see these messages when you are trying to access these services, you should contact your system administrator and ask him or her to add you to the list of authorized users.

There are optional files that do not exist on a system by default. If they do exist, however, they are acted upon. The first is *cron.deny*. If this file exists, then any user named within that file is not allowed to use the cron utility. The second is *cron.allow*. If it exists, then only those users specifically listed within that file are allowed to use the cron utility. These two files are mutually exclusive and only one need be used on a system at a time. Once again, they are optional, and in their absence, all users are given access to cron.

As cron.allow and cron.deny restrict the users who can use the cron utility, so, too, do at.allow and at.deny restrict who can use the at command for running commands at later times.

Summary

The three commands presented here enable the user to exercise some measure of control over the processes he or she has to execute. at enables him or her to schedule a job to be executed once, and batch executes the job when the system's load level permits it to. Finally, cron enables the user to schedule routine jobs and programs that need to be done on a regular basis. It is important to remember that interactive commands cannot be used with any of these commands because the program will have no way to access a terminal for input, and it will abort or hang the system.

Command Summary

at	Submit jobs to be run at a specific time
at -l	List jobs submitted through at and batch
at -r	Remove jobs scheduled through at and batch
batch	Submit a job to be run when the system's load level permits
cron	The system job scheduler
crontab	Submit a job list to cron

crontab -e	On some systems, enables you to edit the current crontab entry
crontab -l	List the jobs that are being processed by cron
crontab -r	Remove the jobs specification list

Program Listing

Listing 1 gtimes.c.

```
/* - - - - - - - - - - - - - - - - - - - - - - - - - - - - - - - - - - - - - - - - - - - - - - - - -
NAME

    gtimes.c - Calculate clock times.

SYNOPSIS

    gtimes [ clock value ]
          - where clock value is a long integer which was previously
          ➡returned
            by the time system call.

DESCRIPTION

    This program without an argument will report the current system time
    both as an ASCII string, and as a long integer which is directly
    reported from time(S).
    Invocation with an argument results in the ASCII time string which
    matches the clock value on the command line.

RETURN VALUE

    Always returns 0.

NOTES

WARNINGS

    There are no provisions for bad data, or overflow.

SEE ALSO
```

```
CHANGE HISTORY
    Initial Version                              01/12/88     ch

    ----------------------------------------------------------------- */
/* Copyright 1988 Chris Hare */

#include <stdio.h>
#include <sys/types.h>
#include <sys/stat.h>
#include <time.h>
#include <errno.h>

main( argc, argv )
int argc;
char *argv[];

    {

    char *ctime(),              /* declare ctime(S) */
         *timestr;              /* storage area for time string */
    long int t_secs,           /* return value from time(S) */
             o_secs,            /* long integer value of command
                               ➡argument */
             atol(),            /* declare atol(S) */
             time();            /* declare time(S) */
        struct tm *mytime;
        struct tm *localtime();
        char *atime_str;

    if ( argc == 1 )
       t_secs = time(0L);
    else
       t_secs = atol(argv[1]);

    timestr = ctime(&t_secs);

    printf( "Clock : %ld\nDate  : %s\n", t_secs, timestr );

    }
```

Chapter Snapshot

Disaster awaits those who cannot or do not save their work.
This chapter discusses the back-up process, including the
following topics:

Understanding archiving strategies and following this
chapter's advice could help save you and your work in
the future.

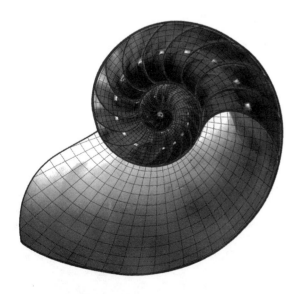

CHAPTER

Archiving and Backup

What good is your data if you can't get at it after your system crashes? In essence, it's worthless! Yes, worthless, unless you care to trust your sensitive information and your accounts receivable to some of the data recovery services that exist in the world. But why chance it? A good backup strategy has saved many system administrators' jobs after the system crashed or some overzealous user chose to delete it. This chapter discusses the issues around backing up your data.

Because this book is not delving into the deep, dark secrets of system administration, the discussion will focus on saving your own data.

Why Back Up Data?

Any number of problems can wipe out or damage your data. Some examples include power failures that scramble the data as it is being written to the disk, or a system crash that bangs the disk heads onto the surface. Program errors, kernel panics, and defective media can all cause loss of data.

The loss of information can be devastating depending upon the information that has been lost. Losing the company's accounts receivable information is much more critical than losing the boss's last memo. Unfortunately, when disaster strikes, it comes either all in one—that is, the system is destroyed—or in small packages, such as when you lose some of your information.

Recall from earlier chapters that once the file is removed, it cannot be recovered. Although there was a version of the Norton Utilities for UNIX, it didn't catch on in the marketplace. Regardless, you need to remember that any deletion of information should be considered permanent.

Now, let me say right now that sometimes your backups are lost causes as well. Having been on the receiving end of fate numerous times, it is possible for the worst to happen: unreadable or broken tapes. Yes, sometimes tapes break or become unreadable over time. Regardless of the backup media being used, care must be taken to store it in conditions suitable for that media. It would be considered wise to make two copies of information that must not be lost and then store the backups separately.

Planning a Strategy

The strategy behind doing backups defines what you will back up, when you will save it, how long you will save it for, and the media you will use. Some examples of backup media are listed in table 26.1.

Table 26.1
Backup Media

Media	Capacity
Quarter Inch Cartridge Tape	Various capacities from 15 MB to 525 MB.
Floppy Disks	Limited capacity, 360 KB to 1.44 MB.
4mm Digital Audio (DAT)	Various capacities, usually 2 to 5 GB. Used often with Hewlett-Packard, DEC Alpha, and Sun systems.
TK50 CompacTape	Single-spool tape used with DEC systems. 95 MB capacity.

Media	Capacity
TK70 CompacTape	Single-spool tape used with DEC systems. 500 MB capacity.
8mm Helical Scan	Large capacity. Can be as high as 25 GB.
WORM	Write Once, Read Many technology. Uses CD-ROM–like technology. Write the data once and read it whenever.
9-Track Tape	Historical value.
Optical Disk	Large capacity, typically around 500 MB, but can be as high as 1.3 GB. Readable and writeable. Works like a hard disk.

The strategy and the media used depends upon what you are going to back up. Saving two 300-kilobyte files to an 8mm video tape could be considered overkill. Consider a strategy that will afford you the most protection. To do this, you need to examine full versus partial backups and backup levels.

Full and Partial Backups

A full backup is usually done by the system administrator as part of his or her duties. It involves a backup of all the files on the system. Most often this is done on a file system basis to make it easier to restore should there be a need to do a complete recovery of a file system.

Partial backups, on the other hand, do not save all the files, but only those defined as necessary by whatever criteria the system administrator decides. For example, they may choose to back up all the files that have changed in the last three days. This can be done easily in a number of ways, as you will see during this chapter. Whenever you back up some number of files, it can be considered a partial backup.

Backup Levels

The concept of backup levels is particularly important to the system administrator who is designing or implementing a backup policy and procedure. A backup level defines what information is backed up. Most backup commands do not have a concept of backup levels: they are a mechanism for you to keep track of what was backed up at what time. Of course, it is also possible that in your situation, the backup media that you have available is capable of backing up all of your data. This means that you would be able to do a complete backup every day if you chose to. In this situation, backup levels are unnecessary.

A few levels and their meanings will be listed. It is important to remember that you can have whatever number of levels you see fit. The examples illustrated here might not work for you in your situation. Three backup levels are discussed, when in fact there are often many more than three.

Backup Level 0

This level refers to an entire backup, or the master backup of a group of files. From the system administrator's point of view, a level 0 backup means that all the files in the system are saved. From a user's perspective, a level 0 backup means all their own files are saved. For example, when you do a level 0 backup of your home directory, back up the entire structure.

Backup Level 1

This is a partial backup, which would include everything that has changed since the last level 0 backup. It would back up all the files in your home directory since you did your level 0 backup.

Backup Level 9

This is also a partial backup, but it includes only files that have changed since the last level 1 backup. The key here is to remember that the current level includes only files that have changed since the next lower level. Here are some examples to make sure you understand this issue.

```
Mon   Tue   Wed   Thu   Fri   Mon   Tue   Wed   Thu   Fri
0     9     9     9     9     1     9     9     9     9
```

This shows a two-week backup cycle. You start (arbitrarily) on a Monday with a level 0 backup, which captures all the files you specified. On Tuesday, you do a level 9 backup, which saves all the files that have changed since the level 0 backup. Wednesday, your level 9 backup saves all of the files that have changed since the previous level 0. This is repeated for the first week. Then on the first day of the second week, you do a level 1 backup, which saves all the files since the level 0. Does this sound like duplication? Well, each day, the list of changed files will be getting longer and longer.

On the second day of the second week, you perform another level 9 backup. This saves all the files that have changed since the previous lower level backup, which is a level 1. So your second Tuesday backup will contain only files that have changed from the previous day when you did your level 1 backup. This process continues for the two-week cycle and is repeated on an ongoing basis.

Backup Levels and Restoring Your Data

You saw in the preceding section a sample backup strategy that you used to create your backups. How do you translate this schedule into a list of tapes to restore? Following are several examples:

```
Mon   Tue   Wed   Thu   Fri   Mon   Tue   Wed   Thu   Fri
0     9     9     9     9     1     CRASH
```

Here you see that the system crashed, which means that you lost the data that you have been backing up. To recover this information to your last backup, you restore the level 0 backup, and then the level 1 backup. You restore the level 0 because it is a complete snapshot of the data. The level 1 backup includes only the files that have changed since the level 0 backup. As you can see, restoring only the level 1 backup would not give you all of the needed files.

```
Mon   Tue   Wed   Thu   Fri   Mon   Tue   Wed   Thu   Fri
0     9     9     CRASH
```

In this example, you lost your data on the fourth day of the first week. To recover in this situation, you again restore the level 0 backup, and then the last level 9 , which you did on Wednesday, the third day in the cycle. Using this type of backup cycle minimizes the number of tapes in use and the number of tapes that must be restored when a failure has occurred.

Choosing the Device

The actual archive device that you will use is dependent upon two things:

> ✔ The devices that are available on the system
>
> ✔ How much data you have to back up

If you have only a tape drive, then the fact that you have only two files to save is irrelevant. But if you have 20 megabytes that need to be saved, using the floppy disk drive is not a good idea. However, if you are lucky enough to have a selection of devices to choose from, then you need to consider which one you will use. Remember that when you are using the device, no one else can access it.

There are some things you should be aware of with some of these devices.

Using Floppy Disks

Floppy disks contain a small amount of data by today's standards. However, they are portable and can easily be mailed to other people around the world. They must be formatted prior to use—failure to do so will result in an error occurring during the backup. If you are on your ninth disk when this happens, your backup must be restarted, and any time spent is lost.

Using Tapes

Tapes should never be used immediately upon being inserted in the tape drive. All tapes should be retensioned using the appropriate command for your tape drive and system. Differing tensions in the tape can cause read or write errors. In addition, all new tapes should be retensioned before use the first time, as well as any tape that has been dropped.

Device Names

The device names for each system are very specific to the vendor. Although there is some commonality between UNIX versions, sometimes the expected device names don't mean the same things. Table 26.2 illustrates the different device names for a quarter-inch cartridge tape drive.

Table 26.2
Path Names to Tape Drives Based Upon Vendor

SCO UNIX System V/386	/dev/rct0
SCO UNIX System V/386 (SCSI)	/dev/rStp0
Sun Microsystems Solaris	/dev/rmt0
Sun Microsystems SunOS	/dev/rst0
Motorola VME Delta UNIX	/dev/rmt0
DEC Ultrix	/dev/rmt0h

As you can see from this limited list, there is no real commonality between device names. Consequently, for the remainder of this chapter, there is a reference to a pseudo-device called /dev/tape. This pseudo-device is used to signify that you should insert the real name of your device.

tar: The Tape Archiver

tar is one of several commands that can be used to save data to an archive device. Typically tar is used with tapes or floppy disks. Of all the commands that can be used to save data in backup archives, tar is the easiest and most user-friendly command of them all. It can save, restore, and list the contents of an archive. The syntax of tar is

```
$ tar key files
```

The key includes any arguments that go along with the options. The actual options that appear on any given version of tar can differ substantially. The key consists of a function that instructs tar what you want it to do, whereas the additional options alter the way that tar does the work. Unlike most UNIX commands, the key, or option list, that is given to tar does not have to contain a leading hyphen. These commands are equivalent:

```
$ tar -x
$ tar x
```

Table 26.3 lists the functions available on tar.

Table 26.3
tar Functions

Function	Purpose
r	The named files are written to the end of an existing archive.
x	The named files are extracted from the archive. If no files are specified, then the entire archive is extracted.
t	The named files are listed. If no argument is provided, all the files are listed.
u	The named files are added to the archive if they are not there or if they have been modified since last written on the archive.
c	Creates a new archive. The write process starts at the beginning of the archive, rather than at the end.

Each tar command will have one of these functions. Without it, tar doesn't know what it is supposed to do. The remainder of the key consists of options. Table 26.4 provides a list of the different options you can find on tar.

Table 26.4
tar Options

Option	Purpose
0-7	This specifies a device as listed in the tar configuration file.
v	Verbose. tar is usually quiet about its work. This option tells tar to tell about everything it does.
w	Causes tar to ask what action should be taken for a specific file, and waits for confirmation from the user.

continues

Table 26.4, Continued
tar Options

Option	Purpose
f file	tar uses the next file as the file name, or device to get the tar archive from. If the file is a dash (-), it reads or writes to standard output.
b num	tar uses num as the blocking factor. This should be used only with raw magnetic tapes.
F file	tar gets any remaining arguments from the named file.
l	tar will display an error if it cannot resolve the links to the files being backed up.
m	Tells tar not to restore the modification times. The new modification time is the time of extraction.
k size	The size argument is the size of the archive in kilobytes.
e	This instructs tar not to split files across tapes or disks. If there isn't enough space on the present archive, a new one is prompted for.
n	This indicates to tar that the archive is not magnetic tape. This is faster because tar can speed over files that it doesn't want. File sizes are printed in kilobytes instead of tape blocks.
p	Indicates that tar should extract the files using their original permissions. Only the superuser may be reliably able to do this.
A	Suppress absolute path names. This is used on restore to eliminate the leading slash (/) on file names.
o	Instructs tar to assign ownership of the files to the user running the program, and not the owner of the files as indicated in the archive.

This is an exhaustive list of options. However, although the list is long, tar accomplishes only one thing: archiving and recovering data. Look now at how to use tar to back up your data.

Doing Backups with tar

Imagine this scenario: You have a lot of data that you want to save to an archive. To do this, you need to use the c option. The other option you will use in the following example is f, which you will use to save the data to a tape.

```
$ cd /usr/spool
$ tar cf /dev/mt0 uucp
$
```

This example is simple in that it illustrates only one option. Try saving the information to a file on the disk, as seen in the following example.

```
$ ls
list       new_file  output    sample
$ tar cvf /usr/tmp/mine *
a list 1 blocks
a new_file 1 blocks
a output 1 blocks
a sample 1 blocks
$
```

In this case, you have added a couple of options. The v option instructs tar to be verbose in what it is doing. The tar command here is writing the archive to a file on the disk. Notice that neither tar nor UNIX makes any complaints that it isn't a device. tar doesn't know that the file /usr/tmp/mine isn't a device, and UNIX doesn't care. This example also illustrates listing file names on the command line.

But how can you tell if the backup was actually successful? Using the t function will cause tar to list the contents of the archive. The following code shows the difference in the output of tar t with and without the v option. Using the v option, the output is similar to that of ls -l.

```
$ tar tf /usr/tmp/mine
Tar: blocksize = 11
list
new_file
output
sample
$ tar tvf /usr/tmp/mine
Tar: blocksize = 11
rw-r--r--105/100     211 Aug 24 18:04 1994 list
rw-r--r--105/100     211 Aug 24 18:05 1994 new_file
rw-r--r--105/100     133 Aug 24 18:05 1994 output
rw-r--r--105/100      36 Aug 24 18:05 1994 sample
$
```

You can also add to the archive, in certain cases, using the r function. This function instructs tar to add files to the archive by going to the end of the archive and enlarging it. This is shown in the following:

```
$ tar cvf /usr/tmp/tape list output
a list 1 blocks
```

```
a output 1 blocks
$ tar uvf /usr/tmp/tape new_file sample
a new_file 1 blocks
a sample 1 blocks
$ tar tvf /usr/tmp/tape
Tar: blocksize = 11
rw-r--r--105/100      211 Aug 24 18:04 1994 list
rw-r--r--105/100      133 Aug 24 18:05 1994 output
rw-r--r--105/100      211 Aug 24 18:05 1994 new_file
rw-r--r--105/100       36 Aug 24 18:05 1994 sample
$
```

If tar can read through the archive, then the archive is okay. However, sometimes tar won't be able to do it. The following example shows what tar does when it can't read an archive. In this case, the tape was defective; in fact, it had no information stored on it. But that information doesn't come from tar. When tar accesses the device and can't find the structure it is looking for, it complains and exists. On occasion, you will find a problem in the middle of an archive. In this case, some of the files will be extracted, and others won't.

```
$ tar tvf /usr/tmp/tape
Tar: directory checksum error
$
```

In the example in figure 26.3, you listed some files on the command line. If the argument is in fact a directory, then the contents of the directory are written to the tape. This is illustrated in the following:

```
$ tar cvf /usr/tmp/tape t
a t/list 1 blocks
a t/output 1 blocks
a t/sample 1 blocks
a t/new_file 1 blocks
$
```

Now you have seen how to get the data into the archive using tar, and how to list the contents. Extraction is no more difficult.

Restoring the Data

Restoring files from a tar archive uses the same command format as the one used to create the archive. The function used is x, and the options that can be combined are the same. The arguments provided on the command line will be extracted if they are part of the archive. This is shown in the following:

```
$ tar cvf /usr/tmp/tape date ls pwd
a date 10 blocks
a ls 17 blocks
a pwd 5 blocks
$ cd /tmp
$ tar xvf /usr/tmp/tape date
Tar: blocksize = 20
x date, 4636 bytes, 10 tape blocks
$
```

The example in the previous code shows the extraction of some files that have been provided on the command line. If the argument specified is a directory, then the entire directory will be restored from the archive, as shown in the following:

```
$ cd /tmp
$ ls -l
total 10
-rwxr-xr-x  1 bin      bin          4636 Sep  1 18:37 date
$ tar xvf /usr/tmp/tape t
Tar: blocksize = 20
x t/list, 211 bytes, 1 tape blocks
x t/output, 133 bytes, 1 tape blocks
x t/sample, 36 bytes, 1 tape blocks
x t/new_file, 211 bytes, 1 tape blocks
$
```

Alternatively, if no arguments are specified on the command line, the entire archive is extracted. Now you can alter the way that tar performs the extraction. The w command is used to prompt the user with the name of the file that is currently being processed and waits for the user to indicate what should be done. The user can enter **y**, which results in the file being extracted, or **n**, which causes tar to skip the file and go to the next one. This is illustrated in the following:

```
$ tar xvfw /usr/tmp/tape
Tar: blocksize = 20
x rw-r--r--105/100    211 Aug 24 18:04 1994 t/list: y
x t/list, 211 bytes, 1 tape blocks
x rw-r--r--105/100    133 Aug 24 18:05 1994 t/output:
x rw-r--r--105/100     36 Aug 24 18:05 1994 t/sample:
x rw-r--r--105/100    211 Aug 24 18:05 1994 t/new_file: y
x t/new_file, 211 bytes, 1 tape blocks
$
```

VI

Administration

Caveat Emptor

Even though tar is user-friendly and capable of both large and small backup jobs, there are several issues to be aware of when using tar. These issues are as follows:

- ✔ File names can be a maximum of 100 characters in length. This includes the path name as well.

- ✔ tar cannot back up empty directories.

- ✔ tar cannot back up special device files, like those found in /dev.

- ✔ There is no real data verification.

Consequently, tar should not be used to back up the root file system, as the resulting backup will not be a complete representation of the data on the file system.

cpio: Copy In, Copy Out

Although cpio accomplishes the same end result as tar, the operation is extremely different. cpio is not as user-friendly as tar. cpio is meant to interact with standard input and standard output to get information on what files should be archived, and where to archive them. The options required to perform a backup are more numerous to be successful. cpio is also more difficult to utilize.

Because cpio doesn't have the same problems as tar, it is frequently used to perform file system backups. It is rarely used by users to save smaller amounts of data because of the difficulty in its use. Consider at the syntax of cpio and its options.

To use cpio, you must specify one of three actions, which direct cpio to create an archive, extract an archive, or copy the source files to another location. Table 26.5 lists these three operations.

Table 26.5
cpio Operations

Option	Purpose
o	Create an archive. This option reads standard input for a list of files and writes them to standard output.
i	Read and/or extract an archive. This accepts patterns on the command line to extract.
p	Pass through. This copies the source file to another directory.

Other options are used with each of these, depending upon which operation you are performing. Each of the options is considered during this discussion.

Performing Backups with cpio

As mentioned, backups are a lot more difficult to perform with cpio. Part of this is because of the command syntax needed and the number of options required. The options that can be used with the o option to create an archive are identified in table 26.6.

Table 26.6
cpio Output Options

Option	Purpose
a	This option resets the access times on the source files once they have been copied to the archive. This has the effect of making the file look like it hasn't been accessed.
c	Writes ASCII headers for each file. This increases the portability of the archive.
B	This causes cpio to block the output records into blocks of 5,120 bytes. Normally output is blocked in 512-byte clocks.
v	This instructs cpio to be verbose in its processing.

cpio reads its standard input to get the list of files that are to be processed into an archive. Normally this is done by finding the files with the find command and passing them to cpio through a pipe. cpio then processes the files, creates the archive, and sends the output to standard out. Consequently, the archive needs to be redirected to a file. Look at the structure of the cpio command line:

```
$ find / -name *shar -print ¦ cpio -oBcv > /dev/tape
```

This example finds all of the files on the system named core and passes the list of names to cpio. cpio will then create the archive, using ASCII headers for the file information and writing the output to the device /dev/tape. This example is shown in the following:

```
$ find / -name "*shar*" -print ¦ cpio -oBcv > /dev/mt0
/u/chare/.pshar.cfg
/u/chare/pshar
/usr/lib/ua/terminfo/tymshare.m
70 blocks
$
```

The list of file names that you see is in fact coming from cpio as it processes each file from find. There are a few options in creating the archive. The major disadvantage when not using the c option during the creation of the archive is that the portability of the archive is reduced to almost nonexistent. Due to the different machine architectures, even if the destination machine could read the tape normally, the binary format for the cpio header might contain information in a form that cannot be understood by the destination machine. For this reason, it is a wise idea to always use the c option for ASCII headers.

Restoring the Data

Unlike the tar command, there is no separate command to list the tape. Listing the tape is considered input, and so the commands to list the contents of the archive are included there. The basic structure of the cpio command to being input is as follows:

```
$ cpio -i[options] [patterns] < /dev/tape
```

Again, cpio reads standard input to determine what files (patterns) should be extracted or listed. The pattern uses the standard filename substitution rules that the shell uses. The default pattern is *, or match all files. To list the contents of an archive, use $ cpio -itcv < /dev/tape as illustrated in the following example:

```
$ cpio -itcv < /dev/mt0
100644 chare        65  Aug 13 00:48:22 1994  /u/chare/.pshar.cfg
100755 chare     33153  Aug 13 00:21:22 1994  /u/chare/pshar
100644 bin         180  Apr  9 21:28:14 1993  /usr/lib/ua/terminfo/
tymshare.m
66 blocks
$
```

The options that are available for use with the input operation of cpio are listed in table 26.7.

Table 26.7
cpio Input Options

Option	Purpose
B	Like the output operation, this option blocks the input records to 5,120-byte blocks before processing them.
c	Uses ASCII header information. If the archive was created with the -c option, then the archive must be processed with -c.
d	Creates the directories as needed.
r	Interactively renames files.

Option	Purpose
t	Prints the table of contents. This prints only a list of file names unless the v option is also used.
u	Copies the files even if the disk copy is newer than the archive copy.
v	Tells cpio to be verbose.
l	When possible, links files rather than copying them.
m	Retains the previous modification time.
s	Swaps bytes within each half word.
f	Copies all the files except those that match the patterns indicated on the command line.
b	Reverses the order of bytes within each half word.

Like the other aspects of tar, similar options must be used. If, for example, the archive was created with the c option for ASCII headers, and the archive is not read with this option, cpio will complain that the archive is out of phase. If the list operation is successful through the archive, then the archive can be considered good. (See the next section, "Caveat Emptor.")

The most commonly used options when restoring from the archive are dependent upon your preferences, but one suggestion follows:

```
$ cpio -iBcdv < /dev/tape
```

This example restores all of the files on the archive, as shown in the following:

```
$ cpio -iBcduv < /dev/tape
lp/member/Epson
lp/model
lp/model/dumb
lp/model/dumb_S
lp/model/dumb-remote
lp/model/imagen_S
lp/model/n450
lp/model/second-remote
lp/model/dumb_sm
lp/pstatus
lp/qstatus
lp/request
lp/request/Epson
```

```
lp/request/Parallel
lp/log
$
```

An important note goes along with the d option. If it is not included on the command line, directories and their files will be skipped. On occasion, you will want to recover only some files. Unlike the command used in the previous example, which restores all the files, you can choose to be more selective, as seen in the following code:

```
$ cpio -iBcdv lp/log < /dev/tape
lp/log
20 blocks
$
```

When being selective like this, it is important to be precise. Unfortunately, many cpio implementations will not properly expand the shell notation of *, ?, and [..], even though they should. If that were the case, then the argument *pshar* should be enough for cpio to find the files that are named pshar. While recovering the files, you can also rename the files should you choose to at that time. This is done with the r option, which is illustrated in the following example using the same list of files.

```
$ cpio -iBcdvr < /dev/tape
Rename </u/chare/.pshar.cfg>

Skipped

Rename </u/chare/pshar>
./pshar
./pshar
Rename </usr/lib/ua/terminfo/tymshare.m>

Skipped

70 blocks
$
```

In this example, the only file copied is uucppublic/pshar, which you have renamed to be pshar in the current directory. With the r option, when the user presses Enter, cpio skips the file.

Copying Directories

On some UNIX systems, the command copy exists to copy directory structures. In fact, on systems that do not have this command, it can be mimicked with cpio -p. The -p instructs cpio to perform the copy on the same pass. It reads standard input for files and copies them to the destination. The following example illustrates using cpio -p to copy a directory and its contents:

```
$ find t -print ¦ cpio -pdlv /usr/tmp
/usr/tmp/t/list
/usr/tmp/t/output
/usr/tmp/t/sample
/usr/tmp/t/new_file
0 blocks
$ ls /usr/tmp
t      tape
$ ls -l /usr/tmp/t
total 4
-rw-r--r--  2 chare    users        211 Aug 24 18:04 list
-rw-r--r--  2 chare    users        211 Aug 24 18:05 new_file
-rw-r--r--  2 chare    users        133 Aug 24 18:05 output
-rw-r--r--  2 chare    users         36 Aug 24 18:05 sample
$
```

What you have done is to create a duplicate directory structure of /usr1/chare in /usr/tmp. This can be verified by using dircmp. (There would actually be some differences because some other files existed in /usr/tmp prior to the example being executed.)

Caveat Emptor

Like tar, cpio also has its problems. The major one is that it is so much harder to use that tar. Because of this unfriendliness, tar is generally chosen over cpio by users, and some new system administrators. cpios other major issues are as follows:

✔ File and path names in some implementations are limited to 128 characters.

✔ There is no real data verification.

✔ Only the superuser can copy the special files in /dev.

The command used depends upon the job and the comfort level of the user involved.

Summary

The tar and cpio backups were discussed in this chapter. Backups can be performed on a variety of media, following any strategy that you determine to be most appropriate for your information. Remember that the time allowed between backups must be equivalent to the amount of data that you are willing to lose in the event of a full system crash.

Chapter Snapshot

Security is one topic that you can never understand enough. The most important asset to most companies is the data contained on their computer system. This chapter examines security as it relates to the UNIX operating system, focuses on the following and in particular:

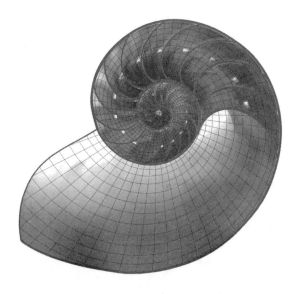

CHAPTER

Security

With the advent of the computer, users found more and more uses for it. As the popularity and the uses for the computer increased, organizations started placing more and more information at the fingertips of their employees through this device. The problem is that people who shouldn't have the information can also often get at it. It is important to remember that security breaches do not always happen from the outside. How many times a year do you hear about thefts that were an "inside job"—that couldn't be accomplished without the help of someone in the organization?

It is safe to say that as many security breaches occur from inside your organization as outside. This is because your employees may be trying to get access to information that they are not entitled to have. If they get it, doesn't that constitute a security breach? Sure it does!

This chapter is about how security works on UNIX systems and how you can better prepare yourself to prevent them from happening by being aware of the common pitfalls that so many people fall into.

When one thinks of security, one often associates it with guards and sophisticated alarm systems. Indeed, some computer installations do have this type of security, but it is more applicable to associate computer security with whether your data will be there later. The following is a potential definition as found in some computer security books on how computer security should really be perceived:

> A computer is secure if you can depend upon it and its software to behave as you expect it to.

Now, bearing in mind that it is possible for buggy software, user error, earthquakes, and lightning to wipe out your data, can you ever say that a computer is totally secure? The U.S. Department of Defense decided that a computer could never be totally secure, so they developed the concept of trustedness. You will look at how a computer is trusted later in this chapter.

Any organization dependent upon computers to store and manipulate the information that is required to operate should be concerned about security—not only from outside attacks, but also from vengeful employees, buggy software, viruses, and hardware failure. To address these issues, a series of policies should be developed to assist in the protection of these computing resources.

Although the policies put into practice are dependent upon the organization, this chapter offers some ideas.

✔ Personal Software Applications

This organization does not permit the installation of personal software. Any user found with personal software on their assigned PC will have said software immediately removed from their PC. This is to assist in the risk reduction of introducing software viruses into your computer systems.

✔ Internet Access

Due to the increased risk that a connection to the Internet brings, and considering that you want your users to have access to this resource, the organization will limit the types of connections that can be made. For an up-to-date list of these connections, please contact your workgroup administrator.

These examples are by no means all-encompassing, but they are two examples of what many organizations are saying in today's networked environment. "Unless we take steps, the Robert T. Morris Internet worm can happen again...."

This chapter presents the types of security, how user controls work, passwords, and more.

Physical Versus Logical Security

You need to address two types of security—physical and logical. The physical is concerned with where the machine is located and the access controls to the machine. The logical security component addresses the issues of security in the software, such as user names and passwords. You need to be concerned about both types because your logical security system will not protect your data if you leave the machine in a place where the thieves can simply carry it off! Following are a list of issues surrounding the physical security.

✔ Location of the Machine

Although it can be considered convenient to have your machine in a "public" place where it is accessible to the people who need it, the danger is that people who shouldn't have access to the machine will be able to affect its operation. If you must use this type of scenario, consider having the keyboard disabled by a keyboard lock or some other security device.

✔ Availability of Removal

If the machine is publicly accessible, it can easily be carried away by someone. This is also true for any PC on a user's desk. In fact, it is advisable to obtain PC locking systems so the PC is attached to someone's desk or workstation and cannot be moved off the desk without the appropriate keys.

✔ Access to Distribution and Backup Media

As more and more software manufacturers are taking a hard line concerning software piracy, it is reasonable to expect organizations to take strict control over the software assets they have purchased. Paying $2,000 for a UNIX license only to have the distribution media disappear is a costly annoyance (especially when the machine is being rebuilt).

The same is true for backup media. If you faithfully back up all of your data and leave the backups available, wouldn't you consider stealing the backups as good as stealing the machine? Sure, the information on the backups might be slightly out of date, but the fact remains that you have lost your data–and to whom, you have no idea.

To address these situations, distribution and backup media should be identified and controlled under lock and key to prevent unauthorized access.

These several points are some of the issues surrounding the physical security of the machine. Although there are more, you will move on to a discussion of logical security. As mentioned, logical security is concerned with the controls and mechanisms that are part of the operating system to control access to the system, and then to the files and data

VI

Administration

stored there. Following are issues around logical security that you should consider. Because this chapter is more concerned with the logical security, many of these issues will be discussed later in the chapter.

✔ User Account Management

When a user leaves the organization, his or her account should be promptly deactivated to prevent access to the system. This is typically done by the administrator; it can be achieved by changing the user's password. This, by itself, however, is not enough. The password must be changed to a value that cannot be matched by any password-cracking program. Most modern UNIX systems provide a mechanism to do this.

It is also important to remember that in a networked environment, users should have the same UID number on every machine they have an account on. When in a networked environment, this applies to every machine on the network that they can access. This will be discussed again later.

✔ Password Management

Are users writing their passwords somewhere because they can't remember them? Are you using a password generator or checker? Passwords are the most commonplace for a security breakdown because the users are the weakest link in the chain.

✔ Education

It is necessary to educate the users on the system that security is not just the administrator's job, but a job for everyone. Regardless of how well the system administrator works to prevent unauthorized access to the system or the data, the sloppy programmer who doesn't consider the impact of some code on the security of the system is guilty of being the cause of the problem. Likewise, the user who leaves her terminal logged in when she goes home leaves an invitation for someone to masquerade as her and do some damage.

It should be fairly obvious at this stage that good security doesn't just happen. It is a complex interaction of policies, procedures, and education for all the system administrators, users, programmers, and management to be aware of and to adhere to at all times.

Security Levels

It was mentioned earlier that the U.S. Department of Defense developed the concept of security levels. These were identified and presented in what is called the Orange Book, or the Trusted Computing Standards Evaluation Criteria. This document presents not only the constraints and operating procedures for the given level of security, but also for what changes must be made for the source code to be approved. Furthermore, the Orange Book also identifies the procedures that a given operating system will be put through to be certified at a particular level.

The Orange Book would lead one to believe that the only system that is secure is the one that is locked in a vault with no users! Although this isn't practical, they have developed the concept of trust. This concept of trust suggests that a trusted system is one that has a higher degree of control over the users on the system and the corresponding data. A trusted system prevents, or at least identifies, unauthorized access to the system.

The three levels mentioned here are the three most common. The other levels, although they are becoming more available, are more suited for extreme security environments such as highly classified information within a government, military, or commercial environment.

The security levels are identified with the letters D, C, B, and A, followed by the number 1, 2, or higher. The letters have been listed here in reverse order because a level D system has lower security than a level C system. The numbers 1 and 2 are also used to identify a sublevel of security within a specific level. For example, there are published standards for levels D1, C1, C2, B1, B2, B3, A1.

A D1 operating system has essentially no security. There is no way for the operating system to know who is sitting at the keyboard, and there is little or no control exercised to prevent access to files. An example of a level D operating system is MS-DOS.

A C1, or Discretionary Security Protection, operating system has more security than a D-level operating system. These operating systems include mechanisms for user authentication and controlling access to files. The most common example of a level C1 operating system is traditional UNIX. However, even traditional UNIX can be improved upon, which is what C2 security does. Discretionary Security means that each user has control over the objects they own. The user can control who can read, modify, and execute the files he or she own. Access is controlled on the fronts: the owner, the group members, and everyone else.

A C2, or Controlled Access Protection, operating system has all the components of a level C1 operating system, plus the ability to further restrict users from executing commands based upon the level of authorization they have, and auditing virtually every event that takes place on the system. Controlled Access Protection means that auditing and increased authentication has been added. Auditing is used to keep records of all security-related events, such as those activities performed by the system administrator. Auditing requires additional authentication because without it, how can you be sure the person who executed the command really is that person? The disadvantage to auditing is that it requires additional processor and disk subsystem resources.

The B1 level, or Labeled Security Protection, is the first level that supports multilevel security, such as secret and top secret. This level states that an object under mandatory access control cannot have its permissions changed by the owner of the file.

The B2 level, also known as Structured Protection, requires that every object be labeled. Devices such as disks, tapes, or terminals may have a single or multiple level of security assigned to them. This is the first level that starts to address the problem of an object at a higher level of security communicating with another object at a lower level of security.

The B3, or Security Domains level, enforces the domain with the installation of hardware. For example, memory management hardware is used to protect the security domain from unauthorized access or modification from objects in different security domains. This level also requires that the user's terminal be connected to the system through a trusted path.

The final level in the Orange Book is level A1, or the Verified Design level. This level requires a mathematically verified design, as well as detailed analysis of covert channels, and trusted distribution. Trusted distribution means that the hardware and software have been protected during shipment to prevent tampering with the security systems.

As you can guess, the higher the level of security, the more expensive it is to procure, implement, and subsequently maintain. However, despite all this, the determining factor regarding what level of security you want to implement is dependent upon three things:

✔ You know what it is you are trying to protect.

✔ You know what you are trying to protect yourself from.

✔ You know how much time, effort, and money you are willing to spend to protect it.

Before moving on to the next topic, it should be pointed out that a higher level of security brings with it its own frustrations and challenges for the users and the administrators. Don't treat it simply as the cure.

Risk Assessment

Any enhancements to policies, practices, or security levels should be considered only after conducting a risk assessment. This is because you will be able to address the issues only by researching, identifying, and understanding the potential problems that could impact the security you want. Furthermore, you are assessing the risk that someone will break into your system. This risk, like many others, is one that you will never be able to reduce to zero. A risk assessment involves measuring the exposure to security violations. No matter how trusted or secure you make your computers, someone somewhere will have the resources to break into them. This affects even systems that are trusted to different levels in the Orange Book. As was mentioned, maintaining a trusted system requires effort. If that effort is not expended, then it becomes easier for that system to be violated.

The next question is, "What do we need to consider when assessing our risk?" Consider the following list of topics:

✔ Physical Security

   Of the machine

   Of the console

   Of the distribution media and license information

   Of the backup media

   Of the network and terminal cables

   Of the documentation

✔ Logical Security

   User names and passwords

   File permissions and ownership

✔ Communications

   Dial-in modems

   Internet access

✔ Programs

   Viruses

   Poorly written code

✔ Policies and Practices

   Do they explain what you want and why?

   Have the users been educated in them and encouraged to follow them?

You cannot easily assess all of these things because many of them are beyond the traditional control associated with users and administrators. Part of the process in assessing a risk is knowing exactly what the network looks like. If there is an up-to-date network diagram, it becomes easier to see some of the mechanisms that people can use to thwart the security systems.

However, the most common problem with security is not the system, or the physical security, or the network, but people. People make mistakes—from writing down passwords, to walking away from a logged-in terminal, to giving their password to someone else.

User Authentication

Many operating systems besides UNIX have user authentication. It involves the user providing some form of identification to the system, and then validation of that identification, typically through a password. Think of it this way—when you use a banking machine, your card has a number encoded on it that identifies you to the banking machine and enables it to retrieve your banking information. However, before you can actually deposit or withdraw money, you must identify yourself, or prove who you are. This is done through your Personal Identification Number, or PIN. After you enter this correctly, the banking machine is convinced that you are who you say you are. (The fact that it still might not be you is being ignored at this stage.)

The same is true for computer operating systems such as UNIX. You must identify who you are through the use of a login name. This login name is associated with a numerical userid, or UID, which is used to uniquely identify you to the system. Each user should have a password associated with his or her user account.

It is also a good idea to limit the use of shared accounts. A shared account enables multiple people to use the same login name. Although this appears to be a good thing, there is no way for a single person to be matched with a single event. In fact, trusted systems highly discourage this type of account.

The Password File

As you saw earlier in this book, the password file is where all the information regarding a user's login account is stored. Although this is true for traditional UNIX, it is not true for enhanced security systems, which make use of the Trusted Computing Base, or TCB. You will look at the TCB in the next section.

Recall the format of a password file entry:

```
chare:u7mHuh5R4UmVo:105:100:Chris Hare:/u/chare:/bin/ksh
username:encrypted password:UID:GID:comment:home directory:login shell
```

When you look at this entry, you see that there are seven colon-separated fields representing the information for this user's account. The password is encrypted so that no one can see what it is when looking at this file. If there are passwords in this file, why should users even be able to see them? The password file is used by the ls command and others to translate the UID on each file to the user name for some meaningful output when the user lists the file. Consider the following output, which shows what the normal output is from ls:

```
$ ls -l rat*
-rwxr-xr-x  1 chare    users       468 Aug  9 22:58 rat
```

```
-rwxr-xr-x  1 chare    users        538 Aug 12 15:16 rat2
```

If you were to change the permissions on /etc/passwd from the default permissions to restrict being able to read the file, the output from ls -l is very different.

```
# ls -l /etc/passwd
-r--r--r-- 1 root     root         595 May  6 13:52 /etc/passwd
# chmod 400 /etc/passwd
# ls -l /etc/passwd
-r-------- 1 root     root         595 May  6 13:52 /etc/passwd
#

$ ls -l rat*
-rwxr-xr-x  1 105      users        468 Aug  9 22:58 rat
-rwxr-xr-x  1 105      users        538 Aug 12 15:16 rat2
$
```

In the first part of the code, root changes the permissions from read-only for all users to read-only for root. When another user ran the ls -l command in the latter half of the code, the user name is now a number. Why is this? It is because the user doesn't have permission to read the /etc/passwd file to get the user name for the associated UID number. Although it is more aesthetic than anything else, commands that look for information in /etc/passwd might not work properly. As a result, the /etc/passwd file should not be writeable by anyone. The passwd program can make the needed modifications to the /etc/passwd file when they are required.

If passwords are the weakest link in the system because people have to know them, why use them? Using the banking analogy, without a PIN to validate the user, anyone could take your banking card to the bank and withdraw all your money. Likewise, in some environments, security is not an issue because of an intensely trusting environment where the doors don't even have locks. Unfortunately, not all of the world is like this, and if a computer has a modem on it, it is likely that someone will try to gain access as soon as they find the connection. Without passwords, you simply invite them, much like handing the thief your bank card that has no PIN. The costs become astronomical in a short period of time.

The Trusted Computing Base

The Trusted Computing Base (TCB) is part of the security system for C2-rated UNIX systems. It adds a significant level of complexity to the operation of the system, and to the administration of it. This system works by moving bits of the /etc/passwd file to other places, as well as adding additional information into the original information. The files that make up the databases for the trusted computing base are scattered in several different directory hierarchies. It is not a good idea to edit these files, however, because serious damage may result to your system.

A system that uses the TCB places an asterisk in the password field of /etc/passwd. This is because the actual user password is stored along with other user information in the Trusted Computing Base. How this is incorporated into the overall operation is beyond the scope of this book. Using the TCB doesn't change the operation of the system so much as how UNIX provides the same services using TCB. On some UNIX systems, such as SCO UNIX, even if you are not using C2 security, the Trusted Computing Base is still being used to provide the security services.

```
chare:u_name=chare:\                 # Actual user name
      :u_id#1003:\                    # User ID
      :u_pwd=MWUNe/9lrPqck:\          # Encrypted password
      :u_type=general:\              # User Type
      :u_succhg#746505937:\          # Last Successful Password Change
      :u_unsucchg#746506114:\        # Last Unsuccessful Password Change
      :u_pswduser=chare:\            #
      :u_suclog#747066756:\          # Last successful Login
      :u_suctty=tty02:\              # Last successful login on tty
      :u_unsuclog#747150039:\        # Last unsuccessful login
      :u_unsuctty=tty04:\            # Last unsuccessful login on tty
      :u_numunsuclog#1:\             # Number of unsuccessful logins
      :u_lock@:\                     #
      :chkent:                       #
```

This example has been modified so comments could be inserted on the entry. The # *text* does NOT appear in the file. This code is included here to illustrate that in the TCB there is in fact other information being tracked. This is not all of it, but that which is contained in one file. For each user, a file named with his or her user name is stored and contains the information shown in the preceding code.

Password Encryption

Password encryption is used to limit unauthorized access to the system by making it harder for people to figure out what a user's password is. The encryption algorithm is based upon the Data Encryption Standard, or DES, algorithm. The exact scheme used is a modified format of the DES. This makes it very difficult to figure out what the password is. In fact, the passwords are considered effectively undecodable. So how is your login validated when you log on to UNIX?

When you enter your password, it is encrypted and compared with the password that is stored. If the encrypted values are the same, then your login has been validated and you are granted access to the system.

The encryption mechanism has been altered through the use of a 12-bit number called salt. This number slightly changes the way that the DES algorithm encrypts passwords. This means that two users can share the same password, and looking at the password file, no one would know it. The salt is stored in the encrypted password as the first two characters. Using this salt, the login program can then compare the user-supplied value with the encrypted value to see if the users are the same.

A password cracker is a program that is used to successively guess passwords. The addition of the salt doesn't make it take longer to find a password, but it forces the bad guy to search for each one individually. Consider the following examples:

```
root:tUazDCY/AyLIw:0:0:Root:/:
chare:7VAVIbHEJ1wzE:105:100:Chris Hare:/u/chare:/bin/ksh
```

Would you believe that these entries show the same password for both root and chare? Of course not! But, in fact they do. The salt in root's password is the characters tU, whereas it is 7V for chare's password. The fact that the salts are different is the reason why the encrypted passwords are different.

Because of the salt, it is possible for a user who has user accounts on multiple machines to be able to use the same password without anyone knowing.

Password Management

Because the passwords are typically the weakest link in the authentication system, you need to consider what makes a good or bad password. It is easy to prove that they are the weakest links: how many of you have written down the combination for a lock simply because you were afraid you would forget it! Chapter 2, "Gain Access," gave recommendations on things to avoid and consider when selecting a new password, and also how to change it.

Password Generators

On many newer versions of AT&T UNIX System V, the ability exists for the user to have the system generate a password for them. Furthermore, the ability exists to prevent users from being able to create their own passwords. Because the generator is more concerned with being able to protect the system, it can generate only a series of characters that meet the password criteria.

The pitfall to generated passwords is that most people don't like them, so they write them down to remember them. Although this can work, it is far better for everyone if users have the choice. The following code illustrates using the passwd generator to change the password.

```
$ passwd
Setting password for user: chare
Old password:
Last   successful password change for chare: Sun Aug 14 16:17:27 1994
```

```
                    Choose password
You can choose whether you pick a password,
or have the system create one for you.
        1. Pick a password
        2. Pronounceable password will be generated for you
Enter choice (default is 1): 2
Generating random pronounceable password for chare.
The password, along with a hyphenated version, is shown.
Press <Return> until you like the choice.
When you have chosen the password you want, type it in.
Note: type your interrupt character or 'quit' to abort at any time.
Password: atapveby  Hyphenation: at-ap-veb-y   Enter password:
Password: hegicyif  Hyphenation: heg-ic-yif   Enter password:
Password: komricam  Hyphenation: kom-ric-am   Enter password:
Password: dydowwai  Hyphenation: dyd-ow-wai   Enter password:
Re-enter new password:
$
```

Here the password generator randomly picks letters with the intent of generating a pronounceable password. It will continue to generate passwords until the user finds one that he likes. When he does, he enters the password (without the hyphens). He is then prompted for it again, and the change is put in place. When looking at this, it is easy to see that these passwords are less likely to be guessed, but they are also much harder to remember. The unfortunate side effect is that this user will be more likely to write down his password to remember it.

Password Aging

Many versions of UNIX provide for password aging. This mechanism controls when users can change their passwords by inserting a value into the password file after the encrypted password. This value defines the minimum period of time that must pass before a user can change his password, and the maximum period of time that can elapse before the password has expired.

This explanation becomes clearer by thinking of a timeline. The password aging control information is stored along with the encrypted password as a series of printable characters. The controls are included after the password, preceded by a comma. There are typically a number of characters following the comma that represent the following information:

✔ The maximum number of weeks the password is valid.

✔ The minimum number of weeks that must elapse before the user can change his password again.

✔ When the password was most recently changed.

There are two special conditions that are recognized by the aging control mechanisms: one that forces the user to change his or her password on next login, and one that prevents the user from being able to change it.

To force a user to change his or her password, such as for a new user, the password field for that user would be modified to include a comma, followed by two periods for the maximum and minimum time periods. In this case, the user will be forced to change his or her password on his next login. Once changed, the "force" control information will be removed from the password entry.

The second special case prohibits a user from being able to change his or her password. This condition is established by setting the maximum value to be less than the minimum value (that is, first < second). In this case, the user is informed that his or her password cannot be changed.

With newer, more secure versions of UNIX on the market currently, you may hear the term "password lifetime." This is a grace period after the maximum time period in which the user can still log in to his account using the expired password. Once the lifetime has been reached, the account would be disabled.

This mechanism doesn't prevent a user from changing his password and then changing it back to the old one later. Only a few UNIX system versions keep track of what passwords a user has used. The actual process of implementing password aging is version-dependent. To implement it on your system, consult your system documentation.

The program in Listing 27.1, pwexp.pl, will advise a user when his password is going to expire so he can be prepared for the day when the system informs him that it has expired. Note, however, that this version of the program is for standard System V UNIX, where a shadow password file is not used.

This program addresses the aging mechanism that has been implemented in versions of UNIX up to System V Release 3.2. At this level, some variations took place in the interests of increasing system security. The AT&T camp moved to using the /etc/shadow file for storing the password information, whereas the SCO camp moved to using the Trusted Computing Base facilities from SecureWare. In SCO's UNIX 3.2v4 product, the aging control information may be in one of /etc/passwd, /etc/shadow, or the Trusted Computing Base files, depending upon which level of security you configure.

Users, Groups, and su

While you are examining security, you need to revisit the concept of user names as well as identify some special users. Each user name on the system can be up to eight characters in length. Although the actual name in use can be more, only the first eight characters are recognized by UNIX, as seen in the following:

```
$ who
chare       tty000       Aug 14 13:06
catherin    w1           Aug 14 18:33
$ grep catherin /etc/passwd
catherine::106:100:Catherine Agent:/u/catherin:
$
```

As this shows, the entry in /etc/passwd has more than eight characters, but when you look at the output of who, only the first eight characters are seen. Consequently, it should be remembered that user names must be unique for the first eight characters. Each user name maps to a unique userid, or UID. This unique UID is used to represent the user to the system. The user name is merely a convenience for us humans.

You have seen that the user information is essentially contained in /etc/passwd, with some variations on the theme. But each user can belong to a group of users. Recall that the permissions field shown in the following code has permissions for the owner of the file, the user in the group, and all other users.

```
r w - r - - r - -
```

In the permissions field, the first three characters represent the permissions for the owner of the file, the second three are for the group, and the final three are for the other users on the system. So, where are the groups of users defined? The groups are defined in the file /etc/group. This file has a format resembling the following code:

```
root:NONE:0:root
other:NONE:1:daemon,lp
bin:NONE:2:root,bin,daemon
sys:NONE:3:root,bin,sys,adm
adm:NONE:4:root,adm,daemon
mail:NONE:6:root,uucp,nuucp,uucpadm
users:NONE:100:tutor,install,chare,catherin,matthew,meagan,terri
```

This file contains the database that lists every group on the system. Each line consists of four colon-separated fields. These fields are shown in table 27.1.

Table 27.1
The /etc/group fields

Field	Definition
users	The name of the group
NONE	The group's password
100	The Group ID (GID)
tutor, install, etc.	The users who belong to the group

The exact group names and configuration are frequently different from one system to another, partially due to the differences in the initial file as provided by the vendor, and the site preferences. If you look in the /etc/passwd file, you find a GID number at the fourth field. This is the user's login group, and consequently the user name might not be included explicitly in the group file entry. This is because the intent of the group file is to identify the additional groups to which the user can belong.

Typically, there has been a difference in how System V and Berkeley UNIX have handled groups. In Berkeley UNIX, when the user logged in, the /etc/group file was scanned, and it placed each user into the group to which he or she belonged. As the user worked, he or she didn't have to worry about group permissions and switching groups like the System V users had to.

The System V users, however, could belong to only one group at a time. Consequently, when they needed to access a file that was not accessible and they belonged to the same group, they could use the newgrp command to change groups. To do this, they provided the name of the group to which they wanted to switch. In order to be successful, the user must belong to the other group. This is illustrated as follows:

```
$ grep "chare" /etc/group
mail:NONE:6:root,uucp,nuucp,uucpadm,chare
$ id
uid=105 gid=100(users)
$ newgrp mail
$ id
uid=105 gid=6(mail)
$
```

If the user is a member of the requested group, the newgrp command is successful. If the user is not a member of the desired group, newgrp prompts the user for a password. This password is encrypted and is interpreted like the password in the /etc/passwd file. The only difference is that there is no easy way for a password to be installed in the file. The following code illustrates using a password to change groups with newgrp.

```
$ cat /etc/group
root:HmILLEJdAnusE:0:root
other:NONE:1:daemon,lp
bin:NONE:2:root,bin,daemon
sys:NONE:3:root,bin,sys,adm
adm:NONE:4:root,adm,daemon
mail:NONE:6:root,uucp,nuucp,uucpadm,chare
users:NONE:100:tutor,install
$ id
uid=105 gid=100(users)
$ newgrp root
Password:
```

VI

Administration

```
id
$ id
uid=105 gid=0(root)
$
```

Here the newgrp command prompts the user for a password because he or she is not already a member of the group. Interestingly enough, many System V vendors are making the needed changes so that the behaviors for groups are more like those of the Berkeley orientation and are moving away from the requirement for newgrp.

Listing 27.5 at the end of this chapter contains a program that originally appeared in *UNIX World* magazine in February 1991. The author is Brian Cartnell, and it was intended to provide a mechanism of inserting passwords into the group file. But it is important to know that there are some good reasons for maybe not using passwords on groups. Consider that a group with a password can be less secure than one with no password, because if the password is discovered, any user can become a member of the group. If there is no password, only the members of the group in the group file can become members of the group.

The group password is likely considered by the users to be less of a security issue than their own passwords. Furthermore, because more than one user knows the password, it is more likely to be accidentally divulged. In addition, because there is no aging mechanism for group passwords like that for passwords, the same group password could be used for the life of the system, thereby increasing the likelihood of a security violation.

Consequently, although the program in Listing 27.5 provides a mechanism for passwords to be inserted into the group file, there is a good argument, as presented here, for not using them at all.

The Superuser

Every UNIX system comes with a superuser account. This account is called root and is the user account from which most of the administrative tasks and system jobs are run. What is so special about the root user is the UID that is assigned to it, which is zero. The password for root is called the root password.

The operating system makes use of this account to perform its own tasks. For example, the following code shows that many processes that run under UNIX in fact belong to the root user—as reflected by the UID column.

```
$ ps -ef
     UID  PID  PPID  C   STIME  TTY  TIME     COMMAND
    root    0     0  0  Aug 11    ? 4829:41   swapper
    root    1     0  3  Aug 11    ?  0:04     init
    root    2     0  0  Aug 11    ?  0:01     pagedaemon
    root    3     0  0  Aug 11    ?  0:57     windaemon
```

```
catherin 1237      1   3 18:33:32  w1   0:07 ua
   chare 1259      1  15 19:28:15  000  0:13 ksh
   chare 1298   1259 64 19:44:08  000  0:01 ps
    root   67      1   3  Aug 11   w4   0:01 wmgr
      lp   59      1   3  Aug 11    ?   0:00 lpsched
    root   64      1   3  Aug 11   w3   0:01 .phclr
    root   71      1   3  Aug 11   w5   5:20 smgr
$
```

Because of this, the root user exercises almost total control over the operating system: all security checks that exist for the safety of the system for other users are turned off for the root account. This means that enabling root access to unauthorized users presents a serious security risk.

However, on some versions of UNIX, the root user cannot log in at the login: prompt. On these systems, the user must log in and then perform an su to root. This enables better tracking, because the su command, which is examined shortly, logs each invocation of the command to a file. Even on systems where root can log in directly, it would be better that the user log in as themselves first, and then su to root.

 In BSD-based versions, whether or not root logins are allowed depends on whether the tty being used is configured to be secure in /etc/ttytab. By default, they are, but many system administrators disable this.

The superuser has virtually unrestricted control over the system. Although in recent times as the move to a more secure UNIX has become prevalent, there have been attempts to compartmentalize control and assign it to different users through authorizations. This means that a normal user could have permission to read all of the files and directories on the system, but only when performing a backup. Here are some of the things the superuser can do:

✔ Change the nice value of any process.

✔ Send a signal to any process.

✔ Turn processing accounting on or off.

✔ Become any user on the system.

✔ Access any working device.

✔ Shut down the system.

✔ Set the system date and time.

✔ Read any memory location.

✔ Access network services on trusted ports.

✔ Reconfigure the network.

✔ Read, modify, and delete any file on the system.

✔ Run any program.

✔ Mount and unmount file systems.

✔ Add, remove, and change user accounts.

✔ Enable or disable disk quotas and accounting.

Although this is a very extensive and impressive list, there are things the superuser cannot do. This is as much to protect the system from unscrupulous super-users as anything else. The superuser cannot do the following:

✔ Make a change to a file on a read-only file system. However, in this case, the superuser could unmount the file system and then mount it again read/write.

✔ Directly modify the contents of a directory.

✔ Decrypt the passwords that are stored in /etc/passwd and /etc/group.

✔ Terminate a process that is in a kernel wait state.

There is an inherent problem with the superuser account. That is that the superuser can do anything. Consequently, if unauthorized root access is acquired, the break-in can be disastrous. Most of the security holes that have been discovered result in the attacker becoming root. Typically, as these are discovered, the vendors repair and issue a patch or advisory to the users of these systems. But getting access to root doesn't solve the attacker's problem, because he or she must devise a way to get continued access to the system without being traced and caught. This can be a difficult job on a well-monitored system.

Other Special Users

Many UNIX systems also provide other special users on the system. These users are to provide access to the system or a certain set of files where root access is not a requirement. Some examples are uucp, which allows access to the files and directories that make up the UUCP communications facilities, and lp, which is used to administer the line printer systems on many UNIX implementations. The following are a few other special users:

root	The superuser account
daemon	Owner of system daemons

bin	Owner of the system commands and files
uucp	UUCP access and administration
lp	Line printer administration account

The exact special users that are on your system are specific to the implementation of UNIX.

/etc/passwd and /etc/group: Impact on Security

The impact that /etc/passwd and /etc/group have on the security of the system can be overwhelming if they themselves are not protected. Because /etc/passwd contains all of the information regarding access to the system, it is imperative that it be a closely guarded file. Under no circumstances should it be writeable by anyone. If someone can alter the contents of /etc/passwd and write the changes back, then they can become root. Likewise with the /etc/group file. If it is left in a position where it can also be edited, an attacker could make changes and slowly work toward having access to the /etc/passwd file, thereby getting unrestricted access. Consequently, in both cases it is imperative that these files remain with permissions that are read-only.

Using su

The su command is a powerful utility that enables one user to become another user. This is a useful utility. Users frequently needing access to something are forced to logout on a terminal when they need only use the su command instead. For example, if you want to change to be another user, all you need to know is his or her user name and the password for his or her account. A sample su session is illustrated in the following code.

```
$ id
uid=105(chare) gid=0(root)
$ su catherine
Password:
$ id
uid=106(catherine) gid=100(users)
$
```

Here you see the user chare using the su command to switch to the user catherine. What in fact happens is that su starts a new shell using the ID of the user that was specified. To return to your previous user name, exit the shell through the exit command, or by pressing Ctrl+D.

```
$ id
uid=106(catherine) gid=100(users)
$ exit
$ id
```

```
uid=105(chare) gid=0(root)
$
```

This is an example of using su to become another user. su is most commonly used to become root. To become root using the su command, no arguments are provided. When prompted for a password, the correct root password must be provided. If the password is incorrect, a message indicating that you didn't become root is printed, and your shell prompt returns. It is a good idea to use the full path name to the command su, which is /bin/su, to ensure that the correct command is being executed. Otherwise, it is possible that a false su command could be executed in its place.

```
$ id
uid=105(chare) gid=0(root)
$ /bin/su
Password:
# id
uid=0(root) gid=0(root)
#
```

If you use the su command to become another user now that you are the superuser, you will not be prompted for that user's password. One of the major advantages of teaching people to use the su command to become root is that su keeps a record of each time it is executed. This enables the system administrator to keep track of who is using su, who is allowed to use it, and who is not authorized to use it.

One nice feature of BSD-based versions is that you can restrict who can use su by making only authorized ones members of a group called wheel. Only members of this group are authorized to use su.

The record is stored in the file /usr/adm/sulog and consists of several fields, as shown here.

```
SU 08/14 19:32 + tty?? root-uucpadm
SU 08/14 19:43 + tty000 chare-root
SU 08/14 20:16 + tty000 chare-root
SU 08/14 20:32 + tty?? root-uucpadm
SU 08/14 20:43 + tty000 chare-catherine
SU 08/14 20:43 + tty000 chare-root
SU 08/14 20:43 + tty000 chare-catherine
SU 08/14 21:02 + tty000 chare-root
SU 08/14 21:06 - tty000 chare-root
```

Each time the su command is invoked, it writes a record to the file indicating the date and time of the su, the terminal port the command was run from, the name of the user running the su, and who he or she wanted to become. Finally, there is a + or a -, indicating success or failure.

Looking for failed su requests is easy using the grep command, as shown here:

```
grep " - " /usr/adm/sulog
```

Here you are looking for the pattern " - ", which indicates that the su command failed. Pay particular attention to the space on each side of the hyphen—in its absence, every line in the file will be returned. Running this command on the sample sulog file, you see the following:

```
$ grep " - " /usr/adm/sulog
SU 08/14 21:06 - tty000 chare-root
$
```

This shows that the user chare failed on an su attempt to root, on August 14 at 9:06 p.m. It is important for users to know that use of the su command is logged, and that unauthorized attempts to become another user will be found.

Implementing Security

You have several things to consider when implementing security, including issues about files and file systems, modems, and networks.

Files and File Systems

The biggest issue in the security of the data on your system is how to keep track of what has been changed and what hasn't. This is a major undertaking. However, through the use of shell scripts, or PERL programs, it becomes a task that can be lessened. Listings 27.2, 27.3, and 27.4 at the end of the chapter provide a series of commands that can be used to keep track of just this: what has changed in your file system.

However, the prominent issue is permissions—not only the regular permissions, but the problem areas of the advanced permissions, the SUID, SGID, and sticky bits. The SUID bit makes the user running the program look like the owner. In many cases, this is not a bad thing, but when the SUID program is owned by root, it can become a potential security hole unless the program has been well-written. Unfortunately, few software vendors distribute the source code for their applications. If this were the case, especially for the SUID sections, many system administrators would probably be happier with having a look at how the vendors are causing potential security problems.

It isn't just the vendors that can be causing file access problems. Most of the time it is programs that are incorrectly installed, or the use of SUID/SGID to solve file access problems without using a more thorough approach. These become a Band-Aid solution that makes the problem worse.

You need a way to be able to find all of the SUID or SGID programs on your system. This can be done using the find program using the -perm option. Finding the SUID programs is shown in the following code:

```
find / -perm -004000 -type f -print
/bin/mv
/bin/mkdir
/bin/rmdir
/bin/df
/bin/newgrp
/bin/passwd
/bin/su
/etc/mount
/etc/umount
/etc/dismount
/etc/lddrv/lddrv
/usr/bin/cancel
/usr/bin/lpstat
/usr/bin/lpsetup
/usr/bin/mailsetup
/usr/bin/setgetty
/usr/bin/uucp
```

This is but a sampling of the actual SUID programs on many UNIX systems. Actually, on this test system, there are 50 commands, which is still a small amount when compared to other UNIX implementations.

SGID files enable the users to assume the same group as the one who owns the file, much like the SUID bit affects the user ID. SGID files can also be located with the find command, as shown here:

```
find / -perm -002000 -type f -print
/bin/mail
/bin/ps
/bin/rmail
/usr/lib/lpadmin
/usr/lib/lpmove
/usr/lib/lpqueue
/usr/lib/lpsched
/usr/lib/lpshut
/usr/lib/reject
/usr/lib/ex3.7preserve
/usr/lib/ex3.7recover
```

Again, this is only a representation of the files that have the SGID bit set. Current implementations have a large number of SGID files because of the attempt to compartmentalize the commands associated with the various major groupings of administration tasks.

For purposes of illustration, it was shown how to use the find command to search the system for SUID and SGID files. Instead of running find twice, you can use the following:

```
$ find / \( -perm -002000 -o -perm -004000 \) -type f -print
```

Again, the administrator needs to be involved in the education of the users on how to protect their own files and data from attack through the careful use of the permissions commands that were discussed thoroughly in Chapter 7, "Controlling Permissions to Files."

Modems

These devices, although great time-saving devices, also present a security problem. With modems, you allow authorized users to access the system from remote locations. From their homes, their cars, and their hotel rooms, users can gain access to their data and networks. The security issue with modems is that the unauthorized users now have a publicly available access point to your system.

Having a modem on your system reduces the level of security because they not only allow unauthorized users in, but they allow authorized users the opportunity to get confidential information out. The first step to protecting the modems connected to your systems is to control their phone numbers. Treat them like passwords—don't give them to anyone who doesn't need them.

There are ways of improving the security with modems—for example, using a callback scheme. This involves having the outside caller dial into your computer system, identify who he or she is, and hang up. Your computer system then calls the remote caller at the predetermined number. Using this format, it is difficult for an unauthorized user to gain access to the system unless he or she is at the predetermined number.

Another form of security enhancement for modems is password modems. These prompt the calling user to enter a password before allowing the connection to the system. If the password provided is incorrect, the connection is not passed through to the UNIX system. This type of connection is not immune to repeated attacks on the password, however.

A third format is to use encrypting modems. These work in pairs to encrypt the data as it is transmitted over the telephone line. The advantage to this is that it makes it very difficult for eavesdropping attackers to intercept passwords and data. The disadvantage is that people who do not have these modems cannot connect to your service, even if they are authorized.

Some other caveats for modems follow. It is important to educate users to be sure to log out of the system prior to terminating the connection. Many systems will properly hang up the phone line when the call is terminated, but this is not the case for all systems. Logging out ensures that the next caller is prompted for a login. If the user doesn't properly log out, the next user calling the system might in fact be greeted by a shell prompt. If the last user was logged in as root, this is a major security issue.

Unfortunately, there will always be someone who tries to access your systems through a modem. Through careful monitoring and control of your phone lines, you can limit or prevent unauthorized access through this source.

Networks

Two types of equivalency are associated with TCP/IP environments: user and host. There are inherent advantages and dangers in each of them. However, before you can read about them, you first need to know what user and host equivalency are.

Equivalence is of most benefit in environments where the BSD "r" commands are supported. These commands are rlogin, rcmd(rsh), and rcp. What is important when using these commands is that the security of any network without user equivalence is highly jeopardized.

For example, consider a user whose login name was simply chris. In one of the remote offices where she worked, through some poor network planning, there turned out to be another user with a login name of chris. These two offices were not connected using TCP/IP. However, when the two offices became connected using TCP/IP, suddenly there were problems. The most obvious one was that the two users with the login chris could each access files belonging to the other.

Once this occurred, the administrator of the central site realized that some form of practice was required to prevent this from happening on an ongoing basis. What the administrator did first was to change the login names for the two users from chris to chrism and chriss. This solved the immediate problem, but in reality all it did was hide the problem with a mirror.

The real issue was one of each user not having an account for each machine on the network, each with the same UID. This is a common problem. Many organizations start out with one or two computers, which then expands and finally erupts into a network.

To minimize the work to be done as the network grows, you should consider the following things:

✔ You should be essentially duplicating the /etc/passwd and /etc/group files on all of the machines in your organization. As a result, each user must have a unique login name and UID.

✔ Group permissions cross system boundaries, so remember to establish the same guidelines for groups. The same groups with the same group IDs (GIDs) must exist on all machines.

While maintaining identical copies of /etc/passwd and /etc/group on all machines on a network will minimize some of the problems mentioned in the text, keeping these files synchronized is extremely difficult. The best solution to this is to use NIS. While NIS is beyond the scope of this chapter, what it enables you to do is maintain only one version of /etc/passwd and /etc/ group for the entire network.

By considering these two things, you have started the journey into Trusted Access. Trusted Access can be configured by the system administrator, meaning that all of the users on the specified system have access to the local system without providing a password. This is called Trusted Host Access, or host equivalency, and is controlled through the file /etc/hosts.equiv.

The second form is controlled by the user, and it enables that user, as well as any others specified, access to that account without providing a password. This is called Trusted User Access, or user equivalency, and is controlled through the user of the file $HOME/ .rhosts.

Configuring Host Equivalency

Host Equivalency, or Trusted Host Access, is configured by the system administrator using the file /etc/hosts.equiv, as illustrated in the following code. This file consists of host names, one per line. It is also a good idea to document in the file who the network administrator is.

```
$ cat /etc/hosts.equiv
oreo
wabbit
ns
ftp
mail
kiwi
ovide
```

Each entry in the hosts.equiv file is trusted. This means that users on the named machine can access their equivalent accounts on this machine without a password. This is not applicable for root, as will be explained later.

As a hypothetical example, consider two machines, oreo and wabbit, which both have a user named chrism. If the user chrism is currently logged into wabbit and issues the following command with Host Equivalency established, chrism will be logged in to oreo, without being asked for her password.

```
rlogin oreo
```

If host equivalency is not there, she will be asked for her password on the remote machine.

There are two things to bear in mind with /etc/hosts.equiv:

✔ It assumes that you trust ALL the users on the remote machine.

✔ Root is NEVER trusted through the use of this file.

There is a second format for the hosts.equiv file, as shown here:

```
$ cat $HOME/.rhosts
oreo chare
wabbit chare
ovide andrewg
$
```

This format lists a system name and a user name. With the addition of the user name, the user is allowed to log in to the named host with any user name that is found in /etc/passwd. For example, consider the following entry found on a machine named ovide:

```
wabbit chare
```

This states that the user with the login name of chare logs into another machine from wabbit. He can use any valid account name from /etc/passwd on the remote machine to log in.

```
rlogin ovide -l andrewg
```

This means that chare on wabbit is being equivalenced to the user andrewg on ovide. This is user equivalency. It is typically configured using methods described later. To use the commands rcmd(rsh) and rcp, host equivalency must be set up and operational.

User Equivalence

User equivalence is a mechanism by which the same user is known to all of the machines in the network. This makes the network administrator's job easier in the long run. It should be considered absolutely necessary for environments in which NFS is being used or is planned to be used.

To configure user equivalence, the user creates a file in her home directory called .rhosts. This file must be writeable only by the owner of the file. If it is not, the file is ignored for validation purposes. As with the hosts.equiv file, this file contains a system name per line, but it generally also includes the name of the user who is being equivalenced.

In the network where chrism works, there are a couple of people responsible for the maintenance and operation of the Usenet news system. To allow those people access to the news server, they have an .rhosts file established in the news home directory, /usr/lib/news.

This .rhosts file looks like the following:

```
wabbit  billho
ovide   andrewg
```

When either of these people log in as news on the news server, they can do so without providing a password, because they are "equivalent" to the user news on that machine.

There is potential for some significant problems in networks where there is host equivalency but not user equivalency. Assume there are two users, Chris McFadden and Chris Skiffle, working on two different machines, but both of them have the same login ID. One day, Chris Skiffle does an rlogin from wabbit to oreo; he can log in without a password. As a result, Chris Skiffle can access all of Chris McFadden's files. In this example, the problem is that there is host equivalence but not user equivalence.

Security Issues with Equivalence

Think of the potential for security breaches in organizations that make extensive use of root equivalency. If the root password on a single machine is found out, access as root to all the machines in the network is possible.

There is a high volume of information shared between the offices of chrism's company. Because they are using only a 19.2-kilobaud PPP link between the offices, it is not highly practical for NFS usage because of the speed and bandwidth limitations.

Consequently, some of the information is sent by way of rdist. In this case, a special user was created on those machines who could write files into the appropriate directories. In this manner, the problem of root equivalence can be prevented, thereby avoiding a significant and dangerous security problem. In addition, simply having host equivalency and no user equivalency can be equally as dangerous, because a host from outside your network might have the same name and therefore be able to access your system almost unrestricted.

Inactive Users

Inactive users are another security hole on a system. Because of their inactivity , it is unlikely that any unauthorized use of their account would go unnoticed. Dormant or inactive accounts should have their passwords set to an unmatchable value. The reason for this is to prevent unauthorized access through these accounts. Many current implementations have a mechanism that enables the administrator to set the password to be unmatchable, or to lock the user's account. On systems that do not have this capability, the administrator can edit the /etc/passwd file and change the encrypted password to a clear text string, and it can never be matched.

```
catherine:ab09/Dbs1ks:106:100:Catherine Agent:/u/catherin:
```

This is a sample inactive account. For this user account to be deactivated, the system administrator can change this password field to an unmatchable value, such as in the following code:

```
catherine:NOLOGIN:106:100:Catherine Agent:/u/catherin:
```

Any user who tries to access the disabled account receives only a `Login incorrect` message. This is to ensure that the attacker doesn't get too obvious a clue.

A second possibility with user accounts is to lock the account. This is typically done through the sysadmsh, or System Administration Shell. To lock a user account, the system administrator chooses the following options, at which point the administrator applies an administrative lock.

Accounts -> Users -> Examine -> Locks

When the user then tries to log in to the system, she gets a message that the account has been disabled. There is no way for the account to be reactivated without the intervention of the system administrator.

Using these two methods, access through inactive or dormant accounts can be effectively locked up and eliminated as a security threat.

What To Do Next

Now that you have taken a wide variety of steps in an attempt to understand what security is and how to protect your users, your data, and your systems from unauthorized attack, how would you know if someone has broken into your systems?

Discovering an Intruder

When you think that there is an intruder on your system, you already have the major tools at hand—tools like ps, who, and process accounting. Use of these tools to see who is on the machine and what they are doing may prove that the user is an authorized person.

There are very distinct rules to follow when you are suspicious of a break-in, and there are several things you want to do:

✔ Identify the person breaking into the system

✔ Determine how he or she got in

✔ Prevent him or her from causing any damage

With this in mind, now examine some possibilities. If you log in to your system and find something unusual, like a user working outside his or her normal work times, you can try using the write or talk command to determine if it really is the user. Of course, this doesn't provide absolute proof, because you can't see them or talk to him or her. Logging the user out by killing his or her login shell may help prevent the attacker from doing any damage, but it doesn't help you find out how he or she got in or who he or she is.

If the user is working on a directly attached terminal, it should be easy to find out where the user is in the building, using a terminal map and the who command. Then it is simply a matter of going to that terminal and finding out who the person is. Often, however, your attackers are not on the premises. They are in another part of the country, coming through a phone line or the Internet.

If the user is on the Internet, you should be able to find out who he or she is. Many versions of the who command print the name of the remote host if the connection is through TCP/IP from a remote host. Be warned, however, that System V UNIX systems generally do not do this. If you have the host name of the remote site, you should be able to enlist the help of the system administrator there in tracking down who made the connection to your host.

Often, however, you don't find out about the break-in until well after it has happened. At this point, all you can do is disaster recovery. Try to find out what files were damaged or compromised, and how the attacker got in, and work to restore or correct the problems. The programs in Listings 27.2, 27.3, and 27.4, were intended to help address these issues. These three programs were originally published in *UNIX World* magazine in September 1990 and April 1991. Authored by Rebecca Thomas of *UNIX World* and Chris Hare, they are used to build a database of files you want to monitor, and they keep track of changes and modifications to those files.

If you think data has been stolen, you can take legal action, but the road is a long and difficult one. You must convince the authorities that a crime may be taking place, and you have to deal with the local and federal laws for the location where you are. For example, the laws on computer crime in the United States are very different from the laws on computer crime in Canada.

Keep very strict control on the evidence that you collect, and ensure that you have signed and dated hard copies of everything. Any magnetic media should be copied and both copies stored for safe keeping. Remember that any action you take will require the use of this evidence in court. Failure to keep track of it properly can result in the case being lost and the attacker going free.

With the widespread wrath of the Internet Worm, the Computer Emergency Response Team (CERT) was established to serve as a collection and distribution point for security-related problems and bulletins regarding the Internet. If you are on the Internet and have experienced a break-in, or suspect that you have, you can contact them for assistance.

Aside from that, the best thing you can do is help your administrator by providing him or her with the support and encouragement to take a stance against lax security. Help train the users to be more aware of security and their part in it.

Summary

In conclusion, the issue of security has become a widespread topic. As the Internet grows, and more and more systems and users are added to it, the likelihood of an increased number of security-related incidents is greater than it was even ten years ago. This means that not only do system administrators need to be more aware of the level of security that is being offered on their systems, but the programmers who write the programs must be convinced that good programming practices will enhance the users' security and further aid in the prevention of data loss or unauthorized access to that data.

As users, you need to push your software vendors to provide more enhanced security tools for the increased protection of the information that we all depend upon to run our businesses, educate students, and run our countries.

Security Tools

Here are some security tools that can help in the monitoring of your security system. The program in Listing 27.1, pwexp.pl, written by Chris Hare, first appeared in the premiere issue of *Sys Admin* magazine, published by R&D Publications as part of the article entitled "How UNIX Password Controls Work." Listing 27.2, mkfilelist, and Listing 27.3, chkfiles, were written by Rebecca Thomas and first appeared in *UNIX World* in September 1990 in the column "Wizard's Grabbag." Listing 27.4, fixfiles, was written by Chris Hare and first appeared in *UNIX World* magazine in April 1991. Your final tool, gpasswd, shown in Listing 27.5, was written by Brian Cartnell and first appeared in the "Wizard's Grabbag" column in *UNIX World* Magazine in February 1991.

The pwexp.pl listing

This is a PERL program that is used to report the status of password aging on your account. To run it, you have the PERL language compiled on your system. Because of the way the aging information is incorporated into the password, this cannot be done in a shell script program.

Running pwexp.pl when you cannot ever change your password will print the following information:

```
$ pwexp.pl
You cannot change your password. Ever.
$
```

Running pwexp.pl when password aging is not turned on will tell you this:

```
$ pwexp.pl
Your password expires in 9 weeks.
Please start thinking of a new one.
$
```

When your password has expired and you must change it, pwexp.pl will print the following:

```
$ pwexp.pl
Your password has expired.
$
```

Here is the PERL code listing for pwexp.pl.

Listing 27.1. pwexp.pl.

```perl
#! perl
eval '(exit $?0)' && eval 'exec perl -S $0 ${1+"$@"}'
& eval 'exec perl -S $0 $argv:q'
if 0;
#
# pwexp.pl - PERL program to check for password expiration times
#
#
#
# get the passwd file entry for this account.  $< is the numerical
# representation of our REAL UID
#
( $username, $passwd, $uid, $gid, $pwage,
  $comment, $gcos, $dir, $shell ) = getpwuid($<);
#
# If passwd aging value is defined
#
if ( $pwage ne "" )
    {
    #
    # extract the maxweeks value
    #
```

```
$maxweeks = &a64l( substr( $pwage, 0, 1 ) );
#
# extract the minweeks value
#
$minweeks = &a64l( substr( $pwage, 1, 1 ) );
#
# extract the last changed value
#
$lastchange = &a64l( substr( $pwage, 2 ) );
#
# what is NOW?
#
$now = time / 604800;
#
# If maxweeks < minweeks, the user can't change his passwd
#
if ( $maxweeks < $minweeks )
        {
        printf "You cannot change your password.  Ever. \n";
        }
#
# The special case where the password must be changed
#
elsif ( ( $minweeks == 0 ) && ( $maxweeks == 0 ) )
        {
        printf "You must change your password.  Now.\n";
        }
#
# if lastchanged is > now, then expired
# if now > lastchanged + maxweeks, then expired
#
elsif ( $lastchange > $now  ||
                ( $now > $lastchange + $maxweeks ) &&
                ( $maxweeks > $minweeks ) )
        {
        printf "Your password has expired.\n";
        }
#
# tell the user when his password expires
#
else
        {
        printf "Your password expires in %d weeks.\n",
```

```
                        $lastchange + $maxweeks - $now;
                printf "Please start thinking of a new one.\n";
                }
        }
    else
        {
        printf "Password aging is not enabled.\n";
        }
    exit(0);
    #
    # the a64l routine was written by Randall Schwartz after a call for
    help
    # in the comp.lng.perl newsgroup.   Thanks Randall!
    #
    sub a64l {
            local($_) = @_; # arg into $_
            die "a64l: illegal value: $_" unless m#^[./0-9A-Za-z]{0,6}$#;
            unless (defined %a64map) {
                    @a64map{'.','/',0..9,'A'..'Z','a'..'z'} = 0..63;
            }
            local($result) = 0;
            for (reverse split(//)) {
                    $result *= 64;
                    $result += $a64map{$_};
            }
            $result;
    }
```

The mkfilelist listing

This program, written by Rebecca Thomas of *UNIX World* magazine, creates a database of files from a sample list. A sample list is shown in Part A.

Listing 27.2.   Part A.

```
/etc
/etc/.nflops
/etc/convert
/etc/convert/SPECIAL
/etc/convert/RENAMED
/etc/convert/formconvert
/etc/convert/convert
/etc/convert/convbydiff
/etc/convert/crontabconv
```

```
/etc/convert/expanddesc
/etc/convert/getdevid
/etc/convert/getdevices
/etc/convert/getmissing
```

To run the program, it must be run as root. A directory called /Secure must be created in the root directory for the filelist database created by mkfilelist. Part B shows a sample run of mkfilelist.

Listing 27.2. Part B.

```
# ./mkfilelist list
Creating the file database...
............................................................
.........................................
...Database complete.
#
```

Part C contains part of the database that was created using mkfilelist.

Listing 27.2. Part C.

```
drwxr-xr-x    root    sys    /etc
-rw-r--r--    root    root   /etc/.nflops
drwxr-xr-x    bin     bin.   /etc/convert
-rwxrwxrwx    root    root   /etc/convert/SPECIAL
-rw-r--r--    bin     bin    /etc/convert/RENAMED
-rwxr-xr-x    bin     bin    /etc/convert/formconvert
-rwxr-xr-x    bin     bin    /etc/convert/convert
-rwxr-xr-x    bin     bin    /etc/convert/convbydiff
-rwxr-xr-x    bin     bin    /etc/convert/crontabconv
-rwxr-xr-x    bin     bin    /etc/convert/expanddesc
-rwxr-xr-x    bin     bin    /etc/convert/getdevid
-rwxr-xr-x    bin     bin    /etc/convert/getdevices
-rwxr-xr-x    bin     bin    /etc/convert/getmissing
```

Here is the actual code to create the filelist.

Listing 27.2. mkfilelist.

```
# Files can be audited for changed owner, group
# owner, or permission modes.  We present two scripts for
# doing so—one creates a database and the other should be run
# periodically to note discrepancies between this database and
# the files on the system disk.
:
```

```
# @(#) mkfilelist  Create system files database
# Author: Rebecca Thomas
# Inspiration: Patrick Wood, Pipeline Associates
# set -x    # Uncomment for debugging
USAGE="Usage: mkfilelist [filelist]"
FILELIST=/Secure/filelist   # Best if on external file system
trap 'echo "$0 interrupted"; exit' 1 2 3 15
#
echo "Creating the file database..."
#
addentry()
{
    PATHNAME=$1
    LISTING='ls -ld $PATHNAME 2>/dev/null'
    if [ -z "$LISTING" ]; then
        ENTRY="# $PATHNAME does not exist"
    else
        set — $LISTING
        MODE=$1
        OWNER=$3
        GROUP=$4
        ENTRY="$MODE\t$OWNER\t$GROUP\t$PATHNAME"
    fi
    echo ".\c"  # Show user we're working
    echo $ENTRY >>$FILELIST
}
#
case $# in
    0)  while read FILENAME ; do
            addentry $FILENAME
        done ;;
    1)  cat $1 ¦ while read FILENAME ; do
            addentry $FILENAME
        done ;;
    *)  echo $USAGE >&2
        exit 1 ;;
esac
echo "\n...Database complete."
```

chkfiles

This is the second part of this three-part command set. The chkfiles program was also written by Rebecca Thomas of *UNIX World*. Its purpose is to read the database created by mkfilelist in Listing 27.2 and validate the current status of those files against the database.

Differences are reported at the command line.

A sample run of chkfiles is shown in Part A of this listing, followed by the code in Part B.

Listing 27.3. Part A.

```
# ./chkfiles
Checking system files ...
...............................................
"/etc/TZ" has users group, should be sys
...............................................................................
#
```

Listing 27.3. Part B.

```
:
# @(#) chkfiles   Check modes, owner, and group owner of files
# Author: Rebecca Thomas, May 1990
# Inspiration: Patrick Wood, Pipeline Associates
# For security, define IFS and PATH and mark for export:
# set -x    # Uncomment for debugging
PATH=/bin:/usr/bin; export PATH
# Define constants:
MAILTMP=/tmp/'basename $0'$$    # Mail message file
FILELIST=/Secure/filelist   # Default file list database
MAILTO=beccat                   # Account name of auditor
TERMINAL=/dev/null          # Initialize for non-interactive use
USAGE="Usage: $0 [filelist]"
# Catch signals, clean up, then exit:
trap 'echo "$0 interrupted"; rm -f $MAILTMP;exit' 1 2 3 15
# If running interactively display messages on terminal:
[ -t 1 ] && TERMINAL=/dev/tty   # if stdout is a terminal
# Define routine to display error message and exit:
abort() {
    if [ "$TERMINAL" = "/dev/tty" ]; then   # Interactive
        echo $1 >$TERMINAL  # write to terminal
    else    # non-interactive so use mail
        echo $1 ¦ mailx -s "System files security audit" $MAILTO
    fi
    exit 1
}
# Process command line arguments, if any:
case $# in
    0)  ;;                  # Use default file list
```

```
    1)  FILELIST=$1 ;;      # Use specified file list
    *)  abort "$USAGE" ;;   # No more than one argument
                            ➡ esac
# Be sure file list database is accessible:
[ -r "$FILELIST" ] ¦¦ # Can't read file list database
    abort "$0: Aborting, because can't access $FILELIST"
# Define function to send and (perhaps) display message:
sendmsg() { echo $1 ¦ /bin/tee -a $MAILTMP >$TERMINAL; }
# Announce our intentions to interactive user:
echo "Checking system files ..." >$TERMINAL
# Loop through all entries in reference file database:
while read LINE ; do
    [ -z "$LINE" ] && continue  # Skip blank lines
    expr "$LINE" : '#' >/dev/null && continue # Skip comments
    echo ".\c" >$TERMINAL   # Show user we're working
    set — $LINE     # Parse reference file entry
    [ $# -lt 4 -o $# -gt 5 ] && {
        sendmsg "Corrupted line: \"$LINE\" in $FILELIST"
        continue ; }
    REFMODE=$1 REFOWN=$2 REFGRP=$3 PATHNAME=$4 EXIST=$5
    # Get current modes:
    LISTING='/bin/ls -ld $PATHNAME 2>/dev/null'
    if [ -z "$LISTING" ]; then
        if [ "$EXIST" != "X" ]; then
            sendmsg "\n\"$PATHNAME\" in database, but not on disk"
        fi
        continue
    fi
    set -- $LISTING
    MODE=$1 OWNER=$3 GROUP=$4
    # If not don't care, check to see if there are discrepancies:
    [ "$REFOWN" != "X" -a "$OWNER" != "$REFOWN" ] &&
        sendmsg "\n\"$PATHNAME\" has $OWNER owner, should be $REFOWN"
    [ "$REFGRP" != "X" -a "$GROUP" != "$REFGRP" ] &&
        sendmsg "\n\"$PATHNAME\" has $GROUP group, should be $REFGRP"
     [ "$MODE" != "$REFMODE" ] &&
        sendmsg "\n\"$PATHNAME\" has $MODE mode, should be $REFMODE"
    done < $FILELIST
#
# Send mail, if necessary:
if [ ! -s $MAILTMP ]; then  # no problem report file
    echo "\nModes, owners, and group owners okay." ¦
    tee $MAILTMP >$TERMINAL
fi
```

```
mailx -s "System files security audit" $MAILTO < $MAILTMP
rm -f $MAILTMP
```

fixfiles

The final command in this set is called fixfiles. It is similar to chkfiles, except that it will correct the problems reported by chkfiles. This program was written by Chris Hare and was originally published in the April 1991 issue of *UNIX World* magazine.

Part A shows a sample run of fixfiles, and Part B contains the source code for the command.

Listing 27.4.   Part A.

```
# fixfiles
Enter file name or control-D to quit: /etc/TZ
Correcting /etc/TZ ...
Enter file name or control-D to quit: #
#
# fixfiles -a
Correcting /etc ...
Correcting /etc/.nflops ...
Correcting /etc/convert ...
Correcting /etc/convert/SPECIAL ...
Correcting /etc/convert/RENAMED ...
Correcting /etc/convert/formconvert ...
Correcting /etc/convert/convert ...
(and so on until the database is completed)
```

Listing 27.4.   Part B.

```
:
# @(#) fixfiles v1.1 - correct discrepancies found by chkfiles
# Author: Chris Hare, Dec. 1990
# Based on chkfiles by Rebecca Thomas, Sep. 1990
# Define constants:
FILELIST=/Secure/filelist   # Secure filelist database
MAILTMP=/tmp/'basename $0'$$    # Mail message file
MAILTO=root                 # Account name of auditor
TERMINAL=/dev/null          # Initialize for non-interactive use
QUIET=No                    # Do we show prompts?
AFLAG="" LFLAG=""           # Initialize option flags
USAGE="Usage: $0 [-q][-f filelist] [-a¦-l listfile ¦ filename...]"
# Trap signals to remove temp file then exit
trap "echo $0 aborted!; rm $MAILTMP 2>/dev/null; exit 0" 1 2 3 15
```

```
# If running interactively display messages on terminal:
[ -t 1 ] && TERMINAL=/dev/tty   # if stdout is a terminal
# Define function to send and (perhaps) display message:
sendmsg() { echo $1 ¦ /bin/tee -a $MAILTMP >$TERMINAL; }
# Function to provide octal equivalent of permission string:
fixperm() {
    echo $1 ¦ awk '{
        count = 0            # loop counter
        LENGTH = 9           # Number of loop iterations
        modestr = substr($1, 2, 9)  # ignore the file type
        while (count++ < LENGTH) {
            symbol = substr(modestr, count, 1)
            if (count >= 1 && count <= 3) { # owner
                s_value = 41;    multiplier = 100
            }
            if (count >= 4 && count <= 6) { # group
                l_value = 200; s_value = 201; multiplier = 10
            }
            if (count >= 7 && count <= 9) { # other
                t_value = 1001; multiplier = 1
            }
            if (symbol == "r") perm_value = 4
            if (symbol == "w") perm_value = 2
            if (symbol == "x") perm_value = 1
            if (symbol == "s") perm_value = s_value
            if (symbol == "t") perm_value = t_value
            if (symbol == "l") perm_value = l_value
            if (symbol == "-") perm_value = 0
            mode_value += (perm_value * multiplier)
        }
        printf "%s\n", mode_value
    }' # end of awk script
} # end of function definition
# Function that (possibly) prompts user:
prompt () { [ "$QUIET" = "No" ] && echo "$1: \c" >$TERMINAL; }
# Function that fixes a specified file
fixfile () {
    FILEPATH=$1 # store for posterity
    [ -z "$FILEPATH" ] && return   # No name, leave function
    set — $FILEPATH     # Place function arg in posn. params.
    if [ $# -eq 1 ]; then   # Reading file path name
        # Specified full path name?:
        if [ 'expr "$FILEPATH" : "^/"' -ne 1 ]; then
```

```
                    sendmsg "$FILEPATH must be full path name"; return
            fi
            ENTRY='egrep "$FILEPATH\$¦$FILEPATH   X\$" $FILELIST'
            if [ -z "$ENTRY" ] ; then
                sendmsg "No database entry for $FILEPATH"; return
            fi
            # Place located database entry in positional parameters:
            set — $ENTRY
        fi
        if [ $# -lt 4 -o $# -gt 5 ] ; then  # invalid field count
            sendmsg "\"$ENTRY\" corrupted in $FILELIST"; return
        fi
        REFMODE=$1 REFOWN=$2 REFGRP=$3 NAME=$4 EXIST=$5
        if [ -f $NAME -o -d $NAME -o -b $NAME -o -c $NAME -o -p $NAME ]
        then
            sendmsg "Correcting $NAME ..."
            chown $REFOWN $NAME 2>&1 ¦ tee -a $MAILTMP > $TERMINAL
            chgrp $REFGRP $NAME 2>&1 ¦ tee -a $MAILTMP > $TERMINAL
            PERMS='fixperm $REFMODE'
            chmod $PERMS $NAME 2>&1  ¦ tee -a $MAILTMP > $TERMINAL
        else
            sendmsg "\"$NAME\" doesn't exist."
        fi
}
# Process command line arguments, if any:
if [ "$OPTIND" = 1 ]; then  # Can use getopts
    while getopts qf:al: flag ; do
        case $flag in
            q)  QUIET=Yes; TERMINAL=/dev/null ;;
            f)  FILELIST=$OPTARG ;;
            a)  AFLAG=Yes; QUIET=Yes; exec < $FILELIST ;;
            l)  LFLAG=Yes; QUIET=Yes; exec < $OPTARG ;;
            \?) echo $USAGE >&2; exit 1 ;;
        esac
    done
    shift 'expr $OPTIND - 1'    # shift options away
else    # getopts not available, so parse manually:
    while [ $# -gt 0 ]; do # while args to process
        case $1 in
            -q) QUIET=Yes; TERMINAL=/dev/null; shift ;;
            -f) if [ -z "$2" ]; then
                    echo "-f option requires an argument" >&2
                    echo $USAGE >&2 ; exit 1
```

```
                    else
                        FILELIST="$2"; shift; shift
                    fi ;;
                -f*)FILELIST='echo $1 ¦ sed 's/^..//''; shift ;;
                -a) AFLAG=Yes; QUIET=Yes; exec < $FILELIST; shift ;;
                -l) if [ -z "$2" ]; then
                        echo "-l option requires an argument" >&2
                        echo $USAGE >&2 ; exit 1
                    else
                        LFLAG=Yes;QUIET=Yes;exec < "$2";shift;shift
                    fi ;;
                -l*)LFLAG=Yes; QUIET=Yes;
                    exec < "`echo $1 ¦ sed 's/^..//'`"; shift ;;
                —) shift; break ;;
                -*) echo "Unrecognized option: $1" >&2
                    echo $USAGE >&2 ; exit 1 ;;
                *)  break ;;
        esac
    done
fi
if [ "$AFLAG" -a "$LFLAG" ]; then
    echo "Can't use both -a and -l options." >&2
    echo $USAGE >&2 ; exit 2
fi
if [ "$AFLAG" -a $# -gt 0 -o "$LFLAG" -a $# -gt 0 ]; then
    echo "Can't use file arguments with -a or -l option" >&2
    echo $USAGE >&2 ; exit 2
fi
# Must abort if there's no database:
if [ ! -f $FILELIST ]; then
    sendmsg "Cannot access file list database" ; exit 3
fi
# Process named files:
case $# in
    0)  prompt "Enter file name or control-D to quit"
        while read FILENAME ; do
            fixfile "$FILENAME"
        prompt "Enter file name or control-D to quit"
        done ;;
    *)  for FILENAME in $* ; do
            fixfile "$FILENAME"
        done ;;
esac
```

```
# (Possibly) make no report if no changes made:
[ ! -s $MAILTMP ] && sendmsg "\nNo changes made."
# Send mail if no terminal notification:
[ "$TERMINAL" = "/dev/null" ] &&
    mailx -s "Fix owner/group/permissions" $MAILTO < $MAILTMP
rm -f $MAILTMP 2>/dev/null
```

The gpasswd file

Listing 27.5.   gpasswd.

```
/*
Even though both the group file (**/etc/group**)
and System V **newgrp** command use group passwords, there's
no standard UNIX utility for installing or changing them.
Here's a program that mimics the **passwd** command user
interface for installing a password for a specified group.
Published in UNIX World Magazine, February 1991
Author : Brian Cartnell
*/
#include <stdio.h>
#include <sys/types.h>
#include <grp.h>
#define GF_PATH     "/etc/group" /* group file */
#define TGF_PATH    "/etc/tmpgroup" /* temporary "group" file */
char *sccsID =
    "gpasswd Install/change group password; Brian Cartmell, 5/90";
char keyspace[] =   /* character set for salt */
  "./0123456789ABCDEFGHIJKLMNOPQRSTUVWXYZabcdefghijklmnopqrstuvwxyz";
char     grppw[9];   /* file scope group password storage */
main(argc, argv)
int argc; char *argv[];
{
    char            membrs[250], mems[250], cgrppw[14], salt[2];
    uid_t           getuid();
    char            **mp;   /* ptr to group member name */
    time_t          time(), now;
    struct group    *grp, *getgrent(), *getgrnam();
    FILE            *tfp;       /* temporary file pointer */
    if (getuid() != 0) {
        fprintf(stderr, "Only the superuser can run %s.\n", argv[0]);
        exit(1);
    }
    if (argc != 2) {
```

```
        fprintf(stderr, "Usage: %s groupname\n", argv[0]); exit(2);
    }
    if ((grp = getgrnam(argv[1])) == NULL) {
        fprintf(stderr,
            "Group %s not found in %s file.\n", argv[1], GF_PATH);
        exit(3);
    }
    printf("Changing password for group %s.\n", grp->gr_name);
    /* call getpass() until user enters two matching passwords: */
    while (getgpass() != 0) /* don't match */
        fprintf(stderr, "They don't match; try again.\n");
    /* Construct "random" salt: */
    (void)time(&now);    /* store time since epoch in now */
    salt[0] = keyspace[now & 077];   /* first char of salt */
    salt[1] = keyspace[(now >> 6) & 077]; /* second char of salt */
    salt[2] = '\0'; /* terminate string */
    /* create encrypted password: */
    sprintf(cgrppw, "%s", crypt(grppw, salt));
    /* attempt to open temporary group file */
    if ((tfp = fopen(TGF_PATH, "a")) == NULL) {
        fprintf(stderr, "Can't open %s for appending.\n", TGF_PATH);
        exit(4);
    }
    /* Process group file entries one at a time: */
    while ((grp = getgrent()) != NULL) {
        for (mp = grp->gr_mem; *mp; ++mp) { /* scan member names */
            if (*(mp+1)) /* there's another member name */
                sprintf(mems, "%s,", *mp); /* copy, add comma */
            else     /* last member name */
                sprintf(mems, "%s", *mp); /* copy, no comma */
            strcat(membrs, mems);   /* build member list */
        } /* end for (mp = ... */
        if (strcmp(grp->gr_name, argv[1]) == 0) /* a match */
            fprintf(tfp, "%s:%s:%d:%s\n", /* copy w/ new password */
                grp->gr_name, cgrppw, grp->gr_gid, membrs);
        else    /* copy over all other entries verbatim */
            fprintf(tfp, "%s:%s:%d:%s\n",
                grp->gr_name, grp->gr_passwd, grp->gr_gid, membrs);
        strcpy(membrs, ""); /* reset for next time */
    } /* end while ((grp = ... */
    endpwent(); fclose(tfp);    /* done with files */
    if (unlink(GF_PATH) != 0) { /* Can't delete group file */
        fprintf(stderr, "Can't unlink %s.\n", GF_PATH); exit(5);
```

```
        }
        if (link(TGF_PATH, GF_PATH) != 0) { /* Can't link to temp file */
            fprintf(stderr, "Can't link %s to %s.\n",
                TGF_PATH, GF_PATH); exit(6);
        }
        chmod(GF_PATH, 0444);    /* make group file r--r--r-- */
        if (unlink(TGF_PATH) != 0) { /* Can't remove temp file */
            fprintf(stderr, "Can't unlink %s.\n", TGF_PATH); exit(7);
        }
        printf("Password change complete.\n");
}
getgpass()  /* get password from user: */
{
    char    *getpass(); /* returns entered password string */
    char    pass1[9], pass2[9]; /* storage for passwords */
    strcpy(pass1, getpass("Group Password: "));
    strcpy(pass2, getpass("Re-enter Group Password: "));
    strcpy(grppw, pass2);   /* copy to file scope storage */
    return(strcmp(pass1, pass2));   /* 0 success */
}
```

Part VII

UNIX Variants and Flavors

Chapter Snapshot

The UNIX operating system has been available on the Intel X86 platform for quite some time. In fact, before releasing DOS, Microsoft ported it there as Xenix. This chapter looks at some of the more popular X86 UNIX and UNIX-like operating systems, and compares the features of each. The topics and operating systems covered in this chapter include the following:

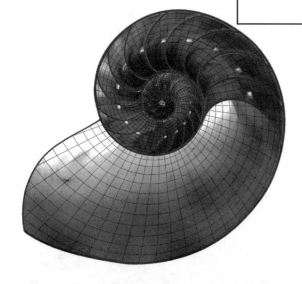

CHAPTER

UNIX Variants on X86 Platforms

UNIX differs from a lot of operating systems in that a lot of flavors of UNIX exist, but they are not all compatible. In the world of DOS, Microsoft has the majority of the marketplace. IBM and Novell each have their own version, however. The versions offered by these other companies are compatible with Microsoft's version, and when you buy WordPerfect 6.*x*, you expect it to work on your desktop PC regardless of which of the three DOSs you are using.

In the UNIX world, however, SCO is not compatible with Linux, and vice versa. UNIX WordPerfect often needs to be purchased for the vendor's UNIX you are running. This chapter attempts to explain some of the differences in the UNIX vendors' products, as well as show what they have in common.

The UNIX Family Tree

Before you learn about the individual products, you should understand how there came to be so many different versions of UNIX. When UNIX was first created within the hallowed halls of Bell Labs, it was referred to as Version 1. As changes and enhancements were made to the operating system, the version number incremented, and UNIX remained within Bell Labs through Version 6.

Version 6 was released to the public—government and schools, primarily—and quickly broke into several different products as enhancements were made by separate entities. Microsoft adapted Version 6 to run on the PC (before the days of DOS) and called it Xenix. The University of California at Berkeley did their modifications and called it BSD. Bell Labs, in the meantime, continued to make enhancements and went to a new numbering system, calling it 2.0. While others made modifications, these were the three main branches that developed. Figure 28.1 illustrates this lineage.

Within Bell Labs

Bell Labs, which became AT&T after the government break-up, continued to work on and refine UNIX. 2.0 became System III, which in turn became System V. (There was no released System IV, though it was rumored to have existed as an internal product.)

System V turned into System V Release 2 (abbreviated SVR2), and then into SVR3, SVR4, and finally SVR4.2. The most current version of the AT&T lineage is SVR4.2. AT&T's UNIX division became Univel, which was sold to Novell, Inc. in 1993.

Xenix's Travels

After porting UNIX to the Intel platform and calling it Xenix, Microsoft focused on a much cruder operating system—DOS. Microsoft continued to offer Xenix for a short while, but never attempted to market it with the same enthusiasm as it did DOS. A start-up company called Santa Cruz Operation, Inc. purchased the right to Xenix from Microsoft, and it became SCO Xenix.

Although remaining a product, SCO Xenix became the basis of a much better operating system—SCO UNIX. An interesting twist of events came several years later, when SCO decided to incorporate the best of AT&T's SVR3 and make SCO UNIX compatible with it. Mixing the best features of SCO UNIX with SVR3 is what gave birth to AT&T's SVR3.2 (see fig. 28.2).

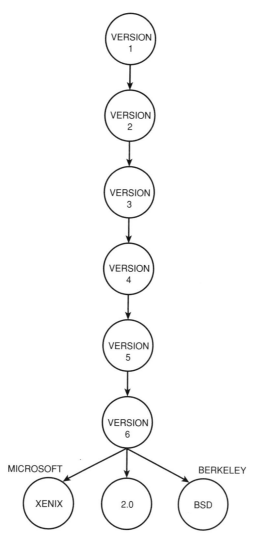

Figure 28.1
When UNIX left
Bell Labs, it broke
into three key
components.

To this day, SCO UNIX is still based upon SVR3.2. Enhancements have continued to be made in the way of utilities and such (to indicate these, SCO uses additional numbering beyond the specified numbers). The current release, for example, is 3.2.4D and is generally referred to as Version 4.

Meanwhile at Berkeley

The University of California at Berkeley continued to add enhancements to the operating system it had modified and used a number preceding the BSD to indicate this. The original BSD UNIX became 2BSD, then 3BSD, and 4BSD. Further modifications were made to 4BSD so that it went to 4.2 and then 4.3BSD.

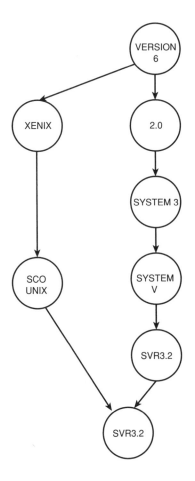

Figure 28.2

Merging the best features of SCO UNIX with AT&T's SVR3 created SVR3.2.

The best of 4.3BSD was also combined independently with AT&T's SVR3, and it became the basis of AIX, as shown in figure 28.3.

After many years of software development, the University of California at Berkeley decided that it was in the business of education, and was not a software company. It therefore announced that no further development of BSD would be done. By this time, BSD had split into two factions—Mach (the basis of NeXT) and V1. The best features of V1 were incorporated with the best features from SVR3.2, and it became SVR4, as shown in figure 28.4.

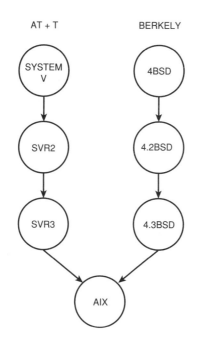

Figure 28.3
Combining
4.3BSD with SVR3
created the AIX
operating system.

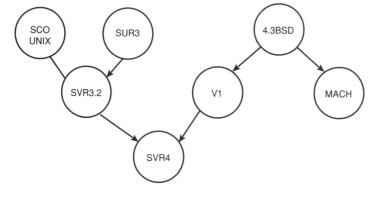

Figure 28.4
Combining
SVR3.2 with V1
created SVR4.

 Berkeley's departure from the software development scene caused a mass exodus of vendors from BSD to System V. Few vendors want to be part of a product that is no longer being refined and enhanced.

For those willing to stick with the tried and true, who are not bothered by the lack of future enhancements, a product currently on the scene is FreeBSD—a UNIX work-alike. Although not 100% compatible with UNIX, FreeBSD incorporates all the features one would expect to find and is available at minimal download cost from many bulletin board systems.

VII

UNIX Variants and Flavors

Other Alliances and Standards

Although several attempts have been made by vendors to take advantage of the best features from two different UNIX versions and incorporate them into one, there have also been many more attempts by standards committees. These committees usually attempt to identify what each UNIX has to offer that is beneficial and combine the best features into one standard. The two most important standards committees are POSIX and X/OPEN.

POSIX was formed in 1985 to define the standards for a UNIX operating system that could be easily ported across multiple platforms (this is somewhat inherent in the dependency on the C programming language). In simple terms, an operating system becomes portable by reducing it to its lowest common denominators. UNIX versions that are POSIX compliant incorporate the most portable features from SVRx (the x is used to denote all versiions of System V) and BSD into one package.

X/OPEN is a European committee aiming at similar standards. Created in 1984, the group consists of 19 vendors (all European) who are trying to define the set of features most needed by users and incorporate them into one standard.

What Comes with System V

Today, the most commonly adhered to standard is System V—especially with the absence of BSD as a future source of change. Before determining whether a vendor's product complies with SV or not, it is important to know the utility set that System V uses. The following offers a list of the System V commands and utilities.

While it is true that Berkeley will not be directly involved with a future release of BSD UNIX, BSD UNIX is alive and well. A company called BSDI, headed by USENIX board member Rob Kolstad, has rewritten BSD and is now releasing BSD 4.4 on multiple platforms. The only major holdout they encountered was that AT&T's USL pressed a copyright infringement suit on Berkeley and BSDI. This suit was dropped by Novell after they purchased USL from AT&T.

It is important to note that your system, regardless of the vendor, will have more utilities than the ones listed here. Those utilities quite often constitute enhancements the vendor has added to make their product more appealing than the competition's. The list shown in the table is only of the generic commands constituting System V Release 4. The majority of these commands are contained within the /bin and /usr/bin directories, as shown in table 28.1.

Table 28.1
The System V Release 4 Command Set

Command	Command	Command
at	find	rm
awk	finger	rmdir
banner	fmt	rsh
basename	fold	ruptime
bc	ftp	script
cal	grep	sdiff
calendar	head	sed
cancel	id	sh
cat	join	shutdown
cd	kill	sleep
chgrp	ksh	sort
chmod	last	spell
chown	line	split
clear	ln	strings
cmp	login	stty
compress	logname	su
cp	lp	sum
cpio	lpstat	tabs
crontab	ls	tail
crypt	mail	talk
csh	mailx	tar
csplit	man	tee
ct	mesg	telnet

continues

VII

UNIX Variants and Flavors

Table 28.1, Continued
The System V Release 4 Command Set

Command	Command	Command
cu	mkdir	test
cut	mknod	time
date	mnt	touch
dc	more	tput
df	mv	tr
diff	nawk	tset
diff3	news	tty
dircmp	nice	umask
dirname	nl	uname
disable	nohup	uncompress
du	od	uniq
echo	pack	unpack
ed	passwd	uucp
egrep	paste	vacation
enable	pcat	vi
env	pg	wait
ex	pr	wc
expr	ps	who
factor	pwd	write
fgrep	rcp	xargs
file	rlogin	zcat

Now that you have an understanding of UNIX heritage and the command set implied by System V Release 4 compliance, it is time to look at the UNIX operating systems currently marketed for the X86 Intel platform.

SCO UNIX

SCO UNIX wants to be the server platform of the future. It is estimated that over 60 percent of the Intel UNIX servers in existence are running SCO UNIX. That amounts to over one million servers around the world. The Santa Cruz Operation believes that users want Windows on their workstations and that fighting the battle to become the desktop operating system is a lost cause—instead their time is better utilized proving the worth of SCO UNIX on the server.

SCO and Intel-based processors are virtually synonymous in the UNIX world. There are two flavors of the product available (in packs of differing user sizes): SCO UNIX is strictly character based and command-line intensive; SCO Desktop is identical to SCO UNIX, except it incorporates a graphical interface environment as well.

Current Version

Although based on SVR3.2, SCO UNIX is currently referred to as 4.2. If spelled out in full, the product would be known as SVR3.2.4.2.

Shells and Graphics

SCO UNIX comes with the three major shells: the standard Bourne shell, the C shell, and the Korn shell. As mentioned earlier, the standard UNIX product does not incorporate a graphical interface with it, although the Desktop product does have Open Desktop and Motif.

Networking

One definite strong point for SCO is the incorporation of a wide range of networking support. This includes support for such protocols as IPX/SPX, TCP/IP, NetBEUI, and NetBIOS—virtually every networking protocol that can be used.

Security

C2 security, discussed in Chapter 27, is built in. A Trusted Computing Base takes security far beyond the standard login and password routine. During installation, you can choose one of four security levels to make the server as secure as you want it.

Requirements

SCO UNIX requires a 386 computer with a minimum of 2 MB RAM and 40 MB free hard drive space. When using the Desktop, the RAM requirement jumps to between 8 MB and 12 MB, while the requirement for free hard drive space climbs to 110 MB.

Downside

The worst complaint that can be lodged against SCO UNIX is that it is based upon SVR3.2 and is not current with 4.2 standards. This works both on behalf of and against SCO. On the positive side, SCO is working with a proven standard that has been in existence for several years. It is also true, for the most part, that software is upwardly compatible—that is, applications written to take advantage of SCO's command set will work with other UNIX versions based on 3.2 or later.

On the negative side, however, SCO UNIX does not have the complete 4.2 command set. Thus, applications written for that set are not always readily suited to SCO.

Other

A great thing about SCO UNIX is its status with application vendors. Currently, there are over 8,000 business applications written for the operating system. Other UNIX vendors recognize the size of this base and, quite often, rather than fighting the battle of trying to get application vendors to do the same for them, they will make their products capable of executing SCO binaries. A classic example of this is UnixWare. Although UnixWare is a new product, there are 8,000 applications that can run on it because it can run applications written for SCO.

Xenix

The basis upon which SCO UNIX was built, Xenix is also marketed by SCO. Xenix is groundbreaking in that it was the first UNIX version ported to the Intel X86 platform. SCO has done little with it in recent years, preferring to make the enhancements to SCO UNIX instead. It is still offered as a product and is supported for reasons of backward compatibility and because it represents a no-frills operating system for users needing little more than multiuser, multitasking UNIX.

Current Version

The current version of Xenix, which has been available for several years now, is 2.3.4.

Shells and Graphics

Xenix ships with no graphical interfaces, but does contain a full set of operating system shells—Bourne, C, and Korn.

Networking and Security

The current release of Xenix does not include enhanced security (C2), nor does it come with networking support built in. TCP/IP can be purchased as an add-on, however.

Requirements

A true strong point of Xenix is its reduced system requirement needs. It will run on a 286 machine with only 2 MB RAM and 40 MB of hard drive space. That is the bare minimum on which it will operate. Running Xenix at the bare minimum is not always such a great idea, however. In reality, you should use a 386 machine with between 4 MB and 8 MB RAM and 100 MB of hard drive space.

Upside

Xenix shines if the user is looking for an inexpensive operating system that can outpower DOS and runs with minimal machine specifications. Xenix offers remarkably fast operation, even on a slower machine, thanks to its capability to multithread and its low overhead.

Other

SCO is no longer developing Xenix, choosing instead to focus on SCO UNIX. Xenix, also, does not include NFS, or Windows and DOS support in the way that most current X86 UNIX versions do. As a standalone operating system with only a command line, it is unparalleled. If you need to connect and interact with other operating systems, however, or prefer a GUI to the command line, there are other choices to suit your needs better.

Linux

If there can be any such thing as a free operating system, Linux is it. Linux was conceived originally as a UNIX-like operating system that would be distributed for free. Several authors have added enhancements to it, through Internet communications, and Linux has grown quickly—both in terms of acceptance and capabilities.

To this day, the Linux operating system remains free—the only thing you have to pay for is the way that you receive it. Linux is available on many bulletin boards; the connect time to download all of it can run upwards of $200. Several businesses have jumped forward and are packaging Linux on floppy disks and CD-ROMs and selling those. In essence, you are paying for the media, but not for the operating system.

Current Version

The most current version of Linux depends on which vendor you purchase it from. Just as with the original UNIX, each vendor is free to add its own enhancements to the product and give value to its version over anyone else's. Currently, the last stable version that all vendors agree on is 1.09. Linux is based on the POSIX standard, consisting of a great deal of BSD with some SVR3.2 tossed in.

Shells and Graphics

Motif and Openwin are available for Linux, and it does include X Windows. Linux really shines, however, with the shells included with it. Not only are the three major shells included, but also two additional ones:

- ✔ **BASH.** The Bourne Again Shell contains additional enhancements to Bourne—adding more regular expression matching, for example.

- ✔ **TCSH.** Tom's C Shell is an enhancement to the C shell, adding additional capabilities.

Networking and Security

Most, but not all, vendor's versions of Linux have TCP/IP support built in, and include NFS tools. At this time, Linux is not certified for C2 security. As Linux is an operating system still under development, this is not out of the ordinary, however.

Requirements

Linux requires a minimum of a 386 machine with 4 MB RAM and 200 MB hard drive space. The minimum RAM requirement should be viewed as being 8 MB, however.

Upside

The best part of Linux is that it provides full source code to everything. If you are interested in the internal workings of an operating system and want to tinker about at the system level, you'll never find a better opportunity to do so than with Linux.

Downside

The downside to Linux is that it resembles UNIX in its origin. Commands work differently in UNIX because they were written by different people working independently of each other. The head and tail commands are the most classic examples of this. To see the first three lines of a file, you should have to specify the following:

```
head -l3 file
```

Instead, the line parameter is implied, and it simply becomes:

```
head -3 file.
```

Linux also is the product of many people making independent contributions. In a way, they are reinventing the wheel.

Other

Linux is a UNIX clone, but is not UNIX compliant—it does not meet the criteria of any UNIX governing body. It will not run SCO applications, significantly reducing the number of applications that will run on it.

FreeBSD

FreeBSD is an offspring of the University of California at Berkeley's decision to devote its energy to education and not to maintaining a software development house. Like Linux, FreeBSD is a 32-bit operating system essentially available for free (you pay for the means by which you acquire it). FreeBSD is available on many bulletin board systems; you can download it for large connect charges, or pay it from a retailer on CD or floppy disks for considerably less.

Current Version and Requirements

Based upon BSD 3.2, FreeBSD will run on a 386 machine with approximately 4 MB of RAM and 200 MB hard drive space. As with Linux, it is highly recommended that the minimum be viewed as a bare minimum, and you should try to avoid that wherever possible.

Networking

FreeBSD comes with TCP/IP networking, SLIP, PPP, telnet, ftp, archie, gopher, and NFS.

Shells and Graphics

FreeBSD comes with X Windows, as well as a wide range of shells. Mirroring those available in Linux, it includes the ksh, tcsh, and bash shells.

Other

FreeBSD and Linux have a great deal in common—both are free 32-bit operating systems based on UNIX. Both include full source code and provide an excellent means by which students, or other interested parties, can experiment with the operating systems and get hands-on experience at a system level.

Additionally, FreeBSD includes several utilities and extras normally only available separately. These include GNU C and C++ compilers, source-level debuggers, and the PERL scripting language.

UnixWare

When Bell Labs dissolved from one entity into many, the UNIX portion was spun into UNIX System Laboratories (USL). In the early 1990s, Novell Inc. agreed to pitch in with AT&T and turn UNIX System Laboratories into another corporation, jointly owned by the two parties, called Univel. UnixWare was the first product this new company released. UnixWare combines the features of UNIX with the capability to connect to NetWare. Before the product was released, Novell purchased all of Univel and the UNIX name.

UnixWare, coming from what once was USL, was one of the first operating systems to incorporate the 4.2 standard. UnixWare, a scaled-down version of AT&T UNIX, is aimed at the portion of the market that needs to incorporate UNIX with the capability to interact with NetWare.

Current Version

The current version of UnixWare is 1.1, although version 2.0 has been in beta testing for quite some time. Both versions are based on SVR4.2.

Shells and Graphics

UnixWare includes both the Motif and Open Look graphical interfaces. It includes only the Bourne shell from the command line, yet offers something called the Windowing Korn shell, in which ksh features can be utilized by opening a command window within one of the GUIs.

Networking

Beyond a doubt, the strength of UnixWare lies in its capability to connect TCP/IP and NetWare (IPX/SPX) networks. By so doing, UnixWare provides an excellent means by which two different networks can be seamlessly integrated by placing one UnixWare machine between the two networks.

Security and Requirements

C2 security is built into UnixWare, and it will run on a 386 machine with 8 MB RAM and 80 MB of hard drive space. To run efficiently, however, 12–16 MB RAM should be considered, and 140 MB should be the minimum hard drive ever considered.

Upside

UnixWare is compatible with SCO applications and will run them whether they are written for SCO UNIX or Xenix. It also will allow access to DOS and Windows applications via emulation (a shell to DOS runs DR DOS 6), and includes Adobe Type Manager with 17 Type 1 scalable fonts.

Downside

Although UnixWare is based on SVR4.2, there are many commands left out of the standard package in an attempt to keep the system requirements as low as possible. Many of these absences can be remedied with the purchase of additional software packages. (It is discouraging that such purchases are necessary, however.)

Such simple things as the man command are left out. The tail command is provided so that you can look at the last lines of a file. You do not get its cousin, the head command, to look at the first lines, however. Table 28.2 shows the standard SVR4.2 commands that you do not get with UnixWare.

Table 28.2
SVR4.2 Commands Not Available with UnixWare

Command	Command	Command
at	head	page
banner	help	paste
batch	join	prof
cal	last	relogin
calendar	login	script
crypt	logname	sdiff
csplit	mesg	spell

continues

Table 28.2, Continued
SVR4.2 Commands Not Available with UnixWare

Command	Command	Command
diff3	more	split
dircmp	nawk	strings
egrep	nice	sum
env	nl	time
expr	nm	timex
factor	nohup	vacation
finger	notify	wall
groups	od	write

Solaris for X86

Sun Microsystems has a software arm responsible for marketing the UNIX operating system. In the X86 ring, they have two contenders: Solaris and Interactive UNIX. Whereas Interactive UNIX can be equated with SCO Xenix as a no-frills package, Solaris competes with SCO UNIX for a full-blown X86 version of the operating system.

One of the founding members of Sun Microsystems/SunSoft is Bill Joy. As a graduate student at Berkeley, Joy created the vi editor, contributed to the C shell, and did a number of great services for the world of UNIX.

Current Version

Originally, the Sun operating system was based upon BSD and was called SunOS. When Berkeley announced that they were no longer developing the product, however, SunSoft quickly converted over to SV, and adopted the moniker of Solaris. Based on SVR4, the current version of Solaris for X86 is 2.4.

Shells and Graphics

Solaris ships with Open Look, but not with Motif. Solaris also includes the three standard shells—Bourne, Korn, and the C shell.

Networking and Security

Complete TCP/IP support is built into the standard Solaris package, as is C2 security. For more details on the levels of security, see Chapter 27.

Requirements

Solaris will run on a 386 machine with 16 MB of RAM and a free space of 200 MB on the hard drive.

Other

Solaris will not run applications written for the SCO family of products. At the same time, there are an impressive number of applications written for Solaris, and SunSoft regularly publishes a guide to these.

Interactive UNIX

The low-end UNIX product from SunSoft is Interactive UNIX. It provides an ideal 32-bit environment for anyone needing an entry-level UNIX operating system without all the features incorporated into Solaris.

Current Version

The latest release of Interactive UNIX is 4.0, and it is based on SVR3.2—the same as SCO UNIX.

Shells, Graphics, and Networking

All three of the major shells are included with the standard product. From that point, what comes with the product depends on the way you purchase it. There is a Base Solution package, which includes nothing more. There also is a Graphical Solution package, which includes X Windows and Motif. Instead of purchasing the Graphical Solution package (or in conjunction with it), you can purchase the Network Solution package. The Network Solution package provides you with the TCP/IP support not included with the Base Solution package.

Security and Requirements

C2 security is built into Interactive UNIX. Interactive UNIX requires a 386 machine with 8 MB of RAM and 120 MB of hard drive space.

Other

Interactive UNIX can run SCO Xenix binaries and applications for either SCO UNIX or SCO Open Desktop. It is tailored for small- to medium-sized offices as a low-cost solution to a 32-bit multiuser operating system.

There is no Windows support to speak of for Interactive UNIX, and it is very much lacking in user friendliness.

NeXTstep

Steve Jobs made history as one of the cofounders of Apple Computers. After leaving that company, he attempted to replicate his success by starting a company that would produce revolutionary computers and put the competition to shame. That company was NeXT Inc.

The original intention was to follow a similar pattern of success as had been established with Apple and produce hardware. The hardware NeXT produced never caught on, but the software they were bundling with the machines did.

Current Version

The current version of NeXTstep is 3.2, and it is based upon Mach—a derivative of 4.3BSD. A newer version, 3.3, is slated for release in the near future.

Shells and Graphics

Based upon Berkeley UNIX (BSD), the default shell is the C shell, although the Bourne shell also is included. The graphical interface is what gives NeXTstep its demand in the marketplace. The 3D interface is proprietary and is not linked with X Windows or anything similar. NeXTstep has become a popular favorite with many computer game developers who use it to write their games before porting elsewhere.

Networking

Out of the box, NeXTstep comes ready to plug and play with TCP/IP, IPX/SPX, or NetBIOS.

Security and Requirements

C2 security is not possible with NeXTstep, given the way it is designed. NeXTstep requires a minimum of a 486 machine, with 16 MB RAM and 200 MB hard drive space. More realistically, 32 MB represents a reasonable amount of RAM, and 300 MB hard drive space more accurately reflects the need.

Other

There is no compatibility with SCO UNIX, leaving a small number of native applications that will run on NeXTstep. Unfortunately, there is also a small hardware compatibility list and a high price point.

On the positive side, however, NeXTstep features superb fonts and is ideal for graphics work.

Summary

There are a good many UNIX or UNIX-like operating systems available for the X86 platform. While some are stripped-down versions of UNIX, others offer all of the features you would expect to find in a full-blown operating system.

The following chapter continues this examination further, and looks at some of the more popular UNIX operating systems available on dedicated platforms.

VII

UNIX Variants and Flavors

Chapter Snapshot

In the last chapter, the history of UNIX and its family tree were explored in terms of how it gave birth to the versions currently available for the Intel X86 platform. In the days before it was available for that processor, and in the days since, UNIX has been a key player in the dedicated hardware platform. This chapter reviews the major players in that arena, and what to expect in the future by including the following:

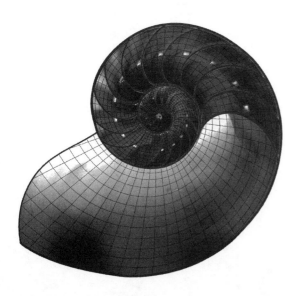

29

CHAPTER

UNIX Variants on Dedicated Platforms

T he previous chapter explored UNIX on the X86 platform, but that is not where it was born, or where it shines brightly. UNIX was written in the late 60s to take advantage of the processor that was available to Thompson and Ritchie at the time. Since then, hardware vendors have ported UNIX to their machines because it makes their machines hum like no other operating system can.

This has created a scenario wherein many sites have UNIX as their operating system, not because they purchased it specifically, but because it came with the hardware they bought. This is what we are referring to as a dedicated platform—the operating system is dedicated to the purchased hardware.

Major Vendors

The following vendors are recognized throughout the world for their continuing enhancements to the UNIX operating system. Although there are others, these are the current key players.

AIX

Advanced Interactive Executive (AIX) is the name of the UNIX operating system offered by IBM. In addition to its normal hardware base, it is one of the few operating systems available for the PowerPC.

AIX fits perfectly into the IBM operating system family, which consists of OS/2 for PCs and AIX for an intensive, client/server environment. OS/2, which goes beyond the graphical interface and an emphasis on one user, bears a great deal of resemblance to UNIX. The file structure utilizes fnodes to serve as indexes, or pointers, to file data, while UNIX calls the same thing inodes. Additionally, OS/2 is multitasking and preemptive multithreading.

HP-UX

Hewlett-Packard is the company behind HP-UX, which is presently available for the HP 9000 series of computers that utilize the RISC processor.

The current version of the product is 9.03, and it comes with all three of the standard shells. It also includes X Windows and Motif, as well as networking support for TCP/IP, NFS, and Lan9000.

C2 security is not built into the operating system, but is presently under development. It is targeted for sites that must maintain large databases.

Solaris

Solaris runs on SPARC-based machines and the PowerPC—in addition to having an X86 version that was previously discussed.

Solaris combines the best features of BSD and SV. Release 2.4, the latest, makes *Symmetrical Multi-Processing* (SMP) available on non-SPARC architectures, as well.

Ultrix

Digital Equipment Corporation markets Ultrix. An interesting side note to UNIX history is that Thompson and Ritchie first ported UNIX to a DEC machine and used the then new C language to do so.

What to Expect in the Future

The dedicated platform vendors for years relied upon the operating system to complement their hardware and used it for little else. Every enhancement to the system was done to keep up with what other vendors were doing or to take advantage of new developments in the hardware.

Currently, however, the emphasis must shift, and more attention is being paid to the need for interaction between UNIX and other operating systems. As with the X86 platform, the push is on to ease the interaction between UNIX and NetWare, DOS, and other operating systems. Not only is it necessary for many users to access DOS, but Windows is the big push in desktop software these days. Being more resource intensive than DOS, and not as fault tolerant as UNIX, Windows access creates problems galore, and has spawned an industry dedicated to providing adequate access.

Summary

UNIX was originally written to take advantage of the hardware available in the machine in which it resided. As a result, it became a favorite operating system with hardware vendors who bundled versions of it with their hardware. Additional enhancements were made by the vendors as they attempted to add routines that utilized their hardware to its fullest potential.

VII

UNIX Variants and Flavors

Part VIII

The Internet and Communications

Chapter Snapshot

The Internet offers almost instantaneous globe-spanning electronic mail communication, archives of powerful free software, powerful online information access tools and data repositories, and something like 4,500 ongoing discussion newsgroups. This chapter introduces you to the Internet and discusses the following topics:

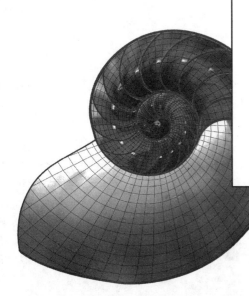

CHAPTER

Accessing the Internet

The Internet—the most widespread computer network on the planet—is the most obvious example of the information realm in which so many white collar professionals evidently wish to spend all their time. The Internet is a seductively attractive realm, with sound and pictures and powerful free software whizzing around, all just waiting to be invited into your own environment. However, you must find your place in the Internet and see how to make it work for you. This chapter looks at some of the tools and practices currently on the Internet.

Internet = Protocols + Culture

The Internet is a community of people who do things their way because, for better or worse, that is the way they like them. A well-known example of this is the Internet's pronounced antipathy to direct advertising. Even the creator of the Internet worm has never been vilified to the degree of the hapless marketeers who send out the e-mail equivalent of junk mail. Sometimes the Internet is the world's biggest small town, with its own narrow way of doing things. But the Internet persists and thrives because of the tyranny of the useful. Its protocols and way of doing things are so useful that people carry on, constantly trying to refine and improve it. Have a look and see if it works for you.

Protocols

Internet Protocols (IPs) are the low-level tools that bind the machines on the Internet into a useful whole. IPs specify the kinds of communications that can occur between machines and how connections can be made to allow those communications. To be on the Internet, a machine must support the IP. One of the most important of these is the *Transmission Control Protocols* (TCP), hence the often-used abbreviation TCP/IP. Among the many others are the *Simple Mail Transport Protocol* (SMTP), *file transfer protocol* (ftp), and *User Datagram Protocol* (UDP).

A *protocol* is an agreement about how something will work. When you see children jumping rope, the rope handlers agree to the speed and intensity with which they will spin the rope. The other kid, the one who gets to jump up and down and have all the fun, is the one who enjoys the benefit of this agreement or protocol. That's you! Because the machines on the Internet use these protocols, you are able to use such services as:

- ✔ electronic mail (e-mail)

- ✔ "white page"-like directories

- ✔ information access tools

- ✔ database queries

- ✔ executable program archives

The Internet basically treats all of its communications as packets of data, each of which has an address. Machines (or their routers) on the Internet maintain tables that describe addresses of local and remote machines, and routes for packets. They deliver packets to addresses by looking up the address, and using the routes, described in the table. (You can use the command netstat to see information about your system's routing table.) Needless to say, with millions of users on the Internet, many complications can arise, but this is the simple version of what happens: packets with addresses get passed from sender to addressee.

For some insight into how the Internet might work, imagine a paper-and-pencil system that people seated in a room might use to send messages to each other. Imagine that each person has two neighbors, one in front and one behind, except for the lucky person who gets to sit up front near the door and always gets a whole graham cracker, and the unlucky person who sits in the back and has to erase rude remarks in math books whenever he has a spare minute. To begin with, participants need a unique name to differentiate themselves from each other, so they write down their unique names on pieces of paper that they can keep.

Each participant can get pieces of paper from each other and read them. To make it easy to read and process each piece of paper, they all agree to put the name of the addressee at the top of the paper. Furthermore, they agree to write their messages with a particular alphabet in blocks of a particular size, say, 64 letters. Now to create a network communications system, they all agree to reach out to their two neighbors every once in a while to see if there are any pieces of paper for them to process. If they get a piece of paper, they read its address. If it is addressed to them, they read the message. If it is not for them, they look up the name of the addressee and the route to use to relay the paper to that name and pass it on.

Imagine that there are many rooms with people doing these paper-shuffling routines. One person from each room is designated as a router to the other rooms. Messages bound for another group are accumulated by the router and periodically handed over to the designated router in one of the other rooms. Of course, the router must keep another table that says what addresses are in use in other rooms. This process continues and the next thing you know, you have an information superhighway.

In our example, each "room" needs its own name in order to be uniquely identified. So all machines and groups of machines on the Internet need unique identifiers. If it were just up to computers, machines would be happy with such memorable labels as "254.253.0.17." Humans prefer names like "whitehouse.gov" and "mit.edu." Tables, such as the file /etc/hosts, contain lists of names and matching Internet addresses. Machines and groups of machines are assembled into a hierarchy described by the Domain Name System. The various levels of the hierarchy are separated by the period (.) in a name like crl.ucsd.edu. The letters after the last period will be one of these:

com	commerce
edu	education
gov	government
mil	military
net	network
org	other organizations

How the Internet Handles the Changing Network Environment

The Internet has its roots in a networking initiative and associated protocols created by the U.S. Department of Defense. Since then, new network issues have arisen—new data types like audio and video, new requirements like real-time response, new hardware, new software, and so forth. How have the protocols used on the Internet kept up?

The Internet and its protocols grow and evolve in response to user needs and currently available resources. Unlike a piece of commercial software that is designed from the top down to accomplish specific things in specific ways, the Internet is adapted to the needs of its users by the users themselves. It grows from the bottom up. Certain ways of doing things prove to be useful and become candidates for the IPs. For instance, the Kerberos protocol allows authentication of packets on a network. That is, it can assure a user, process, or machine that users, processes, or machines are who they say they are. Since its formulation at MIT many years ago, it has been used at many different sites and added to and resold in various commercially available products. The base source code is freely available through ftp from MIT and other sites. Not all machines on the Internet use Kerberos; many machines not on the Internet do. So there is not a necessary relationship between Kerberos use and Internet participation.

Mechanisms are available for formalizing, altering, and replacing (when necessary) IPs. The protocols themselves are stated in documents freely available from various sites on the Internet. You can see a list of the ones used on your machine by entering the command:

```
% cat /etc/protocols
```

The proposal and review process uses a document called a *Request for Comment* (RFC), which describes the protocol. As one RFC puts it, "[An] RFC specifies a standard for the...Internet community. Hosts on the...Internet are expected to adopt and implement this standard."

The Internet Society—a voluntary association—has an Architecture Board and an Engineering Task Force that review and approve technologies as Internet standards. Compliance is voluntary in the sense that if you use the IPs you are on the Internet, and if you don't, you are not. But note that different protocols for networking can coexist with IPs and communicate through gateways. It is not an either/or choice.

Layers and the TCP/IP Stack

The IP is sometimes referred to as the TCP/IP stack because the various constituent protocols are clustered in layers that specify different kinds of interrelated services. Layers are relatively independent of each other. For example, the application layer, which bundles text into a piece of e-mail, does not really know or need to know how the network layer routes the e-mail packets to the destination machine. Similarly, the network layer does not know about the voltage levels that different pins on different connectors use in either machine's hardware.

Classifying Users, Machines, Connections, and Communications

How can users and machines connect and communicate? Some of the most important issues to consider when hooking up people and computers are the following:

✔ How many different machines will each person or machine be connected to?

✔ How much information will be transmitted?

✔ How much autonomy does each user or machine have when connected?

All the different types of connections between machines and users have their own costs and benefits, and each has a place on the Internet.

One familiar connection type is from mainframe computer over a serial line to a simple terminal and keyboard. In this setup, the only machine with any smarts is the mainframe. The terminal can only send and receive characters—letters, numbers, and a few other symbols. This is referred to as character-based communication. The user types in text that appears on the screen. In response, the mainframe computer at the other end of the connection types back some text to the user's screen or performs some other function such as making an entry in a database. The mainframe runs its operating system and other programs and is responsible for all communication. Such a system, for instance a point-of-sale terminal, restricts users to a limited range of interactions.

In UNIX systems, terminals such as the vt100 are typical of terminals used in such a setup. In fact, vt100 has come to be synonymous with *dumb terminal*. Emulation of the vt100 has come to be the sine qua non of dumb terminals, not because they are especially backwards but because they are simply exceedingly numerous. Unfortunately, they can only render about a hundred blocky and hard-to-read characters. Furthermore, they do so in colors that give a vivid visual impression of the words "occupational hazard." Such terminals have some virtues—they are inexpensive, do not require a high bandwidth connection to their computer, and can present readable text.

The Internet version of the dumb terminal is *telnet*, which shares one of the virtues of its hardware cousin—it requires a relatively low bandwidth connection. *Bandwidth* is a measure of a transmission channel's capacity to carry information. For example, letters carried by post are quite low bandwidth; they carry only a few hundred or thousand words and can require several days to deliver. Stepping up another level, telephones transmit sound in real-time, that is, without any appreciable delay, from sender to receiver. Up one more level is television, which carries both sound and pictures. A transmission channel with a given capacity can carry more low-bandwidth than high-bandwidth connections. In other words, it is cheaper to run a low-bandwidth connection.

Using telnet on the Internet, it is also possible to have character-based, peer-to-peer connections in which there are machines on both ends of the line. These machines can communicate in their own rights and "discuss" what functionality they will mutually support. The users of the machines are more autonomous than the users on the point-of-sale terminal example because they can choose from a much wider range of useful commands and actions. Though telnet is still limited to using a bidirectional stream of eight-bit bytes, users can chat in real-time using the *talk* command or its multiuser client/server counterpart, *Internet Relay Chat* (IRC).

Another connection type is peer-to-peer, in which two machines have equal access to resources such as data on a hard disk or printers. These machines are workstations, each with the capability to run its own operating system and other programs. Personal computers in office networks are typically configured as peers. News groups (Netnews or Usenet) are distributed across many different computers. That is, they are not supported or sustained by any single machine anywhere. Any machine that subscribes to them can participate in them.

Client/server connections combine elements of both these types. Autonomous users instruct their workstations to perform a wide range of functions, some of these functions are performed on its own. It, for instance, accepts information from an input device such as a keyboard, mouse, or other pointing device. It also displays information on its screen. However, some instructions are relayed to other machines on the network, which then perform the work that the user actually wants done. For example, one can instruct a television set-top switching box to display a movie. The box relays the request to another machine that bills the user for the movie and returns an "OK" to the set-top box to show the movie. The machine that initiated the request for a service is the client; the machine that provided the service is the server. The automated teller machine, a low-bandwidth example, performs some functions on its own (the desirable ones, like dispensing twenty-dollar bills), whereas another machine on its network performs other functions (undesirable ones mostly, like debiting your checking account).

Other client/server relationships on the Internet range from the *Network File System* (NFS), which allows a machine to access files elsewhere on its network, to the *Domain Name System* (DNS), which specifies the correspondence of machine IP addresses to machine names. Typically, UNIX systems run their servers as daemons, processes which are always running and are not attached to a particular user or terminal.

Security

The security of UNIX systems on the Internet is a specialized and complicated topic. Because of the easy access that the Internet allows, potential threats can occur that may be new to sites more accustomed to allowing much more limited access. Many sites have developed security policies for themselves in which they assess risks and develop methods for minimizing them.

The following are some places to look for more information about security issues.

See the Network Working Group document called *For Your Information (FYI) 8, Site Security Handbook*. This is a text file located on the machine named nic.merit.edu in the directory /documents/fyi.

The Editors' Note from that document reads:

This FYI RFC is a first attempt at providing Internet users guidance on how to deal with security issues in the Internet. As such, this document is necessarily incomplete. There are some clear shortfalls; for example, this document focuses mostly on resources available in the United States.

The preceding Network Working Group document also contains a bibliography.

The Network Working Group document, *For Your Information (FYI) 3, A Bibliography of Internetworking Information*, a bibliography of information about TCP/IP internetworking, mentions:

U.S. General Accounting Office, Computer Security—Virus Highlights Need for Improved Internet Management, 36 pgs., U.S. General Accounting Office, Washington, DC, 1989.

This report (GAO/IMTEC-89-57) describes the worm (the Internet worm of 1988) and its effects. It gives a good overview of the various U.S. agencies involved in the Internet today and their concerns vis-a-vis computer security and networking. The report is available on-line on host nnsc.nsf.net, directory pub, file name GAO_RPT, and on nis.nsf.net, directory nsfnet, file name GAO_RPT.TXT.

Several Netnews groups discuss security issues. Some of these groups are the following:

alt.security	Security issues on computer systems
alt.security.index	Pointers to good stuff in alt.security (Moderated)
comp.security.announce	Announcements from the Computer Emergency Response Team (CERT) about security (Moderated)
comp.security.misc	Security issues of computers and networks
comp.virus	Computer viruses and security (Moderated)
comp.security.UNIX	Discussion of UNIX security

File Encodings

A file might be encoded on the Internet for different reasons: to assure its privacy, to encapsulate it in an archive, to compress it, or to send a binary file using an ASCII transmission method like mail or Netnews. The first issue is not covered in this book. The tar, cpio, and bar commands handle the second issue. The *compress* program handles file compression. This chapter addresses the last issue—sending binary files through ASCII channels.

Binary files represent different kinds of data than plain text. Pictures, sounds, executable programs, the save state of a game, and so on are all different kinds of binary files. They can be transferred around the Internet with a program like ftp. But what if the file's sender or would-be receiver does not have access to ftp? As long as the sender has e-mail or a Netnews feed, the binary files are available by using the uuencode and uudecode commands. These programs convert an arbitrary stream of bytes into ASCII and back again.

To use uuencode, type the following:

```
% uuencode file label > out_file
```

where *file* is the file to be encoded and *label* is the name the file will have when it is decoded with uudecode.

uuencode will first write a header into the encoded version of the file, which is being written to the file out_file. The header contains the label specified on the command line and the ownership and permissions of the original file. uudecode will later produce its output file with that same ownership and permissions.

Once you have the ASCII-encoded version of the binary file, you can send it as an e-mail message or post it to a news group. Anyone who wants to have the file can then copy it to a local disk and type the following:

```
uudecode file
```

uudecode then discards anything that the mail or news program has added to the file and writes a new file. The new file will have the name specified when it was originally uuencoded. It will also have the original file's permissions and ownership, so be sure to use uudecode in a directory in which that user ID has write permission.

Using ping

ping provides the Internet version of a "Hello, are you there?" query. ping sends network packets to a machine on the Internet, which you designate either by name or by address. Use this command when a machine you believe should be present and available on the Internet does not respond to you.

Consider, for example, the following scenario. You try to send e-mail to someone whose address you jotted down on the back of a business card. Unfortunately, you were standing in a crowded shuttle bus at the time and some parts of the address are unclear. You formulate your carefully considered letter (in a word processor, not your mail program, just in case there are problems delivering it later) and send it off. Almost instantly, you receive a message that until you reformulate the address portion of your mail, it cannot be sent. You take a second look at the wrinkled and smeared business card and ask was that "whitehouse.gov" or "whitehouse.gof" you wrote? You can use ping to untangle this mail delivery problem by typing the following command:

```
% ping whitehouse.gov
```

You see the result:

```
Source: [137.110.108.25] —> Destination: whitehouse.gov
[198.137.240.100]

RESULT     PKT#     TIME      LENGTH
success     1        23         56
success     2        22         56
success     3        22         56
success     4        22         56
success     5        21         56
Packets out/in/bad/%loss = 5/5/0/0
Round Trip Time (Ticks) min/avg/max = 21/22/23
~~~~~~~~~~~~~~~~~~~~~~~~~~~~~~~~~~~~~~~~~~~~
```

On BSD versions, if you use ping without any options, ping will return a message that the destination machine is either alive or unreachable. To get the output shown here, you must use ping -s.

Though most of this output from ping is self-explanatory, a few comments are in order. ping sent five packets (at the rate of one per second) and each one arrived at its destination successfully. (Note that you can send as many packets as you wish, but five is probably about right. Sending more than five would not really tell you anything more and would definitely use up some of the network's second most precious commodity: bandwidth.) The % loss in this example is 0, but even if it was something like 20, you don't need to worry. After all, the IP was designed to accommodate packet loss. All the packets seem to take approximately the same amount of time (measured in arbitrary "ticks") to make their trips, and they were all the same length.

If you had typed the following line:

```
% ping whitehouse.gof
```

You would have seen something similar to the following message:

```
whitehouse.gof —> Host not responding (Cannot resolve name)
```

Usage

ping requires the name or IP address of a host. ping will accept a few options to change the rate at which it sends out packets and how those packets will be routed to the destination machine (see table 30.1). The syntax for using ping to detect an Internet machine is as follows:

```
ping host [packetsize] [count].
```

Table 30.1
Using ping To Detect an Internet Machine

Option	Effect
host	Specifies the name or Internet address of the machine to be ping'ed.
packetsize	Specifies the number of bytes in the transmitted packet. The default is 64, which is fine for most uses. Larger packets can hold routing information.
count	Specifies the number of packets to send. Be sure to include this number. Otherwise, ping will emit packets until you press Ctrl+D.

ping sends a special type of packet called ECHO_REQUEST to the host you specify on the command line. You can use a name for a host (such as whitehouse.gov) rather than the IP address (which is 198.137.240.100) as long as you have a table on your machine that translates from the name to the number.

The ECHO_REQUEST packet is part of the *Internet Control Message Protocol* (ICMP), which is, in turn, part of the Internet Protocol itself. Because a machine (or its gateway) can't be on the Internet without supporting these protocols, you can rely on ping to positively identify whether or not a machine is accessible.

Using the finger Command

The finger command can be used over the Internet to show you information about users on other machines. The exact information you receive depends on the command options you use and what the user you are asking about has made available in his or her .plan and .project files. As long as you can overcome any squeamishness you may have about issuing a command like `finger bobr@mrktng.bigbiz.com` or `finger ritaz@finance.soho.com`, you should be able to find out some combination of these information tidbits:

✔ Login name

✔ Actual name

✔ Whether or not you can use the write command to write to the user's terminal

✔ Length of time since the user last issued a command

✔ Length of time since the user logged in

✔ The user's home directory and which login shell is being used for the login

✔ Any information the user wrote in the .plan file in the home directory

✔ Any information the user wrote in the .project file in the home directory

✔ Local location and phone number

You may already be familiar with this command from using it on your own system. The only significant addition of which you need to be aware is that you can include an Internet host name or IP address as part of the user's name you give on the command line.

For example, say you want to see who is currently logged on a machine (called bigbiz.com, for example) on the Internet. You can type the following:

```
% finger @bigbiz.com
```

(Note that you need to include the at sign (@) before the machine name, otherwise, your local finger process will look for a user named (bigbiz.com) and come up empty-...er, -handed.) The output will be a list that looks something like this:

```
[bigbiz.com]

Login      Name            TTY Idle    When     Where
buff       Robin Buffy     p2    1 Tue 19:26  bigbiz.com
bigbiz     Big Business    q3   21: Mon 08:54  bigbiz.com
jps        Jean-Paul Sartorial  q4  20: Mon 15:43  bigbiz.com
```

A few words about the column labeled `idle`. User `buff` has been idle for 1 minute while users `bigbiz` and `jps` have been idle for 21 and 20 hours respectively. Hey, it may not be big-league industrial espionage but at least you get some idea of what is going on over at BigBiz. Note that for a machine with many users, typing finger can yield a long list.

Using finger To See Information about a Specific User

finger can also show information about a specific user whether or not that user is currently logged in.

Typing the following command:

```
finger buff@bigbiz.com
```

might show the following:

```
[bigbiz.com]

Login name: buff                    In real life: Robin Buffy
Directory: /user/mngmnt/buff          Shell: /bin/csh
On since Jan 26 14:31:05 on ttyrc
4 days 23 hours Idle Time
New mail received Tue Jan 30 10:39:23 1994;
   unread since Tue Jan 30 09:37:16 1994
Plan:
Manager, Big Biz Businesses
Mail Code:  2741
Extension:  1212 (phone: 307-555-1212)
```

```
Office:    HQ, 200B
Motto: "If it's big business, it's our business!"
```

Here we see some information about user buff. Everything after the word Plan: is what user buff wrote in a file called .plan. Your site may support the use of a finger daemon (there are some that don't—the White House, for example). You can edit your .plan file to contain the information you would like others to see when they use finger on your account name.

A Noteworthy New Use for finger

As you can see, finger is a tidy, easy-to-use-and-understand Net utility. Some sites use pseudo-users with names like "help" and "info" to enable commands such as the following:

```
% finger help@such-and-such.org
```

This allows for the dissemination of small amounts of information which are not necessarily about an individual user through finger. For instance, typing the following command should show information about a drink vending machine in the Computer Science House of Rennselaer Institute of Technology:

```
% finger graph@drink.csh.rit.edu
```

Usage

finger requires the name or IP address of a remote host machine. Additionally, you can provide a valid user name at the remote machine (see table 30.2). It uses the following syntax:

```
finger [options] [user_name OR @machine_name] ...
```

Table 30.2
Using finger To Get Information about Users on Remote Machines

Option	Effect
user_name	Specifies a specific user at a remote machine. Must be in the form user_id@machine name.
@machine_name	Specifies a specific remote machine and all users currently logged in to that machine.

continues

Table 30.2, Continued
Using finger To Get Information about Users on Remote Machines

Option	Effect
-l	Shows long version of information about the user including login name, name, login shell, how long the user has been logged in or the last time the user was logged in, when the user last read e-mail, and this optional information: location, phone number and the contents of the .plan and .project files.
-s	Shows short version of information about the user including login name, name, the tty connection being used, when the login session began, and from where.
-p	Do not include information from the user's .plan file when showing long version.

When used with a remote machine, finger actually connects you with a finger daemon running on the remote machine. Your finger process passes the information from your command line along to the remote finger process. The remote finger process gathers the information requested and passes it back to your local finger, which then displays it to you.

E-Mail on the Internet

Sending and receiving messages electronically is certainly one of the most visible and attractive benefits of computer networking. Electronic mail occupies a useful niche midway between the telephone call and physical mail. Now if only you knew or could find out anybody's e-mail address! And if only e-mail never bounced!

Whereas the next chapter covers the mail utility, this section covers the role of the Internet in sending mail among various systems. Because there are different addressing schemes in common use, some of them quite complex, not all e-mail gets where it is intended to go. It will also provide some starting points in the search for the complete directory of all e-mail addresses everywhere.

Handling E-Mail

The propagation of e-mail requires different mechanisms than the creation and use of it. Just as with physical mail in which all letter writers are on one side and various national postal services are on the other, e-mail has both user front ends and behind-the-scenes mail transport programs and protocols.

Electronic mail can originate from hand-held computers, home computers, desktops, terminals, mainframes, workstations, fax machines, and possibly the soft drink vending machine at Rennselaer that is on the Internet. Furthermore, all these machines can be on networks other than the Internet such as BITNET or CompuServe. Certainly each one of the machines does not use UNIX and mail. Each uses its own mail programs; some have several from which to choose. That makes the business of addressing and delivering mail quite complex. Even within the UNIX community in the last few years there have been two different methods for addressing mail—the "bang path" and the "domain-based" address, which is currently the preferred one.

Because of the ever-swelling ranks of Internet users who use domain-based addresses of the form userID@machine_name.domain, other networks can sometimes accommodate such addresses directly. To send e-mail from a UNIX system to either CompuServe or America Online, two popular online services, you can use addresses such as the following in which userID_string is converted from the CompuServe ID number by making the comma after the first four digits into a period.

    userID@aol.com

or

    userID_string@compuserve.com

To send to someone on MCIMail, use an address with the following form:

    accountname@mcimail.com

or

    mci_id@mcimail.com

or

    full_user_name@mcimail.com

In other cases, you must explicitly include the gateway between the two networks that you want to use. A *gateway* is a system that understands and communicates with both networks and that can translate messages between them. For example, to send e-mail to a user on the BITNET network, use this style of address:

    userID%site_name.BITNET@BITNET_gateway

Two BITNET gateways are UICVM.UIC.EDU and CUNYVM.CUNY.EDU.

Though it is tempting to imagine that anyone on any computer network can receive e-mail that originates on the Internet, it just isn't so. In that regard, e-mail distribution still lags behind the ubiquitous and easy-going telephone.

VII

The Internet and Communications

Internet E-Mail

Within the Internet, e-mail moves according to the *Simple Mail Transport Protocol* (SMTP). A letter writer uses a program such as elm or mail to create a message. If the address includes a machine.domain part, the mail program hands over the message to sendmail or to some other mail transport program. sendmail interprets the address as written by the user and produces the appropriate IP address. It then relays the e-mail to another mail program for delivery and display to the recipient. However, because of the complexity of generating a valid IP address from whatever the user's mail program hands it, sendmail can have difficulties. Furthermore, e-mail from one point to another may take different routes. If an e-mail address that worked last week suddenly fails this week, this may be part of the explanation.

If It Talks, Is It Still E-Mail?

As long as e-mail consists of nothing more than text, many different machines can read it. But as new data types such as graphics and sound appear in e-mail, incompatibilities can arise. Multipurpose Internet Mail Extensions (MIME) describes some extensions to the earlier standard Internet e-mail. Hardware to enable such technologies as fax, video- and whiteboard-conferencing, and audio is not yet standardized.

E-Mail Address Directories

No single directory can be searched for an individual's e-mail address. Two resources on the Internet might help you locate an e-mail address. They are the *whois* program and the Knowbot Information Service offered by the *Corporation for National Research Initiatives* (CNRI).

Using whois

The whois program searches in a database for matches to a name you type in at the command line. The database to be searched is kept at a *Network Information Center* (NIC). By default, whois looks up records at the machine specific to your site. You can specify another host with the -h option. (In the punning spirit that sometimes seems to run rampant on the Internet, the RFC that describes this service is entitled NICNAME/Whois.)

For instance, what if you meet someone on a bus, but all you can remember is the person's last name. You recall that you were talking about e-mail, so you feel certain that the person has an e-mail address. To search for all records that match the string boulanger, type the following:

```
% whois boulanger
```

The result is the following:

```
% whois boulanger

using default whois server rs.internic.net

Boulanger, Nadia (NB76)          nadboul@SOUTHSTAR.COM
+1 xxx xxx xxx

Boulanger, Paul (PB61)           pwb@FIRST.UP.COM
(xxx) xxxx-xxx

The InterNIC Registration Services Host ONLY contains Internet Information

(Networks, ASN's, Domains, and POC's).

Please use the whois server at nic.ddn.mil for MILNET Information.
```

(I have x'ed out the telephone numbers in the output.) Perhaps this is a start in your search for the person. The Network Information Center that provides directory services has the address internic.net. To get help on the current state of the whois command, you type the following:

```
% whois help
```

The preceding command produces a long display of information about whois. You can also call the InterNIC at (800) 444-4345 or the registration services group at (703) 742-4777.

Using CNRI's Knowbot

The whois program can look up records in any database that conforms to the format it expects. It's possible to type in the target string for which you seek matches just once and have many different databases searched. As CNRI says in the Knowbot manual page, "By submitting a single query to KIS [Knowbot Information Service], a user can search a set of remote "white pages" services and see the results of the search in a uniform format."

Start up a telnet session. At the prompt, enter the Knowbot IP address.

```
% telnet
telnet> open info.cnri.reston.va.us 185
```

At the KIS prompt (>), type the following:

```
> query boulanger
```

You see the output shown previously and much more besides since KIS searches many different databases.

Mail Lists

The Internet supports sending mail to whole groups of users at once. This service differs from USENET news groups because the recipients have the mail list distributions delivered by mail and read them with their mail reader. Typically, a mail list consists of users with a common interest in some topic and a strong desire to read everything that other people have to say on that topic. Of course, some lists are private but many are open to anyone who wishes to join. Most work in the same way:

✔ The contents of the mail list—the e-mail messages—are sent to everyone on the list.

✔ Administrative matters, such as subscribing and unsubscribing, are communicated only to the list administrator.

You subscribe to the mail list by e-mailing the list administrator and saying that you want to be added to the distribution list. List administrators sometimes use a program to assist in managing their mail lists, and so you may want to keep your subscription request rather terse. If your mail program provides a subject line, type in the word subscribe. You might type the same word as the body of the message and include your name. Your e-mail address will already be part of the message. If you do not know the e-mail address to use for the list administrator, try the name of the list with -request appended to it, for example, games-scores-request@sports.report.com. If you want to start your own mail list, the source code for list server programs is available and free.

Mail Servers

Mail servers are programs that distribute files or information. These respond to e-mail messages that conform to a specific syntax by e-mailing files or information requested in the message back to the sender. The information-on-demand can be program archives, documents, digests, indices to other documents, and so on. If, for example, you have an Internet e-mail address, you can request copies of IP *Requests for Comments* (RFCs) by sending a mail message to mailserv@ds.internic.net. The body of the message can include the following:

`rfcnnn`	nnn is the RFC number. (You receive the text of the RFC.)
`file /ftp/rfc/rfcnnnn.yyy`	nnnn is the RFC number and yyy is either txt for the plain text version or ps for the PostScript printable version.
`help`	Get information about using the mail server.

Using mail servers is a convenient way of getting many forms of information, even if you do not have direct ftp or telnet access to it.

Special Text Conventions in E-Mail

In an effort to overcome the drab appearance of text in messages sent through e-mail and to newsgroups, some writers use special configurations of alphabetic characters and punctuation, either in their writing or appended to messages as fanciful signatures.

Smileys, Abrvtns, and Signatures

Viewed sideways, in-line combinations such as :-{) (smiler with mustache) or :-D (laugher) can add emotional overtones to plain text messages that might otherwise be unclear. Possibly their only downside would be the pains you develop trying to puzzle out *-) (happy Cyclops) or :-& (cigarette smoker).

Cn u rd ths? If you can, you are a candidate for using such abbreviations as btw (by the way), fyi (for your information), and rtfm (read the f*ing manual) in your own messages. Guess they save some bandwidth.

Finally, some e-mail writers like to append signatures to their messages. Created with the same character set as smileys, these semi-graphics add something of the character of a hand-written name to the end of a letter or newsgroup posting.

Understanding Netnews/Usenet

Usenet is a network of people and machines that propagate Netnews. Some Internet machines use Usenet, and some do not. Similarly, some Usenet systems are not part of the Internet. Usenet works on networks other than the Internet, for instance, the educational and professional network called Bitnet. Usenet is a happy overlap of content-network news and protocols. TCP/IP now includes the *Network News Transfer Protocol* (NNTP).

Netnews transmits discussions about three-dimensional imaging, movies from Hong Kong, Taiwan and China, pornographic photographs, and chinchilla farming. And that's just newsgroups that start with the letter "a." Netnews is opinion, facts, and rumors, all floating through cyberspace like clouds. Sometimes the range of subject matter in Netnews is so wide that it is hard to remember that most participants in news groups share a common interest—ready access to discussion of topics that are important to them.

You read and write messages to news groups with programs like rn and tin.

Using rn

The very fist time you use rn or any newsreader, the database file .newsrc is initialized for you. The .newsrc file is a resource configuration file that lists, in plain ASCII text, your newsgroups and which messages from the newsgroup you have already read, if any. (Of course, the first time you start reading news, you won't have read any messages.) A default set of newsgroups will be entered, and you can begin reading them.

```
(crl) rn
Trying to set up a .newsrc file--running newsetup...
Creating .newsrc in /user/mbd to be used by news programs.
Done.
```

If you have never used the news system before, you may find the articles in news.announce.newusers to be helpful. A manual entry for rn is also available.

To get rid of newsgroups you aren't interested in, use the u command.

```
Type h for help at any time while running rn.
(Revising soft pointers--be patient.)
Unread news in campus.bulletins                              2 articles
Unread news in campus.buy+sell                              18 articles
Unread news in campus.cs                                     1 article
Unread news in campus.cs.grads                               2 articles
Unread news in campus.grads                                  2 articles
etc.
********   2 unread articles in campus.bulletins--read now? [ynq]
```

When you read an article, the .newsrc file is updated to reflect this. For example, you might have just started rn for the first time. A new .newsrc file has been created for you. You can look at this file with any text viewing program such as more or head, as is shown in the following example:

```
 (crl) more .newsrc
to: 1-270
campus.bad-attitude: 1-9
campus.bulletins: 1-71
```

After you read an article, the database changes. For example, you might see the following:

```
to: 1-270
campus.bad-attitude: 1-9
campus.bulletins: 1-72
```

```
Note that the last message read in the newsgroup
***campus.bulletins*** is now 72.
```

Every time you type in the command rn, there is a pause. The more newsgroups you subscribe to, the longer the pause because rn is reading the .newsrc file.

First, you see a list of unread messages and a prompt line, which asks if you want to begin reading your news.

```
(crl) rn
Unread news in misc.kids                                25
articles
Unread news in sdnet.jobs                                7
articles
Unread news in misc.jobs.offered                       285
articles
Unread news in misc.jobs.contract                      178
articles
Unread news in alt.support.big-folks                     5
articles
etc.
********  25 unread articles in misc.kids—read now? [ynq]
```

Typing **q** quits without any changes being made in your newsgroups database file. Note that what you type in response to these prompt lines does not echo on your screen. Whatever action you specify simply happens.

Responding y shows the first unread article in the group.

```
Article 72 (1 more) in campus.bulletins (moderated):
From: Jan Malden
Subject: (none)
Date: 23 Aug 1994 18:40:23 -0700
Organization: campusgw
Lines: 2
NNTP-Posting-Host: network.campus.edu
jobs
Another test from malden
(Mail) End of article 72 (of 73)—what next? [npq]
```

It is important to note two things about the .newsrc file. First, it grows larger as you add more newsgroups to your list because there will be one new line added for every added newsgroup. Second, it is a single file and should not be subjected to the strain of being used by two programs at once. Only have a single instance of a newsreader at any one time.

The Culture of Netnews

Like any community, even one with such widely varying interests as Usenet, certain standards of behavior evolve by mutual practice and come to be, if not enforced, at least expected. Some groups answer the question of how participants will interact by moderating their newsgroup. A few people read all submissions to the group and decide what will be put in it. Still, many groups are free-for-alls.

As Chuq von Rospach says in *A Primer on How to Work With the USENET Community,* "It is the people on these computers that make USENET worth the effort to read and maintain, and for USENET to function properly those people must be able to interact in productive ways." Here, then, is a modest guide to newsgroup etiquette.

Do participate in your newsgroup when you are pretty certain many other people in the group want to know what you have to say. If you have some thoughts that would be most appreciated by one or two individuals in the group, why not just e-mail them directly?

In most newsgroups, the unmoderated ones anyway, there are the good, the bad, and the rest of us. A large number of newsgroup readers simply *lurk,* Net jargon for "silently watch," rarely, if ever, posting messages of their own. For example, in groups such as misc.jobs that describe job opportunities, most postings are from job providers, not job seekers.

Many newsgroups have questions that are asked every time a new member joins. Most groups have produced a *FAQ,* a list of frequently asked (and answered) questions. These are usually produced as a public service by some long-time participant for whom the pain of maintaining the FAQ is just slightly less than seeing a question about what :-) means. (You already know of course that this is a *smiley,* a sideways collection of keyboard characters organized into a little drawing.) It is always proper to ask for a group's FAQ if you don't see it posted.

Besides civility, another important quality to preserve is bandwidth. The Net, though it may seem to have almost limitless resources, can definitely get clogged up at times. So keep your postings to the point.

Newsgroups are all people talking to people (well, almost all—there are definitely some "robots" out there). Though there is little face-to-face communication, participants on the Net offer ideas and emotions that they care about.

Maximizing telnet Usage

telnet is both a program and a protocol. telnet (the program) uses telnet (the protocol) to provide an interface to remote logins to other machines on the network. A telnet session provides a "virtual" character-based terminal in which the user can type commands and other text and also see the output from processes on the remote machine.

telnet sends all the characters from your side of the connection to the machine on the other side. (By the way, X Window is the way to connect a graphical user interface to remote machines.)

Using telnet, you can login to other machines on the network on which you have an account. For instance, you might have lots of files on another machine. Rather than copying them all over to the machine to which you are currently attached, it might be simpler to switch to the other machine and work on them there. Or take another example: To win a bet, you need to know the billion-and-first digit after the decimal point in the value of pi. But you were planning a night-long session of playing hack on your machine. You know your algorithm for calculating the value of pi will slow your local machine to a crawl. Problem? Not with telnet! Just telnet over to another machine, start your calculations, and exit. While the users on the other machine will be lucky to get a prompt in response to pressing Enter, you'll be duking it out with character-based monsters galore. Take that, fiendish uppercase L!

The basic virtual terminal has a minimal set of features and can conveniently be thought of as a dumb terminal. It reads input from the user's keyboard and displays output on the user's screen. Usually the display shows or "echoes" what is being typed. It can show the 7-bit *ASCII* (American Standard Code for Information Interchange) character set, which includes the English alphabet, punctuation marks, and some control characters. Everything you type is stored locally in a buffer, and then after you enter the * (then press Enter), everything is sent to the remote machine. Some control codes may not be supported on your local machine, even though they are in the 7-bit ASCII character set. Table 30.3 shows some control codes that may produce no effect on your local terminal.

Table 30.3
Some Optionally Supported ASCII Control Codes in telnet

Name	Number	Description
BELL (BEL)	7	Produces an audible or visible signal without showing on the screen.
Back Space (BS)	8	Moves the screen cursor one character position toward the left margin.
Horizontal Tab (HT)	9	Moves the screen cursor to the next horizontal tab stop.

The protocol allows many extensions and options to this basic terminal. For example, you can try to use the 8-bit ASCII character set, which includes many characters used in European languages. Of course, the remote machine to which you connect must be able to interpret characters from that set. You can also specify how the telnet session will interpret such keyboard characters as those you use to backspace over a character, kill a whole line, or send a break to kill the process you started with a command line.

In the simplest case, you use telnet to connect to another machine. To initiate a telnet session with an imaginary machine named oxygen.aco.com, type the following:

```
% telnet oxygen.aco.com
```

Next, you should see the following list:

```
Trying...
Connected to oxygen.aco.com.
Escape character is '^]'.


SunOS UNIX (oxygen)
login:
```

Enter your login and password, and that's all there is to it. You are connected and can begin typing commands as if you were on a terminal physically connected to the remote machine.

There is an equivalent sequence of commands you can use. Type just the following:

```
% telnet
```

You see the telnet prompt:

```
telnet>
```

You can type the telnet program command open followed by the name of the remote machine. Type, for example, the following:

```
telnet> open oxygen.aco.com
```

The connection is made, and you see the login prompt from the remote machine.

```
Trying...
Connected to oxygen.aco.com.
Escape character is '^]'.


SunOS UNIX (oxygen)
login:
```

Getting Help within telnet

If you prefer to use telnet from its prompt, it is easy to get a quick reminder of various commands. Type either:

```
telnet> help
```

or

```
telnet> ?
```

You see the following:

```
Commands may be abbreviated. Commands are:
close      close current connection
display    display operating parameters
mode       try to enter line-by-line or character-at-a-time mode
open       connect to a site
quit       exit telnet
send       transmit special characters ('send ?' for more)
set        set operating parameters ('set ?' for more)
status     print status information
toggle     toggle operating parameters ('toggle ?' for more)
z          suspend telnet
!          shell escape
?          print help information
```

Many of these commands are adequately explained in the table, but a few call for some additional comment. The send command can be used to send special characters or character sequences through to the remote machine. The toggle command turns various attributes on or off. Together, these attributes determine how telnet will respond to certain events or character sequences such as those representing flush, interrupt, quit, erase, and kill.

telnet Variables

After you telnet over to a remote machine, you may need to temporarily interrupt the transmission of characters. But how? Remember, everything you type is being sent by telnet to the other machine. Even typing Ctrl+Z, the signal that would stop a process on your local machine, is simply relayed over. To get the attention of telnet, type the escape character; by default, this is specified to be Ctrl+]. You can specify any key combination you like as the escape character for telnet. From the telnet prompt, set the value of the telnet variable *escape* by typing the following:

```
telnet> set escape ^[
```

By typing Ctrl+], you force telnet to stop sending characters to the remote machine. Instead, it must attempt to process them. In general, you can set the values of telnet variables with a command using the following form:

```
telnet> set variable value
```

There are several telnet variables, as described in table 30.4.

Table 30.4
telnet Variables

Name	Use
echo	Specifies whether or not what you type will appear on your screen. (This is set to a value of "off" when the remote system prompts for your password.)
escape	Specifies the escape character, which halts the flow of characters to the remote machine and forces them to be interpreted by the telnet process running on your local machine.
interrupt	Specifies the Interrupt Process character, which interrupts the user process currently running on the remote machine.
quit	Specifies the character to be used to indicate that the Break or Attention key on the user's keyboard has been entered.
flushoutput	Specifies the character to be used to signify an abort output function on the remote machine.
eof	Specifies the character to be used to send an eof to the remote machine.

You can see the value of telnet variables in your current session by typing the following:

```
telnet> display
```

The preceding command produces something like the following:

```
will flush output when sending interrupt characters
won't send interrupt characters in urgent mode
won't map carriage return on output
won't recognize certain control characters
won't turn on socket level debugging
won't print hexadecimal representation of network traffic
won't show option processing
```

And the following table lists other shortcuts that can be employed to perform other basic tasks:

Shortcut	Command
Ctrl+E	echo
Ctrl+]	escape
Ctrl+?	eras
Ctrl+O	flushoutput
Ctrl+C	interrupt
Ctrl+U	kill
Ctrl+\	quit
Ctrl+D	eof

Sending Special Character Sequences to the Remote Machine through telnet

You can use the send command from within telnet to send certain character sequences to the machine on the other end of your connection. Use the following syntax to do this:

```
telnet> send sequence
```

The variable *sequence* is one or more of the options listed in table 30.5.

Table 30.5
Character Sequences That Can be Sent with the send Command

Name	Use
?	Displays help about the send command.
escape	Sends the escape character (without forcing telnet to stop sending characters).
ip	Sends the telnet protocol IP sequence. (The remote system should abort the process it is currently running for you. Remember that you can specify what is sent by using the set variable command.)
ec	Sends the telnet protocol EC sequence. (The remote system should erase the last character you typed.)

continues

Table 30.5, Continued
Character Sequences That Can be Sent with the send Command

Name	Use
el	Sends the telnet protocol EL sequence. (The remote system should erase the line you are currently typing.)
ao	Sends the telnet protocol AO sequence. (The remote system should flush all output to your terminal.)
brk	Sends the telnet protocol BRK sequence. (The remote system must provide the response.)
ayt	Sends the telnet protocol *AYT* (Are You There) sequence. (The remote system must provide the response.)

Possible Errors

After you have telnet set up so it sends the right characters according to your keyboard preferences, the only likely error will be if telnet cannot connect to the machine you name. You will see an error message like the following:

```
Host unknown
```

The problem here is not with telnet, but with the name you used. Use ping with the machine name to which you are trying to connect. If it is not accessible to ping, then you must have the name and associated address added to your machine's table of hosts.

You do not need to be physically near a system to have a terminal-type connection to it. All you need are a valid IP address and telnet. By providing virtual terminals that can open onto any machine on which you have a login, you can work with data or computational resources anywhere on the Internet.

Employing ftp

ftp is both a program and a protocol. ftp (the program) uses ftp (the protocol) to provide file copying to and from other machines on the network. Note that these other machines are not limited to workstations running UNIX; they can be anything from mainframes to small personal computers, running operating systems from VMS to Macintosh and DOS. One of the virtues of ftp is that it provides a common interface to many different file storage methods and directory structures. ftp (as with all of the Internet protocols) can run over many different kinds of connections. It works over serial (dial-in) lines, Ethernet,

Token Ring, and other connections. However, it is worth noting that ftp does not itself perform any data compression. (Of course, it can copy compressed files.) It also has no "smart restart" features that allow it to pick up where it left off in the event of an interruption to its flow of data.

ftp's many capabilities can be grouped into the following five areas:

✔ **Operation.** How to begin and end ftp sessions, see status, see on-line help, and create macros. Any ftp commands can be entered either at the command interpreter prompt (`ftp>`) or from a command line. This flexibility makes it easy for machine processes, as well as human users, to use ftp.

✔ **Remote accounts.** Accessing your remote accounts. You can use ftp with any account for which you have a password. This does not mean that you must have your own individual account on every machine to which you connect through ftp. "Anonymous ftp" is available on many file archives on the Net. By using the user name "anonymous" and a password (usually your user ID in the form user@machine_name.domain), you can ftp the files placed in the public access directories. For example, the machine nic.merit.edu has a set of public access directories in /document that hold IPs, Requests for Comment, Standards, For Your Information documents, and more.

✔ **Types.** File types. ftp can copy both ASCII (or plain text) files and binary files, that is, any files that have some internal structure of their own such as a spreadsheet, formatted document, or executable program. Binary files are transferred as *images*—a stream of bytes without any modification or interpretation of any kind.

✔ **Names.** File names. You can use regular file names when performing operations on files. ftp also supports *globbing*, "UNIXese" for the use of wild-card characters, single characters that can be used as abbreviations in file names. For example, file?.txt can stand for filea.txt, filer.txt, filez.txt, or file6.txt. Globbing in ftp can be turned on or off.

✔ **Files.** File and directory navigation and management. Once ftp connects to a remote machine and account, you can navigate in the directory structure, make directories, list files, put (send) and get (receive) files, and delete and rename files. There are also versions of commands such as mget and mput that work on multiple files.

Using ftp

Imagine that you receive e-mail from a colleague from whom you have not heard in weeks. She tells you what a great time she had on a faraway island from which she has just returned. But in case you want to know more, she informs you that there is a document called a FAQ, a list of answers to frequently asked questions. The FAQ is available through

The Internet and Communications

anonymous ftp; she gives you the name of the machine and the directory and file name. Perversely, you decide you wish to know more about this island paradise, knowing full well that it would be years before you could get any more vacation time or could possibly save enough money to go. To login to the remote machine and get the FAQ file, type the following:

```
% ftp vacations.bigbux.com
```

If the name vacation.bigbux.com is in your machine's database of known names, you are connected, and you see the following information:

```
% ftp vacations.bigbux.com
Connected to vacations.bigbux.com.
220 vacations.bigbux.com FTP server (Version 4.81 Mon Feb 18
14:33:38 PDT 1994) ready.
Name (vacations.bigbux.com:your_userID): anonymous
331 Guest login ok, send your email address as password.
```

A few comments are in order here. ftp always attempts to login under a name unless you start it up with the -n option). In this example, it will send the name your_userID by default unless you enter something different at the Name prompt. Enter **anonymous**. In response, you see that the remote ftp server will accept that name if you send your user ID and machine name as the password. This should be entered in the form userID@machine.domain, as depicted in the following example:

```
Password:
230- Guest login ok, access restrictions apply.
230- Local time is: Mon Mar 17 17:26:14 1993
230
ftp>
```

Now you can enter the command to list the files in the current working directory, the one you logged in to. Type the following:

```
ftp> ls -F
```

Use the -F option to ls so that directories will be listed with a / after them. You see a list of files in between some other information:

```
ftp> ls -F
200 PORT command successful.
150 Opening ASCII mode data connection for file list.
golf/
islands/
jungles/
tennis/
226 Transfer complete.
57 bytes received in 0.01 seconds (5.6 Kbytes/s)
ftp>
```

The lines about PORT and Opening ASCII and so on are information from ftp. If you don't want to see them and their ilk, enter the following command:

```
ftp> verbose
```

You change directories to islands with the next command:

```
ftp> cd islands
```

If you are curious about what directory you are in, you can type the following:

```
ftp> pwd
257 "/v/public/travel/islands" is current directory.
ftp>
```

Once again, you list the files in the current directory by typing the following:

```
ftp> ls -F
200 PORT command successful.
150 Opening ASCII mode data connection for file list.
beautiful
dismal
impressions/
ok
226 Transfer complete.
32 bytes received in 0.01 seconds (5.6 Kbytes/s)
ftp>
```

The file beautiful is presumably the one you are looking for. To get your own copy of this file, type the following:

```
ftp> get beautiful
```

If you use wild-card file-name expansion, you can just type the following abbreviated version:

```
ftp> beau*
```

Or type enough of the file name to distinguish it from any others in the same directory.

There is another directory listed in our example, impressions. Curious, you change directories to it and, after typing an ls command, find files with names like the following:

```
10on11.28.89

5on3.12.88

7on4.3.90
```

With a little ingenuity, you surmise that perhaps these are files containing impressions that various people have had of the islands listed in the parent directory, with a rating from 1 to 10, followed by the date of their vacation. You decide to add a file of your own impressions. You press Ctrl+Z to temporarily disconnect your terminal from ftp. Opening up a new file with your word processor, you churlishly jot down your impressions of expensive island vacations. After saving the file under the name 0forever, you type fg or the job number to reattach your terminal.

Then, to upload your file, you type the following:

```
ftp> put 0forever
```

You see the following feedback from ftp:

```
ftp> put 0forever
200 PORT command successful.
150 Opening ASCII mode data connection for 0forever.
226 Transfer complete.
local: 0forever remote: 0forever
30 bytes sent in 0.01 seconds (2.9 Kbytes/s)
ftp>
```

You disconnect from the remote machine by typing the following:

```
ftp> quit
```

ftp responds with the following output:

```
221 Goodbye
```

You see your command shell prompt.

Using ftp—Operations

ftp can connect to any host on the Net for which you have a name or IP address. You can get online help at the ftp command prompt ftp>. You can also set *toggles*, variables that are either on or off, to specify what information about its operations ftp will display on your screen (see table 30.6).

Table 30.6
ftp Operations/Connections

Name	Use
open name	Opens a connection using the FTP protocol to the machine specified by name. (ftp defaults to starting the login process on the remote machine. If you do not want this behavior, use the -n option on the command line.)
close	Close the current connection but keep ftp operating.
bye	Close the current connection and terminate ftp.

The machine name for the open command must be of the form machine.domain. Use close when you want to end the connection to a particular machine and start another one with all of your macros still in effect. Table 30.7 shows the ftp operations and the type of help given.

Table 30.7
ftp Operations/Getting help

Name	Use
help, ?	Shows a list of all commands for which on-line information is available.
help command	Shows a short line of information about the named command.

help shows terse descriptions. For example, the following:

```
ftp> help
```

yields this:

```
ftp> help help
help    print local help information
```

The remotehelp command shows you what the remote machine's idea of help is. Table 30.8 shows ftp operations and the returned on-screen information:

A sample response to the status command might look like this:

```
ftp> status
Connected to vacations.bigbux.com.
No proxy connection.
Mode: stream; Type: ascii; Form: non-print; Structure: file
```

```
Verbose: on; Bell: off; Prompting: on; Globbing: on
Store unique: off; Receive unique: off
Case: off; CR stripping: on
Ntrans: off
Nmap: off
Hash mark printing: off; Use of PORT cmds: on
ftp>
```

Table 30.8
ftp Operations/On-Screen Information

Name	Use
status	Shows current settings.
prompt	Switches on or off prompting during operations on more than one file. (Multiple files are specified by using the following wild-card globbing characters: ? for any single character, * for any string of characters. This can be annoying when copying files with mput or mget but reassuring when deleting files with mdelete.)
verbose	Switches on or off verbose mode. (Use this toggle to see file transfer efficiency statistics and also the replies from the remote ftp process. Replies usually show a completion or error code and a text string.)

To abort a file copy in mid-stream, press Ctrl+C. This makes your ftp send the ABOR command, which is defined in the ftp protocol. The file copy interruption might take a while to happen, depending how attentive the remote machine is to your instructions. If the remote ftp *hangs*, that is, does nothing in response to your commands, however patiently you wait, then just kill the local ftp process.

Using ftp—Remote Accounts

After ftp establishes a connection, you need a valid account name and password to begin file transfers. Table 30.9 shows the ftp Remote Accounts.

Table 30.9
ftp Remote Accounts

Name	Use
user name	Provides a user name to ftp on the remote machine. (You are prompted for this name after connecting to the remote machine unless you start your local ftp with the -n option. After you send the name, you are prompted for a password, which will not echo on your screen as you type it.)

Anonymous ftp

Use the user name anonymous when prompted for a user name. You might see instruction about what to type for your password. If not, try your e-mail address in the form userID@machine.domain.

Using ftp—File Types

ftp can copy ASCII text files and binary files. Binary files are copied literally, without ftp adding or subtracting anything from the stream of bits between local and remote machines. To see the different ftp file types, refer to table 30.10.

Table 30.10
ftp File Types

Name	Use
ASCII	Transmits files as 7-bit ASCII. (Lines end with a combination of two characters: Linefeed and Carriage Return.)
cr	Switches on or off the removal of the Carriage Return character. (UNIX uses Linefeed to delimit lines.)
binary	Transmits files as literal images without altering their internal format (if they have one).
type	Shows the current file type.
type name	Sets the type for file transmission to name, which can be either ASCII or binary.

When copying text files that will ultimately end up on a DOS system, you should switch Carriage Return removal off—use cr because DOS uses both Carriage Return and Linefeed to delimit a line. UNIX uses only a Linefeed. Vive la différence.

The binary or image type should be used for everything else. This ensures that however the bytes are lined up in the orginal, they will stay that way in your copy.

Using ftp—File Names

ftp refers to files by name. For convenience, ftp allows the use of wildcard characters to substitute for parts of file names that you do not need to write out in full. Refer to table 30.11 for a listing of ftp file names.

VII

The Internet and Communications

Table 30.11
ftp File Names

Name	Use
glob	Switches on or off filename expansion.
case	Switches on or off the translation of file names that are in all upper-case to all lowercase when using the mget command.
runique	Switches on or off the adding of digits to the end of file names for files being received to ensure that they are unique. (Starts with .1 and goes up to .99.)
sunique	Switches on or off the adding of digits to the end of file names for files being sent to ensure that they are unique. (Starts with .1 and goes up to .99.)

Use runique and sunique to ensure that you do not overwrite a file on either the local or remote machine that already has a name identical to one you propose to use.

Using ftp—File and Directory Navigation and Management

Using ftp you can move within a directory structure, display the names of files within directories on the remote machine, add and delete files, rename them and, of course, copy files back and forth. Table 30.12 shows the methods of navigating in ftp files and directories.

Table 30.12
ftp Files and Directories: Navigation

Name	Use
cd name	Changes the current working directory on the remote machine to name. (On some implementations of ftp, you will be able to add arguments to cd such as ~ for the login directory and .. for the parent directory.)
cdup	Changes the current working directory on the remote machine to the parent directory.
pwd	Prints the working directory of the remote machine.
lcd name	Changes the current working directory on the local machine to name.

Name	Use
ls	Lists files in the current working directory on the remote machine. (Some implementations may accept ls options such as -l and -F.)
dir	Lists files in the current working directory on the remote machine.
dir name	Lists files in the directory name on the remote machine.
rename	Renames the file on the remote machine named "from" to "name to."

You do not know whether or not the remote machine's implementation of ftp will allow options such as ls -F or cd ~ until you try them. No harm is done if the remote machine does not respond to unknown options; it simply ignores them. The management of ftp files and directories is expounded upon in table 30.13.

Table 30.13
ftp Files and Directories: Management

Name	Use
put local-file remote-file	Copies local-file to the remote machine and gives it the name remote-file. (If you don't specify remote-file, it just uses the name local file.)
mput name	Copies all files specified by name, which may include wild-card characters, to the remote machine under the same names.
get remote-file local-file	Copies remote-file from the remote machine and gives it the name local-file. (If you don't specify local-file, it just uses the name remote-file.)
mget name	Copies all files specified by name, which may include wild-card characters, on the remote machine to the local machine under the same names.
delete remote-file	Deletes the file named remote-file on the remote machine.

continues

VII

The Internet and Communications

Table 30.13, Continued
ftp Files and Directories: Management

Name	Use
`mdelete name`	Deletes all files specified by name, which may include wild-card characters, on the remote machine.
`append local-file remote-file`	Adds the contents of local-file on local machine to the end of remote-file on the remote machine.
`mkdir dir-name`	Makes a directory named dir-name on the remote machine.
`rmdir dir-name`	Removes the directory named dir-name on the remote machine.

ftp copies files back and forth, to and from machines anywhere on the Internet and beyond. There are ftp programs that run on machines using many different architectures and operating systems. The fact that ftp works more or less the same for all machines makes it a very useful tool.

Mastering archie

archie is a database search server. The archie database lists files that are available through anonymous ftp from machines on the Internet. You give archie search instructions—text strings or regular expressions that can be expanded to text strings. These strings should be keywords from your topic of interest.

archie Servers

The list of archie servers in table 30.14 is current as of 1994:

Table 30.14
archie Servers

machine name	IP address	location
archie.au	139.130.4.6	Australia
archie.edvz.uni-linz.ac.at	140.78.3.8	Austria
archie.univie.ac.at	131.130.1.23	Austria

machine name	IP address	location
archie.uqam.ca	132.208.250.10	Canada
archie.funet.fi	128.214.6.102	Finland
archie.univ-rennes1.fr	129.20.128.38	France
archie.th-darmstadt.de	130.83.128.118	Germany
archie.ac.il	132.65.16.18	Israel
archie.unipi.it	131.114.21.10	Italy
archie.wide.ad.jp	133.4.3.6	Japan
archie.hama.nm.kr	128.134.1.1	Korea
archie.sogang.ac.kr	163.239.1.11	Korea
archie.uninett.no	128.39.2.20	Norway
archie.rediris.es	130.206.1.2	Spain
archie.luth.se	130.240.12.30	Sweden
archie.switch.ch	130.59.1.40	Switzerland
archie.nctuccca.edu.tw		Taiwan
archie.ncu.edu.tw	192.83.166.12	Taiwan
archie.doc.ic.ac.uk	146.169.11.3	United Kingdom
archie.hensa.ac.uk	129.12.21.25	United Kingdom
archie.unl.edu	129.93.1.14	USA (NE)
archie.internic.net	198.49.45.10	USA (NJ)
archie.rutgers.edu	128.6.18.15	USA (NJ)
archie.ans.net	147.225.1.10	USA (NY)
archie.sura.net	128.167.254.179	USA (MD)

Connecting to archie

You can connect to archie through telnet and conduct sessions interactively. You can e-mail instructions to archie and have any results e-mailed back to you. Also, archie client programs exist that enable direct interactive connections to archie servers.

The telnet interface enables you to type commands at the archie prompt, which looks like `archie>`, and see the results. Connect by typing the following command:

```
% telnet archie_server
```

In the preceding command, `archie_server` is a machine listed in the table. When you are prompted for a user name, type **archie**. No password is required. You can then enter commands at the prompt. Typing **help** will get you started.

To use the e-mail interface, you mail instructions to the address:

```
archie@archie_server
```

In the preceding example, *archie_server* is a machine listed in the table. To get a list of servers, type the word **server** as the body of the message. To get help, type **help** as the body of the message.

Specialized archie clients are available and free. You can ftp source code for them from the servers listed in the table. The code is in the archie/clients of pub/archie/clients directories. Character-based and graphical versions are available.

Finding Files with archie

To find a file when connected to archie through telnet, type the following:

```
archie> find string
```

In the preceding example, the variable `string` is a string of alphanumeric characters that you are interested in. The string can be a regular expression as described in the UNIX ed command. Regular expressions can include pattern matching and wild-card expansion. For example, type the following:

```
archie> find philately
```

You then see the following result:

```
archie> find philately

        # Search type: sub.
        # Your queue position: 2
        # Estimated time for completion: 33 seconds.
        working... 0
        # No matches were found.
```

The following instruction yields about 40 files:

```
archie> find oxygen
```

Here are the first three of about 40 files produced by the preceding command:

```
# Search type: sub.
# Your queue position: 1
# Estimated time for completion: 1 minute, 28 seconds.
working... 0
Host ftp.iro.umontreal.ca    (132.204.32.22)
Last updated 05:12  6 Sep 1994
    Location: /lude-iro/lynx
2.0.11/run/iro/sun4.1_sparc/samples/elements
FILE    -rw-r--r--     185 bytes  20:00 13 Jul 1993  Oxygen
    Location: /lude-iro/lynx-2.0.11/src/iro/samples/elements
FILE    -rw-r--r--     169 bytes  20:00 13 Jul 1993  Oxygen.Z
    Location: /lude-iro/lynx-2.0.11/src/iro_sol/samples/elements
FILE    -rw-r--r--     169 bytes  20:00 13 Jul 1993  Oxygen.Z
```

Notice that the list of code includes sufficient information for you to access the files using ftp. You cannot view them or download them directly using archie.

How Many Files Does archie Know About?

At press time, the archie database lists more than 2 million files at more than 900 anonymous ftp sites on the Internet.

Getting Information about archie

You can get information about topics within archie using the help command. To see the status of all the variables that you can set within a session, type the following:

```
archie> show
```

There is much more. You can get started by addressing an e-mail message to the following:

```
mail archie@archie_server
```

Type the word **manpage** in the body of the letter and send it off. You should receive your reply within a day or two.

archie searches within its huge database of Internet-accessible files to find matches to keywords you type. If any of the found files look interesting, you can copy them using ftp, or use ftp-by-mail service to send them to you through e-mail.

VIII

The Internet and Communications

Comprehending gopher

gopher displays documents, retrieves files, looks up items in databases, plays sounds, shows pictures, runs other gophers—it sings! it dances! It is a very flexible information access tool that uses TCP/IP to create what users call *gopherspace*, the sum of all the documents that gopher can use. gopher has both client and server parts. The clients attach to the servers and request documents. You control what the client "points at" with simple nested menus.

Using gopher

When you use gopher, you see a sequence of menus and sub-menus. You select a menu item using whatever capabilities your gopher access machine (and you thought it was just a computer!) enables. Character-based terminals can select by typing the number of an item and pressing Enter. Graphical user interfaces enable point-and-click access. You start a gopher by typing the following:

```
% gopher
```

You see the beginning menu screen that looks something like this:

```
           Internet Gopher Information Client v1.12S
                CIS: Campus Information Service
    —>   1.   About CIS/
         2.   What's New (February 7, 1994).
         3.   Campus Information/
         4.   The World/


    Press ? for Help, q to Quit, u to go up a menu      Page: 1/1
```

Notice the arrow pointing at menu item 1. You can select another menu item by typing a new number or using the Up or Down arrows. After making your new selection, press Enter. gopher shows you your choice. For example, if you select 1, you see the next screen for the item About CIS. You can tell that About CIS will offer further choices because there is a / after it.

Next you see the following:

```
           Internet Gopher Information Client v1.12S
                            About CIS
    —>   1.   What is CIS.
         2.   How to Access CIS.
         3.   General Internet Access Topics/
         4.   What's New with CIS.
         5.   Send suggestions or comments <TEL>
```

```
        Press ? for Help, q to Quit, u to go up a menu        Page: 1/1
```

Now if you select 5, Send suggestions..., you go to an interactive dialog box in which gopher prompts you to type answers to questions.

```
              Internet Gopher Information Client v1.12S
                   Comments or Suggestions about CIS
        Please enter your remarks here. When you are finished, enter 2
        blank lines to send your message to the CIS staff. Thanks!
```

gopher is actually using the mail program to enable you to enter text and then to send it off to someone who will read it. It does not replicate the functionality already available in the mail program. It uses the other program in the context of a menu-driven interaction guided by you.

Adding to gopherspace

gopher conceals many details of file format, type of machine and operating system, and so on from the user. This enables users to focus on the way their particular user interface works and the information they want, not on the mechanics of access and manipulation. Furthermore, it is quite straightforward to add your own documents to gopherspace. Client versions of gopher are available for the following platforms:

UNIX curses and EMACS

X Windows (athena, Tk, Xview)

Macintosh Hypercard

Macintosh

DOS w/Clarkson Driver

NeXTstep

VM/CMS

VMS

OS/2 2.0

MVS/XA

Microsoft Windows

Server versions are available for the following:

UNIX

VMS

VM/CMS

MVS

Macintosh

DOS PC

OS/2

Specifying Helper Programs for gopher

You can set environment variables to instruct gopher to use particular programs for particular purposes.

Variable	Function
GOPHER_MAIL	Sends mail with this program.
GOPHER_TELNET	Provides telnet services with this program.
GOPHER_PLAY	Plays sound with this program.
GOPHER_PRINTER	Prints with this program.

gopher uses a client/server relationship and the IPs to make a wide array of information and types of data available to users on many different types of machines.

Using the World Wide Web

The *World Wide Web* (or WWW or W3) is considered either a hyperlink, multimedia client/server information access system or the universe of network-accessible information, that is, an embodiment of human knowledge. Though the first definition may seem prosaic, realize that WWW uses TCP/IP and other pieces of technology that are more than 20 years old. If the second definition seems outlandish, remember that the Internet is the largest computer network ever and that you can now use it to transfer music, video, text, executable programs, and real-time data feeds.

The Web consists of resources that have addresses. *Browsers*—programs that can look at a resource and use it—run on systems from character-based terminals to point-and-click graphical user interfaces. A *Uniform Resource Locator* (URL) describes how to find a resource. Resources range from files to commands to access news groups, copy files, play sounds, show pictures, and so on. A Web page, written in a plain ASCII language called *hypertext markup language* (html) links resources. Web server software, also available for many different platforms, handles requests for the resources it knows about.

Using the Mosaic Browser

The Mosaic client displays a screen image on a graphical terminal. Words and pictures contain links to other resources. By default, Mosaic starts up connected to a home page on a machine at the *Center for High-Energy Physics* (CERN), the home of the WWW, in Switzerland.

When you start Mosaic, you see a large logo-like graphic and text occupy most of the page. Some text is underlined. This represents the presence of a link. If you click on the underlined text, you summon up whatever the original author of the document thought you should see. This could be more text, making the link like a footnote, or it could be more elaborate like an entirely different Web page. In the bar above the page, you see several icons and fields that contain text. For example, immediately to the left of the globe are two arrows and a stylized picture of a house. These buttons take you back and forth on the trail of links that you traverse in the current Mosaic session. To the left of these is a small window that shows the text NCSA Home Page. The *National Center for Supercomputing Applications* (NCSA) maintains its home page at the Uniform Resource Locator (*URL*) shown as `http://www.ncsa.uiuc.edu...` and so on. The pointing finger cursor hovers over the link to this URL; it is where you will go if you click the finger down on the link. (By the way, the window next to the button labeled Search is not active now because there is nothing to search. The globe in the upper left corner rotates when Mosaic loads images, text, or other resources over the network.

If you ever tire of waiting for it to load a massive color image, just click on it to interrupt the loading process.

The program HyperCard on the Macintosh and the Help program on Microsoft Windows are examples of this kind of interface to resources. Those programs only work on their own platforms, of course, whereas Mosaic and WWW can work across many different ones anywhere on the Internet.

html Authoring

Users can author their own Web pages in hypertext markup language. An html document looks like the following:

```
<TITLE>My Local Home Page</TITLE>
<H1>My Local Home Page</H1>
```

```
This is a sample page. You may wish to edit this page to
customize it for your own use. This can be done by editing the
file with a word processor, making the desired changes and saving
the file as text only.
<H2>Your Own Stuff</H2>
......
<H2>Places to Surf</H2>
<UL>
<LI> <A
HREF="http://www.ncsa.uiuc.edu/General/NCSAHome.html">NCSA Home
Page</A>
```

html interleaves plain text with *tags* (the things between the < and the >). The tag <L1> introduces a hypertext link to the NCSA home Web page. Mosaic displays the text on the screen and performs whatever action is specified by the hyperlink. The NCSA home page has links to information about html and authoring so you can get to it right away if you want.

Though the World Wide Web does not magically configure all the information you have on your machine by itself, it does provide the tools for you to do it if you wish.

Summary

The Internet offers almost instantaneous globe-spanning electronic mail communication, archives of powerful free software, powerful online information access tools and data repositories, and something like 4,500 ongoing discussion newsgroups. This chapter introduced you to the Internet and some of its key features.

Chapter Snapshot

Electronic mail has become so ingrained in the business world today that it is difficult to imagine there was a time before it existed. The UNIX operating system was one of the first to include such a feature, and this chapter discusses the operations of it, with such topics as the following:

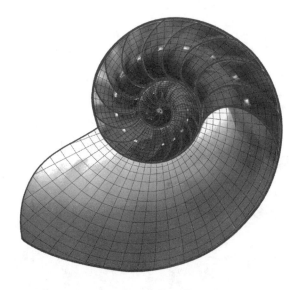

Mail

Electronic mail has become extremely popular and pervasive in the past few years as individuals, workgroups, and companies discover that quick, efficient communication leads to higher-quality work and increased productivity. Without electronic mail, a person who wants to leave a message with a colleague might write a note and leave it on his desk, or if it's important, on his chair, or, if it's really urgent, taped to his computer monitor. There's always a risk that the colleague, no matter how responsible, could lose or misplace the note. There's no way to maintain any accountability for the information actually being received by the intended recipient.

Introducing Mail

Electronic mail, popularly referred to as e-mail, goes beyond workgroup or corporate boundaries to span regions and countries, and provides a convenient means of communicating between individuals thousands of miles apart. Its popularity is tied to the simple but powerful idea that a message, if properly addressed, travels between non-similar computer systems, is handled by a number of unknown intermediary systems in any number of companies, cities or countries, and arrives intact and readable at the destination. Of course, the infrastructure in between the source and destination which consists of the systems, mail programs, and communication links must be maintained properly for this to work. In fact it does work, and quite reliably.

Local electronic mail, that which doesn't pass outside of a local area network, is useful in providing workgroup communication. In many companies or organizations, change is a way of life, deadlines are tight, and the primary hindrance to reaching a goal is not technology, but communication. E-mail is a central part in facilitating communication. Accountability for the communication is inherent in e-mail, as delivery time is stamped with each message. Mail products operating in a homogeneous operating system environment easily provide this capability. UNIX mail, Microsoft Mail, or Lotus cc:Mail, among others, are frequently used as local e-mail tools.

Internet electronic mail is e-mail that passes from a local system into the large, publicly and privately maintained network called the Internet. In the past, much of the mail traffic was generated on and received by UNIX systems, and today many of the systems that process and forward mail on the Internet continue to be UNIX systems. The recent popularity and attractiveness of the Internet in general, and Internet mail in particular, come from the capability to communicate widely and easily with anyone else on the Internet. This popularity is seen in the number of business cards, magazines, and even radio stations that publicly list and advertise their Internet e-mail addresses. UNIX mail in one form or another has been and will continue to be the de facto Internet mail standard.

Computer systems that communicate with each other to pass UNIX mail actually use a language or protocol called *Simple Mail Transport Protocol* (SMTP). As long as the systems "speak" SMTP, it doesn't matter whether the computers or operating systems are similar; the mail will be delivered. Communication between UNIX and non-UNIX mail systems that generally use non-SMTP protocols requires an e-mail gateway. The gateway system acts as a translator speaking both languages, communicating requests for mail between both systems and translating message formats and delivery commands into the appropriate format. E-mail gateways for SMTP mail exist for products such as Microsoft Mail, cc:Mail, or IBM Profs, and these gateways enable the non-UNIX mail systems to communicate on the Internet with UNIX systems.

Using Basic UNIX Mail

All current UNIX operating systems include some form of mail capability. This section describes the basic capabilities and features of UNIX mail. The UNIX System V version of the mail program, mailx, is detailed, and specific differences with the BSD-UNIX mail program, mail, are highlighted.

UNIX Mail Concepts

In order to properly use UNIX mail, some basic mail concepts need to be explained. UNIX mail is built on the concept of a mailbox, which is the repository for your mail messages. New messages addressed to you are put into your mailbox, and messages you delete or file are removed from the mailbox. Sending e-mail is the equivalent of placing the message in the recipient's mailbox.

Messages that you receive and want to keep for later reference are stored in mail files. These mail files are collections of messages that are organized by subject or sender. The directory in which a mail file resides is called a mail folder.

Unlike the Postal Service mail, UNIX mail has no certified mail that certifies that the mail was delivered on a specific date and received by a person whose identity is authenticated. There is no way to know positively that the receiver actually read the mail, because UNIX mail places mail in the receiver's mailbox; however, you can specify a return receipt showing that the message got to the intended mailbox.

There is generally no way to specify urgent or priority mail. Some mail-forwarding systems handling UNIX mail have a lower-priority delivery for bulk or mass e-mailed messages, but this is not universally implemented. Urgent messages must be tagged or highlighted with characters or words that stand out in the recipient's mailbox, somewhat analogous to using a brightly colored envelope to catch the person's attention.

Finally, the standard method for sorting mail in your mailbox or mail files is by the order in which the messages arrive. Other UNIX mail tools such as elm or graphically based mail tools typically have additional sorting and classifying capabilities.

Starting mail

To start mail, enter **mail** at your shell's command line. If you have mail in your mailbox, the mail headers will appear on the screen as in the following example:

VIII

The Internet and Communications

```
% mailx
mailx version 5.0 Mon Sep 27 07:25:51 PDT 1993  Type ? for help.
"/var/mail/steve": 56 messages 6 new 11 unread
 O 41 sun-managers-relay  Fri Aug 26 16:58    41/1869  DLT on Solaris 1.x or 2.x
 O 42 ron                 Fri Aug 26 17:08    17/435   my home phone number
 O 43 Steve Lee           Fri Aug 26 17:45    46/2318  Steve's schedule for next
 O 44 Steve Lee           Fri Aug 26 17:45 8341/515630 netdesign.doc.Z
 U 45 John Smith          Fri Aug 26 21:50    27/542   John's phone number
 O 46 R. Bruce            Mon Aug 29 10:57   173/9006  Hard error
 O 47 Steve Lee           Tue Aug 30 12:57   132/3627  fddi 2.0 performance issue
 O 48 HALLMARK            Tue Aug 30 14:26    69/2010  change of address
 O 49 Ken Lemieux         Tue Aug 30 17:26   127/3309  Re: filesystem layout
 O 50 Ken Lemieux         Tue Aug 30 17:26    45/1775  Re: PCMCIA for NEC Versa
>N 51 sun-managers-relay  Tue Aug 30 17:56    87/3345  SUMMARY: Workman Fix
 N 52 Joe Welfald         Tue Aug 30 19:26    42/1673  Converting audio files
 N 53 Leonardo Serres Pe  Tue Aug 30 20:26    45/2078  Problems when copy a file
 N 54 John Desimond       Tue Aug 30 20:26    41/1896  frame buffer problem?
 N 55 Matthew Stiple      Tue Aug 30 20:56    38/2062  unknown router problem
 N 56 Steve Lee           Tue Aug 30 21:52    22/492   New Address
{mail}&
```

mail displays the version and date of the mail program that you are running, and the name of the mail file you are reading, which in this example is your mailbox. mail then shows a summary of the total number of messages in your mailbox, and the number of new and unread messages. Below these two status lines is a tabular display of the message headers in your mailbox.

The first column indicates the status of the message. The message status is summarized in the following table:

Table 31.1
Mail Message Status Summary

Status	Meaning
N	New, unread message
O	Old message that has been read
R	New message that has been read
U	Unread message

The second column shows the message number. The messages are stored chronologically in your mailbox, with the oldest message set as message number 1. The number of messages that your mailbox can hold is limited only by your system's disk space.

The third column gives the sender's name as specified on his or her system. On BSD-UNIX systems, this column shows the sender's e-mail address. These addresses may take a number of different formats, as shown in the following table:

Table 31.2
Mail Address Formats

Entity	Sample Addresses
Local usernames	ron, martin, john
Internet addresses	slee@unixmail.com
UUCP addresses	denali!ken

The different mail addresses indicate who sent the mail and, to a certain degree, the method by which the message was delivered.

The next column shows the date and time that the message arrived in your mailbox, and the size of the message, both in number of lines as well as number of bytes. For example, the message number 47 from Steve Lee contains 132 lines and 3,627 bytes.

The final column shows a listing of the subject line of the mail message. If the sender of the message provided a descriptive title to his or her message, you can quickly scan the message subjects and determine which message you want to read first.

VIII

The Internet and Communications

You can improve the readability of your mail headers and the chance that the recipient will read the message by including a keyword at the start of the subject line. Words such as URGENT, PRIORITY, or SUMMARY at the beginning of your subject stand out when the recipient scans his or her headers, and make the message content more apparent.

At the end of the header display, the mail program shows the command prompt and waits for you to enter a command. The default prompt is the question mark character, but you may specify a custom prompt in your customization file discussed later in the chapter. In the previous example, the mail prompt is set to {Mail}&.

Reading Your Mail

To read a specific message shown from the mail header display, enter the message number at the command prompt. That message is displayed one page at a time for you to read, as in the following example:

```
{Mail}& 56
Message 56:
From steve Tue Aug 30 21:52:24 1994
Date: Tue, 30 Aug 94 21:52:24 PDT
From: steve (Steve Lee)
To: bob
Subject: New Address

The new address for the company is:

UnixMail, Inc.
1000 Corporate Drive
Seattle, WA  98101
206.555.5550 Voice
206.555.5551 FAX

steve.lee@unixmail.com

{Mail}&
```

Your mail program may be set to use one of a number of paging commands such as more or pg, so the specific key used to move to the next page may be different. The following table summarizes some basic pagination command differences:

Table 31.3
Pagination Command Differences

Pager	Prompt	Next Page	Next Line	Prev Page
more	—More—	Space	Enter	Not Available
pg :	Enter l	-		

When you have finished reading the message, you are returned to the command prompt. To again view the list of mail headers, enter **h**. If you want to read the next message in the mailbox, enter **n**. To redisplay the message you just read, enter the message number.

The displayed mail message consists of two parts, the message header and the body of the message. The message header contains information such as who sent the message, when the message was sent, who the recipient is, what the subject of the message is, and who, if anyone, is on the carbon copy (Cc:) list. Other message header information, such as what other mail systems handled the message as it was being delivered to you, or the original identification number on the sending system, may not be displayed by default. The following example shows a short message with a minimal mail header displayed:

```
Message 53:
From sun-managers-relay@ra.mcs.anl.gov Wed Aug 31 16:26:34 1994
Sender: sun-managers-relay@ra.mcs.anl.gov
Reply-To: c.carreno@bse.org
Followup-To: junk
X-Mailer: WordPerfect Office 4.0
To: SUN-MANAGERS@ra.mcs.anl.gov
Subject:  LISTSERVE

** High Priority **
I'm trying to get listserve running on my SUN
Sparcserver1000.  Could someone tell me where I can
download the Listserve or Majordomo Processes
from.??
Thanks.
c.carreno@bse.org
```

This example shows the same message with the full mail header displayed:

```
Message 53:
From sun-managers-relay@ra.mcs.anl.gov Wed Aug 31 16:26:34 1994
Return-Path: <sun-managers-relay@ra.mcs.anl.gov>
Received: by pnw.unixmail.com (4.1/SMI-4.1)
        id AA25866; Wed, 31 Aug 94 16:26:33 PDT
Received: from ra.mcs.anl.gov by u2.pi.com (5.65b/4.0.071791-PI/PINet)
via SMTP;
```

VII

The Internet and Communications

```
        id AA18858 for sunmgrs; Wed, 31 Aug 94 19:16:42 -0400
Received: (from daemon@localhost) by ra.mcs.anl.gov (8.6.9/8.6.9) id
QAA25485 for sun-managers-outbound; Wed, 31 Aug 1994 16:29:40 -0500
Sender: sun-managers-relay@ra.mcs.anl.gov
Received: from bse.org ([19.7.10.11]) by ra.mcs.anl.gov (8.6.9/8.6.9)
with SMTP id QAA25480 for <SUN-MANAGERS@RA.MCS.ANL.GOV>; Wed, 31 Aug
1994 16:29:37 -0500
From: c.carreno@bse.org
Reply-To: c.carreno@bse.org
Followup-To: junk
Precedence: junk
Received: from BSE-Message_Server by bse.org
        with WordPerfect_Office; Wed, 31 Aug 1994 17:25:39 -0500
Message-Id: <se64bd13.052@bse.org>
X-Mailer: WordPerfect Office 4.0
Date: Wed, 31 Aug 1994 17:25:12 -0500
To: SUN-MANAGERS@ra.mcs.anl.gov
Subject:  LISTSERVE
Status: R

** High Priority **
I'm trying to get listserve running on my SUN
Sparcserver1000.  Could someone tell me where I can
download the Listserve or Majordomo Processes
from.??
Thanks.
c.carreno@bse.org
```

You can specify which mail header fields you want to see or suppress in the mail customization file, .mailrc. The format of this file is discussed in a later portion of this chapter. If the mail message you receive is handled by many systems on its delivery route to you, the complete mail header information may be quite lengthy, and much of it can be ignored or suppressed.

The body of the message contains the text of what the sender wants you to read. The text may be simple ASCII text that you can read, or it may be a series of lines of unintelligible ASCII text, as in the following example:

```
{Mail}& 56
Message 56:
From steve Tue Aug 30 22:43:54 1994
Date: Tue, 30 Aug 94 22:43:54 PDT
From: steve (Steve Lee)
To: steve
Subject: My .cshrc file
```

```
begin 644 cshrc
M(R! *",I0W-H<F,@,2XS(#(#@X+S R%(%%@@=x+U-20HC(R,C(R,C(R,C(R,C
M(R,C(R,C(R,C(R,C(R,C(R,C(R,C(R,C(R,C(R,C(R,C(R,C(R,C(R,C(R,C
M(R,C(PHC"B,@(" @(" @(" N8W-H<F,@9FEL90HC"B,@(" @(" @("!I;FET
M:6%L('-E='5P(&9I;&4@9F]R(&)O=&@@:6YT97)A8W1I=F4@86YD(&YO;FEN
M=5R86-T:79E"B,@(" @(" @("!!#+5-H96QL<PHC"B,C(R,C(R,C(R,C(R,C
M(R,C(R,C(R,C(R,C(R,C(R,C(R,C(R,C(R,C(R,C(R,C(R,C(R,C(R,C(R,C
M(R,C(R,C"@HC(" @(" @(" @<V5T('5P('-E87)C"):"!P871H"@HC(%-E="!O
M<&5N=VEN=&]W(&%S(&UY(&1E9F%U;'0@=VEN9&]W("'-Y<W1E;2 *(W-E="-H
M;VEC93930U0<&5N=VEN="'@HC(" @(" @(" @<V5T('5P('-E87)C"):"!P871H"'@HC
M(&%D9"'!D:7)E8W1O<FEE<R!F;W(@&]C86P@8W5S=&]M"9N9',',"-(.-&'%T
M:"'@](("@@*0HC:68F]"'@(" D>5]M>6-;("9H;96X*"!I('1H96X*(R  @(" @
M(" @:68@*" D>5]VUY8V%O:6--E?2 ]+2 B;W!E;B'E;G]"'@(" @HC"V5T
M(&QP871H(#@#T@*" 0:]"]M92]B<F5S=&)L+V5S;9V9(0"'-R(0:]"]M
M92]S96%T=&)E+VVQO<&5N+")]B:6X@+VV4@<&]L;P<;'C(40;5A-B'LL1.0%4L'#D`]L;1L
M92]R<F&-D+V)V)SB,B('L",$861D(0(1I<F5C=)9R0;CI66((@5.X..!R(.C;VUM
:
```

The unintelligible ASCII text is actually an encoded file that was created using the UNIX uuencode command. The process of encoding a file enables the UNIX mail system to handle non-ASCII files such as programs or data files as normal mail messages. Once received, the encoded mail message must be decoded to extract the file that was sent. The details of encoding and decoding files are discussed in a following section.

Composing Mail

To compose a message to be sent by mail, enter the following where username@mailaddress is the e-mail address of the recipient:

```
{Mail}& mail username@mailaddress
Subject: My new e-mail address
```

You may now type your message, following each line by pressing Enter. Once you finish typing your message, enter either a period on a line by itself or Ctrl+D and press Enter. Depending on how your mail is configured, you may be asked for additional information for delivery of the message, such as who is to be carbon copied (Cc:) on the message. Then your message is delivered and you are back at the {Mail}& prompt.

Once your e-mail message has been completed and sent, it is very difficult or impossible to stop its delivery. Sending your message is analogous to dropping your letter into the mailbox at the Post Office—you can't get it back! Think about the message, its content, and the recipients before you send it.

If you find that you made a mistake while composing the message, you can invoke a full-screen editor by entering on a blank line **~v**. This will start up your editor so you can compose or edit your message. By default, the editor is set to vi, but you can choose another editor, such as emacs. Once you exit your editor, you are returned to composing your message, and you must still end your message by typing a period or a ^D on a blank line.

Listing Mail Headers

At any {Mail}& prompt enter **h** to redisplay the mail headers. To scroll forward one screen of messages, enter **z**. The next group of mail headers is displayed. To scroll backward one screen of messages, enter **z-**. In each case, the current message, as indicated by the > marker, becomes the first message on the header display. If you want to display the headers for a group of messages containing a specific message number, enter **h message_number**. For example, to show the message headers starting with message 28, enter **h 28**.

```
{Mail}& h 28
>  21 steve              Sun Aug 14 19:49   52/1757    Re: equipment list
   22 ron                Tue Aug 16 11:12   23/539     Technical Phone Interview
   23 denali!ken         Tue Aug 16 17:27   51/1545
   24 martin             Wed Aug 17 08:58   30/1037    Account plan
   25 john               Wed Aug 17 11:04   36/951     Re: schedule for aracor
   26 ron                Wed Aug 17 15:16   22/550     Lunch on Wed. 8/24
   27 slee@mailhost      Fri Aug 19 16:31   2058/126570    dcmove.mpp
U  28 denali!don         Mon Aug 22 07:26   28/692     Sendmail security patch
U  29 denali!alaska.open Mon Aug 22 09:29   82/2976    Sendmail security
U  30 denali!alaska.open Mon Aug 22 09:29   158/4634   Sendmail security - adden
   31 owner-baylisa@erg. Mon Aug 22 10:56   52/1852    Announcements from August
   32 larry@wilson.tivor Tue Aug 23 09:57   39/1488    Tivory Customer Support w
   33 metze@cert.org     Wed Aug 24 12:57   185/7571   CERT#18027 Re: attempt to
U  34 ron                Thu Aug 25 07:57   18/421     Coverage
   35 ed.vansdever@tivor Thu Aug 25 11:57   440/26346  Informix Announces DBA To
   36 sun-managers-relay Thu Aug 25 16:56   49/2213    SunNet Manager Discover T
   37 sun-managers-relay Thu Aug 25 20:56   46/2127    strange bootptab messages
   38 rr6@aon.was.com    Fri Aug 26 07:56   74/2405    3rd Annual Puget Sound Su
   39 slee@mailhost      Fri Aug 26 09:56   38/1317    Test Message
   40 sunrise!alaska.ope Fri Aug 26 11:57   83/3100    Re: Sendmail security pat
```

Replying to Mail

After reading a mail message, you may want to reply to the message. The mail program provides a number of choices on how to reply: you may reply to the sender of the message, or you may reply to all of the recipients of the message as well as the sender.

To reply to the sender of a message after you have read it, enter one of the following:

        {Mail}& **r**

or

        {Mail}& **reply**

The Subject: heading automatically takes the current message subject and adds Re: to the begining of it. You then type your reply and send your message. To reply to the sender of a specific message number, enter the message number after the command. For example, to reply to message 13, enter the following:

        {Mail}& **r 13**

If you wish to reply to the sender and all of the recipients of a message, enter one of the following:

        {Mail}& **R**

        {Mail}& **Reply**

As with the reply mail command, the Reply command automatically sets the Subject: heading your reply. In addition, the Cc: header is loaded with all of the recipients of the original message, as shown in the original message's Cc: field. The Reply command also enables you to reply to all recipients of a specific message, as shown in the following example:

        {Mail}& **Reply 15**

Deleting Messages

Your mailbox may grow to be very large in just a short time if you receive many messages. A large mailbox is slower to load when you first start mail, and it makes it more difficult for you to find a specific message. Deleting messages that you have read and don't need to save alleviates this problem.

To delete the message that you have just read, enter the following:

```
{Mail}& d
```

This message is now marked for deletion. The message will be permanently removed from your mailbox when you quit mail. If you view the message headers after deleting messages, you will see that the deleted messages do not show on the screen. The message numbers show a gap in their sequence which implies that the intermediate messages are deleted. If the autoprint mail variable discussed later in this chapter is set, deleting a message causes the next message to be displayed automatically.

Multiple mail messages may be deleted with one command by specifying the message numbers, separated by spaces, on the command line. For example, to delete messages 5, 8, and 13, inclusive, enter the following:

```
{Mail}& d 5 8 13
```

Series of mail messages may also be deleted by inserting a dash between the starting and ending message numbers in the sequence. To delete all of the messages from message 8 to message 23, enter the following:

```
{Mail}& d 8-23
```

Undeleting Mail Messages

Deleting a mail message only marks the message for removal at the end of the current mail session. Luckily, the deleted message can be undeleted using the undelete mail command. To undelete a specific message or messages, type u followed by the message number. For example, to undelete message 11, enter the following:

```
{Mail}& u 11
```

In the same fashion as deleting messages, series of mail messages may be undeleted by specifying the message range on the command line.

Saving Mail Messages in a Mail File

Your mailbox may get very large, even if you regularly delete messages. If you classify your messages along specific categories, such as Personnel, Tech Support, or a specific vendor, you can save similar messages into mail files. Mail files enable your main mailbox to be used for new, incoming mail, and organize the rest of your messages in an efficient manner.

To save a mail message into a specific mail file, type **s** followed by the mail file name. For example, enter the following to save message 6 into a mail file called UNIX:

> {Mail}& **s 6 UNIX**

If the mail file specified on the command line does not already exist, it is created, with this message as its only content. If the mail file does exist, the message is appended to the end of the messages in the mail file. The message is also deleted from the current mailbox, marked for removal at the end of the mail session, and removed from the header display.

To view a mail file instead of your mailbox, you specify the mail file name on the UNIX command line. For example, if you want to view the messages in your Personnel mail file, enter the following:

> % **mail -f Personnel**

When mail brings up the messages in the mail file, you see the mail file name displayed on the second line of the initial display. All of the functions that you can perform to the messages in your mailbox can also be done to the messages in the specific mail file.

Ending Your Mail Session

Once you have finished reading your mail messages and deleting or saving them, you need to end your mail session. At any time during your mail session, you may exit mail immediately without making any changes to your mailbox by entering x at the mail prompt.

> {Mail}& **x**
> %

Exiting mail in this fashion is useful if you made changes to your mailbox and you wish to undo them. This command only restores the mailbox to the state in which it was at the start of the current mail session.

The normal method for ending your mail session is to quit using the q command. Quitting mail commits all of the changes you made during this session. Messages that were deleted are removed from the mailbox. New messages that have not been read have their state changed from new to unread. All messages are renumbered to remove the deleted messages. There is no way to retrieve deleted messages once you have quit the mail session.

Using Advanced Features of Mail

The first section of this chapter deals with the basics of UNIX mail. Further use of mail is explained in the following sections, in areas such as including binary files, compressing files for mailing, and customization of the mail environment.

Using mail from the UNIX Command Line

The preceding section focuses on using UNIX mail as an interactive application for reading and sending mail and for modifying the mailbox. You can also send mail from the UNIX command line by composing a specific mail message, or by redirecting output from another UNIX program or command into mail.

Mailing a Single Message

Mailing a single message from the command line is as simple as running the mail command and specifying the address of the recipients on the command line. The remaining process of composing, editing, and sending the mail message is identical to that in the mail session. The following is a sample session for a user sending a mail message from the command line:

```
% mail steve
Subject: New Office Phone Number
Our new office phone number is 555-3455. Please
update your records.
.
Cc:
%
```

Some mail addresses may have characters that are reserved characters for the shell from which you are running, Bourne, C, or Korn shell. For example, if you are using the C shell, the ! character is reserved for command-line substitution. UUCP style e-mail addresses use the ! character as a delimiter for the message path components. In order to send mail to this style of address, you may need to precede the reserved character with an escape character. For example, to send a message to the address denali!ken from the command line, you enter one of the following to prevent the shell from interpreting the ! character:

```
% mail denali\!ken
```

```
% mail "denali!ken"
```

Mailing from a UNIX Command or Program

There are times when you want the output of a UNIX command or program to be mailed to you, or to a specific user. This capability is used to mail the results of a program to yourself, or another user. If one of your programs is not working correctly, this information could automatically be mailed to your technical support representative. This third form of using UNIX mail enables you to take the standard output from any UNIX command or program and mail it to a specific set of users.

Unlike the previous section in which a user interactively entered the various mail headers and mail text, all information must be specified on the UNIX command line. The output from the UNIX command or program becomes the body of the message text. You must supply additional information such as the recipient, subject, and other information to complete the command.

In this example, the user is sending a directory listing of the current directory to a user joe@sun.com for examination:

```
% ls -al ¦ mail -s "Steve's Home Directory" joe@sun.com
```

The -s option enables a Subject: heading to be added to the message. Any subject description that includes spaces must be surrounded by quotes to prevent the shell from misinterpreting the command line.

Including mail Messages in Your Mail

When you are composing a mail message, you may want to include the text from another message for the recipient to view or reference. You might be composing a response to a question another user has asked, and it might clarify the response to include that question. Similarly, you might be forwarding a mail message to another user and want to add your own comments to it before sending it. In these cases, you can easily add any message in your mailbox to the current message you are composing.

To include a mail message into the current message, enter the following on a blank line:

```
~m message_number
```

In the following example, mail message 53 is sent to user bob. Once that one is read, the mail program reports that it has successfully included that mail message into the currently composed message. Each line in the included mail message will be preceded by a Tab character, by default. If you do not specify a message number, the current number is selected and included.

```
m steve
Subject: Listserve
Do you have information about this issue?
```

```
~m 53
Interpolating: 53
(continue)
.
Cc:
{Mail}&
```

The mail program displays the number of the message that is included. More than one message can be included in your initial one by issuing multiple ~m commands. Once the message is included within the original, you can use your visual editor (~v) to place comments inside the body of the included message.

Including Text Files in Your Mail

Including a text file in your mail message is useful if you need to send a copy of a program listing, memo, or other data to another user. The included file must an ASCII file; the following section describes how to include binary files in your mail messages.

To include a text file in your mail message, enter the following on a blank line:

~r filename

For example, if a vendor's Technical Support Engineer asked you to e-mail her a copy of your .cshrc file, you do this in your message by entering the following:

~r .cshrc

If the file does not reside in the directory where the mail command was started, you need to specify the path to the file, such as in the following example:

```
{Mail}& m steve
Subject: .cshrc file
Here's my .cshrc file

~r .cshrc
".cshrc" 105/2887
.
Cc:
{Mail}&
```

The mail program displays the name of the included file along with the number of lines and bytes. Unlike the condition when you include mail messages in your message, the included file is not indented. You may include multiple files by repeating the ~r command for each file. Once the file has been included into the message, you can edit the included file by invoking your editor (~v).

Including Binary Files in Your Mail

UNIX mail provides a great way to deliver information from one user to another user or group of users, even outside corporate or geographical boundaries. This information is not restricted to simple ASCII text messages, however. The same method of transporting ASCII messages can be used to move binary files, programs, or other non-ASCII files to someone else. These binary files, however, need to be encapsulated and converted into a format that mail can handle. Once received, these files must be extracted and decoded.

The UNIX mail program generally is limited to handling 7-bit ASCII information. Binary or other 8-bit ASCII files must be converted by the uuencode program into a standard 7-bit ASCII format that mail can read. This conversion process increases the size of the file by approximately 35 percent. The uudecode program reverses the conversion process and produces the original file. Both uuencode and uudecode are standard UNIX commands and are generally available on other operating systems, such as MS-DOS, either by the mail vendor or as shareware/public domain software.

Although the process of uuencoding your files makes them unreadable to you, it includes no built-in security or encryption capability. If your uuencoded file is accidentally sent to the wrong person, or if your e-mail is intercepted on its way to the destination, anyone can uudecode the file and extract its original contents. Other security measures for mail encryption and privacy, such as those commercially available from RSI, or the PGP (pretty good privacy) product, use encryption keys to protect the contents of your mail message.

You must run uuencode from the UNIX command line to encode a file. The uuencoded file starts with a begin statement that lists the UNIX file permissions of the file being encoded and a filename descriptor specified on the UNIX command line. This filename descriptor is the name of the recipient's file after it is received and decoded. The encoding process reads the original file and converts the binary information into an ASCII representation that is then formatted into 60-character lines in the encoded file. The uuencode command adds an end command to the uuencoded file once the entire file has been read, which signifies to the decoding program that the encoded file is complete.

The following example shows the process of a sample file being uuencoded, the size of the file after encoding, and the format of the encoded file:

```
%cat Sample.txt
This is a sample file which will be
uuencoded. This does not have binary
data, but will show what the uuencoded
```

```
file looks like.
% ls -al Sample
-rw-rw-r--  1 steve            129 Aug 28 08:14 Sample
% uuencode Sample Sample > Sample.uu
% ls -al Sam*
-rw-rw-r--  1 steve            129 Aug 28 08:14 Sample
-rw-rw-r--  1 steve            201 Aug 28 08:15 Sample.uu
% cat Sample.uu
begin 664 Sample
M5&AI<R!I<R!A('-A;7!L92!F:6QE('=H:6-H('=I;;&P@8F4*=75E;;F-09&5D
M+B4:&ES(&1097,@;F]T(&AA=F4@8F5E;87)Y)Y"F1A=&$L(&)U=")!W:6QL('-H
G;W<@VAA=="!T:&4@=75E;F-09&5D"F9I;&4@;&]O:W,@&EK92X*
```

end
%

The name of the file descriptor does not need to match the original file name. In the preceding example, you would use the following line to make the file descriptor `sample.unix`:

```
uuencode Sample sample.unix > Sample.uu
```

You might want to change the name of the encoded file if you know that the recipient has a file name that duplicates your original file, or if, for security reasons, you don't want your original file name to be known.

In these examples, the encoded file name was chosen by adding .uu to the original file name. Again, this choice is arbitrary, and you can use your own naming convention to designate encoded files.

After the file is encoded, you can include it in your mail message. Because the encoded file might be lengthy, include any information that the recipient needs to know about the encoded file at the beginning of the message. You should include in your message what type of file is the encoded file, why you are sending it, and why the recipient should decode it.

Decoding an Encoded mail Message

If you receive an encoded mail message, its contents are valuable to you only if you can extract the file. If the file has been encoded with the uuencode command, you should be able to read its initial encoding line, which has the following format:

```
begin xyz filename
```

Where *xyz* is the UNIX numerical representation of the file modes, and *filename* is the name of the extracted file. If the file has been encoded with another program, you need that specific program to decode it. (You might need to contact the sender for specific details on how to acquire the decoding program.)

The first step in decoding the mail message is to save the message to a temporary mail file. The choice of the name of the mail file is arbitrary, but it might be useful to use a convention such as appending .uu to the end of the file name listed in the begin statement. Once the temporary mail file is created, you must run the uudecode command from your UNIX shell (use the ~! escape from mail, or exit mail back to your shell prompt). The uudecode command's only argument is the name of the encoded message. The uudecode command will search for the begin statement in the body of the message, discard all of the mail headers, decode the encoded file, and then create a file with permissions and a file name that match those of the begin statement.

The following example shows the process of reading an encoded mail message, saving it to a mail file, and uudecoding it:

```
{Mail}& z
 N 62 steve            Wed Aug 31 19:31   30/796    Listserve
 N 63 steve            Wed Aug 31 19:32   118/3191  .cshrc file
 N 64 steve            Wed Aug 31 19:41   81/4311   my .cshrc file
{Mail}& 64
Message 64:
From steve Wed Aug 31 19:41:10 1994
To: steve
Subject: my .cshrc file

Here's my .cshrc file

begin 644 cshrc
M(R! *",I0W-H<F,@,2XS(#!@:(#%8X+S R;%E(,(#%,(#%+(",(#%*(#%C(D,I,(#%H(#%C(#%C(#%C(#%C(#%C
M(R,C(R,C(R,C(R,C(R,C(R,C(R,C(R,C(R,C(R,C(R,C(R,C(R,C(R,C(R,C
M(R,C(PHC"B,@(" @(" @(" N8W-H<F,@,9FEL90HC"B,@(" @(" @("!I;;4ET
M:6%L*'-E='5P*"\F9I;;4&R9F]R*(&(DT+&@@(#:6YT97)A8W1I=F4@86?Y(&YO;;4E.
M=&4&5R86-T:79E("!B,""!(" @(" @("!!#%M-H1!96QL<('!HC"B,C(R,C(R,C(R,C(R,C
M(R,C(R,C(R,C(R,C(R,C(R,C(R,C(R,C(R,C(R,C(R,C(R,C(R,C(R,C
M(R,C(R,C"D'HC(" @(" @("!<5=T('5P(('-E='5P("!871H"D'HC%-E="!I;
M<&5N=E=.("8E'4IAY(&$E1E9%%U.R!0@=F5N.5F]W("$Y==75E,2 *("!%+2$=-8-H
M;5=%0P3U;3<\=5N=F5N"D'HC(" @(" @("!<5=T('5P(('-E='5P("!871H"D'HC
M(&%-D9"$A1#HW*45H=E=.%F945R$A1%=7RA(;8S@86P*%M-H1!96QL;9Y)S<*("!%+2$=+<&%T
M.B" ]("!00*BTP2$@:-C@Z*B! $#Y36U-N-B!(%2$G26Y497)A8W1I=F4@@(" @
M(" @QEL-96US;Y5=^5D9$%/4%0S3@0Z(& D07<G02 *("!'AJ96QL;PHC(YL;6X\=5T
M*%%0<[I(%1T:D*B!/.B8D%2U3;)B[9B%%4R$]+%9%4SM9;5 I(<$Y$:7H*&TH(VL;;J]
M;92(36TV)5Q4*"DF45E%5E1/73TGW5,K4R1R+%)99E8L,T$\=5=.+"(;;DH:YL2$O8PHC&U-A"$Y,3'
M+92(4X\=+%1"P!);($)("(*+"!@:061$*"8T22\F1C5#"]@%5(B!(#8U4R@F.3PRB@B$P;%D[5B;!+CLA&U-.57
```
--More--

```
{Mail}& s 64 cshrc.uu
"cshrc.uu" [New file] 81/4099
{Mail}& q
% uudecode cshrc.uu
% ls -al cshrc*
-rw-r--r--  1 steve          2887 Aug 31 19:42 cshrc
-rw-rw-r--  1 steve          4099 Aug 31 19:42 cshrc.uu
%
```

Handling Large Files in mail

Many mail delivery systems (both UNIX and non-UNIX) have limits as to the size of a mail message that they will process. Many have a limit of 150 KB; therefore, if you wish to mail binary files larger than this, you must process the file before sending it. If the recipient of your mail uses a different mail system than yours, the message size limit might be smaller than 150 KB. Two common ways of mailing large files are to compress them and to split them.

Using Compression To Compress Large Files

File compression uses various algorithms to detect repeated patterns in files and represent these patterns by shorter character strings. To be valuable, the compression and uncompression must not cause any loss of data. The ratio of the original file size to the compressed file size is called the *compression ratio*. Using most popular file compression programs, many files can be compressed to a compression ratio of 2:1. Some files, such as ASCII text files or sparse raster graphics files, can have compression ratios of 4:1 to 10:1 or greater. Other files, such as those already compressed or GIF graphics files, will not compress further.

The standard UNIX utilities for compression and decompression are *compress* and *uncompress*. Versions for other operating systems such as MS-DOS are available. Other compression programs, such as gzip and gunzip from GNU (which literally means "Gnu not UNIX"), or programs that compress and uncompress files in the MS-DOS PKZIP format, also are available. For compression to be useful, both the sender and recipient must use the same utilities for compression.

Compression uses a smaller file size, enabling large files to fit within the mail programs' message size limits. The smaller file size also reduces the time required to transfer the file from your system to the receiver's system. If you use a method to deliver mail with charges based on connect time (such as a long-distance phone connection) or on the amount of data transmitted (such as some Internet providers), file compression can result in cost savings.

To send a compressed binary file, you must compress the file before beginning the encoding process. The following example shows the compression and encoding process:

```
ls -al csh*
-rw-r--r--  1 steve          2887 Aug 28 09:23 cshrc
% compress cshrc
% ls -al csh*
-rw-r--r--  1 steve          1699 Aug 28 09:23 cshrc.Z
% uuencode cshrc.Z cshrc.Z > cshrc.Z.uu
ls -al csh*
-rw-r--r--  1 steve          1699 Aug 28 09:23 cshrc.Z
-rw-rw-r--  1 steve          2368 Aug 28 09:24 cshrc.Z.uu
```

After the file is in compressed, uuencoded format, you can include it in your mail message and send it. Compressing files using the compress command creates a new file with a .Z extension. Indicating this extension in the uuencode file descriptor alerts the recipient that after uudecoding the message, the resulting file still must be uncompressed using the uncompress command.

Using split To Split Large Encoded Files

File compression might help shrink some files to a size that the recipient's mail program can handle. What can be done about files that still are too large, even after compression? How do you send a file that is 500 KB? The UNIX split command can split the file into multiple files, each smaller than the specified size limit.

The split command divides a file into individual files of a user-supplied length, each of which then can be included in your mail messages. Sometimes it is helpful to run the wc command to count the number of lines in the encoded file so you know how many parts will result from splitting the file.

The following example shows a file being compressed, uuencoded, and then split into 1,000-line sections ready to be mailed:

```
% ls -al testf*
-rw-------   1 steve       1327299 Aug 31 20:55 testfile
% compress testfile
% ls -al testf*
-rw-------   1 steve        430591 Aug 31 20:55 testfile.Z
% uuencode testfile.Z testfile.Z > testfile.Z.uu
% ls -al testf*
-rw-------   1 steve        430591 Aug 31 20:55 testfile.Z
-rw-rw-r--   1 steve        593289 Aug 31 20:56 testfile.Z.uu
% wc -l testfile.Z.uu
    9572 testfile.Z.uu
% split -2400 testfile.Z.uu testfile.Z.uu.
% ls -al testf*
-rw-------   1 steve        430591 Aug 31 20:55 testfile.Z
```

```
-rw-rw-r--  1 steve      593289 Aug 31 20:56 testfile.Z.uu
-rw-rw-r--  1 steve      148759 Aug 31 20:56 testfile.Z.uu.aa
-rw-rw-r--  1 steve      148800 Aug 31 20:56 testfile.Z.uu.ab
-rw-rw-r--  1 steve      148800 Aug 31 20:56 testfile.Z.uu.ac
-rw-rw-r--  1 steve      146930 Aug 31 20:57 testfile.Z.uu.ad
%
```

After the recipient receives all of the split files, the files need to be saved to a mail file. An editor such as vi can remove the header information from each of the messages. The encoded file can be decoded and uncompressed after it has been reconstructed from the individual pieces. Although this process seems like quite a bit of work, and it is, it enables you to send and receive very large files.

Customizing Your Mail Environment

Although the standard, default mail environment enables you to send and receive mail, it might not contribute to your overall productivity with mail. You can customize your mail environment to better suit your specific mail style and habit. You might want to be prompted at the beginning of the message for the Cc: field rather than at the end, for example. Or you might want to view the next message after you delete the current message. Perhaps you want to use emacs for editing your mail message instead of vi. This section provides you with the information necessary to customize your mail environment to suit your needs.

Each system running mail has a global mail startup file (generally called mailx.rc) in a system directory. For Sun Solaris 2, this file, mailx.rc, is located in /etc/mail, but for UNIX it might reside in a different directory. The commands in this startup file apply to all users running mail on this specific system. An administrator who places specific commands in this file will customize the mail behavior globally for all users.

You can create your own individual mail startup file—.mailrc—in your home directory for specific customizations. This file is invoked by mail after the global mail startup file is read. Changes you make to this file affect only you, and not any other user.

When your user account and your home directory were created, the standard user .mailrc might have been copied into your directory for you by your administrator. Using the information in this section, you can modify this file and customize the behavior of mail. If this file does not exist, you can create it using your favorite text editor.

The following section covers the variables most frequently used for customization. For a complete list of all of the customizations available for your version of mail, please consult the man page for mail on your system.

Customizing the .mailrc File

The .mailrc file is a list of mail commands that are run each time mail is started from the command line. The following is a sample .mailrc file:

```
set askcc
set autoprint
set hold
set indentprefix="##>"
set metoo
set record=outmail
set cmd="lpr -p &"
set EDITOR=/usr/ucb/ex
set PAGER=more
set prompt="{Mail}& "
set SHELL=/bin/csh
set VISUAL=/usr/ucb/vi
set folder='Mail'
ignore apparently-to errors-to id in-reply-to message-id precedence
received references remailed-date          remailed-from return-path
sent-by status via
alias archie archie@archie.sura.net
```

The variables listed in this sample .mailrc file and other common mail variables are described in the following sections.

alias

Mail aliases enable you to abbreviate long e-mail addresses into a short format name that is easier to remember and to type. Mail aliases also can be used to set up distribution groups of mail recipients. The mail aliases specified in your .mailrc file are local to you as a user as you send mail; someone else in your office won't be able to use the alias. For system-wide or network-wide mail aliases to take effect, they must be entered into a central file, typically /etc/aliases.

The sample .mailrc file lists an e-mail address archie@archie.sura.net and its alias, archie. When you want to send mail to this address, you can use either the full address or the alias.

You also can set up your own distribution list with an alias. If you want to send your weekly status report to users bob and jan, establish an alias in your .mailrc file as follows:

```
alias statrpt bob jan
```

Each time you send mail to statrpt, both bob and jan get your status report.

VIII

The Internet and Communications

askbcc

Setting the askbcc variable forces mail to prompt for the Bcc: blind carbon copy field after the subject is entered.

askcc

Setting the askcc variable forces mail to prompt for the Cc: carbon copy field after the subject is entered.

autoprint

Setting the autoprint variable enables the next message to be displayed on-screen after the delete or undelete command is issued.

bsdcompat

Setting the bsdcompat variable forces mail to behave according to the default BSD-UNIX mail version. The default pagination command is set to more.

cmd

The cmd variable can be set to a UNIX command that is the default command for the pipe mail command. In the sample .mailrc file, using the pipe command enables the current message to be printed on the printer.

folder

The folder variable enables you to specify the standard directory in which mail files are saved. If the folder variable is set to a relative path and file name, this path is assumed to be off of the user's home directory. There is no default value for this variable, and the standard mail behavior is to save mail files in the user's home directory. Moving mail files to a separate directory can help organize your directory structure. If you want to save all of your mail files in a directory named Mail, for example, enter the following in the .mailrc file:

```
set folder=Mail
```

hold

The default behavior of mail is to place messages that you have read into a mail file specified by the MBOX variable. Setting the hold variable keeps the messages in your system mailbox.

ignore

The ignore command enables you to specify which header fields you want mail to ignore and not display on your messages. This list might get quite lengthy, as is seen in the sample .mailrc file. Many of the header fields are written and duplicated as the mail gets delivered to you. You can specify the particular header field or fields to be ignored on the ignore line, such as in the following example:

```
ignore Received:
```

The header field is the first word in each line in the mail header, and typically ends with a colon. You must use the exact spelling and capitalization when entering the field to ignore in the .mailrc file.

indentprefix

By default, an existing mail message included using the ~m command has each line prefixed with a tab character. If you would like to use a different character or character string, you can set the indentprefix variable accordingly. If you want each message line to start with the characters ###>, enter the following command line:

```
set indentprefix=###>
```

MBOX

The MBOX variable is set to the name of the file to which the messages that have been read are moved. By default, the MBOX variable is set to the mbox file in the user's home directory.

metoo

If you send a message and your login name appears in the list of recipients, mail, by default, will not send you the message. Setting the metoo variable enables you to receive mail that you send to yourself.

PAGER

The PAGER variable specifies the UNIX command used to show long messages on your screen. The System V default PAGER command is pg. If you are using a BSD-compatible version of UNIX, or if the version of mail you are using supports the bsdcompat variable, the default command is more. To explicitly use more as the pager, for example, enter the following in your .mailrc file:

```
set PAGER=more
```

VIII

The Internet and Communications

record

The record variable enables all outgoing messages to be recorded and saved in a mail file. If the variable specifies a relative path to the record file, it is assumed that the path is relative to the record variable name. Record files are useful if you need to have a transcript of the messages you send. Note that record files can grow very large very quickly; therefore, you should monitor the size of the record file frequently. If you want to save all your outgoing messages in a file called outmail, use the following command line:

```
set record=outmail
```

SHELL

The SHELL variable is set to /bin/sh by default. If you want to use another shell, such as the C shell or Korn shell, for command escapes from mail, you can set this in the .mailrc file. To set the shell to be the C shell, use the following command line:

```
set SHELL=/bin/csh
```

sign

The string associated with the sign variable can be considered your autograph, which you can insert into a mail message using the ~a command. Typical autograph strings include the sender's name, company affiliation (if any), address, phone number, and e-mail address.

VISUAL

The VISUAL variable enables you to specify a full-screen editor that is invoked with the ~v command rather than the default vi editor. If your preferred editor is emacs, you can use the following command:

```
set VISUAL=emacs
```

Other UNIX Mail Tools

The UNIX mail command is the basic tool for sending, receiving, and organizing e-mail on UNIX systems. Even though it provides an interactive approach to viewing messages in a mailbox, it is only an ASCII-based tool. In a GUI-based environment such as X Windows, graphical mail tools can be easier to use and provide the user with more intuitive ways of editing, managing, and manipulating mail. With the advent of multimedia tools and capabilities, graphical mail tools also can be a link that users exploit to share sound and image messages as well as the standard text mail. The following are a few mail tools that represent a cross section of the types of products available from vendors and the Internet. This list is not meant to be exhaustive.

Text-Based Mail Products

Text-based mail products generally expand on the capabilities of standard UNIX mail. These products generally are public-domain, noncommercial programs, which, although unsupported, have garnered a wide, loyal following. One of the most popular of these products is elm.

elm is a public-domain product by Dave Taylor that improves on the basic text mail capabilities of UNIX mail. elm provides full-screen mail handling capabilities, as is shown by the sample elm session in figure 31.1.

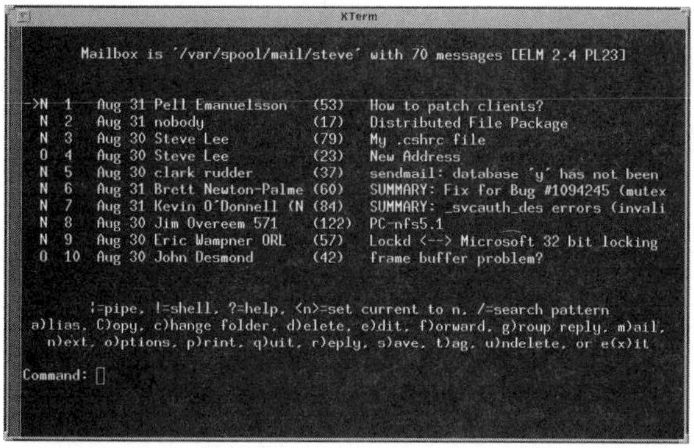

Figure 31.1
A sample screen from elm.

elm enables multiple messages to be tagged for various actions such as mass saving or copying to a mail file, or mass deletion. You can add to the startup file mail aliases that might be extracted from incoming messages, and you can manage these mail aliases interactively. Messages are composed using a visual editor (such as vi by default), and can be searched, sorted, and retrieved.

elm is generally available by anonymous ftp from a number of sites and can be compiled from source code. elm also is available in executable format for a number of popular operating systems.

Graphical Mail Tools

Most vendors' graphical environments based on X Windows, such as those from Sun, Hewlett Packard, or Silicon Graphics, include graphically based mail tools. These tools generally provide windowed interfaces to the basic UNIX mail capabilities such as reading and composing messages. They also might provide additional capabilities such as displaying uuencoded file enclosures and automatic decoding and execution of attached binary files. For instance, an audio file attached to a mail message can be played on the workstation simply by double-clicking on the sound file icon. An example of this type of mail tool is Sun's MailTool.

VIII

The Internet and Communications

Sun's MailTool is shown in figure 31.2 as a windowed application. A message can be selected and displayed from the header window by double-clicking on the message header. A separate section of the viewing window displays any file attachments to the message, and these attachments can be copied out to disk, or displayed or executed directly by double-clicking on the icon. Sun's MailTool is *Multimedia Internet Mail Extension* (MIME) compliant, which means that it can accept and send standard audio and image files to and from other MIME-compliant mail programs.

Figure 31.2

Sun's graphical MailTool uses a windowed approach to sending and receiving mail.

When iconified, MailTool changes its icon image depending on the presence or absence of mail, or to denote the arrival of new mail.

Cross-Platform Mail Tools

Some vendors of mail products such as Lotus and WordPerfect have ported their mail products from platforms such as MS-DOS or MS-Windows to the UNIX operating system. The advantage of these products over other graphical mail tools is that they try to maintain a consistent look and feel across all of the supported platforms and operating systems. A user of cc:Mail on one system should be able to use the majority of functions of the same product on another system. Retraining users to use dissimilar mail products on various systems can be cut back or eliminated.

To provide consistent product operation across all of these platforms and operating systems, these products can supplement or replace normal UNIX mail functions and standards with the vendor's own communication or mail file format or protocol.

Interoperability between the vendor's mail product and UNIX mail can occur through a SMTP gateway that is separately configured and maintained. The selection and evaluation process for these products must take into account the scope of the existing product installation, the mix of various mail products, and how well the product integrates into the UNIX environment.

Summary

This chapter provided you with an overview of UNIX mail, its features, and its usage. You learned how to customize your mail environment also was covered, and how to incorporate alternative mail tools.

You should feel comfortable with the UNIX mail program and how to send and receive e-mail after reading this chapter. Experiment with the features and customizations with mail, and explore the world of communication by e-mail!

Chapter Snapshot

The UNIX operating system is often defined as a multiuser system. By definition, multiple users can be on the same hardware platform at the same time, sharing the operating system. These users can be sitting only feet apart in the same office, or they can be thousands of miles away, connected through phone lines and modems.

Often it is necessary for users to communicate with one another. While most multiple-user operating systems available today offer a mail utility, UNIX goes beyond and offers several other utilities allowing communication to take place—some in real time, and others when a user logs in. This chapter examines the following:

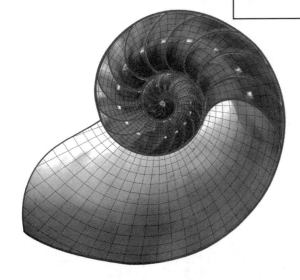

Communicating with Other Users

Today it's hard to imagine an office of computers without electronic mail—the most popular means by which one user can communicate with another. Through e-mail, one user can leave a message for another user on his own system. If they are connected to a network, they can forward messages to users on other systems, and if connected to a service such as the Internet, they can send messages to anyone in the world. While this is an important tool, there are several other ways in which one user, or—more importantly—the system administrator can communicate with another user or users.

This chapter covers the means by which an administrator, or user, can communicate with another user, other than by electronic mail. While some of the methods are useful only under specific conditions, most can be implemented on any UNIX operating system.

write-ing to Other Users

The simplest means by which to send a message to another user currently on the system is with the write command. Use who to find out if a user is on the system (unlike mail, you cannot write to a user unless they are on the system) and then summon write. The following is an example:

```
$ who
hanna        ttya        Aug 27 06:35
evan         ttyb        Aug 31 19:24
$

$ write cliff
cliff is not logged on.
$

$ write evan
```

At this point, the other user's terminal beeps twice and displays the following:

```
Message from {you} on {node name} {terminal} [ {date} ] ...
Message from hanna on NRP (ttya) [ Tue Aug 31 06:41:53 ] ...
```

The prompt disappears from both terminals. Begin typing your message and the write utility copies the lines from your terminal to the terminal of the other user every time the Return key is pressed.

Thus, if you type **how about lunch?** and press Enter, this message appears on his or her screen. If you press Enter on his or her terminal, a prompt reappears, but what he or she types does not show on your terminal. For that to take place, he or she needs to invoke the following:

```
write {your name}
```

To respond to hanna, evan uses the following command:

```
$  write hanna
```

Communication continues, from one terminal to another, until you press Ctrl+D. At that point, your prompt returns, and his or her screen displays <EOT> or <EOF>, indicating the end of the transmission.

If a user is logged into the system more than once, or more than one user is using the same login (never a good idea), you need to follow the name of the user to whom you want to write with his or her terminal identification. For example, assume that two users have logged in as root, but you only want to write to one of them. The following example shows two users logged is as root:

```
$ who
hanna      ttya        Aug 27 06:35
root       ttyb        Aug 31 19:24
root       ttyv008     Aug 27 05:19
$


$ write root
root is logged on more than one place.
You are connected to "ttyb".
Other locations are:
ttyv008
$
```

By not specifying the terminal, the message could not be sent to the intended party. The first occurrence of the designated user in the /etc/utmp file is assumed to be the user with whom you want to commmunicate. Given that there are two users logged in with that name, you are facing a fifty-fifty proposition.

The preferred method of specifying the user with whom you want to speak when more than one is present involves giving the terminal location as well.

```
$ write root ttyb
```

In selecting which of the two users is the one to whom you intend to write, the finger command is of some help, but for the most part, it is up to you to know which terminal a user predominantly uses.

Executing Commands in write

While in the midst of a write session with another user, you can still run shell commands on your terminal. To do so, the first character of the line must be an exclamation mark (!). write will then assume the rest of the line to be a command and will execute that command.

Substituting hello

A non-standard utility that is included with SCO UNIX is hello. hello is a special version of write that displays your typing on the target terminal the minute you press a key. write works in batch mode by waiting until you press <Return> before displaying the message on the target terminal, and hello works in real-time mode.

VIII

The Internet and Communications

Using talk

talk is an interactive form of write that exists in many versions of UNIX—particularly Berkeley. When invoked, it informs the other user that you want to talk to him or her. It continuously retries—sending a message to him or her every two minutes—unless interrupted by you. He or she responds by calling talk and specifying your user name.

On both terminals the screen is divided with a dashed line in the middle. What each user types appears on the top half of his screen, and what the other types appears on the bottom half. After the session has been established, the session is terminated on both ends when either user exits.

talk examines the status of the mesg flag to determine whether or not to enable operation and responds with `Permission denied` if the flag is set to n.

writing and talking to Another Network

If a network is present, you can write or talk to a user on a system other than the one you are on by specifying the user and machine name, separated by the at sign (@). For example, to write to cliff on the NEWRIDER system, the syntax is the following:

```
$ write cliff@NEWRIDER
```

Denying write and talk with mesg

To prevent other users from writing messages to you, and interrupting that very important government job on which you are working, use mesg n. mesg permits or denies messages. When no parameter is given, it tells you the status of the mesg flag, as in the following example:

```
$ mesg
is y
$
```

With an argument of n, it prevents messages by revoking non-user write permission on the terminal of the user. When used with an argument of y, it switches, and reinstates the permission.

The person trying to write to you receives a message informing him or her that permission has been denied.

```
$ write root
Permission denied.
$
```

If you receive the message `Warning: cannot respond, set mesg y`, after you attempt to write to a user, it means that you have mesg set to n. Therefore, you can write to the other user, but they cannot write to you. To correct the situation, set mesg to y. If you are already in the write mode, precede the message with an exclamation mark to invoke the shell, as in the following:

```
!mesg y
```

The other error that can occur, `Can no longer write to user` indicates the other user was accepting messages, but since your initial message, has denied permission (mesg n)—most uncivil of him or her.

The root, or superuser, can send messages to a user whether or not the message flag is on. For all other users, the message flag is examined before messages are accepted.

Seeing to Whom You Can Write

To see who is accepting or denying messaging through the use of write, use the who -T command.

```
$ who -T
hanna    + ttya       Aug 6  08:42
root     + ttyb       Aug 5  19:24
cliff    - tty0       Aug 5  12:40
evan     + tty1       Aug 5  14:56
$
```

A minus sign (-) between the user name and terminal port indicates that he or she is not accepting messages, while a plus sign (+) expresses that he or she can receive messages. In the previous example, the only one who cannot be written to by other users is cliff (the root, or superuser, has precedence over disable messaging).

How mesg *Really* Works

How does the who command know who is logged on? How does who -T know who is accepting messages and who is not? Better yet, why can root always print to another user's terminal, regardless of whether or not his or her mesg flag is enabling messages? The answers to these questions lie in the way terminals are configured.

Terminals are hardware components connected to computers—additional hardware components. The operating system—the software component—holds definitions for the hardware in several places. Actual definitions of what type of terminals are attached and their characteristics are kept in termcap and terminfo databases. A /dev directory off the root directory also contains all the devices for the system.

Performing an ls -l listing on this directory lists all devices attached—drives, printers, and so on. Of interest here are the terminals, which would resemble the following:

```
crw------   1 bin      terminal  0,  0 Aug 26 21:54 tty01
crw------   1 bin      terminal  0,  1 Aug 26 21:45 tty02
crw------   1 bin      terminal  0,  2 Aug 26 21:45 tty03
crw------   1 bin      terminal  0,  3 Aug 26 21:45 tty04
crw------   1 bin      terminal  0,  4 Aug 26 21:45 tty05
crw------   1 bin      terminal  0,  5 Aug 26 21:45 tty06
crw------   1 bin      terminal  0,  6 Aug 26 21:45 tty07
crw------   1 bin      terminal  0,  7 Aug 26 21:45 tty08
crw------   1 bin      terminal  0,  8 Aug 26 21:45 tty09
```

By default, bin is the owner of each file, and terminal is the group. When you login to the system, you become the owner of the terminal device on which you logged in. For example, if karen logs in on terminal 3, kristin on 5, and jenna on 7, the file descriptions change to the following:

```
crw------   1 bin      terminal  0,  0 Aug 26 21:54 tty01
crw------   1 bin      terminal  0,  1 Aug 26 21:45 tty02
crw--w----  1 karen    terminal  0,  2 Aug 26 21:45 tty03
crw------   1 bin      terminal  0,  3 Aug 26 21:45 tty04
crw--w----  1 kristin  terminal  0,  4 Aug 26 21:45 tty05
crw------   1 bin      terminal  0,  5 Aug 26 21:45 tty06
crw--w----  1 jenna    terminal  0,  6 Aug 26 21:45 tty07
crw------   1 bin      terminal  0,  7 Aug 26 21:45 tty08
crw------   1 bin      terminal  0,  8 Aug 26 21:45 tty09
```

Notice that each user becomes the owner of the device they are logged into. terminal can be thought of as a special group of which all users are essentially members (on BSD machines, terminal and daemons are interchangeable). The owner has read and write permissions to their terminal, while the terminal group (all other users) have write permission. This enables all users to write to the terminal and would show up as y in a mesg list.

If mesg n is executed, the write permission is removed for the terminal group. Suppose that kristin turns off messaging, the following lists appears:

```
crw------   1 bin      terminal  0,  0 Aug 26 21:54 tty01
crw------   1 bin      terminal  0,  1 Aug 26 21:45 tty02
crw--w----  1 karen    terminal  0,  2 Aug 26 21:45 tty03
crw------   1 bin      terminal  0,  3 Aug 26 21:45 tty04
crw------   1 kristin  terminal  0,  4 Aug 26 21:45 tty05
crw------   1 bin      terminal  0,  5 Aug 26 21:45 tty06
crw--w----  1 jenna    terminal  0,  6 Aug 26 21:45 tty07
crw------   1 bin      terminal  0,  7 Aug 26 21:45 tty08
crw------   1 bin      terminal  0,  8 Aug 26 21:45 tty09
```

kristin is able to write to the other users/terminals because they still have write permissions turned on for the group. Anyone attempting to write to kristin, however, will be told that he or she does not have permission to do so, since the write permission has been removed for the group.

A UNIX trick that enables you to restrict those who can write messages to you is to use chgrp to change the group from terminal to another group. This new group contains only the members that you are allowing to write messages to you. Those not belonging to that group will receive the permission denied message.

Up Against the wall

Whereas write enables you to send a message to one user, wall sends a message to everyone currently logged on the system—a write all. Because the user sending the message is also a user on the system, he receives the message the same as everyone else. The message, rather than being sent as it is entered, is buffered and not sent until Ctrl+D is pressed.

Typically, the utility is used by a system administrator who needs to send a message to everyone.

Using news and /etc/motd

When there is a message for everyone, you can use wall to send a message, but it only goes to the users who are currently logged on. If they are not currently logged on, you can send mail to them, but that means you have to send mail to everyone. Every person's mail file would grow by the size of the message being sent.

With news, only one file is created and all users read the same file. This reduces the amount of clutter on a system. When a user logs in, if the news command is in her login routine, the contents of any files in /usr/news, or /var/news (depending upon the vendor) are displayed on her screen. Once she sees it, her name is removed from the list of users needing to do so, and the file is not shown to her again, regardless of how many times she subsequently logs in.

If delete is pressed while a news item is being shown, the display stops and the next item is started. Another delete within one second of the first terminates news. news, invoked without any options, prints the current items. Other options that can be used are the following:

VII

The Internet and Communications

Option	Function
-a	Display all items regardless of whether they were already viewed or not.
-n	Show only the names of the current files.
-s	Show only a count of how many current files exist.

It is highly recommended that the system administrator go through the news file and parse old entries, in order to keep the file from growing too large.

The news utility displays a message to a user one time—after he or she reads the message, it will no longer appear unless he or she uses the "-n" option. Some messages, however, bear repeating and need to be displayed on every login. UNIX provides a means to accomplish this with the /etc/motd file.

Whatever the contents of this ASCII file are, they will be displayed to the terminal before the appearance of the prompt whenever the login process is successfully completed. The following is an example of this process:

```
# cat > /etc/motd
****************************************************************
*This weekend, the computer system will be down          *
*from 5:00 Saturday afternoon until                      *
*9:00 Saturday night.  Coincidentally, the boss and      *
*his wife are having a dinner party at that              *
*time, and have asked that all employees be prevented    *
*from logging in and using that as an excuse             *
*for nonattendance -------- have a nice time             *
****************************************************************
<Ctrl><D>
#
```

Now, when a user successfully completes a login, the message appears on his or her screen.

Understanding the /etc/issue File

In addition to motd, which displays messages after the successful login, it is possible to display information prior to login with issue. Many systems incorporate an /etc/issue file that contains the issue—or project—identification printed as a login prompt. It is a standard ASCII file read by getty and then written to all terminals spawned or respawned by the /etc/inittab file.

In the absence of the /etc/issue file, the login prompt is the node name, and the word login, as shown in the following:

```
New Riders Publishing
login:
```

The file can hold any information, and the contents of it will appear between the node name and prompt. The following is an example of this process:

```
# banner `uname -n` > /etc/issue
#

# exit

New Riders Publishing
XX      XX   XXXXXX    XXXXXX
XXX     XX   XX   XX   XX   XX
XXXX    XX   XX   XX   XX   XX
XX XX   XX   XXXXX     XXXXXX
XX   XXXX    XX   XX   XX
XX    XXX    XX   XX   XX
XX     XX    XX   XX   XX

login:
```

More practical uses for this file include storing messages such as System going down at 10:00, do not login past 09:30, or Scan all disks for viruses.

Using echo

One last means of writing to a user (more specifically, a terminal), regardless of the message flag status, is with the echo command and a bit of redirection. To utilize echo, you need to know which terminal the user is using, and how to address it. who will show you where the user is, and tty gives the full address. For example, to send a message to hanna, use the who command to find her device.

```
$ who
hanna       ttya          Aug 27 06:35
root        ttyb          Aug 31 19:24
root        ttyv008       Aug 27 05:19
$
```

Although the terminal is abbreviated ttya, the true address is slightly longer.

```
$ tty
/dev/ttya
$
```

Using this complete address, a message can be sent with the following command:

```
$ echo You had best not be playing games > /dev/ttya
```

Once again, for this to be successful, write permission (mesg y) must be enabled on the terminal to which you, as a member of the terminal group, are writing.

In addition to straightforward echoing, all of the guidelines and possibilities that exist for echoing to your terminal also hold true when going to another terminal. For example, to send the same message and include beeps, enclose the message in quotation marks and add \7's.

```
$ echo "\7\7You had best not be playing games" > /dev/ttya
```

Other escape conventions that can be embedded in the message are the following:

Option	Result
\b	backspace
\f	form-feed
\n	new-line
\r	carriage return
\t	tab

Single quotation marks are used to send the output of executed commands to the other screen. For example, the following clear command clears the receiving screen, while the following date command sends the current date and time to the screen:

```
$ echo `clear` > /dev/ttya
$ echo `date` > /dev/ttya
```

The contents of a memo file can also be sent, but echo views the entire file as a command, and does not see the carriage returns.

Thus you can create a memo file such as the following, and attempt to echo it with the command, $ echo `cat memo` > /dev/ttya:

```
Support will be doing full
system backups tomorrow evening.
Please do not plan on using the
system between 8:30 and 10:00.
Thank you.
```

However, the following is what shows on-screen, and not what you originally typed:

```
Support will be doing full system backups tomorrow evening. Please do
not plan on using the system between 8:30 and 10:00. Thank you.
```

To alleviate this problem, when you create the memo file, add the new line characters directly in the text, and echo will interpret them when it sends the file to the terminal, as in the following:

```
Support will be doing full\n
system backups tomorrow evening.\n
Please do not plan on using the\n
system between 8:30 and 10:00.\n
Thank you.\n
```

Summary

UNIX offers several ways for users to communicate with each other electronically besides electronic mail. These include write, hello, talk, wall, news, echo, and several system files that can be used by an administrator to send messages to users.

VIII

The Internet and Communications

Part IX

Connections

Chapter Snapshot

In the days of old, input went into a computer in the form of punch cards. Those days, thankfully, have passed by and been replaced by the computer terminal. This chapter discusses the software interactions between the operating system and each connected terminal, including the following:

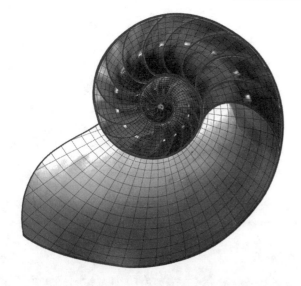

Terminal Interfacing

Having a computer that hums along smoothly does little good if you are unable to interface with it. The days of punch cards and readers are long gone, thankfully, and the terminal screen is the primary interface of choice these days.

Basically, two methods are available for configuring terminals in the UNIX operating system—both using a database-type structure. These two methods involve using either terminfo or termcap entries to create a database of terminal descriptions.

This chapter covers not only the two configuration methods, but also other utilities, such as stty, which make terminals and computers operate together amiably.

Setting and Seeing Options with the stty Utility

In simple terms, a terminal is referred to as a *tty*, and you thus use the *stty* utility to set, or see, tty-related information. To see a quick listing of some of the options currently in effect on the terminal, type stty at a prompt, as in the following example:

```
$ stty
speed 9600 baud; evenp clocal
erase = ^h; swtch = ^`;
brkint -inpck icrnl -ixany onlcr tab3
echo -echoe echok
```

To see an even more detailed listing, use the -a option, as in the following example:

```
$ stty -a
speed 9600 baud; line = 0; intr = DEL; quit = ^|; erase = ^h;
kill = @; eof = ^d; eol = ^`; swtch = ^`
parenb -parodd cs7 -cstopb clocal cread -clocal -hdx -revs_ch
-loblk -ignbrk brkint ignpar -parmrk -inpck istrip -inlcr -igncr
icrnl -iuclc ixon -ixany -ixoff -irts -errbel -extend
isig icanon -xcase echo -echoe echok -echonl -noflsh
opost -olcuc onlcr -ocrnl -onocr -onlret -ofill -ofdel tab3
$
```

Among other things, this semicolon-delimited display reports that the erase, or backspace, character for this terminal is Ctrl+H, the @ character causes the line typed to be ignored, and Ctrl+D is used to signify the end of a file (when creating with cat, for example).

In addition to viewing the options, you can change them with the stty command as well. Just follow the command with the option, mode, and device. To change the baud rate to 1200, for example, use the following command:

```
stty 1200
```

One of the more "clever" commands to try is stty 0, which kills the connection right then and there by setting the baud rate to 0.

Other options shown by the stty -a command can be broken into categories by the operation they govern. The categories are control mode, input mode, output mode, local mode, control assignments, and combination modes.

Setting Control Modes

Table 33.1 shows the control modes and the various values that you can assign to them. Default values are given, with alternatives shown within parentheses.

Table 33.1
Control Modes

Value	Function
0	Immediately hang up the connection.
300, 600, 1200, 1800, 2400, 4800, 9600, exta,extb	Set baud rate.
clocal (-clocal)	Establish a line with or without modem control.
cread (-cread)	Enable or disable receiver.
cs5, cs6, cs7, cs8	Establish character size.
cstopb (-cstopb)	Use two or one stop bit per character.
extend (-extend)	Enable or disable eight-bit transferring.
hdx (-hdx)	Enable or disable half duplexing.
hup (-hup)	Same as hupcl.
hupcl (-hupcl)	Hang up or not hang up connection on last close.
loblk (-loblk)	Block or not the output from a layer.
parenb (-parenb)	Enable or disable parity detection.
parodd (-parodd)	Select odd or even parity.
revs_ch (-revs_ch)	Enable or disable the secondary clear-to-send signal.

Setting Input Modes

Table 33.2 shows the input modes and the various values that you can assign to them. The default values are given, with alternatives shown within parentheses.

Table 33.2
Input Modes

Value	Function
brkint (-brkint)	Signal or not the INTR on break.
err_bel (-err_bel)	Sound or not the alarm on parity error.
icrnl (-icrnl)	Map or not CR to NL on input.
ignbrk (-ignbrk)	Ignore or not the break on input.
igncr (-igncr)	Ignore or not CR on input.
ignpar (-ignpar)	Ignore or not parity errors.
inlcr (-inlcr)	Map or not NL to CR on input.
inpck (-inpck)	Enable or disable parity checking on input.
irts (-irts)	Set and reset or not the request-to-send signal when the input queue is full or empty.
istrip (-istrip)	Strip or not input characters to seven bits.
iuclc (-iuclc)	Map or not uppercase to lowercase.
ixany (-ixany)	Allow any character or only DC1 to restart output.
ixoff (-ixoff)	Have the system send or not send START/STOP characters when queue is full or empty.
ixon (-ixon)	Enable or disable START/STOP output control.
parmrk (-parmrk)	Mark or not parity errors.

Setting Output Modes

Table 33.3 shows the various output mode parameters that are available. Again, nondefault entries are shown within parentheses.

Table 33.3
Output Modes

Value	Function
bs0, bs1	Select style of delay for backspaces.
cr0, cr1, cr2, cr3	Select style of delay for carriage returns.
ff0, ff1	Select style of delay for form feeds.
nl0, nl1	Select style of delay for line feeds.

 Delays relate to how many microseconds the system waits before taking the action. Quite often this defines the repeat rate for the key. If you hold the backspace key down for a short period of time, for example, the cursor should move back one space or two.

ocrnl (-ocrnl)	Map or not CR to NL on output.
ofdel (-ofdel)	Specify whether fill characters are DELs or NULs.
ofill (-ofill)	Specify whether fill characters are used for delays.
olcuc (-olcuc)	Map or not lowercase to uppercase on output.
onlcr (-onlcr)	Map or not NL to CR-NL on output.
onlret (-onlret)	Determine whether NL does or does not do CRs on the terminal.
onocr (-onocr)	Do not or do output CRs at column 0.
opost (-opost)	Post-process output or not.
tab0, tab1, tab2, tab3	Select style of delay for horizontal tab.
vt0, vt1	Select style of delay for vertical tab.

Setting Local Modes

Table 33.4 shows local parameters—those governing operations at your local terminal and keyboard.

Table 33.4
Local Modes

Value	Function
echo (-echo)	Echo back or not every character typed.
echoe (-echoe)	Echo or not ERASE as a backspace-space-backspace string.
echok (-echok)	Echo or not NL after KILL character.
echonl (-echonl)	Echo or not NL.
icanon (-icanon)	Enable or disable ERASE and KILL processing.
isig (-isig)	Enable or disable checking of characters against control characters INTR, QUIT, and SWTCH.
lfkc (-lfkc)	Same as echok.
noflsh (-noflsh)	Disable or enable flush after INTR, QUIT, or SWTCH.
stappl (-stappl)	Use application or line mode on synchronous lines.
stflush (-stflush)	Enable or disable flush on synchronous lines.
stwrap (-stwrap)	Disable or enable truncation of long lines.
xcase (-xcase)	Change or not upper- to lowercase.

Setting Control Assignments

Table 33.5 shows the assignment of control characters. These settings have no true defaults; you can set them to any value.

Table 33.5
Control Assignments

Value	Function
control-character c	Set the control character to c, where the control character is erase, kill, intr, quit, swtch, eof, ctab, min, or time. ^? is interpreted as DEL, and ^- is interpreted as undefined.
line i	Set line discipline to i (must be greater than 0 and less than 127).

Setting Combination Modes

The parameters shown in table 33.6 control various operations in combination with others.

Table 33.6
Combination Modes

Value	Function
-parity, -evenp, or -oddp	Disable parenb, and set cs8.
ek	Reset ERASE and KILL characters back to normal.
evenp or parity	Enable parenb and cs7.
LCASE (-LCASE)	Same as lcase.
lcase (-lcase)	Set or unset xcase, iuclc, and olcuc.
nl (-nl)	Unset or set icrnl, onlcr.
oddp	Enable parenb, cs7, and parodd.
raw (-raw or cooked)	Enable or disable raw input and output (no ERASE, KILL, INTR, QUIT, SWTCH, EOT, or output processing).
sane	Reset all modes to reasonable values.
tabs (-tabs or tab3)	Preserve tabs or expand them to spaces during printing.
term	Set all modes suitable for the terminal type term.

Setting Additional Options

To see the options for a terminal other than the one on which you are presently working, feed the terminal into the stty command. To see the options on tty03, for example, type this command:

```
stty </dev/tty03
```

Additionally, you can use a -g option to generate output in numerical format that you then can use to set another terminal. Consider the following example:

```
$ stty -g
526:1805:9ad:2b:7f:1c:8:40:4:0:0:0
$
```

To use this information to set tty03 identical to the terminal at which you are currently sitting, use this command:

```
$ stty 526:1805:9ad:2b:7f:1c:8:40:4:0:0:0 < tty03
$
```

Using the tabs Command

The tabs command enables you to set tab definitions on a terminal according to the tabspec specification. To work properly, tabs must know the type of terminal, which you can specify by using the -T option. If no -T option is specified, tabs searches the $TERM value in the environment and/or sets the tabs and margins by using the standard output. If no tabspec is given, the default value is -8, and the lowest column number is 1. To invoke tabs tailored to programming languages, use the following tabspecs.

Option	Settings	Standard format
-a	1,10,16,36,72	Assembler, IBM S/370, first format
-a2	1,10,16,40,72	Assembler, IBM S/370, second format
-c	1,8,12,16,20,55	COBOL, normal format
-c2	1,6,10,14,49	COBOL, compact format
-c3	1,6,10,14,18,22, 26,30,34,38,42,46, 50,54,58,62,67	Another version of COBOL compact format
- f	1,7,11,15,19,23	FORTRAN
- p	1,5,9,13,17,21, 25,29,33,37,41,45, 49,53,57,61	PL/I
-s	1,10,55	SNOBOL
-u	1,12,20,44	UNIVAC 1100 Assembler

Additionally, the following three other tabspec types exist:

-*n*   Repeats the tab every *n* columns (1+*n*, 1+2**n, and so on). -0 implies no tabs at all.

*n*1,*n*2,...   Arbitrary format permits specifying any set of numbers, up to 40, separated by commas, in ascending order.

- -*file*   Reads the first line of *file* for tab specifications. If a list is not found, the default of 8 is used.

You can use the following two other options in addition to the tab specification:

-T*type*   Denotes *type* as the terminal type.

+m*n*   Moves all tabs over *n* columns by making column *n*+1 the left margin.

Working with the Termcap Database

Termcap is an ASCII database of terminal descriptions in the /etc directory used by programs that need to customize their operation for the terminal. Classic examples are vi, the visual editor, which must conform to the number of lines and size of the terminal calling it, more, and pg, which must have access to similar information.

Terminal descriptions contain nothing more than initialization sequences, the capabilities of the terminal, a description of how operations are performed, and padding requirements.

Note   UNIX systems use either termcap or terminfo, not both.

The easiest way to generate a terminal description is by copying the description from another entry in the file and making necessary changes to reflect the new terminal. To test the description, set TERMCAP, the environmental variable, to the path name of a file containing the description on which you are working, and the software looks there rather than in /etc/termcap. After you have the definition properly working, move it into the /etc/termcap database.

Entries in etc/termcap are of records separated by pound signs (#) and fields separated by colons (:). The first entry for each terminal gives the known names for the terminal, separated by pipe (I) characters. The first name must always be two characters long and is used by older UNIX systems which store the terminal type in a 16-bit word in a systemwide database.

The second name is the most common abbreviation for the terminal. The third and final name can be a complete description used to identify the terminal fully. It is the only field in any entry that can contain blanks.

Following is an example of a complete entry for a terminal:

```
$ cat /etc/termcap ¦ more
#
na¦vwpt60¦ADDS Viewpoint 60/R40:\
co#80:li#24:bs:am:cl=^L:ti=^X^L:te=^X:\
cm=\EY%+ %+
:ce=\EK:cd=\Ek:kh=^A:kl=^U:bc=^U:kr=^F:nd=^F:ku=^Z:up=^Z:\
kd=^J:do=^J:kb=^H:kc=^M:so=\E0P:se=\E0@:sg#1:ul:us=\E0`:ue=\E0@:u
g#1:\
k1=\E1:k2=\E2:k3=\E3:k4=\E4:k5=\E5:k6=\E6:k7=\E7:k8=\E8:k9=\E9:\
CO=^X:CF=^W:MP=^X^L:MR=^X:\
PU=\E\\+1:PD=\E\\+2:PL=\E\\+3:PR=\E\\+4:NU=\E\\+5:CW=\E\\+6:\
EN=\E\\+7:WL=\E\\+8:WR=\E\\+9:CL=\E\\+0:CR=\E\\+-:DL=\E\\+=:\
CN=^X:CF=^W:RS=\E0@:NM=\E0@:NB=\E0B:NR=\E0P:NS=\E0R:AL=\E0A:AB=\E
0C:\
AR=\E0Q:AS=\E0S:OV#1:
#
```

Notice the first line, na¦vwpt60¦ADDS Viewpoint 60/R40:\, and how it conforms to the description given. All other lines refer to the capabilities of the terminal. These are Boolean capabilities indicating a feature, numeric capabilities giving the size of the terminal or the size of particular delays, and string capabilities, giving a sequence used to perform particular terminal operations.

Capabilities that can appear in an entry are listed and briefly defined in table 33.7.

Table 33.7
Terminal Capabilities in Termcap

Capability	Description
ae	End alternate character set
al	Add new blank line
am	Terminal has automatic margins
as	Start alternate character set

Capability	Description
bc	Backspace if not ^H
bs	Terminal can backspace with ^H
bt	Backtab
bw	Backspace wraps from column 0 to last column
CC	Command character in prototype if terminal can be set
cd	Clear to end of display
ce	Clear to end of line
ch	Cursor horizontal motion only; line stays the same
cl	Clear screen
cm	Cursor motion
co	Number of columns in a line
cr	Carriage return (default ^M)
cs	Change scrolling region (vt100); like cm
cv	Like ch but vertical only
da	Display may be retained above
dB	Number of milliseconds of bs delay needed
db	Display may be retained below
dC	Number of milliseconds of cr delay needed
dc	Delete character
dF	Number of milliseconds of ff delay needed
dl	Delete line
dm	Delete mode (enter)
dN	Number of milliseconds of nl delay needed

continues

Table 33.7, Continued
Terminal Capabilities in Termcap

Capability	Description
do	Down one line
dT	Number of milliseconds of tab delay needed
ed	End delete mode
ei	End insert mode; give :ei=: if ic
eo	Can erase overstrikes with a blank
ff	Hard-copy terminal page eject (default ^L)
hc	Hard-copy terminal
hd	Half-line down (forward 1/2 linefeed)
ho	Home cursor (if no cm)
hu	Half-line up (reverse 1/2 linefeed)
hz	Hazeltine; can't print ~ symbols
ic	Insert character
if	Name of file containing is
im	Insert mode (enter); give :im=: if ic
in	Insert mode distinguishes nulls on display
ip	Insert pad after character inserted
is	Terminal initialization string
k0-k9	Sent by other function keys 0 through 9
kb	Sent by Backspace key
kc	Sent by line termination sequence (such as NEWLINE)
kd	Sent by terminal down-arrow key
ke	Out of keypad transmit mode
kh	Sent by Home key

Capability	Description
kl	Sent by terminal left-arrow key
kn	Number of other keys
ko	Termcap entries for other nonfunction keys
kr	Sent by terminal right-arrow key
ks	Put terminal in keypad transmit mode
ku	Sent by terminal up-arrow key
l0-l9	Labels on other function keys
li	Number of lines on screen or page
ll	Last line, first column (if no cm)
ma	Arrow key map, used by vi version 2 only
mi	Safe to move while in insert mode
ml	Memory lock on above cursor
ms	Safe to move while in standout and underline mode
mu	Memory unlock (turn off memory lock)
nc	No correctly working carriage return
nd	Nondestructive space (cursor right)
nl	Newline character (default \n)
ns	Terminal is a CRT but does not scroll
os	Terminal overstrikes
pc	Pad character (rather than null)
pt	Has hardware tabs (might need to be set with is)
se	End standout mode
sf	Scroll forward

continues

Table 33.7, Continued
Terminal Capabilities in Termcap

Capability	Description
sg	Number of blank characters left by so or se
so	Begin standout mode
sr	Scroll reverse (backward)
ta	Tab (other than ^I or with padding)
tc	Entry of similar terminal; must be last
te	String to end programs that use cm
ti	String to begin programs that use cm
uc	Underscore one character and move past it
ue	End underscore mode
ug	Number of blank characters left by us or ue
ul	Terminal underlines even though it does not overstrike
up	Upline (cursor up)
us	Start underscore mode
vb	Visible bell (might not move cursor)
ve	Sequence to end open/visual mode
vs	Sequence to start open/visual mode
xb	Beehive (F1=Esc, F2=Ctrl+C)
xn	A newline is ignored after a wrap
xr	Return acts like ce \r \n
xs	Standout not erased by writing over it
xt	Tabs are destructive; magic so character

Defining the Sample Entry

Looking at the sample entry for a vwpt60 given at the beginning of this section, you can see that the second line sets the number of columns to 80 and lines to 24. Backspacing and automatic margins are enabled. The screen can be cleared with Ctrl+L. Cursor motion is enabled with Ctrl+X+L and disabled with Ctrl+X. The third line defines cursor motion, and the fourth line covers clearing to the end of the line, end of the display, and so on. The \ character at the end of each line merely indicates that the description is continuing onto the next line.

Examining Other Capabilities

Other capabilities that serve specific purposes and can appear in entries are listed in table 33.8.

Table 33.8
Other Terminal Capabilities in Termcap

Capability	Description
AB	Cobol runtime : alternate blinking
AL	Cobol runtime : change to alternate intensity
AR	Cobol runtime : normal reverse video
AS	Cobol runtime : alternate blinking and reverse
CF	Cobol runtime : make cursor invisible
CN	Cobol runtime : make cursor visible
EN	Multiplan : keystroke to move to end of spreadsheet
MP	Multiplan : terminal initialization on entry
MR	Multiplan : terminal reset on exit
NB	Cobol runtime : normal blinking
NM	Cobol runtime : change to normal intensity
NR	Cobol runtime : normal reverse video

continues

Table 33.8, Continued
Other Terminal Capabilities in Termcap

Capability	Description
NS	Cobol runtime : normal blinking and reverse
NU	Multiplan : keystroke to move to next unlocked cell
OV	Cobol runtime : overhead, same as ug and sg
kA-kZ	SNA communication
lA-lZ	SNA communication (The most critical SNA capabilities are listed in table 33.9.)

Table 33.9 introduces the SNA capabilities available in Termcap entries.

Table 33.9
SNA Capabilities

Name	Function	Hex	Function
lE	FLE	C2	Enter
lI	FLI	C6	Clear
lJ	FLJ	C7	Up; should agree with ku
lK	FLK	C8	Backspace
lL	FLL	C9	Newline
lM	FLM	CA	Tab
lN	FLN	CB	Backtab
lO	FLO	CC	Shiftlock
lP	FLP	CD	Insert
lQ	FLQ	CE	Field mark (FM)
lR	FLR	CF	Attention (ATTN)
lS	FLS	D0	SYS REQ

Name	Function	Hex	Function
lT	FLT	D1	ERASE INPUT
lU	FLU	D2	ERASE EOF
lV	FLV	D3	RESET
lW	FLW	D4	DUP
lX	FLX	D5	QUIT
lY	FLY	D6	Hard-copy
lZ	FLZ	D7	DELETE

To find out the capabilities of your terminal, you should consult the guide to operations that came with the terminal, and, in particular, the emulations tables and addressing charts.

Working with the Second Database: terminfo

If your UNIX system uses termcap databases, making changes to the descriptions are fairly easy because the entries are stored in an ASCII file. If your system uses terminfo, things are a bit more difficult to change.

Instead of having one database file, a file exists for every terminal description. Instead of being ASCII readable, it is compiled and executable (compiling is done with tic, which is discussed later in this section). All files are kept in the directory /usr/lib/terminfo/{first character of the description}/{file}. Thus, the vwpt60 file would be in /usr/lib/terminfo/ v/vwpt60.

Terminfo entries are created from source files having the extension .src. The source files look much like termcap entries in that they consist of one or more device descriptions, with each description consisting of a header and one or more lines listing features for that particular device.

A new twist, however, is that each line in the source file must end in a comma (,), and all lines but the header must be indented. Fields are comma-separated. A partial example of a source file for the vwpt60 entry follows:

```
¦
vwpt60¦na¦ADDS Viewpoint 60/R40,
    alt, am, ul,
    cols#80, lines#24, ma#1, xmc#1,
    bel=^G, clear=\f, cr=\r, cub1=^U, cud1=\n, cuf1=^F,
    cup=\EY%p1%´\s´%+%c%p2%´\s´%+%c, cuu1=^Z, ed=\Ek,
    el=\EK, ind=\n, kbs=\b, kcub1=^U, kcud1=\n, kcuf1=^F,
    kcuu1=^Z, kf0=\E0, kf1=\E1, kf2=\E2, kf3=\E3, kf4=\E4,
    kf5=\E5, kf6=\E6, kf7=\E7, kf8=\E8, kf9=\E9, khome=^A,
    rmcup=^X, rmso=\E0@, rmul=\E0@, smcup=^X\f,
    smso=\E0P^N, smul=\E0`,
```

The header can have as many aliases as you like, but it must contain at least two, separated by pipes (I). The last field is the long name of the device and once again can consist of free text. You can add suffixes to device names—for example, vwpt60-w—to signify special meaning. Valid suffixes include the following:

-am	Automatic margins
-n	Number of lines on-screen
-na	No arrow keys
-nam	Without automatic margins
-np	Number of pages of memory
-rv	Reverse video
-w	Wide mode

As with termcap, the easiest way to create new entries in terminfo is to modify existing source code for terminals. Next, change the TERMINFO variable in the environment to a compiled version of the file on which you are working, and test it before moving it into place.

The capabilities are almost identical to those in termcap, but some are specified differently. One of the biggest changes is that termcap attempts to keep most capabilities to two characters, and terminfo's only restriction is that the capability cannot exceed five characters in length. Table 33.10 lists the terminfo capabilities.

Table 33.10
Terminal Capabilities in Terminfo

Capability	Description
acsc	Graphic character set pairs aAbBcC - def=vt100+
alt	Alternate character set

Capability	Description
am	Terminal has automatic margins
bel	Bell
blink	Turn on blinking
bold	Turn on bold mode
bufsz	Number of bytes buffered printing columns
bw	cub1 wraps from column 0 to last column
cbt	Backtab
chr	Change horizontal resolution
chts	Cursor is hard to see
civis	Make cursor invisible
clear	Clear screen and home cursor
cnorm	Make cursor appear normal
cols	Number of columns in a line
cpi	Change number of characters per inch
cpix	Changing character pitch changes resolution
cps	Print rate in characters per second
cr	Carriage return
crxm	Using cr turns off micro mode
csnm	List of character set names
csr	Change to lines #1 through #2 (vt100)
cub	Move cursor left #1 spaces
cub1	Move cursor left one space
cud	Move cursor down #1 lines
cud1	Down one line

continues

IX

Connections

Table 33.10, Continued
Terminal Capabilities in Terminfo

Capability	Description
cuf	Move cursor right #1 spaces
cuf1	Cursor right
cup	Cursor motion to row #1 col #2
cuu	Move cursor up #1 lines
cuu1	Cursor up
cvr	Change vertical resolution
cvvis	Make cursor visible
cwin	Define window #1 to go from #2, #3, to #4
da	Display may be retained above the screen
daisy	Printer needs operator to change character set
db	Display may be retained below the screen
dch	Delete #1 chars
dch1	Delete character
dclk	Display time-of-day clock
defc	Define a character in a set
dial	Dial phone number #1
dim	Turn on half-bright mode
dl	Delete #1 lines
dl1	Delete line
dsl	Disable status line
ech	Erase #1 characters
ed	Clear to end of display
el	Clear to end of line

Capability	Description
el1	Clear to beginning of line
enacs	Enable alternate character set
eo	Can erase overstrikes with a blank
eslok	Esc can be used on the status line
ff	Hard-copy terminal page eject
flash	Visible bell; locked cursor
fsl	Return from status line
gn	Generic line type
hc	Hard-copy terminal
hd	Half-line down
home	Home cursor
hook	Flash the switch hook
hpa	Horizontal position
hs	Has extra status line
ht	Tab to next eight-space hardware tab stop
hts	Set a tab in all rows, current column
hu	Half-line up (reverse 1/2 linefeed)
hup	Hang up phone
ich	Insert #1 blank characters
ich1	Insert character
if	Name of initialization file
il	Add #1 new blank lines
il1	Add new blank line

continues

Table 33.10, Continued
Terminal Capabilities in Terminfo

Capability	Description
in	Insert mode distinguishes nulls
ind	Scroll text up
indn	Scroll forward #1 lines
invis	Turn on blank mode
ip	Insert pad after character inserted
iprog	Path name of program for initialization
is1	Terminal initialization string
is2	Terminal initialization string
is3	Terminal initialization string
it	Tabs initially every # spaces
ka1	KEY_A1, 0534, upper left of keypad
ka3	KEY_A3, 0535, upper right of keypad
kb2	KEY_B2, 0536, center of keypad
kbeg	KEY_BEG, 0542, sent by beg key
kbs	KEY_BACKSPACE, 0407, sent by backspace key
kc1	KEY_C1, 0537, lower left of keypad
kc3	KEY_C3, 0540, lower right of keypad
kcan	KEY_CANCEL, 0543, sent by cancel key
kcbt	KEY_BTAB, 0541, sent by backtab key
kclo	KEY_CLOSE, 0544, sent by close key
kclr	KEY_CLEAR, 0515, sent by clear-screen or erase key
kcmd	KEY_COMMAND, 0545, sent by command key
kcpy	KEY_COPY, 0546, sent by copy key ... and so on with k and each keyboard key...

Capability	Description
km	Has a meta key
ktbc	KEY_CATAB, 0526, sent by clear-all-tabs key
lh	Number of rows in each label
lines	Number of lines on screen or page
ll	Last line, first column
lm	Lines of memory if > lines
lpi	Change number of lines per inch
lpix	Changing line pitch changes resolution
lw	Number of columns in each label
maddr	Maximum value in micro_address
mc0	Print contents of the screen
mc4	Turn off the printer
mc5	Turn on the printer
mc5i	Printer won't echo on-screen
mc5p	Turn on the printer for #1 bytes
mcs	Character step size when in micro mode
mcub	Like parm_down_cursor for micro adjust
mcud	Like parm_down_cursor for micro adjust
mcuf	Like parm_down_cursor for micro adjust
mcuu	Like parm_down_cursor for micro adjust
mgc	Clear left and right soft margins
mir	Safe to move while in insert mode
mjump	Maximum value in parm_micro
mls	Line step size when in micro mode

continues

Table 33.10, Continued
Terminal Capabilities in Terminfo

Capability	Description
mrcup	Memory relative cursor addressing
msgr	Safe to move in standout modes
ndscr	Scrolling region is nondestructive
nel	Newline
nlab	Number of labels on-screen
npc	Pad character doesn't exist
npins	Number of pins in printhead
nrrmc	smcup does not reverse rmcup
nxon	Padding won't work; xon/xoff required
orc	Horizontal resolution in units per character
orhi	Horizontal resolution in units per inch
orl	Vertical resolution in units per line
orvi	Vertical resolution in units per inch
os	Terminal overstrikes on hard-copy terminal
pad	Pad character
pause	Pause for two or three seconds
pb	Lowest baud rate where padding needed
pfkey	Program function key #1 to type string #2
pfloc	Program function key #1 to execute string #2
pfx	Program function key #1 to xmit string #2
pln	Program label #1 to show string #2
prot	Turn on protected mode
pulse	Select pulse dialing
qdial	Dial phone number #1, without progress detection

Capability	Description
rbim	End printing bit-image graphics
rc	Restore cursor to position of last sc
rcsd	End definition of a character set
rep	Repeat char #1 #2 times
rev	Turn on reverse video mode
rfi	Send next input character
ri	Scroll text down
rin	Scroll backward #1 lines
ritm	Disable italics
rlm	Enable rightward carriage motion
rmacs	End alternate character set
rmam	Turn off automatic margins
rmclk	Remove time-of-day clock
rmcup	String to end programs that use cup
rmdc	End delete mode
rmicm	Disable micro motion capabilities
rmir	End insert mode
rmp	Like ip but when in replace mode
rmso	End standout mode
rmul	End underscore mode
rmxon	Turn off xon/xoff handshaking
rs1	Reset terminal completely to sane modes
rshm	Disable shadow printing
rsubm	Disable subscript printing

continues

Table 33.10, Continued
Terminal Capabilities in Terminfo

Capability	Description
rsupm	Disable superscript printing
rum	Enable downward carriage motion
rwidm	Disable double-wide printing
sam	Printing in last column causes cr
sbim	Start printing bit-image graphics
sc	Save cursor position
sclk	Set time-of-day clock
scs	Select character set
scsd	Start definition of a character set
sdrfq	Set draft-quality print
sgr	Define the video attributes #1 through #9
sgr0	Turn off all attributes
sitm	Enable italics
slm	Enable leftward carriage motion
smacs	Start alternate character set
smam	Turn on automatic margins
smcup	String to begin programs that use cup
smdc	Delete mode
smgb	Set bottom margin at current line
smgbp	Set bottom margin at line #1 or #2 lines from bottom
smgl	Set left margin at current line
smglp	Set left (right) margin at column #1 (#2)
smgr	Set right margin at current line

Capability	Description
smgrp	Set right margin at column #1
smgt	Set top margin at current line
smgtp	Set top (bottom) margin at line #1 (#2)
smicm	Enable micro motion
smir	Insert mode
smso	Begin standout mode
smul	Start underscore mode
smxon	Turn on xon/xoff handshaking
snlq	Set near-letter-quality print
snrmq	Set normal-quality print
spinh	Spacing of pins horizontally in dots per inch
spinv	Spacing of pins vertically in pins per inch
sshm	Enable shadow printing
ssubm	Enable subscript printing
ssupm	Enable superscript printing
sum	Enable upward carriage motion
swidm	Enable double-wide printing
tbc	Clear all tab stops
uc	Underscore one character and move past it
ul	Underline character overstrikes
vpa	Vertical position absolute
vt	Virtual terminal number
widcs	Character step size when in double-wide mode
wind	Current window is lines #1-#2 columns #3-#4

IX

Connections

continues

Table 33.10, Continued
Terminal Capabilities in Terminfo

Capability	Description
wingo	Go to window #1
wsl	Number of columns in status line
xenl	Newline ignored after 80 columns
xhp	Standout not erased by overwriting
xhpa	Only positive motion for hpa/mhpa caps
xmc	Number of blank characters left by smso or rmso
xoffc	X-off character
xon	Terminal uses xon/xoff handshaking
xonc	X-on character
xsb	Beehive (F1=Esc, F2=Ctrl+C)
xt	Destructive tabs; magic smso character
xvpa	Only positive motion for vpa/mvpa caps
zerom	No motion for the subsequent character

As a miscellaneous note, you can use pound signs at the start of a line to indicate labels, but a / character means that padding is mandatory. Padding is the amount of extra time a terminal is given to interpret a command. Both \E and \e map to the ESCAPE character.

Fully describing terminfo entries would require a volume as massive as this book. For more information on specific detail, look for *termcap & terminfo* by Strang, Mui, and O'Reilly (O'Reilly & Associates).

Using the tic Utility

The *tic* utility is the terminfo compiler that translates source code into /usr/lib/terminfo entries. You can use only the following two options:

-c   Checks the file for errors without compiling it.

-v*n*   Uses verbose format. Output of the compile is sent to the terminal, showing the progress. You can specify an arbitrary number from 1 to 10

IX

Connections

(*n*), indicating the level of detail of information. The default level is 1, and higher numbers increase the level of detail given, but no 1-for-1 ratio exists.

If a TERMINFO environmental variable exists, the compiled file is placed in that directory rather than the default /usr/lib/terminfo.

Using the infocmp Utility

A nonstandard utility that many vendors provide is *infocmp*, a utility to print or compare terminfo descriptions. Infocmp converts compiled entries into source code, enabling you to make necessary changes and recompile without having to start from scratch each time.

Options that you can use for comparison between entries include the following:

-c   Lists the capabilities that are the same between the entries or that they have in common.

-d   Lists the differences in capabilities.

-n   Lists each capability in neither entry and provides a quick check to see what was left out of the description.

Options that you can use when obtaining the source code include the following:

-C   Uses termcap names.

-I   Uses terminfo names.

-L   Uses C variable names from <term.h>.

-r   Must be used in conjunction with -C to list capabilities in termcap form.

Other options include the following:

-s   Sorts fields within each type according to the following argument:
         d   the order stored in the database
         i   terminfo name
         l   the long C variable name
         c   the termcap name

-v   Verbosely prints tracing information to the terminal as the program executes.

-V   Program version number is printed on exit.

-w   Changes output to width characters.

-1   Fields are printed one to a line.

Following are examples of the infocmp utility. The first command changes to the terminfo directory and does a listing there. As you can see, there is a subdirectory for each letter of the alphabet with which a terminal type can begin. Following that, a change is made to the v directory and a listing shows all of the terminal types defined for this system that start with v. Lastly, infocmp is used to show the contents of the vwpt60 directory—first altogether, then one line at a time—and compare it to the vwpt78 definition.

```
$ cd /usr/lib/terminfo
$ ls -l
total 224
drwxr-xr-x   2 root      rootgrp        48 Apr  5  1990 1
drwxr-xr-x   2 root      rootgrp        48 Apr  5  1990 2
drwxr-xr-x   2 root      rootgrp        48 Apr  5  1990 3
drwxr-xr-x   2 root      rootgrp       128 Apr  5  1990 4
drwxr-xr-x   2 root      rootgrp       128 Apr  5  1990 7
-rwxr-xr-x   1 root      rootgrp       404 Apr  3  1990 DMV.ti
-rwxr-xr-x   1 root      rootgrp       314 Apr  3  1990 README
drwxr-xr-x   2 root      rootgrp        80 Apr  5  1990 a
-rwxr-xr-x   1 root      rootgrp      2883 Apr  3  1990 adds.ti
drwxr-xr-x   2 root      rootgrp        96 Apr  5  1990 d
-rwxr-xr-x   1 root      rootgrp      6613 Apr  3  1990 dec.ti
drwxr-xr-x   2 root      rootgrp       112 Apr  5  1990 i
-rwxr-xr-x   1 root      rootgrp       881 Apr  3  1990 ibm.ti
drwxr-xr-x   2 root      rootgrp       368 Apr  5  1990 n
-rw-r--r--   1 root      rootgrp      7683 Apr  3  1990 ncr.ti
drwxr-xr-x   2 root      rootgrp        64 Apr  5  1990 p
-rw-r--r--   1 bin       bin         18184 Mar  3  1990 printer.ti
drwxr-xr-x   2 root      rootgrp        96 Apr  5  1990 t
drwxr-xr-x   2 root      rootgrp        64 Apr  5  1990 u
drwxr-xr-x   2 root      rootgrp       160 Apr  5  1990 v
drwxr-xr-x   2 root      rootgrp        96 Apr  5  1990 w
-rw-r--r--   1 root      rootgrp      1783 Apr  3  1990 wyse.ti
$

$ cd v
$

$ ls -l
total 64
-rw-r--r--   2 root      rootgrp      1201 Apr  3  1990 vt100
-rw-r--r--   2 root      rootgrp      1229 Apr  3  1990 vt220
-rw-r--r--   2 root      rootgrp      1256 Apr  3  1990 vt240
```

```
-rw-r--r--   2 root      rootgrp        975 Apr  3  1990 vwpt
-rw-r--r--   2 root      rootgrp       1277 Apr  3  1990 vwpt122
-rw-r--r--   2 root      rootgrp        988 Apr  3  1990 vwpt3a+
-rw-r--r--   2 root      rootgrp        995 Apr  3  1990 vwpt60
-rw-r--r--   2 root      rootgrp        988 Apr  3  1990 vwpt78
$

$ infocmp vwpt60
vwpt60¦na¦ADDS Viewpoint 60/R40,
        alt, am, ul,
        cols#80, lines#24, ma#1, xmc#1,
        bel=^G, clear=\f, cr=\r, cub1=^U, cud1=\n, cuf1=^F,
        cup=\EY%p1%´\s´%+%c%p2%´\s´%+%c, cuu1=^Z, ed=\Ek,
        el=\EK, ind=\n, kbs=\b, kcub1=^U, kcud1=\n, kcuf1=^F,
        kcuu1=^Z, kf0=\E0, kf1=\E1, kf2=\E2, kf3=\E3, kf4=\E4,
        kf5=\E5, kf6=\E6, kf7=\E7, kf8=\E8, kf9=\E9, khome=^A,
        rmcup=^X, rmso=\E0@, rmul=\E0@, smcup=^X\f,
        smso=\E0P^N, smul=\E0`,
$

$ infocmp -1 vwpt60
vwpt60¦na¦ADDS Viewpoint 60/R40,
        alt,
        am,
        ul,
        cols#80,
        lines#24,
        ma#1,
        xmc#1,
        bel=^G,
        clear=\f,
        cr=\r,
        cub1=^U,
        cud1=\n,
        cuf1=^F,
        cup=\EY%p1%´\s´%+%c%p2%´\s´%+%c,
        cuu1=^Z,
        ed=\Ek,
        el=\EK,
        ind=\n,
        kbs=\b,
```

```
                    kcub1=^U,
                    kcud1=\n,
                    kcuf1=^F,
                    kcuu1=^Z,
                    kf0=\E0,
                    kf1=\E1,
                    kf2=\E2,
                    kf3=\E3,
                    kf4=\E4,
                    kf5=\E5,
                    kf6=\E6,
                    kf7=\E7,
                    kf8=\E8,
                    kf9=\E9,
                    khome=^A,
                    rmcup=^X,
                    rmso=\E0@,
                    rmul=\E0@,
                    smcup=^X\f,
                    smso=\E0P^N,
                    smul=\E0`,
        $

        $ infocmp vwpt60 vwpt78
        comparing vwpt60 to vwpt78.
            comparing Boolean.
                ul: T:F.
            comparing numbers.
            comparing strings.
                el:  ´\EK´,´\EK$<25>´.
                kcub1:  ´^U´,´\E`´.
                kcud1:  ´\n´,´\E\^´.
                kcuf1:  ´^F´,´\Eb´.
                kcuu1:  ´^Z´,´\E\\´.
                khome:  ´^A´,´\E=´.
                rmul:  ´\E0@´,´NULL´.
                smso:  ´\E0P^N´,´\E0P´.
                smul:  ´\E0`´,´NULL´.
        $
```

Using the captoinfo Utility

A little utility that is included with many vendors' UNIX systems is *captoinfo*, which converts a termcap description into terminfo (co becomes cols, and so on). Captoinfo looks in the specified file for termcap descriptions and creates an equivalent terminfo description for every one found.

Allowable options include the following:

-v   Verbosely prints out information on the terminal as the transformation is done.

-V   Gives the version of the program in use on exit.

-1   Forces fields to print out one to a line.

-w   Changes the output to width characters.

Understanding gettys and ttymons

While not utilities per se, gettys and ttymons are the daemon processes responsible for establishing connections with terminals using the definitions defined in the termcap and terminfo databases. Older versions of UNIX (Non SVR4) used getty processes to monitor terminal inactivity and wait for a login. Current versions of UNIX have replaced the getty process with ttymon. Both of these methods are discussed in the following paragraphs.

Using the getty Process

A *getty* is a process invoked by the login/init routine (init-getty-login-shell) and responsible for connecting users to the operating system. One getty is spawned for each terminal connected to the system. The getty begins by opening a file in the /dev directory that tells it how to use raw mode, suppress echo, and allow for parity, among other things.

After initialization is complete, getty prints the login message field for the entry, using /etc/gettydefs. After the login message, getty reads the user login name a character at a time, attempting to adapt the system to the speed and type of terminal being used. The login name is checked for lowercase characters. If none are found, getty maps all uppercase characters to lowercase and informs the system to do likewise.

Its job complete, getty calls the login utility, passing the login name as an argument. One getty exists for each inactive terminal, and you can always ascertain the number of terminals configured for login on a system by counting the number of gettys and the current number of logins.

The /etc/gettydefs is nothing more than an ASCII file relaying speed and terminal settings used by getty. It tells what the login prompt should look like and the speed to try next if the user presses the break character to indicate that the current speed is not correct.

IX

Connections

The syntax of each entry follows:

```
label# initial-settings # final-settings # login-prompt
```

Each entry is followed by a blank line. A sample of two listings follows:

```
a# B1800 ECHO ISTRIP CS7 PARENB NL1 CR1 # B1800 CLOCAL CS7 PARENB
TAB3 ECHO SANE CR2 #login:

b# B2400 ECHO ISTRIP CS7 PARENB NL1 CR1 # B2400 CLOCAL CS7 PARENB
TAB3 ECHO SANE #login:
```

The speed flag (2400) is the only one truly required, and SANE serves as a catchall, setting most of the other flags that need to be set for communications.

Using ttymons

Unlike with the getty process, each terminal port does not have a ttymon. Being a STREAMS-based monitor, one ttymon is capable of supporting multiple ports. Aside from this difference, the definition is similar to that of a getty.

ttymon processes are configured by administrators using two utilities: pmadm and ttyadm. Their purpose is to establish terminal modes, baud rates, and variables for each terminal login. They receive such settings from TTY files and attempt different baud rates at the occurrence of break keys.

Using the curses Utility

The *curses* utility is a C-style utility that enables each user a terminal-independent method of updating screens (curses implies cursor). Because the utility is based on the C language, you must include the line # include <curses.h> at the beginning of any file using the curses routines.

A curses library contains routines for managing windows that represent the terminal screen. The default window is called stdscr, and others are created with newwin(). Routines not beginning with w affect stdscr. The refresh() function tells the routines to make the user's terminal screen look like stdscr. When characters are stored, information about the character is also stored, enabling a refresh of exactly what was on-screen before, including video attributes such as underline or reverse.

With a manual page (always the most coherent) of more than 35 pages in length, programming in curses is recommended only for those with nerves of steel and the patience of saints.

Using the tput Utility

The *tput* utility uses the terminfo database to find values of terminal-dependent capabilities and related information and report such to the shell. tput also can initialize or reset the terminal.

The utility returns a string if the attribute in question is of the string type, or an integer if the attribute is of the integer type. If, on the other hand, the attribute is Boolean, all that returns is an exit code of 0 for TRUE (if the terminal has the capability), and 1 for FALSE (if it does not).

You can use an option, -T*type*, to tell the terminal type, but this step is unnecessary under most circumstances because the default is the value of the TERM environmental variable.

Following the name of the utility, specify an attribute, and the value of that attribute is returned. You also can specify `tput init` to initialize the terminal according to the type of terminal in the TERM environmental variable.

Following an attribute, you can pass parameters to execute the string as a command. For example, `tput cup 1 7` moves the cursor up to row 1, column 7, and places the prompt there.

Other examples are given in the following code:

```
$ tput smso          (begins bolding)
$

$ tput cup 20 1      (moves the cursor to row 20, column 1)
$

$ tput longname
ADDS Viewpoint 60/R40
$

$ tput rmso          (stops bolding)
$

$ tput cols
80
$

$ tput lines
24
```

```
$

$ tput smul          (starts underlining)
$

$ tput khome         (moves the cursor home)
$

$ tput rmul          (stops underlining)
$
```

Summary

Several utilities are available for viewing and changing the configuration of terminals
connected to the UNIX operating system, and this chapter covered those utilities. You
can use two methods to define the terminal characteristics within databases: terminfo and
termcap. You also can use a slew of utilities that view these settings or temporarily change
characteristics.

Chapter Snapshot

For all the attempts at memorizing cryptic commands that operating systems offer, nothing is more frustrating than printing. Frustration begins the minute you open a printer box and try to connect the new device to your system, and it remains each time you try to perform an administrative task and remember the commands related to printer management. This chapter looks at the software and operating system side of printer interfacing with topics such as the following:

Printer Interfacing

One of the oldest complaints ever uttered is that a computer (be it for UNIX, DOS, System 7, or any other operating system) can be unpacked, configured, and running in less than a few hours, but properly configuring the printer can take weeks.

That a thing so simple as configuring a printer can have the unparalleled power to create headaches says a great deal for the role of a system administrator. Complaints are constantly lodged against UNIX documentation and its lack of intelligible interpretation. Those users complaining about poor UNIX documentation, however, have obviously never examined the manuals accompanying laser printers, which are even more incoherent.

This chapter does not cover configuration—with so many different types of printer and UNIX machine combinations, the tome that would attempt to do justice to that topic could not be hoisted without a forklift. But the chapter does cover the utilities that enable you to direct output to a printer and manipulate the priorities of operation.

Formatting Documents the UNIX Way

Sending an ASCII file directly from the system to a printer might be fine for obtaining code listings but is rarely required for anything else. Printed documents attract more favorable attention when they have headers, footers, and page numbering. The perception of the information presented is more positive when columns are aligned and the text is appealing to the eye.

UNIX provides two utilities for this purpose, including one for formatting text to the screen, pr, and one for miscellaneous operations, col.

Using the col Filter

The col utility is a filter through which you can pass output to reverse line feeds. An added benefit is that it converts white space to tabs to shorten printing time.

Options that you can use include the following:

-b Strips out all backspacing. This option is particularly useful if you are attempting to print man pages entries. In man pages, emboldening is done by backspacing and printing the character over and over again. This action has a tendency to throw a printer into a spastic fit, which you can avoid by using this option. Consider this example:

```
$ man who ¦ col -b ¦ lp
```

-f Removes reverse line motion while maintaining half-line feeds that might exist.

-p Converts unknown escape sequences to regular characters, leaving them subject to the backspace/overprinting routine from reverse line motions.

-x Does not convert whitespace to tabs.

Printing Files with the pr Utility

The pr utility formats text files and prints them on the terminal. (You can easily divert the output to a printer, however, by piping it to the lp command.)

The first thing pr does is separate the output into pages with a header appearing at the beginning of each page. The header consists of the page number, date, and time associated with the file and the name of the file. By default, the width of the output is 72 characters, and page length is 66 lines (including 10 lines of header and footer). Following the last line, a series of carriage returns is sent to the screen to total 66.

Options that you can use with the pr utility include the following:

+#	Starts printing with page #.
-#	Creates # of columns.
-a	Prints multicolumn output across the page. You must use this option in conjunction with -#.
-d	Double-spaces the output.
-ec#	Places tabs at #+1, 2*#+1, and so on.
-f	Sends a form feed rather than the series of carriage returns after printing a page.
-h	Changes the header to whatever free text you specify in place of the default file name.
-ic#	Changes whitespace in output to tabs at character positions #+1, 2*#+1, and so on.
-l#	Changes the length from 66 to #.
-m	Merges specified files and prints one per column. The maximum number of files specified is eight.
-nc#	Establishes # line numbering.
-o#	Offsets each line by # characters.
-p	Pauses before beginning each page.
-r	Suppresses diagnostics that would normally appear at the end of the operation.
-sc	Separates columns by the character *c* rather than whitespace.
-t	Suppresses the header and footer.
-w#	Changes the width of each line to #.

Spooling Print Jobs with lp

You use the lp command to send print job requests to a line printer. Every system must have a default printer. If you specify no printer with the lp command, the default printer is assumed, and jobs are sent there. Using the -d option, you can route jobs to any other attached printer.

When you request a print job, it is not immediately sent to the printer but rather to a printer spool, where lp associates a unique request ID with each request. Note the following example:

```
$ lp somefile
request id is default-32 (1 file)
$
```

The request to print the file somefile has been assigned an ID of default-32. This name is a unique request ID that you can use to cancel, change, or see the status of the request at any time prior to the completion of it printing.

Options that you can use when sending a print request—these options must always precede file names—include the following:

-c
Specifies the number of copies of the files to be printed. The default is only the requested copy.

-d
Enables you to give a printer destination other than the default printer. If the destination is a class of printers rather than a specific printer, the request is printed on the first available printer in that class.

-f
Prints the request on a specified form.

-H
Prints the request according to the value of a given variable for special handling. Acceptable values for this variable are:

hold
Tells the printer not to print the request until notified. Other jobs print while this one stays in the spool.

immediate
Prints the request now (only the root user or superuser has the permission necessary to invoke).

resume
Resumes printing a held request.

-m
Sends mail to the user after the files have been printed.

-n
Prints the given number of copies.

-o
Enables you to give options specific for the printer to which the request is going. Options are:

nobanner
Suppresses the banner page that normally precedes a printout. The root user or superuser can disallow this option at any time.

nofilebreak
Cancels the form feed between files.

length=	Enables you to specify page length. You can give numbers in terms of the number of lines on the page or the number of inches or centimeters to the page. Valid choices include length=66 (for 66 lines to the page), length=8i (for 8 inches to the page), and length=25c (for 25 centimeters to the page).
width=	Enables you to give a page-width setting that can be in terms of characters, inches, or centimeters.
lpi=	Prints the request with the line pitch set to a number of lines per inch.
cpi=	Prints the request with the character pitch set to number of characters per inch.
-P	Prints only the pages specified. The specified pages can be single page numbers or a range of pages. You can use this option only if a filter is available to process it; otherwise, the entire document is printed.
-q	Places a priority level in the printing queue, with values ranging from 0 to 39, with 0 being the highest priority.
-s	Suppresses return messages to the screen, such as `request id is` `. . . .`
-t	Prints a given title on the banner page. If not used, no title appears.
-w	Writes a message on the terminal after the files have printed. If the requesting user has already logged out, mail is sent to the user's mail file.

Spooling Print Jobs with lpr

lpr is a line printer spooler similar to lp that exists on many systems. It replaces the print command that used to exist on earlier systems and provides an interface to lp. Fewer options are available with this command than with lp, but for most UNIX users, they are easier to use. The utility does not provide pagination options. Options that it does provide include the following:

-b	No banner page is printed.
-cp	Prints a specified number (from 1 to 999) of copies of the file. On some systems, you can specify this option as -#.

-C   Specifies the printer class.

-i   Specifies the number of spaces to indent the output.

-J   Indicates the job name to use on the banner page.

-m   Sends mail upon completion.

-P   Specifies the printer.

-r   Removes the file after it has finished printing.

-T   Adds a specified title.

-w   Specifies the page width.

Understanding Where Spooled Requests Go

When a job is spooled for printing, what becomes of it? The system records the spooling in the /usr/spool/lp/temp directory by creating several files. Following is an examination of that subdirectory and the files within it:

```
$ cd /usr/spool/lp/temp
$

$ ls -l
total 16
-rw------ 1 root      0             0 Aug 12 11:17 32
-rw------ 1 lp        lp           77 Aug 12 10:12 32-0
-rw-rw-r-- 1 lp        lp         1094 Aug 12 11:17 A-0
$

$ file *
32:        empty
32-0:      English text
A-0:       English text
$

$ cat 32-0
C 1
D default
F /usr/acct/karen/somefile
P 20
t simple
```

```
U karen
s   0000
$
```

The spooled entry shows that one copy (the default) is to be on the "default" printer. The file printed is /usr/acct/karen/somefile, the pages are the entire document, the title is standard (simple), the user is karen, and the s value (which determines whether it should return notification to the screen) is null, or 0000.

One additional file that is presently in the temp directory is A-0. This file is the "attempts" file, which is now being created by virtue of the fact that this particular printer is turned off. The following lines of code show the attempts the system makes to print the file:

```
$ more A-0
Subject: Problem with printer default

The printer default has stopped printing for the reason given below.
Fix the problem and bring the printer back on line.
Printing has stopped, but will be restarted in a few minutes; issue an
enable command if you want to restart sooner.
Unless someone issues a change request
        lp -i default-32 -P ...
to change the page list to print, the current request will be reprinted
from the beginning.
The reason(s) it stopped (multiple reasons indicate repeated attempts):
Failed to open the printer port.
(I/O error)
Failed to open the printer port.
(I/O error)
Failed to open the printer port.
(I/O error)
$
```

On each subsequent attempt to print the file, another failure entry is appended to the file. With the exception of this failure log, all other files are removed upon completion or cancellation of the print job.

Viewing the Spool Status with lpstat

Three utilities are available for viewing the status of the print spool, based on how current your operating system is. One of the original utilities for this task is the spool-query command. The output it delivers is, with the exception of one line, identical to that offered by the lpstat command that replaced it. On newer systems, lpq has also been added, but lpstat remains the only standard utility universally recognized for this function.

The lpstat utility prints the status of the line printer operation. If no options are given, the report is of all requests made by the user to lp (or lpr, because it is nothing more than an interface) that are still in the spool. Consider the following example:

```
$ lpstat
default-32              karen              30   Aug 12 10:12
$
```

The status printout shows the request ID, the log name of the requesting user, the total number of characters to be printed, and the date and time the request was submitted. If nothing remains in the spool, no printout is generated, and a prompt is returned.

Following lpstat, you can name a specific printer, and the resulting printout is of all requests for that printer. You also can specify the following options to tailor the output:

-a   Shows the acceptance status of specified printers. If no printer is specified, the status of the default is shown. In the following example, the default printer and its class (cl1) are accepting requests:

```
$ lpstat -a
cl1 accepting requests since Fri Jun 11 23:32:13 1994
default accepting requests since Fri Jun 11 23:32:13 1994
$
```

-c   Shows class names and their members for all specified printers. Consider this example:

```
$ lpstat -c all
members of class cl1:
        default
$
```

-d   Shows the default destination for lp.

-l   Adds verbose qualities to other options.

-o   Shows the status of output requests. You can follow the option by a list of intermixed printer names, class names, and request IDs.

-p   Prints the status of printers. You can follow the option by a list of printer names. Consider this example:

```
$ lpstat -p
printer default waiting for auto-retry. available.
        stopped with printer fault
$
```

-r   Shows the status of the request scheduler. Note the following example:

```
$ lpstat -r
scheduler is running
$
```

-s   Shows a status summary of the print operation, as in this example:

```
$ lpstat -s
system default destination: default
members of class cl1:
        default
device for default: /dev/pp00
$
```

-t   Shows all status information, as in the following example:

```
$ lpstat -t
scheduler is running
system default destination: default
members of class cl1:
        default
device for default: /dev/pp00
cl1 accepting requests since Fri Jun 11 23:32:13 1994
default accepting requests since Fri Jun 11 23:32:13 1994
printer default waiting for auto-retry. available.
        stopped with printer fault
default-32              karen           30   Aug 12 10:12
$
```

-u   Shows the status of output requests for a list of login names (users). -uall is valid to see requests for all users, as is -ubob to see just Bob's, or -u"bob, jan, shannon" to see those three selectively. (Notice the double quotes around the comma-delimited specification.)

-v   Shows the names of printers and the path names of devices associated with them.

Canceling Print Requests

At any time prior to the completion of a print request, you can remove or stop the request. lprm, a nonstandard utility found on many systems, works the same as cancel, the standard SVR4 utility.

To cancel a job, you must know the request ID number. This number was echoed back to the screen when the request was made; you also can see the number with the lpstat command. Using this number, you can cancel your own jobs, or the superuser can cancel any job. In the following example, the default-32 request is canceled.

```
$ lpstat
default-32              karen           30   Aug 12 10:12
$
```

```
$ cancel default-32
request "default-32" canceled
$

$ lpstat
$
```

Instead of specifying a job, you can specify a printer, and the job printing—as well as other jobs spooled up waiting for that printer—is killed . The only option, which is pertinent for the superuser, is -u, which enables the specification of a user for whom all print jobs are to be canceled, as in:

```
cancel -u karen
```

Accepting Print Jobs

The accept and reject utilities enable and prevent lp requests, respectively. accept works on destinations, which can be either an individual printer or a class of printers. The following listing shows the process that transpires in rejecting a printer, then attempting to send a file to it.

```
$ /usr/lib/reject default
destination "default" will no longer accept requests
$
$ lp somefile
UX:lp: ERROR: Requests for destination "default" aren't being accepted.
TO FIX: Use the "lpstat -a" command to see why this destination is not
accepting requests.
$
$ lpstat -a
cl1 not accepting requests since Fri Aug 12 12:22:33 1994 - unknown
➥reason
default not accepting requests since Fri Aug 12 12:23:34 1994 -
➥unknown reason
$
```

Instead of having unknown reason displayed when a user attempts to ascertain why files cannot be printed, you can use the -r option with reject to associate a reason with preventing lp from accepting requests. Consider this example:

```
$ /usr/lib/reject -r"Due to nonpayment of funds" default
destination "default" will no longer accept requests
$
$ lpstat -a
cl1 accepting requests since Fri Aug 12 12:26:44 1994
```

```
default not accepting requests since Fri Aug 12 12:28:53 1994 -
        Due to nonpayment of funds
$
$ /usr/lib/accept default
destination "default" now accepting requests
$
```

Enabling and Disabling lp

As opposed to accept and reject, which work on requests going into the spool, enable and disable affect print jobs going from the spool to the printer. Disabling the printer does not prevent jobs from entering the spool but does prevent them from going to the printer.

When a printer stops with a printer fault (runs out of paper, is offline, and so on), under most circumstances the scheduler attempts to check the status every so often (five minutes is normal). To notify the system that the printer is back in working order sooner, the enable command sets the state to ok.

Options that you can use with disable include the following:

-c   Cancels requests currently printing on the printer.

-r   Attaches a reason that is shown with lpstat queries.

-W   Disables the printers only after the print requests currently printing have finished.

Configuring the Spooling System

The lpadmin utility configures the print service by defining printers and devices. Most vendors include other utilities to simplify matters. Sun provides an Admintool utility, NCR once used Visual Administrator, VA, but now uses System Administrator. But lpadmin is a standard utility across UNIX designed to enable an administrator to add and remove printers from the service and to set or change default destinations.

The -p option enables you to configure a new printer or change the configuration of an existing printer. You must use it with another option; some of the more useful of those include the following:

-c   Inserts a new printer into a specified class. You must follow the option with a printer class. If the class does not exist, it is created.

-D   Enables you to attach a comment for whenever a user does an lpstat operation.

-e   Copies an existing interface to be the new interface program for the printer. Follow the option with the name of the existing interface.

-F   Restores the print service to its default settings after a fault has occurred. You can follow the option with continue to continue printing on the page where the printing stopped, or beginning to restart the print job at the beginning.

-i   Creates a new interface for the printer. You must follow the option with the path name of the new program.

-l   Makes the device associated with the printer a login terminal. lpsched, the print scheduler, automatically disables all login terminals each time it is started.

-m   Enables the selection of a model interface for the printer, where model is one of the interface names supplied with the print service.

-r   Removes a printer from the specified class. You must follow the option with the name of an existing class. If the printer is the only member of the class, that class is removed as well.

-T   Assigns a specified printer type, which is used to extract data from terminfo to initialize the printer before printing each request.

Adding Filters with lpfilter

Filters are responsible for converting files into a data stream suitable for interpretation by the printer. The type of information constituting the data stream includes the following:

1. The file type

2. The destination printer

3. The type of the destination printer

4. The types of content the printer can understand

5. The printing modes requested by the sender

You use the lpfilter command to add, delete, and modify filters used by lp. The syntax is as follows:

```
$ /usr/lib/lpfilter -f {filter name} {option}
```

The allowable options include the following:

-	Enables you to add or modify the filter from the terminal.
-F	Modifies an existing filter.
-i	Resets the filter.
-l	Lists the description.
-x	Deletes a filter.

Using the Brain of It All: lpsched

The print service scheduler is lpsched. It is responsible for maintaining the scheduling of print requests and can be started and stopped only by the root user. The following commands and their associated paths govern lpscheds operations:

/usr/lib/lpsched	Starts the scheduler, usually done in the initialization process.
/usr/lib/lpshut	Stops the scheduler. Any printers that are currently printing stop immediately. If they were in the middle of a job, that job is restarted in its entirety when the scheduler is reenabled.
/usr/lib/lpmove	Enables spooled requests to be moved from one destination to another; can be performed only when the scheduler is running.

/usr/spool/lp, by default, is the directory used for holding requests. If the variable SPOOLDIR exists before the starting of lpsched, however, requests are routed to the directory defined there instead.

Establishing Queue Priorities with lpusers

The lpusers command enables you to define limits on queue priority levels that can be assigned to jobs submitted by users. Priority levels range from 0 to 39, with 0 having the highest priority and 39 the lowest. In the absence of a priority level, the system default is used (default is usually 20).

The following list shows the syntax for each of the available options:

/usr/lib/lpusers -l	Shows the system default and priority levels established for users.
/usr/lib/lpusers -d {level}	Sets the system-wide default.
/usr/lib/lpusers -q {level}	Sets the highest level for users not belonging to any other user list.
/usr/lib/lpusers -u {users}	Removes listed users from any priority level.
/usr/lib/lpusers -q {level} -u {users}	Sets the highest level obtainable by users listed.

Testing the Printer with lptest

lptest is an obsolete command still included on many vendors' UNIX versions. It sends ASCII characters to the printer in chunks of 96 lines, alternating one character per line. In so doing, it succeeds in printing each ASCII character in each position on the page, providing a resourceful test of output capabilities.

The syntax is as follows:

```
$ /usr/ucb/lptest {length} {count}
```

Both the length and count parameters are optional. If not specified, the default length of 79 characters and a count of 200 lines are used.

Summary

UNIX provides a variety of printing functions and facilities. This chapter discussed the concept of spooling print jobs and enabling those print jobs to route to a printer. All utilities regarding those functions were discussed, as well as two utilities useful in formatting the appearance of the finished document.

Chapter Snapshot

It is becoming more and more important each day to learn how to create coexistence and cooperation between dissimilar networks. This chapter focuses on means of interaction between DOS workstations and UNIX machines, including the following topics:

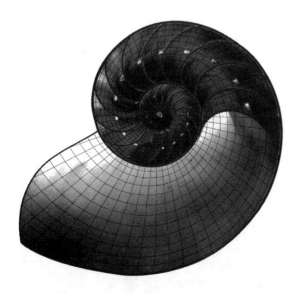

Connecting to MS-DOS

S everal years ago, homogeneous worksites existed where everyone used the same software and operating system platform to do their daily tasks. If the business used UNIX, all the desks were equipped with dumb terminals. If it used DOS, every user had a PC with limited capabilities sitting on top of his or her desk.

As the years have gone by, homogeneity has gone bye. Now the workplace that is confined to only one operating system is the rarity, not the rule. Every involved user has a preference for the application he or she likes to run, and many like certain operating systems. UNIX is beloved for its many capabilities, built-in networking, and multitasking, but it is disdained for its lack of individual user empowerment. In the DOS world, your machine and your data are yours—no administrator slaps restrictions on what you can do.

The ideal solution is a combination of the two, and many sites are going that route. DOS PCs are placed on desktops where users can govern the operations of local data. Connections are then established to centralized UNIX servers where information can be shared. This chapter touches on this connectivity concept and offers insights designed to help you formulate decisions appropriate for your site.

Using Communications Packages

You can connect a PC to a UNIX machine without establishing a network connection in a variety of ways. The easiest of these methods involves the use of a communications package such as ProCOMM or ProCOMM Plus. Several other similar packages are available, but ProCOMM is discussed here as a generic representation of all similar programs.

Making Direct Connections

To connect a PC to a UNIX machine directly, run a cable from the serial port of the PC to a tty port on the UNIX machine. You might need to use a null modem adapter and/or adapters to convert from 25-pin to 9- or 15-pin, depending on the two hardware components involved. You can run a serial cable 75 feet without any noticeable problems in the signal.

Configure the communications package for the com port, 9600 baud, even parity, no parity check, 7 data bits, and 1 stop bit (the most common terminal emulation is VT100). Make certain, by checking the /etc/inittab, that the port on the UNIX machine is configured for a terminal. The following two entries, for example, are for ports a and b:

```
ta::respawn:/etc/getty ttya A vwpt

tb:2:respawn:/etc/getty ttyb d vwpt
```

Both are firing up getty processes to talk to vwpt terminals. (Notice the 2 between the colons in the tb entry; the system must be in run level 2 before the ttyb port initiates. No such restriction exists for ttya.)

On the communications package, you must set the terminal emulation to whatever terminal type the getty is looking for. You also can run a ps - ef command (or ps -aux, if appropriate) to see whether a login is being anticipated, as follows:

```
$ ps -ef ¦ grep tty
root   1738    1  0 Aug  1 ?          0:01 /etc/getty ttya A vwpt
root   1584    1  0 10:11:27 ttyb     0:00 /etc/getty ttyb d vwpt
$
```

The UNIX machine must have the port configured as a terminal for a login to be presented to the workstation. After this connection has been established, the login prompt appears on the DOS workstation as it would on any other terminal. With Windows or DesqView, you can switch between the UNIX session and other applications on the local PC—even cutting and pasting information between the two.

Connecting through Modem Lines

The same terminal emulation/communications software packages that enable you to connect a PC directly to a UNIX machine also enable you to connect through a modem. First, install a modem on the UNIX tower and make certain that the port is properly configured as a getty. Next, configure the software on the PC to dial the number and set the settings to the speed on the UNIX machine's modem: even parity, 7 data bits, and 1 stop bit. (Settings might be slightly different for your setup, but these values are the most common.) Figure 35.1 shows a PCPlus configuration screen in which the appropriate values are being entered.

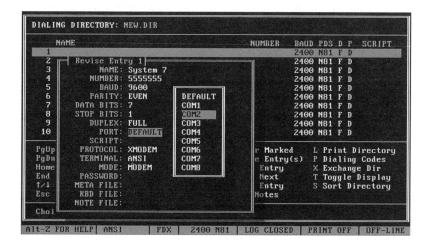

Figure 35.1
Configuring a PC to connect to a UNIX machine using a modem and ProCOMM Plus terminal emulation software.

Lastly, dial the number and establish the connection. You then are operating on the remote PC the same as you would if you were sitting at a dumb terminal directly connected to one of the ports.

Migrating to PC-NFS

The next step, beyond utilizing communications packages and direct connections to go between UNIX and DOS, is to add an NFS package to the PC. Then, instead of having one machine act as a dumb terminal and performing all work on the UNIX machine, you have two machines that are able to communicate with each other in pseudo network fashion. "Pseudo" is implied because, when utilizing such software, DOS machines can mount file systems configured by *Network File System* (NFS) on the UNIX machines and see them as extended DOS disks (virtual).

Currently, several dozen NFS packages are available from a variety of sources and vendors. The important point to note is that it is the PC, in the relationship between host and workstation, that must do all the work. By using daemons, the PC is accessing the UNIX machine, transferring files, viewing them, and so on. The UNIX machine merely acts as host, enabling these transactions to take place.

Great differences exist in the rules assigned to each operating system's file structure, and you need to keep these differences in mind when you're transferring files from one to the other:

1. DOS accepts file names of up to eight characters, with an optional extension up to three characters. UNIX accepts much longer file names (usually 15 characters), and no extensions are used. (What happens when the file kristin_karen_note is copied from the UNIX tower to DOS? Most NFS packages truncate the name.)

2. In DOS, the file name and extension are separated by a period. For this reason, a period is not a valid character within the file name. In UNIX, the period is just another character and might appear once or 15 times. Additionally, it can be the first character or the last. (What happens when .profile is transferred to DOS? Most packages remove the period.)

3. DOS views everything in an uppercase world. CLS and cls mean the same thing. Likewise, type evan.dat means the same as TYPE EVAN.DAT. UNIX, however, views upper- and lowercase as being different. You can have dozens of files on the same system in the same directory called evan.dat, Evan.dat, EVAN.DAT, evan.DAT, and so on. When these files are brought to DOS, they overwrite one another.

If all you need is a way to copy a file occasionally from a UNIX machine to DOS, the process might be easier than you think.

Sun workstations traditionally come with a 3 1/2-inch disk drive. If the file you need to copy resides on one of these workstations, you are in luck. If it does not and one of these workstations is at the worksite, remote copy (rcp) the file to the workstation.

Format a floppy disk on a DOS machine, and then insert the disk into the slot on the workstation. At the workstation, type the following command to mount the PC file system (floppy disk) and begin the appropriate daemons:

```
mount /pcfs
```

Next, type the following to copy the file to the floppy disk in ASCII format, readable by the PC:

```
cp {filename} /pcfs/{new filename}
```

To end the operation, use the following:

```
eject
```

The floppy disk is ejected, and the corresponding daemons are stopped.

Connecting NetWare Networks to UNIX

Novell Inc., from Provo, UT, virtually owns the market in PC networking, with an estimated 65 percent of all networked offices using some form of NetWare. Interestingly enough, Novell purchased UNIX System Laboratories (and the UNIX name). Novell markets its own flavor of UNIX for X86 machines under the name UnixWare. When discussions turn to connecting DOS-based PCs with UNIX machines, considering the products Novell offers is only natural.

The first thing you need to know is that NetWare 3.11 or newer comes complete with the TCP interface needed to connect NetWare to UNIX as a NetWare Loadable Module. Consult the documentation provided with NetWare for information on establishing such connections. These connections give you the ability to have the NetWare server see the UNIX host(s). One can ping another, but no further activity can take place without the purchase of additional software.

Novell markets LAN WorkPlace for DOS and LAN WorkGroup. The WorkPlace for DOS product is also a stand-alone, enabling you to access TCP with or without NetWare. Figure 35.2 shows the iconized options available for starting a TCP connection.

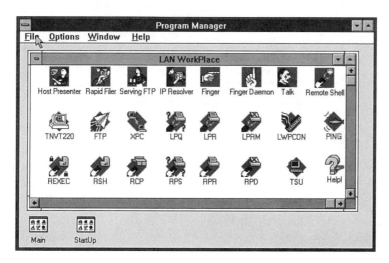

Figure 35.2
The icons available for TCP connections with LAN WorkPlace for DOS (screen shot taken from a Novell demonstration disk).

In addition to connecting to UNIX machines and operating as if there, you can use Rapid Filer, a utility of WorkPlace for DOS, to group files and transfer them from one machine to the other with easy-to-use screen options. Figures 35.3 and 35.4 show the layout of these screens and the steps necessary for file transfers.

Figure 35.3
The Rapid Filer utility screen, showing files on the local machine (top window) and on the UNIX machine (screen shot taken from a Novell demonstration disk).

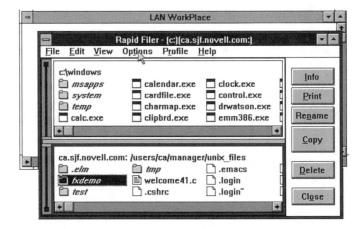

Figure 35.4
The copy options available with the Rapid Fire utility (screen shot taken from a Novell demonstration disk).

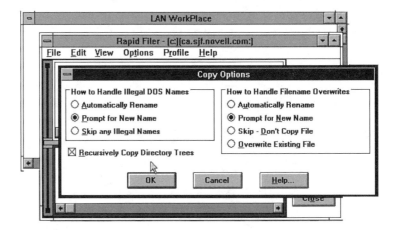

LAN WorkPlace is used for establishing workstation connectivity to NetWare servers or TCP hosts. NetWare NFS is similar, but it enables UNIX users to access NetWare utilities and files from their own environment by mounting the networked drives. (TCP is used to establish the connection between NetWare NFS and the UNIX machines.) To operate on the server, you must have a minimum of 5 MB RAM and a NetWare version of 3.11 or newer.

NetWare for UNIX is a third-product group that you can install in place of TCP\IP on UNIX and non-UNIX machines. It allows the networking features, including file and peripheral sharing, to be available seamlessly to all users and machines.

Summary

This chapter covered basic connectivity between DOS-based computers and UNIX machines. You can use several methods to achieve this connectivity, including direct and indirect connections. The following chapter addresses connectivity between UNIX machines with networking concepts.

IX

Connections

Chapter Snapshot

This chapter introduces you to the basic concepts of UNIX networking, including such topics as the following:

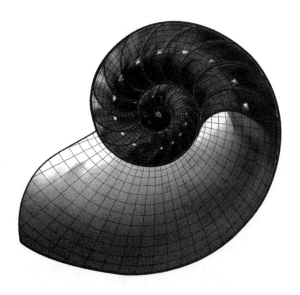

Networking Concepts

The Department of Defense has been a strong UNIX proponent since the early days. The government's interest in the operating system greatly contributed to its growth and acceptance outside its birthplace, Bell Labs.

In 1970, the Defense Advanced Research Project Agency, a division of the Department of Defense, sent out word that if the operating system was to continue to grow, it needed networking capabilities. The agency funded a research project at Stanford University and the consultant firm *Bolt, Beranek, and Newman* (BBN). The goal was to create a set of communication protocols that could provide connectivity between diverse machines.

The result was two different protocols: the Transmission Control Protocol and the Internet Protocol. The two were combined and adopted as military standards in 1983. TCP provides the Host-to-Host communication layer, and IP is strictly the Internet Layer.

Thanks in large part to the military standard, TCP/IP became popular as a networking choice useful for connecting UNIX systems, regardless of manufacturer or vendor. TCP/IP is an open protocol standard available to any vendor and able to run over virtually any type or size of network.

This chapter provides an overview of TCP/IP operations on a UNIX system, as well as many of the utilities available for use after the network is up and running. From an administration standpoint, the space limitations of this book prohibit doing full justice to such a complex topic. Those who must administer a network are advised to consult *Inside TCP/IP* (New Riders Publishing, 1994) for detailed information on every component of the protocol and its installation and maintenance.

Dissecting the TCP/IP Protocol Standard

TCP/IP is defined as a four-level protocol standard, as outlined in the DDN Protocol Handbook.

1. The top layer is the Process Layer, which is where network applications reside.

2. The next layer is Host-to-Host, where TCP is defined.

3. Next comes the Internet Layer, where, as you might suspect, IP's functions and operations are detailed.

4. The bottom layer is Network Access, where the actual interfacing takes place.

Each of these layers has separate processes, utilities, and daemons that are responsible for fulfilling its portion of the process. All are specific and necessary for completing the networking operation.

Installing the Software

Installation of the software is based on the manufacturer and equipment you use, as well as the software brand. Sun workstations and many others, for example, normally ship with TCP/IP already installed. With NCR 3000s, you must purchase additional software and install it with the pkgadd or sysadm utility.

Consult your individual documentation for the installation specifics regarding your hardware/software combination. What follows is a list of variables that you need to set, regardless of how the installation takes place.

Providing the Network Name

The *network name* is a relevant moniker for the site that will be shared by all computers on the network. For a small company, it can be the company name or a portion thereof. For a large company, it can be a division or geographical location. The important thing is to use the same name when installing the software on all machines.

Many vendors also ask for a network alias. This alias amounts to nothing more than another name by which the network can be referred. With a company called Dalton Technology, for example, the name can be DALTONTECH and the alias DALTON. Referring to either name informs the software that this network is the one you mean.

Providing the Host Name

Although the network name is shared by all machines connected to the network, the host name must be unique to each machine. The easiest way to create a host name is to use the node name (uname -n). In some situations, however, this method is not advisable.

The host name is what users use to refer to the physical machine; therefore the name needs to be something that makes sense. If the node name is 030762, those numbers need to make sense to the user in accounting who is trying to access it.

One solution is to use host names that refer to physical location: SALES, MARKETING, and so on. This approach works so long as only one computer is in the sales department. If you're running minis, having only one computer is a possibility; if you're running PCs, there isn't a chance.

Another suggestion is to utilize theme names within the area. All computers in the accounting department, for example, could be pronouns of family members—mother, father, brother, sister, and so on—and all in production could be extended members—stepson, in-law, outlaw, and so on.

Although you can probably think of thousands of ways of coming up with host names, the note to stress is that you need to have uniformity in some sensible way, or a nightmare develops as your site grows.

Many vendors offer host aliases as well as network aliases, thus you can use your node name and a sensible reference. Be very, very certain that you do not use a host name or alias on more than one machine; suffice it to say that you can't and have the network work properly.

Specifying the Internet Address

Here is where the going gets rough. Addresses are a required feature of every network—TCP/IP, NetWare, and so on. They are difficult to understand and implement, but after they're active, they need never be a problem.

An Internet address is a logical address: a 12-digit, 32-bit number required by TCP/IP. The user refers to machines by the host name, which is why host names are so important. When a user refers to a host name, the software converts the name to the address and takes off across the network in search of a match.

The address, like the host name, must be unique for every machine across the network. If the machine is to connect with the outside world and not just an internal network—connect to the Internet, for example—the address must also be unique to all other machines in the world. The *Network Information Center* (NIC) is responsible for assigning unique addresses. Whether or not you intend to connect to the outside world, it is highly recommended that you apply for and receive a unique number from the NIC.

Eventually, every operation grows or goes out of business, and, although connecting to the Internet might not seem like a possibility at this time, predicting what might come down the road is impossible.

The 12-digit number is divided into four sections when written numerically, but has only three components: a network number, a subnet number, and a host number. An example follows:

199.009.200.001

The first three digits are the network number. Three different types of networks can exist, and their type is determined by the network number:

001–127: Class A network

128–191: Class B network

192–223: Class C network

Because 32-bit numbers are used, each numbering scheme can go to 255 (though it is normally reserved). Thus, a class C network has a range from 199.1.1 to 223.254.254. The higher the address number, the fewer machines can be on the network. Class A networks are those with multitudes of machines (up to 16,387,064 machines can be on one network). In the real world, very few class A networks exist. Class B is for large networks not falling into the A category (up to 64,516 machines). Class C is used for a large number of small networks. Up to 254 machines can be on a class C network (256 numbers are available, but 0 and 255 are reserved for broadcasting).

With a class A network, the first three digits depict the type of network. The other nine are used as host addresses. Thus the number of available host addresses is 254 possibilities for the second set of numbers, 254 possibilities for the third set, and 254 possibilities for the last set:

254×254×254 = 16,387,064

With a class B network, the second set of digits is also used to identify the network; thus host addresses are confined to 254 possibilities for the third set of numbers and the last set:

254×254 = 64,516

Finally, with a class C, the first three sets of numbers are used to identify the network, and only the last set is available for host addresses. Hence, the network is limited to 254 machines.

In the example, 199.009.200.001, the address is 199. The host (machine) designation is the last three digits of the number: 001. The numbers in between the address and the host represent the subnet. The subnet enables each machine on the same network to communicate with each other. Thus 199.009.200.001 can communicate with 199.009.200.002, all the way up to 199.009.200.254.

The first three digits of an Internet address are essentially required to tell the system what class of network is being run. The easiest way to think of the subnet is as a zip code.

You can equate the six middle digits, 009.200, to a zip code of 46290, dictating that the machine, like a street address, is in a certain area. The 001 or 254 is equivalent to the four-digit "ZIP plus four" that specifies the actual house in which the person lives. If you want to send a packet of information to a machine, the host name SALES7 must be translated to 009.200.001, then the packet knows where to go.

When (not if) you apply for a unique address from the NIC, you are given the first three fields—199.009.200, for example. You then add the host numbers to the end. The first machine you put on the network does not have to be 001 but certainly should be. The fourth should be 004, and so on.

Testing the Network

After you have installed the software, the first test should be whether the networking software can talk to itself. The /usr/etc directory contains a utility called *ping* whose purpose is to test network applications and connections.

Interestingly, ping allegedly was so named for two reasons. Its operations resemble what maritime submarines do. When the crew of one submarine would sense that another sub might be nearby, they would send out sonar signals to see whether the signals would echo back, a process that was named "pinging."

The second reason, not so dramatic, is that ping is an acronym for ***Packet InterNet Groper.***

When you use *ping me*, a loop is created wherein a signal is sent through the internal networking hardware (ethernet card, and so on) to verify that all is working properly. Two versions of ping are currently in use. One continues to send signals until interrupted with the Ctrl+D key combination, and the other simply tests the connection and returns a response indicating whether it is "alive" or "dead."

Checking Network Status

You can display the current status by using the netstat utility. Several options are available through which you can obtain more detailed information:

Option	Function
-A	Adds associated protocol control block to the display.
-a	Shows all network interfaces.
-i	Displays configured network interfaces.
-n	Shows the output in numeric form.
-r	Gives a routing table display, where applicable.
-s	Displays statistics.

The netstat utility is a powerful tool for ascertaining what is occurring now and what has already transpired, as the following example illustrates:

```
# netstat -s
ip:
        0 bad header checksums
        0 with size smaller than minimum
        0 with data size < data length
        0 with header length < data size
        0 with data length < header length
icmp:
        0 calls to icmp_error
        0 errors not generated 'cuz old message too short
        0 errors not generated 'cuz old message was icmp
        0 messages with bad code fields
        0 messages < minimum length
        0 bad checksums
        0 messages with bad length
        0 message responses generated
tcp:
        844679 packets sent
            572813 data packets (65538263 bytes)
            70 data packets (41381 bytes) retransmitted
            135764 ack-only packets (107991 delayed)
            0 URG only packets
            205 window probe packets
            42166 window update packets
            15539 control packets
```

```
        991658 packets received
                575777 acks (for 65578387 bytes)
                63388 duplicate acks
                0 acks for unsent data
                424440 packets (89243609 bytes) received insequence
                113 completely duplicate packets (110 bytes)
                1 packet with some dup. data (1 byte duped)
                0 out-of-order packets (0 bytes)
                86 packets (39 bytes) of data after window
                39 window probes
                3107 window update packets
                2 packets received after close
                0 discarded for bad checksums
                0 discarded for bad header offset fields
                0 discarded because packet too short
        5637 connection requests
        15834 connection accepts
        21514 connections established (including accepts)
        25485 connections closed (including 4936 drops)
        1021 embryonic connections dropped
        570767 segments updated rtt (of 581429 attempts)
        253 retransmit timeouts
                0 connections dropped by rexmit timeout
        251 persist timeouts
        50223 keepalive timeouts
                50223 keepalive probes sent
                0 connections dropped by keepalive
udp:
        0 bad header checksums
        0 incomplete headers
        0 bad data length fields
        0 packets dropped due to stream Q full
        0 packets dropped due to endpoint not idle
#
```

The ip section deals with incoming packets. Numbers greater than zero can indicate problems with the internal boards or with the cabling leading to the host.

The second section pertains to ICMP, the *Internet Control Message Protocol* that sends error or control messages from one host to another. (This process is the one used with ping.) In the preceding example, no errors have occurred.

The third section is the actual TCP. Important lines to watch include the number of acks for unsent data, as well as the number of out-of-order packets, those discarded for any reason, and the number of packets received after close. Packets received after close are lost for good and should never occur, but often do in the real world.

The `packets sent` value represents the total number of packets TCP has sent to the network board, and `packets received` is the number that has been sent from the board to TCP. The `connection requests` value is the number of times this host has accessed another, and `connection accepts` is the number of times other hosts have accessed this one. The number of `connections closed` is usually a number out of the blue and cannot serve as much reference. The one thing to note is that the number should always exceed the number of connections established.

Examining Important System Files

A handful of files must be maintained either manually or by the network operating system after networking is implemented. This section examines the most important of those files.

Examining the hosts File

The /etc/hosts file is an ASCII database of host numbers, names, and aliases of other machines on the network. With the exception of the Domain Name Service, almost every other network application refers to this file to determine the Internet address of a referenced host. (Domain Name Services act like yellow pages to all hosts on the network.)

Fields are separated by white space that can be either tabs or spaces. Because this file is referred to by almost every networking process, the recommended practice is to arrange the file with the most commonly accessed hosts first, and the lesser accessed last. This arrangement speeds the search time through the data file as the network grows. A sample follows:

```
# SCCS_ID - "@(#)hosts (TWG)        1.1      87/03/23 "
#
#        WIN-TCP HOST TABLE
#
#Internet   Host   Aliases
127.0.0.1        me loopback localhost
# proto
199.9.200.7      SALES7 victor
199.9.200.4      SALES4 nikki
199.9.200.3      SALES3 cole
199.9.200.2      SALES2 victoria
199.9.200.1      SALES1 nicholas
199.9.200.5      SALES5 jack
199.9.200.11     ACCT1
199.9.200.12     ACCT2
```

```
199.9.200.13     ACCT3
199.9.200.14     ACCT4
199.9.200.15     ACCT5
199.9.200.17     ACCT7
```

 Notice the address of 127.0.0.1. Even though this network is a class C network, the address for "me," as in "ping me," is class A. No matter what class network you are running, 127.0.0.1 is always the address of the internal network card.

The aliases are other names by which the system can be referred. If an alias is used more than once, the search stops at the first match because the file is searched sequentially.

On most systems, you need to update this file whenever a new machine is added to the network. On others, a hosttab process is running to scan constantly for new machines added since the last check and automatically add them to the file.

Looking at the Optional hosts.equiv File

An optional file, /etc/hosts.equiv, is a database of machines and users that can log in to the local host without a need for verification. Under normal circumstances, when a user attempts to log in to a machine from another, the user is asked for a password. If the machine from which the user is coming, however, is in the hosts.equiv file, the user is allowed in without the need to supply a password.

An example of this file is the following:

```
SALES1
SALES2
SALES3 amy
SALES4 lisa
SALES4 roger
```

Under this scenario, any user coming from SALES1 or SALES2 is allowed into this machine without being prompted for a password—providing the login the user is using has an entry in /etc/passwd. Coming from SALES3, however, the user is allowed directly in only if the user is logged in over there as amy. Coming from SALES4, both lisa and roger are allowed in, and everyone else must provide a password. Anyone coming from a machine not listed must supply a correct password.

One important concept to keep in mind here is that of security. Although having users able to log in remotely without the bother of supplying a password sounds inviting, it is an open invitation to anyone who can get in one machine to have access to all machines. Think about it long and hard before you allow unlimited remote access.

Examining the .rhosts File

When found within $HOME directories, .rhosts files represent private versions of
/etc/hosts.equiv. When a user attempts to log into a system remotely, the networking
software looks for a /etc/hosts.equiv file entry on the host to which the user is logging in.
If the software can find no such file or cannot find an entry for this user, it looks in the
/etc/passwd file to ascertain what the user's home directory would be. Next, it looks in
that home directory for a .rhosts file to see whether the user has an entry there.

As with the other file, if a host name is specified without a user name, anyone using the
user name for that home directory can log in without being prompted for a password.
The format is identical to that for /etc/hosts.equiv.

Examining Common Utilities

Every vendor supplies a different set of utilities with its implementation of TCP/IP. You
can even purchase a variety of diagnostic tools from third parties, but the UNIX operating
system contains many that do a remarkably competent job, without requiring the outlay
of additional capital.

These utilities are included with almost every vendor's UNIX networking
package. Not only are they of use on a first install, but they also share a common denomi-
nator of starting with an *r*. As a rule of thumb, utilities beginning with that letter work
only when two or more UNIX stations are involved, and not with connected processors
running another operating system.

Using the rwho Utility

The *rwho* utility, much like the who utility but on a larger scale, shows who is logged in to
each host machine attached to the network. This information can be crucial in verifying
that users on other hosts are able to access a machine.

By default, the only users shown are those who have not been idle for an hour or longer.
Idle time is depicted in minutes in the right-most column of the display. Constant activity
is depicted without a time in this column, as with the second entry, user karen, in the
following sample listing:

```
# rwho
jerry     SALES:ttyv00b Aug 29 20:24 :48
karen     ACCTG:ttyv00a Aug 29 21:12
root      MARKT:ttya   Aug 29 17:49 :36
danielle SALES:ttyv008 Aug 29 13:17 :39
danielle SALES:ttyv009 Aug 29 13:53
danielle SALES:ttyv00a Aug 29 16:04 :21
```

```
danielle PRODN:ttyv008 Aug 29 12:54 :30
danielle ACCTG:ttyv008 Aug 29 13:36 :21
danielle ACCTG:ttyv009 Aug 29 14:17 :03
danielle NOBLE:ttyv009 Aug 29 16:45
danielle NOBLE:ttyv00b Aug 29 13:33 :45
danielle JOKER:ttyv008 Aug 29 16:45
danielle JOKER:ttyv009 Aug 29 20:22 :36
danielle JOKER:ttyv00b Aug 29 13:34
#
```

Those users who have been idle an hour or more are not shown. Using the -a option, however, you can view a listing of all users, regardless of idle time, as shown in the next listing. The entries that have been italicized are the ones that did not appear in the regular rwho listing.

```
# rwho -a
jerry    SALES:ttyv00b Aug 29 20:24  :48
karen    ACCTG:ttyv00a Aug 29 21:12
kristin  SALES:ttyv00c Aug 29 17:30 1:39
root     MARKT:ttya    Aug 29 17:49  :36
danielle SALES:ttyv008 Aug 29 13:17  :39
danielle SALES:ttyv009 Aug 29 13:53
danielle SALES:ttyv00a Aug 29 16:04  :21
danielle PRODN:ttyv008 Aug 29 12:54  :30
danielle ACCTG:ttyv008 Aug 29 13:36  :21
hanna    ACCTG:ttyv007 Aug 29 11:42 2:19
danielle ACCTG:ttyv009 Aug 29 14:17  :03
danielle NOBLE:ttyv009 Aug 29 16:45
danielle NOBLE:ttyv00b Aug 29 13:33  :45
danielle JOKER:ttyv008 Aug 29 16:45
danielle JOKER:ttyv009 Aug 29 20:22  :36
danielle JOKER:ttyv00b Aug 29 13:34
#
```

Using the ruptime Utility

As rwho is a who process for the entire network, *ruptime* is an uptime process for each machine on the network, letting you know whether a host machine is up and able to be reached. The following example shows a listing from this command:

```
# ruptime
SALES      up  2+09:49,    4 users,  load 1.07, 1.13, 1.15
ACCTG      up 10+13:43,    1 user,   load 0.18, 0.18, 0.15
PRODN      up 20+11:29,    2 users,  load 1.00, 1.09, 1.14
```

```
NOBLE        up 20+11:28,     2 users,   load 0.03, 0.13, 0.14
JOKER        up 10+13:43,     3 users,   load 0.03, 0.12, 0.14
MARKT        up 20+11:28,     1 user,    load 1.00, 1.00, 1.00
#
```

Each machine's host name is given, as well as the amount of time the host has been on the network in terms of days and hours. PRODN, for example, has been on the network 20 days, 11 hours, and 29 minutes. Following that information is the number of users and the load. Loads are averages in three columns—the last one minute, last five minutes, and last fifteen minutes.

You need to know one critical piece of information: both ruptime and rwho obtain their information from the rwhod daemon process running on every host machine. This daemon maintains files that are traditionally kept in the /usr/spool/rwho subdirectory and updates the information every three minutes. Thus a user could be logged in for two minutes and not show up in an rwho listing if the files have not updated yet.

The rwhod daemon process has the responsibility of producing a list of who is on the current machine, broadcasting that to all other machines, and listening for other rwhod's broadcasts of their status to this host. This information is kept in data files within the subdirectory—one for each host. Listing these files, you can check the last update time and, using the od—octal dump—utility, view the contents.

Using the rlogin Utility

After a host machine is up and talking to the network (as verified with ruptime), the next step is to test access to the machine. To log in to a remote machine as the same user you are on the current machine, use the rlogin utility with a parameter of the remote host name. This action establishes a connection as if your terminal were directly connected to the remote host.

The rlogin process first attempts to log you in without a password by checking for entries in the /etc/hosts.equiv file. If it cannot find the file, or an entry for you in it, next rlogin checks the /etc/passwd file to find your $HOME directory. It looks in there for a .rhosts file that enables you to log in without verification. If rlogin cannot find that file, it prompts you for a password.

Giving the password correctly gets you into the system. If given incorrectly, you must give the login and password combination all over again, but the connection stays live.

After you're connected and successfully logged in, you can perform any UNIX command as if you were sitting at a terminal connected to that host. When you are finished with the session, type exit to close the connection and return to your own machine.

At times, you might want to connect to the remote machine as another user. Suppose, for example, that you are user karen_d on your current machine, but have an account as karen on the other machine. To log in as another user, follow the normal command with -l and the name of the user you will be on the other machine. Consider the following example:

```
$ rlogin ACCTG -l karen
```

When a remote login has been established, it appears in the process table as the rlogind daemon. The user name is not given, though it appears in who listings, but instead the address of the remote host is shown.

When you're remotely logged in to a host, you can jump back and forth between it and the one at which you are truly sitting. To come back to your host, enter a tilde (~) and press the letter z. To return to the remote host, type **exit** on your machine.

The tilde is interpreted as the default escape character. If this arrangement is inconvenient for any reason, you can redefine the escape character by using the -e option. To change the escape character to the dollar sign, for example, you use the following syntax:

```
rlogin ACCTG -e$ -l karen
```

Using the remsh Utility

One of the most useful methods of testing the status of a host in relation to the network is to run a job remotely on that machine. You can accomplish this task without logging in to the remote machine; TCP/IP has a utility for doing so. The name of the utility depends on the vendor who supplied the version, but it usually is rsh or remsh, both indicating that you are remotely running a shell process. In this text, remsh is used to mean either of the two versions.

For remsh to be successful, the local and remote hosts must have proper permissions into each other. /etc/hosts.equiv and/or .rhosts files must enable one machine to access another without password verification.

If one user does not have permission to run the process remotely, the -l option can be used as with rlogin to specify another user. If no command is given following the host name, as in the following example, an rlogin session is initiated:

```
remsh ACCTG
```

Quotation marks become all important with remsh commands. The following command, for example, appends the contents of ACCTG:this file to the MARKT:that file:

```
remsh ACCTG cat this >> that
```

The following command appends the contents of ACCTG:this file to the ACCTG:that file:

```
remsh ACCTG "cat this >> that"
```

You always get what you ask for, so be careful to specify exactly what you want.

Summary

The default networking protocol for the UNIX operating system is TCP/IP. The files and utilities discussed within this chapter are standard with UNIX networking packages. The files enable hosts to communicate with each other, and can be invaluable in enabling an administrator to verify that all networking activities are transpiring as they should. The utilities further verify this information and enable a user to perform tasks remotely on other machines.

Part X

A-Z Command Reference

Command Reference

at/batch

Purpose

Enables you to schedule jobs that are to be executed later. (A job is a set of commands that can be done without your involvement.) For example, you might want to print a file at midnight when the printer is free and your installment is cheaper.

The batch command runs the job with a lower priority when the system utilization is lower. The job or set of commands can run immediately, or it can run later; execution depends on the system load.

Syntax

```
at time
at [options] job-ids
at -qqueue time
```

or

```
batch
```

Options and Variables

-l   Lists the currently scheduled jobs. The list may be limited to specific job IDs. When no job-id is specified, the system lists all jobs. If you are not the superuser, only your jobs are listed.

-r   Removes specified job IDs from the queue. Unless you are the superuser, you can remove only your own jobs.

job-ids   Assigned by the at command as identification codes. When the at command is entered, the system returns the job-id of that request.

time   Specifies the time when the job should start. The format of time is highly flexible and is divided into three basic options: time, date, and increment, of which date and increment are optional.

Option	Function
time	This option can consist of one, two, or four digits. You can use one or two digits to designate hours (that is, at 1, at 10). Four digits designate hours and minutes. (A colon also can be used, that is, at 0815, or at 8:15.) You also may use the suffix am or pm; otherwise, military time is assumed. The at command also accepts the special names noon, midnight, and now.

date   The name of a month, followed by a day and an optional year. If you specify the year, you must precede the year with a comma. Examples are at 9:00am Dec 25 and at 9:00 Dec 25, 1992. You also can express the date as a day of the week spelled out completely or abbreviated, such as at 9:00 Friday or at 9:00 Fri.

increment   Modifies the time and date by an increment of +n units. The n variable stands for an integer, and the units variable may be written as minutes, hours, days, weeks, months, or years. You can use either the plural or singular form of these increments. You also can substitute next for +1.

Rules

The at and batch requests take their lists of commands to execute at the scheduled time from standard input. Commands may be piped to it, redirected to it, or entered interactively.

When invoked, the at command returns a job ID. You can use the ID as the job-id(s) parameter when using the -l or -r option.

Only those users specified in the file /usr/lib/cron/at.allow can schedule jobs. If this file does not exist, the file /usr/lib/cron/at.deny contains the list of users who cannot use at.

If the time specified is earlier than the current time, then the next occurrence of that time is used. That is, if at noon is used, and the command is being issued at 1:00 p.m., then UNIX carries out the command at 1:00 p.m. the next day.

When at issues the assigned set of commands, those commands' results sent to standard output and standard error are mailed to the user.

Message

    at: bad date specification

This message appears if you incorrectly specify the time at which the job is to be executed.

Examples

Suppose that you want to run the set of commands stored in the file my-commands and that you want the commands to be run at noon today. Issue the following form of the at command:

    at noon <my-commands

At noon, the commands will run, and the results will be mailed to you.

If you want to run the job at noon on Wednesday of next week, issue the following form of the command:

```
at noon Wed next week <my-commands
```

Suppose that you want to mail some electronic Christmas cards at 8:00 on December 15. Issue the following form of the at command:

```
at 8:00 Dec 15 <mail-xmas-cards
```

The file mail-xmas-cards contains the set of commands that mails the cards.

Sometimes you want to execute something in the background, but you do not care when it runs. This is referred to as batching a command. Suppose you want to batch a search for some files that end with the characters .old. Issue the following form of the batch command:

```
batch
date
find / -name "*.old" -print
```

This is an example of using batch interactively instead of giving batch a set of commands from a file, as in the previous example. To end this set of commands, press Ctrl+D. You also can use the at command interactively.

See Also

```
cron

date

find

mail

nice

ps
```

banner

Purpose

Takes up to 10 characters and produces a banner by using a series of asterisks (*) to construct the characters. The lp spooler uses banner to print the banner page, typically passing banner the login ID of the user who requests the printout. The output of banner goes to the standard output and may be redirected to a file or piped through another command.

Syntax

```
banner strings
```

Options and Variables

strings   The list of 10 character strings that are used to create a banner. Each string, if separated by a space, creates a banner on successive lines. If you enclose two strings in quotation marks (""), banner places those strings on the same line.

Examples

To produce a banner with the letters "hello," type the following command:

```
banner hello
```

On the screen you will see the word "hello" in large letters constructed with asterisks (*). Issue the following form of the command to print "hello mom" on the default printer:

```
banner "hello mom" ¦ lp
```

On the printer, you find the words "hello mom" on the same line because they were enclosed in quotation marks ("").

See also

```
echo
```
```
lp
```

basename

Purpose

Extracts the file name portion of a path name. You also can optionally strip off trailing characters or extensions, such as .wks. This command is typically used in shell-script programming for advanced file manipulation.

Syntax

```
basename pathname extension
```

Options and Variables

`pathname`   The path name of the file whose base name you want to extract.

`extension`   The extension or suffix to be removed.

Examples

The following example demonstrates the way to use basename to display the word "cliff" out of the path name /usr/acct/cliff.

```
basename /usr/acct/cliff
```

The preceding form of the basename command displays cliff.

Suppose you have a set of spreadsheets created by Lotus 1-2-3, and you want to extract the basename without the Lotus extension. The following example demonstrates this procedure for a spreadsheet of bowling scores.

```
basename /usr/acct/cliff/bowling.wk1 .wk1
```

The preceding form of the command displays bowling. The characters .wk1 are stripped from the output.

When used with the shell's output assignment operator ('), basename can be a powerful tool when writing shell scripts. The following shell script deletes all the files found in the current directory in another directory:

```
for i in /usr/acct/cliff/*
do
rm /usr/acct/pete/'basename $i'
done
```

See Also

```
dirname
```

```
sh
```

bc

Purpose

Enables you to perform simple math operations. The command also offers a programming language that is similar to the C language in structure. The command is particularly useful for base conversions. For a complete list of the bc command's operators and structure, see your system's user manuals.

Syntax

```
bc [options] filelist
```

Options and Variables

-c   Normally, bc acts as a preprocessor for the dc (desk calculator) command. When you use the -c option, bc sends the compiled output to the standard output instead of sending it to dc.

-l   This switch gives you access to the system's math library, which includes trigonometric and logarithmic functions.

filelist   This variable represents the list of files that contain bc functions to be executed. After bc executes the list of files, the command reads from the standard input. When you use the filelist variable, you can load your desired functions from a set of files and then interactively call on these functions.

Rules

The bc command resides in /usr/bin and uses the dc program, which is located in the same directory. The library of mathematical functions is located in /usr/lib/lib.bc. The bc command waits for you to type a math operation, then presents the results. You can continue to enter operations, or you can press Ctrl+D to exit from the bc command.

Message

```
cannot open input file on line 1, badfilename
```

The preceding message appears if you supply a file name that bc cannot open. Badfilename is substituted with the file name you supplied.

Examples

Suppose that you want to use bc to multiply 40 by 512. Issue the command as follows, and note that the result (20480) appears on the next line after the equation:

```
bc
40*512
20480
^D
```

Notice how the Ctrl+D ended your session in bc.

Now, suppose that you want to convert the base 16 (hexidecimal) number 1B to its base 10 (decimal) number. Issue the following form of the bc command, and note again that the result appears after the equation:

```
bc
ibase=16
1B
27
^D
```

The preceding example used a predefined variable to bc called ibase. This variable is used by bc to define in which base the input numbers are.

To convert from base 16 to base 2 (binary), issue the following command:

```
bc
ibase=16
obase=2
1B
11011
^D
```

The preceding example introduced another predefined variable called obase. This variable is used by bc to define what the base of the output numbers should be. 11011 is the binary representative of 1B.

To set scaling to four decimal places and to calculate the result of 1 divided by 3, issue the following form of the command:

```
bc
scale=4
1/3
.3333
^D
```

In the preceding example, the output is limited to four decimals because the predefined scale variable is set to 4.

When setting both ibase and obase, set obase first. Trigonometric functions work in radians. When you enter more than one operation, the usual mathematical order-of-precedence rules apply. Use parentheses to alter this order.

See Also

dc

bdiff

Purpose

Breaks the two large files into smaller chunks before comparing their contents. If you want to compare two files, use the bdiff command on files that are too large for the diff command. The output is then merged; the line numbers adjust as though diff were run directly.

Syntax

```
bdiff file1 file2 lines -s
```

Options and Variables

file1   The first file used in the comparison. If you use a dash (-), bdiff reads standard input.

file2   The second file used in the comparison. If you use a dash (-), bdiff reads standard input.

            Note: You cannot use a dash (-) for both files.

lines   The number of lines to send to diff at a time. The default is 3,500.

-s   Suppresses the printing of bdiff diagnostics. This switch, however, does not stop the printing of diff diagnostics.

Rules

Because the files are broken into pieces, bdiff may not be able to find a minimum number of differences.

Messages

```
ERROR: arg counter(bd1)
```

The preceding message appears if you supply bdiff with the wrong number of arguments.

```
ERROR: 'filename' non-existent( (ut4)
```

The preceding message displays if the specified file does not exist.

Example

Suppose that you want to compare the contents of two very long letters. The first is named letter-to-mom and the second is named letter-to-mom.old. Issue the following form of the bdiff command:

```
bdiff letter-to-mom letter-to-mom.old
```

This command breaks each file into 3,500-line pieces, and then passes the pieces to diff for comparison.

See Also

```
diff
```

```
split
```

cal

Purpose

Displays a calendar on the standard output. The output is small; one year takes up less spaces than an 8 1/2-by-11-inch sheet of paper. This command is useful when you need to compare dates from different years or determine the day of a particular date.

Syntax

```
cal month year
```

Options and Variables

month   May be a number between 1 and 12, or enough letters to represent a unique month. (J is not enough, for example, to distinguish January, June, or July.) The default is the current month.

year   May be any number between 1 and 9999. The default is the current year. You must specify all four digits of the year. That is, 92 refers to the year 92 rather than the year 1992.

Rules

If you do not specify any arguments, the system displays the current month along with the preceding and the following month. The system also displays the current date and time.

Messages

```
cal: bad year 0
```

The preceding message appears if you specify the year 0. The year must be between 1 and 9,999.

```
cal: non-unique month name Ma
```

The preceding message appears if you supply an insufficient number of letters for a month. In this example, the letters Ma have been specified for the month, but cal cannot determine whether May or March is the requested month.

Examples

Suppose you want a quick look at the current month's calendar. You can issue the following command:

cal

The preceding example shows the current month, as well as the preceding and following months.

To display the calendar for the entire year, type the following:

cal 1970

The preceding example shows the calendar for the year 1970.

If you want to see the calendar for a given month, enter the following:

cal 12

The preceding example shows the month of December for the current year.

calendar

Purpose

Produces a things-to-do list by reading the contents of the file named calendar, which should reside in your current directory.

Syntax

```
calendar -
```

Options and Variables

-              This argument causes calendar to search every user's home account
               for the calendar file, and then to mail the results to the user.

Rules

In some vendors' systems, SCO for example, the calendar command already is
correctly set up in the cron file. You should never actually need to use this command;
the mailing should occur automatically.

If you want to receive a mailed things-to-do list, you need a file called calendar in your
home account. In this file, you may list one-line entries containing the date of the task
or appointment. You may specify multiple lines for the same task, but each line must
contain the date or that line is not mailed.

The calendar command accepts the following date formats:

```
12/25/91
```

```
Dec 25 1991
```

```
Dec 25
```

However, `25 Dec` is not acceptable.

The calendar command mails the lines found in the calendar file one day before the
date and on the date. Friday is considered to be one date before Monday. No similar
adjustment is made for holidays.

The calendar file must have public-read permissions, or the calendar utility cannot
access the information.

Example

If you issue the calendar command without the optional argument, the system displays
a list of the to-dos or appointments that reside in your calendar file.

```
calendar
```

See Also

```
cron
```

```
mail
```

cancel

Purpose

Cancels a print request that has been generated by the lp spooler.

Syntax

```
cancel request-ids
```

or

```
cancel printer
```

Options and Variables

`request-ids` Cancels a list of lp spooler request IDs. The lp spooler assigns a unique ID to each print request. Use lpstat to list the request ID.

`printer` Cancels the current print job at this printer location.

Rules

Unless you are a superuser or an lp administrator, you may cancel only the jobs you have requested.

If the job is currently printing, a message regarding its termination is printed on the paper. Also, if someone else cancels one of your print requests, you are notified of the cancellation and receive the request ID of the job that was canceled. If a print request is canceled by someone other than you, you are mailed by the system that canceled the job and informed as to what request ID was canceled.

Messages

```
cancel: "bad-id" is not a request id or a printer
```

The preceding message appears if you try to cancel a print request that does not exist, or if you specify a bad printer name when you issue the cancel command.

```
cancel: request "bad-id" is non-existent
```

The preceding message appears if you give cancel a nonexistent ID.

Examples

To cancel the print request that is going to go to the mailroom printer, issue the following form of the cancel command:

```
cancel mailroom-107
```

The previous example canceled request number 107 on the mailroom printer.

To cancel the current printing job on the mailroom printer, issue the following form of the command:

```
cancel mailroom
```

The previous example cancels the current job on the printer, no matter what number it was.

If you cancel a job while it is printing, the system prints your termination message and then immediately begins printing the next job. The paper, however, does not advance to the top of page. A good practice to adopt is first to disable the printer; this stops printing the current request and stops printing all jobs on that printer until enabled again. You may then cancel the request, realign the printer to the top of page, and then enable the printer.

See Also

```
disable

enable

lp

lpstat
```

cat

Purpose

Concatenates or joins files together. You also can use this command to display a file.

Syntax

```
cat [options] filelist
```

Options and Variables

-s   Suppresses messages about unreadable files.

-u	Causes the output to be unbuffered.
-v	Displays control characters with a caret (^); the caret appears before the character. For example, an end-of-text character-hex 04 displays as ^D.
-t	Causes tabs and form feeds to be displayed in the -v format. The -t switch is valid only with the -v option. If the -t switch is used, tabs appear as ^I and form feeds appear as ^L.
-e	Causes newline characters to be preceded by a dollar sign ($). The -e switch is valid only with the -v option.
filelist	This is an optional list of files that are to be concatenated. If you do not specify any files, or if you do specify a dash (-), cat reads the standard input.

Rules

The file name used to store the output cannot be the same as any of the input names, unless the output file is a special file.

Messages

```
cat: illegal option — -badoption
```

The preceding message indicates that you invoked cat with an invalid option (that is, an option not included in the preceding list). The -badoption variable is replaced with the option you specified.

```
cat: cannot open badfile
```

The preceding message indicates that you invoked cat with the name of a file that cannot be opened.

```
cat: input filename is output
```

The preceding message means that you specified an output file that was used in the input (such as cat myfile hisfile >myfile).

Examples

If you want to view the letter you wrote to mom on the screen, type the following:

```
cat letter-to-mom
```

The preceding command concatenates the file named letter-to-mom with nothing and sends the output to the screen.

Suppose you have a standard file containing your signature and you want to add it to your letter before you sent it. You can enter the following command:

```
cat letter-to-mom signature >send.let
```

The preceding command appends the file named signature to the file letter-to-mom and creates a new file named send.let.

The cat command can be used to capture printouts from a machine for which no other suitable media exchange exists. You can simply substitute a UNIX computer for the printer and issue a command similar to the following:

```
cat </dev/tty1a >my-file
```

See Also

cp

echo

more

pg

pr

cd

Purpose

Changes the current working directory.

Syntax

```
cd dirname
```

Options and Variables

dirname   The name of the directory you want to make current. If you do not specify a directory when you issue the cd command, then the system automatically changes to your home account.

Rules

You must have execute permissions on the directory you want to make active. Two special directories exist:

.   Refers to the current directory.

..   Refers to the parent directory.

Messages

baddir: bad directory

The preceding message indicates that you specified a nonexistent directory.

cd /*dir*?

If you mistype the new directory's name, cd prompts you with the name of a directory that you might have meant. You can press any key to make the /dir? directory current; press N to cancel the command.

Suppose you wanted to change your working directory to /usr/cliff. You can enter the following:

cd /usr/cliff

After typing this, you are in Cliff's home account. From here, you can issue the following:

cd ..

The preceding example changes to this directory's parent directory (/usr/cliff is a subdirectory of /usr). Use this command repeatedly to back out of the directory hierarchy one level at a time.

When you are finished, type the following command:

cd

Typing cd alone always returns you to your home account.

See Also

chmod

ls

pwd

sh

chgrp

Purpose

Changes the group ownership of a file.

Syntax

```
chgrp group filelist
```

Options and Variables

group   The group to which you want to change. For this variable, you may substitute either the numerical value of the group ID or the name as found in the file /etc/group.

filelist   A space-separated list of files whose group ownership you want to change.

Rules

You may not change a file's group ownership unless you are the file's owner or the superuser.

Messages

```
chgrp: unknown group: badgroupid
```

The preceding message indicates that you entered a group ID that does not exit. In the actual message, the system substitutes badgroupid with the bad group ID you supplied.

```
badfile: no such file or directory
```

This message means that you supplied chgrp with the name of a nonexistent file.

Example

The directory /usr/local/bin is created by the system administrator to keep loosely created commands separate. These commands often need ownership established, simply as a way of confirming the command practice. The following example does this:

```
chgrp bin /usr/local/bin/*
```

This command changes all of the files found in the local/bin directory to the group ownership of bin.

See Also

chmod

chown

chmod

Purpose

Changes the mode of files. A file's mode controls the access permissions associated with that file.

UNIX has three levels of security: ownership, group, and everyone else. Within each of these three levels are three permissions: read, write, and execute. On standard files, the read permission enables you to read a file's contents, the write permission enables you to modify the file, and the execute permission enables you to execute it.

Directories behave in only a slightly different manner. The read permission enables you to view the contents of the directory; that is, you can use the ls command. The write permission enables you to create new files in the directory and to delete files from the directory. Finally, the execute permission enables you to make the directory your current working directory; that is, you can use the cd command.

Syntax

chmod *mode filelist*

or

chmod *level action permission filelist*

Options and Variables

The preceding syntax lines show the two formats of the chmod command. The first format also sets the permissions at all levels. The second format is more complicated than the first, but enables you to use symbols to specify the permissions. The second format sets the permissions incrementally.

filelist   The list of files to be affected by the chmod command.

mode   The numeric mode (in octal form) of this file's permissions for all levels. Each octal number sets a bit in the mode field stored in the inode table of the file system; adding the numbers together sets the combination of the permissions. The permissions at the user/owner, group, and other/world levels all follow the same pattern. There is an additional level that controls some special handling. The mode is in the following form: SUGO, where S=special, U=user/owner, G=group, and O=others/world. Each number may be any from the following table.(Consult the user's reference provided with your system for the S meaning of the number because they differ from the U, G, and O meanings.)

Value	Permission
0	None!
1	Execute
2	Read
4	Write

level   The level to be affected by the rest of the command. The level may be any of the following characters:

Character	Meaning
u	The user/owner of the file
g	The group level
o	Others or the world level
a	All the levels

action   Specifies the action that is to take place on the file's mode. The action may be any of the following characters:

Character	Meaning
+	Adds the permission
-	Removes the permission
=	Sets the permission to be only what is specified

permission   The permission to apply to the file. The permission may be one or more of the following characters:

Character	Permission granted
r	Read
w	Write
x	Execute

Message

```
chmod: ERROR: invalid mode
```

This message indicates that you did not specify the mode correctly. Check each portion of the command again. The second form of the command must use the rules described earlier. If this message appears, it can mean that you simply mistyped a character.

Examples

The following command enables the file letter-to-mom to have all permissions at all levels:

```
chmod 777 letter-to-mom
```

Notice that the special level is not specified; this is an implied 0 and no special permissions are granted. Although the execute permission is nonsensical in this case, it demonstrates the use of the 7 to mean all possible permissions.

To enable any user to read a file, but not change it, type the following:

```
chmod 644 letter-to-mom
```

Now all users may read the letter to mom, but only the owner has the right to change the file.

To open the file to any user to make changes, enter the following:

```
chmod a+w letter-to-mom
```

The preceding command enables all users to modify the letter.

Another possibility is as follows:

```
chmod o-wr,g-wr letter-to-mom
```

The preceding command removes the read-and-write permissions at both the group and other levels.

The last sample command sets the other level to allow read-only permission:

```
chmod o=r letter-to-mom
```

All other permissions at this level are removed.

See Also

```
ls

umask
```

chown

Purpose

Enables you to change the ownership of the file. In a sense, chown enables you to give a file to someone else.

Syntax

```
chown user filelist
```

Options and Variables

user   A numerical user ID or a valid user name as found in the /etc/passwd file.

filelist   A space-separated list of files, whose ownership you want to reassign.

Rules

Only the superuser or a file's owner can change the ownership of a file. Remember, however, that if you are not the superuser and you assign a file to another user, you are no longer the owner of the file. Therefore, you cannot change your mind and reassign the file back to yourself.

Messages

```
badfile: No such file or directory
```

The preceding message indicates that you specified a nonexistent file. In the actual message, the system substitutes badfile with the name of the file you specified.

```
chown: unknown userid baduserid
```

This message means that you specified a user name that is not found in /etc/passwd. In the actual message, the system substitutes baduserid with the user name you specified.

Example

As with the chgrp command, you can ensure that all of the commands found in /usr/local/bin are owned by bin.

```
chown bin /usr/local/bin/*
```

This example changes all the files found in the local/bin directory to the ownership of bin.

See Also

```
chgrp
```

clear

Purpose

Clears the screen. If a printer is being used as the standard output, the clear command advances the paper.

Syntax

```
clear term
```

Options and Variables

term   The name of the terminal type to be cleared. If you do not specify a terminal type, the environment variable TERM is used. The terminal name you specify must match a valid entry in the file /etc/termcap.

Rules

The cl termcap type should be defined in the /etc/termcap file. If not, then a series of newlines are sent.

See Also

```
echo
```

cmp

Purpose

Compares two files to determine whether they are different.

Syntax

```
cmp -l -s file1 file2
```

Options and Variables

-l   Causes cmp to list the offset (in decimal) where a difference is detected between the files. This switch also causes cmp to display the numerical representation of the differing bytes (in octal).

-s   Tells cmp not to produce any output. Only an exit status is set, using the following values:

                     0 = No differences

                     1 = The files are different

                     2 = Inaccessible or missing file

file1   A valid file name. You also can specify a dash (-) to have cmp read from the standard input.

file2   A valid file name.

Messages

```
cmp: EOF on file
```

The preceding message indicates that one of the files was shorter than the other. In the actual message, the system substitutes file with the name of the shorter file.

```
cmp: cannot open file
```

This message means that the file cannot be accessed, the file may not exist, or you do not have read permissions. In the actual message, the system substitutes *file* with the name of the file you specified.

Example

Suppose that you have a letter that you are planning to send, letter-to-mom, and another letter named letter.save. You need to compare the two files to determine whether their contents are the same. Issue the following command:

```
cmp letter-to-mom letter.save
```

The cmp command is best suited for binary files; the diff command is best suited for text files. If you want to know only if two files are identical, however, and if you do not care why the two files might be different, cmp works fine.

See Also

```
comm

diff

diff3

sdiff
```

comm

Purpose

Finds the lines that are common between two sorted files. The command generates three columns of information. The first column lists the lines found only in the first file, the second column lists the lines found only in the second file, and the third column lists the lines found in both files.

Syntax

```
comm [options] file1 file2
```

Options and Variables

-1	Tells comm not to produce the first column.
-2	Tells comm not to produce the second column.
-3	Tells comm not to produce the third column.
file1	The name of the first file to use in the comparison. You can specify a dash (-) if you want comm to read the standard input.
file2	The name of the second file to use in the comparison.

Rules

Only sorted files may be used with this command.

If all three options are supplied (-123), no output appears.

Message

```
comm: cannot open badfilename
```

This message means that you specified a nonexistent file, or that you do not have permission to read the file. In the actual message, the system substitutes badfilename with the name of the file you specified.

Examples

Suppose two users (Cliff and Amy) work on similar projects. Each project has its own file name to track what Cliff and Amy are working on. You want to know what projects have the same name. The following example shows a way to accomplish this task:

```
ls /usr/amy >amy.dir

ls /usr/cliff >cliff.dir

comm amy.dir cliff.dir
```

The first line of the example built a list of the files found in Amy's home account; the second did the same for Cliff's. The last line issued the comm command to those two files, displaying what was in common between the two lists and which files were only in one or the other.

```
comm -12 amy.dir cliff.dir
```

Using the same directory lists from the preceding example, this example limits the output to those files which are in common only.

See Also

```
cmp

diff

dircmp

sdiff

sort

uniq
```

copy

Purpose

Copies files or entire directory structures, keeping the same ownership, permissions, and modification times intact.

Syntax

```
copy [options] sources destination
```

Options and Variables

-a	Tells the system to prompt for confirmation before making each copy. Any response beginning with a Y is assumed to be a yes; any other response is assumed to be a no.
-l	Tells UNIX to use links rather than copies whenever possible. This is not possible with directories. (This option, if links are possible, is significantly faster because copies are not made of the data.)
-n	Copies file only if it is new. The -n option is meaningless when used with directories. Two directory names may be shared, and copy still copies their contents if used with the -r option.
-o	Keeps the original owner and group ownerships of the copied files. Otherwise, the file's owner and group become the user who is running the copy procedure.
-m	Causes the copied files to keep their modification and access times. Otherwise, the files' modification times are set to reflect the time the copy is made.
-r	Recursively traverses directories, copying each file and directory encountered. In other words, as copy encounters a directory, it traverses any subdirectories until the entire directory tree has been copied.
-v	Tells UNIX to display the copied files verbosely. Each file name is displayed as it is copied.
sources	A list of the files or directories to be copied. The list is space-delimited.
destination	The directory or file to be copied to.

Rules

The copy command behaves like the cp command when used with files or when the destination is a directory. You can use the copy command in place of the cp command in these instances.

Message

```
copy: cannot open badfilename
```

This message indicates that you tried to copy a file that is nonexistent or for which you do not have permission to read. In the actual message, the system substitutes badfilename with the file name you specified.

Examples

Suppose you are about to make some major revisions to the files found in your current working directory. Use the following command:

```
copy * /tmp/test
```

The preceding example makes a copy of all the files in the current directory, and places the copies in the /tmp/test directory. It also copies the first files found in any subdirectories within the current directory.

Suppose that the current directory contains a subdirectory called play, and that the play subdirectory contains one file called rules and a second-level subdirectory named games. The preceding command copies the file rules, but does not copy the contents of games; you must add the -r flag to copy the subdirectory's contents. The following form of the command does the trick:

```
copy -r . /tmp/test
```

With the -r switch in place, copy recursively copies the current directory to the directory /tmp/test. The command creates a duplicate of the directory structures.

The UNIX documentation states that you can copy entire file systems. In a general sense, however, this is not true. Links may be created within the file system, but they are not preserved across file systems. If you use the copy command to move a file system, the links are lost. By using the cpio command as follows, however, you preserve the links:

```
find . -depth -print | cpio -pamdlv /my-new-filesytem
```

This command copies all the files found in the current directory to the new file system.

The copy -r * * command is dangerous because it copies all directories to themselves in an endless loop. The user can press Ctrl+C or Del to stop the command.

See Also

```
cp
```

```
cpio
```

```
dircomp

ln

mv
```

cp

Purpose

Copies files. You can copy one file to another file or copy a list of files to a directory.

Syntax

```
cp source-file dest-file

cp source-list dest-directory
```

Options and Variables

source-file	The file to copy.
dest-file	The destination name.
source-list	A space-separated list of files to copy.
dest-directory	The destination directory.

Examples

Suppose you want to work on a letter to your mother, but you want to make sure that the original letter remains intact. To copy a letter to Mom to a file called letter.save, issue the following command:

```
cp letter-to-mom letter.save
```

The preceding example saves the current letter to a file name that can be referenced later.

To copy all files starting with the word letter to a directory called old-letters, issue the following command:

```
cp letter* /old-letters
```

No verification is done for a file that already exists with the same name in the destination directory. Be careful when copying files to a directory—there may be a file in that directory with the same name. The cp command writes over the existing file, and all information in that file is lost.

See Also

    copy

    ln

    mv

    rm

cpio

Purpose

Stands for copy in/out. The cpio command copies a list of files to a backup archive (copy out) or copies from an archive to the file system (copy in). It is useful not only for creating and restoring backups, but also for moving files about in the file system.

Syntax

    cpio -o [*options*]

    cpio -i [*options*] *filelist*

    cpio -p [*options*] *dirname*

Options and Variables

-o	Creates the archive or backup (generates the output).
-i	Copies in from a restored archive.
-p	Accepts a list of files from the standard input and passes them to the specified directory. This switch is useful for copying whole directory structures on the file system.
-B	Signifies a blocking factor of 5,120 bytes-per-record. Otherwise, default block size is 512 bytes. This switch is used with the -o and -i options and is used only when sending the output to, or reading the input from, a character-special device.
-a	Resets the access times of the files after the copy is completed. If it is used with the -l option, the files with links are not affected. This switch also is used with the -o or -i options.

-c	Creates or reads the header information in the archive in an ASCII-character format, which creates headers that are readable on other platforms. For example, you can move an archive created on an X86 Intel-based machine to a 68X Motorola-based machine. This switch is used with the -o or -i options.
-d	Creates the directories as needed. If the directories do not exist, the cpio command creates them. This switch is used with the -p or -i options.
-f	Enables you to change the interpretation of the filelist variable. The filelist variable is generally a list of files to extract, but when the -f option is used, filelist becomes the list of files not to extract. This switch is used with the -i option.
-K *volsize*	Specifies the size of the source or destination volume. This variable is a number representing the size in kilobytes, and it is useful when reading or writing to removable media (tapes or floppies).
-l	Links files instead of copying them, if possible. This switch is used with the -p option.
-m	Retains the modification times of the files as found in the archive. Normally, modification times change to the current time, which has no effect on directories. This switch is used with the -i and -p options.
-r	Renames the files in filelist. You are prompted for each file in filelist for the new name. If none is given, the file is skipped. This switch is used with the -o or -i options.
-t	Prints a list of the files in the archive. This switch is used with the -i option.
-u	Extracts the files from the archive unconditionally. The cpio command usually only extracts the file from the archive if the file in the archive has a newer modification time than the one on the file system. This switch is used with the -p or -i options.
-v	Signifies verbose mode and tells the cpio command to give a status report to the screen. This switch is used with the -i option.
filelist	A space-separated list of files to extract from the archive. This list can contain wild cards. The wild cards supported are the same as the simple regular expression expansion provided by the shell (sh). If you use wild cards, enclose filelist in quotation marks; otherwise, the shell expands them. A weakness of another archiver, tar, is that it does not support wild cards; it relies on the shell to expand its list of files.

Character	Meaning
!	A metacharacter that means "not"
?	Matches a single character
*	Matches any number of characters
[ ]	Matches the set of characters specified between the brackets
dirname	The destination directory for the files given by the cpio command by using the -p option.

Message

The message usually displayed is a usage clause that shows you the necessary syntax for using cpio. If you see this message, you probably did not provide a necessary option, and you should check your command line again.

Examples

```
ls ¦ cpio -oBc >/dev/rfd096ds15
```

The preceding example lists the current directory that passes the list through the pipeline to cpio. The cpio command uses the input from the pipeline as its list of files to copy. The command copies this list of files to the standard output with a blocking factor of 5120, and the header information is written in a portable ASCII format. This output is then redirected to the character-special device /dev/rfd096ds15 (a high-density, 5 1/4-inch floppy disk).

```
cpio -iBcdm "*.ltr" </dev/rfd096ds15
```

The preceding example extracts only the files ending in .ltr from the floppy disk, placing them in the current directory. Any subdirectories are created as needed. The file's modification times are the same as they were at the time the archive was created.

```
ls -A ¦ cpio -pdl /usr/newdir
```

The preceding example takes the list generated by ls and copies it to the directory /usr/newdir. It creates any needed directories, and it uses linking instead of copying whenever possible.

The cpio command, with the -i and -o options, is a filter program—it accepts its input from the standard input and directs its output to the standard output. This means that the command can be anywhere in the pipeline, as long as the input to the -o option is a list of file names, and the input to the -i option is the result of a previous -o option. The -p option is not a true filter—output is the specified directory.

See Also

```
copy

find

tar
```

cron

Purpose

Manages the system's scheduled execution of programs. The system comes installed with this program in place; it should run at all times in the background—you should never need to type this command. This command enables you to schedule jobs by reading a file in /usr/spool/cron/crontabs/username (username is substituted with the name of a user running the job). This is the mechanism that executes at, batch, and crontab requests.

Syntax

```
cron
```

Rules

In order to use the cron command, you must have your user name in the /usr/lib/cron/cron.allow file. Some sites may have the file /usr/lib/cron/cron.deny, which is the list of users who cannot use the command.

See Also

```
at

batch

crontab
```

crontab

Purpose

Shows the cron command the way to run the scheduled job. By setting up the appropriate file, you can have jobs executed routinely, for example, a nightly unattended backup.

Syntax

```
crontab sched-file

crontab -l

crontab -r
```

Options and Variables

-l   Lists what you told the cron command to do.

r   Removes jobs from the cron tables (the jobs are no longer executed).

sched-file   The name of a file containing the schedule and programs to run. If no file is given, crontab reads from the standard input. The file must be in the following format:

Character	Meaning
M	Minute of the hour (0-59)
H	Hour of the day (0-23)
D	Day of the month (1-31)
m	Month of the year (1-12)
d	Day of the week (0-6; 0=Sunday)
cmd	Program to run—the string passed to sh.

The first five fields can contain a single digit, a list of digits separated by commas, a range of digits using a dash, or an asterisk that means all legal values.

Rules

All jobs are executed with sh from your home account ($HOME). The environment is set up with HOME, LOGNAME, SHELL=/BIN/SH, and PATH=/bin:usr/bin. If you need to run your .profile to set additional environment variables, do this specifically in the crontab sched-file. Only one sched-file is allowed at a time—the new one overwrites the old one.

Messages

```
crontab: you are not authorized to use cron. Sorry.
```

The preceding message means that you tried to use cron when you were not allowed to. Check the cron.deny and cron.allow files.

```
crontab: can't open your crontab file
```

The preceding message indicates that you do not currently have a crontab file defined. You either tried to list it, by using the -l flag, or you gave a bad flag and crontab thought it was a file name.

```
* * * * echo hello
crontab: error on previous line: unexpected character found in
line.
```

The preceding message means that your sched-file is not properly defined. In the example, the file contains a line without enough fields. When this happens, cron ignores the entire file. You must make the change and then resubmit the file.

Examples

```
0 8 * * * echo "Good Morning"

0 8 25 12 * echo "Merry Christmas"

0 8 * * 1 echo "Not Monday again"
```

The preceding lines are examples of messages the sched-file can contain. The first line gives the message Good Morning every day at 8:00 a.m. The second line sends the message Merry Christmas once a year, on the 25th of December at 8:00 a.m. (Hopefully, you will not be at work to get it.). The last line complains about Monday once a week, on Monday morning at 8:00 a.m.

```
crontab exmpl-crontab
```

The preceding example reads a file called exmpl-crontab in the current directory and informs cron that the jobs found in it are to be executed.

```
crontab -l
```

The preceding example lists the jobs you asked cron to execute.

```
crontab -r
```

The preceding example informs cron to remove your jobs from its list of jobs to schedule. You have to resubmit a sched-file in order for cron to execute anything for you.

See Also

```
at/batch

cron

sh
```

crypt

Purpose

Encrypts a file. The crypt command uses a password to store a file in an encrypted form and requires the same password to decode the file. The crypt command reads from standard input and writes to standard output.

Syntax

```
crypt password
```

Options and Variables

password   Gains access to the file (also referred to as the encryption key). If password is not supplied, crypt prompts for it.

Rules

The crypt command generates files that are compatible with the editors ed, edit, ex, and vi when in encryption mode.

Although documented, the crypt command is not bundled with some UNIX products because the distribution of crypt libraries is regulated by the U.S. Government. (They are not available outside of the United States and its territories.) Contact your dealer to obtain these tools.

Two or more files encrypted by the same key are concatenated. In any attempt to decrypt output, only the first file will be correctly translated.

Examples

Suppose you have a secret that you want nobody to know, and you want to send it in a letter to your mother. You can encrypt it with the following command:

```
crypt pickles <letter-to-mom>let.crypt
```

The preceding example encrypts the letter by using the password/key of pickles and stores the result in the file let.crypt.

When your mother receives the letter through electronic mail, she can save it to a file, let.crypt, and then print it with the following command:

```
crypt pickles <let.crypt ¦ lp
```

The preceding example decodes the previously encrypted file and prints it.

See Also

```
ed
```

```
vi
```

csh

Purpose

Initiates the C shell—a command interpreter like sh. (It is named C shell because its syntax resembles that of the C programming language.) Like the sh command, csh is itself a complete programming language. To take advantage of csh, consult the reference manual and user's guide supplied with your system or consult a book that covers csh exclusively.

Syntax

```
csh
```

Example

Suppose you want to do some work, but you must preserve your current shell environment and directory setting. You can issue the following command to launch a new shell for this temporary work:

csh

You may now make changes to the environment and change directories. When you exit this shell, your environment returns to its original condition.

See Also

```
sh
```

cu

Purpose

Dials into other systems through a modem or by a direct connection. The cu (call UNIX) command also provides a set of tilde commands to enhance its usefulness. (See the Rules section for description of tilde commands.)

Syntax

```
cu [options] system-name

cu [options] -lline -sspeed telno

cu [options] -lline -sspeed dir
```

Options and Variables

-x*debug-level*	Sets cu into a debugging level to give diagnostics on its progress. Normally, cu operates silently—you do not know what it is doing. The debug-level can be any digit between 0 and 9; 9 gives the most information.
-n	Prompts for a telephone number.
-o	Makes connection with odd parity.
-e	Makes connection with even parity.
-oe	Makes connection with seven data bits and no parity.
system-name	The name of the system to call, requiring that system-name be set up in the file /usr/lib/uucp/Systems. The speed, line, and phone number are pulled from this file.
-l*line*	The device to which the modem is attached.
-s*speed*	The baud rate at which to make the connection. If this option is not used, the speed is pulled from the file /usr/lib/uucp/Devices.
telno	The telephone number to dial.
dir	The keyword used to inform cu that you want to talk directly with the modem. This is useful when you need to program the modem.

Rules

The system administrator must have properly installed the modems and configured the uucp subsystem to use them. As a minimum, the devices connected to the modems need to be set up in the file /usr/lib/uucp/Devices.

The cu command offers several tilde commands, which can be used while running cu. Each command is preceded by a tilde (~). If you call one machine, and then use that machine to call another machine, two tildes are needed to make a tilde command work on the third machine. The following list contains a few of the available commands:

Command	Meaning
~.	Disconnects from the machine or quits cu. This command is useful if you need to abort a program running on the remote system or if you cannot log in for some reason.
~!	Runs a subshell on the local system.
~!*command*	Runs the command command on the local system.
~%*command*	Runs the command command on the local system and sends the results to the remote system.
~%break	Sends a break signal to the remote system. This command is useful when the speed at which you dialed in is not the speed the at which the port is currently set. A break on UNIX systems causes a new baud rate to be selected.
~%b	Same as ~%break.

Messages

```
Connect failed: SYSTEM NOT IN Systems FILE
```

The preceding message means that you gave cu a system name it does not recognize. (Use uuname to obtain a list of valid system names on your system.)

```
Connect failed: NO DEVICES AVAILABLE
```

The preceding message indicates that all of the modems are in use.

Examples

Suppose you have several machines connected by modem and the machine called valley is where some of the applications you need to work on are found. Type the following command:

```
cu valley
```

The preceding example calls the system valley.

If you have difficulty making the connection, type the following:

```
cu -x9 valley
```

The preceding example calls the system valley and sets a debugging level of 9.

Sometimes you may not know the machine name or the name is not yet in the system file. You can use the following command:

```
cu -l/dev/tty1A -s2400 555-5309
```

The preceding example calls the phone number 555-5309 by using the modem attached to the port /dev/tty1A at 2400 baud.

Periodically, you need to connect to the machine itself to program or debug it. To do this, enter the following:

```
cu -l/dev/tty1A -s2400 dir
```

The preceding example makes a connection with the modem to program it or test it.

The cu command opens devices for exclusive use. If cu terminates abnormally, the device can remain locked.

See Also

cat

echo

stty

tty

uname

cut

Purpose

Extracts fields from a list of files. Fields can be defined as character positions, or they can be defined relatively with a field separator.

Syntax

```
cut -cchar-pos filelist

cut -ffields -dfield-sep -s filelist
```

Options and Variables

-cchar-pos	The character position to cut out. It can be a list separated by commas (,), a range separated by dashes (-), or a combination of both (for example, 1,4,5, or 1-4, or 1-4,5-10,25 are all valid).
-ffields	The fields to cut out. It can also be a list. Fields are denoted by a one-character separator. If the separator repeats, the fields are not treated as one separator. The fields option uses the same syntax as char-pos.

`-d`*field-sep*	Specifies the field separator. A tab character is the default. The field-sep can be any character.
`-s`	If a line contains no field-sep, do not include it. Normally lines without any field separators are passed through.
filelist	The list of files to cut from. If no files are specified, cut reads from the standard input.

Rules

The -c and -f options are mutually exclusive.

Messages

```
line too long
```

The preceding message means that one of the input lines from one of the files was longer than 511 characters.

```
bad list for c/f options
```

The preceding message indicates that you did not supply cut with either a -c or -f flag or that the char-pos/fields were incorrectly specified.

```
no fields
```

The preceding message means that you didn't supply char-pos or fields.

Example

```
cut -f1,5 -d: /etc/passwd
```

This example extracts the user ID and names from the password file.

See Also

```
grep
```

```
paste
```

date

Purpose

Displays the system date and time (the superuser can set the date and time). You can control how the date is displayed.

Syntax

```
date MMDDhhmmYY

date +format
```

Options and Variables

MMDDhhmmYY   This is the format used to set the date and time. The following list explains each part (containing two digits).

MM	The month (01-12)
DD	The day (01-31)
hh	The hour (00-23)
mm	The minute (00-59)
YY	The year (00-99) (optional)

+format   Controls how the date is displayed; consists of a % followed by the following:

n	Inserts a newline
t	Inserts a tab
m	Month (digits)
d	Day of month (digits)
y	Last two digits of year
D	Date as mm/dd/yy
H	Hour
M	Minute
S	Second
J	Julian date (001-366)
W	Day of week (0-6, 0=Sunday)
a	Sun, Mon, Tue, and so on
h	Jan, Feb, Mar, and so on
r	am/pm notation for time

Messages

```
no permission
```

The preceding message means that you are not the superuser and you tried to set the system date.

```
bad conversion
```

The preceding message indicates that you did not give the date setting syntax correctly.

```
bad format character
```

The preceding message shows that you did not use a format character from the above table.

Examples

```
date 0826130094
```

The preceding example sets the date and time to 08/26/94 at 1:00 p.m.

```
date "+Date = %D   Time = %H:%M"
```

The preceding example displays something like the following:

```
Date = 08/26/94   Time = 13:00
```

This line shows the output of the command with the date and time set.

dc

Purpose

Uses postfix notation, which is also referred to as reverse polish notation. If you are not familiar with this format, you should use the bc command. The dc (desk calculator) operates on decimal integers, but you can specify a base and fractions.

Syntax

```
dc progfile
```

Options and Variables

progfile   An optional file name containing a set of dc commands.

number   Pushes the value number on stack.

+-/*%^   Top two values are operated on by popping them off the stack and pushing the result on the stack in their place.

c	Clears stack
d	Duplicates top value
i	Removes top value
p	Prints top values
f	Prints all values
q	Quits program

Messages

```
O is unimplemented
```

The preceding message means that the O is replaced with the octal number of the character you typed in. The character you typed has no meaning in dc.

```
stack empty
```

The preceding message indicates that the stack is empty—you did not push enough arguments to perform the task you want done.

Example

```
4 5 + p
```

This example adds four to five and prints the result.

See Also

bc

df

Purpose

Reports the amount of space that is free on the disk.

Syntax

```
df [options] [filesystems]
```

Options and Variables

-t	Reports the total allocated size of the file system.
-f	Causes df to actually count the number of free blocks, instead of reading the number from the mount table. This option is used to check for memory corruption.
-v	Causes df to report the percentage of free blocks (not available in all systems).
filesystems	This is an optional list of file systems from which free disk space can be reported. If this is left blank, all currently mounted file systems are reported.

Rules

The df command reports in blocks of 512 bytes each.

The -v option cannot be used with the other options.

Message

```
df: illegal arg badarg
```

This message means that you specified an option that is not in the list above. The badarg option is replaced by the bad option you supplied.

See Also

du

mnt

diff

Purpose

Compares two text files and reports what must be done to the one to make it look like the other. It can also be used to create a script usable by the editor ed to re-create the second file from the first. To compare binary files, use the cmp command.

Syntax

```
diff [options] oldfile newfile
```

Options and Variables

-b	Causes strings of blanks and tabs to be equal (for example, the big tree is the same as the big tree).
-e	Generates a script suitable for the editor ed.
-f	Produces a script in the opposite order. It is not usable by ed, however.
oldfile	This is the name of the file that the diff command compares with newfile.
newfile	This is the name of the file you use to compare with oldfile. In a sense, newfile is the control file because the diff command reports what it takes to make oldfile look like newfile.

Rules

The output of diff can take any one of the following forms:

> *lineno* a from-*lineno* to-*lineno*

The preceding form says that the text in the first file at lineno needs to have the text in the second file from the line number from-lineno to the line number to-lineno added to it.

> from-*lineno* to-*lineno* d *lineno*

In the preceding command, the text in the first file found between line number from-lineno and line number to-lineno must be deleted. If they existed, they would fall after the line number in the second file lineno.

> from-*lineno* to-*lineno* c from-*lineno* to-*lineno*

In the preceding command, diff shows how two sets of lines are different, and how they need to be changed from the first set of line number ranges to match the second set of line number ranges.

Example

> **diff old-letter letter-to-mom**

This example reports what you have to do to the file old-letter to make it look like letter-to-mom.

See Also

cmp

```
comm

diff3

ed

sdiff
```

diff3

Purpose

Compares three files at a time. Similar to the diff command.

Syntax

```
diff3 [options] file1 file2 file3
```

Options and Variables

-e	Produces a script for ed to change file1 to reflect the differences between file2 and file3.
-x	Produces a script for ed to change file1 to reflect the differences in all files.
-3	Produces a script for ed to change file1 to reflect the differences in file3.
file1	The first file used in the compare (usually the oldest of the three).
file2	The second file used in the compare.
file3	The third file used in the compare.

Rules

On most systems, diff3 does not work on files larger than 64 KB characters.

Example

```
diff3 old-letter letter-to-mom new-letter
```

This example compares the three letters and displays the results of the comparison.

See Also

cmp

comm

diff

ed

sdiff

dircmp

Purpose

Compares the contents of two directories. Lists the files that are only found in one or the other and runs diff on each of the files that share the same name.

Syntax

dircmp [*options*] *dir1 dir2*

Options and Variables

-d	Runs a "full" diff on the files named the same. Normally, dircmp reports if the contents are the same or not.
-s	Suppresses the diff pass on the file that has the same name. Only a comparison of the file found in either directory is done.
-w*width*	Sets the width of the output to width characters; the default is 72.
dir1	The name of the directory to use in the comparison. If you want the current directory, use a period (.).
dir2	The name of the second directory; may also be a period.

Example

dircmp /usr/bin /bin

The preceding example compares the two executable paths /usr/bin and /bin.

See Also

cmp

diff

dirname

Purpose

Enables you to extract the directory portion of a path name, which is useful in shell scripts.

Syntax

dirname *pathname*

Options and Variables

pathname   The path name for which you want to know the directory portion. If no slashes (/) are used in the string provided, a period (.) is returned.

Examples

dirname /usr/bin/test

The display result of the preceding example is /usr/bin.

dirname /usr/bin

The preceding example results in /usr. Even though bin is a directory, dirname does not look at the file system to determine what the directory portion of the string is—it looks for the last slash and assumes everything before that.

dirname usr

The result of the preceding example written to standard output is a period (.).

See Also

basename

sh

disable

Purpose

Disallows terminals to be logged on to, or print jobs to be applied to, the printer. When you disable a printer, jobs may still be queued for that printer. The jobs will not be placed on the printer, however. This command is useful for clearing paper jams or swapping out the printer for servicing.

Syntax

```
disable terminals

disable -c -rreason printers
```

Options and Variables

-c	Cancels the current print job.
terminals	The list of terminals you want to disable.
-rreason	If the printer is disabled for an extended period of time, you can alert users by specifying a reason for the printer being disabled. reason must immediately follow -r; if it is more than one word, enclose it in quotes.
printers	The list of printers to disable.

Rules

When you disable a printer, any current print job stops. When you enable the printer again, the job starts from the beginning, unless you use the -c flag.

Examples

```
disable tty12
```

The preceding example disables the twelfth console terminal.

```
disable mailroom
```

The preceding example disables the printer called mailroom.

```
disable -c -r"servicing, back up in 1 hr." mailroom
```

The preceding example disables the mailroom printer, cancels the current print job, and notifies users checking on the status of this printer why it is disabled and when it will be back in service.

See Also

cancel

enable

lp

lpstat

du

Purpose

Displays the amount of space being used by the specified directories or files. The information is reported in 512-byte blocks.

Syntax

du [*options*] *names*

Options and Variables

-s	Causes only a total for each of the specified names. Normally, a number for every subdirectory is displayed.
-a	Causes each file encountered to be displayed with its size.
-f	Traverses only the directories in the currently mounted file systems; other file systems are ignored.
-u	Causes files with more than one link to be ignored.
-r	Causes du to produce a message about this fact (it is usually silent) if a directory cannot be read.
names	The list of directories or files for which you want the space requirements calculated. If left blank, the current directory is used.

Rules

Files with more than one link are only counted once. However, du has a maximum number of links it can table, so when this maximum is exceeded, the sizes used by these files are included in the total. The native block size for SCO UNIX, for example, is 1,024 bytes, whereas the du command block size is 512 bytes. Thus, files having fewer than 512 bytes are still regarded as 2 blocks.

Examples

```
du -s /usr/bin /bin
```

The preceding example reports the total space, in 512-byte blocks, used by the directories /usr/bin and /bin.

```
du
```

The preceding example reports the space usage of the current directory and gives a number for each subdirectory encountered.

See Also

```
df
```

echo

Purpose

Takes the arguments pasted to it and writes them to standard output. The echo command is useful in shell scripts to prompt users for input or inform them of the status of a process.

Syntax

```
echo -n string
```

Options and Variables

-n   Normally, echo follows all output with a newline; this option suppresses that.

string   The string of characters you want to output. The following special characters are recognized to produce special output sequences:

Sequence	Meaning
\b	Backspace
\c	Don't print a newline at the end
\f	Form feed
\n	A newline

\r	A carriage return
\t	A tab
\v	A vertical tab
\\	The backslash itself
\0n	n is a 1-, 2-, or 3 -digit octal number, representing a character.

Rules

Arguments are best surrounded by quotation marks (" "). You can make echo print the value of a shell environment by placing a dollar sign ($) in front of the variable within the string.

Examples

```
echo Hello
```

The preceding example prints Hello on the standard output.

```
echo "enter Y or N \c"
```

The preceding example prompts the user for a Y or N response without echoing a newline.

```
echo
```

The preceding example produces a newline.

```
echo 'Can you hear this \07\07\07?'
```

The preceding example demonstrates the use of octal digits. In this example, the shell script is used to sound the terminal bell three times.

The echo command is built into the Bourne shell. It behaves differently in any other shell, based on that shell's options for echo. Use /bin/echo in the C shell to avoid getting its built-in echo.

See Also

```
cat
```

```
sh
```

ed

Purpose

Edits lines; useful on systems or terminals that do not support full-screen editors, such as vi.

Syntax

```
ed - -p prompt filename
```

Options and Variables

-	Suppresses the messages produced by the e, r, w, q, and ! commands.
-p *prompt*	Enables you to specify your own prompt string.
filename	The name of the file you wish to edit. You can only edit one file at a time.

Rules

The ed command reads the specified file into its buffer. All changes and additions are made to the data in the buffer, not to the original file. You must write out a new copy of the file to save your changes. The ed command is driven by commands (arguments) entered while in command mode. You cannot enter text in command mode—you must switch to text-input mode. When in command mode, editing is performed on a line-by-line basis.

Because ed is rather complex and powerful, see the user's guide and reference provided with your system or refer to a book dedicated to the usage of ed.

Example

```
ed letter-to-mom
```

This example starts up the editor ed to edit a letter to Mom.

See Also

```
vi
```

enable

Purpose

Enables terminals to be logged on to, and print jobs to be applied to, the printer.

Syntax

```
enable terminals

enable printers
```

Options and Variables

terminals   The list of terminals you wish to enable.

printers   The list of printers to enable.

Examples

```
enable tty12
```

The preceding example enabled the twelfth console terminal.

```
enable mailroom
```

The preceding example enabled the printer called mailroom.

See Also

```
cancel

disable

lp

lpstat
```

env

Purpose

Modifies the environment for the execution of a command without affecting the current environment. It can also be used to display the current environment. The environment is a set of variables that are accessible by programs (PATH, for example).

Syntax

```
env - name=value command
```

Options and Variables

-	Restricts the environment to only be those values to follow in the name=value list. Normally, env adds the list to the environment.
name=value	A list of assignments to pass the command to be executed. It may be repeated one or more times to specify multiple passings.
command	The name of command and its arguments to be run with the specified environment.

Examples

env

The preceding example prints the current environment in a name=value format, one per line.

env HOME=/usr/frank sh

The preceding example runs a new shell with the home account set up as /usr/frank.

file

Purpose

Determines the type of file. It can recognize whether the file is 386-executable, 286-executable, commands text, ASCII text, or c-source. Many of the UNIX commands are only shell scripts; file can report which ones are scripts.

Syntax

```
file [options] [filelist]
```

Options and Variables

filelist	An optional space-separated list of files.
-f	Checks the files within filelist.

Messages

> `filename: cannot open`

The preceding message shows that you asked file to "type" a file that does not exist; `filename` is replaced by the file you requested.

> `filename: cannot open for reading`

The preceding message shows that the file you requested exists, but you do not have read permission; `filename` is replaced by the file you requested.

Example

> **`file /xenix`**

This example examines the file /xenix and reports its file type.

See Also

The internal `type` command of `sh`.

find

Purpose

Traverses the specified directories, generating a list of files that match the criteria specified. Files can be matched by name, size, creation time, modification time, and so forth. You can even execute a command on the matched files each time a file is found.

Syntax

> `find dirlist match-spec action`

Options and Variables

`-name file`	Causes find to match the specified file, `file`. If enclosed in quotation marks (" "), file can contain wild cards (* and ?).
`-perm mode`	Matches all files whose mode (see chmod) matches the numeric value of mode. All modes must be matched—not just read, write, and execute. If preceded by a negative (-), mode takes on the meaning of everything without this mode.

`-type x`	Matches all files whose type of file is *x*, in which *x* is the following:

c	Character device
b	Block special
d	Directory
p	Named pipe
f	Regular file (not the preceding types)

`-links n`	Matches all files with n number of links.
`-size n`	Matches all files of size n blocks (512-byte blocks). n, if preceded by a +, matches all files larger than n blocks. a - matches those smaller than n blocks.
`-user user-id`	Matches all files whose user ID is user-id. May be the numeric value or the log-name of the user.
`-atime days`	Matches all files last accessed days ago.
`-mtime days`	Matches all files last modified days ago.
`-newer file`	Matches all files that have been modified more currently than the last file.
`-exec cmd`	Executes cmd for each file matched. The notation {} is used to signify where the file name should appear in the command executed. The command must be terminated by an escaped semicolon (\;).
`-ok cmd`	Prompts user for confirmation before the command is executed.
`-print`	Prints the names of the files found.
`dirlist`	A space-separated list of the directories you want to search for a file or set of files.
`match-spec`	The matching specification for the files you want to find.

Rules

The match-specs can be grouped together and combined to limit the criteria. Multiple specs are assumed to be "AND"s, meaning that both criteria must be met. To offer more control over selection, the following list describes other options:

( )	Parentheses can be used to group selections together. Because the parentheses are special to the shell, they must be escaped (\\()).

-o   The "OR" operator that overrides the default "AND" assumption.

!   The "NOT" operator that negates the expression that follows it.

The n and days arguments can be preceded by a plus (+) or a negative (-) to denote either more than or less than, respectively.

Messages

```
find: bad option -badoption
```

In the preceding message, you gave find a match-spec that is not valid; badoption is replaced with what you specified.

```
find: incomplete statement
```

In the preceding message, you didn't give find enough arguments for it to understand what you wanted.

Examples

```
find . -name letter-to-mom -print
```

The preceding example searches the current directory and its subdirectories for a file called letter-to-mom. When it finds the file, the full path name is shown on the screen.

```
find . -name "letter*" -print
```

The preceding example looks for all files starting with the character letter.

```
find . -name "letter*" -exec ls -l {} \;
```

In the preceding example, you search for the files starting with letter and execute a long list of them. Notice the placement of the brackets {} and the escaped semicolon \;.

```
find . ! \( -name "letter*" -o -name "*mom" \) -print
```

The preceding example is quite a bit more complicated—it looks for a list of files that do not start with letter or end with mom.

finger

Purpose

Displays information about users on the system.

Syntax

```
finger [options] users
```

Options and Variables

-b	Displays a brief output.
-f	Suppresses header lines.
-i	Displays a quick list with idle times.
-l	Forces the long (extended) output.
-p	Does not print the .plan file.
-q	Displays a quick list of users.
-s	Displays a short format.
-w	Displays a narrow format of specified users.
users	An optional list of user names giving extended information about the user is displayed.

Rules

The finger command reads the information in the comment field of the /etc/passwd file. The comment field is divided up into three subfields, each separated by a comma. The second field requires two commas. For example, if the comment field contains Frank Burns, Swamp, Mash, and 555-2939, Frank Burns is displayed under "In real life," Swamp, Mash are displayed under "office," and 555-2939 is displayed under "home phone."

The extended information about users includes the comment field described above and two files found in their home accounts (.plan and .project). The contents of these files are displayed on the screen.

Idle time is the elapsed time since something was displayed on the screen or since the user has typed something. This is not necessarily true idle time, however; it is possible for a program to be doing useful work without requiring the user's intervention.

An asterisk (*) before the terminal name indicates that the user is not allowing others to write to his terminal.

Examples

```
finger
```

The preceding example lists all users on the system.

```
finger frank susie
```

The preceding example lists extended information about frank and susie.

See Also

w

who

grep/egrep/fgrep

Purpose

The grep command stands for Global Regular Express Printer; the egrep command stands for Extended Global Regular Express Printer; the fgrep command stands for Fast Global Regular Express Printer.

These commands are the text search tools of UNIX. They look for patterns found in files and report to you when these patterns are found. The name of the command comes from the use of regular expressions in the ed family of editors.

Syntax

    grep [options] reg-expres filelist

or

    egrep [options] reg-expres filelist

or

    fgrep [options] string filelist

Options and Variables

-v	Lists the lines that do not match string or reg-expres.
-c	Displays only the count; counts the matching lines.
-l	Displays only the names of the files containing a match.
-h	Suppresses the name of the file the match was found in from being displayed (grep and egrep only).
-n	Displays each matching line with its relative line number.
-y	Eliminates case-sensitive matching. Does not work with egrep.
-e reg-expres	Denotes that the phrase following the -e is a regular expression. Useful when the regular expression or string starts with a dash (-). (Works with grep and egrep only.)

-f *file*	The file file contains the strings or expression to search for. (Works with egrep and fgrep only.)
filelist	An optional space-separated list of files to search for the given string or reg-expres. If left blank, the standard input is searched.
reg-expres	The regular expression to search for. Regular expressions are in the form used by ed (see the man page for the definition of regular expressions).
string	The string you want to find in the files.

Rules

The fgrep command can only search for fixed strings. Multiple strings can be searched for by separating each by a newline or by entering them in the -f file file.

The egrep command can search for combinations of regular expressions. It accepts the following enhancements to regular expressions defined by ed:

+	If this trails a regular expression, it matches one or more of that occurrence.
?	If this trails a regular expression, it matches 0 or 1 occurrences.
¦	Denotes multiple regular expressions.
( )	Groups expressions.

Enclose all phrases and patterns containing special characters (brackets, slashes, pipes) in quotation marks.

Messages

```
grep: illegal option — badoption
```

In the preceding message, you gave grep an option/flag that it does not understand; badoption is replaced by what you specified.

```
grep: can't open file
```

In this message, you tried to search a file that does not exist or for which you do not have read permission; file is replaced by the file you specified.

Examples

```
grep hello letter-to-mom
```

The preceding example searches for the word hello in the file letter-to-mom.

```
fgrep hello letter-to-mom
```

The preceding example does the same thing.

```
grep "[hH]ello" letter-to-mom
```

The preceding example searches for the word hello or Hello.

```
fgrep "hello
Hello letter-to-mom
```

The preceding example does the same thing.

```
egrep "([Ss] ome¦[Aa]ny)one" letter-to-mom
```

The preceding example looks for all the words someone, Someone, anyone, or Anyone in the file.

```
vi 'fgrep -l hello *'
```

The preceding example generates a list of file names in the current directory that have the word hello in them and passes this list to the editor vi.

See Also

ed

sh

head

Purpose

Prints out the first number of specified lines of a file.

Syntax

```
head -lines filelist
```

Options and Variables

-lines	Sets the number of lines from the beginning of the file to print. The default is 10.
filelist	A space-separated list of file names you want printed. If left blank, the standard input is read.

Example

```
head letter-to-mom
```

The preceding example prints the first ten lines from the file letter-to-mom.

See Also

```
cat

more

pg

pr

tail
```

id

Purpose

Displays your identification to the system. It reports your user name, user ID number, group name, and group ID number. If you change user IDs frequently with the sw command, id is especially helpful because it informs you of what you are currently using.

Syntax

```
id
```

Example

```
id
```

Shows the id information.

join

Purpose

Extracts common lines from two sorted files. Only one line of output is produced for each pair of lines in the two files that match, based on the specified keys.

Syntax

```
join [options] file1 file2
```

Options and Variables

-a*n*	Places the lines that do not match from file1 or file2 on the output; the n file can be 1 or 2.
-j*n m*	Joins the two files on the mth field of file n. If n is not specified, the mth field of each file is used.
-t *char*	Causes char to be used as the field separator. All instances of char are significant. Multiple instances of char and the default are treated as one. To use the tab as the field separator, enclose it in apostrophes. By default, the field separators are tabs, newlines, and spaces.
-e *string*	Replaces an empty output field with string.
file1	The first file used in the join; can be a dash (-) that tells join to read from the standard input (thus, join can be a filter in a pipeline).
file2	The second file used in the join.

Rules

Each file must be sorted by its join field, which, by default, is the first field.

Example

join to-do-list old-do-list

This example reports those lines that the two lists have in common.

See Also

```
comm

sort

uniq
```

kill

Purpose

Sends the specified signal to the specified process. Normally, this command is issued to stop execution of the process.

Syntax

```
kill -signal pid
```

Options and Variables

`-signal`	An optional signal that can be sent. The default is 15, which stands for SIGTERM (Software Termination Signal). Two other popular signals are 1, which is the equivalent of hanging up the phone as if on a modem; and 9, which is referred to as a sure kill because the process cannot trap this signal.
`pid`	The process ID of the process you want to send the specified signal-pids are numbers used by the system to keep track of the process. The ps command can be used to report these.

Rules

The process to be killed must belong to you, unless you have superuser permissions. The list of signals used by the kill command is located in /usr/include/sys/signal.h.

Message

```
kill: permission denied
```

You tried to kill a process that you do not own, or you are not the superuser.

Examples

```
kill 29
```

The preceding example sends signal 15 to process 29.

```
kill -1 29
```

The preceding example sends signal 1 to process 29.

```
kill -9 29
```

The preceding example sends signal 9 to process 29 (it should work if no others do).

Although signal -9 is the sure kill, you should try -15 and -1 first. These signals can be caught by the applications, which can, upon receipt of these signals, properly clean up after themselves. Because -9 cannot be caught, you may have to do some housecleaning after the process terminates.

Sometimes even signal -9 does not kill the process. This happens when the process is using a kernel service and cannot receive signals. Periodically, processes get locked up in this mode. The only way to resolve this is to do a system shutdown.

Do not kill the following processes: swapper, init, logger, update, cron, or lpsched.

See Also

```
ps
sh
```

last

Purpose

Reads from the /etc/wtmp file and reports the history of logins and logouts from the system. This command can be used to report who has logged in or what terminals have been used.

Syntax

```
last -n limit -t tty user
```

Options and Variables

-h	No header.
-Wwtmpfile	Uses wtmpfile instead of wtmp.
-n limit	Limits the output to limit lines.
-t tty	Reports the login activity on the terminal device tty.
user	Reports the login activity of the user.

Rules

The last command reads the /etc/wtmp file, which grows until cleared. On many systems, this file is cleared daily. On these systems, last can only report the information within the last 24-hour period.

Examples

```
last frank
```

The preceding example reports the login activity of the user frank.

```
last
```

The preceding example reports all information; it is not restricted to a user or terminal.

See Also

```
finger

ps

w

who
```

line

Purpose

Reads a line (a string of text up to a newline character) from the standard input and writes it to the standard output. This command is useful within a shell script program to read a user's input or to read a file and examine its contents.

Syntax

```
line
```

Example

```
while INPUT='line'
do
echo $INPUT
done
```

The preceding example does not do anything interesting, but it demonstrates the usefulness of the line command.

See Also

echo

sh

ln

Purpose

Creates a link between two files, enabling you to have more than one name to access a file. A directory entry is simply a name to call the file and an inode number. The inode number is an index into the file system's table, in which the real information of where the file is found on the disk, including the owner, the mode, and so on, is located. Therefore, it is easy to have more than one name to inode reference in the same directory or multiple directories.

A link is better than a copy because when using a link, only one copy exists on the disk with two names (no additional storage space is required). The associated drawback is that modifications made to the one are realized on all the links. Any file can have multiple links.

The ln command acts as a link to the cp and mv commands and behaves in a very similar manner. All rules for these two commands apply here as well, except that invoking the ln command just makes a link.

Syntax

ln *source-file dest-file*

ln *source-list dest-directory*

Options and Variables

source-file	The file to copy.
dest-file	The destination name.
source-list	A space-separated list of files to copy.
dest-directory	The destination directory.

Example

```
ln letter-to-mom my-letter
```

This example enables you to edit either the file letter-to-mom or the file my-letter and to modify both of them at the same time.

The ln verylong.name v causes verylong.name and v to be names for the same file. The example ln/usr/jim/data/chart jims.chart creates a new name, jims.chart, in your current directory, pointing to its other location.

See Also

```
cp

ls

mv
```

logname

Purpose

Reads the /etc/utmp file to report the name you used to log in to the system.

Syntax

```
logname
```

Example

```
logname
```

This command reports the name you use to log in to the system.

If you are using the Bourne shell, you can place the following in your profile file:

```
PS1="'logname'>";export PSI
```

This causes your prompt string, which is normally the dollar sign ($), to be your user name, followed by the greater than sign (>), that is, $frank> instead of just $.

lp

Purpose

Submits a print request, or changes the options of a previously entered request. Print requests are spooled, enabling you to move on to other work.

Syntax

```
lp [options] filelist

lp -i id [options]
```

Options and Variables

-c	Makes a copy of the original file. Without this option set, a link is established between the original file and the working area of the lp spooler. Changes to the original file do not affect current printing.
-ddest	Specifies the destination of the print request; dest can be an individual printer or a class of printers (a group of printers accessed under one name). See the lpstst -v command to obtain a list of printers to use as dest.
-f formname	Causes the spooler to print the request only.
-d any	When the specified formname is mounted on the printer. With the -d any option set, the request goes to any printer with formname mounted.
-H spec_H	Denotes special handling of the request. Valid values for spec H are: hold, resume, and immediate.
-m	Notifies user by mail when printing is complete.
-n number	Prints number of copies of the request.
-o option	Dependent on the printer-dependent or class-dependent interface script chosen by your system administrator when the printer was defined.
-q priority	Assigns the request priority of priority. The range of priority is 0 to 39, with 0 being the highest priority.
-s	Tells lp to be silent. Normally lp responds with the print request ID.

| -t *title* | Prints title on the banner page. |
| -w | Writes a message to the user's terminal when the request is printed. |

Rules

If the environment variable LPDEST is set and no -ddest is set, the request goes to the dest defined by LPDEST; otherwise, the request goes to the system default printer. If you use the same printer regularly, set up LPDEST with that printer's name.

Messages

```
request ID is mailroom-100 (2 files)
```

The preceding request sends two files to the mailroom printer.

```
lp: destination "mailrom" non-existent
```

The preceding request to print to a printer called "mailrom" was not granted because the system does not know any printers named "mailrom."

```
lp: can't access file "monday_repots"
lp: request not accepted
```

The preceding message was an attempt to print a file named "monday_repots." No file existed by that name (in this case, it looks like a typo for monday reports).

Examples

```
lp myfile
```

The preceding example prints the file myfile to the default printer.

```
lp -dmailroom myfile
```

The preceding example prints the file myfile to the printer named mailroom.

```
lp myfile my_other_file
```

The preceding example prints the two files myfile and my_other_file.

```
date ¦ lp
```

The preceding example sends the date to the default printer. It demonstrates the way lp can be used at the end of a pipeline to facilitate a hard copy of the work done by the pipeline.

Use the -s option when defining printers for applications. This relieves the user from being bombarded with request IDs on his screen to confuse him.

See Also

```
cancel

disable

enable

lpstat

mail

write
```

lpstat

Purpose

Shows the status of the lp spooler system and print requests.

Syntax

```
lpstat [options]
```

Options and Variables

-a *list*	Shows the acceptance status of the printers in list.
-c *list*	Shows the class names of the printers in list and their members.
-d	Shows the lp spooler's system default destination printer.
-f *list*	Verifies that the forms listed in list are defined to the lp spooler.
-o *list* -l	Shows the status of the print request queued for the printers in list. The -l flag gives more detail on the request.
-p *list*	Shows the status of the printers in list—usually used to make sure the printer is enabled and why.
-r	Shows whether the scheduler is running or not. If the scheduler is not running, no print jobs can be scheduled to print.
-s	Shows a status summary of the spooler. Lists whether the scheduler is running, the default printer and printer names, and the devices associated with them.
-t	Shows all status information.

| -u *list* | Shows the status of the printer request. Similar to -o, but shows a list of users instead of printers. |
| -v *list* | Shows a list of printers and the devices associated with them. |

Rules

Leaving list blank causes the flag to respond with all the entries that apply to that flag.

Message

```
mailroom-100    frank    245     Sep 15 20:13 on mailroom
```

This message is a sample of the output generated by lpstat with no options, issued by the user frank after making a print request. The first field is the request ID, the second is Frank's user name, the third is the size of the request in bytes, and the fourth is the date and time the request was made. The last field is the status message, reporting that the request is currently on the printer and is being printed.

Examples

```
lpstat
```

The preceding example shows the outstanding print request for the user entering the command.

```
lpstat -u
```

The preceding example shows the outstanding print request for all users. Notice how the list parameter, which causes all users to show, is not supplied.

```
lpstat -t
```

The preceding example shows all status information.

```
lpstat -s
```

The preceding example shows whether the scheduler, the system default printer, and the devices for each printer on the system are running.

When you use the -t option and you have more than four printers, your information may scroll off your screen. Pipe it to lp or a pager, such as more.

See Also

```
cancel
```

```
lp
```

ls

Purpose

Lists the contents of directories in the file system.

Syntax

```
ls [options] filelist
```

Options and Variables

-A	Shows all files, including hidden files. Hidden files start with a period. Does not show the current directory (.) or parent directory (..).
-a	Shows all files, including current directory and parent directory.
-C	Creates columnar output, sorted down the columns.
-x	Creates columnar output, sorted across the columns.
-d	Lists only directory names, not their contents. Typically used with -l to get the status of a directory.
-l	Gives a long listing. A long listing gives the following details about the files: type of file, permissions, link/directory count, owner, group, size in bytes, file name, and when the file was last modified. The file types are as follows:

-	Normal file
d	Directory
b	Block special device (disks)
c	Character special device (terminals)
p	Named pipe
s	Semaphore
m	Shared memory

The permissions are three clusters that each contain three bytes. Each cluster represents the permissions for the owner, group, and other, respectively. The permissions are as follows:

r	Indicates read permission.
w	Indicates write permission.
x	Indicates execute permission (directories use this to control traversal through them).
-t	Sorts by the time last modified. Used with the -l option.
-u	Sorts by the time last accessed. Used with the -t option.
-c	Sorts by the time the inode information last changed. Used with the -t option.
-r	Reverses the sort order.
-i	Shows the inode number of the file in the first column.
-F	Places a / after directory entries and an * after executable programs.
-R	Indicates recursive listing of subdirectory contents.

Message

```
/bin/ls: arg list too long
```

This message asks ls to process an argument list that has more characters than it can handle. The maximum number of characters in an argument list is 5,120.

Examples

```
ls
```

The preceding example lists the files in the current directory in one long column.

```
ls -C
```

The preceding example lists the files in the current directory, broken up into columns.

```
ls -l
```

The preceding example gives a long listing of the files in the current directory.

```
ls -ltr /usr/lib/sco
```

The preceding example gives a long listing, sorted by modification time and in descending order, of the files found in the directory /usr/lib/sco.

Use -d to find the characteristics of a directory. Otherwise, the contents of the directory are shown and not the directory itself.

lc is a link to ls, which assumes the option of -C.

l is a link to ls, which assumes the -1 option.

lx is a link to ls, which assumes the -x option.

See Also

chmod

mail

Purpose

Enables you to communicate with other users, not only on your local machine, but also with connections to the larger computing community. This is the electronic mail facility, an extremely powerful tool. E-mail provides a way to pass messages throughout the office without having to wait for a scheduled mail run. Furthermore, users can catalog incoming mail and use the mail system as a to-do list and filing system to track correspondence.

Syntax

mail [options] [usernames]

Options and Variables

-e	Tests to see if there is any mail in your incoming mailbox. There is no visible output when this option is used.
-f *file*	Opens file to read mail. If file is omitted, the file mbox is used.
-F	Stores outgoing mail in a file name the same as that of the first recipient of the message.
-H	Shows a header summary of the mailbox contents only.
-i	Causes mail to ignore interrupts while constructing mail messages; can be useful while working over noisy dial-up lines.
-n	Does not initialize from the system mailrc file. The mailrc file sets various options to customize the mail environment for each site; a user can also have the mailrc file. This is typically called .mailrc in the user's home account.
-N	Does not print a summary header of the mailboxes' contents.
-s *subject*	Sets the subject line in the mail header to subject.
-u *user*	Reads user's incoming mailbox.

Rules

The -u user option is only possible if the system administrator has set the permissions on the incoming mailboxes to allow this. Your system can use enhancements to basic mail called mailers. Many remote features of mail work only if UUCP is installed on the system.

Message

```
No messages.
```

The preceding message shows that you invoked the mail utility with no options set and that your incoming mailbox is empty.

Examples

```
mail
```

The preceding example invokes the mail utility and enables you to read your mail.

```
mail -u frank
```

The preceding example invokes the mail utility to read the user frank's mailbox.

```
mail frank -s "fishing trip"
```

The preceding example invokes the mail utility to send a message to frank on the subject of a fishing trip.

```
mail frank -s "fishing results" < fishweights
```

The preceding example sends a message to frank on the subject of "fishing results" from a prepared file called fishweights.

```
date ¦ mail frank -s "date"
```

The preceding example shows how mail can be used at the end of a pipeline to mail the results of the pipeline to a user. This example shows the date to mail to frank.

```
mail kim john sally
```

The preceding example invokes the mail utility to start construction of a message to three people: kim, john, and sally.

You must be deliberate when setting up a good structure for cataloging your mail files. Otherwise, you may have mail files throughout the file system. If you want to catalog or save messages, talk to your system administrator about a good approach—he may already have the structure in place for you.

To use this command, read the user's guide and tutorial provided with your system; the power and intricacies of electronic mail are beyond the scope of this reference.

See Also

```
write
```

mesg

Purpose

Controls the accessibility of your terminal to others for messages to appear on your screen; also sets permissions.

Syntax

```
mesg n y
```

Options and Variables

n   Does not enable users to send messages to your terminal.

y   Enables users to send messages to your terminal.

                If no option is specified, shows the status of the mesg command.

Rules

The default state of your terminal enables users to write to your terminal. The superuser always is allowed to write messages that override your permission setting. Write permission has no effect on mail.

Messages

```
is y
```

The preceding message shows that your terminal enables others to write to it.

```
is n
```

The preceding message shows that your terminal does not enable others to write to it.

Examples

```
mesg
```

The preceding example shows whether users can or cannot write to your terminal.

    `mesg n`

The preceding example disallows writing messages to your terminal.

    `mesg y`

The preceding example enables users to write to your terminal.

It is a good idea to set root's .profile file to include the command mesg n. Many terminals have an escape sequence that puts them into an echo command mode. That is, what is supplied by the user writing to root's terminal is, in effect, executed by root. This is a grave security hole.

See Also

    `write`

mkdir

Purpose

Creates new directories in the file system.

Syntax

    `mkdir [(options)] dirname`

Options and Variables

`-m mode`	Sets the directory permissions to mode at the time of creation.
`-p`	Makes all nonexistent child directories.
`dirname`	The name of the new directory.

Message

    `cannot access letters/`

In this command, you tried to create a directory, and a parent in the list did not exist. In this example, the parent is letters; use the -p option.

Examples

    `mkdir letters`

The preceding example creates a directory called letters.

```
mkdir -p letters/personal letters/work
```

The preceding example creates two directories: letters/personal and letters/work. If the directory letters did not exist, the -p option would create it to avoid an error message.

See Also

chmod

rm

rmdir

mknod

Purpose

Makes special files, which consist of devices, named pipes, semaphores, or shared memory.

Syntax

mknod *file_name* [*options*]

Options and Variables

b *major minor*	Makes a block special file with major device number major and minor device number minor.
c *major minor*	Creates a character special file, with major and minor device types, instead of a block special file.
p	Makes a named pipe.
s	Makes a semaphore.
m	Makes a shared date (memory) file.

Rules

Only the superuser can make block and character special files. Because mknod is not normally in the user's path, you must include mknod's path name, as shown in the example that follows.

Message

```
mknod: must be superuser
```

This message shows that you attempted to make a block or character special file and you do not have superuser privileges.

Example

```
mknod my_pipe p
```

This example creates a named pipe called my pipe.

mnt/umnt

Purpose

Enables regular users to mount file systems, similar to those offered to the system administrator through mount. The system administrator can limit access to some or all of these file systems.

The umnt command enables regular users to unmount file systems, similar to those offered the system administrator through umount.

Syntax

```
mnt -tu dirname
```

or

```
umnt dirname
```

Options and Variables

-u   Causes mnt to behave as umnt, and unmounts the file system.

-t   Prints a table of information about the file system.

Rules

The directory you want to mount must be defined by the system administrator in the file /etc/default/filesys, with an entry of mount=yes, or the command fails.

Message

```
Device busy
```

This message shows that an attempt was made to either mount a device that is already in use, or unmount a device that is currently in use (an open file, the current directory, and so on).

Examples

```
mnt /mnt
```

The preceding example mounted a device to the default mount directory /mnt.

```
umnt /mnt
```

The preceding example creates an unmounted device that was mounted to the default mount directory /mnt.

more

Purpose

Views files one screen at a time. Use more to view text that scrolls off the screen. The more command also provides some handy text-search capabilities by using regular expressions.

Syntax

```
more [options] [+linenumber] [+/pattern] filenames
```

Options and Variables

-c	Draws each line from top to bottom by clearing the line and then drawing the next line. Normally, more clears the screen and then draws each line.
-d	Displays the prompt Hit space to continue, and Rubout to abort in place of the default more prompt.
-f	Counts logical lines instead of screen lines; long lines that wrap around the screen are not counted.
-l	Does not treat the ^L (form feed) character in a special manner. Normally treats ^L in the same way as the window filling up—by pausing.

-n	Sets the window size to n lines long. The window size is the number of lines that show on the screen.
-r	Shows carriage returns as ^M.
-s	Condenses multiple blank lines into one.
-v	Shows all control characters as ^C, in which C is the character used to generate the control character. Those above DEL are shown as M-C, in which C is the character without the high-bit set.
-w	Waits at the end of the file for user-supplied control of quit. Normally, more quits at the end the file.
+*linenumber*	Indicates which line to begin with in the file.
+/*pattern*	Searches for the specified pattern or phrase; begins displaying the file at that point.

Rules

For the -c option to work, the terminal must support the clear-to-end-of-line capability.

Messages

```
filename: No such file or directory
```

The preceding message shows that you tried to view a file that does not exist.

```
******** filename: not a text file ********
```

The preceding message shows that you tried to view a file that is not a text file. The more command tries to determine if a file is a text file or not before enabling you to view it. The filename variable is then replaced by the name you specify.

```
*** dirname: directory ***
```

The preceding message shows that you tried to use more to view a directory file. The dirname variable is then replaced by the name you specify.

Examples

```
more letter-to-mom
```

The preceding example looks at a text file called letter-to-mom.

```
ls -l /dev ¦ more
```

The preceding example demonstrates the way more can be used at the end of a pipeline to control the output of the pipeline.

While using the more utility, press h for a list of other possible actions to use.

Set more option defaults with the environment variable MORE. For example, if you always want the -v and -w options set, enter the following line in your .profile:

```
MORE="-v -w"; export MORE
```

If, while viewing a file, you realize you want to change something, enter the v command. This command boots the vi text editor, enabling you to make the changes you want. Exit the editor, and you return to the more utility.

If you want to look at a section of the text that contains a certain set of characters, enter the / command, then type regular expression. This command searches for the regular expression you entered. See the ed command in your reference manual for more information on regular expressions; they are powerful tools.

The more command is a Berkeley command and is usually available only on Berkeley UNIX. If more is not available, use the pg command.

See Also

```
cat

ed

pg

pr

vi
```

mv

Purpose

Moves or renames files or directories.

Syntax

```
mv -f file1 file2

mv -f dir1 dir2

mv -f filelist dir
```

Options and Variables

-f	Overwrites existing files, regardless of permission settings.
file1	The source file name.
file2	The destination file name (new name).
dir1	The source directory name.
dir2	The destination directory name (new name).
filelist	A space-separated list of file names. When this option is used, files retain their names but are moved to the new directory dir.
dir	The destination directory.

Rules

The mv command cannot physically move a directory; it can only rename it.

Messages

```
mv: filename: mode mode
```

The preceding message shows that filename already existed and the mode of the file did not permit it to be overwritten. A response to this prompt with any word starting with a y causes the move to take place. If the -f option is used, the prompt does not show and the move takes place.

```
mv: filename and filename are identical
```

The preceding message shows that you tried move a file to itself.

```
mv: cannot access filename
```

The preceding message shows that you tried to move a file that did not exist.

Examples

```
mv letters letter
```

The previous example changes the file name letters to letter.

It is easy to remove files by mistake. One way to deal with this is to create a directory to move files to, instead of deleting them. Then type a command like the following:

```
mv letter $HOME/trashcan
```

In the previous example, trashcan is a directory in the user's home account. This can be a useful way to remove files because they have a better chance of being recovered if necessary.

The mv command does not prompt for confirmation of the move unless the destination file already exists and the mode of the file prohibits writing. Because mv first removes the destination file, you can lose the file.

Consider the following directory listing from the lc command:

```
customer.dat   inventory.dat

customer.idx   inventory.idx
```

An accidental entry of mv customer*, in which you forget to supply a destination directory, causes the customer.idx file to be wiped out. When a wild card expands to only two files and you forget to give the destination directory, you wipe out the second file in the expansion.

Because mv first removes the destination file before performing the move, any links established with the destination file are lost. If you need to maintain those links, copy the file to the destination name and then remove the original file.

The ln, cp, and mv commands are linked to each other; they determine their actions based on how they are invoked.

See Also

```
chmod

copy

cp

ln

rm
```

newgrp

Purpose

Changes group affiliation of each user.

Syntax

```
newgrp - group
```

Options and Variables

- Logs in the user under this default group ID.

group This is the group ID under which you want to become active. The group must be set up in /etc/group and the user must be in the list, otherwise access is denied.

With no options, newgrp returns you to the group you are in when you log in. The newgrp command terminates your current shell and then executes the shell associated with your new group.

Rules

When using the C shell, you cannot use the logout command; use Ctrl+D.

Messages

```
unknown group
```

The preceding message shows that you asked to change to a group ID that does not exist.

```
Passwd:
```

The preceding message shows that you asked to change to a group ID for which a password exists. You must enter the correct group password or access to the group is denied.

```
Sorry
```

The preceding message shows that access to the group is denied. Either your user name is not in the list of valid users for the group or you entered an incorrect group password.

Example

Suppose that you are a member of several groups, each of which is designed around a specific task. One of those tasks is to edit personnel data. To do this, however, requires special access to the personnel data files. You can issue the following:

```
newgrp personnel
```

This example changes your group ID to personnel.

See Also

```
id
```

```
su
```

news

Purpose

Reads posted news in which news articles are simple text files that have been placed in the /usr/news directory. The directory /usr/news is a publicly accessible directory for posting information to be shared with other users.

Syntax

```
news [options][items]
```

Options and Variables

-a	Shows all news items, no matter how current.
-n	Shows just the names of the articles, not their contents.
-s	Reports whether there are any articles to read.
items	Enables you to specify which articles (news items) you want to read. Use a space to separate each item from the next.

Rules

The news command places a file named .news_time in your home directory. It uses the time and date of this file to compare to the articles in the /usr/news directory to determine whether an article has been read yet.

Message

```
cannot open item
```

The preceding message appears if you have asked to read a specific article, but that article does not exist.

Example

To print current articles only, type the following at the shell prompt:

news

See Also

```
mail
```

```
write
```

nice

Purpose

Lowers the scheduling priority level of a process. By so doing, other processes receive more computing time, enabling them to finish earlier. The name of this utility comes from the fact that you are being "nice" to other users on the system if you use it.

Syntax

```
nice -increment command [argument...]
```

Options and Variables

-increment   The amount to change the scheduling priority. Processes normally are given a scheduling priority of 20. Increments may be any integer in the range 0-39.

command   The command (with its arguments) you want run with the specified nice factor.

Rules

When you use the C shell, this command does not apply—the C shell has its own nice command.

Examples

The nice command is usually applied to a large batch job that is expected to take a long time to complete. In order to not degrade system performance for others, a considerate user lowers the priority of the batch operation by using nice.

Suppose you want to run a large batch job called mass-update. Running the following command lowers the priority from the default value of 20 to 30:

```
nice -10 mass-update
```

Note that the minus before the 10 in the preceding example denotes an argument, not a negative number. End users may only lower a process's priority by entering positive increments; the superuser may enter a negative increment to increase the priority of a process.

If the superuser wants to increase the priority of this mass-update process, he does so by entering the following command:

```
nice -- 20 mass-update
```

The preceding example increases the priority of the process to 10. Note the two minus signs. The first alerts the nice command that an increment follows; the second indicates that the increment is negative.

nl

Purpose

Adds line numbers to a file. This utility is particularly useful when viewing program source code, such as a C program.

Syntax

```
nl [options] file
```

Options and Variables

-b*type*	Specifies the way in which the body of the text is to be numbered. The type variable may be any of the following:

a	All lines
t	Printable text only (default)
n	No lines (no numbering)
p*str*	Only those lines containing the pattern called str

-h*type*	Same as -b for the header. n is the default type.
-f*type*	Same as -b for the footer. n is the default type.
-p	Does not restart numbering at logical page breaks.
-v*init*	init is the number at which to start logical page numbering (default is 1).
-i*incr*	incr is the amount to increment the page numbering (default is 1).
-s*char*	char is the character used to separate the numbering from the text of the file (default is a tab).
-w*width*	width is the number of characters in a line number (default is 6).

Rules

If file is left blank, the standard input is assumed, enabling nl to be used as filter program in a pipeline.

The output of nl is always to the standard output.

The nl command views text as logical pages. Each page consists of a header, a body, and a footer section. Logical pages are indicated by lines that contain only the following to denote the beginning of a section:

Section	Indicated by
header	\:\:\:
body	\:\:
footer	\:

Message

```
INVALID OPTION (-C) - PROCESSING TERMINATED
```

The preceding message appears if you give the nl command with the C option because C is not an option that nl recognizes. The -C flag stands for the option letter you tried to use.

Example

To number all lines in the file called first-draft and send the output to the default printer, type the following:

```
nl first-draft ¦ lp
```

See Also

pr

pack/pcat

Purpose

The pack command compresses (packs) files so their storage requirements are reduced by up to 40 percent. This command is useful when you send files by using a modem; smaller files take less time to transfer.

The pcat command works like cat, but it works on packed files (enabling you to view the files).

Syntax

```
pack - filenames
```

or

```
pcat - filenames
```

Options and Variables

- If specified, more statistical information about the packing of the files is shown.

`filenames` A space-delimited list of the files to be packed.

Rules

The pack command obtains a reduction of 40 percent on text files and of only 15 percent on binary files. (This is a rough estimate; compression rates vary for each file.)

Messages

```
pack: filename: xx.xx% Compression
```

The preceding message appears if you can compress the file filename by xx.xx percent.

```
pack: filename: cannot open
```

The preceding message appears if a file by this name does not exist, or if it exists but you do not have permission to access it.

```
pack: filename: already packed
```

The preceding message appears if the file you try to pack appears to already be packed.

```
pack: filename: cannot pack a directory
```

The preceding message appears if you mistakenly try to pack a directory—you cannot pack directories.

```
pack: filename: file name too long
```

The preceding message appears if filename is more than 12 characters long (without room to append the .z). The maximum length for a file name is 14 characters.

```
pack: filename: has links
```

The preceding message appears if you try to pack a file that has links. You cannot pack a file with links.

```
pack: filename.z: already exists
```

The preceding message appears if you try to pack a file whose name already includes the .z extension. The pack command does not overwrite the file.

```
pack: filename: no savings - file not changed
```

The preceding message appears if running pack on the file does not result in any savings. Nothing is done to the file.

```
pcat: filename: cannot open
```

The preceding message appears when you issue the pcat command and filename does not exist, or if filename exists but you do not have permission to access it.

```
pcat: filename.z: not in packed format
```

The preceding message appears if a file with the .z extension exists, but the file is not in a packed format.

Examples

Suppose you have a group of files in a directory called old-letters that you do not access very often. If you pack the files, you save storage space and are still able to access the files when needed. To pack all the files in the directory old-letters, type the following:

pack old-letters/*

After running this command, all files in the directory old-letters are compressed. The original file names now have a .z extension, indicating that they have been compressed. To look at the packed file letter-to-mom.z one screen at a time, type the following:

pcat old-letters/letter-to-mom.z ¦ pg

See Also

cat

unpack

passwd

Purpose

Enables an end user to change his password. Although system administrators can use this command to administer user accounts, using the system administrator's shell (sysadmsh) to administer user accounts is strongly recommended.

Two of the password-management features are as follows:

locks An account may have a lock on it. Locks can be applied automatically if more than a system-defined number of tries are made to log in under a specific user name.

expiration A password can expire after a certain amount of time has passed (sometimes referred to as password aging).

Syntax

```
passwd
```

Rules

You can change only your own password. To change someone else's password, you must be an administrator. Passwords should be easy to remember but hard to guess.

Messages

```
Permission denied
```

The preceding message appears when you attempt to change the password for a user who does not exist, or if you are not a system administrator but attempt to change a password other than your own.

```
Sorry
```

When you try to enter a new password, the passwd command prompts you for your old one. The preceding message appears if you enter your old password incorrectly. You need to invoke passwd again to change your password.

Example

If you want to change your password, type the following:

passwd

This command places you into the password-change program.

paste

Purpose

Produces columnar output from one or more files, with each file contributing a column of the output. The paste command often is used with cut to reorder columns in a file.

Syntax

```
paste -s -ddelim filelist
```

Options and Variables

-s   Causes paste to behave differently. Joins columns serially. This option causes paste to traverse each file separately, using lines in the file for each column. The first line is the first column, the second line is the second column, and so on.

-d*delim* Specifies which character will be used to delimit each column (tab is the default). The -ddelim argument can use the following characters to separate columns: \n (newline), \\ (backslash), c (extended), \t (tab), and \0 (empty). Any special characters normally recognized by the shell must be enclosed in quotation marks.

filelist A list of files to paste together. If filelist consists simply of a dash (-), paste reads from standard input rather than a file.

Rules

The output of paste is always standard output.

Output lines are restricted to 511 characters. Use no more than 12 input files at one time, unless you use the -s option.

Messages

```
line too long
```

The preceding message appears if the output of using paste with the files supplied is a line that has more than 511 characters.

```
too many files
```

The preceding message appears if you asked to paste together more than 12 files. You need to use two or more passes to do the job.

Examples

Suppose you have information in two files that you want to combine and display as a single report. The first file, stock_nums, contains stock numbers, one per line. The second file, stock_desc, contains descriptions of each item, again one per line.

```
Contents of file stock_nums:
32154
19856
```

```
67833
78906

Contents of file stock_desc:
Envelopes
Paper
Pencils
Staples
```

To combine these two files into one file with two columns of information, type the following command:

paste stock_nums stock_desc > report

To view the contents of the file report, type the following command:

cat report
```
Envelopes       32154
Paper           19856
Pencils               67833
Staples               78906
```

Suppose you have a file named phonenums, which has a person's name and 10-digit phone number on each line. The file looks like the following:

```
phonenums
Bill Ding          313-275-1000
Rocky Heads        303-555-2000
Bertha Baby        201-664-3000
Ray Don Gazz       214-323-4000
```

To display this file with two names and numbers on each line, type the following:

paste -s -d"\t\n" phonenums

The preceding command produces the following output:

```
Bill Ding      313-275-1000    Rocky Heads    303-555-2000
Bertha Baby    201-664-3000    Ray Don Gazz   214-323-4000
```

See Also

```
cut

gre

join

pr

tee
```

pg

Purpose

Enables you to view text files; unlike more, pg enables you to go backward in the file.

Syntax

```
pg [options] filelist
```

Options and Variables

-	Specifies that text should be read from standard input.
-number	Sets window size to number. That is, number lines are shown at one time (default is 1 less than the li parameter in /etc/termcap, or 23 lines for a 24-line screen).
-p *message*	Uses message as the prompt at the end of each screen of information. An optional %d may be used in message to show the current page number. Enclose message in quotation marks (" ") to ensure that the shell does no wild card expansion. (The default prompt is :.)
-e	Does not pause at the end of each file.
-f	Does not split lines at the end of the line, but wraps them to another line.
-n	Causes pg to recognize the end of the command as soon as a letter is pressed.
-s	All messages and prompts use standout mode (usually reverse video).
+*number*	Starts showing text only after number lines have been encountered.
+/*pattern*/	Starts showing text when pattern is found; pattern uses the rules of regular expressions.
filelist	A list of space-delimited file names. If filelist is not supplied, pg reads from the standard input.

Rules

If the terminal type defined by the environment variable TERM cannot be found in /etc/termcap, the terminal type of dumb is used.

Messages

> pg: dirname is a directory

The preceding message appears if you invoke pg to read a file that was a directory. dirname represents the name with which you invoked the pg command.

> pg: No such file or directory

The preceding message appears if you try to view a file that does not exist, or if you do not have permission to read the file.

Examples

Suppose you have created a file called letter-to-mom that contains a letter to your mother, and you want to browse it without editing it. Enter the following command:

pg letter-to-mom

The preceding example displays the file letter-to-mom one screen at a time.

Suppose you have a directory that contains many files. When you use the ls command by itself to display the contents of the directory, the file names can scroll quickly off the screen. Pipe the output of the ls command to pg, which displays the file names one screen at a time. As an example, look at the contents of the /dev directory, one screen at a time, by entering the following command:

ls -l /dev ¦ pg

The preceding example demonstrates how to use pg at the end of a pipeline to control the output of the pipeline.

While using the pg utility, press h (help) at the prompt to view a list of commands available within pg.

Pressing / while using pg places you in forward search mode; pg searches forward to the bottom of the file for the regular expression you specify. Similarly, pressing either ^ or ? places you in reverse search mode; pg searches backward to the top of the file for the regular expression you specify. Regular expressions are as described for pattern.

Commands preceded by a negative number cause pg to do the option backward the specified number of times. For example, typing the following at the pg prompt causes pg to display the previous page:

-1

See Also

cat

ed

grep

more

pr

Purpose

Enables you to format a file while printing it to the standard output. Some of the functionality of paste and nl is built into pr also.

Syntax

pr [options] *filelist*

Options and Variables

+page	Begins printing with page page.
-col	Specifies col columns of output. This option assumes the options -e and -i.
-a	Prints multicolumn output across the page.
-m	Merges the files, printing each file in a column, and overrides the -col option.
-d	Double-spaces the output.
-eccol	When reading the input, tabs are replaced with character c and expanded to positions (col + 1), ((2 * col) + 1), ((3 * col) + 1), etc. Note that c can be any nondigit character and col defaults to every 8 positions.
-iccol	Works on the output of pr (as -e works on the input), replacing white space with the character c. (White space is spaces, tabs, and so on.)
-ncwidth	Selects line numbering. c is the character to place between the line number and the normal output (the default is a tab). width is the number of character positions the number will occupy + 1. (The default is 5).

`-wlength`	Sets the width of the page to length characters. For columnar output, the default is 72; no limit is assumed otherwise.
`-ooffset`	Offsets each line of output from the left margin by offset character positions. (The default is 0.)
`-llines`	Sets the length of the page to *lines* number of lines. (The default is 66.)
`-h string`	Uses string as the header rather than the file name.
`-p`	Causes pr to page the output, pausing at the end of each page. (Waits for the user to press Enter only if the output is associated with a terminal.)
`-f`	Uses a form feed character between pages. Normally, pr fills the remaining lines with newline characters to cause a page break.
`-t`	Does not print the header or the footer. Normally, pr prints a five-line header and footer.
`-schar`	Separates multicolumn output with char.
`filelist`	A space-delimited list of files. If left blank, the standard input is read. A dash (-) may be used as a file name to tell pr to read from the standard input. Combining file names and a dash (-) causes pr to read from both the standard input and the listed files.

Messages

```
pr: can't open filename
```

The preceding message appears if pr cannot access filename. Either that file does not exist or you do not have permission to read it.

```
pr: bad option
```

The preceding message appears if you specified an option that pr does not understand.

Examples

When the C compiler finds errors, it references the line number in the C source-code file where the error occurred. Thus, it is helpful to have a printout of the C source file, which includes line numbers. Entering the command formats the file program.c with line numbers and sends the output to the printer:

```
pr -n program.c ¦ lp
```

Suppose you have a 132-column printer on which you want to print the output of the ls command. Enter the following command:

```
ls ¦ pr -8 -i\ 6 -w132 -l51 ¦ lp
```

The preceding example takes the output of the ls command and produces an 8-column report, in which the columns are separated by a space every six character positions, sending it to a printer that probably holds 11-by-8 1/2-inch paper (132 columns-by-51 lines).

See Also

cat

fgrep

grep

lp

more

nl

paste

pg

ps

Purpose

Reports the status of processes currently running on the system. Because processes progress rapidly in their execution path, this report is only a snapshot view of what happened—the results of subsequent invocations of ps may be quite different.

Syntax

```
ps [options]
```

Options and Variables

The command with no options shows you a picture of the currently executing processes on your terminal. The following columns are reported:

PID   The process ID number used by the kernel to keep track of the process.

TTY	The terminal with which the process is associated.
TIME	The accumulated time spent running the process (CPU time, not "wall clock" time).
CMD	The name of the process that is running.
-e	Shows the status of every process.
-d	Shows the status all processes, except group leaders.
-f	Gives a full list. A full list gives you the user name that invoked the process and shows you the original command line used to invoke the process. If ps cannot get the command-line information, it places the name of the process in square brackets []. The following also are shown:

PPID	The process ID of the parent process (the process that invoked this one).
C	Used for scheduling purposes.
STIME	The time at which the process started.

-l	Gives you a long list, which gives you a snapshot of the following:

F	The status flag of the process (for example, 01 = in core, 10 = being swapped).
S	The state of the process (for example, S = sleeping, R = running, Z = terminated, B = waiting).
PRI	The current priority of a process. The lower the number, the higher the priority. Usually, a process with a priority of less than about 24 is in the kernel, and signals cannot be caught. This situation results in an unkillable process.
NI	The nice factor used in scheduling.
ADDR1, ADDR2	The address of the process, in memory or on a disk.
SZ	The size of the user area (not including the size of the text portion).
WCHAN	The kernel event for which the process is waiting.

-t*ttys*	Reports the status of the process associated with the terminals listed in ttys. ttys may be comma-delimited or space-delimited and enclosed in quotation marks. (You do not need the tty portion of the tty name.)

-p*pids*	Reports the status of the processes with PID numbers of pids. The format for pids is the same as for ttys.
-u*users*	Reports the status of the processes invoked by the users in the list users. The format for users is the same as for ttys.
-g*glist*	Reports the status of the processes whose group leaders are in the list glist. The format for glist is the same as for ttys.

Message

```
ps: illegal option
```

The preceding message appears if you give ps an option it does not understand.

Examples

The following example shows you the processes running on your terminal:

```
ps
```

If you are the system administrator, you might be interested in the processes running terminals tty01 and tty02. To view this information, type the following:

ps -t01,02

The system outputs the process information for these two terminals—it looks something like the following:

```
    PID TTY      TIME COMMAND
7525 tty01
```

To see what jobs the user named frank is running, type the following:

ps -ufrank

ps -elf ¦ more

The -t and -u options are useful for system administrators who need to kill processes for users who have gone astray.

See Also

```
kill

more

nice

w
```

who

whodo

pwd

Purpose

Reports your present working directory (the current directory).

Syntax

pwd

Messages

Cannot open ..

or

Read error in ..

Both of the preceding messages indicate a problem with the file system. Contact a system administrator.

Example

pwd

This example shows the directory you last changed to, which is your current working directory.

See Also

cd

rm

Purpose

Removes files, file links, and whole directory structures from the file system.

Syntax

```
rm [options] filelist
```

Options and Variables

-r   Deletes recursively the directories specified in filelist. Directories are not deleted unless this option is used. -r can delete only up to 17 levels of subdirectories.

-i   Specifies interactive mode. Asks for an affirmative (y) response before removing an item.

-f   Specifies forced mode. Normally, rm prompts you if you do not have permission to delete a file. This option forces the deletion; you are not involved.

--   Indicates the end of all options. Useful if you have to delete a file name that is the same as the name of an option. Suppose, for example, that a file named -f is created by accident and you want to delete it.

filelist   A space-delimited list of files you want to delete; may contain directory names as well.

Messages

```
rm: filename nonexistent
```

The preceding message appears if you tried to remove a file that does not exist; filename represents the name of the file.

```
rm: illegal option — ?
```

The preceding message appears if you supplied rm with an option it did not understand. You may be trying to delete a file that starts with - -. Refer to the - - option, earlier in this section.

Examples

```
rm letter-to-mom
```

The preceding example deletes the file named letter-to-mom.

```
rm -r oldletters
```

In the preceding example, oldletters is a directory. The command deletes all the files in this directory substructure.

```
rm -i frank*
```

The preceding example finds all files that start with the letters frank and prompts you to delete the file.

To delete a file, you must have a write permission on the directory in which the file resides.

See Also

copy

cp

ln

mv

rmdir

rmdir

Purpose

Removes directories.

Syntax

```
rmdir [option] dirlist
```

Options and Variables

-p   Causes rmdir to delete any parent directories that also become empty after the directories specified in dirlist have been deleted. A status message lists what was deleted and what was not deleted.

-s   Suppresses the messages when the -p option is active.

dirlist   A space-delimited list of directory names. Directories must be empty to be deleted.

Rules

If the sticky bit is set on a directory, the directory is deleted only if at least one of the following is true:

The parent directory is owned by the user.

The user owns the directory in dirlist.

The user has write permissions to the directory in dirlist.

The user is the superuser (root).

Messages

```
rmdir: dirname non-existent
```

The preceding message appears if the directory you tried to remove does not exist.

```
rmdir: dirname not a directory
```

The preceding message appears if you used rmdir on a file name that is not a directory.

```
rmdir: dirname not empty
```

The preceding message appears if you tried to delete a directory that still contains some files.

Example

```
rmdir letters.1970
```

This example deletes a directory that used to hold some very old letters.

You must have write permission on the parent directory to remove any subdirectories.

See Also

```
rm
```

rsh

Purpose

This restricted version of the shell sh limits the capabilities of users set up with sh. Users can run any command found in their path, but cannot do any of the following:

✔ Change a directory

✔ Redirect output to a file, using > or >>

✔ Set the $PATH or $SHELL environment variables

✔ Invoke a command that contains slashes (/)

These restrictions are enforced after the user's .profile file is executed.

This command should not be confused with the Berkley rsh (remote shell) command. If you purchase TCP/IP from SCO UNIX for example, remote commands are implemented by using the command rmd.

Syntax

```
rsh [options]
```

Options and Variables

The options for rsh are the same as for sh.

Rules

Unless rsh is the user's login shell, no real restrictions apply. Invoking rsh as a shell script to lock the user into the current account does not work; when the user gains access to the shell, a simple entry of the command sh turns off any restriction. When rsh is the user's login shell, however, rsh does not let the user invoke sh.

Example

```
rsh
```

This example invokes the restricted shell. (This is effectively useless as a security measure.)

The rsh command does not provide any real security because rsh launches sh to execute any shell scripts giving that script full rights. Although the launch of sh enables the script to execute without restrictions, it also allows the script to contain the following:

```
SHELL=/bin/sh; export SHELL
sh
```

If a user could access a shell script with these two simple lines, the security would be discounted because that user is no longer running under rsh, but under the full-blown sh.

See Also

```
csh
```

```
sh
```

sdiff

Purpose

Runs diff, comparing the files side-by-side. This command can be extremely useful when you try to compare two versions of a file. The output is more suited to the human eye than that of regular diff.

Syntax

```
sdiff [options] file1 file2
```

Options and Variables

-w*width*	Specifies that the output line is to be width characters. The default is 130.
-1	Identical lines appear only on the left side of the output.
-s	Suppresses identical lines.
-o*filename*	Enables you to merge the two files into a third file specified by filename. The sdiff command prompts with a percent sign (%) after displaying the set of differences. Identical lines are copied automatically to filename. Valid responses to the % prompt include the following:

	l	Appends the left column to filename.
	r	Appends the right column to filename.
	s	Silent mode, doesn't print identical lines.
	v	Turn off silent mode.
	e l	Invokes ed with the left column.
	e r	Invokes ed with the right column.
	e b	Invokes ed with both columns.
	e	Invokes ed with neither column.
	q	Exits sdiff.

Changes made in the editor are transferred to filename.

file1	The file in the left column of the output.
file2	The file in the right column of the output.

Rules

Output is divided into three columns. The left column is file1; the right column, file2; and the middle column is one of the following:

Symbol	Meaning
	A space (no symbol) means that the lines are identical.
<	These lines are in file1 only.
>	These lines are in file2 only.
¦	These lines are different.

Messages

```
sdiff: cannot open: filename
```

The preceding message appears if you supplied sdiff with a file name, that does not exist.

```
sdiff: Illegal argument: arg
```

The preceding message appears if you supplied sdiff with an argument, arg, it does not understand.

Example

```
sdiff letter-to-mom letter.bak
```

This example compares the two files letter-to-mom and letter.bak, to see how they differ.

See Also

```
diff

diff3

ed
```

sh

Purpose

Invokes the UNIX system shell, specifically the Bourne shell. One of many command interpreters available under UNIX, the Bourne shell is the most commonly used. The sh command is also a programming language of sorts; it provides all the control structures found in most high-level languages.

Syntax

```
sh [options] args
```

Options and Variables

args
: What you supply for args varies, according to the options you supplied. Typically, you use the name of a shell script or the name of a shell script and arguments to that script.

Rules

Several files are affected by the sh command: /etc/profile holds the shell variables and is executed before executing commands in your profile. Then $HOME/.profile is read and executed by the shell.

Messages

```
-c: bad option(s)
```

The preceding message appears if you invoked a shell with an option sh did not understand. The c flag is replaced with the bad option.

```
script: script: cannot open
```

The preceding message appears if you asked sh to run a script that does not exist, or if you do not have permission to read the file.

Examples

To invoke a new shell, type the following:

```
sh
```

You may now change directories, set environment variables, and so on. When you return to the original shell by pressing Ctrl+D or typing **exit**, you are returned to the directory from which you launched the new shell; any environment variables you changed are returned to their former values.

```
sh install.prog
```

This example runs their installation script.

```
EDITOR=/usr/bin/emacs; export EDITOR
```

The preceding example sets the environment variable EDITOR to a popular public-domain editor called Micro-Emacs. Applications can access variables such as EDITOR and alter their behavior based on the variables' values.

The next example is a bit trickier. Formatting floppy disks is a common task, but who wants to type the format command repeatedly? This example shows how to take advantage of the programming capabilities of sh by using a while loop.

```
while :
do
format /dev/rfd096ds15
done
```

The commands listed on the lines between do and done are executed as long as the last line between the while and the do returns a zero value. Because the colon (:) always returns a value of zero, this loop executes forever. When you finish formatting all the disks, press the interrupt key (usually the Del key).

The following example introduces the echo and read commands of sh. This example is useful when the software product you just bought has an assortment of floppies that need to be extracted. Who wants to type tar up to 20 times?

```
while :
do
echo "Next floppy? \c"
read yn
tar xvf /dev/rfd096ds15
done
```

The echo command displays the prompt Next Floppy, without moving the cursor to the next line (\c). The read command pauses so that you can enter something and stores the result in the made-up variable yn. Pressing Enter at the prompt causes tar to begin extracting the files. When you have finished, press the interrupt key.

See Also

```
cd

csh

echo

env

rsh

tar
```

shutdown

Purpose

Brings the system safely to a point at which the power may be turned off. You need to tell UNIX that you want to turn off the operating system. The shutdown command enables you to control when shutdown occurs, and it also notifies the users on a regular basis. It performs vital management services and gracefully shuts off the multiuser portion of the system.

Syntax

```
shutdown [options]
```

Options and Variables

`-y`	Without this flag set, shutdown asks throughout each subprocess if you really want to shut down the system. This forces a **yes** response to each question, and you are not prompted with it.
`-gtime`	Specifies the grace period before shutdown; time is expressed as hh:mm, with hh: the number of hours and mm the number of minutes to wait before shutting down.
`-fmesg`	Specifies the message to write to the user's terminal, informing the user that the system will be shutting down. Be sure to enclose mesg in quotation marks (as in -f"shutdown soon").
`-Fmesgfile`	Specifies that the message to send to the users' terminals is in the file mesgfile.
`-i state`	Specifies a new state for the system. The -i option shuts down the system completely. The -:i option enters single-user maintenance mode.
`su`	After the system goes through the shutdown process, it enters single-user mode without completely shutting down the system.

Rules

It is a UNIX convention that the shutdown command should be invoked from the root (/) directory.

Only the superuser can execute the shutdown command. Messages are sent to the users' terminals at intervals, based on the amount of time remaining until the shutdown, as shown in the following:

Time remaining	Message sent every...
More than 1 hour	hour
More than 15 minutes	15 minutes
More than 1 minute	minute

In the preceding scheme, each line is closer to shutdown time.

Messages

```
shutdown: not found
```

The preceding message probably appears because /etc is not in your search path (PATH), which means you probably are not the superuser, and you cannot invoke the command.

```
device busy
```

The preceding message appears if some users ignored the messages about the shutdown and are using one of the mounted file systems. Part of the shutdown process is to unmount all file systems. If a file system is still in use when shutdown occurs, umnt "complains."

Examples

The simplest way to invoke shutdown is to type the following:

shutdown

After asking whether you really want to do this, shutdown asks for the grace period and then asks whether you want to send a message other than the default.

In the following example, you tell shutdown not to prompt for confirmation on the shutdown scheduled to take place in one hour:

shutdown -y -g1: -F/etc/shutdown.msg su

The contents of the file /etc/shutdown.msg are sent to all users logged on the system. After the hour has passed, the system goes through the shutdown process and changes to single-user mode.

See Also

```
mnt/umnt
```

```
wall
```

sleep

Purpose

Suspends execution for an interval of time.

Syntax

```
sleep seconds
```

Options and Variables

seconds   Specifies the number of seconds to sleep (must be an integer).

Rules

The sleep command is not guaranteed to wake up after exactly the number of seconds specified.

Example

The following example gives a list of the file called my-file every 10 seconds:

```
while :
do
l my-file
sleep 10
done
```

Do not issue a sleep command of more than 65,536 seconds. If this time is exceeded, time sets an arbitrary value less than this period of time.

sort

Purpose

Enables you to sort and merge text files. Sorts may be based on character fields or numeric fields, and multiple sort keys may be specified.

Syntax

```
sort [options] files
```

Options and Variables

-c	Checks whether the files are sorted. If they are, no output is generated.
-m	Merges the specified files. The assumption is that the files are already sorted.
-u	Makes sure that only unique lines go to the output. A line's uniqueness is based on the sort keys.
-o*file*	Specifies the output file name; may be the same as one of the input file names. Normally, the output of sort is the standard output.
-y*kmem*	The amount of memory (expressed in kilobytes) to use for the sort area. Normally, sort grows in memory size to meet its needs. Use this option to specify an amount known to be optimal for this sort.
-z*reclen*	The length of the longest output line. Although sort normally determines the longest line while sorting the input files, the -m and -c options may need this option to avoid abnormal termination.
-d	Sorts in "dictionary" order. Only letters, digits, and blanks are used for ordering.
-f	"Folds" lowercase letters to uppercase for sort purposes. Both cases are considered equivalent.
-i	Ignores nonprintable characters in the sort keys.
-M	Treats sort key as if it were a month. "JAN" is less than "FEB," which is less than "MAR," and so on. This option implies the -b option.
-n	Specifies that the key is a numeric key; implies the -b option.
-r	Reverses the sort (descends).
-t*fld-sep*	Specifies that the field separator is the character fld-sep, not tabs or blanks.
-b	Ignores leading blanks when determining the start and end position of the sort keys.
+*keybeg*	Specifies that the sort key starts at field number keybeg. Fields start counting at zero; the fifth field is a 4. The variable keybeg accepts the format M.NO, in which M is the field number and N is the character offset in that field. The absence of .N assumes zero. F may be any of the following options: **b, d, f, i, n,** or **r** (all of which have the meanings described earlier, but apply only to this key).

-*keyend*	Specifies the field number on which the key ends, and follows the same format rules as +keybeg. If no ending field number is specified, the end of the line is assumed.
files	An optional list of files to be sorted or merged. If no files are specified or - is used as the file name, the standard input is read.

Rules

The sort command reorganizes files according to a portion of each line called the sort key. Any portion of a line can be specified as the sort key. If no key is specified, the entire line is used.

When multiple keys are used, the keys specified later on the command line are compared when the earlier ones are equal. All comparisons are governed by the locale of the system, enabling support for international usage.

Because sort distinguishes records by looking for the newline character, the command is not suitable for binary files.

Messages

```
sort: invalid use of command line options
```

The preceding message appears if you specify an option that sort does not understand.

```
sort: can't open filename
```

The preceding message appears if you specify a file name that does not exist.

```
sort: can't create filename
```

The preceding message appears if you specify the -o option with a file name in a directory in which you do not have permission to write, or if the file name exists but you do not have permission to write to it.

Examples

```
ps -e ¦ sort
```

Because the first column of ps is the PID number, the preceding example gives you (in PID order) the processes running on the system.

```
ps -e ¦ sort +3
```

Because the last column of ps is the name of the command, the preceding example lists (by command name) the processes running.

```
ps -e ¦ sort -u +3
```

The preceding example strips out any duplicate process names.

```
ps -e ¦ sort -r +2 -3
```

In the preceding example, the third column is the CPU time the process has had. The sort is reversed by using -r.

Lines longer than 1,024 characters are truncated.

See Also

```
join

ps

uniq
```

spell

Purpose

Checks spelling of a text file. A facility to add and remove words from the dictionary also exists.

Syntax

```
spell [options] +userdict filelist
```

Options and Variables

-v   Shows all words not literally in the dictionary, along with a list of possible correct spellings.

-b   Uses the British spelling.

-l   The spell command supports the troff macros, .so, and .nx, which are used to chain files together to create a complete document. Normally, spell does not follow these chains when a path that begins with /usr/lib is used . The -l causes spell to look at these files as well.

-i   Causes spell to ignore all chaining requests.

-x   Displays (in the form =stem) every plausible word stem for each word checked.

+userdict   Contains a list of words that, although not found in the system dictionary, should be considered correctly spelled. userdict should have one word per line.

> filelist   The list of files to read and check for correct spelling. If no files are specified, spell reads from the standard input.

Example

If you want to impress your mother with your excellent spelling, type the following:

```
spell letter-to-mom
```

This example examines the file letter-to-mom and displays any misspelled words.

split

Purpose

Breaks a text file into smaller pieces. Periodically, files become too large to load into an editor or some other utility. The split command enables you to handle the file in more manageable pieces.

Syntax

```
split -numlines file tagname
```

Options and Variables

> -numlines   Specifies the number of lines to include in each piece. The default is 1,000.
>
> file   The file to be split into smaller pieces. If left blank, or if - is used, standard input is read.
>
> tagname   By default, split builds the output pieces by creating the following files: xaa, then xab, then xac, and so on. If the variable tagname is specified, it replaces the x in the previous list, thus building the list: tagnameaa, tagnameab, tagnameac, and so on.

Rules

There must be enough room in the current file system for two copies of the file.

Message

```
cannot open input
```

The preceding message appears if you gave split the name of a file that does not exist.

Examples

That last letter to Mom was a long one. The following example breaks that letter into 1,000-line pieces, which is small enough to fit into the vi editor.

```
split -1000 letter-to-mom momletter
```

The output files are named momletteraa, momletterab, and so on.

```
cat momletter* >letter-to-mom
```

The preceding example takes all the pieces and puts them back together and into the file letter-to-mom.

See Also

```
cat
vi
```

strings

Purpose

Extracts the printable strings from an object module or binary file. Strings are any sequence of printable characters, ending with a newline or null character.

Syntax

```
strings [options] filelist
```

Options and Variables

-	Normally, strings examines only the initialized data space of an object file. The - option tells strings to examine the whole file.
-o	Shows the byte offset in the file where the string was found.
-number	Normally, the length of a valid string is four consecutive printable characters. This option enables you to control the minimum length of a string.
filelist	A space-separated list of file names to be examined for strings.

Example

```
strings /bin/ls
```

This example shows all the strings in the program ls.

stty

Purpose

Sets the terminal device driver (tty) line controls. The stty command provides many options for controlling the tty driver. You may set the character size, parity, baud rate, input preprocessing of special characters, and output processing of special characters.

Syntax

```
stty [options] [settings]
```

Options and Variables

-a   Shows all current settings of the currently logged-in terminal. Normally, stty gives a reduced version of all the settings. Because stty actually reads from the terminal driver, you can find out what the terminal settings are for another tty by redirecting the input to stty (see the example that follows).

-g   Produces 12 hexadecimal numbers, separated by colons. This output is suitable for input to stty.

settings   The settings may either be the output of a previous -g flag or a series of stty commands.

Rules

The stty command changes the way the system's tty driver behaves, in reference to how your terminal is physically set. There are two ways that terminals communicate: the physical settings on the device and the way the system thinks it should talk to the device. If these are not equal, the communication breaks down. The stty command affects only how the system thinks the device is talking. You use stty to allow the system to talk to tty devices with different communication needs.

Examples

The following example shows all the settings on this tty:

```
stty -a
```

This next example shows all the settings on the second console:

```
stty -a </dev/tty02
```

Occasionally a program crashes, leaving your terminal in a state in which it does not seem to be accepting your input. In this case, enter the following command to return your terminal to a usable state:

```
<^J>stty sane<^J>
```

Do not type the parentheses or press Enter. The <^J> notation simply indicates that you should hold down the Ctrl key while pressing J.

See Also

```
tty
```

SU

Purpose

Substitutes another user ID for yours, enabling you to "become" someone else on the system so that you can access their files; you need to know the correct password to do this.

Syntax

```
su - user [arguments]
```

Options and Variables

-	Logs you in as this user, running through /etc/profile and his .profile file.
user	The user you want to become. If left blank, root is assumed.
arguments	Any arguments specified are passed to the program invoked by the shell. One common use is to specify -c, followed by a command to be executed; this causes the command to run (as if you were that user) and then returns. You become that user only for the time it takes to execute the command.

Rules

The superuser may su to anyone else without needing a password. If you are not the superuser, you are prompted to supply the user's password you want to become. Press Ctrl+D to resume your previous identity.

Messages

```
Unknown id: baduserid
```

The preceding message appears if you asked to become a user that does not exist on your system. (The baduserid variable represents the file name of the user you asked to become.)

```
Sorry
```

The preceding message appears if you did not enter the correct password at the prompt.

Examples

```
su - frank
```

In the preceding example, you become the user frank, going through the same login process you would go through had you logged on as frank in the first place.

In the following example, you become the accounting user and run a program called close-month.

```
su - accounting -c "close-month"
```

sync

Purpose

Flushes system disk buffers. Make sure that the buffers are flushed before you shut down the machine. Otherwise, a correct image of the information is not written to the disk. Because both shutdown and haltsys do a sync, the need to use sync is limited.

Syntax

```
sync
```

Example

The following example causes the system disk buffers to be flushed:

sync

See Also

shutdown

tabs

Purpose

Sets the tab stops on the terminal or workstation.

Syntax

tabs *tabstops* [*options*]

Options and Variables

tabstops   Specifies where the tab stops should be. May be any of the following four constructs:

    -code   A predefined set of common programming languages' conventional tab settings. If you do not use these languages or do not like the settings, this option is not helpful. See your reference guide for specifics.

    -every-n   Specifies that the tab stop should be every-n + 1 characters.

    -list   A comma-separated list of the tab stops. If a number, other than the first one, is preceded by a plus sign (+), the number is considered to be an increment of the first.

    -file   Specifies that the tab stops are found in file file, and conforms to the rules outlined in fspec(F).

-Tterm   Specifies which terminal type to use to obtain the codes used to program the terminal's tab stops. If term is not specified, the environment variable TERM is used.

+mlmrgn   Specifies the left margin; tab stops is expressed relative to lmrgn.

Rules

The terminal must support having its tab stops set from the host.

Messages

```
illegal tabs
```

The preceding message appears if you have used the list form to specify the tab stops, and this list is not in the correct order.

```
illegal increment
```

The preceding message appears if, using the list format, you did not specify the increment value correctly.

```
unknown tab code
```

The preceding message appears if you attempted to specify a predefined tab stop that does not exist.

Examples

The following example sets the tab stops to 5, 9, 13, 17, and so on:

```
tabs -4
```

```
tabs 1,5,9,13,17
```

Another way to accomplish the same thing is to type the following example:

```
tabs 1,+4
```

tail

Purpose

Enables you to view the end of a text file or track the growth of a text file. The default is the last 10 lines.

Syntax

```
tail [options] file
```

Options and Variables

beg-offset   The offset within the file to begin viewing. If beg-offset is preceded by a -, the offset is relative to the end of the file; if a + is used, the offset is relative to the beginning of the file. The following qualifiers may be used to specify beg-offset's unit of measure:

b   The offset is expressed in blocks.

l   The offset is expressed in lines. (This is the default.)

c   The offset is expressed in characters.

If beg-offset is left blank, 10 lines are assumed.

-f   When this option is used, and the input is not standard input, tail monitors the growth of the file. This is an endless loop of output. To end the loop, use the interrupt key.

file   The name of the file for which you want to view the end or whose growth you want to track. If file is left blank, the standard input is used.

Message

```
tail: illegal option — option
```

The preceding message appears if you tried to invoke tail with an option other than -f.

Examples

The following example looks at the last 10 lines of letter-to-mom:

tail letter-to-mom

The following example looks at the last 10 characters of letter-to-mom:

tail -10c letter-to-mom

The following example begins showing letter-to-mom after the first 10 lines have been read.

tail +10 letter-to-mom

Assuming that a file called growing-file is being built by some other process, the next example shows you what has been built so far and what is being generated on an ongoing basis. You pipe the output through the pager more, to keep it from generating too fast to view on-screen.

tail -f growing-file ¦ more

See Also

    more

    pg

tar

Purpose

Saves and restores files to and from an archive medium, typically floppy disks or tape. Creates tape archives, that is, backups of your file system.

Syntax

    tar [*key*] [*argument*] [*drive*] [*options*] *filelist*

Options and Variables

key
: A string of characters containing a function letter and function assignments. Specifies what action to take as to the archive. A key consists of one of the following function letters:

: c
  : Creates a new archive, or overwrites an existing one.

: r
  : Writes the files named in filelist to the end (rear) of the archive.

: t
  : Gives a table of contents of the archive.

: u
  : Updates the archive. If the files named in filelist are not found in the archive or if they have been modified since the last write, adds them to the end of the archive. (May take quite a bit of time.)

: x
  : Extracts the files named in filelist.

argument
: When an option requires an argument, the arguments are delayed until after all the options have been specified. Then the arguments are listed on the command line in the same order as the options.

drive
: A number between 0 and 9999. This number is a key to the file /etc/default/tar, which specifies default options for the device name, blocking factor, device size, and whether the device is a tape.

b *block*
: Specifies the blocking factor, block. May be any integer between 1 and 20. The default is 1. Use only with raw tape or floppy devices.

f name	Specifies the file name name to be used as the archive. May be a regular file or a special character device (such as /dev/rfd096ds15 for a high-density floppy disk). If -is used, standard input is read from or written to, depending on the action specified. (You cannot pipe a filelist to tar as you can with cpio).
l	Tells tar to complain if it cannot resolve all the links to a file. Normally, tar is silent about archiving a set of files when not all the links are specified. Used only with the c, r, and u actions.
m	Tells tar not to restore the modification times. The modification time is the time of extraction.
v	Places tar in verbose mode. That is, the file names are displayed on the terminal while tar processes them. When used with the t option, tar gives you a list similar to the long list of the ls command.
w	Causes tar to wait for you to respond with a y or an n before taking action on the file. (Any response that starts with the letter y means yes; any other response means no.) Not valid with the t action.
F	The next argument is a file that holds a list of files to be manipulated.
k	The next argument is the size in kilobytes of the device. This enables tar to know when it has filled the device and needs to prompt for the next floppy disk or tape.
n	Tells tar that the device is not a tape drive. For floppy devices, this enables tar to seek to the files it wants.
A	Changes all absolute file names to relative file names.
filelist	The list of files to manipulate; may contain wild cards (see warning later in this section). If filelist is a directory, that directory is traversed recursively, matching all files in that directory's substructure.

Rules

When you list the file names, be careful about whether you use absolute or relative path names. Files are extracted from the archive in the same way they were created. Furthermore, if you request that only one file be extracted, you must specify that file name on the command line, exactly as you did when you created the file. For example, suppose that you created an archive by using the following:

```
tar cvf /dev/rfd096ds15 /usr/frank
```

This line created an archive of all the files in the directory hierarchy /usr/frank. To retrieve a file called letters-to-mom, you enter the following:

```
tar xf /dev/rfd096ds15 /usr/frank/letters-to-mom
```

If you specified only letters-to-mom in the filelist, tar does not find the file.

Messages

```
tar: tape write error
```

The preceding message usually means one of two things: either you do not have a floppy disk or a tape in the drive, or the floppy disk or tape is full.

```
tar: tape read error
```

The preceding message usually appears if you do not have a floppy disk or tape in the drive.

```
tar: directory checksum error
```

The preceding message usually means one of two things: either you have specified the wrong media type for the floppy disk or tape drive, or the tape needs to be rewound. Specifying the wrong media type is a common error. Users have been known to place a 360 KB floppy in the drive and then try to access it by using the /dev/rfd096ds15 device.

Examples

The following example creates (when using a high-density floppy drive) an archive of the current directory, showing all the file names it encounters:

```
tar cvf /dev/rfd096ds15 .
```

The following example extracts all files found on the floppy disk, showing you the names of the files it encounters:

```
tar xvf /dev/rfd096ds15
```

The following example demonstrates the syntax used to combine options that require arguments. The example creates an archive of frank's home account, using a blocking factor of 20, and places the archive on the high-density floppy disk:

```
tar cvbf 20 /dev/rfd096ds15 /usr/frank
```

The following example shows how to use - to send output to standard output. It creates an archive of frank's home account, piping the output through wc to get a count of the characters. As a result, you learn how big the archive is.

```
tar cf - /usr/frank ¦ wc -c
```

Special devices are not placed on the archive.

Although you can use wild cards in filelist, the tar command does not do any wild card expansion. The shell does the expansion and passes the result to tar. This can be a problem for novice users who delete files and then want to extract them from the archive. Because the file does not exist on the file system, the shell cannot expand the wild cards to match the nonexistent files. Suppose that you have a series of files, all with names ending in .ltr. You can create the archive of the whole directory by using the following:

```
tar cf /dev/rfd096ds15 .
```

Then, realizing that you somehow had messed up all the files ending with .ltr, you can extract them from the archive with the following command:

```
tar xf /dev/rfd096ds15 *.lst
```

The preceding command would then restore the fouled .lst files. If the files are deleted, however, tar does not find any files to extract.

If files have been deleted, you need to specify each one fully without using wild cards. Alternatively, you can use a prepass, with the t option redirected to a file, as follows:

```
tar tf /dev/rfd096ds15 >list.tmp
```

Then use the following to get back all the files ending in .lst:

```
tar xf /dev/rfd096ds15 'grep ".lst$" list.tmp`
```

See Also

```
cpio

grep

ls

tar

wc
```

tee

Purpose

Splits the output in a pipeline to one or more files. This command enables you to capture what is going to standard output and place that output into a file while still allowing the output to flow through standard output.

Syntax

```
tee [options] filelist
```

Options and Variables

-i   Causes tee to ignore interrupts.

-a   Appends the output to the files in filelist instead of overwriting them.

-u	Causes the output through tee to be unbuffered.
filelist	The space-separated list of files into which you want to capture the output.

Example

The following example places a copy of the filelist generated by ls -l in the file listing, while you view the list through the pager more:

```
ls -l ¦ tee listing ¦ more
```

See Also

ls

more

test

Purpose

Tests a variety of conditions by asking true/false questions. Returns a zero exit status if what it tests was true. The test command is most commonly used in if and while statements. The if and while statements are sh control constructs used when programming in the Bourne shell.

Syntax

test [*expression*]

Options and Variables

expression	The true/false question to be tested. (The command indicates its findings by means of a return code.) The following may be used to build a valid expression:

-r *file*	True if file has read permissions.
-w *file*	True if file has write permissions.
-x *file*	True if file has execute permissions.
-f *file*	True if file is a regular file.
-d *file*	True if file is a directory.
-c *file*	True if file is a block special file.

-u *file*	True if file has the set-user-ID flag set.
-g *file*	True if file has the set-group-ID set.
-k *file*	True if file has the sticky-bit set.
-s *file*	True if file has a file size greater than zero.
-t *fd*	True if the file with file descriptor fd is opened and associated with terminal device. The default fd is 1.
-z *str*	True if the length of the string str is zero.
-n *str*	True if the length of the string str is nonzero.
str1 = *str2*	True if string str1 equals string str2.
str1 != *str2*	True if string str1 does not equal string str2.
str	True if string str is not a null string.
int1 -eq *int2*	True if the integer int1 equals the integer int2. The following may also be used instead of -eq:

-ne	Not equal.
-gt	Greater than.
-ge	Greater than or equal to.
-lt	Less than.
-le	Less than or equal to.
!	Negates the expression.
-a	A logical AND.
o	A logical OR.
( )	Used for grouping.

Rules

All file-oriented tests test false if the file does not exist.

Examples

The following example tests whether the file letter-to-mom exists and is a regular file:

```
if [ -f letter-to-mom ]
then
echo "letter-to-mom exists"
fi
```

The next example tests to see whether both a letter to mom and letter to dad have been written:

```
if [ -f letter-to-mom -a -f letter-to-dad ]
then
echo "both letters written"
fi
```

time

Purpose

Determines how much time a program takes to execute.

Syntax

```
time command
```

Options and Variables

command   The command you want to time.

Rules

The time command reports the following three times:

real   The total elapsed time since you invoked the command (sometimes referred to as wall-clock time, referring to time that elapsed on the clock in your office).

user   The amount of time spent on the CPU (outside of sys time).

sys   The amount of time spent in the kernel. The amount of time spent fulfilling system requests.

Adding user time to sys time gives you the total CPU time. The difference between this and real time is the amount of time the CPU spent on other tasks.

Example

This example reports the amount of time compressing the file letter-to-mom took:

```
time compress letter-to-mom
```

touch

Purpose

Changes the access and modification times of a file or creates a new file with specified times.

Syntax

```
touch [options] MMDDhhmmYY filelist
```

Options and Variables

-a	Specifies the time for changing the access time of the specified files.
-m	Same as -a, but for modified time.
-c	Tells touch not to create a file that does not exist in filelist.
MMDDhhmmYY	The time to which to set the file. The format is as follows:

MM	The month
DD	The day
hh	The hour
mm	The minute
YY	The year

filelist	A space-separated list of the files you want to have the specified time.

Rules

The options -am are the default. You cannot modify a file's creation time. (The term creation time is somewhat misleading. A file's creation time is not really the time at which the file was created; rather, it is when the inode information—file size, mode, owner, and so on—changed.)

You can only update a file by using the touch command if you have write permission on that file.

Message

```
touch: illegal option — badoption
```

The preceding message appears if you tried to specify an option (represented here by badoption) that touch does not understand.

Examples

The following example sets the modification and access times of letter-to-mom to the current date (maybe you want to make it look like you wrote to her resentfully):

touch letter-to-mom

The example that follows sets the modification and access times of letter-to-mom to 01/01/91 at 12:01 p.m.:

touch 0101120191 letter-to-mom

See Also

```
date
```

tr

Purpose

Copies standard input to standard output, substituting or deleting selected characters. The tr command translates or maps characters in a file, and enables you to do some rather robust character-handling with a simple structure.

Syntax

```
tr [options] from-string to-string
```

Options and Variables

-c   Restricts the output to the characters specified in from-string and effectively appends those characters in to-string. Normally, tr substitutes the characters in from-string for the characters in to-string, with the output showing the original contents of the file with the substitution applied.

-d   Deletes the characters specified in from-string.

-s   Strips repeated characters generated in the output by those specified in to-string, leaving only one of the repeating characters in the output.

from-string   The string of characters to map from; the characters you want translated. The following special notations may be used and repeated:

[c1-cn]   Specifies a range of ASCII characters, from c1 to cn.

[c*n]   Specifies that character c repeats n times. The n may be zero or left blank, which assumes a huge number of the character c. This is useful for padding the to-string (see the Rules for this command).

\octal   Specifies the octal value of a character. This is useful for manipulating the nonprintable characters (control characters).

to-string   The string of characters to map into; the character the from-string should translate to. The special notations noted previously may be used here as well.

Rules

The to-string must be the same number of characters as the from-string.

Message

```
bad string
```

The preceding message appears if the number of characters in from-string and to-string are not equal.

Examples

The following example is one way to translate DOS text files into a format more suitable in UNIX. It deletes the carriage returns and the DOS end-of-file marker Ctrl+Z:

```
tr -d "\015\032" <dosfile >unixfile
```

The next example, a significantly more complicated way of accomplishing the task done by the preceding example, demonstrates two features of tr. This example replaces all the carriage returns and end-of-file markers with the UNIX newline character. The -s strips the duplicate newlines, producing only one. To ensure that the lengths of the two strings are equal, to-string uses the "padding" option described earlier.

```
tr -s "\015\032" "[\012*]" <dosfile >unixfile
```

Be sure to enclose from-string and to-string in quotation marks, as shown in the examples, to ensure that the special meaning of any characters recognized by the shell are escaped and passed to tr instead of being expanded by the shell.

Although you can use the range notation with characters that represent digits, such as [0-9], such notation refers strictly to the digits themselves and not to the value they may represent. You cannot use this to replace all tens with nines, for example, because 10 has two digits and 9 has only one.

See Also

ed

sed

true/false

Purpose

The true command returns a zero exit status (which means true in the shell). When you are programming in the shell, the true command is useful for creating continuous loops.

The false command returns a nonzero exit status.

Syntax

true

Example

Formatting floppy disks is one of the rituals of computer use. Instead of typing the format command repeatedly, you can have the computer do the repetition for you, as the following example demonstrates:

```
while true
do
format /dev/rfd096ds15
done
```

When you finish formatting the stack of floppy disks, you can kill the loop by pressing the interrupt key at the format prompt.

In the Bourne shell, the colon (:) character yields the same results as true, does not require executing a program, and is easier to type.

See Also

sh

tty

Purpose

Reports the name of the currently logged-in terminal device or tests whether standard input is a terminal.

Syntax

tty *option*

Options and Variables

-s   Causes tty to test whether the standard input is a terminal device. No output is generated. The result code is set to zero if standard input is a terminal, and the code is set to one otherwise.

Message

not a tty

The preceding message appears when you try to invoke tty without using the -s option, and the standard input is not a terminal.

Examples

The following example simply reports the terminal's device name:

tty

The next example tests whether the standard input is a terminal:

```
if tty -s
then
echo "This is a terminal"
fi
```

umask

Purpose

Sets permission codes automatically on newly created files. Specifies what the default permissions of files you create will be, or reports what the current defaults are.

Syntax

```
umask mask
```

Options and Variables

mask   The mask applied when generating the permissions for the files you may create. If mask is left blank, umask reports the current setting. The mask is composed of three digits, each of which is taken from the following table:

         0   You do not want to restrict any permissions.

         1   You want to restrict execute permissions.

         2   You want to restrict write permissions.

         4   You want to restrict read permissions.

The digits represent the permissions for the owner of the file (you), the group, and the rest of the world, respectively.

Adding any of these digits together restricts the combination of the permissions. Thus, a 7 restricts all permissions.

Rules

The umask command is the opposite of the chmod command, in that it specifies permission to turn off. Note that cp and mu are not affected by umask.

The term mask is derived from the fact that the value specified here is actually masked at the bit level to generate the permissions. Simply think of the mask as the permissions you do not want to give.

Examples

The following example reports the current mask setting:

```
umask
```

The next example gives everyone on the system complete access to every file you create:

```
umask 000
```

The following example gives you complete permissions on the files you create, but everyone else can only read and execute those files:

```
umask 022
```

The last example gives you and the people in your group complete permissions and does not allow anyone else to do anything:

```
umask 007
```

See Also

chmod

uname

Purpose

Reports the name of the computer and operating system and other catalog information.

Syntax

uname [*options*]

Options and Variables

-s	Reports the system name. (This is the default.)
-n	Reports the nodename of the system, identifying the system to a network. (Used in communications.)
-r	Reports the release number of the operating system.
-v	Shows the version number of the operating system.
-m	Reports the hardware name of the machine currently in operation.
-a	Reports all the preceding information.
-X	Like -a, except that -X behaves like XENIX's -a option, giving the description of each piece of information, and printing one piece-per-line with its description.

Rules

Use the -r, -s, and -v options together to display all the system information at once. Some systems also enable the system administrator to use -S to name the computer.

Message

```
uname: illegal option - badoption
```

The preceding message indicates that you invoked uname with an option that the uname command does not recognize.

Examples

The following example reports the system name of the currently logged in machine:

uname

The next example produces a table of all the information:

uname -X

uniq

Purpose

Compares adjacent lines of a file and strips out lines that are identical, producing only one unique line.

Syntax

```
uniq [options] input output
```

Options and Variables

-u   Causes uniq to output only the lines that are not repeated.

-d   Causes uniq to output only the lines that are repeated (one copy only). Lines occurring only once are not in the output.

-c   Produces a report in which the left column is the count of the number of times the line repeats and then the line itself.

-fields   During the comparison for uniqueness, the first fields count of fields is skipped. Fields are separated by tabs or spaces.

+chars	After skipping any specified fields, chars skips number of characters also.
input	The name of the file to read from. If left blank, the standard input is read.
output	The name of the file to create with the results of the uniq command. If left blank, standard output is used. If specified, output must not be the same as input.

Rules

The default operation is to output all lines in the input file, but with only one copy of any repeated lines.

The uniq command assumes that the input file already is sorted.

Examples

The following example shows a list of users currently logged in to the system. Anyone who logged in more than once is shown only once:

```
who ¦ cut -d" " -f1 ¦ uniq
```

The next example is a slight twist on the preceding one. It shows only users who logged in more than once:

```
who ¦ cut -d" " -f1 ¦ uniq -d
```

The following example shows only users who are not logged in more than once:

```
who ¦ cut -d" " -f1 ¦ uniq -u
```

The last example lists users on the system, as well as a count of the number of times they are logged in:

```
who ¦ cut -d" " -f1 ¦ uniq -c
```

See Also

```
comm
```

```
sort
```

unpack

Purpose

Uncompresses a file, restoring the file to its original form.

Syntax

```
unpack filelist
```

Options and Variables

filelist   The space-delimited list of files to unpack. Because all packed files end in .z, you do not need to specify the .z.

You can only unzip a file with the unpack command if you have read permission on that file.

Messages

```
unpack: filename.z: cannot open
```

The preceding message appears if you have asked unpack to unpack a file that does not exist with a .z appended.

```
unpack: filename.z: not it packed format
```

The preceding message appears if a file name with .z appended exists but is not in packed format. The .z at the end of the file is a coincidence; it does not mean that the file is packed.

Example

Having written a long letter to mom and packed it to reduce its storage requirements, you now want to unpack it to modify or print it. The following example gets the job done:

```
unpack letter-to-mom
```

See Also

```
pack
```

vi

Purpose

Stands for visual editor. That is, vi is the same editor as ed, except that vi is full-screen, and you can see the changes you make. The visual editor is such a powerful tool that this description can only provide rudimentary information about the command and its usefulness.

Syntax

    vi *filename*

    view *filename*

    vedit *filename*

Options and Variables

The three preceding forms all invoke the same editor. The first is the normal form. In the second form, view invokes the editor in read-only mode, thus allowing vi to act somewhat like the pagers more and pg; view cannot be piped to, however. In the third form, vedit places the editor in novice mode, which can be useful for beginners.

filename   The name of the file to edit.

Once in vi, the following are but a few of the commands available:

ESC	Returns you to command mode, enabling you to enter a new command
r	Replaces one character
R	Unlimited replacement in the line
i	Insert mode
dd	Deletes the line
x	Deletes a character
$	End of the line
^	Beginning of the line
:x	Writes the file and exits vi
:q!	Quits vi without saving file
/	Allows entry of a search pattern

Rules

The vi command works modally, with editing commands entered in command mode and text entered in input mode. Press Esc to switch between insert mode and command mode, and use either an a or an i to append text before or after your current position.

Example

The following example starts vi, so that you can work on a letter to your mother:

```
vi letter-to-mom
```

See Also

ed

W

Purpose

Reports who is logged in to the system and what they are doing. The w command also reports how many users are on the system, how long the system has been up, and the load averages (the average number of processes in the last 1, 5, and 15 minutes).

Syntax

```
w [options] users
```

Options and Variables

-h   Does not show the header information. Normally, w prints a heading line showing the current date, how long the system has been up, the number of users currently logged in, and the load averages.

-l   The default, this option specifies the long format. It produces the following columns:

         User   The user logged in.

         Tty   The terminal the user is on.

         Login@   Time at which the user logged in on this terminal.

         Idle   Number of minutes that the user has not typed anything at the terminal. This does not mean that the processes on the terminal are not doing something useful. The user may have launched a process that takes a long time to execute but requires no interaction (a large sort, for example).

         JCPU   The cumulative CPU minutes used by all jobs run during this login session.

	PCPU	The number of CPU minutes the present process is taking.
	What	The name of the currently running process with its arguments.
-q		The quick output. Lists only the following from the preceding table: User, Tty, Idle, and What.
-t		Prints only the heading line. This command is equivalent to uptime.
users		A space-separated list of users to which to limit the output of w. Normally, w reports all users.

Message

```
w: illegal option — badoption
```

The preceding message appears if you invoked w with an option it does not support.

Examples

The following example reports all possible information:

```
w
```

The next example reports just the uptime, number of users, load average information, and so on:

```
w -t
```

The following example reports the information on the users Frank and Sue only:

```
w frank sue
```

See Also

```
finger

ps

who

whodo
```

wall

Purpose

Writes to all users currently logged in on the system. It is a broadcast message.

Syntax

```
/etc/wall
```

Options and Variables

The wall command reads from standard input until an end-of-file (Ctrl+D) is reached. This command then broadcasts this message to all users on the system.

Rules

You must be the superuser to execute wall to override any protection users may have on their terminals to avoid being written to. Furthermore, the file is in the /etc directory, and the system default is to not enable regular users to execute permissions.

Some installations do not permit end users to use wall. Even at sites allowing end users access to this command, end users can only write to terminal devices on which they have write permission.

Examples

```
wall
Please get off the system in 10 minutes^D
```

The preceding example invokes an interactive version of wall. A one-line message ending with the end-of-file keystroke (Ctrl+D). The message does not go out until the end-of-file is encountered.

The next example redirects the file shutdown-note to wall and sends the contents of that file to all users:

```
wall <shutdown-note
```

See Also

```
write
```

wc

Purpose

Counts the number of characters, words, or lines in a file.

Syntax

```
wc [options] filelist
```

Options and Variables

-c	Counts only the number of characters.
-w	Counts only the number of words. Words are any string of characters separated by a space, tab, or newline.
-l	Counts only the number of lines. (More precisely, counts the number of newline characters encountered.)
filelist	A space-separated list of files to count the contents of. If left blank, the standard output is read.

Rules

Any combination of the preceding options may be used; the default is all of the options. When more than one option is specified, output is in the following order: lines, words, characters.

Message

```
wc: can't open filename
```

The preceding message appears if you invoked wc by asking it to count in a file it cannot open. Either the file does not exist or you do not have permission to read it.

Examples

```
wc letter-to-mom
```

The preceding example tells you how many lines, words, and characters are in the letter-to-mom.

```
dd if=/dev/rct0 ¦ wc -c
```

The preceding example counts the number of characters on the tape. In other words, it tells you how much data is on the tape. (It is also a useful way of validating that the tape is readable.)

what

Purpose

Searches files for the character sequence @(#), and prints the characters following that sequence until a ~, >, <, \, null, or newline symbol is found. The file name is shown, followed by a colon. On the subsequent lines, the string between @(#) and terminator is also shown. The what command is intended to be used by get in the SCCS (source code control system).

Syntax

```
what filelist
```

Options and Variables

filelist   The space-separated list of files to search.

Rules

The what command is intended to be used with the get command, which automatically inserts identifying information.

Example

This example looks at the file my-file; if it finds the sequence @(#), it reports those lines:

```
what my-file
```

who

Purpose

Reports who is currently on the system, as well as other user and login information.

Syntax

```
who [options] file

who am i
```

Options and Variables

-u	Reports users currently logged in to the system and the last occurrence of activity on the tty.
-am i	Lists the name of the user invoking the command, the logged-in user, and the login time.
-A	Shows UNIX accounting information.
-T	Indicates whether the terminal enables users to send messages to it. A + just before the LINE column indicates that the terminal may be written to; a - indicates no; and a ? may indicate a problem with the terminal.
-l	Shows only the lines waiting for someone to log in.
-H	Prints the header line.
-q	Shows a space-separated list of user names and a count.
-d	Shows the processes that have expired and have not been respawned by init.
-t	Shows when the system date or time last changed (both the old and new values).
-a	Shows all available information.
-s	Limits the output to form like -u, but only the NAME, LINE, and TIME columns are provided.
file	An alternative file to read to obtain login information, this file usually is /etc/wtmp (a history of the contents of the /etc/utmp file). Because /etc/wtmp grows over time, it must be cleaned up periodically.

The who command produces the following columns:

NAME	The name of the user.
LINE	The terminal to which user is logged in.
TIME	When user logged in.

IDLE	The number of minutes since user has typed something at the terminal. A dot (.) indicates that some activity has occurred during the last minute.
PID	The process ID of the login shell.
COMMENTS	The comment field, as defined in /tcb/files/inittab.

Examples

The following example gives the columns: NAME, LINE, and TIME:

who

The next example shows when the system time changed:

who -t

See Also

ps

w

whodo

whodo

Purpose

Sees who is on the system and what they currently are doing.

Syntax

/etc/whodo

Options and Variables

The whodo command produces a merged output from the ps and who commands.

Example

whodo

The preceding example produces a list of who is on the system and what that user is doing.

See Also

```
finger

ps

w

who
```

write

Purpose

Communicates interactively with a user who is otherwise inaccessible.

Syntax

```
write user tty
```

Options and Variables

user   The user name of the person to whom you want to send a message (to the screen).

tty   When the user is logged in to more than one terminal at a time, you may specify the terminal to which you want the message to go.

Rules

The write command reads from standard input. Whenever you press Enter, write sends that line to the user. When you press the end-of-file key (Ctrl+D), write exits.

Messages

```
Message from sending-user sending-tty
```

The preceding message appears if someone is writing to you. The write command lets you know who is sending the message and the terminal from which write is running.

```
(end of message)
```

The preceding message appears if the user sending you a message has finished.

```
user is not logged on.
```

The preceding message appears if you tried to write to a user who is not currently on the system.

```
permission denied
```

The preceding message appears if the user you want to write to does not want to be written to right now. That user probably issued the mesg n command.

When you have finished a line of thought and want the person you are communicating with to respond, it is common practice to use the notation (o) to signal "over." And when you have finished the conversation, use (oo) to signal "over and out." Others use multiple newlines. When using this convention, you press Enter at least twice to signal to the other user that your turn is over.

If the user has a telephone, simply picking up the telephone and calling is probably just as easy to do. Although write is extremely useful when a telephone is not available, it can be quite cumbersome because one person cannot respond until the other user has completed a line of thought.

Novice users tend to get frustrated if they are written to because they are not comfortable enough with the system to respond. Usually, they believe that the writing is messing up the application currently running—and yes, some applications available on UNIX do not provide a redraw or shell escape function. This, in essence, cripples that user, even though no real damage has taken place.

If a user is logged in to more than one terminal, write assumes the terminal with the most recent login, which may not be the user's current terminal. This presents a problem because you have to track down the current terminal, or it may appear as though the user is not able to respond. This is a real-life problem, due to the multiple consoles and multiscreen capabilities of UNIX.

See Also

mail

mesg

who

yes

Purpose

Continuously outputs a given string or the letter y. The yes command can be used when programs that require a yes response to some prompts are running, but you cannot be there to answer the prompts.

Syntax

```
yes string
```

Options and Variables

string   The string to output continuously. If left blank, the letter y is generated.

Rules

The yes command continues to output the given string until it is aborted or killed. In a pipe, yes terminates when the program to which it is piping terminates.

Example

If my-file does not enable write permissions, the rm command prompts for a yes or no response. The following example gives the yes response. This duplicates the -f option to rm.

```
yes ¦ rm my-file
```

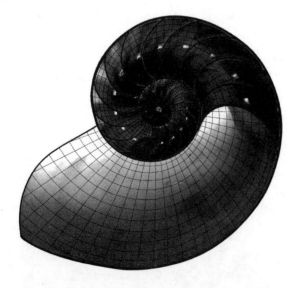

APPENDIX

Differences between UNIX and DOS

O perating systems are everywhere you look. Every computer, workstation, host, mini-tower, or mainframe that boots up has one. Microsoft brought DOS to the marketplace in the early 1980s, and it quickly gained popularity as it became intrinsically linked to the personal computer. Today it is one of the most-used operating systems in existence—quite an accomplishment when you contemplate how young it is.

Many beginning UNIX users who have computer experience have gained it on DOS-based machines. This appendix compares and contrasts key components of each, detailing the differences.

File Names

DOS adheres to strict rules about file names. To begin with, they can be only up to eight characters long, with a three-character extension. In UNIX, some systems allow file names of 14 characters, but most allow 255. Additionally, extensions have meaning in DOS; .EXE, .COM, and .BAT make a file executable. You cannot run a file named TEST.KAD. With UNIX, extensions mean nothing, and any file, under any name, can run. The period is also treated like any other character and has no special meaning—it is possible to have a file named Karen.Kristin.And.The.Crew. The only special meaning in UNIX is if the period is the first letter of the file name, in which case the file is "hidden" from directory listings. Additionally, listings are always shown in ASCII order. When listing a directory, those files with names starting with numbers are listed first, followed by uppercase A through Z, and finally lowercase a through z.

Case Sensitivity

UNIX is case sensitive. Three separate files can be under the same directory with one named "karen," another named "Karen," and the third "KAREN." They are all treated as separate entities because upper- and lowercase characters are differentiated.

All commands are in lowercase, and typing **AWK** results in a message that the command is not found, when awk is sitting right there.

File Separators

DOS uses the backslash character (\) to distinguish directories and subdirectories (as in cd \junk\stuff). UNIX replaces the backslash with the slash character (/) (as in cd /junk/stuff).

There's some history behind the file separator difference between DOS and UNIX. DOS was originally based on the CP/M operating system and it used "\" as file separators. UNIX was mostly written in the C language and the backslash key (\) has special meaning when used with other characters. For example, \t is a tab, \n is a newline character.

Options

DOS uses the / to signify an option to a command. For example, to get a windowed view of the files in your directory, you would use dir /w. UNIX uses the hyphen (-) in place of this. For example, to count the number of lines in a file, the command is wc -l filename.

Deletions

When files are deleted in DOS, the first character of the file name is removed in the file allocation table, marking the space it occupied as being available for other files. This is why a deleted file can be recovered—all you have to do is respecify the first character. In UNIX, a deleted file is really removed from the system, and it cannot be recovered. The only recourse is to hope someone saved it on a backup.

Multitasking

Only one command can be specified at a time on the DOS command line. Multiple commands can be given in UNIX, separating each with a semicolon if they are completely separate commands (clear ; pwd), or placing multiple requests on the same line if the same command is performed on each of them (ls -l *.exe *.com *.bat).

Multiuser

DOS is based on a one-user scenario. One user sits at the computer, so everything on the computer must belong to him or her. UNIX is based on a multiple-user scenario. Each user is required to log in before he or she can begin any work. Once logged in, he or she can access only files to which he or she has permission.

Prompts

The standard DOS prompt reflects the drive and/or subdirectory (prompt pg). The standard UNIX prompt is based on the shell you are using—a $ for most shells, or a % for the C shell.

Command Interpreters

There is only one command interpreter in DOS: the command.com file. In UNIX, there are three primary ones, known as shells. Most vendors offer more than one with their software and users can take their pick of which one they like best. The three choices are Bourne, Korn, and C.

Consistency

DOS maintains some consistency throughout the command process. For example, if you want to use an option, you always precede the option with a slash (/). In UNIX, sometimes you use letters for options, and sometimes you do not. For example, to see how many lines are in a file, you use `wc -l filename`. But to see the last line of a file, you use the number 1, as in `tail -1 filename`. If UNIX maintained consistency, it would be `tail -l1 filename`.

APPENDIX

Sample Programs

The programs listed here are examples of routines written in languages other than the shell programming language. Viewing them, you can see that the constructs and syntax are very similar to those used by the shell itself.

Both of the programs are of a shell archive routine, with the first written in the C language and the second in PERL. As they are included on the disk attached to this book, you don't need to type them to use them!

Listing B.1   cshar.c

This is a C program. If you have no C programming experience, then you should find a copy of Larry Walls PERL program, and use the program in Listing 2.

```
/* ------------------------------------------------------------------

@(#) cshar.c v2.1 - Create a shell archive      (C) 1988 Chris Hare

NAME
        cshar - Create Shell Archive Files

SYNTAX
        cshar FILELIST archive

DESCRIPTION
        cshar is a program to create shell archive files for transfer to
        another system, or for compacted archive on the same machine.

        The shell archive created by cshar is portable across SCO XENIX
        systems, AT&T UNIX systems, and Motorola UNIX Systems.

        The Filelist can be a source file containing a list of files, or
        they can be passed on the command line.  Any directories which are
        passed on the command line are searched, and any directories, and
        files located there are also processed.

NOTES
        The shell archive also contains information regarding the number of
        characters expected when the file is reassembled.  This is verified
        by using the UNIX command 'wc' to check the number of characters in
        the file.

        The same source code file is used for both UNIX and XENIX systems
        The determining factor is which -Ddefine is used on the compiler
        command line.
        -Dx286 - SCO XENIX 286
        -Dx386 - SCO XENIX 386
        -DATT  - ATT UNIX 68010
        -DMCS  - Motorola UNIX System V (VME 680x0 )

        Other systems can be supported on this command simply by adding the
        appropriate defines.
```

```
WARNINGS
        This routine expects to find two UNIX commands on the target
        system:
                wc
                sed

        If neither of these two commands is found, then the archive cannot
        be unpacked.

--------------------------------------------------------------------------*/
#include <sys/types.h>
#include <a.out.h>
#include <fcntl.h>
#include <string.h>
#include <stdio.h>
#include <memory.h>
#include <errno.h>
#include <sys/utsname.h>
#include <sys/stat.h>
#include <sys/dir.h>
#include <time.h>

long int char_out = 0;
long int dir_out = 0;
long int files_out = 0;
long int dir_skip = 0;
long int file_skip = 0;
long int skip = 0;
long int files_in = 0;
long int dirs_in = 0;
long int oth_in = 0;
int rec = 0;
FILE *output,
     *fopen();
char record[BUFSIZ-2], new_rec[BUFSIZ];
char id[] = "@(#) cshar.c Copyright 1988-1991 Chris Hare";
#define ID "cshar"
#define VERSION "2.5"
#define LASTDATE "Mon Aug  5 23:35:28 EDT 1991"
#ifdef XENIX
#define SYSTEM "XENIX System V"
   char id2[] = "@(#) XENIX System V";
#endif
```

continues

Listing B.1   cshar.c, Continued

```
#ifdef ATT
#define SYSTEM "AT&T UNIX System V"
#define ARCMAGIC 0177545
    char id2[] = "@(#) AT&T UNIX System V";
#endif
#ifdef MCS
#define SYSTEM "Motorola UNIX System V"
    char id2[] = "@(#) Motorola UNIX System V";
#endif

main( argc, argv )
int argc;
char *argv[];
{
    int count;
    char outfile[256];
    char *ctime(),              /* declare ctime(S) */
         *timestr;              /* storage area for time string */
    long int t_secs,            /* return value from time(S) */
             time();            /* declare time(S) */
    char *user_buf;
    struct utsname utsname;
    char *user_name;
    user_name = (char *)0;

    if ( argc < 2 )
       {
       fprintf( stderr, "%s %s\n", ID, SYSTEM );
       fprintf( stderr, "Usage : %s files outfile\n", argv[0] );
       exit (1);
       }
    strcpy( outfile, argv[ argc - 1 ] );
    if ( ( access( outfile, 0 ) ) == 0 )
       {
       fprintf( stderr, "The named output file %s exists.  Aborted.\n",
          outfile );
       exit(1);
       }
    output = fopen( outfile, "w" );
    if  ( output < 0 )
       {
       perror("");
```

```
        exit    (2);
        }

    t_secs = time(0L);
    timestr = ctime(&t_secs);

    fprintf( stderr, "Writing output to %s\n", outfile );
    rec = fprintf( output, ":\n");
    char_out = char_out + rec;
    rec = fprintf( output, "#\n# To Recover Files, type \"sh
sharfile\"\n");
    char_out = char_out + rec;
    rec = fprintf( output, "#\n# %s \n", id );
    char_out = char_out + rec;
    rec = fprintf( output, "# Version %s on %s (%s)\n",
          VERSION, SYSTEM, LASTDATE );
    char_out = char_out + rec;
    user_buf = cuserid(user_name);
    uname(&utsname);
    rec = fprintf( output, "# Wrapped by %s!%s on %s#\n",
                  utsname.nodename, user_buf, timestr );
    char_out = char_out + rec;
    rec = fprintf( output, "#\n# ---- Contents of this archive ----\n#\n" );
    char_out = char_out + rec;
    for ( count = 1; count <= argc - 2; count++ )
        chk_args( argv[count] );
    rec = fprintf( output, "#\n# ----------------------------------\n#\n" );
    char_out = char_out + rec;
    fprintf( stderr, "%s : Request List\n", argv[0] );
    fprintf( stderr, "Number of Files to Process : %ld\n", files_in );
    fprintf( stderr, "Number of Directories to Process : %ld\n", dirs_in );
    fprintf( stderr, "Number of Objects Likely Skipped : %ld\n", oth_in );
    fprintf( stderr, "\n");
    for ( count = 1; count <= argc - 2; count++ )
        proc_entry( argv[count] );
    fprintf( stderr, "Archive Complete.\n");
fprintf( stderr, "\nShell Archive Statistics\n");
fprintf( stderr, "------------------------\n");
fprintf( stderr, "Number of Files to Process           : %ld\n",
files_in );
fprintf( stderr, "Actual Number of Files Processed     : %ld\n",
files_out );
fprintf( stderr, "Actual Number of Files Skipped       : %ld\n",
```

```
      ➥ file_skip );
      fprintf( stderr, "Number of Directories to Process       : %ld\n",
      ➥ dirs_in );
      fprintf( stderr, "Actual Number of Directories Processed : %ld\n",
      ➥ dir_out);
      fprintf( stderr, "Actual Number of Directories Skipped   : %ld\n",
      ➥ dir_skip );
      fprintf( stderr, "Number of Objects Likely Skipped       : %ld\n",
      ➥ oth_in );
      fprintf( stderr, "Number of Unknown Entries Skipped       : %ld\n", skip );
      fprintf( stderr, "Number of Characters Written (Bytes)    : %ld\n",
      ➥char_out);
         exit (0);
      }
/****** proc_entry *****/
int proc_entry( fname )
char *fname;
{
   int type;
   type = stat_file( fname, 0 );
   if ( type == 2 )
      pack_file( fname );
   else if ( type == 1 )
      pack_dir( fname );
   else
      {
      fprintf( stderr, "Skipping %s\n", fname );
      skip++;
      }
}
/****** stat_file - determine if file is regular file or directory *****/
int stat_file( fname, record )
char *fname;
int record;
{
   struct stat statbuf;
   int ret;
   ret = stat( fname, ( struct stat *)&statbuf );
   if ( ( statbuf.st_mode & S_IFMT ) == ( S_IFDIR ) )
      ret = 1;
   else if ( ( statbuf.st_mode & S_IFMT ) == ( S_IFREG ) )
      {
      if ( record > 0 )
```

```
          {
          ret = chk_bin( fname, 0 );
          if ( ret == 0 )
             {
             fprintf( output, "#\t%-40s\t(%d bytes)\n", fname,
             ➥statbuf.st_size );
             ret = 2;
             }
          }
       else
          ret = 2;
       }
    else
       ret = -1;
    return( ret );
}
/****** chk_bin - determine if file is binary *****/
int chk_bin( fname, report )
char *fname;
int report;
{
#ifdef XENIX
    struct xexec execbuf;
    int bfile;
    bfile = open( fname, O_RDONLY );
    read( bfile, (char *)&execbuf, sizeof(execbuf) );
    close( bfile );
    if ( ( execbuf.x_magic == X_MAGIC ) ¦¦
         ( execbuf.x_magic == ARCMAGIC ) ¦¦
         ( ( fname[(strlen(fname) - 2)] == '.' ) &&
         ( fname[(strlen(fname) -1)] == 'o' ) ) )
       {
       if ( report == 1 )
          {
          fprintf( stderr, "Skipping %s - not a text file\n", fname );
          file_skip++;
          return (-2);
       else
          return (-2);
          }
       }
    return(0);
#endif
```

```
#ifdef ATT
   FILHDR execbuf;
   int bfile;
   bfile = open( fname, O_RDONLY );
   read( bfile, (char *)&execbuf, FILHSZ );
   close( bfile );
   if ( ( execbuf.x_magic == MC68KPGMAGIC ) ¦¦
         ( execbuf.x_magic == ARCMAGIC ) ¦¦
         ( ( fname[(strlen(fname) - 2)] == '.' ) &&
         ( fname[(strlen(fname) -1)] == 'o' ) ) )
      {
      if ( report == 1 )
         {
         fprintf( stderr, "Skipping %s - not a text file\n", fname );
         file_skip++;
         return (-2);
      else
         return (-2);
         }
      }
#endif
#ifdef MCS
   /*
      The file header structure is not defined in /usr/include/a.out.h, but
      in one of the files which is included in a.out.h,
   */
   FILHDR execbuf;
   int bfile;
   bfile = open( fname, O_RDONLY );
   read( bfile, (char *)&execbuf, FILHSZ );
   close( bfile );
#ifdef DEBUG
   fprintf( stderr, "(chk_bin) processing file %s magic = %d\n",
         fname, execbuf.f_magic  );
#endif
   if ( ( execbuf.f_magic == MC68MAGIC ) ¦¦
         ( ( fname[(strlen(fname) - 2)] == '.' ) &&
         ( fname[(strlen(fname) -1)] == 'o' ) ) )
      {
      if ( report == 1 )
         {
         fprintf( stderr, "Skipping %s - not a text file\n", fname );
         file_skip++;
```

```
         return (-2);
            }
      else
         return (-2);
      }
#endif
   return(0);
}
/***** pack_file - fix the file and send to output *****/
int pack_file( fname )
char *fname;
{
   FILE *infile;
   int ok, bytes, eol = 0;
   long eof = 0;
   ok = chk_bin( fname, 1 );
   if ( ok == -2 )
      return( ok );
   infile = fopen( fname, "r" );
   if ( infile == (FILE *)0 )
      {
      fprintf( stderr, "Skipping %s - can't open file for reading.\n",
               fname );
      file_skip++;
      return( -1 );
      }
   fprintf( stderr, "Archiving %s\n", fname );
   rec = fprintf( output, "if test -f %s \n", fname );
   char_out = char_out +rec;
   rec = fprintf( output, "then\n" );
   char_out = char_out +rec;
   rec = fprintf( output, "echo will not overwrite %s 1>&2\n", fname );
   char_out = char_out +rec;
   rec = fprintf( output, "else \n" );
   char_out = char_out +rec;
   rec = fprintf( output, "echo Extracting %s 1>&2\n", fname );
   char_out = char_out +rec;
   rec = fprintf( output, "sed 's/^X//' > %s << \\!!!EOF!!!\n", fname );
   char_out = char_out +rec;
   while ( eol = fgetline( infile ) != 1 )
      {
      sprintf( new_rec, "X%s\n", record );
```

```
            rec = fprintf( output, "%s", new_rec );
            char_out = char_out +rec;
            memset( new_rec, 0x00, sizeof(new_rec) );
            memset( record, 0x00, sizeof(record) );
            }
        rec = fprintf( output, "!!!EOF!!!\n");
        char_out = char_out +rec;
        bytes = fseek( infile, 0L, 2 );
        if ( bytes == -1 )
           fprintf( stderr, "Error seeking to EOF in %s.  Err# is %d.\n",
                    fname, errno );
        eof = ftell( infile );
        rec = fprintf( output, "if test \"\`wc -c %s\`\" -ne \"%ld %s\" \n",
        ➡fname,
                eof, fname );
        char_out = char_out +rec;
        rec = fprintf(output,
            "then\n  echo \\007WARNING %s : Extraction Error\nfi\nfi\n",
            ➡fname );
        char_out = char_out +rec;
        fclose( infile );
        files_out++;
        return(0);
        }
/***** pack_dir - process directory *****/
int pack_dir( fname )
char *fname;
{
    int dirp;
    struct direct dp;
    int status = 0;
    char new_name[256];
    dirp = open( fname, O_RDONLY );
    if ( dirp < 0 )
        {
        fprintf( stderr, "Skipping : can't access directory : %s.\n",
        ➡fname );
        dir_skip++;
        return( -1 );
        }
    rec = fprintf( output, "echo creating directory :  %s 1>&2\n", fname );
    char_out = char_out + rec;
```

```
   rec = fprintf( output, "mkdir %s 1>&2\n", fname );
   char_out = char_out + rec;
   while ( ( status = read(dirp, (char *)&dp, sizeof(dp) ) ) ==
sizeof(dp) )
      {
      if ( ( strcmp( dp.d_name,".") != 0 ) &&
         ( strcmp(dp.d_name,"..") != 0 ) )
         {
         sprintf( new_name, "%s/%s", fname, dp.d_name );
         if ( dp.d_ino != 0 )
            proc_entry( new_name );
         }       /* end strcmp if */
      }          /* end while */
   close( dirp );
   dir_out++;
   return(0);
}             /* end pack_dir */
/***** fgetline - get a line from a FILE stream *****/
int fgetline(fp)
FILE *fp;                        /* FILE pointer for stream    */
{
   int c,i,eofflag;
   eofflag = 0;
   i = 0;
   while ( ((c=getc(fp)) != EOF) && (c != '\n') )
      record[i++] = c;
   record[i] = '\0';
   if (c == EOF)
      eofflag = 1;
   return(eofflag);
}                                /* end of fgetline */
/* ***** chk_args ******************************************************** */
int chk_args( fname )
char *fname;
{

   int type;
   int ok;

   type = stat_file( fname, 1 );
```

```
        switch ( type )
           {
           case -1:
               return(0);
           case 1:
               dirs_in++;
               return(0);
           case 2:
               files_in++;
               return(0);
           default:
               oth_in++;
           }
        return(0);
    }
```

Listing B.2   pshar

This is a PERL language program. As a result it is much more portable than a C language program, which typically requires some measure of tweaking on every system. When running pshar for the first timne, you see the following:

```
$ pshar -o /tmp/test fi*
pshar Version 4.02
Copyright 1989-1993 Chris Hare, UniLabs Research Group
Configuring ....
Checking for /u/chare/.pshar.cfg ...
   Checking for /etc/default ...
   Checking for /etc/pshar.cfg ...
Oops! I can't find any configuration files.  Because you aren't the
system administrator, I will create one for you in your home directory.

Thank you for using pshar.  This configuration will only be run once,
unless the configuration file is removed.
Please answer the following questions.  Default values
are enclosed in [].

Operating System Type [Generic UNIX] :
Domain Name [.UUCP] :
Default Archive Size [128K] :
Creating pshar configuration file : /u/chare/.pshar.cfg
                Oh drat, I can't create >14 char filenames here.
Loading Configuration file ... /u/chare/.pshar.cfg
```

```
Archive Size set to 131072 bytes...
pshar Copyright 1989-1993 Chris Hare, UniLabs Research Group
Version 4.02 for Generic UNIX
Surveying ...
Survey Results
    Number of text files to process   : 8
    Number of binary files to process : 0
    Number of device files to process : 0
    Number of directories to process  : 0
    Number of unknown entries skipped :
    Total Size of Archive             : 461 bytes
    Size of each part                 : 131072 bytes
    Number of Parts                   : 1

    Output File Base Name             : /tmp/test

Starting Archive ...
Creating Part 1
Archiving file : fi1    text file, 94 bytes
Archiving file : fi2    text file, 38 bytes
Archiving file : fi3    text file, 35 bytes
Archiving file : fi4    text file, 54 bytes
Archiving file : fi5    text file, 22 bytes
Archiving file : fi6    text file, 58 bytes
Archiving file : fi7    text file, 80 bytes
Archiving file : fi8    text file, 80 bytes
Assembling Archive part 1 (file is /tmp/test.1)
Archive Complete.
```

The shell archive file itself appears as follows:

```
#!/bin/sh
#
# pshar Copyright 1989-1993 Chris Hare, UniLabs Research Group
# Version 4.02 for Generic UNIX
#
# This archive was wrapped on Sat Aug 13  0:48:32 EST 1994
#                               by chare@UNIXPC..UUCP
#
# Part 1 of 1
#
# This sharchive was created using PERL.  To recover the files
# in this archive, run the command 'sh filename', where filename
# is the name of the file which contains this archive.
```

```
# As in
#                   sh /tmp/test.01
#
# This archive will not overwrite a file by the same name
# unless a -c is given as an option as in :
#                   sh /tmp/test.01 -c
#
# For a copy of this program, please contact chare@unilabs.org
#
#
# ---------------------------------
# This archive contains :
#    fi1                                    (       94 bytes/text)
#    fi2                                    (       38 bytes/text)
#    fi3                                    (       35 bytes/text)
#    fi4                                    (       54 bytes/text)
#    fi5                                    (       22 bytes/text)
#    fi6                                    (       58 bytes/text)
#    fi7                                    (       80 bytes/text)
#    fi8                                    (       80 bytes/text)
#
# ---------------------------------
#
#
echo "pshar Copyright 1989-1993 Chris Hare, UniLabs Research Group"
echo "Version 4.02 for Generic UNIX"
if test -f fi1 -a "$1" != "-c"
then
   echo "shar : will not overwrite fi1 "
else
   echo "extracting fi1 (94 bytes)"
   cat > fi1 << \!END_OF_FILE!
:
if [ -f "$1" ]
then
        echo "$1: regular file"
else
        echo "$1: not a regular file"
fi

exit 0
!END_OF_FILE!
fi # end of overwrite test
```

```
    if test "`wc -c fi1`" -ne "94 fi1"
    then
        echo "WARNING fi1 : Extraction Error"
    fi
if test -f fi2 -a "$1" != "-c"
then
    echo "shar : will not overwrite fi2 "
else
    echo "extracting fi2 (38 bytes)"
    cat > fi2 << \!END_OF_FILE!

if test -n "$1"
then
    echo "$1"
fi
!END_OF_FILE!
fi # end of overwrite test
    if test "`wc -c fi2`" -ne "38 fi2"
    then
        echo "WARNING fi2 : Extraction Error"
    fi
if test -f fi3 -a "$1" != "-c"
then
    echo "shar : will not overwrite fi3 "
else
    echo "extracting fi3 (35 bytes)"
    cat > fi3 << \!END_OF_FILE!

if test "$1"
then
    echo "$1"
fi
!END_OF_FILE!
fi # end of overwrite test
    if test "`wc -c fi3`" -ne "35 fi3"
    then
        echo "WARNING fi3 : Extraction Error"
    fi
if test -f fi4 -a "$1" != "-c"
then
    echo "shar : will not overwrite fi4 "
else
    echo "extracting fi4 (54 bytes)"
```

```
    cat > fi4 << \!END_OF_FILE!

if test -z "$1"
then
   echo "no value was given"
fi
!END_OF_FILE!
fi # end of overwrite test
   if test "`wc -c fi4`" -ne "54 fi4"
   then
      echo "WARNING fi4 : Extraction Error"
   fi
if test -f fi5 -a "$1" != "-c"
then
   echo "shar : will not overwrite fi5 "
else
   echo "extracting fi5 (22 bytes)"
   cat > fi5 << \!END_OF_FILE!
:
echo "$# arguments"
!END_OF_FILE!
fi # end of overwrite test
   if test "`wc -c fi5`" -ne "22 fi5"
   then
      echo "WARNING fi5 : Extraction Error"
   fi
if test -f fi6 -a "$1" != "-c"
then
   echo "shar : will not overwrite fi6 "
else
   echo "extracting fi6 (58 bytes)"
   cat > fi6 << \!END_OF_FILE!

if [ ! "$testvar" ]
then
        echo "testvar has no value"
fi
!END_OF_FILE!
fi # end of overwrite test
   if test "`wc -c fi6`" -ne "58 fi6"
   then
      echo "WARNING fi6 : Extraction Error"
   fi
```

```
   if test -f fi7 -a "$1" != "-c"
   then
      echo "shar : will not overwrite fi7 "
   else
      echo "extracting fi7 (80 bytes)"
      cat > fi7 << \!END_OF_FILE!
if [ $# -lt 2 -a $1 -ne 1 ]
then
      echo "Sorry, you cannot run this command."
fi
!END_OF_FILE!
fi # end of overwrite test
   if test "`wc -c fi7`" -ne "80 fi7"
   then
      echo "WARNING fi7 : Extraction Error"
   fi
if test -f fi8 -a "$1" != "-c"
then
   echo "shar : will not overwrite fi8 "
else
   echo "extracting fi8 (80 bytes)"
   cat > fi8 << \!END_OF_FILE!
if [ $# -lt 2 -o $1 -ne 1 ]
then
      echo "Sorry, you cannot run this command."
fi
!END_OF_FILE!
fi # end of overwrite test
   if test "`wc -c fi8`" -ne "80 fi8"
   then
      echo "WARNING fi8 : Extraction Error"
   fi
echo "You have unpacked Part 1 of 1.   "
echo "You have unpacked all parts."
echo "extraction complete."
```

Finally, the following is the actual PERL source code for this shell archive maker:

```
#!/usr/local/perl
eval '(exit $?0)' && eval 'exec /usr/local/perl -S $0 ${1+"$@"}'
& eval 'exec /usr/local/perl -S $0 $argv:q'
if 0;
#---- PROGRAM IDENTIFICATION -----------------------------------
#
```

```
# PROGRAM NAME  : pshar
# PROJECT       : A Better Shell Archiver
# AUTHOR        : Chris Hare
# DATE          : PERL Version : August 1992
#
#---- PROGRAM ENVIRONMENT -----------------------------------------
#
#---- DESCRIPTION -------------------------------------------------
#
# A Little bit of History
# ---------------------
#
# In the effort to build the better shell archiver, I started building
# C versions after my first shell based version back in 1987, and some
# discussions with Rebecca Thomas of UNIX World about it.  Since then, the
# C version has been ported to Motorola UNIX, AT&T UNIX, SCO XENIX, SCO
# UNIX, DEC Ultrix, and SunOS.
#
# The major problem with porting the C version was the inconsistent manner
# in which different UNIX versions determined if a file was a binary
# executable image.  In the C version, it was not possible to capture a
# binary into the shell archive.  With the PERL version it is.
#
# This is a very robust shell archiver program.
#
# Copyright
# --------
# This program is NOT in the public domain, although it may become (or be)
# publically available.  The copyright owner retains all rights however
# insignificant to the application code presented here.
#
# Features
# --------
# The features of this program include
#
#       * Configuration file to specify the maximum archive size
#
#       * can handle multiple part archives
#
#       * can include all types of text files
#
#       * can include binary files after being uuencoded
#
```

```
#          * can include character special files by using the mknod command
#            on the target system.
#
#          * can include block special files by using the mknod command on
#            the target system.
#
#          * detects and reports extraction errors
#
#          * uses /bin/sh for reconstruction.  uudecode, and mknod will be
#            called as needed.
#
#          * More portable than C - all you need is PERL.
#
# Bugs
# ----
#
# This may not be the cleanest PERL code in the world, but what the hey!
#
#---- MODIFICATION HISTORY ----------------------------------------------
#
# MOD    DATE    WHO     DESCRIPTION
#        YYMMDD
# ====   =======  =======  ============================================
# 1.0    ?        C.Hare   Initial C Version
# 1.1    ?        C.Hare   C version Ported to SCO XENIX
# 2.0    ?        C.Hare   C version Ported to SCO UNIX
# 2.1    ?        C.Hare   C version Ported to AT&T 3B1
# 2.5    ?        C.Hare   Added a lot of functionality under Motorola UNIX
# 2.52   ?        C.Hare   C version Ported to DEC DECStation 3100 (Ultrix)
# 2.53   ?        C.Hare   C version Ported to Sun Sparc SunOS 4.1.1
# 3.0    920803   C.Hare   First PERL port under PERL 4.035
# 3.01   920804   C.Hare   Added Combine function to assemble the archive
# 3.02   920805   C.Hare   Corrected recursiveness errors
# 3.03   920805   C.Hare   Added overwrite protection
# 3.04   920805   C.Hare   Corrected header code for the top of the archive
# 3.05   920805   C.Hare   Added a lot of source code comments
# 3.10   920805   C.Hare   Added a call to the PERL subroutine, flush, as some
#                          of the stuff at the end of the file wasn't
#                          appearing.
# 3.11   920805   C.Hare   Added a call to the PERL subroutine ctime, so
#                          that the date in the top of the file makes a
#                          little more sense.
# 3.20   920807   C.Hare   First useable release
```

```
# 3.21   921103   C.Hare   Changed the directory searching routines to use
#                          a pipe from ls.  This resolves the "." & ".."
#                          restriction noted in bug # 920805-02
# 3.30   930411   C.Hare   Added comments to the code
#                          Corrected end of file and continuation of file
#                          processing for regular files.
# 3.31   930411   C.Hare   Corrected bug 930411-005, so that the proper
#                          handling of binary files through uuencode/
#                          uudecode is
#                          performed on small binaries.
# 3.32   930411   C.Hare   Corrected code for binary file support in multiple
#                          part archives.
# 3.33   930906   C. Hare  Added code to set defaults in the event that the
#                          base system configuration file isn't found.
# 3.34   930913   C.Hare   Added code to allow for the exclusion of binary
#                          files from the sharfile.
# 3.35   930913   C.Hare   Added code for the support of DEBUG tracing
# 3.36   930913   C.Hare   Added code to support on report only.
# 3.37   930913   C.Hare   Added code to allow for exclusion of directories
# 3.38   930913   C.Hare   Added code to allow for exclusion of special files
# 3.39   930913   C.Hare   Added code for an option to list the output file
# 3.40   930930   C.Hare   Added code to change the operation of GetUser
#                          to get the domain name from the command line, or
#                          default to .UUCP in the archive.
# 3.41   930930   C.Hare   Added support to allow for archive size to be
#                          entered in bytes, Kbytes, or Mbytes
# 3.42   930930   C.Hare   Added support to correct bug #930929-02, which
#                          insures that directory structutres are created.
# 3.43   930930   C.Hare   Added support to abort archiving files which
#                          cannot be read.
# 3.44   930930   C.Hare   Added support to create temporary files in the /tmp
#                          directory.  This corrects bug #930929-03
# 3.45   930930   C.Hare   Corrected bug #930804-01, which corrected testing
#                          for long filename, and shortened the filename to
#                          fit in 14 characters.
# 3.46   931002   C.Hare   Added code to build a single shell script which
#                          will run all of the others in sequence.
# 3.47   931002   C.Hare   Added code to default the output filename to
#                          "part", but it isn't fully implemented yet.
# 3.48   931002   C.Hare   Added code to create a "done" file for each part
#                          as it is extracted.  This is only done on multi-
#                          part archives.
# 4.00   931002   C.Hare   First Official Release
```

```
# 4.01  931002  C.Hare  Added support for config files
#                               Default in /etc or /etc/default
#                               User in $HOME/.pshar.cfg
#                               Added code for self-config of pshar on
#                               first execution of the command.
# 4.02  940418  C.Hare  Corrected code to uuenode binary files to use
#                               temporary files in /tmp which are the current PID
#                               followed by .u.  Also did some ethesthic cleanup.
#
#---- PROGRAM MAINLINE ----------------------------------------
#
$Program="pshar";
$Version="4.02";
$Copyright="Copyright 1989-1993 Chris Hare, UniLabs Research Group";
$Part = 1;
$MaxPart = 1;
$total_size = 0;
$run_size = 0;
$rFileCount = 0;
$bFileCount = 0;
$sFileCount = 0;
$DirCount = 0;
$NormalDir = "";
select(STDOUT);
$¦ = 1;


#
# Load in the configuration file
# Redefine the location of this file if you want it somewhere else!
# DO NOT USE THIS LINE.  pshar will not auto-configure itself using config
# files which could be in sevral different places.
# $Config = "./pshar.cfg";
#
$Config = &CheckConfig;

if ( $#ARGV < 1 )
   {
   printf STDERR "Usage : pshar [-b] [-d] [-r] [-s] [-x] -o output
filelist\n";
   printf STDERR "$Copyright\n";
   printf STDERR "Supported Options are :\n";
   printf STDERR "\t-b\tDo not process binary files\n";
   printf STDERR "\t-d\tDo not process directories\n";
```

```
        printf STDERR "\t-o\toutput file\n";
        printf STDERR "\t-r\tReport Only, do not create the archive\n";
        printf STDERR "\t-s\tDo not process special files\n";
        printf STDERR "\t-x\tReport Everything as you do it\n";
        printf STDERR "\t-S\tArchive size in bytes\n";
        printf STDERR "\t-D\tHostname Domain\n";

    if ( -r $Config )
        {
        printf STDERR "\nConfiguration files exist : $Config\n";
        }
    else
        {
        printf STDERR "\nNo configuration files exist\n";
        }
    exit(1);
    }

require "flush.pl";
require "ctime.pl";
require "getopts.pl";

# check on how long our max filename length is
#
# This only affects the creation of the shell archive files, not the
# files being archived
$MaxLen = &FileNameLenCheck;
$MaxNameLen = 14 if ( $MaxLen == 1 );
$MaxNameLen = 255 if ( $MaxLen == 0 );
#
# process arguments
#       set the output file to be the first argument, and shift the
#       list over
#
&Getopts('dbsrxo:S:D:');
if ( $opt_o eq "" )
    {
    $BaseOutputFile = "part";
    }
else
    {
    $BaseOutputFile = $opt_o;
    }
```

```
#
# retrieve and load the configuration file which will identify the user
# customizable options
#
if ( -r $Config )
   {
   printf STDOUT "Loading Configuration file ... $Config\n";
   require "$Config";
   }
else
   {
   $OS="Generic UNIX";
   # $OS="AT&T UNIX 3.51m/UNIXPC";
   # $UseDomain = "unilabs.org";
   if ( $opt_S ne "" )
      {
      $ArchiveSize = $opt_S;    # Size set by the user
      # &ValidateSize;
      # printf "Archive Size set to $ArchiveSize bytes...\n";
      }
   else
      {
      printf "No config file found.  Using System defaults ...\n";
      $ArchiveSize = 131072;    # 128K
      }
   }

&ValidateSize;
printf "Archive Size set to $ArchiveSize bytes...\n";

#
# Get the date and time
#
&GetDate();
&GetUser();
#
# Calculate the total archive size
#
printf "$Program $Copyright\nVersion $Version for $OS\n";
printf "Surveying ...\n";
$run_size = &CheckArgs( @ARGV );
$MaxPart = int( $run_size / $ArchiveSize );
$Rem = $run_size % $ArchiveSize;
```

```
$MaxPart++ if ( $Rem > 0 );
printf "Survey Results \n";
if ( $run_size <= 0 )
   {
   printf "   No files in the list to process.\n";
   exit(0);
   }
printf "   Number of text files to process   : $rFileCount\n";
if ( $opt_b == 1 )
   {
   printf "   Binary files are being skipped\n";
   }
else
   {
   printf "   Number of binary files to process : $bFileCount\n";
   }
printf "   Number of device files to process : $sFileCount\n";
if ( $opt_d == 1 )
   {
   printf "   Directory files are being skipped\n";
   }
else
   {
   printf "   Number of directories to process  : $DirCount\n";
   }
printf "   Number of unknown entries skipped : $Skipped\n";
printf "   Total Size of Archive             : $run_size bytes\n";
printf "   Size of each part                 : $ArchiveSize bytes\n";
printf "   Number of Parts                   : $MaxPart\n\n";

$MaxPartLen = length( $MaxPart );
# we add two because the filename is NAME.p###
$MaxPartLen = $MaxPartLen + 2;
if ( length( $BaseOutputFile ) > ( $MaxNameLen - $MaxPartLen ) )
   {
   # OK, so we can't use long file names, so chop it down ....
   $newName = substr( $BaseOutputFile, 0,( $MaxNameLen - $MaxPartLen ) );
   $BaseOutputFile = $newName;
   }
printf "   Output File Base Name             : $BaseOutputFile\n\n";

if ( $opt_r == 1 )
   {
```

```
        printf "Analysis Complete.\n";
        exit(0);
        }

printf "Starting Archive ...\n";
&OpenFile;
&StartTrackFile;
#
# capture the file type and size
#
for ( $Loop = 0; $Loop <= $#ARGV; $Loop++ )
    {
    $arg = $ARGV[$Loop];
    if ( -d $arg )
            {
            &ProcessDir( $arg );
            }
    elsif ( -f $arg )
            {
            &Normalize( $arg );
            &ProcessFile( $arg );
            }
    elsif ( -b $arg )
            {
            &ProcessBlockNode( $arg );
            $sFileCount++;
            }
    elsif ( -c $arg )
            {
            &ProcessCharNode( $arg );
            $sFileCount++;
            }
    else
            {
            $Skipped++;
            }
    }

close( OUTPUT );
&Combine();
printf "Archive Complete.\n";
close(TRACER);
exit(0);
```

```perl
#---- PROCEDURE : CheckArgs -----------------------------------------
#
# Usage : CheckArgs( files );
#
sub CheckArgs
{
   #
   # save the list of files to be processed
   #
   local( @fileargs ) = @_;
   if ( $opt_x == 1 )
      {
      printf STDERR "sub CheckArgs: @fileargs\n";
      }
   #
   # set some local variables : this will likely be recursive
   #
   local( @moreargs, $Loop, $ArgLoop );

   #
   # loop around each entry in the list
   #
   for ( $ArgLoop = 0; $ArgLoop <= $#fileargs; $ArgLoop++ )
      {
      $entry = $fileargs[$ArgLoop];
      if ( $opt_x == 1 )
         {
         printf STDERR "Analyzing $entry \n";
         }
      #
      # get the size of the file
      #
      $size = -s $entry;
      #
      # and process based on the file type
      #
      if ( -b $entry )
         {
         next if ( $opt_s == 1 );
         $sFileCount++;
         }
      elsif ( -c $entry )
```

```
            {
            next if ( $opt_s == 1 );
            $sFileCount++;
            }
        elsif ( -d $entry )
            {
            #
            # we have a directory, so get the filenames in that directory,
            # and call CheckArgs to process them.
            #
            next if ( $opt_d == 1 );
            &GetFileNames( $entry );
            @moreargs = @allfiles;
            &CheckArgs( @moreargs );
            $DirCount++;
            }
        elsif ( -T $entry )
            {
            #
            # simply increase the size of the archive for text files
            #
            $run_size = $run_size + $size;
            $rFileCount++;
            }
        elsif ( -B $entry )
            {
            next if ( $opt_b == 1 );
            #
            # increase the size of the archive for binary files, but use a
            # factor of 1.5 times their normal size, in order to account
            # for the increase in size during the uuencode
            #
            # NOTE THAT THIS SIZING IS APPROXIMATE
            #
            $run_size = $run_size + ( $size * 1.5 );
            $bFileCount++;
            }
        }
    return( $run_size );
}


#---- PROCEDURE : GetFileNames -----------------------------------------
#
```

```perl
sub GetFileNames
{
   local( $dirname ) = @_;
   local( $Count );
   $Count = 0;
   undef @allfiles;
   if ( $opt_x == 1 )
      {
      printf STDERR "Processing DIRECTORY : $dirname\n";
      }
   open( dir, "ls $dirname ¦ " );
   while (<dir>)
      {
      chop;
      $allfiles[$Count] = "$dirname/$_";
      if ( $opt_x == 1 )
         {
         printf STDER "   Found entry : $allfiles[$Cont]\n";
         }
      $Count++;
      }
   close( dir );
   return( @allfiles );
}

#---- PROCEDURE : ProcessDir --------------------------------------
sub ProcessDir
{
   local( $dirname ) = @_;
   local( $Loop, $entry, @args, $dir_arg );
   if ( $opt_d == 1 )
      {
      if ( $opt_x == 1 )
         {
         printf STDERR "Directory processing is turned off :
         ➡$dirname\n";
         }
      return;
      }

   printf STDOUT "Archiving directory : $dirname\n";
   printf OUTPUT "if [ ! -d $dirname ]\nthen\n";
   printf OUTPUT "echo \"creating directory $dirname\"\n";
```

```
        printf OUTPUT "mkdir $dirname\n";
        printf OUTPUT "fi\n";
        &GetFileNames( $dirname );
        @args = @allfiles;
        for ( $Loop = 0; $Loop <= $#args; $Loop++ )
            {
            $dir_arg = "$args[$Loop]";
            if ( -d $dir_arg )
                    {
                    &ProcessDir( $dir_arg );
                    }
            elsif ( -f $dir_arg )
                    {
                    &ProcessFile( $dir_arg );
                    }
            elsif ( -b $dir_arg )
                    {
                    &ProcessBlockNode( $dir_arg );
                    $Skipped++;
                    }
            elsif ( -c $dir_arg )
                    {
                    &ProcessCharNode( $dir_arg );
                    $Skipped++;
                    }
            else
                    {
                    $Skipped++;
                    }
            }
}
#---- PROCEDURE : ProcessBlockNode -------------------------------
sub ProcessBlockNode
{

    local( $filename ) = @_;
    $type = "blockdev";

    if ( $opt_s == 1 )
        {
        if ( $opt_x == 1 )
            {
            printf STDERR "Special file processing is turned off :
```

```
➡$filename\n";
        }
    return;
    }

    printf STDOUT "Archiving block device file : $filename   \n";
    &WriteDevice( "b", $maj, $min );
}
#---- PROCEDURE : ProcessCharNode -------------------------------
sub ProcessCharNode
{
    local( $filename ) = @_;
    $type = "chardev";

    if ( $opt_s == 1 )
        {
        if ( $opt_x == 1 )
            {
            printf STDERR "Special file processing is turned off :
            ➡$filename\n";
            }
        return;
        }

    printf STDOUT "Archiving char device file : $filename   \n";
    &WriteDevice( "c", $maj, $min );
}
#---- PROCEDURE : ProcessFile ------------------------------------
sub ProcessFile
{
    local( $filename ) = @_;
    ( $type = "text" ) if ( -T $filename );
    ( $type = "binary" ) if ( -B $filename );
    ( $type = "directory" ) if ( -d $filename );
    ( $type = "blockdev" ) if ( -b $filename );
    ( $type = "chardev" ) if ( -c $filename );

    if ( ( $opt_b == 1 ) && ( $type eq "binary" ) )
        {
        if ( $opt_x == 1 )
            {
            printf STDERR "Binary file processing is turned off :
            ➡$filename\n";
```

```
        }
    return;
    }

if ( ! -r $filename )
    {
    printf STDERR "\007*** $filename is not readable\n";
    return;
    }
printf STDOUT "Archiving file : $filename    ";
#
# if the file we are to process is a regular one, the do this code
#
if ( -T $filename )
    {
    #
    # talk to the user
    #
    #
    # calculate the file size, and open the input file
    #
    $size = -s $filename;
    printf STDOUT "text file, $size bytes\n";
    open( INPUT, "$filename" );
    #
    # Write the top of the file details
    #
    &WriteFileStart();
    #
    # while there is input to process ...
    #
    while ( <INPUT> )
        {
        #
        # calculate the length
        #
        $length = length( $_ );
        #
        # if the current size of the archive, plus the length of this
        # line will exceed the desired archive size, then stop the
        # current part, and continue the file in the next part
        #
        if ( ( $total_size + $length ) > $ArchiveSize )
```

```
            {
            &WriteFileNotDone();
            &OpenFile();
            &WriteFileContinue();
            $total_size = $length;
            }
        #
        # write the output line, and increment the total_size counter
        #
        print OUTPUT $_;
        $total_size = $total_size + $length;
        }
    #
    # write the end of file information
    #
    &WriteFileEnd();
    }
else
    {
    #
    # the specified file is of the binary persuaion, and therefore
    # needs a little for fiddling with in order to get it into the
    # archive
    #
    # talk to the user, and compute the file size
    #
    $size = -s $filename;
    printf STDOUT "binary file via uuencode (binary $size bytes)\n";
    #
    # do the uuencode - hopefully the filename isn't more than 12
    # characters - if it is? Oh well!
    # Because of problems if the file is in a subtree, the temporary file
    # name is now the process ID number followed by .u
    #
    system( "cat $filename ¦ uuencode $filename $filename > /tmp/
    ➥$$.u" );
    sleep(2);
    #
    # get the size of the uuencode file
    #
    $u_size = -s "/tmp/$$.u";
    open( INPUT, "/tmp/$$.u" );
    #
```

```perl
# Write the top of the file details
#
&WriteBinaryFileStart();
#
# while there is input to process ...
#
while ( <INPUT> )
   {
   #
   # calculate the length
   #
   $length = length( $_ );
   #
   # if the current size of the archive, plus the length of this
   # line will exceed the desired archive size, then stop the
   # current part, and continue the file in the next part
   #
   if ( ( $total_size + $length ) > $ArchiveSize )
      {
      &WriteBinaryFileNotDone();
      &OpenFile();
      &WriteBinaryFileContinue();
      $total_size = $length;
      }
   #
   # write the output line, and increment the total_size counter
   #
   print OUTPUT $_;
   $total_size = $total_size + $length;
   }
#
&WriteBinaryFileEnd();
system( "rm -f /tmp/$$.u" );
}
#$total_size += $size;
}
#---- PROCEDURE : Combine ----------------------------------------
#
sub Combine
{
for( $Part = 1; $Part <= $MaxPart; $Part++ )
   {
   $OutputFile = "$BaseOutputFile.$Part";
```

```perl
$InputFile = "$BaseOutputFile.O$Part";
$HeaderFile = "$BaseOutputFile.H$Part";
&TrackFile;
printf STDOUT "Assembling Archive part $Part (file is
➥$OutputFile)\n";

open( OUTPUT, ">$OutputFile" );
open( HEADER, "$HeaderFile" );
open( INPUT, "$InputFile" );

while (<HEADER>)
   {
   print OUTPUT $_;
   }
printf OUTPUT "#\n# ---------------------------------\n#\n#\n\n";
printf OUTPUT "echo \"$Program $Copyright\"\n";
printf OUTPUT "echo \"Version $Version for $OS\"\n";

while (<INPUT>)
   {
   print OUTPUT $_;
   }
printf OUTPUT "echo \"You have unpacked Part $Part of $MaxPart.
➥ \"\n";
if ( $Part < $MaxPart )
   {
         $temp = $Part + 1;
   printf OUTPUT "echo \"You must unpack Part $temp next.\"\n";
   printf OUTPUT "touch done.$Part\n";
   }
if ( $Part == $MaxPart )
   {
   printf OUTPUT "echo \"You have unpacked all parts.\"\n";
   printf OUTPUT "echo \"extraction complete.\"\n";
   }

close( OUTPUT );
close( HEADER );
close( INPUT );
unlink( "$HeaderFile" );
unlink( "$InputFile" );
   }

}
```

```
#---- PROCEDURE : OpenFile --------------------------------------
#
sub OpenFile
{
   printf STDOUT "Creating Part 2---------------------
sub WriteFileContinue
{
   printf STDOUT "   continuing $filename\n";
   printf OUTPUT "echo \"Continue extraction of $filename \"\n";
   printf OUTPUT "cat >> $filename << \\!END_OF_FILE!\n";
}


#---- PROCEDURE : CheckArgs --------------------------------------
sub WriteBinaryFileContinue
{
   printf STDOUT "   continuing $filename\n";
   printf OUTPUT "echo \"Continue extraction of $filename \"\n";
   printf OUTPUT "cat >> $filename.u << \\!END_OF_FILE!\n";
}


#---- PROCEDURE : WriteDevice -----------------------------------
sub WriteDevice
{
   ( $mode, $maj, $min ) = @_;
   printf OUTPUT "if test -f $filename -a \"\$1\" != \"-c\" \n";
   printf OUTPUT "then\n";
   printf OUTPUT "   echo \"shar : will not overwrite $filename \"\n";
   printf OUTPUT "else \n";
   printf OUTPUT "   echo \"creating device file $filename ( $maj/$min
                ➥)\"\n";
   printf OUTPUT "   echo \"** IF the mknod fails, execute the
                ➥command\"\n";
   printf OUTPUT "   echo \"      mknod $filename $mode $maj $min\"\n";
   printf OUTPUT "   mknod $filename $mode $maj $min\n";
   printf OUTPUT "fi\n";
}
#---- PROCEDURE : WriteFileStart ---------------------------------
#
# This procedure creates the preamble at the top of the data for the
# file which puts the file name in the archive header, and tests to see
# if the file already exists on extraction.
#
sub WriteFileStart
```

```
     {
        printf HEADER "#   %-40s  (%8d bytes/text)\n", $filename, $size;
        $OverTest = 1;
        printf OUTPUT "if test -f $filename -a \"\$1\" != \"-c\" \n";
        printf OUTPUT "then\n";
        printf OUTPUT "   echo \"shar : will not overwrite $filename \"\n";
        printf OUTPUT "else \n";
        printf OUTPUT "   echo \"extracting $filename ($size bytes)\"\n";
        printf OUTPUT "   cat > $filename << \\!END_OF_FILE!\n";
     }
#---- PROCEDURE : WriteFileNotDone -------------------------------
#
# This procedure is called when the maximum size of the archive is reached
# before the end of the file.
#
sub WriteFileNotDone
     {
        printf OUTPUT "!END_OF_FILE!\n";
        printf OUTPUT "echo \"$filename continued in the next part.\"\n";
        if ( $OverTest == 1 )
           {
           printf OUTPUT "fi # end of overwrite test\n";
           $OverTest = 0;
           }
        printf STDOUT "   splitting $filename\n";
     }
#---- PROCEDURE : WriteFileEnd -------------------------------------
sub WriteFileEnd
     {
        printf OUTPUT "!END_OF_FILE!\n";
        if ( $OverTest == 1 )
           {
           printf OUTPUT "fi # end of overwrite test\n";
           $OverTest = 0;
           }
        printf OUTPUT "   if test \"`wc -c $filename`\" -ne \"$size
                        ➥$filename\"\n";
        printf OUTPUT "   then\n";
        printf OUTPUT "      echo \"\007WARNING $filename : Extraction
                        ➥Error\"\n";
        printf OUTPUT "   fi\n";
     }
```

```
#---- PROCEDURE : WriteBinaryFileStart -------------------------
#
# This is the processing done in the shell script to create the binary
# file.
# NOTE: The overwrite test is currently not implemented.
#
sub WriteBinaryFileStart
{
        printf HEADER "#   %-4lled when the maximum size of the archive
                        ➥is reached
# before the end of the file.
#
sub WriteBinaryFileNotDone
{
   printf OUTPUT "!END_OF_FILE!\n";
   printf OUTPUT "echo \"$filename continued in the next part.\"\n";
   if ( $OverTest == 1 )
      {
      printf OUTPUT "fi # end of overwrite test\n";
      $OverTest = 0;
      }
   printf STDOUT "   splitting $filename\n";
}
sub GetDate
{
   $Date = &ctime(time);
   #
   # This hack is here because the ctime.pl library formats the date with a
   # newline at the end of the string - we don't want one there, thanks.
   #
   chop( $Date );
}


sub GetUser
{
   $User = getlogin;
   $Hostname = 'uname -n';
   chop( $Hostname );

   if ( $opt_D ne "" )
      {
      $User = "$User@$Hostname.$opt_D";
      }
```

```
        elsif ( $UseDomain ne "" )
            {
            $User = "$User@$Hostname.$UseDomain";
            }
        else
            {
            $User = "$User@$Hostname.UUCP";
            }
    }
#
# this subroutine we will examine a filename and normalize it into a series
# of directories and filenames.  The purpose of this is to ensure that all
# of directories are included in th2++$#NormalDir] = $dir;
                printf STDOUT "NormalDir[++$#NormalDir] = $dir\n";
            }
    }


#
# This routine checks the variable $NormalDir to see if the directory
# name we are processing has been made in the archive already.
#
sub CheckNormalized
{
    local( $WantDir ) = @_;
    local( $Loop );
    for ( $Loop = 0; $Loop <= $#NormalDir; $Loop++ )
        {
        if ( $opt_x == 1 )
            {
            printf("have $NormalDir[$Loop] want $WantDir\n");
            }
        if ( $NormalDir[$Loop] eq $WantDir )
            {
            printf STDERR "Directory $WantDir already in archive\n";
            return(1);
            }
        }
    return(0);
}

sub ValidateSize
{
```

```
#
# We want to look for the key letters 'K', and 'M' to mean kilobytes and
# megabytes respectively.
#
   $[ = 0;
   $LastChar = substr( $ArchiveSize, -1, 1 );
   $LastChar =~ y/a-z/A-Z/;
   if ( $LastChar eq "M" )
      {
      $Value = substr( $ArchiveSize, 0, (length($ArchiveSize) - 1) );
      $ArchiveSize = $Value * 1024000;
      }
   elsif ( $LastChar eq "K" )
      {
      $Value = substr( $ArchiveSize, 0, (length($ArchiveSize) - 1) );
      $ArchiveSize = $Value * 1024;
      }
}
#
# This module checks to see if we fail on creating a 15 character file
# filename.
#
sub FileNameLenCheck
{
   $testName = "/tmp/longfilenametes";
   $testName2 = "/tmp/longfilenamete";
   open( test, ">$testName" );
   close( test );
   if ( -r $testName2 )
      {
      # > 14 charactre filenames are TRASH
      'rm $testName2';
      printf STDOUT "                    Oh drat, I can't create >14 char
                                 ➡filenames h
ere.\n";
      return(1);
      }
   elsif ( -r $testName )
      {
      # >14 character filenames are OK
      'rm $testName';
      return(0);
      }
```

```
}
sub StartTrackFile
{
   open( TRACER, ">>$TraceFile" );
   printf TRACER ":\n";
   printf TRACER "#\n#This was created using pahsr, and it will\n";
   printf TRACER "# automatically unpack all of the archives.\n#\n";
}
sub TrackFile
{
   printf TRACER "# This is the next archive to run\n";
   printf TRACER "if [ -r $OutputFile ]\nthen\n";
   printf TRACER "/bin/sh $OutputFile\n";
   printf TRACER "else\necho \"Your are missing $OutputFile.\"\n";
   printf TRACER "exit 1\nfi\n#\n#\n";
}

sub CheckConfig
{
   printf "$Program Version $Version\n$Copyright\n";
   printf "Configuring ....\n";
   $HOME = $ENV{'HOME'};
   $User = getlogin;
   #
   # If the user has one - use it.
   #
   printf "   Checking for $HOME/.pshar.cfg ...\n";
   if ( -r "$HOME/.pshar.cfg" )
      {
      return("$HOME/.pshar.cfg");
      }
   # if not, then check for system ones.
   else
      {
      printf "   Checking for /etc/default ...\n";
      if ( -d "/etc/default" )
         {
         #
         # this is probably an SCO system
         #
         if ( -r "/etc/default/pshar.cfg" )
            {
            return("/etc/default/pshar.cfg");
```

```
                 } # endif
            else
                {
                if ( $User eq "root" )
      g");
                    } #endif
                } #end else
            }
        else
            {
            printf "   Checking for /etc/pshar.cfg ...\n";
            if ( -r "/etc/pshar.cfg" )
                {
                return("/etc/pshar.cfg");
                }
            else
                {
                if ( $User eq "root" )
                    {
                    &SelfConfig( "/etc/pshar.cfg" );
                    return("/etc/pshar.cfg");
                    }
                }
            }
        }
    printf "Oops! I can't find any configuration files.  Because you
            ➥aren't ";
    printf "the\nsystem administrator, I will create one for you in your ";
    printf "home directory.\n\n";
    #
    # if we get to here, then there isn't a user config file, or a
    # system config file.  Sooooo, create a user config file.
    #
    &SelfConfig( "$HOME/.pshar.cfg" );
    return("$HOME/.pshar.cfg");
}


sub SelfConfig
{
    local( $config_file ) = @_;
    select( STDOUT );
    printf "Thank you for using pshar.  This configuration will ";
    printf "only be run once, \nunless the configuration file is ";
```

```
   printf "removed.\n";
   printf "Please answer the following questions.  Default values\n";
   printf "are enclosed in [].\n";
   printf "\nOperating System Type [Generic UNIX] : ";
   $op_sys = <STDIN>;
   chop ( $op_sys );
   if ( $op_sys eq "" )
      {
      $op_sys = "Generic UNIX";
      }
   printf "\nDomain Name [.UUCP] : ";
   $dom = <STDIN>;
   chop ( $dom );
   if ( $dom eq "" )
      {
      $dom = ".UUCP";
      }
   printf "\Default Archive Size [128K] : ";
   $size = <STDIN>;
   chop ( $size );
   if ( $size eq "" )
      {
      $size = "128K";
      }
   printf "Creating pshar configuration file : $config_file\n";
   open( config, ">$config_file" );
   select( config );
   printf "\$OS=\"$op_sys\";\n";
   printf "\$ArchiveSize = \"$size\";\n";
   printf "\$UseDomain = \"$dom\";\n";
   close( config );
   select( STDOUT );
   return(0);
}
```

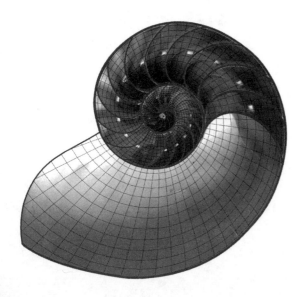

INDEX

INDEX

INDEX

INDEX

INDEX

INDEX

INDEX

INDEX

INDEX

INDEX

INDEX

INDEX

INDEX

INDEX

INDEX

INDEX

INDEX

INDEX

INDEX

INDEX

INDEX

INDEX

INDEX

INDEX

INDEX

INDEX

INDEX

INDEX

INDEX

INDEX

Inside UNIX
REGISTRATION CARD

Fill out this card to receive information about future OS/2 books and other New Riders titles!

Name _____ **Title** _____

Company _____

Address _____

City/State/ZIP _____

I bought this book because: _____
_____

I purchased this book from:
☐ A bookstore (Name _____)
☐ A software or electronics store (Name _____)
☐ A mail order (Name of Catalog _____)

I purchase this many computer books each year:
☐ 1–5   ☐ 6 or more

I currently use these applications: _____
_____
_____
_____

I found these chapters to be the most informative: _____
_____

I found these chapters to be the least informative: _____
_____

Additional comments: _____
_____

☐ I would like to see my name in print! You may use my name and quote me in future New Riders products and promotions. My daytime phone number is:_____

New Riders Publishing 201 West 103rd Street • Indianapolis, Indiana 46290 USA

Fold Here

PLACE
STAMP
HERE

New Riders Publishing
201 West 103rd Street
Indianapolis, Indiana 46290
USA

WANT MORE INFORMATION?

CHECK OUT THESE RELATED TITLES:

	QTY	PRICE	TOTAL

Inside Windows NT. A complete tutorial and reference to organizing and managing multiple tasks and programs in Windows NT! This book focuses on integration capabilities and networking options of Windows NT—an inside look at the operating environment of the future! ISBN: 1-56205-124-5.   ____ $34.95   _____

Integrating Windows Applications. This is the intermediate-to advanced-level Windows user's no-nonsense guide. Readers will learn how to create sophisticated documents through Dynamic Data Exchange and Object Linking and Embedding. This book contains several extras, including a disk loaded with examples, database files, and macros. ISBN: 1-56205-083-4.   ____ $34.95   _____

Inside OS/2 2.1, 3rd Edition. Get the inside story on OS/2, from the industry's best-selling book, on the latest version of this powerful operating system! Completely updated and revised, this book covers installation, memory management, and compatibility—plus detailed coverage of the OS/2 Workplace Shell. With lots of techniques for integrating DOS and Windows applications under OS/2, this book has everything readers need. ISBN: 1-56205-206-3.   ____ $39.95   _____

Ultimate Windows 3.1. If you're looking for the most up-to-date and comprehensive reference on Windows 3.1, your search is over! Loaded with tips, features, bug-fixes—plus coverage of sound boards, CD-ROMs, and video—you'll find only the latest and most relevant information available. A bonus disk includes a hypertext application with "2000 Windows Tips." ISBN: 1-56205-125-3.   ____ $39.95   _____

Name _____

Company _____

Address _____

City _____ State ____ ZIP _____

Phone _____ Fax _____

☐ Check Enclosed   ☐ VISA   ☐ MasterCard

Card # _____ Exp. Date _____

Signature _____

Prices are subject to change. Call for availability and pricing information on latest editions.

Subtotal   _____

Shipping   _____

$4.00 for the first book and $1.75 for each additional book.

Total   _____
Indiana residents add 5% sales tax.

New Riders Publishing   201 West 103rd Street • Indianapolis, Indiana 46290 USA

Orders/Customer Service: 1-800-428-5331
Fax: 1-800-448-3804

Fold Here

- -

PLACE
STAMP
HERE

New Riders Publishing
201 West 103rd Street
Indianapolis, Indiana 46290
USA